RENEWING
The Laboratory Approach

ORGANIZATIONS
to Planned Change

Robert T. Golembiewski

UNIVERSITY OF GEORGIA

F. E. PEACOCK PUBLISHERS, INC.

ITASCA, ILLINOIS

Copyright © 1972
by F. E. Peacock Publishers, Inc.
Library of Congress
Catalog Card Number 72–79876
ISBN 0–87581–129–9
Printed in the United States of America

To that tiny stranger

> who first came and stayed to fill our home and hearts
> and minds

To that microscopic self

> which wondrously reveals an expanding crowd within:
> Dump and 'bott,' Bumbumniecki and the Mad Gerbel,
> Mrs. Dettelson and Allison

To that mega-package of will and want

> that seeks to mark increasingly more of the world
> as her own

In short, to Alice herself

CONTENTS

viii

INTRODUCTION

The title of this book was selected only after long deliberation. Still, *Renewing Organizations* falls far short of revealing the precise goals of this book. Some such title as "Toward Continuous Renewal for Organizations and Individuals" captures more of its flavor. Certainly the thrust suggested by the key word "toward" is appropriate, but even that may suggest too much; that is to say, the alternative title implies more than can presently be delivered. We are but a little way down the road of understanding what continuous renewal implies, for individuals or for organizations. And although we are beginning to see a little more daylight about how one goes about accomplishing "continuous renewal" for individuals and organizations, now is definitely not the time to rest on those tentative laurels.

Better the pedestrian if less revealing title, then, providing that the full scope of this volume is made clear. This book deals with how individuals and organizations can go about making more effective choices, as well as coping better with change if that is what we choose or have thrust on us. The technology is new and only beginning to develop, and there is a very real doubt as to whether what we know is already far too little, far too late. But we still must try, even if only the attempt is possible, even if change is our contemporary Armageddon. Alvin Toffler put the necessity in perspective in his discussion of "future shock," the "shattering stress and disorientation that we induce in individuals by subjecting them to too much change in too short a time." He came away from his research "with two disturbing convictions":

> First, it became clear that future shock is no longer a distantly potential danger, but a real sickness from which increas-

ingly large numbers already suffer. This psychobiological condition can be described in medical and psychiatric terms. It is the disease of change.

Second, I gradually came to be appalled by how little is actually known about adaptivity, either by those who call for and create vast changes in our society, or by those who supposedly prepare us to cope with those changes. Earnest intellectuals talk bravely about "educating for change" or "preparing people for the future." But we know virtually nothing about how to do it.[1]

This book accepts the first of these two propositions and attempts to show how the state of the art extends beyond the limits sketched by Toffler in the second proposition. The flood of contemporary history, as Toffler documents it, certainly is attacking man and his institutions at their most vulnerable point. Beyond that, this volume attempts to provide some guidance for men in their institutions to generate constructive adaptation to historical challenges, which task Toffler did not undertake.

Three Perspectives on a Central Dilemma

Three perspectives help develop much of the sense of the central dilemma that history is challenging man and his institutions at their most vulnerable point. *First,* the thrust of contemporary history can be characterized by a related set of words: change, revolution, turmoil, rootlessness, and so on. As one popular author expressed it: once-reliable constants have now become galloping variables.[2] In effect, almost as much has happened in the past 50 years of man's history as happened in all of his earlier history. The pace of happening is implicit in one fact. There have been approximately 800 lifetimes of 62 years each in the past 50,000 years. Of these 800 human lifetimes, some 650 were spent in caves.[3] Of these 800 human lifetimes, also, one or at most two have been spent with blood transfusions, air conditioning, first-generation mass transportation systems, television, medical services that can lay meaningful claim to improving the quality of human life, and formal education that extends beyond some small elite.

Second, and perhaps even more significant, the total effect is less and less a case of history just happening to us. More and more, we trigger deliberate change and conscious innovation, perhaps even lust after it, even as we more clearly recognize the many unanticipated and some-

---

1. Alvin Toffler, *Future Shock* (New York: Random House, 1970), pp. 3, 4.
2. Warren G. Bennis, "Beyond Bureaucracy," *Trans-Action,* Vol. 2 (July–August, 1965), p. 31.
3. Toffler, *op. cit.,* p. 15.

times overwhelming effects we thereby set in motion. We have met the enemy and they is us, as Pogo put it. And no truce seems likely between the two faces of man.

The only real alternative is to get better and better at minimizing the negative effects of deliberate change and innovation, short of urging that some idyllic state of nature once existed and can be regained. And the state of the art has been getting better and better in some areas, as in controlling physical pollution. Major advances still have to be made in mastering people effects. Clearly people effects there are, massive ones. For example, rigorous research confirms what intuition had suggested all along. The more change-episodes an individual experiences, the greater the likelihood that he will become ill and that he will have a more severe illness. An index of change has been developed, and it helps significantly in predicting the amount and severity of illnesses experienced by people in diverse populations.[4] We still must develop the fulsome technologies to cope with what clearly exists.

It is as if man has become more a traveler in time than to places, and in the process he has exponentially raised the costs of his traveling. Travel to new places often results in "culture shock," as the individual finds himself in a new environment without the old cues that guided his life. The new cues tend to be strange or incomprehensible or even abhorrent. As Toffler notes, they account "for much of the bewilderment, frustration, and disorientation that can plague Americans in dealing with other cultures. The common consequences are breakdowns in communication, misreadings of reality, and inability to cope."[5]

These consequences of culture shock are mild compared to the costs of rapid travel through time, the costs of future shock. Some contrasts between future shock and culture shock may be sketched briefly. A traveler in space usually can look forward to returning home, as one antidote to his culture shock. A traveler in time, even when he stays in the same place, finds his sense of a cultural home kaleidoscopically changing just as he gets familiar with it. Future shock is reliefless in this basic sense. It can be seen in the grief that follows the disbanding of a project team or in the depression of a professional who no sooner has gained his training than he must think about its imminent obsolescence. Perhaps future shock is best reflected in the sense of things happening so evermore quickly that the brief encounter must do it all, even in romantic dalliance. The moment becomes increasingly all, especially for what Staffan Lindner calls the "harried leisure class." As he explains, "We had always expected one of the beneficent results of economic affluence to be a tranquil and harmonious manner of life. . . . What

---

4. See, generally, the *Journal of Psychosomatic Research*, esp. Vol. 10, pp. 355–66, and Vol. 11, pp. 213–47.
5. Toffler, *op. cit.*, pp. 12–13.

3

has happened is the exact opposite. The pace is quickening, and our lives in fact are becoming steadily more hectic."[6] Warren Bennis and Philip Slater capture the sense of it in an arresting book title: *The Temporary Society.*[7]

Third, humankind is, unfortunately, far less adept at dealing with galloping variables than with reliable constants, whether as individuals or groups. Henry Ford, for example, had learned that lesson well as it applied to organizations. "You can have any kind of Ford you want," he is reputed to have said, "as long as it's a black Model T." Ford reflected both an ideal and practicality, even if unknowingly.

Ford's dictum was consistent with the classical theory of bureaucracy. Its ideal was a precisely defined set of duties and responsibilities, an elegant watchworks that once set running would regularly and continuously produce the intended effects. Stability and order were its dominant themes; and the mass production of identical items was its *raison d'être.* Building only black Model T Fords was its forte. Certainly in the forefront of Ford's thinking was a compelling practical consideration. Identical end-items implied minimum complexity and fewest managerial problems. So black Model Ts it was, then.

Mr. Ford had things the easy way for awhile, but only for a brief while, as the affairs of men are reckoned. Changes in consumer demands and industrial competition forced Ford to "have a better idea" and, consequently, to get in the business of dealing with galloping variables. As it was with Ford, so it is increasingly with all of us. The thrust of history leaves us with fewer and fewer reliable constants, at least constants that are reliable for very long.

The thrust of history and the skills of mankind are at cross-purposes, in sum, and significantly so. The results are most clear in the dry rot of our cities, but the effects are ubiquitous in all our institutions—political, social, and economic. These institutions are being sorely tested to provide the things that more and more people are seeking or demanding. Hence our institutions now must not only catch up to these expanding demands, but they also can look forward to continuous renewal throughout the foreseeable future so as to meet and hopefully anticipate the demands to come. Moreover, institutions from one point of view reflect the spirit of man, and from another they mold his quality of life. Consequently, the ideas and attitudes of men also must catch up with today's expanding demands, as well as stand ready for continuous renewal in the tomorrows that can now be only dimly envisioned.

---

6. Staffan B. Lindner, *The Harried Leisure Class* (New York: Columbia University Press, 1970), p. 1.
7. Warren G. Bennis and Philip Slater, *The Temporary Society* (New York: Harper & Row, Publishers, 1968).

Renewal and Revolution as Alternate Strategies

There is no way of putting off either individual or organizational renewal, but a major choice must be made. Beyond a pollyannish hope that matters will get better if they are left alone, that is to say, two alternative approaches are available: rebellion against our institutions, with the goal of destroying them; or renewal of the institutions, with the goal of making them more effective. It is a question of burning or learning, in short, if we reject the alternative of lapsing into a growing irrelevance.

Some would argue that it is only through revolution against our institutions that they will ever be renewed. In some cases this is no doubt true. At the very least, however, massive efforts at renewal should precede that last resort, revolution. The thesis of this volume is that this last resort in today's organizations is far too premature, for we have only recently begun attempts at major organizational renewal, at least with any real sophistication. The technology for renewal is becoming increasingly available, and a profession for specialists in that technology is only now emerging.

There are numerous additional reasons for stressing renewal. Consider only that revolutions seem generally better for smashing than creating, better for permitting a massive emotional orgasm than for constructive social action. One of the key reasons seems to be that revolution is oriented to the *ultimate end*. Any action that achieves the noble end may seem appropriate in revolution, that is to say. This often enormously complicates putting the pieces back together again. In contrast, renewal should be more *means-oriented*. Not just any action is appropriate for approaching the goals of a program of renewal, in short. And there can be a world of difference in the two basic questions that rebellers and renewers tend to emphasize:

- "How do we destroy this need-depriving institution?" asks the revolutionary.
- "How can we improve on an imperfect but existing institution?" asks the renewer.

To revolt or renew poses serious dilemmas, then. I illustrate only. The problem for the revolutionary is that his zeal to change what exists can encourage him to neglect the issues of what is to take its place, and when, and how. The problem for the renewer is that his concern for having a working institution, even if imperfect, might make him over-timid where he should be bold. The cop-out temptation is clear: the certain, even if imperfect, institutions of today may become paralyzingly attractive when compared to the practical uncertainties of some hoped-for brighter new world.

This book attempts to slip between the horns of such dilemmas. For example, this book urges changes in today's organizations, while it seeks to do so within a more or less specific framework of values. At the same time, this book urges caution in simply replacing what exists because it is imperfect, like all works of men. Change should follow only clear need, in short, and then only when the probability of success is high.

This is a radical book, to put it directly, written from what is hopefully a disciplined perspective. In short, this approach accepts Harvey Cox's challenge. "If we choose to live responsibly in the world," he noted, "then we must face the issue of how we can harness organizational power for authentic human purposes."[8]

Overchoice or Underchoice?

This book also is dedicated to enlarging the *manageable and meaningful choices* open to individuals and organizations, via emphasis on a technology for renewal and change. Basically, that is, this volume is dedicated to helping men survive their modern freedom, to helping them take advantage of the richness and diversity that is increasingly available and that, not incidentally, will be increasingly necessary in modern business and government organizations. The position here is that, despite the patent problems it has brought and will bring, our continuing technological development has (in the words of Harvey Cox) "opened up new possibilities not present before." He concludes:

> In the world of work, . . . secularization is not the Messiah. But neither is it the anti-Christ. It is a rather dangerous liberation; it raises the stakes, making it possible for man to increase the range of his freedom and responsibility and thus to deepen his maturation. At the same time it poses risks of a larger order than those it displaces. But the promise exceeds the peril, or at least makes it worth taking the risk.[9]

The concern about man surviving freedom distinguishes this volume from the vast bulk of social commentary whose depressed theme is that man is increasingly coerced by repressive standardization and regimentation. In the orthodox commentary, man was far freer in some past time. Then, in the words of the French mystic Jacques Ellul, "Choice was a real possibility for him."[10] The only issue in orthodox social com-

---

8. Harvey Cox, *The Secular City* (New York: Macmillan Co., 1965), p. 173. (Copyright © Harvey Cox, 1965, 1966.)
9. *Ibid.*, p. 167.
10. Jacques Ellul, *The Technological Society* (New York: Vintage Books, 1967), pp. 77, 83, and 90.

6

mentary is how chronic the condition is, and even there the usual agreement is that man's condition is very chronic indeed.[11] The death throes may even now be upon us, some commentators tell us.

In contrast, the view here is that overchoice is more the modern problem than is underchoice. The kaleidoscopic profusion of today's life styles, and their substantial mutual tolerance, implies such an expanded range of choice, for example. Hence the balanced view. This is no call to slack off on efforts at combating repression or standardization or homogenization of human choice at every turn. But the dominant emphasis here is that equipping individuals and organizations for expanded choice deserves at least equal attention. That attention is focused on two basic questions. What are the attitudes and values that permit an individual to constructively test the choices open to him, as opposed to those attitudes and values that wall him off from what he might become? And what skills does an individual need in order to exploit choices available to him, with some growing probability that change will have bearable costs?

Stressing overchoice does not mean, however, that all is clearly for the best in this best of all possible worlds. The present view is a more complex one. That is, this volume sees today's and tomorrow's man as having a great and growing potential for choice, both as individual and as organization member. For example, the choices open to the American poor or to blacks, however far short of parity they remain, have been enormously enlarged in the past few decades. But enlarged choices are not necessarily manageable or meaningful. Thus one can be coerced into change or face being discarded into some social refuse pile. There is precious little choice in offering such "alternatives," for example, as: "You can choose to be retrained, or to go hungry." Moreover, even if real choices are possible, the choices may be so numerous as to coerce the individual into an escape from freedom. No choice means no failure, from another point of view, while numerous choices imply correspondingly greater challenge and risk in the pursuit of heightened expectations. And there's the rub.

Hence the dedication of this volume to enlarging *manageable and meaningful* choices open to individuals and organizations, defined here in terms of an approach to change and renewal that is scaled to human dimensions. Simply, the dedication here is toward improving the odds that Everyman can adapt to his choice-filled world while minimizing the future shock inherent in the effort.

The increased range of choices to be considered below can be sketched here. Within an overall ethical or moral framework, the focus below on

---

11. Roderick Seidenberg, *Post-Historic Man* (Boston: Beacon Press, 1957).

personal renewal will have several dominant emphases. The several thrusts toward increased choice for individuals include:

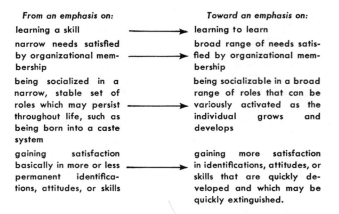

From an emphasis on:	Toward an emphasis on:
learning a skill	learning to learn
narrow needs satisfied by organizational membership	broad range of needs satisfied by organizational membership
being socialized in a narrow, stable set of roles which may persist throughout life, such as being born into a caste system	being socializable in a broad range of roles that can be variously activated as the individual grows and develops
gaining satisfaction basically in more or less permanent identifications, attitudes, or skills	gaining more satisfaction in identifications, attitudes, or skills that are quickly developed and which may be quickly extinguished.

Several kinds of expanded choices to guide organization renewal are also stressed below, and they are at once clearer and more elusive. Their diversity can be suggested here, if at the expense of brevity and perhaps vagueness. The several thrusts toward expanded choices for organizational renewal include:

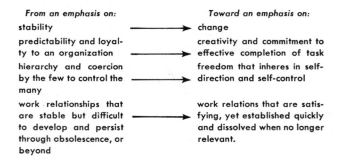

From an emphasis on:	Toward an emphasis on:
stability	change
predictability and loyalty to an organization	creativity and commitment to effective completion of task
hierarchy and coercion by the few to control the many	freedom that inheres in self-direction and self-control
work relationships that are stable but difficult to develop and persist through obsolescence, or beyond	work relations that are satisfying, yet established quickly and dissolved when no longer relevant.

The Laboratory Approach and Organization Development (OD)

The discussion below will describe ways to manage large and growing potentialities for change and choice, within two related conceptual frameworks. The "laboratory approach" provides the all-encompassing framework, while Organization Development (OD) is the more specific focus. The former begat the latter, as it were, to facilitate coping with change and choice in organization contexts. Four themes will help sharpen the complementarities and distinctions between our two basic points of reference.

1. Laboratory Approach as Genus: Internal Logic, Values, Interventions

The laboratory approach may be considered as a *genus,* as one way of learning which is at once convenient and potent. In brief, the laboratory approach has a common base and aim. Thus the approach is an educational strategy which rests primarily on the experiences of the learners themselves in various social encounters. Commonly, also, the aim is to develop attitudes and competencies that aid learning about human relationships. In these basic commonalities, the laboratory approach involves "learning how to learn." "Essentially, therefore," we are told, "laboratory training attempts to induce changes with regard to the learning process itself and to communicate a particular method of learning and inquiry."[12] The diverse forms and consequences of this "particular method of learning and inquiry" constitute the targets of this volume.

The first four sections below (Part I) will consider this genus from two basic and related points of view. They will detail what may be called the *internal logic* or *broad theory* of the laboratory approach, what it seeks to do via which specific dynamics under which conditions. These sections also will stress the *values* or *normative agreement* on which the laboratory approach rests, the "why" of what it seeks to accomplish. The first sections thus seek not only to be clear on what and when, to paraphrase "Jesus Christ, Superstar," but are keenly concerned with why.

The laboratory approach is also conceived here as generating a number of species for learning or change. These species include *strategies, designs,* and *interventions for change* that are consistent with the laboratory approach. Explicating these species will be the burden of Parts II and III of this volume. Each species will be treated in a similar way. It will be:

- defined and described
- illustrated in applications relevant to individual or organization renewal, as appropriate
- evaluated in terms of research relevant to its impact and consequences

These strategies, designs, and interventions deal with the *practicum* or the *techniques* of the laboratory approach and constitute the bulk of this book. As such, they are the necessary complement of the emphases in the first four sections on the *internal logic* and the *values* or *normative* agreement underlying the laboratory approach.

Genus and species interactions thus constitute the vitals of this book. Together, they—the laboratory approach and its derivative strategies

---

12. Edgar H. Schein and Warren G. Bennis, *Personal and Organizational Change through Group Methods* (New York: John Wiley & Sons, 1965), p. 4.

for change, learning designs, and interventions—constitute the technology for renewal of concern.

2. Organization Development as Value-Loaded: Some Perspectives

The keenness below for "why" issues, issues concerning the quality of organizational processes and products, has a direct motivation. Paramountly, Organization Development is squarely in the business of dealing with both "desired" and "desirable" values, to use Solomon's revealing terminology.[13] Thus an organization's executives typically seek such outcomes as high output, low turnover, and so on, and these desired values usually are significant goals of OD programs. At the same time, however, OD programs must deal with desirable values which should increasingly come to guide organization processes. These desirable values are part of the theoretical and personal framework within which the OD specialist works. At the broadest level, for example, it will be argued below that OD has an ontological relevance to human development. Not only are values relevant to OD, then. But OD is seen as facilitating movement toward important goals of human development which are in effect meta-values defining *the* desirable and progressively human condition. OD is also seen as contributing to narrower organization goals that are managerially desired.

The commingling in OD of desired and desirable values cannot be neglected, patently. This makes life complicated, as Ross forcefully demonstrates in one particular.[14] That is, values are relevant not only to how an organization goes about its business, but also to what an organization's business is. Ross powerfully illustrates the relevance to OD of broad values defining the desirable, the good life. If an organization is engaged in an immoral enterprise, it is for Ross a matter of moral irrelevance whether that organization is managed despotically or benignly. He notes convincingly that ". . . no aspect of organizational or procedural humaneness could justify the product of Auschwitz." The only moral OD approach to such organizations, Ross argues, is to neutralize or destroy them. "The behavior of these organizations is such," he concludes, "that to make their products neutral or benign would entail making these organizations less effective, increasing waste, and encouraging discontent and disruption within them."[15] By "these organizations" Ross means not only those whose purpose was mass extermination, but also those which make napalm, despoil the environment, exploit the consumer, aggregate tremendous social power, and so on.

13. Lawrence N. Solomon, "Humanism and the Training of Applied Behavioral Scientists," *Journal of Applied Behavioral Science,* Vol. 7 (September, 1971), esp. pp. 531–32.
14. Robert Ross, "OD for Whom?" *Journal of Applied Behavioral Science,* Vol. 7 (September, 1971), pp. 580–85.
15. *Ibid.,* pp. 581–82.

This book will certainly not settle the moral issues about which Ross writes, but neither will it permit readers to take the easy way out. It is Ross's view that many, or even most, OD practitioners do in fact seek that easy way. He observes that: "the OD professional is either unconcerned with, or supportive of (in value terms), what the client organization actually does. Evidently, process is seen as more important than purpose."[16] So it may be, although Ross's view is overstated from this writer's perspective. But as that view does apply, to that degree are OD professionals suffering (or perhaps, shortsightedly profiting) from a technical myopia.

This book provides no support for that myopia, but neither does it provide magic spectacles that can correct shortsightedness. This in-betweenness can be circumscribed in terms of three propositions. First, OD efforts must be judged in terms of two kinds of moral frameworks: the "internal" values related to organizational processes that inhere in the OD practitioner's theoretical framework, and "external" values that relate to organizational purposes. As OD becomes more potent, so does the interfacing of internal and external values become more critical. Second, the ethical burden of OD practitioners is particularly heavy because, for good or ill, they have become identified as major modern carriers of humane values, they are widely seen (in Ross's words) as seeking to move "corporate and other bureaucracies from punitive hierarchies toward nurturant commonwealths." Third, OD applications acquire awesome moral relevance because they typically relate to the quality of life in our major contemporary engines of power and purpose. OD applications consequently are suffused with issues of value.

3. An OD Cube: Focus, Locus, Designs

There is a third convenient way of illustrating the prime thrusts of this volume in dealing with Organization Development, or OD, which is a specific vehicle for bringing to bear the power of the laboratory approach on organizational change and choice. Figure 1 suggests the sweep and range of this volume from the OD perspective. Overall, OD is a corpus of techniques that are consistent with the internal logic and the normative agreement of the laboratory approach as applied in organizations. In more detail, to explain the sense of Figure 1, OD programs *focus* on one or a variety of diagnosed problems. Moreover, each diagnosed problem has a *locus* at one or more levels of social organization, extending from the several roles that each individual plays to the complex social systems that encompass large numbers of actors. Finally, OD programs rely on a broad range of laboratory *learning designs or interventions,* intended to cope with various diagnosed problems, typically at several levels of social organization. Later sections will develop the sense

---

16. *Ibid.*, p. 581

Figure 1. A Schema of Organization Development, or OD

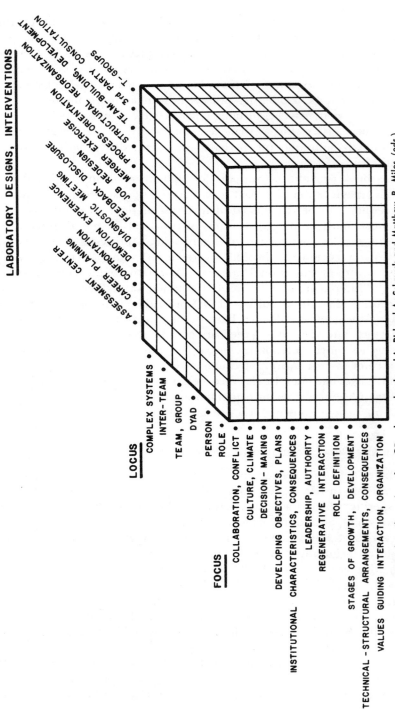

LABORATORY DESIGNS, INTERVENTIONS

- ASSESSMENT CENTER
- CAREER PLANNING
- CONFRONTATION
- DEMOTION
- DIAGNOSTIC MEETING
- FEEDBACK EXPERIENCE
- FEEDBACK, DISCLOSURE
- JOB REDESIGN
- MERGER EXERCISE
- PROCESS-ORIENTATION
- STRUCTURAL REORGANIZATION
- TEAM-BUILDING, DEVELOPMENT
- 3rd PARTY CONSULTATION
- T-GROUPS

LOCUS

- COMPLEX SYSTEMS •
- INTER-TEAM •
- TEAM, GROUP •
- DYAD •
- PERSON •
- ROLE •

FOCUS

- COLLABORATION, CONFLICT •
- CULTURE, CLIMATE •
- DECISION-MAKING •
- DEVELOPING OBJECTIVES, PLANS •
- INSTITUTIONAL CHARACTERISTICS, CONSEQUENCES •
- LEADERSHIP, AUTHORITY •
- REGENERATIVE INTERACTION •
- ROLE DEFINITION •
- STAGES OF GROWTH, DEVELOPMENT •
- TECHNICAL-STRUCTURAL ARRANGEMENTS, CONSEQUENCES •
- VALUES GUIDING INTERACTION, ORGANIZATION •

Source: Based on the notion of an OD cube as developed in Richard A. Schmuck and Matthew B. Miles (eds.), *Organization Development in Schools* (Palo Alto, Cal.: National Press Books, 1971), p. 8.

and meaning of the various labels in Figure 1, and especially of the several laboratory designs or interventions. Here note only that each topic in this volume can be located at one or more of the 858 coordinates of Figure 1. For example, Subsection 3 of Section C, Part I, introduces process orientation, the core intervention of the laboratory approach. Process orientation is defined there as a shared commitment by interdependent persons to mutually examine all aspects of their interdependence, an examination with a technology guided by a common set of values. That introduction would have coordinates (0,0,9) on the three axes of Figure 1: focus, locus, and designs. Later in this volume, applications of this basic intervention will be illustrated at a variety of loci as they focus on a range of diagnosed problems. For example, Section E, Part II, will detail how the process orientation can be applied at the locus of a complex system of organization so as to focus on and, hopefully, change that system's culture or climate. This concern of that section may be indexed as (10,6,9) on the OD cube in Figure 1.

4. The Basic OD Bias: Group-Oriented Strategies

A fourth and final theme comprehensively characterizes this volume. OD basically reflects a variety of group-oriented strategies for conscious and deliberate change in social systems. In essence, changes in group-level phenomena such as social norms and values are seen as the primary motivators of organizational change, via their influence on the behavior of individuals. This basic OD bias is hardly the only approach to change. Other approaches place their emphasis elsewhere. Alternatively,

- Technological or environmental conditions are seen as prime determiners of systemic change.
- Changes in individuals are seen as the basic intended mediators of organizational change.
- Change is seen as largely unplanned and uncontrollable, whether it is serendipitous or calamitous.
- Change is seen as the basic product of an elite which seeks to generate unknowing and even unwilling change in large systems, as by guerrilla activities.

The bias here toward group-oriented strategies is dominant, then, but it is hardly an exclusive one. The position here is simply that group-oriented strategies have a variety of general advantages for many OD purposes, a number of which are illustrated below. Other convenient sources also detail those advantages, especially with respect to individual-oriented strategies.[17]

---

17. Harvey A. Hornstein, Barbara Benedict Bunker, and Marion G. Hornstein, "Some Conceptual Issues in Individual and Group-Oriented Strategies of Intervention into Organizations," *Journal of Applied Behavioral Science*, Vol. 7 (September, 1971), pp. 557–68.

Toward A Heightened Individual ←→ Organization Exchange

The laboratory approach and its derivative learning designs are truly a significant modern phenomenon, and perhaps as some claim they are even the most important learning technologies developed in the past three decades or so.[18] We shall see. In any case, two of the basic learning designs—"T-Groups" and "encounter groups"—have become notable parts of the contemporary culture, for good or ill, and probably for two basic reasons. First, one major goad seems to be the common frustration of psychological and social needs, the impersonality and dehumanization that so many people feel is the modern legacy. Second, the new affluence no doubt has encouraged more attention to the satisfaction of psychological and social needs. Hence the characterization of some learning designs derived from the laboratory approach as a kind of middle-class hippiedom.[19]

Whatever the diverse catalog of reasons underlying the prominence of the laboratory approach, however, one fact seems constant. More and more people seem to be demanding more and more from their relationships and institutions. Two contributing forces seem involved: many people are more explicitly needful than ever before, and many institutions and organizations are less and less successful in responding to those needs. Carl Rogers provides useful perspective on why so many people have been drawn to the laboratory approach. He asks:

> . . . what is the psychological need that draws people. . . ?
> I believe it is a hunger for something the person does not find
> in his work environment, in his church, certainly not in his
> school or college, and sadly enough, not even in modern family
> life. It is a hunger for relationships which are close and real;
> in which feelings and emotions can be spontaneously expressed
> without first being carefully censored or bottled up; where
> deep experiences—disappointments and joys—can be shared;
> where new ways of behaving can be risked and tried out;
> where, in a word, he approaches the state where all is known
> and all accepted, and thus further growth becomes possible.
> This seems to be the overpowering hunger which he hopes to
> satisfy through his experiences in an encounter group.[20]

18. For a brief and incisive introduction, see Arthur Blumberg, *Sensitivity Training: Processes, Problems, and Applications* (Syracuse, N.Y.: Syracuse University Publications in Continuing Education, 1971). Jane Howard, *Please Touch: A Guided Tour of the Human Potential Movement* (New York: McGraw-Hill Book Co., 1970), provides insightful personal reactions to some 20 learning experiences based on the laboratory approach, if in widely varying degrees.

19. Donald Thomas and Thomas Smith, "T-Grouping: The White-Collar Hippie Movement," National Association of Secondary Schools, *Bulletin* (February, 1968), pp. 1–9.

20. Carl R. Rogers, *Carl Rogers on Encounter Groups* (New York: Harper & Row, Publishers, 1970), pp. 10–11.

From this perspective, the laboratory approach is more an effort to cope with freedom than it is an escape from sameness or isolation. Certainly, in any case, coping with freedom is a critical theme in the material below. In important senses this book is the necessary counterpart and logical consequence of the earlier interests reflected in my *Men, Management and Morality*.[21] The earlier book emphasized that a real choice exists between two concepts for organizing, one that is in place virtually everywhere and an alternative concept that is attractive in theory but has few real-life applications. This volume emphasizes ways of approaching one of those organizing concepts, so as to make the choice between the two concepts meaningful and manageable. Similarly, the earlier book stressed the relative usefulness of alternative models for organizing work under different conditions; this book begins to sketch how an organization can change from one model to the other.

The theme of increased meaningful choice binds this book to the earlier *Men, Management, and Morality*. It is appropriate, then, to introduce this book with a paraphrase of Rousseau that highlighted one of the dominant themes of that earlier one:

> Men can be free within wide limits in organizations, but almost everywhere they are in unnecessary and ineffective bondage. This is a revolutionary tocsin, but it is more restrained than ringing pronouncements that men have only to break the chains of bondage. A great deal more, in point of fact, requires doing; and the doing requires a moral discipline and technical awareness beyond that of a simple call for unshackling man in organizations.
>
> This study details how men can be more free in organizations, but it has no vision of the end of the particularly human condition, the tension between the self and the social order. Freedom is not viewed as "free and easy," then. Rather, the emphasis is upon freedom as "free, responsible, and responsive."[22]

The words above are the same as in the earlier book, but their usage here is different. The earlier book, at best, could *describe* alternative ways of organizing work *that have existed at various worksites*. This book, at best, can suggest the ways in which a specific structuring of work *can be realized at specific worksites*. The difference is enormous.

ROBERT T. GOLEMBIEWSKI
Athens, Georgia

---

21. Robert T. Golembiewski, *Men, Management, and Morality* (New York: McGraw-Hill Book Co., 1965). For a kindred and broader work, see George E. Berkley, *The Administrative Revolution: Notes on the Passing of the Organization Man* (Englewood Cliffs, N.J.: Prentice Hall, 1971).
22. *Ibid.*, p. 7.

15

Some Orienting Perspectives

Part I. Some Orienting Perspectives

A. THE LABORATORY APPROACH
TO LEARNING:
SCHEMA OF A METHOD

This and the following section provide a primer on the laboratory approach to learning. Their focus is at once commonplace and complex. That is, this section develops the initial complexities in the commonplace events of establishing contacts between human beings, as we go about making a livelihood or just living. That complexity is both wonderful and awesome. It is wonderful in its common intricacies and awesome in relation to the infrequent sophistication with which Everyman copes with those intricacies.

The primer on the laboratory approach in this section attempts to work toward the goals of increasing the effectiveness and richness of life for individuals in their organizations. While the approach is easily sketched, its execution is subtle. The initial subsection below briefly describes and illustrates the laboratory approach. Two subsequent subsections will elaborate on this first-order description and illustration, the first by detailing some intended consequences of the laboratory approach, and the second by sketching some of its basic dynamics.

1. SOME OVERALL FEATURES:
LEARNING HOW TO LEARN

The first step in the implementation of the goal of providing an introductory overview of the laboratory approach will focus on four perspectives on the theme "learning how to learn." Four major characteristics of the approach will first be sketched, followed by a brief illustration of the laboratory approach in action. In addition, two basic processes of the approach will be detailed. Finally, the range of target phenomena within the scope of the laboratory approach will be outlined.

a. Four Characteristics of the Laboratory Approach: Some Initial Features of Learning How to Learn

Four characteristics suggest how the laboratory approach is oriented toward helping individuals "learn how to learn." *First,* the approach basically is an educational strategy for learning and inquiry. In this sense, the laboratory approach prescribes how a person goes about investigating and understanding complex social and psychological realities. Chris Argyris describes the several emphases that distinguish the laboratory approach in these terms:

> The primary reason for the creation of laboratory education was to help human beings to deal more effectively with complex human relationships and problems. As such, laboratory education shares the same goals with many other types of education. What distinguishes laboratory education from most other education is its basic assumptions concerning the process of education. The traditional educational methods primarily emphasize substance, rationality, the inappropriateness of feelings, direction and control by the teacher, and so on. Laboratory education assumes that these emphases are not adequate by themselves. New ones need to be added such as the importance of maintaining the effectiveness of the learning group, the admission of all data that are relevant, including feelings, and the enlargement of responsibility by giving the students greater direction and control over their education.[1]

The emphases on feelings, group maintenance, and learner control, then, paramountly characterize the learning strategy that is the laboratory approach.

Second, the laboratory approach directs attention to a very special focus for learning and inquiry, the experiences of the learners themselves. Thus much traditional learning is centered "out there," as in subject matter like geometry which is in several senses external to the learner. In contrast, the focus of the laboratory approach is "in here," on what goes on within and between the learners themselves. The learning derivable from the laboratory approach is at once potentially threaten-

1. Chris Argyris, "On the Future of Laboratory Education," *Journal of Applied Behavioral Science,* Vol. 3 (April, 1967), p. 153.

ing and rewarding. One can fail to understand geometry, and make it all right. Failure to develop an increasing understanding of self is likely to have harsher consequences.

Third, the laboratory approach seeks to focus on the "in here" of interpersonal and intergroup relations in several very specific ways for quite discrete purposes. Section B below will take a thorough look at these ways and purposes, but several key words will make the point with sufficient force for present purposes. The key words for the laboratory approach are: attitudes, values, and skills. That is, the laboratory approach seeks to encourage certain attitudes about interpersonal and intergroup relations, and it also attempts to induce respect for certain values that should guide the relations of men with their fellows. Moreover, the laboratory approach provides experience with a range of behavioral skills consistent with these attitudes and values.

Fourth, the laboratory approach tends to emphasize learning in social contexts. The general goal is the creation of a society of learners whose combined resources can encourage and enrich the learning of individual members. Such learning communities can facilitate inquiry in a variety of ways. These include developing an atmosphere congenial to search and experimentation, generating emotional support for the efforts of individuals, and providing enthusiasm when a learner succeeds or offering encouragement when he can only lay claim to struggle. In addition, a learning community permits vicarious learning. That is, an individual can identify aspects of himself in others and profit from observing the learning attempts of others. The progression is something like this. I see aspect X of myself in Jim. In Jim, X leads to certain problems, such as his rejection by others. I wonder if X in me has the same effects. And if so, what can I do about it?

b. A Cameo of the Laboratory Approach in Action: Bob and His Work Team

These four features leave many gaps in understanding which must be tolerated as this volume unfolds, but note here that the laboratory approach can generate powerful and involving learning experiences about interpersonal and intergroup relations. Some sense of this power and involvement in learning can be suggested by, in effect, looking in on a group that is learning how to learn via the laboratory approach. The learning group is in fact composed of the members of a work team who are trying to improve their functioning on the job. The main speaker is Bob, an individual who was "drowning in responsibility" at work and who was so distant from his colleagues that they reported difficulty communicating with him. And Bob himself had begun to talk and act as if his productive life, and even enjoyable living, were over for him. His colleagues learned something about the man Bob, and he in turn learned something about them, when he talked about how "I saw myself inside . . . a loneliness." An observer provides this report of a brief sequence:

The room was still. "It's like being out on my boat, alone, surrounded by the sea. I go out at night when it is pitch black, with only the moon on the water to light the way.
. . . "I have a fine, sturdy craft," he said proudly. "It's sixteen foot, fully equipped, and I know what to expect of her. I take her out sixty-five miles—that's our limit."
Some people in the group shuddered. It was a big risk in a small boat.
"Don't think that I'm an old fool for taking her out so far," Bob said. "Some crackpot. I know what she'll do. I've tested her, first 10 miles, then 25 miles, then 35 . . . 45 . . . 55 . . . then 65. No more, no less. Exactly 65 miles—our point of no return. Once I took my wife out. It was quiet and dark. She was frightened. I said, 'Don't worry, honey, I know what I'm doing. I've figured everything out to the last detail. I'm master out here.' She calmed down, but I never took her out again. I go alone. I've never taken anyone else on my boat but her, that one time —and I never will."
Some people were sitting on the floor by their chairs, listening to his loneliness and courage, like children gathered at a story-teller's feet, urging him to go on.
"Don't think I wasn't frightened when I first went out. It's dark and quiet, and the only sound is the water splashing against the side of the boat. A clear, cool spray hits my face. All around me darkness. Nothing . . , At first the sea is rough, but then—far out—the sea is calm. I'm not frightened anymore. 25 miles—I'm following the stars. 35 miles—the moon glistens on the water. 45 miles—a fish jumps out of the sea—I'm startled! . . . It's quiet again. 55 miles—I can feel the excite-ment in me. I'm almost there—65 miles. I made it. I stand up in the boat and stare into the darkness, then up to the sky. Some-thing surges over me. I throw my arms open wide and scream into the darkness. . . . I wait . . . listen . . . Nobody hears me."
People were crying for the lonely old man. There was the look of peace on Bob's face and slowly, somehow, the loneliness was leaving. He looked young, strong.
Softly, I said, "Do you realize you've taken us with you? You've given us the privilege of being the first on your boat."
People said, "Thank you, Bob." "You're a poet." "You've

got great courage." "I could listen to you all night." "I've never known what a wonderful person you are."

Jim asked, "How old are you, Bob?"

"Forty-nine," Bob replied.

Jim exclaimed, "Is that all! You've been acting like you're an old man—like your life's over, like your career with the company was finished. You've even looked old."

Jack said, "You're a young, powerful person, Bob. Look at yourself."

Bob's smile was young. He seemed to be overwhelmed with the adulation of the group—with the love that came by letting people in. . . .[2]

c. Two Basic Processes of the Laboratory Approach: Feedback and Disclosure

Two basic processes—feedback and disclosure—help generate much of the impact of learning sequences such as the powerful touching of persons just illustrated. Complex definitions are not necessary for present purposes. Feedback refers to information we give to others about themselves; and disclosure involves telling something about ourselves to others. Greater subtlety in these definitions will be introduced later.

The Jo-Hari Window[3] in Figure 1 provides a convenient vehicle for demonstrating the centrality of the two processes. The Window divides all interpersonal and intergroup reality into one of four cells, depending upon whether the datum is known or unknown to the Self or to Others. If there is something about me or my behavior that is known to others but not to me, for example, in that regard it can be said that I have a blind spot. The more blind spots I have, the larger is my Blind Area, and the more difficulty people will have in relating to me. I may think myself a great raconteur, for example, while others perceive me as a boor. The relational problems are more or less obvious. I will be puzzled when I am not invited to parties by people I am convinced find me an attractive conversationalist. Still others initially will be frustrated that I do not pick up their signals that I should modify my behaviors. Sooner or later, no doubt, even the long-suffering will give me up as too far out of touch with them to bother with over the long run.

Elementally, the aim of the laboratory approach is to increase the size of the Public Arena, and the emphasis below is on the rationale for such enlargement, as well as on strategies for achieving it. The rationale for

2. Arthur H. Kuriloff and Stuart Atkins, "T-Group for a Work Team," *Journal of Applied Behavioral Science*, Vol. 2 (January, 1966), pp. 84–85.
3. Joseph Luft, *Group Processes* (Palo Alto, Cal.: National Press Books, 1963), pp. 10–15.

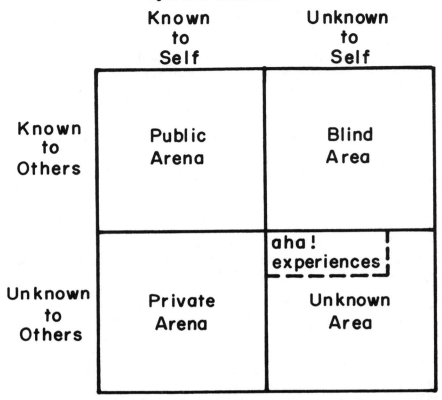

Figure 1. The Jo-Hari Window

Source: Based on Joseph Luft, *Group Processes: An Introduction to Group Dynamics* (Palo Alto, Cal.: National Press Books, 1963), pp. 10–15.

enlarging the Public Arena is direct: it permits individuals to isolate major areas of concern with dispatch and efficiency, which raises the probability of successful problem-solving. To the degree that the Public Arena is cramped and narrow, individuals will be restricted in solving interpersonal and intergroup problems so that they remain solved. The strategies for enlarging the Public Arena require more attention. These strategies include:

- aha! phenomena, or flashes of insight
- reducing the size of the Blind Area by giving feedback
- reducing the size of the Private Arena by self-disclosure

Aha! Phenomena, or Reducing the Unknown Area

The Public Arena can be enlarged by flashes of insight that illuminate for both Self and Others material previously in the Unknown Area.

These aha! phenomena can be the specific targets of psychoanalysis and the various psychotherapies, which seek the genetic roots of severe emotional disorders in experiences that an individual has suppressed into his unconscious mind. Somewhat similar learning opportunities can occur in the laboratory approach, when the individual assembles data of which he is aware at the conscious or preconscious levels and "puts it all together."

The case of a minister in a volunteer agency provides an example of an aha! experience. He and his colleagues met to do some work on their interpersonal relationships before beginning a new project, and, almost from the start, the minister was locked in intense conflict with a new female staff member. All were surprised by the constant attacks of the minister, such behavior being decidedly out of character for him. But the minister's colleagues encouraged him to work through his relationship with the woman and were ever alert to remind him "there you go again" when his attacks resumed. The minister himself was surprised, puzzled, and not a little ashamed of what he was doing. And he was unnerved because he realized the woman provided little provocation. Early one morning on arising, he had an aha! experience. The woman, he realized, reminded him of a parishioner from his early ministry. The other woman had created a major dilemma for the young minister: she demanded his wife and daughter in a lesbian relationship, and threatened suicide if the minister did not assent. He did not; and she did. The minister's anger and resentment toward this early parishioner apparently lurked within him, unresolved these many years, to be directed at the new staff member, who, he reported, bore a striking resemblance to his young parishioner. The minister was left with a major question. How many other women in the past had also served as surrogates for the suicide victim, meeting a need which neither they nor the minister were aware of? The insight would help him manage such situations in the future, he hoped.

Reducing the Blind Area

Fortunately, increasing the Public Arena does not depend on massive insights alone. Consider the approach of reducing the size of the Blind Area, of eliminating a person's blind spots. Feedback is the basic vehicle here, as Figure 1A suggests. We can decrease the blind spots of others by telling them how we perceive their behavior. In the learning episode above, for example, Jim gave Bob some direct feedback. "You've been acting like you're an old man—like your life's over, like your career with the company was finished. You've even looked old." Feedback is the process by which Self learns how he appears to Other. And feedback is one thing we cannot do for ourselves, no matter what our skills and resources. Our fellow men must help us intricately adjust our actions and

25

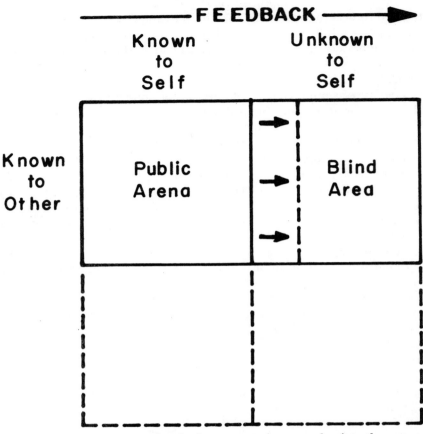

Figure 1A. Simplified Role of Feedback

behaviors, as they report on whether our actions are having the consequences for others that we intend.

The bare illustration above must suffice here, but giving effective feedback is so important that extensive attention will be given to this art form later in this book. A set of ground rules for giving feedback will be described and illustrated at that point.

Reducing the Private Arena

The Public Arena also can be increased by decreasing the Private Arena, as Figure 1B implies. Here disclosure is the vehicle. In the learning episode above, again, Bob is disclosing much about himself to colleagues on his work team. He talks about his loneliness and his great need for human contact, in the context of his efforts to prove himself. Recall his struggle against the sea, alone, in going as far out to sea as his craft would permit. And then when he reaches his limit, he is starkly reminded of what it means to be so alone and so far from others, whether at sea or in everyday life. "I made it. I stand up in the boat and stare into the darkness, then up to the sky," he exults. But solitary triumph has its costs, and Bob cannot totally bear them. "Something surges over me. I throw my arms open wide and scream into the darkness. . . . I wait . . . listen . . . Nobody hears me."

Figure 1B. Simplified Role of Disclosure

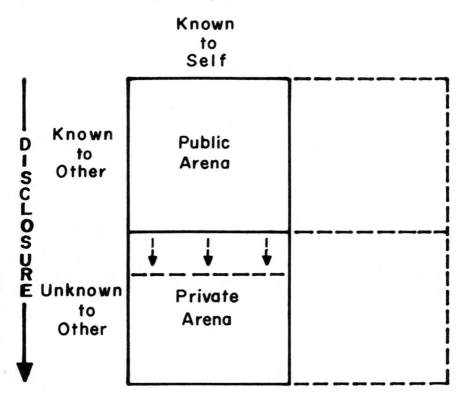

Extended attention also will be given later to this second basic process of the laboratory approach, but two cautions are appropriate at this point. Not every disclosure is useful, be it noted. Some kinds of disclosure can inhibit the development of relationships, for example. At a minimum, the timing and relevance of a disclosure are critical. Too much disclosure too early can be as damaging as too little, too late. Consider the announcement by a very junior executive at a meeting announced as a first step toward more honest work relationships between the invitees. He was a homosexual, the junior executive revealed as soon as the meeting convened, apparently to show his commitment to greater honesty with his work colleagues. The announcement was not particularly helpful in improving relationships at work. The disclosure came very early, and its relevance to the matter at hand was questionable in any case.

It may be useful to counterbalance the dramatic quality of the examples of feedback and disclosure. Be it seriously noted, therefore, that neither feedback nor disclosure need be accompanied by figurative cymbal clashes. "I don't understand what you just said," for example, also is a piece of disclosure. And at various times, that piece of disclosure can be highly relevant, even critical.

d. The Scope of the Laboratory Approach: Some Boundaries

Whether dealing with dramatic or everyday events (and the difference between the two can be deceiving and vague), the laboratory approach extends the two basic processes of feedback and disclosure into broad areas of life. Table 1 should be self-explanatory in its essentials, although later discussion will add perspective and depth to this skeletal description. Note here, then, only that the table provides three kinds of data. It elaborates some basic goals of the laboratory approach, by way of providing some perspective on the overall goal of aiding the development of more humane relationships between more effective human beings. Moreover, Table 1 outlines some common target data for the laboratory approach. The list is not exhaustive, of course, but it should illustrate the phenomena that are of central concern in the approach. Finally, Table 1 indicates three kinds of learning which can be aided by the laboratory approach.

2. SOME INTENDED CONSEQUENCES: CONFRONTING AS THE BASIC GOAL

Learning how to learn, after the model of the laboratory approach, implies a tension between two needs. Perhaps dramatically, this tension can be viewed as a contrast of the Need to Know and the Need for Privacy. To be effective and adaptive, we need to know about our blind spots, and we need to tell others how we perceive them. In short, we need to confront and to be confronted. Oppositely, we also need to preserve some sense of a private self, a domain that may be all the more precious because it is the basic existential proof that we are in an ultimate sense unique beings who control some portion of our lives. Diversely, the tension ebbs and flows from situation to situation, but it is seldom absent from the human drama.

The tension between the Need to Know and the Need for Privacy is

Table 1. Some General Areas of Concern in the Laboratory Approach

Basic Goals for Outcomes	Kinds of Target Data	Kinds of Learning
Laboratory programs enhance authenticity in human relations by seeking to increase:	The focus is on public, here-and-now data, as they are experienced. These data include:	The laboratory approach generates three basic kinds of learning by participants, to varying degrees in individual cases:
■ individual awareness about self and others	■ the specific *structures* developed, such as the leadership rank order	■ learning that is largely cognitive and oriented toward techniques, as for effective committee functioning
■ acceptance of others	■ the *processes* of group life, with special attention to getting a group started, keeping it going, and then experiencing its inevitable death	■ learning that highlights deep emotional needs of which the participant was variously aware and that shows how such needs can be satisfied
■ acceptance of self		
Laboratory programs seek to free individuals to be more effective while they are more themselves, both as persons and as members of organizations, by seeking to enhance the development of:		
■ sensitivity to self and others	■ the specific *emotional reactions* of members to one another's behavior and to their experiences	■ learning that demonstrates the significance of "unfinished business" and illustrates how and with what effects the press against the consciousness of such matters may be relieved
■ ability to diagnose complex social situations and to conceptualize experience in behavioral science terms	■ the varying and diverse *styles* or *modes* of individual and group behavior, as in "fighting" or "fleeing" some issue that has overwhelmed group members	
■ action skills and attitudes required to capitalize on increased sensitivity and enhanced diagnostic skills		

perhaps best illustrated by personal relationships in an urban setting. Relationships there—as contrasted with small-town life—are based on free selection and common interests, with proximity being a minor consideration. As a result, the urban apartment dweller may go for years without developing a close acquaintance with his physical neighbors, or even perhaps without knowing their names. This does not mean that urban dwellers have no need of others. Rather, they have to protect substantial privacy in order to really develop those selected relationships they need just as much as small-town inhabitants do. Otherwise, they would be swamped with inevitably shallow and unsatisfying relationships. Harvey Cox explains:

> Urban man . . . must have more or less impersonal relationships with most of the people with whom he comes in contact precisely in order to choose certain friendships to nourish and cultivate. This selectivity can best be symbolized perhaps by the unplugged telephone or the unlisted number. A person does not request an unlisted number to cut down on the depth of his relationships. Quite the opposite; he does so to guard and deepen the worthwhile relationships he has against being dissolved in the deluge of messages that would come if one were

open on principle and on an equal basis to anyone who tried to get through. . . . Those we want to know have our number; others do not. We are free to use the switchboard without being victimized by its infinite possibilities.[4]

The purpose here is to begin developing the position that managing this tension between the Need to Know and the Need for Privacy is the ultimate human concern. That is, the option of neglecting the tension between the two basic needs is not really open. The only alternatives are to be more or less effective in balancing the two needs in opposition.

a. The Essence of the Laboratory Approach: Toward Competence through Regenerative Systems

The laboratory approach in its essentials deals with balancing the Need to Know and the Need for Privacy. The point will be supported first by considering a simple interaction model of four variables, two combinations of which may be called "regenerative" and "degenerative."[5] Figure 2 suggests the sense of two self-fulfilling systems of interaction, defined roughly in terms of high versus low profiles of four variables. For simplicity, Figure 2 refers only to the interaction system that develops between any two people. Commonsense understandings of risk and trust will suffice for now, but openness and owning must be distinguished. For one can be open without owning; and one can own up to a fib and hence not be open on that point. For example, Jim may tell me that some of my friends regard some of my behavior as reprehensible. If Jim is one of my friends, and if he feels that my behavior is reprehensible, then Jim is being open about that attitude, but he is not owning it. He lets me judge which of my friends he is referring to.

In the degenerative pattern, one cannot win for losing. Consider the husband and wife whose relations are degenerative. During a long business trip away from home, the husband has second thoughts about the relationship. He decides to take a risk, to trust that his wife will understand if he openly talks about and sincerely owns his true feelings toward her. On the way home from the airport, the husband buys an extravagant bouquet of flowers to help begin a new era of good feelings. His wife has not gone through the same thoughts and feelings as her husband, however, and she perceives the flowers in the context of her low trust and high risk. "Well, what have you been up to now?" she

---

4. Harvey Cox, *The Secular City* (New York: Macmillan Co., 1965). p. 41. Copyright © Harvey Cox, 1965, 1966.
5. The model is a synthetic one, but supported by a variety of research. See, for example, the relationship of risk and trust sketched in John Lillibridge and Sven Lundstedt, "Some Initial Evidence for an Interpersonal Risk Theory," *Journal of Psychology*, Vol. 63 (1967), pp. 119–28.

reflexively and bitingly greets her husband. This increases the risk perceived by the husband and discourages the owning and openness he had planned on. "Why, you bitch," he blurts out. And so the best of intentions were interpreted so as to confirm a degenerative pattern. As was said, you cannot win for losing in degenerative systems.

A similar bouquet no doubt would have had more pleasant consequences, given a somewhat more healthy interaction system. In a real sense, regenerative systems increase the probability that two interacting persons cannot lose for winning. This is meant in two senses. First, there is less likelihood that misunderstandings and misperceptions will de-

Figure 2. A Simple Model of Two Systems of Interaction

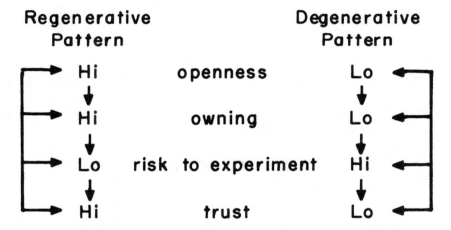

velop in regenerative systems, trivial events often being the materials out of which major impasses develop. Second, even if major issues do develop between a pair of individuals interacting in a regenerative system, the prognosis is still good. At worst, the trust is there to confront the issues, and the risk of doing so is low enough to discourage the continued festering of the issue in the closedness of silence.

Two summary points can be made. The laboratory approach attempts to provide experience and to develop skills for heightening regenerative systems, as well as for reversing degenerative ones. Moreover, the existence of a regenerative system depends upon the careful and conscious managing of the tension between the Need to Know and the Need for Privacy.

To extend the argument an important step, regenerative systems are critical aids to individuals as they seek to establish and augment their

31

interpersonal competence. This is no small matter. Directly, the drive to substantial and growing interpersonal competence is a major determinant of the emotional health of individuals. To hurry a patent conclusion, then, the laboratory approach is where it's at in significant senses in the matter of interpersonal and intergroup relationships. That significance motivates the use of the laboratory approach to find more fulfilling balances of the Need to Know and the Need for Privacy.

Once asserted hurriedly, however, two aspects of this argument urging the centrality of the laboratory approach can usefully be dealt with in more detail. First, a mini-theory of trust will suggest its complex role in regenerative systems and will also help establish the specific senses in which the quality of interpersonal and intergroup life can be affected in critical ways by high-trust versus low-trust conditions. Then the relevance of regenerative systems to emotional health and interpersonal competence will be outlined.

A Mini-Theory of Trust and Its Consequences

The dynamics of regenerative systems are usefully elaborated by a focus on interpersonal trust, one of the four variables in the two basic illustrative models introduced above. The choice is not whimsical, for at least two basic reasons. First, the centrality of trust in helping, or growthful, relations has long been emphasized.[6] Second, recent empirical research helps establish some of the specific connections implied by the centrality of trust in various theoretical formulations.[7]

The role of trust can be suggested briefly. Overall, as Jack R. Gibb convincingly argues,[8] low trust induces defensive behavior, which is perhaps the basic block to any learning. That is, learning or growth depends essentially on acceptance of self and others, and defensiveness inhibits that acceptance. To a similar point, Carl Rogers concluded that initial and continuing trust plays a major role in a variety of significant outcomes for growth or learning, as in more rapid intellectual development, enhanced originality, and so on.[9] A variety of separate studies can be marshaled in support of this efficacy of high trust, whether between

---

6. See, especially, Carl R. Rogers, "The Interpersonal Relationship: The Core of Guidance," *Harvard Educational Review,* Vol. 32 (Fall, 1962), pp. 416–29.
7. Frank Friedlander, "The Primacy of Trust as a Facilitator of Further Group Accomplishment," *Journal of Applied Behavioral Science,* Vol. 6 (October, 1970), pp. 387–400; and Dale Zand, "Trust and Managerial Effectiveness," *Administrative Science Quarterly* (in press).
8. Jack R. Gibb, "Climate for Trust Formation," in Leland P. Bradford, Jack R. Gibb, and Kenneth D. Benne (eds.), *T-Group Theory and Laboratory Method* (New York: John Wiley & Sons, 1964), pp. 279–309.
9. Carl R. Rogers, *On Becoming a Person* (Boston: Houghton Mifflin Co., 1961), esp. pp. 39–58.

therapist and client,[10] members of either problem-solving groups or of sensitivity training groups,[11] or parent and child.[12] Recently, Dale Zand has successfully extended the test for the centrality of trust to managerial effectiveness, in a very useful and revealing way.[13]

Zand's theoretical network is sketched in Figure 3, especially because it breaks new ground while it is clearly consistent with work having a long developmental history. Basically, Zand develops a fourfold concept of trust, drawing on the contributions of Morton Deutsch[14] and Jack Gibb,[15] especially. Zand distinguishes the *intention* of a sender, as well as his *behavior*. The model thus admits the commonplace slippage between intent and action. The receiving actor, as it were, at once *expects* a certain level of trustworthiness from the sender and also *perceives* a specific level of trustworthiness in various behaviors. The possible richness encompassed by these components of the model should be patent. For example, a low expectation about trustworthiness might lead to a congruent perception of the sender's behavior and intention, even though the sender and other observers might read high trustworthiness into both intention and behavior of the sender. In this regard, also, the model seems faithful to major features of social life.

Further, Zand's model provides that the character of the problem-situation involving sender and receiver is relevant. Specifically, some issues involve a high degree of what Zand calls "objective uncertainty," and it is on such issues that the effects of high trust versus low trust are likely to be most pronounced. Zand notes that low trust adds a "social uncertainty" to whatever degree of objective uncertainty exists in a problem-situation. The implied dilemma merely requires statement. It is precisely problem-situations with a high objective uncertainty that tend to induce low trust. So nature is not kind in this regard, and applied behavioral science must labor to increase trust so as to facilitate effective responses to situations with a high objective uncertainty.

Figure 3 also sketches a number of major consequences that might be expected of high-trust conditions where the problem-situation has a substantial objective uncertainty. Those consequences clearly touch much that is central in social and organizational life.

Two points about Zand's model deserve special note. First, in a clever

10. Melvin J. Seeman, "Counselor Judgments of Therapeutic Process and Outcome," in Carl R. Rogers and R. F. Dymond (eds.), *Psychotherapy and Personality Change* (Chicago: University of Chicago Press, 1954), pp. 99–108.
11. Friedlander, *op. cit.*
12. Alfred Lee Baldwin, Joan Kalhorn, and Fay H. Breese, "Patterns of Parent Behavior," *Psychological Monograph*, Vol. 58, No. 268 (1945), pp. 1–75.
13. Zand, *op. cit.*
14. Morton Deutsch, "Cooperation and Trust: Some Theoretical Notes," in Marshall R. Jones (ed.), *Nebraska Symposium on Motivation* (Lincoln: University of Nebraska Press, 1962), pp. 275–319.
15. Gibb, "Climate for Trust Formation."

Figure 3. A Schema of the Components and Consequences of Interpersonal Trust

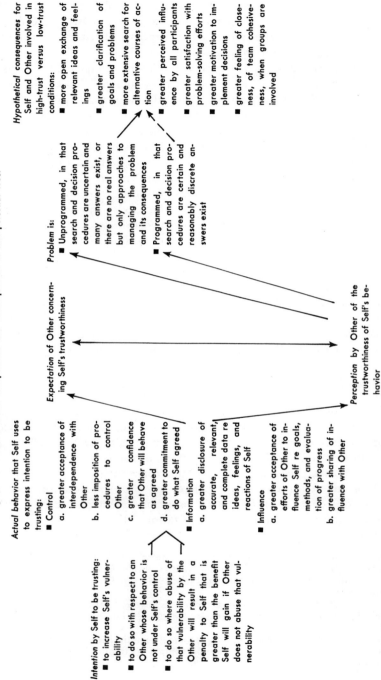

Intention by Self to be trusting:
- to increase Self's vulnerability
- to do so with respect to an Other whose behavior is not under Self's control
- to do so where abuse of that vulnerability by the Other will result in a penalty to Self that is greater than the benefit Self will gain if Other does not abuse that vulnerability

Actual behavior that Self uses to express intention to be trusting:
- **Control**
  a. greater acceptance of interdependence with Other
  b. less imposition of procedures to control Other
  c. greater confidence that Other will behave as agreed
  d. greater commitment to do what Self agreed
- **Information**
  a. greater disclosure of accurate, relevant, and complete data re ideas, feelings, and reactions of Self
- **Influence**
  a. greater acceptance of efforts of Other to influence Self re goals, methods, and evaluation of progress
  b. greater sharing of influence with Other

Expectation of Other concerning Self's trustworthiness

Perception by Other of the trustworthiness of Self's behavior

Problem is:
- **Unprogrammed,** in that search and decision procedures are uncertain and many answers exist, or there are no real answers but only approaches to managing the problem and its consequences
- **Programmed,** in that search and decision procedures are certain and reasonably discrete answers exist

Hypothetical consequences for Self and Other involved in high-trust versus low-trust conditions:
- more open exchange of relevant ideas and feelings
- greater clarification of goals and problems
- more extensive search for alternative courses of action
- greater perceived influence by all participants
- greater satisfaction with problem-solving efforts
- greater motivation to implement decisions
- greater feeling of closeness, of team cohesiveness, when groups are involved

Source: Based upon Dale Zand, "Trust and Managerial Effectiveness," *Administrative Science Quarterly* (in press).

Note: ——— indicates dominant relationship
- - - - indicates less-dominant relationship

simulation, high-trust and low-trust conditions were successfully induced. The two conditions generated patterns of consequences that were sharply different, as judged by the chi-square test. The high-trust condition generated consequences like those sketched in Figure 3, on all nine variables that Zand employed. The low-trust condition generated opposed consequences in all cases. That is, the low-trust condition encouraged significantly less open exchange of relevant ideas and feelings, and so on. Of major significance, the results were exactly the same in data from two sources: self-reports from the actors in the simulation, and reports from observers who were unaware of which specific actors had been exposed to high-trust instructions and which had experienced the low-trust induction.

The second point is that Zand's model clearly shares substantial conceptual ground with the regenerative/degenerative models above. For example, Zand notes the "spiral reinforcement" feature of his model, which is similar to the self-heightening features attributed to both regenerative and degenerative models. For example, assume the interaction in Zand's model of a high-trust sender and a low-trust receiver. Because of his low expectations about the trustworthiness of the sender, the receiver is likely to misperceive the trustworthiness reflected in the behavior of the sender, and he is very likely to consistently read malice into the intentions of the sender. The sender not only tends to get that message; in addition, he might be concerned enough about misperceptions of his behavior and misjudgments of his intentions to punish the receiver. As sender becomes defensive, or hostile, or noncommunicative, clearly he is also drawn into contributing to the intensity of the low-trust condition. This is the essence of spiral reinforcement. One can't win for losing, as was noted earlier. High-trust conditions trend toward opposite consequences, as should be clear from the dynamics of Zand's model as well as from the regenerative model.

Regenerative Systems: Emotional Health and Interpersonal Competence

A second perspective on regenerative systems can be gained by tracing their interactions with emotional health, in broad terms, and with interpersonal competence, more specifically. The development by Argyris[16] of Robert White's[17] basic concept will be relied on heavily. The concept of interpersonal competence is a central one for the laboratory approach, related closely to its goal of heightening or inducing regenerative systems between individuals. To begin suggesting this close relationship, White

---

16. Chris Argyris, *Intervention Theory and Method* (Reading, Mass.: Addison-Wesley Publishing Co., 1970), pp. 16–20, 38–39.
17. Robert W. White (ed.), *The Study of Lives* (New York: Atherton Press, 1963), pp. 72–93.

defined interpersonal competence as the "capacity, fitness, or ability" of an individual to carry on those transactions that result in the individual maintaining himself, growing, and flourishing. White also argues persuasively that interpersonal competence is a basic human concern. Argyris develops this conceptual beachhead by proposing three measures of interpersonal competence. Interpersonal competence tends to increase, Argyris proposes,[18]

- as one's awareness of relevant factors increases
- as the problems are solved in such a way that they remain solved
- as the solutions involve a minimal deterioration of the problem-solving process

The relevance, if not the necessity, of a regenerative system for maintaining and extending interpersonal competence in the Argyrian sense should be patent. That relevance can therefore be sketched briefly. A regenerative system will help insure that relevant factors are considered in problem-solving, especially as those factors involve feedback or disclosure from other persons, as they often do. Moreover, a regenerative interaction system between individuals will help assure that problems are solved in such ways that they remain solved, as by taking into account the preferences of relevant parties or by providing feedback early in the implementation of any solution should it prove to have unanticipated consequences. Finally, a regenerative system will raise the probability that individuals are content that their inputs have been made and heard. Such a heightened probability can help maintain the viability of a problem-solving process. Even an objectively correct solution, that is, may prove a failure if it is arrived at or implemented in ways that strain the processes or persons through which subsequent solutions will have to be made. This is the case even where an objectively correct solution exists, and there are very many cases in which one does not exist. Particularly in interpersonal relations, in sum, it is often the specific way you skin a particular cat that really counts.

The relevance of regenerative systems, and thus the relevance of the laboratory approach, to the development of interpersonal competence also can be suggested in another way. That is, there are ample reasons to imply a strong relationship between interpersonal competence or effectiveness and four conditions:

- self-acceptance
- confirmation
- essentiality
- psychological success

18. Chris Argyris, "Explorations in Interpersonal Competence," *Journal of Applied Behavioral Science*, Vol. 1 (January, 1965), p. 59.

Self-acceptance clearly relates to the balance of regenerative/degenerative systems that an individual has developed. Specifically, self-acceptance refers to the confidence that an individual has in himself and to the degree that he regards himself highly. Self-acceptance depends on knowledge about self, then, and the clarity of that knowledge will be influenced in significant senses by the quality of the interaction systems in which an individual operates.

The more regenerative are the interaction systems within which an individual operates on balance, to make a crude extension, the greater the individual's probable interpersonal competence. The point holds in two major senses. That is, a regenerative system implies that valid information will be available to parties in interaction, and each needs that information to know how the Other sees him. More significantly, a regenerative system affects two crucial probabilities. It reduces the probability that feedback or disclosure will be perceived as hurtful or punitive. Moreover, a regenerative system increases the probability that feedback or disclosure will lead to the development of new values or attitudes or behaviors. The high trust and low risk to experimentation in regenerative systems are the two factors which most directly raise these two crucial probabilities. Low trust and high risk can make any feedback or disclosure pointless and even punishing.

In conclusion, it is not always easy to learn how others see us, to accept ourselves as others see us, or to change ourselves in ways that make our perception by others more acceptable to us. And degenerative systems complicate all three of these paramountly human concerns.

Confirmation of an individual occurs to the degree that others experience him as he sees himself. To the degree that an individual sees himself as different than others experience him, his interpersonal competence is likely to be reduced. The rationale is both clear and compelling. Such an individual is not likely to be effective in gaining his objectives, or at least in gaining them for the reasons he expects. In a more fundamental sense, an individual who is more or less consistently disconfirmed may experience major problems associated with who he is or, to say much the same thing, with how he is perceived by others. The two major alternatives for coping with consistent disconfirmation are difficult to sustain. Thus, an individual can deny the validity of the disconfirming cues, or he can accept his ineffectiveness in revealing himself to others as he intends. The implicit conclusion merely requires stating. Regenerative systems are important vehicles via which an individual can either gain this critical confirmation or can begin working to reduce the degree of disconfirmation he experiences.

The quality of an individual's interaction system also affects confirmation in a more subtle and insidious way. In degenerative systems, an individual may experience a kind of bogus confirmation. This is perhaps even worse than getting confirmation from others concerning aspects of himself which an individual prefers to forget. Others may report they perceive the individual as a poet, for example, and he indeed sees himself as a souped-up if undiscovered Keats. In fact, these others really feel he is clumsy even in ordinary conversation, and a disaster with ballpoint in hand. But the others do not feel free to be open enough to own such a sentiment. And the individual may scribble on, uninformed by the kind of reactions he needs, or suspects, or may even want.

Essentiality refers to the condition under which an individual is able to express his central needs as well as to utilize his central abilities. The very term implies the sense of the concept. "What am I doing involved in this?" is one way we can express feelings of a low degree of essentiality. The underlying concept of the personality is one of many layers, with preferences or abilities or values somehow ranked in order. Continued need to activate low preferences will induce feelings of low essentiality. The common vernacular refers to "scraping the bottom of the barrel," I believe.

Regenerative systems clearly would be more likely to induce feelings of essentiality than would a degenerative system of interaction. In the latter, for example, an individual who preferred to be collaborative might find himself unavoidably relating with another with a narrowly competitive style. The individual would be caught in a condition of low essentiality. There might be no way to avoid the interaction, and there would be no easy way to improve it. The high risk level in a degenerative system, to illustrate, could inhibit raising the issue of the unsatisfactory pairing of the collaborative style preferred by the one person with the win/lose competitive style he actually experienced. This describes a vicious circularity, which is demeaning in an ultimately human sense.

Psychological success is a complex of the three conditions above, as can be established briefly. It is a function of the degree to which an individual can define his own goals or meaningfully participate in their definition. Responding only to the goals set by others can generate feelings of failure, even when objective successes are achieved. Psychological success is also probable to the degree that goals are related to an individual's central needs, or abilities, or values. In addition, as the individual defines paths to attain his goals, the possibility of psychological success is heightened. Finally, attaining a realistic level of aspiration will induce psychological success. The point applies in two major senses. An aspiration level that is set too high can generate feelings of psychological failure, no matter what the actual performance. One can fail even as he does quite well, that is to say. A level of aspiration that can be attained very comfortably also can generate feelings of failure, it being an "easy piece" in today's cinematographic language, and consequently too available to be motivating over the long run. In fact, the individual may despise himself for succeeding in such a facile way.

Regenerative systems are crucial for inducing the condition of psychological success, it should be clear. Such a system will facilitate an individual setting his own goals or participating in their definition, for example.

The linkages above, in sum, are intended to suggest how the laboratory approach contributes to interpersonal competence, as well as to emotional health. Two idealized and simple systems of interaction were used to help make the point. But the subject matter is as big and complex as the study of man.

b. The Thrust of the Laboratory Approach: Toward Confrontation through Competence

Interpersonal competence, further, is ineluctably linked to confrontation in the logic of the laboratory approach. Some of the interfaces are straightforward. The competent are more able to confront; and successful confrontation contributes to competence. Other aspects of this interfacing are more subtle and need further analysis here.

The sense of this topic will be put down simply first and examined in its particulars later. The laboratory approach basically seeks to increase the incidence of a particular style of behavior—confronting. Confrontation is relatively rare, however, especially because it requires substantial interpersonal competence.

As a first step in building content into these two summary propositions, consider some "new business" between two individuals. Assume the new business is the unexpressed warmth that Joe feels for Jim. How is this new business to be handled? In order, these four modalities are characteristic means of responding to new business:

- pairing
- flight
- fight
- confrontation

The first two modalities are by far the most probable. Unfortunately, these modalities are the least likely to manage the new business. Indeed, all but the last modality can compound the initial business. At the very least, in addition to the initial business, the first three modalities raise questions of the individual's lack of courage and/or competence in facing new business with which he must contend. The "new business" often begets a more complicated bit of "unfinished business."

The generation of unfinished business, which remains as a press against

39

the conscious mind or may even get deeply repressed, is not a trivial matter. Unfinished business is at the heart of herniated interpersonal and intergroup relationships, for reasons that can be sketched briefly. The working concept of unfinished business is that of a burden or excess baggage to which the individual can add and from which he can subtract, and which requires correspondingly variable energies to carry. Common usages suggest the point. "That's a load off my mind," we might say as we give a friend a piece of feedback that we consciously suppressed, that was unfinished business. The greater the energies devoted to unfinished business, crudely, the less energy an individual has to manage his socioemotional life. Hence, the less interpersonally competent he is likely to be. More subtly, unfinished business in the socioemotional realm can become so great that it inhibits rational-technical performance.

Take the four modalities individually. *Pairing* is perhaps the most common way of dealing with new business. Picture an impassioned sales director concluding an announcement of a new program with a request for questions or reactions. No response is forthcoming, and the sales director is left with his own fantasies. No sooner is the audience outside of the meeting room, however, than reactions begin tumbling forth. Friends "pair," they get together to discuss informal reactions. "It'll never work," some say. "A great idea," is the sentiment others share. The sales director gets neither kind of input.

Pairing is at once understandable and perhaps even necessary, but it nevertheless avoids dealing with the new business generated by the request of the sales director. Pairing is especially understandable in degenerative systems, where the risk may be too great for public feedback or disclosure. And pairing may be necessary, as a way of comparing notes or perhaps even of preserving the handhold on sanity inherent in the fact that other people see things in the same terms. The issue avoided, of course, is why the questions and reactions that flowed so easily in the informal pairings were not shared with the sales director when he requested them. And this can cut many ways.

Flight is also a common response to new business. In this modality, the provoking stimulus is somehow avoided. In contrast, pairing deals with the stimulus, but not in the environment within which it was generated.

There are numerous ways to flee. One can observe the provoking stimulus, for example, and consciously choose to suppress it. Less directly, one can misperceive the stimulus to see what one wanted to see instead of what existed. Or, more often, selective perception takes over, and the individual does not respond to stimuli because he has been socialized or conditioned to see only parts of the reality about him. The selective perception of specialists has been much noted with vengeful humor, for example. There is the story of a consultant to a hospital who was

40

touring the wards to learn something of the problems of doctors and nurses. The consultant made some note about a particular person-patient. A doctor corrected him. "You may see a person in that bed," the doctor noted, "but I see a case of myocardial infarction." More or less, we all have trained incapacities that incline us to perceive selectively.

Flight can have much to recommend it under various conditions, in the sense of strategically retreating to fight or confront another day. The interpersonally competent person certainly will have flight responses in his repertoire. Strategic retreats can be both useful and necessary. Just as clearly, however, flight neglects the new business. The especial danger of flight is that the accumulation of such unfinished business can begin to overburden interpersonal systems and perhaps lead to unforeseen blowups between people that apparently derive from the straw that broke the camel's back. This is a classic case of little s and big R, where s stands for stimulus and R refers to response. One after another, s_1, s_2, and s_3 are perceived, but flight is the mode and no overt response is made ($R = 0$). A little r would have been an appropriate response to each little s, but the responses are in a sense "saved up." Their whole often can be far larger than the sum of its parts, as when s_4 triggers a massive R all out of proportion either to that stimulus or to the ones before. Schematically,

$$s_1 \longrightarrow 0$$
$$s_2 \longrightarrow 0$$
$$s_3 \longrightarrow 0$$
$$s_4 \longrightarrow R$$

Such events can leave all parties puzzled. "Now how did that little s_4 lead to that huge R?" is the characteristic question. Unless the parties have the skill and willingness to work backward to put the R in perspective, such sequences can pollute relationships. And individuals will feel a reduced interpersonal competence as minor stimuli unexpectedly lead to massive responses. Better to suffer silence than to risk a verbal explosion, in short. These are clear limitations on the usefulness of the flight response to new business.

Fight is an infrequent mode of dealing with new business. The low incidence of this mode is understandable, even though it may sometimes help clear the air between people. Basically, the approach directly threatens relations and, consequently, this tends to be a last-ditch strategy. The mode implies win/lose competition, which often means that the approach creates as many problems as it solves. If nothing else, the resentment of the loser may be a factor to contend with sooner or later.

41

My own experience generates an example of a more-or-less polite fight response. I was a very-junior faculty member at a prestigious university, only recently arrived on campus, at once confident and unsure. Strolling on the campus one day, a senior faculty member clearly drew a bead on me from a distance and rushed over. "Are you going to the luncheon for Charles de Gaulle, Bob?" he asked. I responded quickly, but I believe I recalled what flashed through my mind beforehand. "What's this guy up to?" I reflected. "He knows that I am not much interested in foreign affairs and, even if I were, as a very-junior faculty person I certainly would not be among the 100 or so guests that at a maximum could be accommodated at the luncheon site." I took an uncharitable tack, responding to his one-upsmanship. "Go to the luncheon, you say," I responded in a way that reflected my irritation and defensiveness. "Well, I'm not sure. It depends on what the main course is." What he valued, in short, I ridiculed. There is no better way to rupture a relationship, especially a new one.

Confrontation, a fourth mode of dealing with new business, is at once quite rare and also the goal of the laboratory approach. The necessary and interacting amalgam is one of personal skills and appropriate environments. In terms of the vocabulary introduced thus far, confrontation requires interpersonal competence and regenerative interaction systems. Moreover, the interpersonally competent person will tend to be successful at developing regenerative systems, and regenerative systems also will contribute to the interpersonal competence of the parties involved in them.

Confrontation has developed quite a recent popular reputation, and the usage here must be sharply distinguished from the confrontations in today's mass media. Negatively, confrontation does not mean defecating in the desk drawer of a university president. Rather, confrontation as used here implies four interacting skills and attitudes in people.

First, the confronting person must "know where he is." That is, he must know what he is thinking or feeling, he must know how he is reacting. In the common vernacular, a confronting person must "be in touch with himself." This assumes certain skills, as well as attitudes that call for the application of such skills as a part of daily life. For most people, at least much of the time, this first requirement for confronting behaviors is well within their normal reach.

Second, confrontation requires that a person know why he is where he is. If he is angry, for example, he needs to know what induced or triggered his anger. More dynamically, the individual needs confidence and experience that he can trace his reactions or thoughts back to some precipitating stimuli, at least in substantial part. If he feels warm and accepting, the same requirement holds. Self-insight and analysis are required, in short. Without such insight and analysis, catharsis may result, but confrontation is unlikely. "I'm angry with you when you make fun of me," is a good enough opener. "There is just something about you that bothers me," is not particularly helpful, however. It is difficult to modify or change "just something," and the common goal of confrontation is to get the Other to modify or intensify or change something.

Third, the confronting person must be able to express where he is, as well as why he is there. In part, personal courage is required. In part, also, regenerative systems are called for. There will be precious little confrontation, in sum, if we have to wait on courageous heroics. Environments must permit, encourage, and even reward confronting behavior. Otherwise it will remain in critically short supply.

Fourth, the person intent on confronting must master a difficult balance. He must be able to achieve the three conditions described immediately above, while permitting and even encouraging others to do the same. The point applies particularly to those in positions of power or authority. They may be able to achieve the first three conditions with ease, while complicating or prohibiting a similar achievement by others. Consider the psychiatrist who allegedly told one of his patients: "Jack, there's something I'd like to tell you. No," he quickly reflected, "I better not. The last patient I did that with ended up committing suicide." Presumably, the psychiatrist knew where he was, why he was there, and he certainly was not inhibited in communicating about those two elements. But his approach, to put it mildly, was not likely to encourage his patient to attempt to achieve the first three conditions for confronting behavior.

Despite the emphasis above on interpersonal confrontation, note in addition that at least two other types of confrontation can be distinguished. Vicariously, first, a person may engage in self-confrontation as he recognizes in others an aspect of himself that he has previously denied or not explicitly acknowledged. Very often, interpersonal confrontations between others will trigger such self-confrontation. Second, situations may generate dilemmas that encourage the individual to take stock of himself and his competencies. Again, interpersonal confrontation may trigger this second variety of self-confrontation. Indeed, interpersonal confrontation may be the situational dilemma that induces stock-taking.

That the thrust of the laboratory approach is toward confrontation through interpersonal competence should give it a particular quality— "a very real toughness," in Sheldon Davis's words—which is too little noted. "In dealing with one another, we will be open, direct, explicit," Davis notes as he develops his view. "Our feelings will be available to one another, and we will try to problem-solve rather than be defensive. These values have within them a very tough way of living—not a soft way." Davis sees too little of this view in the behavioral sciences, which often seem to him to value the building of happy teams of employees who "feel good about things." He prefers concentration on building such relationships between individuals and groups that they "can function well and can zero in quickly on their problems and deal with them rationally, in the very real sense of the word." Davis concludes:

> There is no real growth—there is no real development—in the organization or in the individuals within it if they do not confront and deal directly with their problems. They can get together and share feelings, but if that is all they do, it is merely a catharsis. While this is useful, it has relatively minimal usefulness compared with what can happen if they start to relate differently within the organizational setting around task issues.[19]

3. SOME BASIC DYNAMICS: TWO TYPICAL ILLUSTRATIVE MODELS

It is now possible to get somewhat more specific about the basic dynamics of the laboratory approach, despite the real theoretical elusiveness of our quarry.[20] These dynamics relate to both group and personal development, each of which will be illustrated below by considering a typical developmental model. The examples are chosen from a large set of possible models, presented here as of unusual value in understanding the basic behavioral dynamics of interest to the laboratory approach.

a. Orientations toward Authority and Intimacy: A Model of Group Development or Learning

A particular influential approach to group development focuses on the orientations to authority and intimacy brought to a group by its members. These orientations significantly both shape the style of group development and help determine the effectiveness with which a group evolves into a miniature society whose members are related by ties of

---

19. Sheldon A. Davis, "Organic Problem-Solving Method of Organizational Change," *Journal of Applied Behavioral Science,* Vol. 3 (March, 1967) , pp. 4–5.
20. C. Gratton Kemp observes of the T-Group that it "is an amalgamation of several theories of learning and of behavioral change. At certain stages, . . . it relies upon the association theory of learning. At other times, especially in the initial stages of heightened ambiguity and frustration, it relies upon gestalt and field theories of learning. In the final stage, which is marked by more acceptance and permissiveness, there is a movement toward self theory.

    "It has in effect no consistent theoretical basis. Various theories and therefore various methods are used by the same leader if he deems them useful. The T group is not, however, eclectic; it does not presume to take the best from each theory and unite them into one theory. Rather each theoretical basis is emphasized when it is considered to be useful." C. Gratton Kemp, *Perspectives on the Group Process* (Boston: Houghton Mifflin Co., 1970) , p. 183.

mutual support, affection, and valid communication. Conceptually, these two orientations are seen as interrelated in complex ways that determine group and individual outcomes. The two orientations have mutual interactions and also relate in complex ways to two other central group problems or concerns, those of identity and of goals or needs.[21] The arrows in Figure 4 suggest these complicated relationships.

Figure 4. Four Central Problems in Group Development

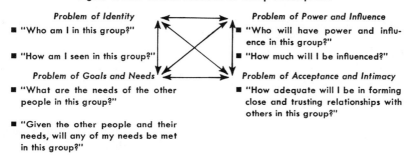

Problem of Identity
- "Who am I in this group?"

- "How am I seen in this group?"

Problem of Goals and Needs
- "What are the needs of the other people in this group?"

- "Given the other people and their needs, will any of my needs be met in this group?"

Problem of Power and Influence
- "Who will have power and influence in this group?"

- "How much will I be influenced?"

Problem of Acceptance and Intimacy
- "How adequate will I be in forming close and trusting relationships with others in this group?"

Source: Gordon L. Lippitt, *Organization Renewal* (New York: Appleton-Century-Crofts, 1969), p. 118.

The model developed by Warren Bennis and Herbert Shepard[22] reflects the authority/intimacy approach and is rooted in the work of William Schutz[23] and Wilfred Bion.[24] Bennis and Shepard focus on what they call the "dependence" and "personal" aspects. As they explain:

> The dependence aspect is comprised by the member's characteristic patterns related to a leader or to a structure of rules. Members who find comfort in rules or procedure, an agenda, an expert, etc. are called "dependent." Members who are discomfited by authoritative structures are called "counterdependent."
>
> The personal aspect is comprised by the member's characteristic patterns with respect to interpersonal intimacy. Members who cannot rest until they have stabilized a relatively high degree of intimacy with all the others are called "overpersonal."

21. Gordon L. Lippitt, *Organization Renewal* (New York: Appleton-Century-Crofts, 1969), pp. 118–20.
22. Warren G. Bennis and Herbert Shepard, "A Theory of Group Development," *Human Relations,* Vol. 9 (November, 1956), pp. 415–37.
23. William Schutz, *FIRO-B* (New York: Holt, Rinehart & Winston, 1958).
24. Wilfred Bion, "Experiences in Groups: I–VII," *Human Relations,* Vol. I, No. 3 (1948), pp. 314–20; No. 4 (1948), pp. 314–20, and 487–96; Vol. II (January, 1949), pp. 13–22, and (October, 1949), pp. 295–304; Vol. III (February, 1950), pp. 3–14, and (November, 1950), pp. 395–402; and Vol. IV (August, 1951), pp. 221–27.

Members who tend to avoid intimacy with any of the others are called "counterpersonal."[25]

Elaboration of this basic schema in three ways proves revealing. *First,* any individual may evidence any one of the four behavioral modes in more or less extreme form from time to time. Some individuals will compulsively and consistently adopt one or another of the extreme modes, however. They are considered to be "conflicted." The "unconflicted" or "independent" person may be highly dependent or incorrigibly rebellious at times, but he is more able to respond to situational differences. Hence, he creates fewer problems in communication. That is, a person who is compulsively counterdependent will attack authority figures more or less constantly, under most conditions. The person characterized as independent would respond more to the quality of particular authority figures. Behavior in the independent mode can be critical to effective group functioning.

Second, depending upon the specific mixes of these various orientations, group development takes one tack or another. A group of overpersonals would trend toward pleasantness and away from a high level of performance on rational-technical tasks. Similarly, a group balanced between extreme dependents and counterdependents is in for some stormy times, for the very structure needed by the one is the bondage resented by the other.

Third, although some people can be classified as dominantly reflecting one orientation or the other, many people can expose different orientations as situations change. They may have primary and backup orientations, for example. Thus a person might be quite dependent when he is anxious, but quite personal as his anxiety falls below some threshold level.

The developmental sequence of Bennis and Shepard can be useful, especially if one keeps in mind that the pattern is not invariant and also that many groups return again and again to various developmental phases.[26] The model below is best viewed as a somewhat stylized sequence of completed phases. Many actual groups do not complete all phases, but most groups do deal variously with each phase. The groups from whose

---

25. Bennis and Shepard, *op. cit.*, pp. 417–18. Their concept overlaps substantially with other sets of developmental sequences, such as that of B. W. Tuckman, who identifies "forming," "storming," "norming," and "performing," parallel to the stages of Bennis and Shepard. B. W. Tuckman, "Developmental Sequences in Small Groups," *Psychological Bulletin,* Vol. 63 (1965), pp. 384–99.

  For some evidence supporting these phases, see Evan R. Powell and Leellen Brigman, "An Analysis of Change of Classroom Group Structure" (Paper presented at the Annual Meeting, American Educational Research Association, Los Angeles, Cal., 1969).

26. Warren G. Bennis, "The Relationship between Some Personality Dimensions and Group Development" (unpublished MS, Boston University Human Relations Center, 1956).

46

experience the developmental sequence was developed were new ones composed of strangers. Their purpose was to develop and maintain an effective system of communication among themselves. The groups included a "trainer," an expert in group dynamics who was committed to the goal of maximizing the control by group members of their learning environment. Presumably, these groups contained members with more or less normal distributions of the several orientations noted above.

The stylized developmental sequence of Bennis and Shepard is built around two phases, Dependence and Interdependence, each of which has several subphases. Overall, the phases move from a preoccupation with power to an emphasis upon love, from a fixation on the superficial roles of its members to a deeper concern with individualized behaviors and reactions. The six subphases are sketched below, while Table 2 provides greater detail on Phase I: Dependence, or Power, Relations.

Subphase 1: Dependence—Flight

The two sets of behaviors which dominate this subphase characterize it as "dependence—flight." The dominant concern of group members is with authority, their basic behavioral mode is dependent, and their preoccupation is with the professional trainer and his failure to provide specific direction. As Bennis and Shepard conclude:

> The search for a common goal is aimed at reducing the cause of anxiety, thus going beyond the satisfaction of immediate security needs. But just as evidencing boredom in this situation is a method of warding off anxiety by denying its proximity, so group goal-seeking is not quite what it is claimed to be. It can best be understood as a dependence plea. The trainer, not the lack of a goal, is the cause of insecurity. This interpretation is likely to be vigorously contested by the group, but it is probably valid. The characteristic expectations of group members are that the trainer will establish rules of the game and distribute rewards. He is presumed to know what the goals are or ought to be. . . . The pretense of a fruitless search for goals is a plea for him to tell the group what to do, by simultaneously demonstrating its helplessness without him, and its willingness to work under his direction for his approval and protection.[27]

In the initial group meetings, at both conscious and unconscious levels, members attempt to deal with the anxiety of their goalless existence. Members can seek a common goal to achieve security, or they can withdraw into boredom, and much else besides. The trainer's verbal claims are that he wishes the group to control its learning environment in ways

---

27. Bennis and Shepard, *op. cit.*, pp. 419–20.

Table 2. A Stylized Developmental Sequence for a Group Dealing with Phase I: Dependence, or Power, Relations

	Subphase 1 Dependence—Submission	Subphase 2 Counterdependence	Subphase 3 Resolution
1. Emotional modality	Dependence—Flight	Counterdependence—Fight: Off-target fighting among members; distrust of staff member; ambivalence	Pairing; intense involvement in group task
2. Content themes	Discussion of interpersonal problems external to training groups	Discussion of group organization; i.e., what degree of structuring devices is needed for "effective" group behavior?	Discussion and definition of trainer role
3. Dominant roles (central persons)	Assertive, aggressive members with rich previous organizational or social science experience	Most assertive counterdependent and dependent members; withdrawal of less assertive independents and dependents	Assertive independents
4. Group structure	Organized mainly into multi-subgroups based on member's past experiences	Two tight subcliques consisting of leaders and members, of counterdependents and dependents	Group unifies in pursuit of goal and develops internal authority system
5. Group activity	Self-oriented behavior reminiscent of most new social gatherings	Search for consensus mechanism: voting, setting up chairman, search for "valid" content subjects	Group members take over leadership roles formerly perceived as held by trainer
6. Group movement facilitated by:	Staff member abnegation of traditional role of structuring situation, setting up rules of fair play, regulation of participation	Disenthrallment with staff member coupled with absorption of uncertainty by most assertive counterdependent and dependent individuals; subgroups form to ward off anxiety	Revolt by assertive independents (catalysts) who fuse subgroups into unity by initiating and engineering trainer exit (barometric event)
7. Main defenses	Projection; denigration of authority		Group moves into Phase II

Source: From Warren G. Bennis and Herbert Shepard, "A Theory of Group Development", *Human Relations*, Vol. 9 (November, 1956), p. 431.

that may be new and unprecedented for them. Group members tend not to accept such claims at face value, and perhaps they see the "expert" as being cleverly hard to get.

However, the authority concern is usually covert and is dismissed quickly when it surfaces. The wished-for dependence on the trainer does not receive explicit and extended treatment and—even though few members are deluded by what they are doing—the focus is on external matters such as the "outside" roles of members in the real world. This subphase is dominated by the true dependents, as well as by those group members whose dependence is triggered by the ambiguity and anxiety of early meetings. Dependence is a backup mode for many people, especially under conditions that are threatening.

Subphase 2: Counterdependence—Fight

In most groups of the kind described above, a stressful and unpleasant second subphase develops. This subphase belongs to the counterdependents, as well as to primary dependents whose backup mode is to reject uncooperative authority figures.

Two developments dominate this second subphase of dealing with authority issues. First, the trainer is likely to be a focal person, and his continued failure to guide the group becomes a matter of extended public criticism. A power vacuum develops, but efforts of members to assume leadership often are checkmated when they do occur, which is relatively seldom. Seeing what happens to the first "leader," the trainer, most members are reticent about getting in line for the same treatment. The few more persistent and perhaps less subtle members usually can be controlled by the others.

In the second subphase of development, the group tends to polarize into subgroups on some issue, often into two subgroups on the question of how much structure is appropriate. Some hold out for agendas, a chairman, and so on; but those in a counterdependent mode will have little or none of it. Most members are likely to identify basically with one of the subgroups, inflexibly and stereotypically contesting, for example, for "much structure" or "no structure." The independents are more mobile and often are bemused with the intense polarization they observe but do not share. Members in the independent mode, however, are at this stage neither able to resolve the conflict nor to assume leadership.

Subphase 3: Resolution—Catharsis

The third subphase associated with the power modality is critical, and it occurs mercurially when it happens. The independents, who are

49

the critical actors, function effectively to the degree that they are joined by group members who had been expressing dependent or counterdependent modes.

The catharsis can come in several ways. A direct challenge to the trainer may precipitate the catharsis, as via an invitation or request that he leave the group. Or somehow the polarization of the group can provide such an integrative opportunity. Thus the very survival of the group may encourage the "building of bridges" between subgroups, the threat being that otherwise all will fail. Independents often trigger such integrative efforts. But this comes later rather than sooner, because it usually takes considerable time for the independents to build relations with members of such subgroups. Similarly, one of the members in a strong dependent or counterdependent mode may have a learning experience. "God," he might announce, "this is just the way I am at work. And we always fight there too. What am I doing to you people? And what am I doing to myself?"

Not all groups achieve resolution of their power concerns, but resolution is quite common, and it trends toward certain similar features. Whatever the trigger, it suddenly becomes clear how the group members can help one another while they succeed as a group in "really communicating" with one another. This is heady stuff indeed. Intense involvement in task is likely, and group members "come alive." The Resolution —Catharsis subphase is not likely to last long in terms of physical time, probably because so much is done so rapidly that group members soon need some time for consolidating their experiences and sharing their achievement.

The exposition above may appear too tidy, and that impression needs to be counterbalanced somewhat. Blocking and regression do occur. That is, a group can remain for extended periods of time at one level of development, or even drop back to a concern with lower levels. Moreover, several developmental emphases can coexist at the same time, for all or many members of a group. Finally, some member may be fixated at primitive developmental levels, while most of his colleagues are in the Resolution—Catharsis subphase. But beyond these complexities and complications, some common developmental highlights of a group working on issues of internal authority or influence are evident. And the word "developmental" is deliberately used, in the sense of a definite order of progression over time.

Much the same complexities and qualifications apply as a group begins to turn more attention to Phase II, toward the resolution of problems of interdependence or intimacy. Again, also, there are some common regularities.

Subphase 4: Enchantment—Flight

Should a group attain subphase 4, a "honeymoon period" is almost certain. Most or all members take part. This is Everyman's subphase, but the overpersonals have a field day.

The subphase can be characterized with unusual definiteness. Sweetness and light prevail, joy abounds, and laughter—above all, laughter—characterizes a group's interaction. Patently, the gains of subphase 3 are not to be jeopardized. The group has known past conflict and values its present solidarity. Members tend to be pleased with the group achievement and often revel in their new intimacy with yesterday's strangers. Any mention of unfinished business is buried, quickly and subtly if possible. Only a very persistent and unaware member could fail to perceive the operating norm in this subphase.

Subphase 5: Disenchantment—Fight

Sooner or later, the honeymoon ends. The trigger episode can take various forms. The independents may become bemused with how suddenly members in contrasting dependent and counterdependent modes were able to patch over their differences and how zealously they rejected any attempts to rock their particular boat. This may cause regression to subphase 2. More likely, counterpersonal modes will become dominant. The specific forms are varied. Someone may note that he hopes there will be more to his group experience than "holding hands," which was nice enough, but enough is enough. This may be an innocent signal that one member has enjoyed his experience and feels the group has stagnated, if pleasantly so. The overpersonals may sense the potential loss of satisfaction of their needs and an abhorrent return to subphases 1 or 2, however, and hence they will resist. Their resistance will grow to the degree that subphase 4 has threatened members with a dominant counterpersonal orientation. The counterpersonals may openly acknowledge their low needs for personal intimacy, or they may adopt such postures as concern over someone "tampering with their psyche." Matters can get more complicated, obviously, the more subtle the posturing.

In short, polarization around the intimacy issue characterizes subphase 5. Two or more subgroups will develop, probably with different memberships than the subgroups organized around the authority issue. Bennis and Shepard describe and interpret polarization about intimacy in this revealing way:

> Subphase 5 belongs to the counterpersonals as subphase 4 belongs to the overpersonals. Subphase 4 might be caricatured as hiding in the womb of the group; subphase 5 as hiding out of sight of the group. It seems probable that both of these modali-

51

ties serve to ward off anxieties associated with intimate interpersonal relations. A theme that links them together can be verbalized as follows: "If others really knew me, they would reject me." The overpersonal's formula for avoiding this rejection seems to be accepting all others so as to be protected by the others' guilt; the counterpersonal's way is by rejecting all others before they have a chance to reject him. Another way of characterizing the counterpersonal orientation is in the phrase, "I would lose my identity as a member of the group." The corresponding overpersonal orientation reads, "I have nothing to lose by identifying with the group."[28]

Subphase 6: Resolution—Catharsis

A variety of forces act to induce some resolution concerning the intimacy issue. Thus the group has the successful experience with its authority issue to rely on, which can suggest a model for problem-solving. Moreover, if members are open about their differential needs for intimacy, a mutual tolerance can develop even between people with different needs for sharing intimacies and different capacities for developing intimate relationships. Or in some groups the imminence of a final meeting may encourage the appropriate mobilization of group resources to urge a livable resolution.

Again, complications and qualifications are appropriate. Some groups might have an abortive subphase 6, which could signal that the earlier resolution of authority issues was only superficial. Perhaps the basic additional point, however, concerns the probability that any group will develop not only through the six subphases, but also at various levels of insight and probing. That is to say, a group might go through the six subphases more or less at a superficial level. The work accomplished then would become the basis for a higher (or deeper) level of analysis, for another go-around with greater intensity and comprehensiveness.

b. Cycles of Accumulating Human Experience: A Model of Individual Development or Learning

There are numerous possible ways of viewing the laboratory approach as it applies to individual development or learning.[29] In such a choice,

---

28. *Ibid.,* p. 431.
29. For extensive summaries of a variety of models of learning, see Ernest R. Hilgard, *Theories of Learning* (New York: Appleton-Century-Crofts, 1966). More conveniently, see Fremont A. Shull, Jr., Andrew L. Delbecq, and L. L. Cummings, *Organization Decision-Making* (New York: McGraw-Hill Book Co., 1970), esp. pp. 78–81.

some insights are gained at the expense of others obscured by the model chosen. This section follows up on the suggestions about the cyclical character of learning in the discussion above.

The vantage point here views the laboratory approach in the context of a model of developmental plateaus, each of which provides a socio-emotional base for a possible cycling to a new and higher level of understanding and awareness of self. Success is not certain, of course, and even hurtful regression is possible. Perhaps too simplistically, the individual may find that understanding and being aware of himself is intolerable. Or the learner may find that his initial socioemotional base is not adequate to support the kind of great leap forward he seeks. If the individual is successful in attaining any higher level of understanding, however, that achievement in turn becomes the base for another potential round of cycling. And so on and on, as the individual continues to develop or learn. As Leland Bradford notes: "One way of looking at the [laboratory approach] is to see it as a cyclic process in which learning recurs in increasing depth. . . . As learning increases . . . so a cycle of growth continues."[30]

C. M. Hampden-Turner has developed one such cyclic model of special value.[31] He proposes an "existential learning theory" in the form of a "cycle of accumulating human experience," which is sketched in Figure 5. The "base" in this model is provided by three aspects of an individual's past developmental cycles:

- The quality of his cognition, or that universe which includes the breadth of an individual's understanding, his sensitivity to the needs of others, or his ability to develop effective strategies for satisfying needs
- the clarity of his identity, or the quality of the ways in which an individual sees himself: e.g., his awareness of self in relation to others, his consciousness of his behavior in various roles, and his growing differentiation from other people as a responsible individual actor
- the extent of his self-esteem, or the degree to which an individual values himself and others, the degree to which he can accept himself and others as needing to grow and to help others do so

These three factors in combination, Hampden-Turner notes, determine a person's level of overall interpersonal competence. See stage 4 in Figure 5, which proposes that the individual orders these three factors into a

---

30. Leland P. Bradford, "Membership and the Learning Process," in Bradford, Gibb, and Benne (eds.), *op. cit.*, pp. 200–205.
31. C. M. Hampden-Turner, "An Existential 'Learning Theory' and the Integration of T-Group Research," *Journal of Applied Behavioral Science*, Vol. 2 (October, 1966), pp. 367–86.

resultant state labeled "experienced and anticipated competence." This is the plateau from which an individual can attain greater development or learning. Conceivably, also, these three factors combine to form a plateau from which regression is possible.

As previous discussion should suggest, even at this early stage in examining the cyclic model the laboratory approach seeks to improve the probability of a new and higher level of insight and understanding. Hampden-Turner takes pains to establish, specifically, that the labora-

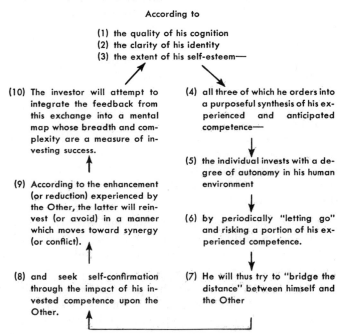

Figure 5. A Cyclical Model of Individual Development or Learning

According to

(1) the quality of his cognition
(2) the clarity of his identity
(3) the extent of his self-esteem—

(10) The investor will attempt to integrate the feedback from this exchange into a mental map whose breadth and complexity are a measure of investing success.

(4) all three of which he orders into a purposeful synthesis of his experienced and anticipated competence—

(9) According to the enhancement (or reduction) experienced by the Other, the latter will reinvest (or avoid) in a manner which moves toward synergy (or conflict).

(5) the individual invests with a degree of autonomy in his human environment

(8) and seek self-confirmation through the impact of his invested competence upon the Other.

(6) by periodically "letting go" and risking a portion of his experienced competence.

(7) He will thus try to "bridge the distance" between himself and the Other

Source: C. M. Hampden-Turner, "An Existential 'Learning Theory' and the Integration of T-Group Research," *Journal of Applied Behavioral Science*, Vol. 2 (October, 1966), p. 368.

tory approach intends to improve the three components of overall competence he outlines—quality of cognition, clarity of identity, and extent of self-esteem. Early research implies that the approach can lay substantial claim to succeeding in this intention. For example, the laboratory approach emphasizes the development of increasing self-awareness in individuals, as well as an appreciation of the impact of their behavior on others.[32] A growing research literature suggests that this is achieved more

---

32. Bradford, Gibb, and Benne, *op. cit.*, p. 279.

often than not.[33] Subsequent chapters will deal with this literature in detail.

Given a certain level of "experienced and anticipated competence," as in Hampden-Turner's model, a cycling experience may begin. As stages 5 and 6 in Figure 5 represent, the individual willingly offers some part of his self-related "base" to others for acceptance or rejection. As his interaction systems are regenerative, to that degree will the individual be willing to expose himself to test his self-concepts at any particular plateau of his understanding.

Stages 5 and 6 are critical in human growth or development; perhaps they are even the ultimately human act, and such potential loss of self in order to find one's self does not just happen. Consider four points which establish the relation of the present model with the previous discussion of regenerative systems. First, the individual must act with a substantial degree of autonomy if he is to really *own* the results of the testing of self. As the individual is forced into such an investment, so will he be likely to resist any possible learning. Indeed, he may even feel psychological failure as he succeeds in learning. Second, the individual must strive to be *open* in dealing with others about self. That is, his base of experienced and anticipated competence will be meaningfully tested only to the degree that openness characterizes his interaction with others. By not informing others, in sum, he may only be handicapping himself. Third, the individual also must *risk* by "letting go." Hampden-Turner expresses the point with a penetrating directness: "I discover that I am valuable and meaningful to the Other only through risking that I am worthless and meaningless."[34] Fourth, such letting-go will be a function of the *trust* that the individual experiences in the situation he invests in. The sense of the critical nature of stages 5 and 6, and hence of regenerative systems, is captured in this summary statement by Jack and Lorraine Gibb:

> The central dynamic of the growth process is a movement from fear to trust. Latent fear predisposes individuals to build social structures around role relations, develop strategies for mask maintenance, attempt to manage motivations by various forms of persuasion, and maintain tight control systems. The individual camouflages his fears to himself by building role barricades; he camouflages his humanness with an idealized presenting self; he reacts to imposed motivations by attempting to impose motivations on others; and he protects himself from intimacy by defending or rebelling. With experience in high

33. Douglas R. Bunker, "Individual Applications of Laboratory Training," *Journal of Applied Behavioral Science,* Vol. 1 (April, 1965) , pp. 131–47.
34. Hampden-Turner, *op. cit.,* p. 376.

trust environments, however, he tends to be more personal; he replaces facades with intimacy and directness; he becomes more search-oriented and self-determining; and he develops the capacity for making interdependent relationships with relevant and significant others.[35]

In the very act of letting-go, the individual exposes himself to feedback which could imply rejection or modification of his base of experienced and anticipated competence. The process is delicate because of the inevitable differentiation of Self and Other, as stages 7 and 8 in Figure 5 attempt to suggest. To use the feedback of the Other, the individual must somehow "bridge the distance" between Self and Other. Dynamic counterforces are involved. Thus the individual strives to preserve his differentiated Self, to maintain a gap between Self and Other. Paradoxically, the differentiation of Self requires the confirmation that only Other can supply. Hence the need to bridge the Self/Other gap. Martin Buber expressed the point powerfully. "The basic of man's life is two-fold, and it is one," he explained. That basic includes "the wish of every man to be confirmed as to what he is, even as what he can become, by men; and the innate capacity in man to confirm his fellow men in this way."[36]

A number of metaphors come to mind. The kind of thinking required conveys a sense of patting your head and rubbing your tummy. Intimacy requires some distance, and to be individual implies association. Moreover, to find yourself really means risking the loss of some part of yourself to others. In Kenneth Benne's words, the process "involves some of the deepest dilemmas of personal and social life, the dilemma of self and society . . . of conservation and of apartness partially overcome in an association which, while firm and security-giving, yet enhances and affirms rather than eclipses and derogates individual variation and difference."[37]

We have no really good metaphors to express the process of "bridging the distance," however, and hence the attempt at explanation above must fail. But some necessary conditions can be specified with some certainty. When we expect others to be just like ourselves before we can learn from them, for example, we are assured of learning little. This will preserve our sense of experienced and anticipated competence, but only in a bogus way. Moreover, it also prohibits the test that alone can provide a stable platform for cycling to higher levels of competence. Paradoxically, moreover, we need Other to be differentiated from us if he is

35. Jack R. Gibb and Lorraine M. Gibb, "Role Freedom in a TORI Group," in Arthur Burton (ed.), *Encounter* (San Francisco: Jossey-Bass, Inc., Publishers, 1969), p. 43.
36. Martin Buber, "Distance and Relation," *Psychiatry*, Vol. 20 (May, 1957), p. 101.
37. Kenneth D. Benne, "From Polarization to Paradox," in Bradford, Gibb, and Benne, *op. cit.*, pp. 235–36.

to provide us this essentially human service. Consequently, what we call tolerance plays an important role in bridging the gap between Self and Other. On the other hand, the Self cannot be surrendered to the Other. The common idiom suggests how valueless such surrender is to development or learning. "If that's the way you say I am," goes the idiom, "then that's how I am." This is at least a statement of dependence, which limits the degree to which an individual can accept any learning as his own. The idiom also may disparage the feedback from the Other, depending on the tone of voice and inflection. Consequently, what we commonly call conformity cannot play a major role in bridging the Self/Other gap.

The subtleties of the latter point have escaped some critical observers,[38] and perhaps even many devotees of sensitivity training. For example, some observers see in sensitivity training a vehicle for the development of consensus and for the subjugation of the individual to it. Commitment to any interpersonal relationship does imply a loss of individual freedom, but the *quid pro quo* is personal development. There are pitfalls aplenty in bringing off this paradoxic exchange, to be sure. But just as surely, there is no alternative to taking the risk, short of arrested development. Ashley Montagu sensitively captures the point in his discussion of an individual's identification with a group:

> In this process the consciousness of self may actually increase, the sense of personal identity may become even more vivid, and one's ties to one's society more firmly established than ever. Individuation, as the development of personal identity, is neither the contrary nor the contradictory of social identification, it *is* social identification.[39]

To return to Figure 5, the developmental payoff for individuals occurs at stages 9 and 10. Both Self and Other can grow individually while they facilitate each other's growth. Basically, the differentiated Self and Other provide insights or aspects that can be integrated into Other and Self, respectively. Tolerance of the initial differentiation, that is to say, facilitates further differentiation while it intensifies the sense of shared contributions to development or learning. Such dual effects magnify the results of the separate investments of Self and Other and encourage additional investments.

The cycle of learning then can feed on itself, finally, on the products of stages 9 and 10. A complementary enhancement of Self and Other, that is, will contribute to raising the plateau of "experienced and anticipated competence" symbolized by stages 1, 2, and 3 in Figure 5.

---

38. William Gomberg, " 'Titillating Therapy': Management Development's Most Fascinating Toy," *Personnel Administrator*, Vol. 12 (July–August, 1967) , pp. 30–33.
39. Ashley Montagu, *On Being Human* (New York: Abelard-Schuman Ltd., 1950) , p. 76.

The outcomes are not necessarily happy ones, although they dominantly tend to be. The process of individual development or learning also can come unglued at stages 9 and 10 in Figure 5. The result could be a reduced sense of overall competence, perhaps even a seriously impaired sense. The probability of such a consequence is, in large part, a function of the sophistication of the technology underlying various species of the laboratory approach. The next chapter turns to three aspects of this technology. The chapter will consider, in turn, common values underlying the laboratory approach, several possible illustrative learning designs, and several alternative learning theories. In effect, these aspects of the laboratory technology deal with the issue of increasing the probability that sanguine effects will result from applications of the laboratory approach.

B. THE LABORATORY APPROACH TO LEARNING: VALUES THAT GUIDE APPLICATIONS

As with any technology for learning, the laboratory approach has to face some critical and complex issues. The relevant questions can be posed easily enough. Are the effects attributable to the technology worth achieving? If so, with what confidence can specific effects be expected? What safeguards exist or can be developed to raise that confidence and to minimize the exceptions that prove the rule? And what of the potential side effects of the technology? Or given the legitimacy of early experimentation with any promising technique, is the cost/benefit ratio for the laboratory approach favorable enough to encourage running the risks over the longer run?

Answers to such questions come but grudgingly and haltingly, however, and it will take all of this volume to attempt to develop relevant working answers. In this section the effort is begun, in full awareness of a major challenge. Perhaps the dominant norm among early students of the laboratory approach was the development of new methods and the cultivation of differences, as well as, hopefully, innovations. There was (and is) strength in this, especially as it adds to knowledge or inhibits a premature closure on methods or concepts. However, diversity can also create confusion and disintegration, which can inhibit the accumulation of theory and practice. This section, in effect, will be swimming against the current of the norm of diversity and its burgeoning contemporary products.

4. SOME COMMON GOALS:
TOWARD AUTHENTIC, HELPING, RELATED MAN

Basically, this section accepts one piece of the complex action. It focuses on factors that guide the application of the laboratory approach, on constraints expressed in terms of explicit values as well as those that are implicit in the properties of the learning technology. Therefore, this section has a strongly prescriptive orientation. It cannot be otherwise. As far as possible, the aim is to present the essence of the laboratory approach, basing the presentation on the consensus of aficionados. There will be points at which consensus does not exist or where debate is the order of the day, of course. At those points, this section becomes an intensely personal product.

a. Meta-Values of Laboratory Approach: Toward Open Interpersonal Systems

Every technology dealing with humans rests on some set of meta-values, or basic goals. They may be explicit, or they may be what Alvin Gouldner called a "metaphysical pathos" of implicit understandings, hopes, and aspirations. In effect, these meta-values constrain applications of the technology. Sometimes in unambiguous terms, and sometimes via what one can call "spirit," these meta-values help determine what should be done and what should be avoided, how it should be done, and when it should be done.

The laboratory approach is not different on this score, except perhaps in the degree of attention given to its meta-values. Overall, these basic values may be characterized as diversely contributing to a sense of open interpersonal systems. Or perhaps the concept of mutually helpful and vulnerable systems more fully suggests the total spirit of the laboratory approach. The following discussion of five meta-values will help the reader make his own choice. Column A of Table 1 (page 68) summarizes these meta-values.

Acceptance of Inquiry

The first of the five meta-values providing significant constraints for applications of the laboratory approach rests on a deep acceptance of inquiry as the norm in relationships with others. "It is what we don't know that can destroy our relationship" could well serve as a motto. The opposed meta-value is perhaps more common and is reflected in such maxims as: "Familiarity breeds contempt." The difference between these two guiding values is profound. The true acceptance of inquiry involves a mutual accessibility of persons to one another, as well as a potential vulnerability to each other and a real commitment to the possibility of being influenced by the other. The opposed meta-value legitimates a more distant relationship and, if only in a superficial sense, a safer relationship.

The acceptance of inquiry, if not the rejoicing in it, has two basic logical consequences. Thus the laboratory approach as applied is preoccupied with "testing out" reactions or perceptions or interpretations. The tentativeness recognizes only two absolutes: the certainty of the complexity of the observed phenomena, and the inevitability that reactions to the phenomena will be diverse. The laboratory approach has a significant place for "subjective truth," then. Considerable attention is devoted to how various people differently perceive the same stimuli and to how the same stimulus generates diverse responses. And in such matters there are often as many truths as there are observers. A hypothetical spirit is very useful for eliciting this diversity of human responses. Hence also the incidence of statements in applications of the laboratory approach such as "from where I sit," versus statements like "you are competitive." In addition, experimentalism also is a logical consequence of the acceptance of inquiry, especially in the sense that a perceived need may motivate an innovation. Inquiry would be a contraceptive experience were it not linked closely with experimentation. For example, assume I learn I do not communicate effectively with X. That is important enough, but the major personal payoff comes when I learn how to overcome that inadequacy. Working toward this payoff implies experimentation.

Expanded Consciousness and Recognition of Choice

A second meta-value—an expanded consciousness and recognition of choice—also is implied by the acceptance of inquiry. Patently, experimentation would be sterile in the absence of a consciousness of the diversity of choices that exist. The linkages are direct: an expanded consciousness or awareness generates wider choices; choice permits experimentation that could lead to change; and freely made choice also helps assure that the individual will own the change rather than (at best) accept its imposition. These linkages constitute a circular process that seeks to enhance the potential for learning, as well as the owning of and commitment to its consequences.

The role of choice is an especially major one in the laboratory approach, that is to say. As Warren Bennis expressed his own emphasis on expanding the sense and reality of choice:

> . . . I care much less about a participant's learning that he
> talked too much and will, in the future, talk less, than I do

about his recognizing that choice exists and that there are certain clear consequences of under- or over-participation. I care much less about producing a "cohesive" group than I do about members' understanding the "costs" and gains of cohesiveness, when it's appropriate and worth the cost and when it may not be. I care far less about developing shared leadership in the T-Group than I do about the participants' recognizing that a choice exists among a wide array of leadership patterns. In short, I care far more about developing *choice and recognition of choice points than I do about change.* Change, I think, is the participants' privilege, but choice is something trainers must emphasize.[1]

Hence it is that the T-Group or sensitivity training group—the ideal learning vehicle of the laboratory approach—offers the ultimate choice: being a contributor, from the very beginning, to the development of a special learning community that never existed before and that will cease to exist when the experience concludes. More or less, other learning vehicles based on the laboratory approach have the same goal of maximizing responsibility for, and commitment to, the consequences of any learning experience.

Collaborative Concept of Authority

Consistent with an expanding sense of choice, the laboratory approach also reflects a collaborative concept of authority, the third meta-value. This is meant in two senses. In laboratory learning situations, first, the role of the participant is by design a far more influential one than in traditional learning situations. In some variations of the laboratory approach, indeed, this ability to influence extends to all details but the scheduling of the time and place of the initial meeting. Beyond that, the participants share responsibility with any professional staff concerning all future planning, even as to living accommodations for the rest of the experience, if indeed it is not canceled at the outset by mutual consent! Second, laboratory learning situations provide an experience with collaborative authority relations that provide analogs for relations in the real world. Even though extreme forms of mutual influence may be seldom applicable outside of designated learning situations, more or less mutual patterns of influence usually are open alternatives.

A complex rationale supports this collaborative concept of authority. For example, the political and social heritage of Western civilization rests on a substantial and growing sense of popular influence over the environment. "No taxation without representation" and "Power to the

---

1. Warren G. Bennis, "Goals and Meta-Goals of Laboratory Training," *NTL Human Relations Training News,* Vol. 6, No. 3 (1962), p. 4.

people" are merely two forms of the same heritage. More narrowly, the collaborative concept of authority is rooted in a desire to improve the quality and efficiency of the learning process. Specifically, learning can be considered a form of the broader process of influencing behavior, and the various forms can have profoundly different consequences. To illustrate, Herbert Kelman has argued that it is useful to distinguish at least three forms of influence:[2]

- *compliance,* in which case the influence is accepted to receive some reward or avoid some punishment controlled by the influencing agent
- *identification,* in which case the influence is accepted so as to maintain or develop a satisfying relationship with the influencing agent
- *internalization,* in which case the influence is accepted because it is congruent with the learner's own value system

These three modes can interact in complex ways. For example, influence or learning based on compliance that is accepted can become a part of an individual's own value system, in which case future acceptance of similar influence attempts can be based on internalization.

The three modes for influencing behavior also imply distinct effects. The laboratory approach attempts to induce identification and especially internalization as the basic processes in its influence or learning attempts. Clearly, these two forms of influence imply an increasingly collaborative sense of authority. In part, the emphasis in the laboratory approach rests on very deep value preferences about the quality or style of learning processes. In some part, also the emphasis on identification ⟶ internalization (read: identification trending toward internalization) rests on beliefs-*cum*-evidence of the greater resultant effectiveness on such a learning situation. In terms of our operating vocabulary, learning based on identification ⟶ internalization will increase the probability that learners will own their experiences. Consequently, the individual is both more likely to retain the learning and more likely to apply it outside the specific learning situation.

The basic qualities of this concept of authority are a pervasive sense of cooperation and collaboration and a commitment to resolve conflicts openly in a problem-solving sense. The collaborative concept of authority, in words reminiscent of Mary Parker Follett, allows the problem-situation to determine which skills and resources are appropriate and, consequently, who should influence decisions. An opposed style might rely on command/obedience, for example, with problems being solved by authority figures who are presumed to have the skills appropriate to the generality of problems-situations.

2. Herbert C. Kelman, "Processes of Opinion Change," *Public Opinion Quarterly,* Vol. 25 (Spring, 1961), pp. 57–78.

Mutual Helping Relationships in Social Settings

Reinforcing this concept of shared authority, the laboratory approach emphasizes the development of mutual helping relationships in social or community settings. This fourth meta-value has at least two major components. Helping is seen as perhaps *the* distinctive human attribute that requires cultivation and development. Relatedly, the social setting is seen as an optimal (perhaps even natural) locus for mutual helping. This world view assumes a diversity of notions, among them the classical concept of man as a social animal. In addition, the emphasis upon community reflects a reasonable belief that social units can facilitate learning because of the extraordinary and perhaps unique capacity of groups to induce massive forces to reinforce learning or change.[3]

Numerous social adhesives help bond together the helping relationships stressed by the laboratory approach. For example, learning designs based on the approach tend to generate substantial (even unparalleled) exchanges of warmth, or support, between members. Such exchanges can help cement a community of learners. Consider what an individual can obtain from such a learning community. All but universally, for example, psychosocial growth is seen as depending upon some degree of warmth or nurturance. The effects of lack of maternal nurturance can be profound[4] and, more or less, the need persists even through old age.[5] Similarly, the laboratory approach rests on acceptance of the Other as he is, on what has come to be called "unconditional positive regard."[6] Acceptance does not imply approval, but rather a valuing of the Other, a respect and a concern for him. Relatedly, designs based on the laboratory approach attempt to stress the psychological safety of participants. As two careful students note:

> People must certainly differ greatly in their ability to accept the guarantee of psychological safety. To the extent that the feeling of safety cannot be achieved—and quickly—the prime basic ingredient for this form of learning is absent. Its importance cannot be overemphasized, nor can the difficulty of its being accomplished.[7]

It should not be necessary to gild the lily with the note that most of us need unconditional regard and psychological safety.

3. Robert T. Golembiewski, *The Small Group* (Chicago: University of Chicago Press, 1962), esp. pp. 9–26.
4. R. I. Watson, *Psychology of the Child* (New York: John Wiley & Sons, 1959).
5. Gerard Egan, *Encounter: Group Processes for Interpersonal Growth* (Belmont, Cal.: Wadsworth Publishing Co., 1970), p. 260.
6. Carl R. Rogers (ed.), *The Therapeutic Relationship and Its Impact* (Madison: University of Wisconsin Press, 1967).
7. John P. Campbell and Marvin D. Dunnette, "Effectiveness of T-Group Experiences in Managerial Training and Development," *Psychological Bulletin*, Vol. 70 (August, 1968), pp. 73–104.

Authenticity in Interpersonal Relations

This fifth, and final, meta-value of the laboratory approach is the equivalent of the hackneyed "tell it like it is." Its focus is on the expression of feelings as well as on the analysis of the behaviors inducing them, in sharp contrast to traditional technologies for learning.

The rationale for the meta-value of authenticity has two kinds of roots. First, there are the clearly moral precepts on the theme "To thine own self be true; thou canst not then be false to any man." Second, authenticity is seen as empirically critical in communication. Only a sketch of

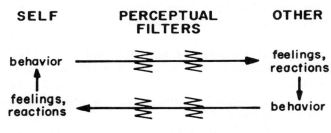

Figure 1. Two Contrasting Patterns of Communication Linkage

1A. A Complete Linkage

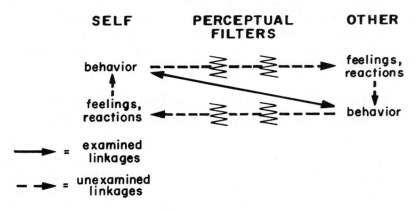

1B. A "Shorted" Linkage

the issue is possible here. Minimally distorted communication is seen as critical to group development, for example. That is, failure to be authentic in the senses of "leveling" and "expressing feelings" so as to elicit similar behaviors from others can accumulate so much unfinished business as to overburden interaction. The simple model in Figure 1A elaborates the point. A complete communication linkage takes this form: Some behavior by Self is perceived and variously distorted through the perceptual filters of Other, in whom they trigger feelings and reactions; Other responds with behaviors that may or may not be congruent with his emotional reactions to the (mis) perceptions of what Self is communicating; and these behaviors of Other have some impact on Self, after they are passed through Self's perceptual filters. All of this gets extremely chancy in a "shorted" linkage, as sketched in Figure 1B. Here neither Self nor Other are open about their feelings or reactions, so both have to guess about the intentions behind behaviors and about the impact that their own behaviors have on the other person. The dangers of miscommunication are great. Thus Other may misinterpret the motives behind the behavior of Self, even if he perceives that behavior without major distortion. Consequently, Other may respond in ways inexplicable to Self, or unexpected by him. Since Self does not reveal these reactions or feelings, his resulting behaviors toward Other are in turn likely to be seen as unrevealing, if not as puzzling or inappropriate. Similarly, the individualized perceptive filters of both Self and Other may result in misperception of behaviors, which would often become manifest if feelings or reactions were dealt with, as in Figure 1A. Hence the stress in the laboratory approach on authenticity, on reporting feelings and reactions as well as behaviors.

Authenticity seems critical in broader senses as well. For example, contemporary constructs of mental health tend to emphasize outcomes in which the individual as he is known to himself is much the same person known to others.[8] This congruence of the person and the person perceived by others has generated some empirical research that implies the value of the concept.[9] Clearly, this congruence rests squarely on the ability of both Self and Other to be authentic.

b. Some Operating Values of Laboratory Approach: Toward Development of Specific Competencies

A second major set of value constraints on applications of the laboratory approach may be called operating values. The term "operating" may be awkward, but the core of the meaning is that they are value-loaded guidelines or rules of thumb consistent with the meta-values. The operating values are also oriented toward helping to guide the development of specific competencies, such as attitudes or behavioral skills. There can be a number of such operating values, applying to various processes central to the laboratory approach.

The focus here is on one particular set of operating values, a set of

8. Marie Jahoda, *Current Concepts of Positive Mental Health* (New York: Basic Books, 1958).
9. G. T. Barrett-Lennard, "Dimensions of Therapist Response as Causal Factors in Therapeutic Change," *Psychological Monographs*, Vol. 76, No. 43 (1962).

guidelines for giving constructive and helpful feedback. Column B in Table 1 (page 68) summarizes the constraints that should guide effective feedback. In short, not just any reaction to another person constitutes effective feedback for him. Hence the concern of two observers that the laboratory approach not be seen as legitimating the "concept that anything goes regardless of consequences." They note of that concept that:

> Instead of creating interpersonal awareness it may foster personal narcissism. If an individual says anything he wishes, then he may come to assume that just because he feels like expressing himself is justification enough to do so. This may preclude effective communication, for he then ignores whether the other person is receptive to his message, and he ignores the effect of his message on the other person. Communication may not be seen as an interpersonal event but merely as the opportunity to express oneself. The principle of "optimal communication" is ignored for the principle of "total communication."[10]

The basis for feedback prescribed by Table 1 will be illustrated here only briefly, since a full treatment will be attempted later. Consider the emphasis on here-and-now phenomena in column B, for example. It limits applications of the laboratory approach in several senses. For example, the here-and-now emphasis focuses attention on ongoing events to which all present have more-or-less equal access. Similarly, the operating value directs attention away from there-and-then probing and interpretation, which are more appropriate for psychoanalytic or psychotherapeutic experiences.

A convenient approach will be taken here to considering the other operating values. Each of these values will be illustrated in Topic d below, along with the immediate goals of the laboratory approach, in a way that is revealing enough at this stage of analysis.

c. Some Immediate Goals of Laboratory Approach: Toward Transfer of Specific Awareness

Column C of Table 1 can be used to permit similarly convenient treatment of some immediate goals under the topic below. These goals refer to the specific foci of the laboratory approach, awareness or learning about which can be transferred outside of an immediate learning situation. For example, increased insight and self-knowledge gained in a

10. Louis A. Gottschalk and E. Mansell Pattison, "Psychiatric Perspectives on T-Groups and the Laboratory Movement," *The American Journal of Psychiatry*, Vol. 126 (December, 1969), p. 835.

learning environment should be transferable to other situations, in whole or in part.

d. Some Illustrations in Action:
Meta-Values, Operating Values, and Immediate Goals

The laboratory approach is not narrowly means-oriented. Quite the opposite is the case, in fact, as the sections above should suggest. The specific contribution here[11] to reinforcing the sense of the value-loaded quality of the laboratory approach builds on the content of Table 1,

Table 1. Three Sets of Normative, or Value, Constraints on Applications of the Laboratory Approach

(A) Meta-Values of Laboratory Approach	(B) Operating Values of Laboratory Approach	(C) Immediate Goals of Laboratory Approach

1. An attitude of inquiry reflecting (among others):
  a. a hypothetical spirit
  b. experimentalism
	1. Emphasis on here-and-now occurrences	1. Increased insight, self-knowledge

2. Expanded consciousness and recognition of choice	2. Emphasis on the individual act rather than on the total person acting	2. Sharpened diagnostic skills at (ideally) all levels, i.e., the levels of the:
		  a. individual
		  b. group

3. A collaborative concept of authority having as two core elements:
  a. spirit of collaboration
  b. open resolution of conflict via a problem-solving orientation
	3. Emphasis on feedback that is nonevaluative in that it reports the impact on the self of other's behavior, rather than feedback that is judgmental or interpretive	c. organization
		  d. society
		
		3. Awareness of, and skill practice in, creating conditions of effective functioning at (ideally) all levels

4. An emphasis on mutual "helping relationships" as the best way to express man's interdependency with man, or man's basic social nature and connectedness	4. Emphasis on "unfreezing" behaviors the trainee feels are undesirable, on practice of replacement behaviors, and on "refreezing" new behaviors	4. Testing self-concepts and skills in interpersonal situations
5. An emphasis on "authenticity" in interpersonal relations, a high value on expressing feelings and their effects	5. Emphasis on "trust in leveling," on psychological safety of the trainee 6. Emphasis on creating and maintaining an "organic community"	5. Increased capacity to be open, to accept feelings of self and others, and to risk interpersonally in rewarding ways

Source: Adapted from Edgar H. Schein and Warren G. Bennis, *Personal and Organizational Change through Group Methods* (New York: John Wiley & Sons, 1965), pp. 30–35; and Leland P. Bradford, Jack R. Gibb, and Kenneth D. Benne, *T-Group Therapy and Laboratory Method* (New York: John Wiley & Sons, 1964), pp. 10, 12.

11. This section is based on Robert T. Golembiewski, "The Laboratory Approach to Organization Development," *Public Administrative Review*, Vol. 27 (September, 1967), pp. 215–17.

which lists meta-values, operating values, and immediate goals of the laboratory approach. Disagreements among practitioners may exist about details in the table, but not about its essence.

There is no easy way of illustrating the complexity of Table 1, but some of its uses can be established. Consider a competitive exercise in a learning design based on the laboratory approach which uses groups. Individual A, who has suffered with the muddling-through characteristic of early meetings, seizes the opportunity provided by the time pressure of the exercise to whip his group into shape. He is well pleased with his efforts initially, but in the end his group loses badly. Moreover, he learns soon thereafter that the commitment he thought he had been instrumental in developing existed largely in his own mind. This news comes from the postexercise analysis of questionnaire data gathered at various stages of the game about the involvement of group members, members' confidence in their team strategy, and so on. These data showed that most members of A's group privately reported low involvement and lack of confidence in their team, and hence in A.

Table 1 provides a way of classifying the reactions of our hypothetical individual A. His reactions will be compared to the table via a shorthand, such as reference to (A–1) to indicate that the postexercise analysis encouraged A to take a critical and experimental approach toward his own behavior, as designated by item 1 in column A.

Let us assume that (like most of us) A did not enjoy losing the competitive exercise, particularly in the presence of prestigious peers. But A is disturbed that his group "held out on him" and "let him down" by failing to communicate their feelings and expectations to him. In terms of the vocabulary introduced earlier, his sense of his own experienced and anticipated competence has been disconfirmed. If the level of trust is high enough (B–5), and if group members generally accept the meta-values of laboratory work (A–1 through A–5), A can begin learning from this disturbing challenge to his skill and to himself (C–4). This will particularly be the case to the degree that both A and his colleagues are able to act authentically and to share their feelings and reactions (A–5).

Individual A can take diverse tacks to learning, to increasing his awareness. What did he do that encouraged other group members to lead him down the primrose path (C–1)? What cues did he miss that he might be sensitive to in similar situations (C–2 and C–3)? These are among the questions dealing with the here-and-now (B–1) that A can raise.

Only other group members can provide answers to such questions in their own reactions and feelings about the here-and-now, however, and A soon learns he will receive roughly in proportion to his giving of himself. He has somewhat opened (C–5) his Private Area by disclosing that he is troubled about his role in the exercise. That revelation may earn him some constructive feedback (B–3) that shares with him the impact his behavior had on others (A–4). His initial openness also may save A from the no-feedback that essentially rejects A as well as his specific actions (B–2) during the competitive exercise. Indeed, perhaps paradoxically, A can only gain acceptance as a person as his actions are considered significant enough to react to, whether positively or critically, and as the atmosphere permits him to be himself with minimal feelings of risk and defensiveness (B–5 and B–6).

But A must go further still if he wants to learn more. For example, he must be able to accept the integrity of the feelings of his colleagues (C–5), rather than deny them or search for underlying motives. This is a mutual enterprise, clearly. And the mutual giving and accepting of reactions, in turn, will contribute to the cohesiveness of the group (B–6). For it signals to other group members that they need not withhold their reactions (B–5) for fear that they will be disparaged or discounted. The results are generally happy, for the hiding of reactions not only creates unfinished business but also deprives everyone of data and thus inhibits everyone's learning. Moreover, as the sense of community in his training group grows, so will A feel more free to risk further exploration (A–1 and C–5) of the dynamics of the competitive exercise. And when A acknowledges that even the "strong man" can be free only as he acknowledges his interdependence with those about him (A–4 and B–6), as well as his independence of them, then a really firm foundation will have been established for learning.

Learning can take a variety of directions, once this foundation for true exchange has been established. Two basic directions can be distinguished. From that foundation, group members can collaboratively (A–3) help A survey the range of alternatives open to him (A–2), help him to work toward modifying awkward behaviors (B–4), and reinforce his efforts to experiment with other behaviors (A–1 and B–4). Also from that foundation, A may decide that change is not appropriate, given his back-home setting. The climate at his work may violate such values as those in Table 1, for example, or the individual may not feel able to integrate the new behaviors into his repertoire. In that case, A may have gained insight about the consequences he might expect from how he must behave. In addition, A has made a conscious choice among alternatives, and that act in itself may make it easier for him to understand and accept that part of himself.

These notes are sketchy and may seem lifelessly stilted in the bargain, but they illustrate the dynamic linkages that underlie the static picture in Table 1. Meta-values, operating values, and immediate goals will simultaneously if variously serve to constrain the laboratory approach, and thereby they will shape its products.

At least two questions are begged by this illustration, however. First, why should any individual A expose himself to such a learning situation? Bernard Lubin and William Eddy provide a multiple rationale that responds to this question. In their view, the laboratory approach meets a variety of needs that encourage exposure to it:[12]

- Participants have been conditioned to inhibit the expression of the emotional aspects of their communications, which reduces interpersonal effectiveness.

  The laboratory approach legitimizes feelings and facilitates experiencing, expressing, and examining the emotional aspects of communication.

- Participants, however well they may function interpersonally, have developed resistances against attending to certain classes of cues about the effects of their behavior on others. This inhibits their potential for learning newer, more functional behaviors.

  The laboratory approach provides an opportunity for each participant to receive information about how his behavior is seen, as well as to learn about his impact on others.

- Even though participants might have opportunities in everyday life to receive information about their interpersonal performance, it is difficult to practice new behaviors because of the real or imagined risk.

  The laboratory approach encourages and provides opportunities for the practice and analysis of new behavior.

- Although participants function more or less effectively in leadership and membership roles in a variety of groups back home, such factors as the need to meet a schedule make it likely that individuals will have neither the opportunity to examine decision-making, communication, or problem-solving processes, nor the leisure to analyze their roles in these back-home processes.

  The laboratory approach to learning provides opportunities to learn about the many forces at work in groups, as well as to study one's own performance in relation to these forces.

- Participants may have considerable cognitive knowledge about the "principles" of leadership, communication, group dynamics, etc. However, they may not be able to translate this knowledge into action, for a variety of reasons.

  The experience-based laboratory approach may help them to act on their knowledge.

Even granting the motivation for exposure to the laboratory approach inherent in such factors, a second question remains. Should certain individuals avoid learning designs based on the laboratory approach? The

---

12. Bernard Lubin and William B. Eddy, "The Laboratory Training Model: Rationale, Method and Some Thoughts for the Future," *International Journal of Group Psychotherapy*, Vol. 20 (July, 1970), pp. 315–16.

unqualified answer is: Yes. A more helpful answer rests on the description of the kinds of individuals who seem to learn via the laboratory approach. In sum, they are relatively healthy individuals who are capable of interacting with others and who have an interest in improving their degree of effective coping. Chris Argyris emphasizes three prime attributes of relatively healthy individuals. Such individuals have:[13]

- a relatively strong ego that is not overwhelmed by conflicts and doubts, but can entertain them
- defenses that are "low" enough, or "porous" enough, to allow the individual to hear what others say about him, with accuracy and minimal threat and without the major mediation of a therapist or educator
- an ability to communicate thoughts and feelings with minimal distortion

e. Some Guiding Implications for Learning Designs: Toward Maximizing Ownership

The various value-loaded considerations implicit in Table 1 come to an especial point as they are applied to the design of specific learning experiences. Argyris has done us the service of developing the senses in which such values specifically guide or constrain specific applications of the laboratory approach. He develops four implications for learning designs, which are presented in the form of direct quotations in Figure 2.

Argyris's implications for learning design stand on their own, and the temptation to redo his competent work will be resisted. The implications will become part of the frame of reference that will help understand and evaluate various applications of the laboratory approach.

5. SOME ALTERNATIVE LEARNING DESIGNS: DIVERSE MEANS TO COMMON GOALS?

To this point, the focus has been on the genus "laboratory approach" rather than on its several species. Deliberately, the treatment has been vague about specific learning designs. The time has come to do more fine tuning and less broad describing.

Basically, the laboratory approach seeks to get valid feedback into groups or individuals in order to improve their functioning. It is just that simple, and just that complex. There are any number of possible learning designs for attempting the task. Sometimes these alternative

---

13. Chris Argyris "T-Groups for Organizational Effectiveness," *Harvard Business Review*, Vol. 42 (March, 1964), p. 67.

Figure 2. Some Implications Guiding the Design of Laboratory Experiences Based on the Laboratory Approach

Implication I
1. All participants who attend laboratory programs of any type will have a certain degree of self-awareness, self-acceptance, and interpersonal competence.
2. These qualities will greatly influence and be influenced by the laboratory program.
3. The faculty should strive to plan activities that will tend to maintain (or increase) the present degree of self-awareness, self-acceptance, and interpersonal competence.
4. The faculty may strive to plan activities that will tend to increase the present degree of self-awareness, self-acceptance, and interpersonal competence.
5. Since man is incomplete without others, the faculty should not plan any educational activities that erode or deteriorate man's basic need for human connectedness or his responsibility toward others (in order that they and he can help themselves become more self-responsible).

Implication II:
1. The faculty should strive not to plan any activities that encourage unnecessary dependence, psychological failure, withdrawal, conformity, and mistrust.
2. The faculty should strive to plan activities that will increase the participants' knowledge of and skill in developing more effective groups, intergroups, and organizations.
3. Since the laboratory program is a system, the faculty should strive not to create one that is close to the traditional organizations, with their closedness, group inefficiencies, and intergroup rivalries.

Implication III:
No matter what the central learning target is (individual, group, organization), the learning processes used should not damage the targets that have been made peripheral. Learning, for example, that has the group as its primary target should be planned so that those types of educational activities be used that minimize damage to aspects of the individual and vice versa.

Implication IV:
Learning activities, no matter what their target, that create conditions for psychological success, confirmation, and essentiality are to be maximized. Learning activities that create conditions for psychological failure, disconfirmation, and nonessentiality are to be minimized.

Source: Chris Argyris, "On the Future of Laboratory Education," *Journal of Applied Behavioral Science*, Vol. 3 (April, 1967), pp. 155–59.

learning designs are merely more-or-less equivalent approaches; sometimes they differ significantly in terms of the risk they imply, the degree of reinforcement they provide for any changes in behavior or attitudes or values, and so on. The purpose here is to sample this diversity of learning designs, and to sketch their features and consequences.

a. The Matrix Learning Vehicle: T-Groups, or Sensitivity Training Groups

In a very real sense, the laboratory approach began with the forerunners of what are today called "T-Groups" or "sensitivity training groups." With real justice, then, the T-Group can be considered the matrix learning vehicle of the laboratory approach. Two varieties of the matrix learning vehicle need to be distinguished for some purposes, although the description below usually will apply with equal force to both varieties. They are:[14]

- *Basic T-Group*—or "stranger sensitivity training group"—composed of individuals who are strangers and do not normally work together. Focuses on expressing and unfreezing old attitudes, on developing interpersonal trust, on increasing trust and openness between group members, and on practicing new skills and behaviors.
- *Variant T-Group*—variously called "core group," "action group," or "family group"—composed of individuals who normally do work together and have a past and a future. Encourages discussion of members' working relationships. The tradeoffs are clear: there may be somewhat more risk in openness and in experimenting with new behaviors or skills; but any learning occurs in an environment that will persist after the training and which can serve to reinforce learning outside of the immediate training situation.

Some Basic Commonalities

The Basic T-Group or sensitivity training group deals largely with personal learning about the self in interpersonal and group situations.[15] In roughest terms, the Basic T-Group ("T" is for "training") may be defined as a small group of a dozen or so "normals," generally strangers who meet in an "unstructured setting" for an extended period of time with a "trainer" having a strong background in the behavioral sciences. By "unstructured setting" is meant that Basic T-Groups typically have no specific task to perform, and the focus is on learning from the interactions generated in whatever activities they engage in. The trainer plays a critical role in this purposive early nondirectedness. Hence the stock complaint is that the trainers do not even try to help. The reality is that the active intention of trainers is to maximize the sense of participant ownership of what will occur. The effect is to create dilemmas which participants must labor to resolve. The unstructured situation provides an unusual opportunity for group members to unfreeze old behavioral patterns, to look at them analytically and with low defensiveness. That situation also provides an opportunity basically to help members develop their own individualized learning society. The implied initial unhingedness can be unsettling to some individuals, but the experience

---

14. This section draws heavily on Golembiewski, "The Laboratory Approach to Organization Development," pp. 212–14.
15. For a detailed review of typical T-Group dynamics, see Carl R. Rogers, *Carl Rogers on Encounter Groups* (New York: Harper & Row, Publishers, 1970), pp. 14–42.

seems well within the thresholds of normal anxiety or stress-producing situations.[16]

Each T-Group as a learning community has its own distinctive texture, then, but commonalities abound. Overall, members of T-Groups typically have experiences that develop insight and behavioral skills which surprise the learners. The fascination of learners with T-Group processes is both common and reasonable, for the apparently unstructured T-Group is so designed as to focus on issues that are at the heart of life. Alexander Winn well captures the sense of how the Basic T-Group design generates these vital issues. He explains:

> The participants learn to the extent they change their fundamental attitude to the learning process itself. To acquire some insight, to obtain new awareness of himself, the participant must accept the raw data which the here-and-now experience generates. This acceptance implies willingness to express and deal with feelings as legitimate data for exploration. The T-Group members thus become both explorers and objects of their own exploration and study. To paraphrase Fromm-Reichmann: a successful participant, as he knows himself at the end of his T-Group experience, will be much the same person as he is known to others.
>
> The absence of structure and familiar patterns of role, status, and authority creates a dilemma which the participant must resolve. The authority vacuum must be explained (or denied) and the two main issues, i.e., our relationship to authority and our relationship to peers must be confronted. These issues epitomize our historical ambivalence toward power and love, dependency and interdependency, distance and intimacy. In existential terms, the T-Group widens considerably our range of choices and increases our awareness of freedom we may wish to enjoy. The final choice and responsibility for it remains our own.
>
> The T-Group then is a different medium of communication, a qualitatively different one from a lecture, the printed word, a seminar, or a case discussion.[17]

16. The unstructured situation seems to induce some regression in participants, usually a kind of regression in the service of the ego that facilitates learning by challenging the efficacy of previous patterns of behavior. Severe regression may explain the ego breakdowns that occasionally occur in T-Groups. Cyril R. Mill, "A Theory for the Group Dynamics Laboratory Milieu," *Adult Leadership,* Vol. 11 (November, 1962), pp. 133–34, 159–60.
   See also Section A of Part II below.
17. Alexander Winn, "The Laboratory Approach to Organization Development: A Tentative Model of Planned Change," *Journal of Management Studies,* Vol. 6 (May, 1969), p. 157.

More specifically, T-Groups have two major purposes. First, their members analyze the data generated by their own here-and-now interactions. These interactions cover a broad range. Thus T-Group members:

- explore the impact of their behaviors, values, and attitudes on others
- determine whether they want to change their behaviors, values, or attitudes
- experiment with new behaviors, values, or attitudes, if individuals consider changes desirable
- develop awareness of how groups can both stimulate and inhibit personal growth and decision-making

The second goal of T-Group members is to work to develop insight and behavioral skills that facilitate both analysis and action in the T-Group, as well as in back-home situations. Sensitivity training seeks, in the words of William G. Scott, to

. . . accomplish the end of behavior change through a philosophy and technique of training which is best described as a concern with "how"—how a trainee appraises himself, how a group behaves, how another would react in a given situation. In short, sensitivity training has as its purpose the development of [the trainee's] awareness of himself, of others, of group processes, and of group culture.[18]

Unlike the "deep" analysis of psychoanalysis and psychotherapy, T-Groups consider mostly the public, here-and-now data available to all members. The range of these target data is very wide. They include:

- the specific *structures* members develop in their interaction, such as the leadership rank order
- the *processes* of their group life, with special attention to getting a group started, keeping it going, and then experiencing its inevitable death
- their specific *emotional reactions* of warmth or anger or whatever to one another's behavior and to their experiences
- the varying and diverse *styles* or *modes* of individual and group behavior, as in fighting the trainer or in fleeing some issue that has overwhelmed group members

The overall goal is to increase the level of trust among group members so that each will provide the others with timely and unambiguous feed-

18. William G. Scott, *Organization Theory* (Homewood, Ill.: Richard D. Irwin, 1967), p. 332.

76

back concerning perceptions, feelings, or reactions. Hence the incidence of such conversational fragments: "I feel that . . ."; "the way you come across to me . . ."; "I believe that . . ."; and "what I hear you saying is. . . ." Briefly, each individual is *the* expert about his own perceptions, reactions, and feelings. Being open about these gives group members data vital for acting effectively and efficiently. In contrast, failure to risk being open implies the creation of roadblocks to group and individual development.

The typical design of a laboratory experience also provides for developing and testing insight and behavioral skills. Much of this work goes on in the Basic T-Group, but specific exercises which can cover an extremely broad range—from improving listening skills to more visceral experiences dealing with an individual's specific reactions to warm interpersonal contacts—are common. Ideally, such exercises are tailored to the specific needs of a specific Basic T-Group. Consequently, their design makes great demands on the experience and ingenuity of the trainer, for sensitivity groups can develop in an incredible diversity of ways.

Variant T-Groups have been developed to facilitate back-home learning, that is, to ease the transfer of learning from the temporary environment in which the learning occurs to other environments in the learner's life space. Variant T-Groups are intended to increase the probability that their members will experiment at the worksite with new behavioral skills or insights, so as to create more satisfying work relations. These Variant T-Groups may be called family groups, core groups, or action groups. They differ from Basic T-Groups in two senses. They are composed of individuals who typically work together and who consequently have past relationships with which to contend. In addition, members of such groups will continue their relationships outside of the specific learning situation. The rationale supporting their use essentially proposes that members of a Variant T-Group can rely on their common experience to support being open in the broader company of organization peers and superiors, where great forces probably inhibit behavioral change or experimentation. Variant T-Groups tend to range widely between the group's here-and-now and the organizational there-and-then. That is, their members often have long and intricate common histories that do not so enrich or burden Basic T-Groups. In groups of both kinds, however, the aim is to help liberate the individual from socioemotional impediments to his effective functioning, whether as a person or as an organization member.

The diversity of T-Groups extends far beyond these elemental distinctions, but the underlying unity of laboratory programs of organization change is nonetheless real and marked. Although what follows is oversimplified, it illustrates that unity. The immediate analysis stresses three kinds of learning possible in both Basic T-Groups and Variant

T-Groups, which variously tend toward the same end: to free individuals to be more effective while they are more themselves. The three kinds of learning are not mutually exclusive.

First, some individuals may extract learning from the lab experience that is largely cognitive and technique-oriented. Thus, some participants may emphasize after training that their committees function more smoothly because of their sensitivity to, and increased skills in dealing with, the processes of their own functioning. Both increased sensitivity and skills in process analysis are common products of laboratory programs.[19]

Second, for many participants, T-Groups or sensitivity training experiences highlight needs that previously went unmet or unrecognized. Very little of this learning may properly be called cognitive. The learning is emotional, making the individual more aware of who he is, what he needs to function wholly, and how he can get it. Very often, the core issue is the feeling of personal repression and confinement in life or in organizations. The consequences are multiple: the individual feels restricted, his levels of trust and comfort are low, and his personal effectiveness and perhaps his interpersonal competence and task efficiency suffer. His sense of confinement is likely to grow, consequently, and the stage is set for a new and more regressive cycle. The laboratory approach can help break this cycle by allowing the individual to work on issues which are real to him, but which tend to be shunted aside in organizations. One highly placed executive in a federal agency expressed the point in these terms:

> Many times in the last four years, I wanted to get up and walk out of a staff meeting. I asked myself what am I doing here with all these strangers. Now, after all these years, I feel a little like starting to talk to A. . . . Staff meetings have become more open. That makes the big difference.

Third, experiences in T-Groups may primarily tap varying levels of unfinished business. The term was introduced earlier. By way of a brief refresher here, note that if an issue keeps intruding itself and inhibits work on other issues, it is a piece of unfinished business. At least two cases must be distinguished. The more devilish variety of unfinished business is that to which the involved parties are but dimly alert. Much effort often is necessary to surface this business and to relate it to some inducing stimulus. There is a second variety of unfinished business, about which all parties are more or less consciously aware but which they withhold, and even this variety has its subtle aspects. Two parties may share some specific information with a third party, and each may know, or guess, that the other knows. If the issue is of mutual interest, however,

19. Chris Argyris, "Interpersonal Barriers to Decision-Making," *Harvard Business Review,* Vol. 44 (March, 1966), pp. 84–97.

the business remains unfinished until the two parties publicly exchange that piece of information and work on it. The issue presses on the consciousness and inhibits both individuals as they continue to suppress it.

Unfinished business covers a wide range. Thus a continuing wrangle between a trainer and T-Group member about authority may come to be seen by the latter as a symbol of unresolved tensions between him and his father, for example. The appropriate here-and-now response by the trainer to that disclosure is: "It's hard to deal with that business here, because your father is not here. But I can tell you how this authority figure reacts to you; and the other group members also have seen the interaction between us. Looking at our interaction may help in other situations; and it certainly should help here." Or an individual may reveal (as he has perhaps long yearned to do) that his organizational aloofness hides a tormenting loneliness. The manager quoted in Section A above provided such testimony, for example, as he explained what happened to him during his only recreation, solitary sailing far out into the ocean. "I stand up in the boat and stare into the darkness. then up to the sky," he concluded. "Something surges over me. I throw my arms open wide and scream into the darkness . . . I wait . . . listen . . . Nobody hears me."[20] If such disclosure occurs in a Variant T-Group, the work team might be able to provide continuous support at work. In the case of the lonely manager, for example, this typical deluge of emotional support from his workmates followed his soliloquy about the sea and his loneliness.

> People were crying for the lonely old man. There was the look of peace on Bob's face and slowly, somehow, the loneliness was leaving. . . .
>
> People said, "Thank you, Bob." "You're a poet." "You've got great courage." "I could listen to you all night." "I've never known what a wonderful person you are."
>
> Jack said, "You're a young, powerful person, Bob. Look at yourself."
>
> Bob's smile was young. He seemed overwhelmed with the adulation of the group—with the love that came by letting people in.[21]

Family groups composed of individuals with close organizational ties can extend such support into the worksite, which is one basic reason for their usefulness. Basic T-Groups have major limitations in this regard.

The consequences of raising unfinished business may be diverse, but

20. Arthur H. Kuriloff and Stuart Atkins, "T-Group for a Work Team," *Journal of Applied Behavioral Science*, Vol. 2 (January, 1966) , p. 85.
21. *Ibid.*, p. 85.

usually the consciousness of all concerned is liberated. As an example of the worst (and highly improbable) result: A serious issue is raised prematurely and with little skill by a member of a T-Group. Here, the consequences may be harmful, if time and will are short. One effective safeguard against such an eventuality—and, in addition, against a willful mischiefmaker—is the highly cohesive character of the typical T-Group, whose members cannot be divided and conquered as easily as in the "real world" because of the participants' commitment to evaluate the processes of their own interaction. The presence of a trainer also is an important safeguard.

The most effective safeguard against hurtful feedback in T-Groups, however, is built into the dynamics of the laboratory approach by the value-loaded constraints introduced in the previous section. These constraints aid in the development and testing of mutual confidence and trust among T-Group members. And as confidence and trust grow, so also does the capacity to state, to hear, and to work through weighty issues. This may seem a fragile defense against the inopportune raising of difficult issues, until one sees it in action. The successful T-Group, in short, tends to develop a helping and (when necessary) healing community of learners that creates an unusually strong probability of regenerative interaction. The T-Group which does not progress beyond early stages of development, in addition, is not likely to induce the authentic and intense behavior that we normally anticipate might be hurtful to group members.

Last-ditch defenses against deeply hurtful feedback are seldom needed, however. Very often, the public raising of unfinished business will suffice to extinguish its press on the consciousness. Or at least the group is free to work on the issue, and in a supportive way that eases the task.

Openly raising unfinished business is no cure-all. Some unfinished business cannot be settled. But raising such issues mutually and publicly at least signals the inappropriateness of overloading organizational or interpersonal relations with that piece of unresolved business. Some unfinished business may even require therapy. One of the T-Group trainer's important functions, indeed, is to intervene decisively when it is necessary to encourage group members to concentrate on their immediate feelings and reactions, thereby avoiding the temptation to provide amateur psychiatric services. Group members are *the* experts about their own feelings, reactions, and perceptions. But few group members are qualified therapists.

Some Differences between T-Groups and Group Therapy

T-Groups also can be distinguished in terms of what they are not, although only imprecisely. For example, T-Groups are not therapy groups in the usually accepted sense, even though they share some common features.

Patent commonalities exist between T-Groups and therapy groups, as Jerome Frank conveniently establishes for us.[22] Overall, both kinds of groups experience some tension in early sessions; initial uncertainty and lack of trust in each method are characteristic; the focus is on assisting members in evaluating the need for changes in behavior, attitudes, or values; and minimally distorted communication is their common goal. In addition, both T-Groups and therapy groups can have similar developmental histories involving authority and affection issues like those sketched in Section A above. Even more, some users of each approach have adopted the traditional stance of the other.[23] Indeed Irwin Yalom concludes that a significant number of T-Group practitioners aim at "not only the acquisition of interpersonal skills but the total enhancement of the individual."[24]

The distinctions between the two approaches to learning, however, are such as to mark them as members of a distinct genus. Frank details several major differences. The intensity of the emotional arousal is often greater in therapy groups; members of therapy groups have relatively serious functioning inadequacies that require major attention, while T-Group members are relatively healthy persons who are seeking to augment their effectiveness; and the trainer in therapy groups is deliberately a more central figure than his counterpart in the T-Group.[25] To this impressive collection of differences, Lubin and Eddy add several significant ones. They note that the T-Group

> . . . deals almost exclusively with the "here and now" of group development and transactions among members, to the exclusion of genetic material. The therapy group, on the other hand, frequently searches for the factors associated with conflicts and perceptual distortions in the patient's past life experiences. Dreams, fantasy and discussion of patients' relationships with people not in the group are very legitimate for the work of the

22. Jerome D. Frank, "Training and Therapy," in Leland P. Bradford, Jack R. Gibb, and Kenneth D. Benne (eds.), *T-Group Theory and Laboratory Method* (New York: John Wiley & Sons, 1964), pp. 442–51.

23. Gottschalk and Pattison, *op. cit.*, p. 826, note: "Some T-Group trainers disdain group process or group growth, for they see their goal as solely personal change. On the other hand, many group therapists see individual change as accomplished only through effective group process. Hence their therapeutic effort is directed at maximizing group process. In this instance the T-Group and the therapy group have reversed the traditional stances from both fields."

24. Irwin D. Yalom, *The Theory and Practice of Group Psychotherapy* (New York: Basic Books, 1970), p. 8.

25. See on this point, Leonard Horwitz, "Transference in Training Groups and Therapy Groups," *International Journal of Group Psychotherapy*, Vol. 14 (March, 1964), pp. 203–33.

therapy group. The patient in group therapy is not interested in and does not attend in order to learn about "groups." For him the therapy group mainly exists as the medium through which the amelioration of his suffering or help with personal problems takes place. Conversely, the group emphasis T-Group member has a high investment in learning about groups and improving his leadership and membership skill.[26]

Beyond such elemental and relatively sharp differences, distinctions between T-Groups and therapy groups tend to become differences in degree. But those differences in degree can be significant, and the need to develop and maintain a delicate uniqueness is correspondingly important. For example, the easy approach is to note that T-Groups are for normals, while the diseased require therapy. But T-Groups have been used with apparent success for psychiatric populations. Moreover, the plain fact is that normal/diseased are not polar-opposite categories[27] into which individuals can be sorted. The only rule of thumb for the use of T-Groups, then, is to discourage reliance on them as a therapy substitute as far as that is possible beforehand, and to be prepared to cope initially with symptoms of disease as that may become necessary.

Similarly, it is only superficially definitive to note that therapy deals with removing more-or-less gross developmental abnormalities, with psychopathology as an explanation for dysfunctional behaviors. In contrast, T-Groups can then be said to deal with enlarging human potentialities, which is the traditional province of education.[28] Irving Berger makes the distinction when he observes that both therapy and education "rely largely upon developing and encouraging the maturing capacities within individuals," and that this common reliance creates problems in differentiating therapy from education. "A way to resolve our dilemma," Berger concludes, "would be to consider therapy specifically oriented toward solving intrapersonal problems, with consideration of resistances, transferences, and the unconscious drives and their derivatives. References then to therapeutic changes in educational groups could best be stated as *ego development* or improvement in one's self-image."[29]

This approach does not question the validity of the clinical model, but challenges its exclusivity. Basic to this challenge to the clinical model are a number of key assumptions about man as interested in growth

---

26. Lubin and Eddy, *op. cit.,* p. 328.
27. Arthur Burton, *Modern Psychotherapeutic Practice* (Palo Alto, Cal.: Science and Behavior Books, 1965) , pp. 383–85.
28. Most observers also note that formal education has failed in this job of putting the individual in meaningful and growthful contact with others. See Egan, *op. cit.,* p. 12.
29. Irving L. Berger, "Resistances to Learning Process in Group Dynamics Programs," *American Journal of Psychiatry,* Vol. 6 (December, 1969) , pp. 852–53.

despite his relative well-being, as contrasted with a model of man in more rather than less acute difficulty. As Frederick Stoller details these assumptions that challenge the clinical model:[30]

- At any given moment, the human adult possesses a complex variety of possibilities or potentialities which are latent in substantial part but which also are available to him under appropriate conditions.
- People invest energy in some aspects of themselves at the expense of others, with the consequence that one facet of the individual often becomes more fully explored and developed than others.
- Latent responses within the individual's hierarchy of responses are often available and can emerge when the more frequent responses cease to occur with regularity.
- All exploration involves risk-taking and courage.
- Dulled perception about one's course in the world is probably the rule rather than the exception.

At some point, despite the general attractiveness of this challenging model, "enlarging human potentialities" will overlap with "removing gross developmental abnormalities." Again, the need is to distinguish the two end points of the underlying continuum, to limit the number of cases in the area that overlap, and to develop skill and competence in dealing with the inevitable but hopefully few and decreasing number of residual cases.

Some Differences between T-Groups

While differences are being drawn between therapy groups and T-groups, note that significant differences also exist among T-Groups. Given that each laboratory experience is somewhat *sui generis,* Lubin and Eddy distinguish T-Groups with three more-or-less distinct emphases: Group-Oriented T-Groups, Intergroup T-Groups, and Personal and Interpersonal T-Groups. These are described briefly in Table 2, in shorthand terms that should be generally understandable.

The three types of T-Groups distinguished in Table 2, in effect, reflect the impact of two main trends in laboratory education. These trends, in Lakin's terminology,[31] emphasize the use of the T-Group for enhanced interactional awareness, and for expanded experiencing.

---

30. Frederick H. Stoller, "A Stage for Trust," in Arthur Burton (ed.), *Encounter* (San Francisco: Jossey-Bass, Inc., Publishers, 1969), pp. 82–84.
31. Martin Lakin, *Interpersonal Encounter* (New York: McGraw-Hill Book Co., 1972), esp. pp. 20–23, provides a revealing summary of the two trends. For an early and prominent statement of the transition between the two trends, see Irving R. Wechsler, Fred Massarik, and Robert Tannenbaum, "The Self In Process," esp. pp. 34–35, in Irving Wechsler and Edgar Schein, *Issues in Human Relations Training* (Washington, D.C.: National Training Laboratories, Selected Reading Series No. 5, 1962).

Table 2. Basic Emphases in T-Groups

Design Focus	Individual Relevance	Organizational Relevance	Experiences
Personal and Interpersonal	More openness and honesty in dealing with self and others Reduced defensiveness and game-type behavior Increased capacity to learn from one's own behavior Expanded awareness to growth potential Increased awareness of racially conditioned feelings and attitudes	Improved communication with others Development of new ways of working with others Locating feelings that block satisfactory and effective relationships, and bringing these out for examination Working for creative resolution to conflict	T-Groups Nonverbal exercises Painting Improvisation and fantasy Body movement Interpersonal confrontation Racial confrontation
Intergroup	Effects on your behavior when your group is working with another group Looking at your loyalties in multigroup operations Diagnosing intragroup problems brought on by intergroup work Examining the effects of different racial mixtures	Examining intergroup consultation, cooperation, and competition (corresponds to interdepartmental relationships in a firm) How changes can be made between groups Looking at payoffs for collaboration and competition Conceptualizing and confronting conflict, including that generated by racial differences	T-Groups Competitive and collaborative exercises Observation of groups Conflict models Multiple loyalty simulations Construction of conceptual models
Group	Increasing ability to act in different ways in a group and to live with different types of group climates, including that in which race is a problem Getting feedback on your ground style and work methods Using your own feelings to help understand group processes Feeling freer in groups	Understanding stages of group life and development Leadership and membership in groups (such as departments, task forces, teams, classes) Learning why some problems get "solved" over and over, and why some decisions don't stick Constructive methods for dealing with problem members Experimenting with different methods for handling racially generated problems	T-Groups Role analysis Cluster and large groups Team building Consultation Helping relationships Construction of conceptual models Group problem-solving exercises

Source: Adapted from Bernard Lubin and William B. Eddy, "The Laboratory Training Model: Rationale, Method, and Some Thoughts about the Future," *International Journal of Psychotherapy*, Vol. 20 (July, 1970), p. 314.

These main trends in the use of the T-Group are not mutually exclusive; but they can easily come into conflict. When the goal is enhanced interactional awareness, as in Group-oriented and Intergroup T-Groups, much attention will be devoted to the individual in context: decision-making processes, leadership styles, subgroup formation, and so on, as well as to the emotional reactions associated with such topics. Much of this may be seen as pointless and even counterproductive, given the goal of expanded experiencing. Consequently, several elements of technique and emphasis have evolved that enhance the narrowing and deepening of focus. For example, the trainer's role in Personal and Interpersonal T-Groups becomes far more central and directive. Moreover, the focus of attention in Personal and Interpersonal T-Groups at least shifts decidedly toward the intrapersonal and toward unconscious processes, and that focus may be more or less exclusively on "self-awareness." Perhaps most characteristic, finally, emphasis on the individual level of analysis in "personal growth" experiences is facilitated by heavy reliance on a range of mini-designs for learning, very often "nonverbals," that are used to trigger various emotions and reactions in individuals. As Lakin observes, "talking and thinking are somewhat deemphasized" in the experiencing trend, and a "few trainers . . . go so far as to castigate the uses of language and thinking as inhibiting entrapments of the spirit or as manipulative 'head work.' " Such designs also include trainer-directed "body movement" exercises that attempt to involve more of the large muscles. The goal is to get the "whole man" involved in learning, as it were, to involve the peripheral nervous system in learning as well as the autonomic and central nervous systems.

Lines are notoriously difficult to draw, but such differentiating tendencies have the potential for generating differences in kind as well as degree. As the following section will show, for example, spin-offs from the Personal and Interpersonal T-Group—especially the "encounter group"—sometimes extend these differentia so markedly as to imply a genus distinct from the laboratory approach. These extensions tend, as it were, to reach back to the origins of group methods, when individuals were dealt with in a group, but not by and with a group. The extensions consequently forfeit some variable part of the distinctiveness of group processes and methods.

b. Some Spin-off Designs:
Highlighting and Intensifying T-Group Dynamics

The T-Group, or matrix learning vehicle of the laboratory approach, has had a profound and wide-ranging impact on developing technologies for socioemotional learning. And no wonder. For the T-Group not only intimately touches the core issues of life and living, but it does so in convenient ways. As Kenneth Benne explains, the T-Group triggers

> . . . some of the deepest dilemmas of personal and social life, the dilemmas of self and society, of authority and freedom, of conservation and change. It involves the odyssey of human loneliness and of apartness partially overcome in an association

which, while firm and security-giving, yet enhances and affirms rather than eclipses and derogates individual variation and difference. Although such dilemmas are part of the lot of all men, in the T-Group they can be dramatized on a stage small enough so that they can be enacted as well as seen, worked through to some acceptable outcome, and the experience of their working out criticized and evaluated in terms of personally significant ideas.[32]

Consequently, the T-Group has spawned a range of designs that variously seek to exploit its potential for diverse learning. These designs differ both in degree and in kind, having in common the basic desire to utilize the major forces inherent in group situations for learning and development. Basically, these spin-off learning designs of the T-Group take two forms. First, some such designs seek to highlight dynamics typical of T-Groups, while other spin-offs from the basic T-Group technology seek intensification and speeding-up of the learning experience in major ways. Both of these varieties are illustrated below. Second, some of these designs can even be used to generate these dynamics outside of T-Group contexts, as will be developed under Topic C below.

Highlighting T-Group Dynamics and Isolating Their Analogs

Various designs have been developed to highlight and heighten the basic T-Group processes of feedback and disclosure, for example. These designs vary significantly in impact and risk, and no doubt in potential contribution to learning.

Consider feedback. Three types of designs can be illustrated, which run the gamut of risk as well as potential for learning. One benign example gently uses the Jo-Hari Window as a vehicle for encouraging feedback. After two or three T-Group meetings, a general session is held. Participants are first introduced to the Window and its supporting rationale, then asked to anonymously write on sheets of paper some information they have not shared in the group, either feedback or self-disclosure. For the former, for example, the individual is asked to indicate some behavior or attitude or reaction to another member which the writer feels is in the Blind Area of that member's Window. These samples of feedback or disclosure are then read aloud to the participants by a presenter, for the purpose of indicating how much data are still in the Blind Area or the Private Arena. Names typically are not used.

The purpose of the design built around the Jo-Hari Window is direct: to encourage feedback under conditions that encourage safety. Typically,

---

32. Kenneth D. Benne, "From Polarization to Paradox," in Bradford, Gibb, and Benne (eds.), *op. cit.*, pp. 235–36.

groups will spend the following session exploring who wrote what about whom and why, as intended. Numerous safeguards clearly are also built into this design. Primarily, the writer has an anonymous chance to observe the impact that his feedback or disclosure has on the listeners, perhaps on his specific target.

Some generically similar designs may not be so benign, whether used in T-Groups or other contexts. Thus members of a group of married couples are encouraged to write on a slip of paper three things they would never dream of telling their spouses.[33] To encourage disclosure, members are then challenged as to who will be the first to publicly share one of the items on his or her list with wife or husband. Such designs are in a different class than the one above.

Somewhere between the Jo-Hari Window design and the one for married couples is the basic interview/report model used to increase feedback to all kinds of systems, from couples to members of large organization units. In this model, a change agent first interviews those involved and then variously reports back the results of his investigation. The purpose is to increase the valid information available to the system, while preserving some margin of safety for the participants.

A wide variety of designs also has been developed, some of which explore relatively specific emotions or processes and others whose consequences are more difficult to predict or control.[34] In the former category, for example, feelings associated with trust may be explored in a well-known set of nonverbal exercises. Thus an individual may stand with his back to a cluster of people and be instructed to hold himself rigid while he allows himself to fall backward. In the interim, he may trigger feelings associated with his trust in the cluster of people behind him to arrest his fall. A few people cannot bring themselves to place even this minimal trust in others, while most experience a moment of doubt about

---

33. George B. Leonard, "The Man and Woman Thing," *Look,* December 24, 1968, pp. 62–68.
34. William C. Schutz, *Joy: Expanding Human Awareness* (New York: Grove Press, 1967) and B. Gunther, *Sense Relaxation: Below Your Mind* (New York: P. F. Collier, 1968) both describe a number of high-impact designs, often non-verbal. A broader range of designs is surveyed in J. William Pfeiffer and John E. Jones (eds.), *A Handbook of Structured Experiences for Human Relations Training* (Iowa City, Iowa: University Associates Press), Vol. 1 (1969), Vol. 2 (1970), and Vol. 3 (1971). Pfeiffer and Jones make a useful distinction, treating designs that emphasize fantasies, awareness expansion, and nonverbal communication with "a specific caution." Such designs are often used to heighten awareness of self and others, and also to stimulate affective response. Pfeiffer and Jones emphasize the safeguarding of participant voluntarism in the use of such high-impact designs, to reduce the probability that a learner will be put in a situation which he cannot handle and which he would generally avoid. Most of the learning designs in the Pfeiffer and Jones volumes, they note, "can be used by facilitators with limited experience and limited formal training in the behavioral sciences." (Vol. 1, p. 1.)

the risk and the relief of the invariably successful efforts by the people behind to gently break the fall.

Intensifying T-Group Dynamics: Encounters

Various designs are oriented toward intensifying normal T-Group dynamics in major ways, and perhaps the most prominent is the encounter group. Encounter groups differ enormously among themselves, basically as a function of the style or personality of the professional leader or facilitator. For example, the encounter groups of Carl Rogers clearly are very much like the Basic T-Group described above.

A certain class of "encounter" is usefully distinguished from T-Groups, however. The differences are shadings, sometimes of emphasis and sometimes of essence. The common belief underlying some encounters is that "the therapeutic process can be viewed not as treatment but as resumption of the humanizing or psychological growth process where it has been blocked off, re-experiencing dissociated parts of the self, converting structures of flexible exploratory human relationships, redefining self through current relationships."[35] The underlying rationale takes some such form.[36] Human beings function at some small fraction of their potential; releasing blockages to this potential will enable individuals to break through to more effective levels of the Self, and to a greater fluidity and efficiency in such activities as communication.[37]

Depending on the degree of emphasis and extension of these core notions, encounter groups are either similar to T-Groups or significantly different from them. Both learning vehicles, for example, attempt to contribute to more effective interpersonal functioning. Five properties of one class of encounter suggest the character of the significant differences between the learning vehicles.

First, despite a range of emphases,[38] encounter groups concentrate on primary thought processes, via the extensive use of a broad range of exercises. Lubin and Eddy make the point fully:

> Such strategies as increasing sensory awareness, relaxation methods, fantasy and dream study, nonverbal games, physical con-

---

35. Bertram R. Forer, "Therapeutic Relationships in Groups," in Burton (ed.), *Encounter*, p. 35.
36. Bernard Lubin and William P. Eddy, "The Laboratory Training Model: Rationale, Method, and Some Thoughts for the Future," *International Journal of Group Psychotherapy*, Vol. 20 (July, 1970), pp. 329–30.
37. C. Moustakas, *Creativity and Conformity* (Princeton, N.J.: D. Van Nostrand Co., 1967), p. 45.
38. Compare, for example, the mainly verbal encounter groups described by Rogers with the emphasis on somatopsychologic methods described by Schutz: Carl R. Rogers, "The Process of the Basic Encounter Group," in J. F. T. Bugental (ed.), *Challenges of Humanistic Psychology* (New York: McGraw-Hill Book Co., 1967), pp. 261–78; and Schutz, *op. cit.*

tact, meditation, etc., are utilized to circumvent the restrictions maintained by the censoring ego, to enable participants to get in contact with early "feeling memories," to experience feelings at deeper levels, and to make the unconscious conscious.[39]

Encounter group members may explore fantasies and daydreams or engage in free association. The purpose is to make individuals more aware of their primary thought processes and, perhaps, more skillful in extracting meaning from their productions. Or members may be encouraged to explore their sensations during body-movement sessions or to analyze their body styles in expressing various emotions and reactions.

A primitive contrast between what may be called the "intended depth" of encounter groups and T-Groups helps make the present point. Encounters intentionally seek to plumb the psychic depths.[40] Although T-Groups as here conceived have shifted somewhat toward greater personal insight in their developmental history, in Leonard Horwitz's terms, they "do *not* typically aim at uncovering and resolving unconscious conflict." Rather, they attempt to help the individual perceive more clearly his own mode of interaction which may impair his effectiveness. Horwitz concludes: "Perhaps one could say that T-Groups aim to impart insights concerning the more conscious or preconscious levels of personality functioning."[41] In related terms, Gerard Egan stresses that psychotherapy deals primarily with experiencing, "with the client's struggle with his directly felt experiencing [in which] the individual's inward data are more important than words." In sensitivity groups, however, Egan observes, "it is rather a question of getting participants to verbalize the more or less integral *pathos* experiences they *do* have and *are* in contact with."[42] From another point of view, sensitivity training allows the individual to test his "assumptive world," and especially as it refers to interpersonal relations.[43] Encounter groups are likely to strike deeper, to stress and to seek to change the "internalized parents" of taboos and prescriptions learned by individuals earlier in life that complicate or conflict with the realities of adult relationships.[44] At the same time, both T-Groups and encounters assume that persons need interpersonal relationships for growth. It is their approach to this agreement that differs.

Second, the encounter group is often distinguished from the T-Group in two significant and related ways, differences that are sometimes one of degree and most times of kind. That is, the encounter group is less in-

---

39. Lubin and Eddy, *op. cit.,* p. 330.
40. Forer, *op. cit.,* pp. 38–40.
41. Horwitz, *op. cit.,* p. 204.
42. Egan, *op. cit.,* p. 183.
43. Jerome D. Frank, *Persuasion and Healing* (Baltimore, Md.: Johns Hopkins University Press, 1961), pp. 18–34.
44. Forer, *op. cit.,* p. 32.

terested in group phenomena, and the role of the trainer or leader is far more central than in T-Groups. Specifically, encounter groups take place in group situations, but their dominant focus is on leader-member relations rather than on member-member relations, as in the T-Group. That is, there is less emphasis in encounter groups on the consensual validation that is such a powerful force for learning in T-Groups, as members compare perceptions and reactions. This individuation in encounter groups may encourage a kind of emotional narcissism and privatism, as some critics fear, and it may forfeit powerful reinforcers of change. Moreover, and there is little doubt about this point, the kind of group development sketched in Section A above is not likely to occur in some encounter groups.

Perhaps the major difference is that the trainer in the class of encounter group of interest here does not behave so as to create a "leadership vacuum." Far from it, in fact. Despite clear exceptions,[45] the trainer in an encounter group seems to behave more or less consciously in ways that trigger major processes characteristic of psychotherapy, such as transference.[46] As Lubin and Eddy compare the trainer roles in the two situations:

> The centrality of the encounter group leader and his prerogative to structure the experience of participants are accepted by participants. In contrast, participants in laboratory training are encouraged to examine their feelings about and their perceptions of the various roles that the trainer takes during the laboratory as part of the learning process.
>
> . . . In the encounter group, since the role of the leader is so central to what takes place in the group, the occurrence of feedback from peers is variable and depends upon the leader's style. In the gestalt encounter group, for example, the leader may work in a one-to-one manner with an individual for an extended period of time. It might be quite awhile before other group members have the opportunity to share impressions and feelings with the protagonist.[47]

---

45. Hobart F. Thomas, "Encounter—The Game of No Game," in Burton (ed.), *Encounter*, p. 78, notes: "I am very much in accord with those who view the encounter group leader as a facilitator rather than one who directs and tells people what to do. As I see it his main responsibility lies in his ability to allow for the maximum possible development of the forces lying fallow within the group. There is immense potential for healing relationships between people, and I feel that in a climate such as the one I am attempting to describe, that people manifest a natural tendency to seek out others who meet their needs at the moment. This is indeed a type of therapeutic community."

46. Horwitz, *op. cit.*

47. Lubin and Eddy, *op. cit.*, p. 330.

In a T-Group, the basic trainer style is intended to facilitate group development, as well as to intensify the sense of ownership among participants of the learning experience. Literally, and by design, the group dynamics engaged by the normal T-Group are at least not encouraged to develop in some encounter groups.

Third, encounter groups tend not to be characterized by the here-and-now emphasis of T-Groups. There seems considerable searching for genetic materials in some of the available descriptions,[48] although the range is broad.[49] John Mann reflects this range when he notes that

> . . . it would be premature to conclude that the major or sole function of an encounter group is to provide psychotherapy for relatively healthy people. Psychotherapy can be the point of concentration, and many of the practitioners take this focus, but such an interpretation is not inclusive of the encounter group phenomenon.[50]

The variety is consistent with the observation of Arthur Burton, a friendly observer. "Encounter groups," he noted, "have been so busy being expressive that they have had little time to look to their theories."[51]

Fourth, encounter groups have broader ambitions for change than T-Groups, and they typically meet for shorter periods of time. The ambitions show through clearly. Carl Rogers is quoted as saying that "the encounter movement is the most significant social movement of our time." And encounters are offered as a "secularized psychotherapy for Everyman," with the group by and large not being led by "psychoanalysts or psychiatrists but by people trained in the social and behavioral sciences," as well as by group leaders who are "in vast numbers teachers, ministers, publishers, artists, housewives, students, and a laity imbued with a certain call to rescue humanity."[52]

These ambitions are often sought in brief time frames. A weekend is a more or less typical duration for an encounter group. Techniques—such as the "marathon"—have been developed to make full use of the brief period allotted.[53]

48. John Mann, *Encounter: A Weekend with Intimate Strangers* (New York: Grossman Publishers, 1970) .
49. Thomas, *op. cit.*
50. Mann, *op. cit.,* p. x.
51. Burton (ed.) , *Encounter,* p. ix.
52. *Ibid.,* pp. 2, 8.
53. Not all proponents of encounter sanction such techniques. For example, Burton (ed.) , *Encounter,* p. 24, lets go this broadside: "The marathon encounter experience, as a special form of encounter, seems to imply that intensity and forced confrontation is an important factor in growth. The term marathon . . . implies seeing things to a conclusion and this fits the American temperament. The marathon encounter, by the bye, is also very lucrative for the group leader and often goes along with his usually insistent temperament. But the principle of spaced

Fifth, in many senses the differences between the target class of encounters and T-Groups involve the point when each says: Stop. Encounter group ideology is far the less restrained. A report of the American Psychiatric Association makes the point with some force. That report notes:

> The part has been equated with the whole; the naive assumption has been made that if something is good, more is better. If involvement is good, then prolonged continuous marathon involvement is better. If expression of feelings is good, . . . then total expression—hitting, touching, feeling, kissing and fornication—must be better. If self-disclosure is good, then immediate, prolonged exposure in the nude (culminating in the members of the group "eyeballing" each others' crotch area) must be better.[54]

All of these themes, and more, are reflected in the following extended portion of a dramatic enactment of an encounter group. Richard is the trainer, and Restas is the central member. Restas is a drug user, and Richard's interpretation is that Restas uses drugs to numb himself to his experience, to freeze out other people and to keep from feeling. Restas, indeed, reports that he feels "frozen in a block of ice," and one group member raises the question of whether there is "any way we could warm [Restas] up." The narrative begins with a reaction and a question to Richard:

> RESTAS: Leave me alone. All of you. I don't want your help. I don't want anything from any of you. I must have been out of my mind to come here. You bunch of amateur head-shrinkers. You don't know what you are doing. It is terribly dangerous. Do people ever commit suicide?
>
> . . . . .
>
> RICHARD: Really, Restas. I am concerned that your anger may trigger the unfreezing process. I wouldn't want to be responsible.
>
> RESTAS: You wouldn't want to be responsible! What the hell do you want? All you do is stir people up and then you step back with a picture of mock horror on your face and say, "I am not responsible."
>
> Let me tell you, you tin god . . . let me tell you the truth . . . You are a coward like the rest . . . You are a hollow

---

learning still applies to growth experiences and we know that much occurs between treatment sessions. Marathon encounter seems at present a hysterical form of encounter."

54. American Psychiatric Association, *Encounter Groups and Psychiatry* (Washington, D.C., April, 1970), pp. 15–16.

balloon . . . a caricature of a person . . . You are not real
. . . Take away the group and what would you be? . . . a
man caught with his pants down . . . I know you. You look
good here . . . but I have seen your weaknesses, I have
smelled your fear . . .

RICHARD: Are you feeling any tingling in your fingers?

. . . . .

RESTAS: You know how I feel. There are steel pins digging into
my nerve endings.

RICHARD: Ann, run into the kitchen and get all the ice they have
. . . and bring back some towels.

RESTAS: You want to freeze me up again.

RICHARD: Hurry!

. . . . .

RICHARD: You don't have to be a hero, Restas. You can cry out
if you want to.

RESTAS: I—don't—want—to. Stop trying to make me weak. Just
because I showed you up doesn't mean you have to castrate
me.

RICHARD: Nobody here will think less of you. You don't have to
suffer silently.

. . . . .

ANN: I have the ice.

RICHARD: I am going to give the ice cubes to everyone and ask
them to press them to different parts of you. They won't
touch you, only the ice will. If it is too cold, they can wrap it
in towels. Is that all right?

RESTAS: Hurry. Maybe it will help.

ANN: Let me try on your forehead. Is that any better?

RESTAS: Yes! It doesn't feel cold. It is warm. What a blessing.
Yes, everybody. Do it! Cover me from head to toe in ice. Let
me take off my shirt and my pants. Cover me. Please, oh
please.

For five minutes the group members apply ice, moving it
slowly around to leave no spot untouched. Restas breathes
deeply, mutters, moans.

ANN: There is no more ice in the kitchen.

RESTAS: That is enough. I feel better, very weak, but better.
You can stop. I just want to lie down here. . . .

JOHN: How did you know to use ice?

RICHARD: I don't know how I knew.

ANN: I am so thankful you didn't blow your cork. I don't know
what would have happened without you.

RICHARD: I don't mind saying that I have had it. I would love to collapse.

FRANK: Why don't you?

RICHARD: What I would really like is to be passed around the group.

MARCIA: How?

RICHARD: You form a circle. I stand in the middle and then I relax and you pass me around the circle from one person to another. Then after a minute or so you lift me up, trying to keep my body more or less straight. Then you rock me. Then you slowly put me down. Then, if you want, you keep your hands on me for a minute or two and slowly take them away. Can you remember all that?

MARCIA: If we forget, we'll improvise.

RICHARD: That's what I am afraid of. I'll have to take my chances. I am yours.

Richard is passed around, lifted, rocked, lowered. The group remains around him. Ann begins to cry. A few tears run down Thurston's face. Bill looks very somber. . . .

RESTAS: What is happening? What are you all doing? Where is Richard? There is something I must tell him.

RICHARD: I am under here. What is it?

RESTAS: I think I am all right generally.

RICHARD: That is good.

RESTAS: Are you sick?

RICHARD: No, just collapsed.

RESTAS: Did I do that to you?

RICHARD: There is such a thing as creative collapse.

RESTAS: Can I do anything for you?

RICHARD: Rest and get your own strength back. . . .

MARCIA: John and I want to do something for you. We want to work on you from top to bottom. We want to massage you. Get undressed.

RICHARD: Yes, ma'am.

MARCIA: And enjoy it.

RICHARD: I'll try.[55]

c. Some Tests of Spin-offs:
Where Differences in Degree Become Differences in Kind

All of these spin-offs of the laboratory approach imply a cost/benefit ratio, in greater or lesser degree. The benefits may be calculated in terms

55. Mann, *op. cit.*, pp. 167–72. From *Encounter* by John Mann. Copyright © 1970 by John Mann. All rights reserved. Reprinted by permission of Grossman Publishers.

of "getting to it" faster, or of highlighting processes as they occur. The cost may be expressed in terms of the neglect of developing a supportive and effective group which is characteristic of the T-Group experience, or in terms of the risk of setting up conditions of psychological failure for the learner. Blending design elements so as to generate favorable cost/benefit ratios is a major art form.

Some of the design spin-offs raise broad questions, since they imply differences from the laboratory approach as described above that are so great as to become differences in kind rather than degree. The point will be demonstrated briefly and narrowly. The purpose is to develop a model for testing particular learning vehicles against the laboratory approach, as defined above. The illustrative focus will be on encounter groups or other variations that make the role of trainer-leader a continually central one and that, relatedly, also rely heavily on various subdesigns introduced by the trainer to place the participant in learning situations he can accept but which are basically trainer contrived. The conclusions apply especially to large encounter groups, which may reach 100 or so participants, guided by a single trainer through a rapidly paced sequence of subdesigns. At some point, the basic argument runs, it is necessary to distinguish sharply the laboratory approach and some of its spin-offs as qualitatively different experiences. Every learning design should be subjected to such tests, since apparent extensions in degree can generate differences in kind. The distinction is not between better or worse, merely between approaches that differ in kind.

The senses in which differences in degree become differences in kind can be illustrated in several ways. *First,* at some point, some degree of centrality of a trainer-leader so violates important features of the laboratory approach as to create a different learning experience. Recall that the laboratory approach strives to create learning situations that maximize the psychological success, confirmation, and essentiality experienced by participants. As Argyris explains:

> . . . a T Group usually begins with the withholding of the expected directive leadership, agenda, power and status. These factors are withheld less to teach the persons how to deal with stress and more to communicate that the educator really means it when he says their re-education is going to be their own responsibility. In terms of our model, the educator attempts to create conditions where the individuals can define their own goals, the paths to their goals, and the strength of the behavior that they wish to overcome.[56]

More rather than less, the central leader in most encounter groups negates or threatens such conditions. He may, as Argyris also charges, create

56. Chris Argyris, "On the Future of Laboratory Education," *Journal of Applied Behavioral Science,* Vol. 3 (June, 1967) , p. 158.

a dysfunctionally high degree of dependence on the trainer. Such dependence may reduce the sense of the learner's ownership of the experience and, perhaps, his ability to transfer the learning to other situations.

Second, the emphasis in encounter groups seems to be on full expression or catharsis that is expected to well up from the unconscious. Far less is the emphasis on integration of any learning with a participant's more immediate defenses, or perceptions, or value structures, which will remain basically intact after the learning experience and which are the basic focus of attention in T-Groups. This position must be tethered in two major senses. There is a wide variation in encounter experiences and T-Groups, so global generalizations are always inappropriate. However, the unconscious clearly plays a crucial role in individual development. For example, because repressed childhood experiences can impair an individual's ability to communicate as an adult, it is appropriate that some learning technologies focus on the unconscious. And some material from the unconscious will penetrate into T-Groups, as it does into everyday conversation.

Third, the issue is the point at which a difference in degree blurs into a difference in kind. Several such points can be illustrated here. As an encounter purposively and massively seeks to elicit unconscious materials, for example, to that degree does it depart from the model of constraining values that circumscribe the laboratory approach. Relatedly, emphasis on the unconscious implies a there-and-then versus a here-and-now emphasis, which is critical in the present concept of the laboratory approach. Moreover, relatedly, the encounter group tends to emphasize diagnosis. The T-Group emphasizes both how individuals see one another and the inexpertness of participants as therapists. Finally, emphasis on the unconscious implies a more privatizing experience, in which less attention will be paid to the mutual and even laborious checking-out among participants of reactions or judgments or observations that is so characteristic of T-Groups. That is, the T-Group is learning in interaction, where insight derives from the contrasts or similarities of differentiated personae in a group. The intent is to trigger "consensual validation," which is apparently a major motivator and reinforcer of change.[57] The focus in an encounter group is more on the individual in depth than in relation.

Such comparisons could be extended, but two major points have already been sustained. That is, the T-Group and the class of encounter groups defined above basically *do* differ in major ways, whatever value one places on one or the other. Moreover, some of the differences in learning vehicles are such as to be differences in kind more than degree.

---

57. Golembiewski, *The Small Group,* pp. 19–25.

6. SOME ISSUES ABOUT CONSTRAINTS ON LABORATORY TECHNOLOGY: A MATTER OF THEORIES OF LEARNING OR CHANGE

A final basic constraint on the laboratory approach is its underlying theory of learning or change, for more-or-less obvious reasons. For example, an appropriate theory of change would guide the design of learning experiences capable of generating increasingly predictable consequences. Such a theory or model also would help the practitioner make specific interventions within the context of some learning design, an aid of considerable consequence because such interventions typically have to be made on the fly.

Progress toward the development of a learning theory or model has been mixed. Agreement generally exists about a global model that explains the intended effects of the laboratory approach. But that model leaves open important issues which are still unresolved, or which are still the subjects of basic disagreement.

The purpose here is to describe the agreement (as well as to indicate the points of contrast and issues of disagreement) about theories of learning or change relevant to the laboratory approach. The description suggests what is available in the way of guidance and what still requires further development and clarification.

a. A General Model of Change: Agreement about Global Processes

The classic Lewinian model of change has received wide acceptance as reflecting the global processes of the laboratory approach. Lewin proposed three stages of attitudinal change: (1) unfreezing, (2) changing, and (3) refreezing. With some elaboration, that three-phase model has proved serviceable in describing the broader processes of learning or change in the laboratory approach.

The appropriate elaborations on Lewin's model deal with key mechanisms operating at the several stages. They may be sketched briefly.[58]

Stage 1. Unfreezing

(1) Some stimulus points up an unexpected feature of an individual's coping mechanisms, his defenses, self-concepts, or whatever.

---

58. Lubin and Eddy, *op. cit.*, pp. 316–17; and Edgar Schein and Warren G. Bennis (eds.), *Personal and Organizational Change through Group Methods* (New York: John Wiley & Sons, 1965), pp. 275–76, provide the basic model for this description.

The unstructured nature of a T-Group is often noted as providing an unsettling experience which brings into question an individual's capabilities to adapt and hence helps motivate looking at Self with the minimal defensiveness and distortion to which the term "unfreezing" applies. Generally, disconfirmation or lack of confirmation about some aspect of the Self is the trigger, and especially so if (for example) the disconfirmation is consensually validated by several observers. ("You say you are not anxious, but we all see you as terrified and seeking support from the authority figure.")

(2) The stimulus induces a potentially motivating concern, perhaps anxiety, guilt, shame, or anger.

At least initially, such feelings may induce defensiveness, or avoidance of the meaning of the stimulus-situation as applied to the Self. Such reactions or feelings also may prove motivators right from the start, however, for they can trigger a concern to change or to understand in people whose defenses are appropriately low. In either case, agreement exists about the conditions required to activate such potentially motivating concerns:

(3) The concerns—perhaps anxiety, guilt, shame, or anger— become motivators as the person experiences a sense of psychological safety for Self and others, and as barriers to experimentation and change are removed.

This suggests the development of a regenerative system, where trust is high enough and risk low enough to induce openness and owning. Low openness and owning may be considered the primary barriers to change. ("The guy you describe isn't me; I'd tell you people if he were. Honest.")

Stage 2. Changing

(4) The individual openly scans his interpersonal environment for new information about himself.

As a person feels psychologically safe, he is open to the inputs of others. These inputs clarify, modify, or perhaps even change the focus of the original stimulus. ("Now I see. You said I wasn't cooperating at first. Now I hear you saying that you felt I rejected you.") As Edgar Schein and Warren Bennis explain, the "changee . . . may begin to view himself from the perspective of an array of others. As his perspective, his frame of reference, shifts, he develops new beliefs about himself which, in turn, lead to new feelings and behavioral responses."[59]

---

59. Schein and Bennis, *op. cit.*, p. 276.

(5) If some change seems appropriate to him after scanning, the individual seeks to identify some model to guide his change.

In a T-Group, the trainer very often provides such an early model. Especially at later stages in a group's development, the range of possible models will widen. As the individual experiences the other group members as differentiated, he can isolate a broad range of specific attributes as models. An individual can then decide whether or not to try to integrate these attributes into his existing behaviors and attitudes.

(6) The individual practices replacement behaviors or attitudes implied by, or deduced from, the model.

Here, a supportive T-Group can be very useful. Its members can confirm or disconfirm progress, provide emotional support for experimentation, and encourage continued effort. True mutual learning may take place. ("I beamed when you said you were angry, just when I perceived you to be angry. We're on the same wave-length at last. You used to deny you were angry when I was certain I perceived the signs. That induced my distrust of you, and my mistrust in my own radar. I couldn't help you much, then, even really talk with you.")

Stage 3. Refreezing

(7) The replacement responses must be integrated with the rest of the learner's personality, defenses, and attitudes.
(8) They must be integrated as well into his significant on-going relationships outside of the immediate learning situation.

The issue is particularly relevant when the learning occurs in a Basic T-Group and the individual wishes to transfer the replacement responses into his real-world relationships. The "transfer issue" will receive major attention below.

As useful as this three-stage model is, however, it has serious inadequacies. Thus the model gives inadequate attention to the process of change from the changee's perspective. A more adequate model also would specify the sources of tension or discomfort proposed by the model that give initial impetus to unfreezing. Schein and Bennis suggest the required elaboration on the basic three-stage model by listing some of the sources of tension in early T-Group sessions:

(1) dilemmas created by the unfreezing forces—how to establish a viable identity in the group, how to control others, how to insure that the group goals will include his own needs, and

how to keep the group discussion at an appropriate level of intimacy; (2) the heightened consciousness of self that brings with it the possibility of discovering something within himself that will prove to be unacceptable; (3) the actual possibility of getting honest reactions to himself from others, which have always been relatively unavailable and may prove to reveal unacceptable parts of himself, or worse, may prove himself to be entirely unacceptable; (4) defensive reactions to feedback already obtained, either because it was hostile and retaliatory or because it was too threatening; (5) the belief or assumption that he may not be able to change behavior which is unacceptable to others (therefore it may be better not to learn about it in the first place) ; (6) the belief or assumption that feedback is always evaluative and always deals with inadequacies or things that are wrong.[60]

Moreover, the three-stage model is moot on many significant questions which often begin with: "How much. . . ?" Specifically, if some unfreezing is useful, is there some point beyond which additional unfreezing is not especially conducive to learning or is, in fact, positively detrimental to learning? Similarly, given that some feedback is a good thing, in what strengths should it be given? The following section suggests a range of possible theoretical answers to such critical questions.

b. Three Specific Models of Change: Disagreement about Optimum Discrepancies

In some senses, "how much?" questions can be avoided safely. That is, although exceptions exist, by far the stronger tendency is to withhold feedback rather than to come on too strong. Typical fantasies about the fragility of others in the face of our inevitably incisive feedback are enough to tether short the overwhelming proportion of us, especially in view of the threat of retaliation to the giver of feedback. More or less, it is a case of people who do not throw glasses because they live in stone houses. Typical also are the massive defensive forces that most people can bring to bear in fending off even literal thunderbolts of feedback— denial, mishearing, misinterpretation, accusations of projection, and an even larger battery. An experienced trainer in a T-Group should be able to provide somewhat insightful guidance in cases in which these powerful and primary defenses against "too much" are not operating. Again, however, he is more likely in the usual situation to be encouraging feedback than to be inhibiting it. So he also is likely to have a major

---

60. *Ibid.*, p. 301.

margin for error built into the resistances of the normal learning experience.

Such common hedges against fallibility, however, are no real substitute for a guiding theory or model of learning or change. And the available literature does not provide much of a guide, as can be illustrated by sketching three competing models. The models have certain commonalities. They postulate that a motive force for change inheres in "discrepant situations," in cases of a difference between some stimulus and a person's "internal anchors" of attitudes, perceptions, or whatever. The obvious question is confronted in three different ways by three different models of change.[61] That question is: What degree of discrepancy is optimum for inducing learning or change?

Model I. Greater Discrepancy ⟶ Greater Change

Roughly, this model provides that the greater the discrepancy between a stimulus and an individual's internal anchors, the greater the probable change in his attitudes and opinions so as to reduce that discrepancy. The tension induced by discrepancy acts as a motivator. Many studies[62] report such an effect, which has been incorporated in theoretical syntheses like Leon Festinger's theory of cognitive dissonance. As he notes: ". . . the discrepant reality which impinges on a person will exert pressures in the direction of bringing the appropriate cognitive elements into correspondence with that reality . . . The strength of the pressures to reduce the dissonance is a function of the magnitude of dissonance."[63]

Model II. Greater Discrepancy ⟨ Greater Change or Lesser Change

Model II also rests on the motivational properties of discrepancy, but it introduces a major intervening variable in the discrepancy/change sequence, the degree of "ego involvement." Roughly, high ego involvement means that the person experiencing a discrepancy feels strongly about the stimulus-issue, that the issue is a central one for him in a psychologic sense.

Model II includes two general cases. The first general case applies when ego involvement is high. In this case, Model II predicts a contrast

---

61. The following discussion is based on Robert T. Golembiewski, "Organizational Properties and Managerial Learning," *Journal of the Academy of Management,* Vol. 13 (March, 1970), esp. pp. 18–21.
62. John R. P. French, Jr., "A Formal Theory of Social Power," *Psychological Review,* Vol. 63 (1957), pp. 181–94.
63. Leon Festinger, *A Theory of Cognitive Dissonance* (Evanston, Ill.: Row, Peterson and Co., 1957), p. 18.

effect when discrepancy is great and an assimilation effect when the discrepancy is smaller. That is, a great objective discrepancy is likely to be perceived as even more discrepant than it is, given a high ego involvement. A contrast effect will inhibit change in the direction of the stimulus. This prediction contradicts Model I, as Figure 3 shows. When ego

Figure 3. Two General Cases in Change Model II

	Discrepancy	Ego Involvement	Probable Effect	Change toward the Discrepant Stimulus
General Case 1:	Smaller ⟶	High ⟶	Assimilation ⟶	Greater
	Greater ⟶	High ⟶	Contrast ⟶	Smaller
General Case 2: (Model I Modified):	Smaller ⟶	Low ⟶	Assimilation ⟶	Smaller
	Greater ⟶	Low ⟶	Assimilation ⟶	Greater

involvement is low, however, as in the second general case as shown in Figure 3, Model II predicts the same effects as Model I. When a person experiencing a discrepancy does not feel strongly about a stimulus-issue, that is, Model II predicts an assimilation effect, whether the discrepancy is greater or lesser. In either case, the course of least resistance for the person experiencing the discrepancy is to move attitudinally toward the discrepant stimulus or to perceive it as less discrepant than it is. Observed change will be greater toward the more discrepant stimulus, but change toward the less discrepant stimulus also will occur. General Case 2 in Figure 3 depicts these relations.

In addition, the second general case of Model II is limited by some students to narrow ranges of discrepancy. Increases in discrepancy will yield linear attitudinal change only up to a point, they argue. Beyond that point, the rate of change decelerates and then turns negative. As James O. Whittaker explained:

> . . . the relationship was curvilinear. Small discrepancies yielded small change, moderate discrepancies yielded the maximum change, and the degree of change tended to diminish as the discrepancies became even larger.
> . . . We suspect that on issues that are low in involvement, the discrepancies would need to be much greater than those we employed before decreasing change would result.[64]

---

64. James O. Whittaker, "Resolution of the Communication Discrepancy Issue," in Muzafer Sherif and Carolyn Sherif (eds.), *Attitude, Ego-Involvement, and Change* (New York: John Wiley & Sons, 1967), pp. 168–69.

Model III. Balance Hypothesis

Model III emphasizes the balanced state rather than the degree or direction of change. Thus Fritz Heider writes of the interaction of "sentiments" and "units" in terms in which the concept of balanced state

> . . . designates a situation in which the perceived units and the experienced sentiments co-exist without stress; there is thus no pressure toward change, either in the cognitive organization or in the sentiment. . . . That sentiment, unit formation, and balanced state have something to do with each other can be stated as a general hypothesis, namely: the relationship between sentiments and unit formation tends toward a balanced state.[65]

Model III also is distinguished in two other major senses. Thus Model III—unlike Model I—admits both assimilation and contrast effects. Unlike Model II, moreover, the intervening variable is not the ego involvement of the subject confronted by the discrepancy. Rather, the intervening variable is the character of the object of the discrepancy. As Fritz Heider explains: "It has been assumed, and with good support from experimental findings, that 'Assimilation appears when the differences between the substructures [of a unit] are small; contrast appears when the differences are large.' "[66]

An example may clarify the significant differences between the three models. Assume A does not like B, whom A later discovers is the anonymous author of a sensitive and moving poem of which A has said: "Only a beautiful spirit could have written it." How does A handle the discrepancy?

- Model I. A would come to like B more in direct proportion to the degree of the discrepancy between A's original sentiments about B and about the poem.
- Model II. It would depend on A's degree of ego involvement with B:
  a. If A is ego-involved with B, the larger the discrepancy between A's original sentiments about B and about the poem, the less likely A is to favorably change his sentiments toward B (General Case 1 in Figure 3).
  b. If A is not particularly ego-involved with B, the larger the discrepancy between A's original sentiments about B and about the poem (at least up to some undetermined point), the more

---

65. Fritz Heider, *The Psychology of Interpersonal Relations* (New York: John Wiley & Sons, 1958), p. 177.
66. *Ibid.*, p. 211.

likely is A to favorably change his sentiments toward B (General Case 2 in Figure 3).

- Model III. A new balance would develop between A's sentiments toward B and his original definition of B as a unit. The initial unbalanced combination of positive sentiments about the poem and negative evaluation of the author as a unit could be resolved in several ways:

  a. by A seeing the person-author B as a total positive unit; consequently, A comes to like B more

  b. by A deciding he really does not like the poem, thereby creating a balance with B seen as a totally negative unit; consequently, B is disliked at least as much as originally

  c. by A doubting or denying B's authorship of the poem; in which case B is disliked as much or more than originally; and so on

    The choice between these alternative resolutions presumably will depend on the magnitude of the differences between B's "substructures," that is, B as person and B as author. The greater the difference, the more likely are alternative resolutions like b and c above.

The three models above derive from simple experiments in which discrepancy is induced by design. But they also seem relevant to the laboratory approach, many of whose central dynamics involve the highlighting of discrepancies. These discrepancies include, for example, differences between how a person sees himself and how others perceive him to be.

The choice of an optimum discrepancy, by extension, is an important consideration in the processes of both feedback and disclosure, which are both central processes of the laboratory approach. Some data suggest the special value of the balance model, which subsumes Models I and II as special cases. But the basic issues are in major doubt at this stage of the game. All that is clear is that some critical questions go unanswered, while these theoretical issues are in doubt. For example, consider the issue of who should give a piece of feedback to a particularly resistant member of a T-Group, so as to maximize the chances of learning or change on the part of the target. The usual prescription is: the more people, the better, with the underlying process of consensual validation being justly considered as central. The usual prescription is wise-enough counsel, but not sufficient if one persists in the original question. The three models imply different answers. They are:

- Model I. Any member, so long as he comes on strong in the sense of a discrepancy between his feedback and the internal anchors of the target; in fact, the stronger the better, at least up to the point at which the feedback is too strong to be valid.

104

- Model II. Any member, so long as his feedback is not so vitiated as to be neglected or so strong as to be overpowering; the somewhat-varnished truth is what it takes.
- Model III. A very specific member, probably an "independent" not too closely identified with the target: the purpose is to avoid the low-change condition, when A and B are ego-involved and when A sees the two "structures" of B (as positive relational object and as giver of specific negative feedback) as highly discrepant.

The choice of a guiding model does make a difference. This should be clear in the humble case of who should give feedback, and in what strength. The same conclusion seems to hold in the case of such macroscopic interventions as the design of a total learning experience.

7. SOME DISTINCTIONS RELEVANT TO AFFECTIVE MAN: THE GENERAL REACH OF THE LABORATORY TECHNOLOGY

As the diverse considerations above should establish, the laboratory approach emphasizes learning via an affective entree. Roughly, the individual is seen as a valuing and feeling entity and, as such, his behavior is significantly influenced by his valuations of experience and the feelings associated with those valuations. Moreover, the individual may be variously unaware of these affective and value bases for his behavior or of their impact on others with whom he interacts. This will especially be the case in degenerative relationships. In simple terms, it is necessarily incomplete to think about the impact of one's behavior on others, and it may be illusory in that some of the best evidence is in the values and feelings of the Other. Hence the basic learning progression for the laboratory approach is:

$$\text{Affective} \longrightarrow \text{Behavioral} \longrightarrow \text{Cognitive}$$

This basic progression does not imply that cognition or behavior are without influence on valuation or feeling. The progression does reflect the basic assumption that the affective emphasis is strategically impactful, at least in many cases. But behavioral and cognitive learning need not always be based on affective entree. Subsection 5 under Section D below, for example, sketches one type of situation in which laboratory values can be approached in another way, at least initially.

The interaction of affect, behavior, and cognition may be made somewhat more explicit. The laboratory approach helps and encourages individuals to determine what they need and want affectively to meet their own needs and motives. In turn, this sensitization should induce the search for appropriate behavioral skills, as well as thought concerning those skills and the life situations in which they can be applied. In organizations, for example, cognitive concerns often center around the design of structures, procedures, or policies that can reinforce the behaviors that are considered desirable by the organization's members.

The general reach of the laboratory technology may be indicated more directly. The outline below sketches eight affectively-relevant levels of a generalized life span,[67] all of which can serve to activate behavior.

- *Basic needs,* or *drives,* are generically inferred from states of well-being/threat experienced by the individual. That is, the need for food is defined as basic because of the consequences for the organism's integrity and survival when that need is unsatisfied, or poorly satisfied.

  Two sets of these needs may be distinguished. First, there are the well-known physical states based on biochemical processes, imbalances in which induce behavior. The visceral states—hunger, thirst, and so on—are the clearest illustrations.

  Second, evidence also strongly suggests an ontological set of social and psychologic needs. In the theoretic work of Maslow[68] and Argyris,[69] for example, the individual is seen either as trending from the satisfaction of lower level needs toward the

---

67. The approach is suggested by David G. Bowers, *Perspectives In Organizational Development* (CRUSK–Institute of Social Research, University of Michigan, n.d.), pp. 21–22.

68. "Self-actualization" is the *summum bonum* of needs in such concepts, and it has often been rooted in a framework of a "hierarchy of needs." For a conceptual wellspring, see Abraham H. Maslow, *Motivation and Personality* (New York: Harper & Row, Publishers, 1954).

   In his latest (and posthumous) work, Maslow calls for a "humanistic biology" to deal with the ontological goals or needs for individuals he posits to exist. Just as deprivation of the need for food can cause disease, Maslow argues, so also does the deprivation of "the basic-need satisfactions of safety and protection, belongingness, love, respect, self-esteem, identity and self actualization. . . ." He sees such needs as related to the "fundamental structure of the human organism itself," in the same ways and via the same logic that established the more strictly biologic needs. He explains: ". . . the classical way of establishing a body need, as for vitamins . . . has been first a confrontation with a disease of unknown cause, and *then* a search for this cause. That is to say, something is considered to be a need if its deprivation produces disease." His list of social-psychological needs was inferred in a similar manner, if in a preliminary way, as explanations for "spiritual or philosophical or existential ailments" that are seen as deriving from deprivations of basic social-psychological needs, or what Maslow calls "instinctoids." *The Farther Reaches of Human Nature* (New York: Viking Press, 1971), pp. 22–23.

69. Chris Argyris, *Personality and Organization* (New York: Harper & Row, Publishers, 1957, esp. pp. 49–53, provides a specific model of the dimensions of self-actualization.

satisfaction of higher level needs or as paying the costs in frustration, fixated behavior, and so on. Basically, the laboratory approach essentially constitutes a set of values that increase the probability that an individual can increasingly become aware of and satisfy these basic social and psychological needs.

- *Basic affective states* are associated with various degrees of well-being/threat, such as fear, satiation, anxiety, anger, comfort, and so on. Evidence suggests that these subjective states can be influenced by learning, as when an organism develops defenses that permit managing the impact of an affective state, or that even mask an affective state. The evidence also suggests that these affective states are somehow primal. In sum, they are not merely learned responses, although the individual typically learns acceptable ways to express them and even to experience them.[70]

- *Motives* are conceived of as powerful if usually derivative activators of behavior. They refer to the specific modalities in which the individual seeks satisfaction of his basic needs or drives. Scott[71] distinguishes two basic motives—psychological and social. Psychological motives activate specific patterns of quest for maintenance of mental integrity and balance. Social motives induce behaviors that seek to develop stable patterns of association with other men. Thus an individual's basic social motivation[72] might be toward patterns of association that stress affiliation, achievement, or power, or various combinations thereof.

  Such social motives are seen as learned.[73] This learning can occur in the process of meeting the basic needs or drives, as well as in the process of seeking to avoid undesirable affective states (e.g. anxiety) and/or to approach subjectively desirable affective states.

- *Values* are in effect higher order attitudes which are valuational "shoulds."[74] In Scott's[75] words, a "value, or moral ideal is . . . an individual's concept of an ideal relationship (or state of affairs), which he uses to assess the 'goodness' or 'badness,' the 'rightness' or 'wrongness' of actual relationships that he observes or contem-

70. Ezra Stotland, *The Psychology of Hope* (San Francisco: Jossey-Bass, Inc., Publishers, 1969), p. 31.
71. William G. Scott, *Human Relations in Management* (Homewood, Ill.: Richard D. Irwin, 1962), pp. 80–82.
72. David C. McClelland, John W. Atkinson, Russell A. Clark, and Edgar L. Lowell, *The Achievement Motive* (New York: Appleton-Century-Crofts, 1953).
73. A similar notion has been the key one in a number of theoretical systems, as in Harry Stack Sullivan, *Conceptions of Modern Psychiatry* (New York: W. W. Norton & Co., 1953), pp. 19–23.
74. Milton Rokeach, *Beliefs, Attitudes, and Values* (San Francisco: Jossey-Bass, Inc., Publishers, 1968).
75. William A. Scott, *Values and Organizations* (Chicago, Ill.: Rand McNally & Co., 1965), p. 3.

plates." For example, a person may have compassion or pity toward the disadvantaged, a lower order attitude. His or her behavior will depend, in part, on values concerning how that person should respond to those for whom he has compassion.

- *Beliefs* refer to purported existential states, some of which can be proved or disproved in a direct sense, and others of which are at least temporarily beyond proximate proof or disproof. Some negative beliefs about various categoric groups, for example, can be tested rather directly. Belief that the sun rotated around the earth was first challenged on deductive grounds, however, and only recently by direct observation. Belief in an ultimate moral order escapes such proof or disproof, finally, at least within a human context.

  Beliefs can activate behavior, it is important to note, whatever their potential for being proved or disproved. Indeed, some have argued that beliefs will be motivators in direct proportion to the degree that any belief, or logical deductions from it, are not testable or provable. In any case, the term belief suggests an intensity which distinguishes it from attitudes and opinions, which intensity also can significantly influence behavior.

- *Attitudes,* or the inferred bases of behavior, in Allport's classical definition[76] are a "mental and neural state of readiness organized through experience, exerting a directive or dynamic influence upon the individual's response to all objects and situations with which it is related."

  Attitudes can have cognitive aspects, then, and they can trigger behavior. The thought component is most prominent in the organization of experience underlying attitudes. Thought may also intervene in decisions to behave consistent with the attitude.

  Attitudes also are affective vectors, as it were. As Kiesler notes:[77] "The principal aspect of an attitude is the degree to which it is positive or negative toward something."

- *Opinions* are usefully distinguished from attitudes, as by the Hartleys.[78] "Many situations are problematical in that they involve new and strange objects or new combinations or arrangements of familiar objects. . . In this process of assessing the situation, participants draw on past experience, bring to bear attitudes

76. Gordon W. Allport, "Attitudes," in C. Murchison (ed.), *A Handbook of Social Psychology* (Worcester, Mass.: Clark University Press, 1935), p. 798. See also Charles A. Kiesler, *The Psychology of Commitment* (New York: Academic Press, 1971), p. 4.
77. Kiesler, *op. cit.,* p. 4.
78. Eugene L. Hartley and Ruth E. Hartley, *Fundamentals of Social Psychology* (New York: Alfred A. Knopf, 1952), p. 657.

that seem to be relevant; but they cannot rely, except tentatively, upon these attitudes to carry them through the situation. With a greater or lesser degree of rationality, a definition of the situation, a conception of the kind of action appropriate to it, will be worked out; it is just such a definition that seems to be referred to, on both the practical and the scholarly level, as opinion."

- *Set, or frame of reference,* refers to the general structure that an individual tends to impose on his experience.

By extension, then, a person's behavior can be influenced in two major ways via an affective approach. For example, a changed attitude or value can motivate behavioral change, or consideration of such change. Moreover, if no value or attitudinal change occurs or is even considered, major learning is possible. Thus an individual can become more aware of his affective life, of interactions between what he desires and how he behaves, and so on. Major potential for behavioral change inheres in such enhanced awareness.

Three points highlight significant interactions of the laboratory technology and the eight affectively relevant levels in the outline above. *First,* various learning designs based on the laboratory approach can tap the full affective range. For example, a T-Group design could help a person realize that one of his sets or stereotypes is wildly inapplicable. Or such an experience might sensitize an individual to the strength of his affiliative motives, of which he had become increasingly unaware over time. Or an individual might learn something about the subtle range of defenses he has developed to avoid being in touch with his own feelings or affective states, as well as those of others.

Second, the affective range in the outline has differential potential for change, both practically and ethically. Sets or attitudes, for example, have a substantial potential for change. Change in them may be simple, as a practical matter. And change may also be desirable in that it enhances the individual and his associations. In contrast, the laboratory technology is oriented toward pointing up the character and impact of basic affective states or motives, rather than toward changing them. These "higher" affective levels are "givens," in critical senses. That is, they are not only more difficult (or perhaps, impossible) to change, as a practical matter. Moreover, change at such levels implies serious ethical issues about tampering with the essential person, playing God, and so on. In complex ways, in addition, the laboratory technology also has various interactive links with the several affective levels. Thus various laboratory designs could highlight inconsistencies between a person's motives or values and his expressed attitudes or opinions.

Third, to risk a simplification, the laboratory approach implies a basic test relevant to the affective range. The test has two components for each individual. Thus each participant in a laboratory experience should:

- try to compare the values of the laboratory approach as described above, with his normal complement of "lower" affective levels: values, beliefs, attitudes, opinions, and sets, in the language of the outline
- try to test whether or not the values of the laboratory approach enhance meeting his "higher" affective levels—basic needs, basic desired affective states, and social needs—as he hopefully comes to recognize the latter more clearly as a result of a learning design based on the laboratory approach.

Based on such a dual test, the prudent individual makes his choices. It is just that deliciously simple, and just that maddeningly complex.

C. THE LABORATORY APPROACH
TO ORGANIZATION DEVELOPMENT:
PERSPECTIVES ON THEORY
AND PRACTICE

The special genius of each age is reflected in its distinctive ways of organizing work. If the preceding age stressed stability and consistency, roughly, the emphasis today is on organizing for change and variability. The specific implications are diverse and still obscure, but the general point is overwhelming. John W. Gardner reflects both the certainty and the caution. "What may be most in need of innovation is the corporation itself," he notes. "Perhaps what every corporation (and every other organization) needs is a department of continuous renewal that could view the whole organization as a system in need of continuing innovation."[1]

The major contemporary response to the need for planned organizational change is the burgeoning emphasis on Organization Development, or OD. At least four levels of meaning—philosophic, operating, strategic, and tactical—are required to give some initial working content to the term. At the philosophic level, OD is nothing less than "a reorientation of man's thinking and behavior toward his organizations," in the words of Lyman K. Randall. He adds that OD also

> . . . views man and change optimistically. It applies a humanistic value system to work behaviors. It assumes people have the capability and motivation to grow through learning how to im-

---

1. John W. Gardner, *Self-Renewal* (New York: Harper & Row, Publishers, 1965).

111

prove their own work climate, work process, and their resulting products. It accepts as inevitable the conflicts among the needs of individuals, work groups, and the organization but advocates openly confronting these conflicts using problem-solving strategies. Its goals are to maximize the utilization of organization resources in solving work problems through the optimal use of human potential.[2]

In an operating sense, OD programs have several major distinguishing features. They are: (1) *planned* programs, that (2) involve some meaningful *system* of work, (3) that are managed by the *top responsible officials* who are both aware of and committed to the program and its objectives, (4) which are conceived as *long-term efforts,* (5) whose thrust is to improve *organizational effectiveness* by (6) *planned interventions* that focus on interpersonal and group processes via (7) the applications of behavioral science knowledge basically through *experiential learning* which (8) is *action-oriented* rather than concerned only with increases in knowledge, skills, or understanding.[3]

What are the major directions in which these operating features are applied? Strategically, OD efforts have three thrusts. Thus Alexander Winn explains that OD "implies a normative, re-education strategy intended to affect systems of beliefs, values and attitudes" that will permit more timely and effective responses to technological or broader social changes. In turn, these normative and behavioral changes may also trigger, facilitate, and reinforce compatible restructuring of formal work and reporting relationships.[4] Such restructuring constitutes the formal organization of responses to technological or broad social changes. Changing attitudes or values, modifying behavior, and inducing change in structure and policies, then, are the three strategic objectives of OD programs.

Tactically, and last on the list of levels of initial meaning of the concept of Organization Development, OD programs can be used to induce a broad family of organizational changes. Only a huge list could exhaustively catalog those uses. Illustratively, however, OD programs can analyze and help change or review:[5]

- managerial strategies
- organization climates that are inconsistent with individual needs or changing environmental demands

2. Lyman K. Randall, quoted in Warren H. Schmidt (ed.) , *Organizational Frontiers and Human Values* (Belmont, Cal.: Wadsworth Publishing Co., 1970) , p. 22.
3. Richard Beckhard, *Organization Development: Strategies and Models* (Reading, Mass.: Addison-Wesley Publishing Co., 1969) , p. 9.
4. Alexander Winn, "The Laboratory Approach to Organization Development: A Tentative Model of Planned Change," *Journal of Management Studies,* Vol. 6 (May, 1969) , p. 161.
5. Beckhard, *op. cit.,* pp. 16–19.

- organization structures and related job roles
- an organization's culture or associated norms
- ineffective patterns of intergroup collaboration
- communication systems that block or distort the flow of information
- inadequate planning processes
- the motivation of a workforce
- policies and procedures that were adaptations to an environment which is changing
- patterns of relationships between individuals and groups, as in mergers or unmergers

The bulk of this volume will describe representative OD applications that have this panoply of tactical goals.

These four levels of meaning demonstrate that OD contrasts pointedly with the reorganization literatures in public and business administration. Those literatures are concept-oriented and give little attention to changes in attitudes and behavior necessary to implement its guiding concept. This is something like a theoretical architecture which designs buildings to have frameworks of spaghetti riveted together by candy drops.

1. SOME OVERALL FEATURES: TOWARD SELF-RENEWING ORGANIZATIONS VIA OD

Some impressive strides toward continuous organization renewal have been taken of late, using the laboratory approach to organization development (OD). The immediate purpose is to sketch some overall features of OD, in a deliberately limited way. That is, the focus here is on general characteristics of OD programs—how and why they seek to induce greater openness, trust, and shared responsibility. Their goal is to increase interpersonal competence via regenerative interaction systems. In Beckhard's terms, this involves enhancing the attitudes and skills of organization members that relate to "self-awareness, communication skills, ability to manage conflict, and tolerance for ambiguity—all essential requirements for the organization leader in today's and tomorrow's world."[6] Resting on such common social and psychological foundations, OD programs can flower diversely. For example, greater openness in an organization might highlight critical needs for changes in policies, procedures, structure, or technology. An OD program then would seek to meet these needs through such methods as training programs, changes in policies and procedures, or the redesign of tasks as well as the restruc-

6. *Ibid.*, p. 40.

turing of organizations.[7] Later sections, beginning with Part II, will provide specific detail on this diversity within the context of common socio-emotional preparation.

The overall features of OD are approached here in terms of two base-line descriptions. Somewhat generally, OD can be described as an educational process, following John Sherwood,[8] which constitutes a new way of looking at the human side of life in organizations. The most general objective of OD is, according to Sherwood, "to develop self-renewing, self-correcting systems of people who learn to organize themselves in a variety of ways according to the nature of their tasks, and who continue to cope with changing demands the environment makes on the organization." The underlying educational process is one which identifies applicable human resources in the organization, expands them, and allocates them so as to improve the problem-solving capabilities of the organization. Somewhat more specifically, again relying in part on Sherwood, the laboratory approach to OD can be described as:

- a long-range effort to consciously introduce planned change into an organization in ways that involve its members, both in diagnosis of problems and prescriptions of change,
- which effort involves an entire organization, or some relatively coherent and meaningful subsystem of an organization,
- working toward the goal of greater organizational effectiveness by enlarging the array of reasonable organizational choices and by increasing the probability of self-renewal and constructive adaptation, by
- intervening in the ongoing activities of an organization in ways that facilitate learning by broad segments of its members and that also facilitate the making of choices from among alternative ways to proceed,
- with the common resultant need to change behaviors or values or attitudes, which must be distinguished from "changing personality," which has the flavor of changing men into angels, and
- with the common need to deal with "system problems" and "structure problems," as well as with "people problems."

Sheldon Davis provides useful perspective on OD as process from the experience of TRW Systems. He characterizes an "organic approach to

7. Sheldon Davis, "An Organic Problem-Solving Method of Organizational Change," *Journal of Applied Behavioral Science*, Vol. 3 (January, 1967), pp. 3–21.
8. John J. Sherwood, *An Introduction to Organization Development*, Experimental Publication System. Washington, D.C.: American Psychological Association, No. 11 (April, 1971), Ms. No. 396–1. Also reprinted in J. W. Pfeiffer and J. E. Jones (eds.), *1972 Annual Handbook for Group Facilitators*, Iowa City, Iowa: University Associates Publishers, 1972.

organizational change" in terms of three elements.[9] *First,* improvement in any social system requires a dual approach. The analyst must be able to understand what goes on in some cultural system, while he avoids being entrapped by that culture and its values. Yet analytical detachment cannot mean leaving the culture of the system. "This ability to step out of the culture and yet not leave it, not become alienated from it," Davis concludes, "is a very important one."

Second, it is necessary to take a systems engineering approach to the OD effort, to look at a total system so as to consider the probable effects of a change in one part on other parts. The organization is seen as a network of interacting and overlapping individual and group systems. The OD goal is to bring about a more effective integration and meshing of these systems.[10]

Third, Davis notes that direct confrontation of relevant situations is perhaps the essential element. "If we do not confront one another," he explains, "we keep the trouble within ourselves, and we stay in trouble."

a. Five Characteristics of Organization Development: Some Features of Self-Renewal

Five characteristics in these two descriptions of OD deserve spotlighting. *First,* the basic OD learning strategy is experiential. As in the T-Group, that is to say, the locus is "in here" rather than "out there." For example, one consultant was asked to help a management group of an executive and his major subordinates to improve its decision-making. The consultant observed the group in action and was asked by the executive for his reactions when a rather important decision had been reached, at least in the eyes of the executive. The consultant responded characteristically, encouraging the group to seek both diagnosis and solution from its own resources. To this end, he suggested that group members rate their commitment to the decision on a low/high scale of 1 through 5. The executive rated his commitment 5; his subordinates' ratings ranged from 2 to 4. The diagnosis of that decision-making effort was patent, and the group began to work on ways to help the executive avoid being led down the primrose path of his own wishes by the silence of his subordinates.

Second, the laboratory approach to OD emphasizes the "how" as contrasted with the "what." The dominant initial focus is on action, on processes or methods for achieving, testing, and (if necessary) changing interpersonal and intergroup relationships required for effective per-

---

9. Davis, *op. cit.,* pp. 12–13.
10. Samuel A. Culbert and Jerome Reisel, "Organization Development: An Applied Philosophy for Managers of Public Enterprise," *Public Administration Review,* Vol. 31 (March, 1971), p. 161.

formance. Far less central are the specific action goals, or the specific policies, procedures, or structures for achieving them.

This broad statement requires tethering in two senses. Paramountly, the laboratory approach to OD is not a gun for hire for any purpose. In sharp contrast, applications of the laboratory approach are to be constrained by broad ranges of values that define the essentials of the philosophy and internal logic of this specific technology for change. Relatedly, the laboratory approach to OD is not essentially a technology for "management by consensus," as some critics take pains to contend.[11] The technology's primary stress is on the quality of interpersonal and intergroup relationships, and on the adequacy of communication networks to isolate and resolve current problems. The technology is compatible with many organization structures and mechanisms for decision-making. Management by consensus is only one possible mechanism for making decisions, and (if taken literally) it is applicable only under very limited conditions.

A broad consensus does motivate the laboratory approach to OD, but it is more elemental than some decision-making mechanism or structure. That primal consensus, in the words of Kenneth D. Benne, is that men in organizations must go beyond "the conventional and parochial certainties of unquestioned group identifications and loyalties." He concludes that:

> . . . contemporary men cannot achieve a viable combination of "freedom" and "security," both of which they claim to prize, through rejection of group and organizational life in a spree of romantic individualism. But their affirmation of its practical necessity must not be a blind acceptance of the contemporary and traditional patterns in which their lives happen to be set historically.
>
> In affirming the inescapability of grappling with the demands of groups and organizations, contemporary men must at the same time learn how to alter, how to build and rebuild group and organizational patterns, even as they participate in them, with an eye to the values of personal freedom and spontaneity. Such learning is facilitated by the kind of clear-eyed and socially supported look into the abyss which T-Group experience provides.[12]

In its dominant focus on action, on methods *for achieving, testing,* and *changing* interpersonal relationships for effective performance, the

---

11. William Gomberg, " 'Titillating Therapy': Management Development's Most Fascinating Toy," *Personnel Administrator,* Vol. 12 (July–August, 1967), pp. 30–33.
12. Kenneth D. Benne, "From Polarization to Paradox," in Leland P. Bradford, Jack R. Gibb, and Kenneth D. Benne (eds.), *T-Group Theory and Laboratory Method* (New York: John Wiley & Sons, 1964), p. 243.

laboratory approach to OD constitutes a truly revolutionary departure from much organizational analysis. For example, proponents of Scientific Management were *concept-oriented*. Realizing that their utopia could never really exist anywhere until it existed everywhere, they desired to reform society so as to create the kind of people who could live in the scientifically managed society and love it. However, they were muddled about how to achieve what that concept required, beyond the stopwatch, the micro-motion camera, and other technical appurtenances. In contrast, the laboratory approach concentrates on behaviorally preparing individuals to decide upon and to achieve *their* definition of the desirable organizational life. In the laboratory approach, one may almost say that there is no such thing as a bad concept for change. Only more or less adequate behavioral commitment to a concept determines success or failure, to exaggerate the point somewhat.

Basically, a concept-oriented approach encourages win/lose games, which the mixed record of conventional attempts at administrative reform suggests is awkward.[13] To be sure, win/lose games sometimes may be necessary. Perhaps, illustratively, President Franklin D. Roosevelt was tactically correct in setting up a win/lose situation by neglecting to represent Congress on the 1937 committee that studied the restructuring of the federal executive.[14] The costs of win/lose games tend to be substantial, at the very least. Moreover, in any case, there is another way.

Third, the laboratory approach to OD fixates on increasing valid information, generating additional and reasonable choices, and developing active resources in the host organization. In principle, these may seem reasonable fixations, and benign ones in the bargain. In practice, however, this appearance often vanishes quickly. Increasing information and choices, for example, usually requires raising issues that some power wielders may prefer to leave undisturbed. Consider an organization member with high rank and low capabilities who was a roadblock to other members with low rank but high capabilities. Generally, he would feel it awkward to increase information and enlarge choices relevant to his own case. Almost by definition, that is to say, the laboratory approach to OD can raise issues that strike to the heart of the organizational ties that bind. These are not tasks for the faint-hearted: increasing information, raising alternatives, and developing resources.

Fourth, the development of a truly collaborative relationship is the goal of the laboratory approach to OD. That is, the OD approach does not merely seek to generate valid information and to expose alternatives for action. Organization members must also be able to use the information to make choices among alternatives, choices that are both informed

---

13. Karl A. Bosworth, "The Politics of Management Improvement in the States," *American Political Science Review,* Vol. 47 (March, 1953), pp. 84–99.

14. Barry Dean Karl, *Executive Reorganization and Reform in the New Deal* (Cambridge, Mass.: Harvard University Press, 1963).

and uncoerced. In addition, the choices must be made and the underlying information gathered in ways that enhance the commitment of organization members to the decision.

There is considerable tightrope walking in OD applications related to this point. The subtleties can be illustrated. Essentially, OD works with existing organizational centers of power. But OD programs will at least increasingly challenge these centers of power to become more open to a wide variety of influence attempts. Indeed, an OD program may fundamentally alter the distribution of power. Hence OD programs do not seek "management by consensus." But they do seek to involve the widest relevant range of information and resources, while they are also realistic about where power is. As Samuel Culbert and Jerome Reisel note:

> OD works essentially with the power influence systems in an enterprise. It attempts to influence opinion leaders and thereby multiply its impact. This means that OD processes are involved initially and continually with the top and uppermost levels of management, although eventually all managerial segments can be involved in some measure.[15]

The situation has inherent in it a broad range of possible perversions. This range includes OD practitioners serving as lackeys of the power wielders or acting as quiet subverters of all authority. The *media via* is a hard road.

Fifth, OD programs have a relational thrust. Overall, they seek to relate individual needs and organization goals, to increase their congruence for mutual benefit. The tendency to attempt to make a whole from some set of parts, to relate several sets of needs or demands, is also common in OD efforts. These common missions include helping an organization adapt to new or changing environments, to develop collective identities to replace those shattered by change, and to vitalize an organization to seek its mission with new zest and efficiency.

b. Some Broad Values Guiding Self-Renewal via OD: Toward the Open Organization

That the laboratory approach to OD is action-oriented and emphasizes processes to develop or change interpersonal and intergroup relations does not imply that the goal is just any development or change. The laboratory approach is not narrowly means-oriented, in sum. If the discussion in the preceding two sections did not establish that point, this and the following section should.

---

15. Culbert and Reisel, *op. cit.,* p. 162.

Both antecedent and subsequent analyses elaborate the ways in which the laboratory approach to OD is value-loaded, but there is no way to overemphasize the point. For convenience, its guiding values may be thought of as trending toward the evolution of an "open organization." This is not to say that differences in authority and status will disappear. Rather, these differences will be conditioned in diverse ways by a set of values such as the one below. As a first approximation, approaches to these guiding organization values are consistent with the laboratory approach to OD:[16]

- full and free communication
- greater reliance on open confrontation in managing conflict, where participants psychologically own at least the causes of the conflict and its consequences as well as (hopefully) agree on approaches to managing the conflict, as contrasted with a reliance on coercion or compromise
- influence based on competence rather than on personal whim or formal power
- expression of emotional as well as task-oriented behavior
- acceptance of conflict between the individual and his organization, to be coped with willingly, openly, and rationally

It will be the burden of the rest of this book to develop the specific senses in which approaches to such values pervade OD programs, both in concept and in application. That is, these central values serve two purposes. Thus they can generate more specific sets of values or goals to guide OD efforts. Moreover, these broad values condition the development of specific learning designs that can induce corresponding behaviors in organizations.

c. Two Paradigms in Organization Development: Worksite as End Point or Starting Point?

Given such broad OD values, the next logical concern is their implementation in organizations, a task complicated by the fact that OD designs consistent with the laboratory approach can generate at least three levels of learning. First, an organization member will gain *personal learning,* that is, information about himself in interaction. Second, some of that personal learning can be extended to the worksite to increase understanding or to improve functioning. This may be called *transfer learning.* Third, organization members might attempt some *environmental learning,* as they seek to restructure a worksite or an organization

---

16. Philip E. Slater and Warren G. Bennis, "Democracy Is Inevitable," *Harvard Business Review,* Vol. 42 (March, 1964), pp. 51–59.

so as to permit them to perform more satisfying behaviors at work. Patently, this last type of learning is the critical payoff of OD.

Which level of learning is to receive prior emphasis in effective OD designs? Major questions remain unanswered about phasing the several levels of learning. Two basic macro-designs will be distinguished. Presently, the safest position is that these two macro-designs are alternatives available for any specific OD effort. Circumstances will encourage the choice of one or the other alternative, although no clear guidelines exist for making the choice.

Stranger Experiences ⟶ Family Experiences

The orthodox entree into the laboratory approach to OD begins with stranger experiences in a Basic T-Group. There organization members get safe experiences with values, attitudes, and behaviors consistent with the laboratory approach, safe in the sense that participants can savor the experience without concern about preserving appearances with organizational peers or superiors. Note that sometimes "cousin" groups are used. They are composed of people from the same parent organization who have not worked closely together and are not likely to do so.

The orthodox entree then builds toward family designs that involve individuals who are associated at work. The general intent is that, at some point, enough persons trained at off-site locations will be seeded into the organization so that they can begin to spearhead changes at work. The system will "go critical," in effect, when some unspecified proportion of an organization's membership has a positive experience with laboratory values. The proportion need not be very large, if it includes enough organizational influentials. The power calculus is imprecise, but only a few people might do for starters.

Several details are sufficient to describe this orthodox macro-design. First, organization members go hither and thither for separate experiences. They work on *personal learning,* which they may later apply individually and gingerly as *transfer learning* at work. They probably will make more aggressive attempts at transfer in family or marriage relations, and success there may increase the motivation to make applications at work. In such diverse ways, an increasing number of an organization's members may have a "positive experience" with laboratory values, which means that those values are dually seen as contributing to personal growth and as applicable at work, realistically as well as ideally. At some point, "enough" members have a positive experience and begin to deliberately emphasize transfer learning in the host organization, as well as begin to work on *environmental learning.* "Team development" is a common vehicle for extending laboratory learning to the worksite, as Sections C and D of Part II will show.

120

The rationale for the orthodox progression is transparent. Organization members can gain experience with the laboratory approach under anonymous conditions which encourage experimentation and risk-taking, while they reduce the costs of "failing" or "losing face" in front of workmates with whom continuing relations are necessary. Overall, the high degree of voluntarism possible via the initial reliance on stranger experiences is no doubt also a major motivator for individuals to extract benefit from the experience. As voluntarism decreases, the tendencies to fight the experience, or to deny it, will grow. Conveniently, the rationale presumes that the personal learning from the stranger experience will variously penetrate into work. For example, a Basic T-Group experience can be of varied usefulness in inducing personal learning that can generate organization change. Consider only that:

- The Basic T-Group can provide an arena to develop and to test new skills and insights applicable to interpersonal situations that may be modified for use at work.

- The experience in the basic T-Group can reveal the nature and importance of differences between "public" and "private" attitudes. A positive experience in the stranger experience can encourage an organization member to confront similar differences at work in such ways as to own them, analyze them, and perhaps reduce them so as to enhance performance in the organization.

- The stranger experience can point up the limitations of existing organization norms.

- The experience in the Basic T-Group at least can illustrate in life that some alternatives to common organizational norms are available.

- The Basic T-Group can help generate new norms for work and help enforce them as well, as by inducing a desire in individuals to try to achieve at their work some of the gratification of needs they experienced in a Basic T-Group.

Family Experiences ⟶ Possible Stranger Experiences

Particularly of late, some proponents have stood the usual phasing of the laboratory approach to OD on its head, as it were. They prescribe that learning experiences for the immediate work group should initiate an OD program. These initial experiences may be T-Groups or any number of variously circumscribed spin-offs which will be described and discussed below. If individual organization members prefer, after the initial experience with their work team they may subsequently arrange for a stranger experience to deepen insights that they begin to develop in their family experience.

121

Alexander Winn has been the major proponent of this alternative macro-design for OD. Based on his experience of a decade at Alcan: Canada, he concludes that ". . . programmes of team development contribute substantially to individual growth but . . . the reverse is not necessarily true."[17] Hence Alcan:Canada moved from a massive reliance on stranger T-Group experiences through semistranger experiences in "cousin" T-Groups composed of Alcan's diverse workforce who did not work together and probably never would. The firm finally came to rely more and more on sensitivity training experiences for work teams as the basic opener for OD effects. Winn explains that the family experience differs from a stranger T-Group in important ways:

> Quite frequently, it becomes a variation of a work conference in which, in addition to the manifest, overt topic or agenda, the covert, the hidden, the process and the here-and-now are explored. The explorations of the family T-Group are obviously not limited to the data the group generates in its confrontation at the meeting. Their past experiences, the "carry-overs," the "hang-ups," their anxiety and frustration, their feelings of hostility as well as of warmth, become the here-and-now data as well. The real authority figure, not a surrogate, is present along with one's work partners from one's own as well as other functionally related departments. By making explicit the many blocks to inter-personal, intra-group, and inter-group communication, and by seeking to break through these, it becomes the most powerful way to affect the social system.[18]

The rationale for this second macro-design is less straightforward than for the stranger ⟶ family progression, as a sampling of the fuller rationale suggests. *First,* beginning with stranger experiences resulted in personal learning, but transfers into the workplace were unsatisfyingly slow at Alcan:Canada, according to Winn.

> As should have been expected, the stranger and semi-stranger T-Group experience affected the individual where he was most involved in a deep personal sense and where his ambivalent feelings had the strongest resonance—in his home. It is thus in the nuclear family, i.e., in a culturally prescribed environment of lesser mobility and greater trust that the individual has found a more receptive ground for experimentation with his own behavior than in an affectively neutral industrial organization.[19]

---

17. Alexander Winn, *op. cit.*, p. 163.
18. *Ibid.*, p. 160.
19. *Ibid.*, p. 158.

Directly, the question of transfer was not solved by the stranger ——————➤ family progression. Trainees slowly transferred into work the insights, the understanding of the complexities of group phenomena, or the enhanced sense of their impact on others that they gained in stranger T-Groups.

Second, in part, this lack of transfer reflects a translation difficulty. Alcan:Canada trainees apparently had great problems seeing how they could translate into work the often-profound learning gained in stranger T-Groups. The stranger T-Group can be so emotionally charged or can deal with such novel topics that the organization member is at once caught up in the dynamics and very unclear about how it all applies back home. Indeed, Winn proposes that stranger T-Group experiences in cases can hinder rather than facilitate OD efforts. He speculates that the fantasied costs of transfer may seem too high, especially in the case of organization members who participated in an all-male stranger T-Group where the expression of feelings was accompanied by displays of crying, hugging, or whatever. Organization transfer might appear remote, at best. At worst, as Winn concludes, homosexual anxieties may inhibit organization members "from being close to another man, whether it be his superior, peer or subordinate. He may select the fight-flight modality which will support, by distance or contradiction respectively, his individuality in the back-home environment."[20]

When the work team together experiences a sensitivity training experience, patently, there is no such great need to translate or transfer experiences from one context to another. The situation implies a discipline, or holding-back, that is at once bane and boon. Family T-Groups may have "shallower experiences," and defenses may be higher. On the other hand, the experience has a "what you see is what you get" quality which, at its best, implies a realistic tethering of expectations about change and learning. As Winn suggests:

> The organizational family T-Group experience does not have to reshape the individual's underlying personality characteristics, but it does alter his expectations of himself and others about what is legitimate behaviour. The group reaches the point in its team development when the members begin to behave in a more open and authentic way, and when they can resolve conflicts more effectively. The organizational T-Group establishes a frame of reference for working through and managing conflicts. Resolution is not a Utopian answer but a workable solution to immediate issues. In a way, conflicts are accepted as a price we all have to pay for living in a complex industrial society. As new

---

20. *Ibid.,* p. 159.

issues arise, they are again confronted openly. Effective and continuous conflict resolution is but the basis of an effective decision-making process so central to our organizational lives.[21]

Third, even if the organization member clearly sees the applicability at work of his learning in a stranger T-Group, he often is not able to act on his insight. This reflects a practical and theoretical issue. Practically, the learner later faces the problem of somehow getting his work colleagues to the learning plateau he reached. Theoretically, Alcan:Canada's experience reflects the critical gap between insight and action. This will especially be the case where the learner moves from the supportive and warm environment of the stranger T-Group to the more affectively neutral if not hostile environment of the worksite.

A Critical Open Question

To the betting person, the considerations above suggest that you make your choice and pay the price. Winn sees only enough evidence to make a negative conclusion, for example. He concludes:

> There is not enough evidence that the "seeding" and saturation with stranger or semi-stranger T-Groups is a prerequisite for an effective organizational family lab. There were as many instances when past T-Group experience triggered off the individual's defenses against an organizational family lab as there were examples when such prior exposure to stranger T-Groups was pertinent and helpful.[22]

The shape of the evidence necessary to permit finer decisions about beginning with stranger or family experiences can be sketched in terms of the unique approach of Reed M. Powell and John Stinson.[23] They compared the differential impact of standardized T-Group experiences in family and stranger settings on the performance of simulated business firms.[24] Each firm had five members. The research time schedule is complex. Essentially, however, 15 firms first had six to eight hours of experience with the simulation. After matching the firms for performance in these initial trials, three clusters of firms were distinguished:

- five Family-Trained firms whose members had a T-Group experience together

---

21. *Ibid.,* pp. 159–60.
22. *Ibid.,* pp. 159–60.
23. Reed M. Powell and John F. Stinson, "The Worth of Laboratory Training," *Business Horizons,* Vol. 14 (August, 1971), pp. 87–95.
24. The simulated business environment is from E. T. Hellenbrandt and John F. Stinson, *The General Business Management Simulation* (Athens, Ohio: Follett Book Co., 1965).

124

- five Stranger-Trained firms whose members each had a separate T-Group experience
- five Control firms whose members had no training

Subsequently, each firm spent 12 to 16 additional hours in further trials on the simulation. The basic experimental data involve comparisons of the initial 6 to 8 hours of simulation time with the final 12 to 16 hours.

The findings of the Powell-Stinson experiment can only be considered as tentative at this time, but they are suggestive of the complex issues involved in the question: Should the initial experience be in a stranger or in a family experience? Three highlights emphasize those findings. *First,* although the T-Group experience was a brief one and was oriented

Table 1. Selected Impacts of Laboratory Training on Operations of Simulated Firms

	Mean Scores on Selected Dependent Variables		
	Five Family-Trained Firms	Five Stranger-Trained Firms	Five Control Firms
1. Average accumulated profit	$186,600*	$445,380	$440,080*
2. Average increase in stock price	$.12*	$5.75†	$10.25*
3. Average change in cohesiveness	+.349*†	−1.39†	−1.484*
4. Average change in leader-initiating structure behavior	−5.304*	−3.826‡	+3.17*‡
5. Average change in task-oriented behavior by leader	−3.41	−3.096	−.91

Source: Reed M. Powell and John F. Stinson, "The Worth of Laboratory Training," *Business Horizons,* Vol. 14 (August, 1971), p. 92.

* difference between family-trained and control firms was statistically significant by Mann-Whitney U test.

† difference between family-trained and stranger-trained firms was statistically significant.

‡ difference between stranger-trained and control firms was statistically significant.

toward task rather than relationships,[25] the experience tended to be impactful. The decrease in leader-oriented behavior[26] in rows 4 and 5 in Table 1 supports this conclusion, when either Family-Trained or Stranger-Trained firms are compared to Control firms.

Second, Family-Trained firms seemed more able to transfer the effects of their training into their simulated worksite. Rows 4 and 5 in Table 1 suggest the point. Relatedly, row 3 shows that the cohesiveness of Family-Trained firms increased, while Stranger-Trained and Control firms experienced sharp decreases. This is expected. Given that cohesive-

25. Powell and Stinson, *op. cit.,* p. 91.
26. For the measuring instrument, see Andrew W. Halpin, *Manual for the Leader Behavior Description Questionnaire* (Columbus: Bureau of Business Research, Ohio State University, 1957).

ness is a measure of the resultant attraction of a group for its members,[27] the data imply that the family T-Group experiences helped induce more satisfying and enjoyable interpersonal relationships that persisted throughout the simulations.

Third, the Family-Trained firms did not work together as productively on the technical task as the other two kinds of firms. See rows 1 and 2 in Table 1. Powell and Stinson see clear cause and effect. They note: ". . . it seems reasonable to assume that the participants had a limited amount of time to devote to the simulation; as more time was devoted to improving interpersonal relationships, less was available for productive activities."[28]

These findings suggest numerous issues which Powell and Stinson cannot resolve, which is not to demean this seminal research but only to describe its limits. One of those issues is perhaps most central: Why bother with T-Groups at all when in this case the Control firms were at least as effective as trained firms in performing their task? Several factors indicate why the available data do not resolve such central issues. Consider only four factors.

First, the simulations were sharply time bounded, and it is an open question whether the effects sketched above would have been maintained over a longer period. Major questions are moot in the absence of such longitudinal data. For example, would the decreases of cohesiveness in stranger-trained and control firms over the longer run have caused a deterioration in task performance?

Second, and relatedly, the interpretation of the data assumes that as cohesiveness increases, productivity decreases.[29] Other research strongly suggests, in contrast, that the actual relationship is more complicated. Low cohesiveness implies low productivity on tasks that require collaborative effort, in this alternative view. Up to a substantial point, increases in cohesiveness are associated with increases in productivity. At very high levels of cohesiveness, however, either very high productivity *or* very low productivity may be expected. High cohesiveness implies substantial group control over member behavior. And both very high and very low productivity require that behaviors of all group members be narrowly distributed, which is to say highly controlled.[30]

27. The cohesiveness subscale of the Work Group Description Questionnaire was used in the present case. See Ralph M. Stogdill, *Managers, Employees, and Organizations,* Monograph No. 125 (Columbus: Bureau of Business Research, Ohio State University, 1965).
28. Powell and Stinson, *op. cit.,* p. 93.
29. Ralph M. Stogdill, "A Behavioral Model of Organization" (Paper presented at Annual Meeting, American Psychological Association, Washington, D.C., 1969).
30. Robert T. Golembiewski, "Small Groups and Large Organizations," in James G. March (ed.), *Handbook of Organizations* (Chicago: Rand McNally & Co., 1965), esp. pp. 88–94 and 101–6.

Given this alternative concept of cohesiveness, the patterns in Table 1 might change substantially over the longer run.

Third, the reward schedule for participants is not clear. Specifically, participants were told that their academic grades would be affected by their performance on the simulations. Apparently, this potential reward was not great enough to engage the high cohesiveness of the family-trained firms. Or, alternatively, their socioemotional needs were stronger than their aspirations for grades, or that portion of them which would be affected by their simulation performance. Note that the data in Table 1 are also consistent with that variety of cohesive group which uses its control over member behavior to defy management.

Whether more attractive reward schedules, over longer periods of time, would have the same effects in most or all cases are the major unknowns. Depending on those specific effects, the high cohesiveness generated in family-trained firms will be viewed as either troublesome or as facilitative, from the perspectives of such authority figures as executives or professors.

Fourth, the training in this case seems to have been skewed more toward love than truth, to risk a revealing simplification. The broad point gets major attention at a number of other points, especially in Section B of Part III. Here note only that the present training experience may have encouraged an extreme emphasis on a homogenized social inclusion, as contrasted with membership that acknowledges differential abilities and interests. The "honeymoon period" which characterizes the early stages of many T-Groups is based on homogenized social inclusion, as is illustrated in Subsection 3 of Section A above.

It is not known whether the Powell-Stinson groups happened to be caught at such an early stage of development. But the available data do not urge rejection of this possibility. Thus the T-Group experience was a brief one. Moreover, its design seems congenial to the possibility suggested above. As Powell and Stinson explain their T-Group design:

> Throughout . . . there was a considerable emphasis on developing consensus in decision making. Compromise and one-man decisions were discouraged. Rather, T-Group participants were encouraged to ensure that all points of view were heard and thoroughly discussed, that all members contributed to the decisions as much as possible, and that the groups arrived at a consensus on their decisions.
>
> It is probable that this concentration on participation and consensus encouraged [the appointed] formal leaders to reduce the strength of their leadership.[31]

---

31. Powell and Stinson, *op. cit.,* p. 93.

Yes, indeed.

The laboratory approach is also oriented toward truth as well as love, however, despite the likely early fixation on warmth, inclusion, and so on.[32] If the truth is that various differentiations among a group's membership are appropriate because of their varying knowledge and skills, the longer-run goal of the laboratory approach is to facilitate that differentiation and to help cope openly with its inevitable fallout. Such differentiation can be risky for a group's members, but it is a risk necessary to progress beyond early stages of development.

d. The Scope of Organization Development: Some Boundaries

Wherever an OD program may be started, substantial agreement exists about the boundary conditions that circumscribe a successful application. Specifically, some greater sense of the scope of the laboratory approach to OD can be gained by detailing three kinds of boundaries. These boundaries, as it were, help stake out the territory of OD. The three kinds of boundaries are: (1) the typical set of objectives underlying OD programs; (2) some assumptions implied by these typical objectives; and (3) some broad agreements about the linkages of individual learning with organization change, as well as about the inadequacies of the available research as it relates to these agreements.

Major Objectives of Typical OD Programs

OD programs typically reflect several common major objectives, or goals. Overall, the goal is to release the human potential within an organization. Specifically, the goals of individual OD efforts can cover a broad or narrow range. One cannot go very wrong in expecting that any specific OD effort will emphasize major objectives such as these:[33]

- to create an open, problem-solving climate throughout the organization so that problems can be confronted, rather than fought about or fled from
- to build trust among individuals and groups throughout the organization, whether the linkages are vertical ones between superiors and subordinates, horizontal ones between peers, or diagonal ones between individuals of different ranks in different units of organization

---

32. Section B of Part III describes how such an unbalanced concept of the laboratory approach creates problems for Organization Development and prescribes ways to avoid that outcome.

33. These objectives derive from a variety of sources, primarily from Sherwood, *op. cit.*, and NTL Institute for Applied Behavioral Science, "What Is OD?" *News and Reports*, Vol. 2 (June, 1968), p. 1.

- to supplement the authority associated with role or status with the authority of knowledge and competence
- to locate decision-making and problem-solving responsibilities as close to the information sources as possible
- to make competition where it exists contribute more to the meeting of work goals, as where organization units compete in producing a good or service more efficiently and effectively, as opposed to win/lose competition
- to maximize collaboration between individuals and units whose work is interdependent
- to develop a reward system which recognizes both the achievement of the organization's mission (profits or service) and human development (growth of people)
- to increase the sense of ownership of organization objectives throughout the work force
- to help managers to manage according to relevant objectives rather than according to "past practices," or according to objectives which do not make sense for one's area of responsibility
- to increase self-control and self-direction for people within the organization
- to create conditions where conflict is brought out and managed
- to increase awareness of group "process" and its consequences for performance—that is, to help persons become aware of what is happening between and to group members while the group is working on the task, e.g., communication, influence, feelings, leadership styles and struggles, relationships between groups, how conflict is managed, etc.

These common OD objectives come to a sharp focus in which, basically, the organization is seen as a system in need of continuing innovation. An OD program begins by stressing the development of attitudes, behaviors, and skills that will support such continuing innovation. And the goal is nothing less than the creation of a more humane and effective organization.

Some Assumptions of Typical OD Efforts

Typical OD objectives rest on similar conceptual foundations. These foundations are a mixed bag, including relatively hard empirical findings and plausible hypotheses. These foundations of OD programs also prescribe how organizations ought to be so as to be effective, "healthy," or morally acceptable.

As with all systems of social theory and practice, the conceptual founda-tions of OD also include a variety of more-or-less explicit assumptions about how the world is or ought to be. That such assumptions are in-cluded in theoretical principle or in practical precepts is neither good nor bad, it is simply inevitable. The prudent person can only be as clear as possible about these assumptions. In that spirit, Figure 1 is a con-

Figure 1. Some Assumptions Underlying Typical OD Objectives

- Work which is organized to meet people's needs as well as to achieve organiza-tional requirements tends to produce the highest productivity and quality of production.
- Most members of organizations are not motivated primarily by an avoidance of work for which tight controls and threats of punishment are necessary—but, rather, most individuals seek challenging work and desire responsibility for ac-complishing organizational objectives to which they are committed.
- The basic building blocks of organizations are groups of people; therefore, the basic units of change are also groups, not simply individuals.
- The culture of most organizations tends to suppress the open expression of feel-ings which people have about each other and about where they and their organization are heading. The suppression of feelings can adversely affect problem-solving, personal growth, and satisfaction with one's work.
- Groups which learn to work in a constructively open way by providing feedback for members become more able to profit from their own experience and become more able to fully utilize their resources on the task. Furthermore, the growth of individual members is facilitated by relationships which are open, supportive, and trusting.
- "People support what they help create." Where change is introduced, it will be most effectively implemented if the groups and individuals involved have a sense of ownership in the process. Commitment is most assuredly attained where there is active participation in the planning and conduct of the change.
- The basic value underlying all OD theory and practice is that of *choice*. Through the collection and feedback of relevant data—made available by trust, open-ness, and risk—more choice becomes available to the organization and to the individual, and hence better decisions can be made.

From John J. Sherwood, *An Introduction to Organization Development,* Experimental Pub-lication System. Washington, D.C.: American Psychological Association. No. 11 (April, 1971), Ms. No. 396–1. Also reprinted in J. W. Pfeiffer and J. E. Jones (eds.), *1972 Annual Handbook for Group Facilitators.* Iowa City, Iowa: University Associates Publishers, 1972.

tinuation of the persistent effort in these early pages to make the founda-tion of organization development as explicit as possible. The figure details a number of assumptions that support OD efforts, with some of the assumptions having various degrees of empirical support and others being more in the nature of value preferences.

Some Agreements and Inadequacies

The linkage of individual change in a Basic T-Group with organiza-tional change was made casually above, but this does an injustice to reality. Let us begin remedying this injustice in two ways: (1) by sketching three broad areas of agreement about the nature of the complex linkages which OD programs seek to make and (2) by detailing the inadequacies of existing theory to act upon these points of agreement.

Agreement I. OD efforts based on the laboratory approach stress the "organic" versus the "mechanistic" nature of organizations.[34] As opposed to traditional organization theory, that is, the emphasis is on assembling the competencies necessary to do the job, on team development, and on problem-solving. As opposed to traditional organization theory with its emphasis on functional specialization, similarly, OD applications stress organizing around flows of work, projects, or matrix overlays, as Section A of Part III, especially, will demonstrate.

Unfortunately, comparative testing of such alternative ways of organizing has barely begun, despite the convincing case that can be made by syntheses based on a disparate research literature.[35] Line-staff relations in this regard are like the weather. For example, despite torrents of criticism, little comparative work of even a semicontrolled kind exists on the basis of which the organization analyst can with confidence set himself to doing something constructive about line-staff relations.

Agreement II. Points of organizational fragmentation are strategic points for applications of the laboratory approach in organizations. The fragmentation may set department versus department, line versus staff, headquarters versus the field, or labor versus management. Various designs based on the laboratory approach to OD can help clarify the sources of tension and set the stage for reducing them. For example, desired changes in attitudes and behaviors resulted from an effort based on the laboratory approach to confront some very complex interactions within one firm—between headquarters and a field-sales force, as well as between several hierarchical levels.[36]

These strategic targets for change, however, impose correspondingly great demands on the adequacy of the theory underlying OD applications designed to remedy matters. Candidly, that theory is still in its early stages of development. Practically, however, waiting on the development of some eventually mature theory is the best way to assure that development will be slow or even stagnant. Prudent aggressiveness is necessary to extend the art and science of OD, to get us from here to there, wherever that is.

---

34. Herbert A. Shepard, "Changing Interpersonal and Intergroup Relationships in Organizations," in March (ed.), *op. cit.*, pp. 1115–43.
35. Robert T. Golembiewski, *Men, Management, and Morality* (New York: McGraw-Hill Book Co., 1965).
36. Robert T. Golembiewski and Arthur Blumberg, "Confrontation as a Training Design in Complex Organizations," *Journal of Applied Behavioral Science*, Vol. 3 (December, 1967), pp. 525–47.

Agreement III. Applications of the laboratory approach stress the ideal of a change program simultaneously affecting behavior, task, and structure.[37] The ideal of simultaneous change is seldom as closely approached in such organizations as Non-Linear Systems, but simultaneity comprises a major theme in many programs of organization change and development.

Although simultaneity is a major goal of OD, it largely exceeds our present theoretic and practical grasp. The reigning Iron Law of Organization Life is that shackling of the personality and repression of the self are the major consequences of organizing. OD stands in marked contrast, arguing that major complementarities are possible. Given the imprecision of our existing knowledge of behavior-task-structure linkages, the ideal is a lofty one.

The demands implied by these three points of agreement highlight the inadequacies of the laboratory approach to organizational change and development. The summary conclusion may be driven home in terms of three particulars. *First,* we lack appropriate empirical theory to guide OD efforts, as later discussion will help establish. Epigrammatically, the classroom reflects a complexity that more than matches the capacity of existing theory. So much more ill-equipped are applications in incredibly more complex formal organizations.

Second and relatedly, the lack of theory is tied to the inadequate volume of research dealing with applications of the laboratory approach to organization change. Thus Edgar Schein and Warren Bennis note that:

> Discouragingly, but not unexpectedly, the research effort seems weakest in those situations where the risks are highest and the tasks are most complex. We are referring to the uses of laboratory training in inducing change in organizations. In some organizational change programs, a great deal of attention is being paid to research, but not enough research is yet being done.[38]

Subsequent chapters will illustrate the improvements since 1965 in this puny state of the literature. But the generalization still applies, and in uncomfortable degree, at this later date.

Theory and research about the application of laboratory methods to individual learning are in much better shape, in contrast. Much is known

---

37. Richard Beckhard, "An Organization Improvement Program in a Decentralized Organization," *Journal of Applied Behavioral Science,* Vol. 2 (January, 1966), pp. 3–26.
38. Edgar Schein and Warren G. Bennis (eds.), *Personal and Organizational Change through Group Methods* (New York: John Wiley & Sons, 1965), p. 323.

about who is likely to learn what in which laboratory designs, and certainly no one can doubt the considerable power of laboratory experiences to change attitudes or to modify behavior. More generally still, research on the personal and interpersonal aspects of laboratory training reflects all the signs of robust activity. Later sections will review this research.

Third, existing research about organizational applications of the laboratory approach has important design limitations. Generally, much research about learning in laboratories has a strong focus on outcomes, such as the before/after change in an individual's ability to empathize with others. Commonly, input or process variables receive less attention. Exceptions to this generalization exist both early and late in the short history of sensitivity training. But the generalization still holds rather more than less, as will be demonstrated in detail in later sections.

The outcome bias also characterizes research on OD applications based on the laboratory approach, although with several interesting reservations. For example, the outcomes emphasized most in research about change programs in organizations tend to cover a narrow range and/or to be restricted to the feeling realm. Of course, many narrow measures of the success of OD efforts can be cited. For example, attitudes of both headquarters and field officials in a large organization have been changed via a modified laboratory design, as one small part of a long-run program of change.[39] As the criteria for success are broadened, however, so also does the validation of change become more elusive and problematic. Whether the attitudinal changes noted above also produced more effective work relations, for example, is just such an elusive and problematic issue. Highly placed organization members have reported that they feel their work relations are freer and more productive. Such reports are a significant outcome, to be sure, and for some purposes even the most important one. But other outcomes also are of scientific and practical interest.

Finally, the complexity and chancy nature of crucial events in organizations often leave change agents exhaustedly satisfied if "things seemed to work out pretty well, on balance." This gross outcome bias I can well understand, as a participant in several major efforts in which events far beyond the change program affected it substantially.

Straightforward summary is possible concerning the third problem with the laboratory approach to organization change. With rare exceptions,[40] laboratory approaches to organization change have not been validated in the broader sense of tracing their influence on such desirable states as high productivity or low employee turnover. Complexity and

---

39. Golembiewski and Blumberg, *op. cit.*
40. Louis B. Barnes and Larry E. Greiner, "Breakthrough in Organization Development," *Harvard Business Review*, Vol. 42 (November–December, 1964), pp. 139–64.

confounding variables make it very difficult to support rigorously the compelling circumstantial evidence of the value of laboratory programs for change. Similarly, very few change programs in large organizations have looked closely at input variables or the specific processes of the groups involved.[41] It has been, in short, "outcome" bias.

2. SOME INTENDED CONSEQUENCES: TOWARD MUTUALITY AS THE BASIC GOAL

The laboratory approach to OD has engendered some schizoidlike reactions, in the absence of a research literature of such scope and clarity as to inhibit all but the most foolhardy and ill-informed critic. On the one extreme, OD is sometimes seen as the contemporary substitute for the Christendom of yesteryear, whose derivative moral order has grown increasingly inadequate as a guide for men in large organizations. At the other extreme, the laboratory approach is seen as just another new if extremely powerful tool by which top management can manipulate the psyche of organization members.[42] Proponents of the one extreme see salvation, while those of the opposite persuasion see enslavement.

Whatever history will reveal in its own good time, this volume neither seeks salvation nor expects enslavement from the laboratory approach. And this volume doubts that much is gained from such dramatic counterpositioning. Moreover, it assigns a very low probability to either extreme outcome. At the same time, the character of human affairs is such that one extreme or the other might evolve. Hence the choice is to dwell on the normative and design constraints that influence the several species of the laboratory approach, with the goal of seeking more salvation and less enslavement.

This volume does not wait on history, perhaps impatiently. The view here is that the laboratory approach is a useful way of contributing to a heightening mutuality of organization demands and satisfaction of member needs. The basic model is an exchange model, and the governing concept is a delayed double spiral.

Reference to a delayed double spiral is not meant to be either obscure or profound. The probable obscurity can be dealt with briefly. From the organization's point of view, more and more has been demanded of its members over historical time: The organization's spiral of needs loops outward and upward, decisively. In the early days of industrialization,

---

41. For one exception, see Chris Argyris, *Interpersonal Competence and Organizational Effectiveness* (Homewood, Ill.: Dorsey Press, 1962).
42. William G. Scott, "Schmidt Is Alive and Enrolled in a Sensitivity Training Program," *Public Administration Review*, Vol. 30 (November, 1970), pp. 621–25.

for example, its logic required large numbers of hands at a central location, the term "hands" mutely testifying to what the organization needed from almost all of its members. But even to get the "hands," it was necessary to revolutionize agriculture, move people to central cities, and destroy the home as a center of commerce. Today, again from the organization's point of view, far more of man is needed than his hands. Increasing skills, longer periods of socialization and training, and especially greater tolerance for change, instability, and tension: these characterize the broadening spiral of today's organization demands. Of paramount significance is the sharp increase in these demands, more or less in the last decade.

For the individual his spiral of need satisfaction has also broadened, but probably always at a delayed rate. Today may be characterized as one of those times when the gap between organization demands and satisfaction of member needs is considered critically large by enough people to make a significant difference. Cries by the young that they "want more than a job" may be viewed sardonically by those for whom "just any job" in 1935 would have answered their most urgent prayer. Similarly, demands by many Catholic priests and nuns that their needs can only be met by changes in the Church's prohibition of marriage may be dismissed by those for whom the opportunity to serve God in a special way is the only needed incentive. And the examples could be multiplied, but they all make the same point. Clearly, the stakes required to induce playing various organization roles have been sharply raised in the period of a few decades. The view here, perhaps primitive, is that these stakes have increased just as have the demands that organization life makes on more and more people.

From the point of view of an exchange model, two possibilities exist. First, new incentives can be developed to insure that organization demands will continue to be met, even as they spiral outward at unprecedented rates. Second, individual expectations can be lowered. This General Bullmoose strategy is at best a temporary expedient. At worst, the strategy conjures up images of depressions or garrison states or Great Leaps Forward that go backward in major respects.

From a major perspective, then, this volume seeks to contribute to the development of the satisfaction of individual needs that will help assure that organization demands will be met. Overall, the laboratory approach aims to identify major human needs, and to suggest how they may be met in organizations. The specific immediate contributions here to that overall aim are two: (1) to sketch one way of viewing the linkages of individual needs and organization demands and (2) to use the notion of regenerative communication systems to suggest the ways in which the laboratory approach can contribute to mutuality in organizations.

135

a. The Essence of Organization Development:
Toward Linking Individual and Organization Needs/Demands

The essence of OD programs is to link individual needs/demands with those of their organizations. The usage "needs/demands" is clumsy and will be discontinued after this initial paragraph. But the clumsy usage deals with a critical notion. My need as an organization member can be viewed as a demand upon the organization for satisfaction and organization needs often will be expressed or perceived as demands by its members. Needs/demands it is, then.

Figure 2 presents one model of how the laboratory approach can serve to link individual and organization needs in crucial ways. "Needs" are to be understood broadly as prerequisites for effective functioning, or at least aids to such effective functioning. The assumed contribution to effective functioning of each of the items mentioned, in turn, rests on empirical findings[43] as well as on (hopefully reasonable) hypotheses when research is inconclusive or is lacking.

The schema in Figure 2 is simple in its concept. It begins with a basic premise, that mutuality in meeting individual and organization needs will be associated with high output and member satisfaction. This basic premise is supported in two ways. First, some individual and organization needs are outlined, for the purpose of showing how satisfaction of these needs implies competence in interpersonal and intergroup relations. In turn, the common consequences of these learning designs—such as increased openness and individual commitment—can clearly be related to the satisfaction of individual and organization needs. The intent is to depict a self-heightening system.

b. The Thrust of Organization Development:
Toward Mutuality through Regenerative Systems

The thrust toward mutuality in organization development can be established in a somewhat more specific way, as in Figure 3, which sketches how degenerative communication systems can create serious problems in organizations. The usefulness of regenerative systems for individuals was (hopefully) established in an earlier section. The purpose here is to suggest the mutual value of regenerative systems to organizations as well as to individuals.

Figure 3 is an ideal construct, relating how two self-heightening sets

---

43. Newton Margulies, "Organizational Culture and Psychological Growth," *Journal of Applied Behavioral Science,* Vol. 5 (October, 1969), pp. 491–508; and John D. Aram, Cyril P. Morgan, and Edward S. Esbeck, "Relation of Collaborative Interpersonal Relationships to Individual Satisfaction and Organizational Performance," *Administrative Science Quarterly,* Vol. 16 (September, 1971), pp. 289–96.

of relations can explain the genesis of what are offered as common problems in organizations. Because Figure 3 attempts to impose some order on complex observations, it is in this sense far more a low-level clinical description of a syndrome of effects than it is a "theory." But the figure has the virtue of suggesting why organizational changes are so complex, while it mirrors what seem important aspects of reality. Note, for example, the circular reinforcement of effects suggested by Figure 3. To illustrate, increases in unfinished business between individuals and organization units can lead to the development of organization norms that restrict the interaction which alone can support the communication and decision-making processes necessary to reduce the unfinished business. Moreover, Figure 3 also implies another wheels-within-wheels construction. That is, the model allows that organization norms restricting interaction can reinforce degenerative systems which exist between individuals or can induce degenerative systems even in cases where individuals have the best of collaborative intentions. This is the essential meaning of the abortive romance between a Hatfield and a McCoy, or a Montague and a Capulet.

The reader should find Figure 3 more or less self-explanatory, except for the comment on fragmentation of organization units, and it will take all of this volume (especially Section A of Part III) to sketch that point with even minimal clarity. As a first step here, note that in a major sense every organizing effort has integrating and fragmenting consequences. Philip Selznick eloquently made the point for that primal organizational act, delegation of authority. The intended consequence of delegation is manifest, to factor the elements of some task so as to take advantage of specialized competencies and also to control their integrated performance. So far, so good. But the very isolation of specialized competencies sets fragmenting forces in motion. Thus differential training creates different interests; the specialized competencies may be organized into separate departments, thereby encouraging the development of subgoals which overlap only partially; and such differentiating and potentially fragmenting forces begin to influence the content of decisions in subtle ways.[44] The only way out is a kind of running faster to stand still.

Every organizing effort has integrating and fragmenting consequences, in short, and the name of the usual game is to maximize the former and to minimize the latter. Hence the crucial significance in Figure 3 of the hypothesized tendency of degenerative communication systems to encourage the fragmentation of organization subunits.

The point of this topic can be stated tersely. OD has as one of its major purposes the development and maintenance of regenerative sys-

---

44. Philip Selznick, *TVA and the Grass Roots* (Berkeley, Cal.: University of California Press, 1949).

Figure 2. A Simplified Model of Findings-Hypotheses Underlying An Organization Development Program Based on the Laboratory Approach

Basic Premise: To the degree that individuals can meet their own needs while meeting organizational needs, two simultaneous conditions become increasingly probable:

- satisfaction of organization members will heighten
- output will increase, both in terms of quality and quantity

Individual

An individual's basic needs center around self-realization and self-actualization. The former involves a person seeking himself as he is in interaction with others, with the goal of increasing the congruence between his intentions and his impact on others. Self-actualization refers to the processes of growth by which an individual realizes his potential.

An individual whose basic needs are being met experiences corresponding psychological growth, the prime conditions for which, and consequences of which, are:

- a growing awareness of the needs and motivations of self and others
- a lessening of the degree to which his relationships and actions are distorted, especially via more actively inducing feedback from others and by more effectively interpreting it
- an increasing ability to modify behavior in response to feedback about its impact on others, to respond appropriately rather than stereotypically
- a growing tendency to seek or develop conditions that promote psychological growth for self and others
- an expanding capacity to determine goals and internal motivations for self

An individual who experiences psychological growth will be correspondingly motivated to search for work, challenge, and responsibility.

Organization

An efficient organization will develop an appropriately shifting balance between institutionalization and risk-taking. The former refers to infusing with value the activities of the organization, so as to elicit member support, identification, and collaboration. Risk-taking is necessary in innovating more effective ways to deal with existing activities and in adapting to environmental changes in society, markets, technologies, and so on.

An organization's successful balancing of institutionalization and risk-taking will depend upon:

- the increasingly complete use of people as well as nonhuman resources
- the development and maintenance of a viable balance between central control and local initiative
- fluid lines of communication—vertically, horizontally, and diagonally
- decision-making processes that solve problems that stay solved without creating other problems
- infusing the organization with values that support its existence as a stable institution and that also motivate its developmental change as an adaptive structure

An organization with such a working balance of institutionalization and risk-taking will develop appropriate norms that support efforts of organization members to search for work, challenge, and responsibility.

Satisfaction of both individual and organization needs will be facilitated by, if such satisfaction does not in fact crucially depend upon, *skill and competence in interpersonal and intergroup situations.*

Organizational family teams can be exposed to such learning designs derived from the laboratory approach as sensitivity training, with the intention of *increasing confidence, trust, and responsibility* that can be applied directly to solving organizational issues. Skill and competence in interpersonal and in intergroup situations can be increased in sensitivity training groups composed of strangers, that is, but the real test is the application of such learning in life-relevant situations. Such application will require that substantial numbers of organization members learn appropriate interpersonal skills, as well as that they internalize a set of values which support and reinforce such learning.

An individual's growth and self-realization are facilitated by interpersonal and intergroup relations that are *honest, caring, and non-manipulative.* Individuals can gain convenient experiences with these personal needs and with ways of satisfying them in such learning designs derived from the laboratory approach as sensitivity training. This is a managed process of gaining experience with attitudes and skills for inducing greater openness about positive and negative feelings, attitudes, or beliefs. Such openness leads to greater trust and reduced risk in communicating and is intended to suggest possible transfers into other environments.

Persons in groups which develop greater openness tend to *identify strongly* with other members and with the goals of the group.

Groups characterized by strong identification with members and goals become *increasingly capable of dealing* with issues facing their members, and hence increasingly *capable of influencing their environment* in desired ways.

Groups whose members identify strongly and who can influence their environment are likely to be effective reinforcers of decisions about change. Such groups also can provide emotional support necessary to sustain required changes in the values, attitudes, or behaviors of their members.

Source: Adapted from Robert T. Golembiewski and Stokes B. Carrigan, "Planned Change in Organization Style Based on Laboratory Approach," *Administrative Science Quarterly*, Vol. 15 (March, 1970), p. 81.

Figure 3. A Degenerative System and Some of Its Typical Outcomes in Organizations

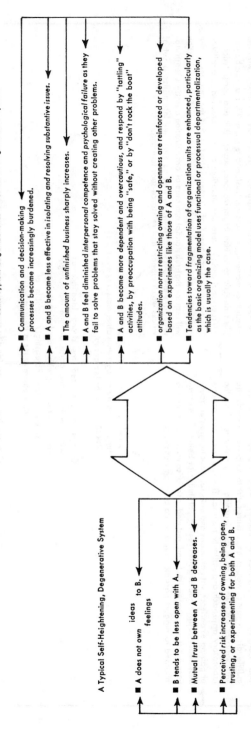

Some Typical Organizational Outcomes of Degenerative Systems

■ Communication and decision-making processes become increasingly burdened.

■ A and B become less effective in *isolating and resolving substantive issues.*

■ The amount of *unfinished business* sharply increases.

■ A and B feel diminished *interpersonal competence and psychological failure* as they fail to solve problems that stay solved without creating other problems.

■ A and B become more dependent and overcautious, and respond by "tattling" activities, by preoccupation with being "safe," or by "don't rock the boat" attitudes.

■ *organization norms* restricting owning and openness are reinforced or developed based on experiences like those of A and B.

■ Tendencies toward *fragmentation* of organization units are enhanced, particularly as the basic organizing model uses functional or processual departmentalization, which is usually the case.

A Typical Self-Heightening, Degenerative System

■ A does not own ideas to B. feelings

■ B tends to be less open with A.

■ Mutual *trust* between A and B decreases.

■ Perceived *risk* increases of owning, being open, trusting, or experimenting for both A and B.

tems between individuals and groups. The intended outcome is to reduce organizational consequences like those sketched in Figure 3 which contribute to the organizational fragmentation that is so much with us. In this sense, OD attempts to develop greater centripetal forces in the face of growing centrifugal forces. These centrifugal forces can be conceived of as the major resultant of the delayed double spiral referred to above: expanding organization demands, and lagging satisfaction of individual needs in organizations. The prime consequence is to impair the exchange relationship between many organizations and many of their members.

3. SOME BASIC DYNAMICS:
TOWARD A PROCESS ORIENTATION

In its most elemental intent, an OD application based on the laboratory approach seeks to induce two conditions. The first is an awareness among organization members of a sense of their own processes of relating with one another as they go about their work. The second is a commitment to analyze those processes, regularly. In effect, a process orientation reflects a shared norm. In Herbert A. Shepard's words, that norm involves "a joint commitment among interdependent persons to 'process analysis,' i.e., to shared examination of their relationship in all aspects relevant to their interdependence."[45] Shepard calls it "observant participation." The awareness of process, plus the commitment to analyze it, is here referred to as a process orientation.

In concept, the process orientation is directly related to a system's competence. The implied centrality of the process orientation can be established briefly, following Chris Argyris.[46] He distinguishes three "core activities" of any system, such as an organization. A system must be able to achieve its objectives, to maintain its internal environment while doing so, and to adapt to its relevant external environment so as to exert necessary control over it. In the competent organization, its processes of carrying on these core activities are such that five outcomes tend to occur:

- The information needed to cope with the diverse factors relevant to the core activities will be both available and understandable to organization members who need that information.
- The information needed to cope is in such a form as to be usable.
- The system can afford the cost of gathering, understanding, and using the information.

45. Herbert A. Shepard, "Explorations in Observant Participation," in Bradford, Gibb, and Benne (eds.) , *op. cit.*, p. 379.
46. Chris Argyris, *Intervention Theory and Method* (Reading, Mass.: Addison-Wesley Publishing Co., 1970) , esp. pp. 36–37.

- Problems are solved and relevant decisions are made and implemented in ways that neither create additional new and similarly grave problems nor induce the recurrence of the original problem.
- The four consequences above are accomplished while increasing—or at least while not decreasing—the capacity of system members to solve problems, make decisions, or take implementing actions.

Commonly, it is difficult to determine whether a specific attempt to induce a process orientation produces all these consequences. For example, a consultant was asked to observe a decision-making meeting in a manufacturing concern. He accepted, but arrived so late that the group was just about to adjourn, the decision having been "made." The person presiding at the meeting, in a more or less friendly way, noted: "Well, we did it without you." To which the consultant replied: "I can't be sure, since I wasn't here. And I'm not clear on all the details, but you say you made a decision. I'm willing to test it. Are you?" The gauntlet having been mutually tossed, the group quickly agreed to a brief test, after a micro-design was described. On an index card, each group member would make two quick ratings using a 1–5 scale which sought to ascertain low versus high "commitment to the decision just made." Each person rated a score for Self and one for All Others. The consultant would be scorekeeper, to increase openness by eliminating the risk that a person's handwriting might be recognized by one of the participants. It was a very long time before the group of seven men adjourned, once they saw a compilation of the responses. The scores for Self were 1's and 2's and one 3; for All Others, the scores were all 5's, except for one 4. Moreover, one index card contained this carefully lettered question: "What decision? I thought we were just getting a first reading about where we all stood." The presiding official was crushed, but he ordered lunch and suggested that all afternoon appointments be canceled in the prospect that "it will take us awhile to get ourselves out of the mess we almost got me in."

In sum, this attempt at inducing a process orientation generated the first three consequences above. The jury was out on the last two consequences for quite a long time.

a. Some Characteristics of Process Orientation: Integrative Applied Behavioral Science

Just what is this process orientation, specifically? A summary way of putting it is that it is integrative applied behavioral science designed to improve the quality and effectiveness of human interaction. That probably does not answer the question very directly. And it will be necessary to take two approaches to outlining even a skeletal framework of a more satisfactory answer. These approaches to "process orientation" involve: (1) describing its several major properties and (2) sketching some guidelines that will facilitate a process orientation.

Six Major Properties of a Process Orientation

As a first step in adumbrating the notion of process orientation, six major properties can be distinguished. *First,* and this must by now be a conditioned response when one thinks of any species of the laboratory approach, process orientation is experiential. Its basic learning stimulus is not a case study or a theoretical presentation. The stimulus is, for example, that decision we may have just made, and how we made it.

Second, the process orientation presumes collaborative relationship in both diagnosis and prescription between a consultant and some client, whether the consultant is internal or external to the organization of his client. The purpose, then, is not only to "get the patient well." Far more is the purpose to develop interests and skills in the client that provide him with diagnostic skills which will permit him to help judge his own interactional health, as well as that of his own organization. Even more is the purpose to involve the client so intimately in joint problem-solving that his defensiveness is low and that, ideally, he internalizes the solution as his own. Perhaps paramountly, the goal of the process orientation is to develop attitudes and skills that encourage the client to enter into true helping relationships with others and that also raises the probability of his success in doing so. Basically, from this perspective, a process orientation requires developing the principle and practice of the values sketched in Section B above.

Third, as the emphasis on creating resources internal to the organization implies, the process orientation is a continuous one. Short of collaborative death, there is no alternative to it. One can only do it better or worse, do it most often or hardly at all.

Fourth, the process orientation ideally operates simultaneously at individual, interpersonal, and intergroup levels. Moreover, several complex processes can simultaneously operate at each level. Schein describes in detail six such processes, which are listed here to suggest the reach of the process orientation. These human processes are:[47]

- *communication,* as in who talks to whom
- *member roles and functions in groups,* which can emphasize self-oriented behavior, performance of task, or maintenance activities associated with preserving viable relations between members
- *group problem-solving and decision-making*

47. Edgar H. Schein, *Process Consultation* (Reading, Mass.: Addison-Wesley Publishing Co., 1969), pp. 15–75.

143

- *group norms and group growth,* as in the developmental stages sketched in Section B
- *leadership and authority,* as in issues of who influences whom
- *intergroup cooperation and competition*

The awareness and analysis of the complex interaction of such human processes at multiple levels constitutes a demanding task, but nature comes that way and must be confronted for what it is. Consider the manager addressing two sections subordinate to him. "I am really proud of section A," he might say. At the individual level, that may be exactly what the manager is feeling. Instead of warmth in return from some members of section A, however, he may at the interpersonal level receive embarrassment, rejection, or even hostility. For the manager may have triggered some feelings of competition between sections A and B, and his kindly pat on the head may be liked by some members of section A who at another level resent his comments as a rattling of section B's cage that might later generate some unpleasantness.

Fifth, the process orientation can be enriched by contrasting "process" with "content" and with "structure." In a rough sense, for example, process deals with how a decision is made and implemented; content refers to the "what" of a decision—its quality, its logical or technical basis; and structure deals with issues like who will formally implement the decision and what the procedures will be. The three levels variously interact. Consider structure and process. As Schein observes: ". . . the roles which people occupy partly determine how they will behave. It is important to have the right structure of roles for effective organizational performance." But structure does not predetermine process. Schein concludes: ". . . people's personalities, perceptions, and experiences also determine how they will behave in their roles and how they will relate to others."[48]

The richness of human interaction lies in the subtle blending of these three levels of meaning. For example, early sessions of a sensitivity training group are likely to fixate on issues of content and structure, as in Figure 4. Later, the same issues of structure and content can generate major additions to knowledge as individuals also respond to the process associated with those issues. The heightened learning possibilities of a process orientation inhere in the fact that issues of structure and content are relatively determinate and invariable. In contrast, the processes associated with raising them will vary with individuals, stages of group development, and a wild panoply of other variables.

Sixth, process orientation is an additional path to increased organizational effectiveness, not an exclusive one. Both contribution and limita-

---

48. *Ibid.,* p. 11. Reprinted by special permission from Schein, *Process Consultation: Its Role in Organization Development,* 1969, Addison-Wesley, Reading, Mass.

Figure 4. Richness in Interaction and Issues of Content, Structure, and Process

Early in Training:

Bill: Don't you think—after the way we have ←——→ been floundering—that . . . maybe we ought to have a chairman?

Mary: I agree—maybe a chairman can put ←——→ some order into what's going on here.

Jack: Quite so—we've got to have some or- ←——→ ganization to get things done around here.

Later in Training:

Bill: Earlier I suggested that we have a chairman and well . . . some of you agreed that it was a good idea. But . . . we never got around to doing it. Now— I'm suggesting it again.

Mary: I think, Bill, I was one of those that agreed with you then, but now I get a feeling that you are uncomfortable if things aren't done in a highly organized way . . . I mean, just for the sake of organization.

Jack: Bill, I feel Mary really has a point here. Besides—the way you've acted on other things gives me the impression that you're annoyed if people don't pick up your suggestions. Maybe you want a chairman so that it's easier for you to get your own way. What do you think?

Source: Robert Tannenbaum, Irving R. Weschler, and Fred Massarik, *Leadership and Organization* (New York: McGraw-Hill Book Co., 1961), pp. 202–3.

tion are implicit in this property. Schein captures the flavor of both features. He explains that:

> Obviously there is room in most organizations for improved production, financial, marketing, and other processes. I am arguing, however, that the various functions which make up an organization are always mediated by the interactions of people, so that the organization can never escape its human processes. As long as organizations are networks of people, there will be processes occurring between them. Therefore, it is obvious that the better understood and better diagnosed these processes are, the greater will be the chances of finding solutions to technical problems which will be accepted and used by the members of the organization.[49]

To which balanced position only one note needs to be added. Improvements in manufacturing and financial processes have long received major attention, while interpersonal and intergroup processes have received significant attention only in recent years.

These six properties suggest a working definition, in conclusion. The process orientation is one approach to augmenting personal and system effectiveness. It has an experiential thrust which encourages attention to a broad range of events at all levels in interpersonal and intergroup

---

49. Reprinted by special permission from Schein, *Process Consultation: Its Role in Organization Development,* 1969, Addison-Wesley, p. 9.

situations. The purpose of process orientation is a continuous one, to help individuals observe and understand events around them, and to develop skills of diagnosis and prescription in persons who consequently can act more effectively in coping with their environment. The stimuli to be learned from are primarily those of everyday life—human actions and their impact on others in the full gamut of formal and informal relationships. A process orientation draws from life, in sum, and can contribute to it.

Guidelines and Methods for a Process Orientation

Within the broad context of the values of the laboratory approach and of organization development sketched above, the process orientation implies a more specific set of "shoulds," or "oughts." These operational guidelines could take a variety of forms, but Jack Fordyce and Raymond Weil have presented an unusually useful set that they extract from their own OD efforts. They highlight a number of guidelines applicable to the process orientation as conceived here:[50]

- We pay attention to individual as well as group needs.
- We pool the widest possible range of opinion.
- We systematically question established ways of doing things.
- We emphasize feedback and ongoing critique.
- We clarify interpersonal relationships by deliberately digging out garbage—that is to say, concealed feeling that blocks simple man-to-man understanding.
- We stress responsibility for sharing management of the enterprise.
- We encourage exploration of oneself and one's connection to others.

Numerous methods for action on these guidelines are available, and they are usefully reviewed to flesh out the notion of process orientation. The methods are listed in order of their probable threat or confronting qualities. An important generalization should be kept in mind. "As a rule of thumb," as Fordyce and Weil express the point, "the more confronting the method, the richer the response and the stronger the impulse to change. But groups [and individuals] vary considerably in their readiness to work with immediate methods."[51]

For convenience, the assumption is made below that an OD external consultant or an internal staff man is seeking process-oriented informa-

---

50. Reprinted by special permission from Jack K. Fordyce and Raymond Weil, *Managing with People*, 1971, Addison-Wesley, Reading, Mass., p. 77.
51. *Ibid.*, p. 137.

tion at the request of some line executive. That person would have available to him such methods for collecting information.

Questionnaires and Instruments Soliciting Written Responses. Depending on the information required, various questionnaires and instruments can be used to generate data about processes. Typically, such devices are used with the assurance that only aggregate data will be reported to superiors, with the intent of increasing openness by reducing risk. Some of these devices can be improvised on the spot, as was the test mentioned above of the commitment of a group to a decision. Others may have to be painfully developed for ad hoc use. Fortunately a great many questionnaires and instruments have been developed and are "on the shelf," as it were.[52]

Interviews. These can provide great flexibility for the OD man, especially for probing and exploratory purposes. Again, respondents typically are guaranteed anonymity.

Upward Feedback Devices. This set of designs uses groups of employees to generate information. The groups may be work teams, or they may be assembled *de novo* by the OD man to get representation of specific interests or classes of workers. The group itself does the reporting, either in writing or via tape recording of a discussion, thus removing the OD man from the role of interpreter he must play in the two methods above. This method tends to raise the credibility of the product to the executive, coming as it does directly from the employees in whom he is interested. Obviously, however, the method makes greater demands on the time of the executive, especially in reading reports or in listening to tape recordings. Groups may be assured anonymity, or they might identify their products. One especially interesting version of this method is an edited tape recording of a real-time discussion, with the voices understandable but disguised.[53]

Questionnaire/Instrument/Interview Followed by Feedback to Contributing Parties. This is a classic OD method used, for example, as a first step in team-building projects. In the typical case, an OD consultant interviews a manager and his immediate subordinates, or he might use a questionnaire or some instrument to gather the needed data. Then the consultant reports his summary findings and observations to all those interviewed in a total session. The goal is to facilitate public coping of the "now that the consultant mentions it" variety with material that was in a group's Private Arena, to use Jo-Hari Window terminology. The consultant also may unearth data in the Blind Area. The method is intended to be quite confronting, of course, but if participants feel the

---

52. Subsequent sections will review the use of several questionnaires and instruments. Generally, see Schein, *op. cit.*, pp. 42–43.
53. Alton Bartlett, "Changing Behavior as a Means of Increased Efficiency," *Journal of Applied Behavioral Science*, Vol. 3 (July, 1967), pp. 381–403.

risks are too high they can manage the level of risk to tolerable levels by a variety of possible devices. All participants can agree that the OD consultant had a very bad interviewing day, for example, or that he has no real grasp of their working world.

Clearly, the method also can be a risky one for the OD consultant. Consequently, he cherishes even the one interviewee who can accept enough risk to say: "Well, since no one else here will validate what the OD consultant is reporting to us, I will. He's reporting a number of matters of concern to me, and I'll bet they are of concern to others on our managerial team. I feel threatened in saying this, even. What have we done to ourselves? Or at least what have I done to myself to make it so risky to reveal what is bugging me to men I have worked with for years, when I spilled the beans to a consultant I hardly know."

Pictorial Representations. Sometimes pictures or collages can provide revealing information, perhaps due to the greater legitimation of fantasy or perhaps to the regression encouraged by working with paste, scissors, and glue. I recall one case in which two groups were asked to make physical representations of themselves as a work unit during an evening session, which representations would serve as vehicles for mutual analysis the next morning. The issue to be explored was a typical "us good guys" and "them bad guys" one. Almost all members of both groups acknowledged the halo over their own group and saw the pitchfork in the hands of "them." Both representations were impressive and revealing enough, and much polite and mutually congratulatory small talk was exchanged over nightcaps. Who contributed what to the intergroup conflict at work was brought into sharp focus when some members of one group variously amended the product of the other group in the wee hours of the morning, after first secreting their own product away overnight in a safe location to protect it from retaliation.

Representations in Life. This method of gathering data can be impactful. Members of one work group, for example, seemed to be having real problems concerning influence, involving issues of competition and of techniques used in that competition. Most members acknowledged the problem but found it difficult to deal with in any but veiled and abstract terms. They agreed to a micro-design in which they were to occupy a vertical position in space corresponding to their influence in the group. Two stimuli were used. The first was an "is" stimuli: What level of influence does each individual exert? There was much mirthful relative arranging of selves in space after this first cue: some crouched, others stood tall, some lay on the floor, some stood on chairs, etc. The ensuing discussion was animated, but not particularly revealing. "Are you really happy down there?" one member on a chair might ask a member on the floor. "Most times," might come the answer. "But you rubbed it in on that X contract."

148

The second stimulus was a "want": How much relative influence did individual members want to assert? Again, vertical position in space was to indicate the degree of influence which each individual desired to exert. Considerable confusion followed, with one member seeking in some way to express his impressive desire for influence. Finally, he forcefully positioned one of his colleagues and proceeded to use him as an unwilling platform to reach a fortunately sturdy wagon-wheel lighting fixture. There he hung, head and shoulders above his colleagues in his need to exert influence. Literally, there was no way this man could satisfy his need for influence without stepping on someone, in this case an unwilling someone.

Direct Confrontations: Groups. The OD consultant can generate *in vivo* data by confrontations between groups having problems or merely intent on improving their relationships. The basic vehicle for generating data is a Three-Dimensional Image, which each group develops in private. The Three-Dimensional Image is a response to these three questions by (to make it simple) groups A and B:

- How do we see ourselves?
- How do we see the other group?
- How do we believe the other group sees us?

Description and analysis are at the group level only. Although the 3-D Images are developed in private, the groups are told they will later be shared publicly.

A later section will detail the design and results of one such confrontation; this bare sketch can suffice here.

Direct Confrontations: Meetings for Two. These meetings are for any organization pairs, such as a manager and one of his subordinates, who wish to work toward some common goal more effectively. Usually a third party, a skilled resource person, sits in to help work on process. One effective way to conduct such a meeting for two is to have each party make three lists:[54]

- positive feedback list: things the person values in the way the two people have worked together
- "bug" list: things he has not liked or cannot tolerate in their relationships
- empathy list: a prediction of what the other party has on his lists

The lists then become the focus for analysis by the pair, aided by the third person. The procedure "is highly structured," Fordyce and Weil note, "but it is also foolproof."

---

54. Fordyce and Weil, *op. cit.,* p. 114.

The design and the results of a specific meeting for two will be discussed in a later section so, again, brevity is possible here.

b. Some Consequences of Viable Processes: Toward the Healthy Organization

The attention to interpersonal and intergroup processes rests on a simple model that has been verified in some part. Specifically, the model has three components:

Human processes intervene in critical ways between inputs and outcomes, and any improvement in these processes will result in the liberation of energy. That energy can be converted to various uses, such as the facilitation of change. The failure to implement a decision that was made only by disrupting interpersonal or intergroup processes illustrates the lack of energy and the resistance that can be attributed to inadequate processes.

Within this broad input/output model, the quality of interpersonal and intergroup processes is seen as having critical linkages with individual and organizational effectiveness. For example, adequate organizational processes will facilitate individual growth; and growing individuals can improve the quality of organizational processes. Moreover, ineffective organizational processes are associated with chronic symptoms. Fordyce and Weil, for example, stress three such symptoms. Dependency and/or rebelliousness by subordinates can develop in response to "chiefs [who] play at being powerful fathers [and] Indians [who] obey submissively or revolt or run away." Defensiveness and narrowness of perspective are two other chronic symptoms of inadequate processes.[55]

Nor very far below the level of such conceptions involving the quality of interpersonal and intergroup processes, and sometimes even explicit in them, is the notion of organizational health or illness. Such notions are largely metaphorical at present, but attempts are being made to specify content for the metaphor. The content-filled metaphor then can be subjected to empirical test, and thus to rejection or to amendment. One useful approach is that of Fordyce and Weil, who propose a number of indicators of organizational health/illness. To illustrate, they define "unhealthy" and "healthy" in terms of a large number of descriptive statements. These statements are illustrated in Figure 5.

55. *Ibid.*, p. 8. Broadly, see Louis C. Schroeter, *Organizational Elan* (New York: American Management Association, 1970).

Despite a variety of problems, such an approach has its values. Consider the problems of measuring the degree to which various organizations possess the several characteristics. And no doubt no organization ever existed that fulfilled all the characteristics of a "healthy organization." But the approach does provide useful descriptions of the typical outcomes toward which the process orientation trends. And the approach does imply at least the possibility of empirical testing and verification, on the basis of which some more measurable typologies might be built. Some research in this direction will be reviewed in later chapters, in fact, using another set of measures on the adequacy of an organization's processes.

At another level, organization health can be estimated in terms of a variety of other criteria. John Gardner provides an intriguing illustration in his focus on "organizational dry rot."[56] A checklist of diagnostic

Figure 5. Some Indicators of Organizational Health

Unhealthy Organizations	*Healthy Organizations*
■ There is little personal investment in organizational objectives except at top levels.	■ Objectives are widely shared by the members and there is a strong and consistent flow of energy toward those objectives.
■ People in the organization see things going wrong and do nothing about it. Nobody volunteers. Mistakes and problems are habitually hidden and shelved. People talk about office troubles at home or in the halls, not with those involved.	■ People feel free to signal their awareness of difficulties because they expect the problems to be dealt with and they are optimistic that they can be solved.
■ Extraneous factors complicate problem-solving. Status and boxes on the organization chart are more important than solving the problem. There is an excessive concern with management as a customer, instead of the real customer. People treat each other in a formal and polite manner that masks issues—especially with the boss. Nonconforming is frowned upon.	■ Problem-solving is highly pragmatic. In attacking problems, people work informally and are not preoccupied with status, territory, or second-guessing "what higher management will think." The boss is frequently challenged. A great deal of nonconforming behavior is tolerated.
■ People at the top try to control as many decisions as possible. They become bottlenecks and make decisions with inadequate information and advice. People complain about managers' irrational decisions.	■ The points of decision-making are determined by such factors as ability, sense of responsibility, availability of information, work load, timing, and requirements for professional and management development. Organizational level as such is not considered a factor.
■ When there is a crisis, people withdraw or start blaming one another.	■ When there is a crisis, the people quickly band together in work until the crisis departs.
■ Conflict is mostly covert and managed by office politics and other games, or there are interminable and irreconcilable arguments.	■ Conflicts are considered important to decision-making and personal growth. They are dealt with effectively, in the open. People say what they want and expect others to do the same
■ Minimizing risk has a very high value.	■ Risk is accepted as a condition of growth and change.

Source: Selected from Jack K. Fordyce and Raymond Weil, *Managing with People* (Reading, Mass.: Addison-Wesley Publishing Co., 1971), pp. 11–13. Reprinted by special permission.

---

56. John W. Gardner, "How to Prevent Organizational Dry Rot," *Harper's Magazine,* October, 1965, p. 21.

questions permits some judgment of the degree to which any organization has the disease. The following selected questions suggest the fuller range of the questions that Gardner would ask of any organization, questions that all bear on the effectiveness of coping with change. Gardner asks:

- Does the organization have an effective program for the recruitment and development of talented manpower?
- Has the organization an environment that encourages individuality and releases individual motivations?
- Is there an adequate system of two-way communication in the organization?
- Does the organization have a fluid and adaptable internal structure?
- Are there ample opportunities and situations where the organization provides a process of self-criticism?
- Does the organization have the ability to cope with vested interests?
- Has the organization developed effective face-to-face groups for accomplishment of work goals?
- Does a climate of trust exist between individuals and groups in the organization?

As Gardner suggests, moreover, it is not only that the answers to such questions are significant. More paramountly are the processes of raising such questions—frequently and willingly—as an organization's members review their purposes, policies, and procedures.

c. An Illustration of Process Analysis:
The Manager Who Loved So You'd Never Really Know It

The process orientation can help remove a variety of blockages to organized effort, as the following dramatic illustration suggests. The background is relatively simple. A new manager was appointed to head a field marketing group, after a short but astounding record as a salesman. Almost from the start, by his own admission and from the complaints of his men, it was clear that his managerial problems were mounting. Some difficulties in adjustment had been expected, especially since the new manager was picked over several other salesmen with greater seniority and fine records. But the difficulties lasted longer than the new manager or his superiors either expected or felt comfortable with. A two-and-a-half-day "process conference" was called to see if relief were possible. The manager and his men were to arrive in time for Sunday dinner, and the conference would conclude at Wednesday noon.

From the earliest stages of the process conference, the new manager reflected behaviors and attitudes that created cross-pressures for his men. Four points deserve special emphasis. First, the new manager reflected a strong desire to win every point even when the relevance of the issue was obscure and the manager's position was a tenuous one; and he assiduously kept selling his role and himself even when they did not seem at issue. Second, the new manager was "helpful," in his view, or "needlessly dominant," as his subordinates saw it. His concern included keeping the water pitchers full and iced. "You guys want cold water. Right?" And perhaps his favorite expression was: "I know you all like to do things in ways you are accustomed to, but you ought to do it this way." "This way" was, of course, his way. Third, he expressed dislike of, and even contempt for, most blacks. The company had an Affirmative Action program, but the new manager would have none of it. He would not voluntarily attempt to seek out potential black salesmen, he announced, although he might be a "good soldier" if a "lot of pressure" were put on him. If blacks were so lazy and unmotivated that they did not answer his help-wanted ads for salesmen, he explained, too bad. His generalizations did not extend to all blacks. Fred, one of his salesmen, was an exception to the new manager. Fred was black, but he had "worked his way up by his own efforts, and not by looking for handouts." Fourth, with it all, the new manager expressed a strong need for acceptance by his men, even for their love.

The potential dilemmas in these behaviors and attitudes of the new manager were triggered constantly in the first day of the conference, one might even say deliberately. For example, the manager might push very hard to get his men to accept some position. They often would resist, sometimes out of annoyance at being badgered, and often for what they considered sufficient technical or market reasons. The new manager would read lack of personal acceptance or rejection in the group and would then emphasize how difficult it was for him to work under conditions where he was not accepted as a person.

Considerable attention was focused on the quality of the processes generated by the new manager in the sessions of the first and second days, attention that carried into the early morning hours over cards and drinks. The subordinates confirmed that their reactions at the conference were like those at work, and for the same reasons. And the new manager gave increasing signs of awareness of the impact of his behaviors and attitudes. "I'll be damned," he commented several times in effect, "there I go damning you if you do and cursing you if you don't."

During a long session on Tuesday night and early Wednesday morning, the new manager organized much of the data into a new level of insight. No verbatim report is available, but during Wednesday's regular session the new manager spelled out his understanding. This summary contains the sense of his new understanding of himself and of his work relations:

> None of this stuff is entirely new, but it fits together now. I put it all together last night.
>
> I like all of you, and I probably even would like your love, but I have been pushing that need too much in this group. I have been jumping all over to be helpful, and I know I alienate people by doing what they don't want to do, or want to do in their own way. I've got to let things be. And I know I have tried to win every point, even the very doubtful ones. I really don't need to be a big man that way.
>
> I have been bad-mouthing all blacks, too, and saying that if others before them could work their way up, they could too. I know only a small percentage are the welfare chiselers and revolutionaries. And I know that it is tougher to work your way up today if you don't have skills, or the cultural background.
>
> How does all this go together? I love my father, I realize, and need his love. He has always held back from me, and that made me feel unworthy. I have tried to make it all up with you guys, and my subordinates, and probably my family too. It's that simple, and that complex.
>
> But I really don't need all from you that I have been asking. I like you guys, and respect you. But I have been asking too much from you. I want you to accept me, but I have been forcing myself on you. I want you to consider me a competent guy, but I have been trying to do it all.
>
> Hell, Fred, I don't even hate blacks.
>
> I just love my father, who worked his way up from the bottom. My business is basically with him, not you.
>
> I'm ready to get to work. I feel like a big weight has been lifted. I'll try not to impose it on you guys again.

The evidence indicates that both the manager and his men did in fact subsequently get to work in mutually satisfying ways. They cite the value of the process conference in "getting over the hump." But only a continuous attention to their own processes will conquer similar humps as the sense and sentiment of that one meeting fade in memory and possibly get violated in practice.

This illustrates a major breakthrough via a process orientation and goes as far in the laboratory approach as it is advisable to go. In some cases, follow-up with individual therapy might be indicated. In this case, the new manager seemed thoroughly in command of the learning situation. Indeed, only he had the relevant data, which he had assembled and organized. Revealingly, the manager notes that it was easier for him to

154

recognize and reorganize that data because he was "so tired" from all the late talking and card playing that his "conscious controls were weakened." Since the late-night activities were not usual ones for the manager, one might also say that he also controlled or even created that aspect of his own learning environment.

D. THE LABORATORY APPROACH TO ORGANIZATION DEVELOPMENT (II): FURTHER PERSPECTIVES ON THEORY AND PRACTICE

This section attempts to provide three kinds of counterpoint to the general themes stressed in Section C above, as a brief overview suggests. *First,* two major and specific senses will be emphasized in which the laboratory approach to OD trends away from the bureaucratic model, as developed by scholars like Max Weber. It is not overly dramatic to describe the common goals of OD efforts as moving toward the nonbureaucratic organization, or perhaps even toward antibureaucracy.

Second, several alternative OD designs will be sketched. In effect, these learning designs are extensions into organization contexts which derive from the basic learning vehicle of the laboratory approach, the T-Group. Sometimes these learning designs make direct use of T-Groups, and sometimes the designs attempt to engage specific processes analogous to those observed in T-Groups, as in the case of designs that increase the feedback available to members of an organization. Whether they use the T-Group directly or as an analog, however, such designs are all constrained by the values and guidelines elaborated in the first three sections of this volume. In common, also, such designs seek to meet the basic challenge of transfer learning: How to transfer into large technical organizations the learning that is most conveniently generated in small social groups?

If the first emphasis of this section stresses specific OD goals, the second outlines the variety of designs that can lead to achieving these specific goals. The counterpoint of objectives and techniques will characterize much of the essence of this section, in fact.

Third, a final emphasis attempts to detail some limitations on applications of OD designs. Not all organizations are convenient hosts for OD efforts, in short. In individual cases, not all organizations are "culturally prepared" for the laboratory approach to OD. Some conditions for cultural preparedness will be hazarded, as a step toward some satisfactory statement that will be developed later in the maturation of OD. More specifically, diverse technologies and institutional contexts also serve as constraints on applications of the laboratory approach to OD. The illustrative focus below will be on how OD efforts can be affected by the growth strategy of a specific organization, as well as on how public agencies face special problems in being receptive to OD programs.

4. SOME COMMON GOALS: TOWARD THE NONBUREAUCRATIC ORGANIZATION

The common core goals of OD efforts derive from essentially the same base observation. Rousseau expressed an early form of this observation when he noted that men are born free but are everywhere in bondage.[1] The irony was a delicious one for him, and he clearly saw that this bondage would not exist in only one very special case, where the "I" and the authoritative "They" were one and the same. Rousseau held out little hope that this case ever would or could exist. For the "They" would be somehow differentiated from "I" even in very simple societies, and perhaps even within each person as id and ego vs. supergo, in Freudian terms. And, Rousseau saw, this primitive differentiation carried within itself the potential for the development of the bondage of constraints on the Self imposed from outside. Man at once needs the bondage to live more securely, and he variously chafes under it. Bertram Forer made the same point:

> The fact of his structuring indicates that [man] has relinquished some freedom to experience, wish, and act in order to maintain continuity, recognizability, stability, and predictability and in order to insure continuing relationships with important persons. Self-maintenance and relationship maintenance are both essential to life but are often at odds. He has become a person whose sense of self, whatever it has happened to be, is his most important possession and often his most threatened one. A major issue in his life, then, has to be how to maintain

1. Jean Jacques Rousseau, *Du contrat social.*

the sense of self through the sequential events of his life, both directing the course of life and dealing with uncontrollable assaults and repercussions, and at the same time retain other persons. For there are continual threats to the continuity of the experience of self and to successful accomplishment of those activities and relationships that represent the expression of self.[2]

Two common OD goals derive from the base observation of the difficulties for interpersonal and intergroup relations that inhere in any structuring in organizations, especially if the structure is based on the "bureaucratic model." Basically, the bureaucratic model is seen as a dysfunctionally restrictive "They" which constrains the "I" in ways that increasingly frustrate organizational as well as personal needs/demands. Two possible OD strategies inhere in this basic notion. The first seeks to ameliorate the difficulties in interaction resulting from the bureaucratic model and its organization values. The second strategy seeks new models for organizing work, so as to preclude the very emergence of the difficulties that are attributed to the bureaucratic model. Patently, these two goals are variations on the same point. They orient OD toward the development of nonbureaucratic organizations, or even antibureaucratic organizations.

a. Some Dysfunctions of "Pyramidal Values": Modifying Traditional Organizing Concepts

Chris Argyris has argued that the laboratory approach to OD should modify the "pyramidal values" common in today's organizations. These values are listed in Figure 1. In practice, the values clearly underlie much behavior in organizations, and they encourage a variety of consequences that constrain spontaneity, adaptability, and effectiveness. Figure 1 suggests some of those consequences, toward whose understanding we can take an immediate step. Consider one revealing illustration:

Q.: Have you ever been in a meeting where there is a lot of disagreement?

A.: All the time.

Q.: Have you ever been in a meeting when the disagreement got quite personal?

A.: Well, yes, but not very often.

Q.: What would you do if you were the leader of this group?

---

2. Bertram R. Forer, "Therapeutic Relationships in Groups," in Arthur Burton (ed.), *Encounter* (San Francisco: Jossey-Bass, Inc., Publishers, 1969), p. 28.

Figure 1. "Pyramidal Values" and Some of Their Typical Consequences in Organizations

Pyramidal Values Common in Organizations

■ The significant human relationships at work are those directly related to getting the job done; they have a task or technical preoccupation.

■ Effectiveness in human relationships increases directly as behavior is rational and logical, as communications are unambiguous. Conversely, effectiveness decreases as behavior becomes more emotional and nonrational.

■ Human relationships are most efficiently motivated by consciously and clearly defined directives, authority, and controls. Rewards and penalties are used to reinforce rational behavior and achievement of objectives.

Some Typical Consequences of Pyramidal Values

■ Individuals get and give less direct information about their interpersonal impact on each other. Such information may be suppressed at various levels of consciousness, where it cannot be dealt with. Or the information may be communicated in veiled ways, in which case:
  a. it will be disguised or raised in the context of rational, technical, or intellectual issues
  b. it will be difficult to deal with

■ Increases occur in the denial of feelings or reactions, in closedness to new ideas, and in demands for stability.

■ Interpersonal competence will decrease as individuals:
  a. are less likely to be open about and own their reactions, ideas, and feelings
  b. experience reduced trust in one another
  c. react to increased risk by reducing their willingness to experiment or change
  d. are less effective in solving problems.

■ As interpersonal competence declines, increases are probable in pressures toward conformity and toward dependence on authority figures, both of which circularly lead individuals to get and give less information about their interpersonal impact on each other; etc.; etc.

Source: Based on Chris Argyris, "T-Groups for Organizational Effectiveness," *Harvard Business Review*, Vol. 42 (March, 1964), pp. 61–63.

A.: I would say, "Gentlemen, let's get back to the facts" or I
would say, "Gentlemen, let's keep personalities out of this."
If it really got bad, I would wish it were five o'clock so I
could call it off, and then I would talk to the men individually.[3]

In capsule form, these responses imply anticonfrontation. The responses
suggest flight and pairing; and they either imply the existence of degenerative interaction systems or contribute to their development in major
ways.

Without denying in all cases the virtue of the intervention strategy
above, the pyramidal values have a broad potential for mischief as prevailing guides for behavior. "What causes dynamic, flexible, and en-
thusiastically committed executive teams," Argyris asks rhetorically, "to
become sluggish and inflexible as time goes by?" He sees a major cause in
the buildup of consequences like those in Figure 1, beyond some tolerable but easily surpassed limit that exists in all human systems. The
pyramidal values, concludes the Argyrian rationale, must be modified
so as to avoid a variety of awkward consequences.

Argyris prescribes a two-pronged approach to avoiding the consequences detailed in Figure 1, consequences which can generate substantial barriers to collective effort. Thus Argyris argues that a modified set
of organization values should guide collective effort. These values provide that:[4]

- The important human relationships do involve those related to
  achieving organizational objectives, but these important relationships also include those necessary to sustain or develop the organization's socioemotional system as well as those related to adapting
  to the external environment.
- Human relationships increase in effectiveness as both technical
  and interpersonal data become conscious, discussable, and increasingly controllable.
- Directives, authority, and controls can influence human relationships, but the most effective influences will occur through authentic relations between individuals, internal commitment, and feelings of psychological success.

The induction of this modified set of values is seen as a problem in reeducation, purely and simply, for which required reeducation the laboratory approach is a prime learning vehicle. Argyris outlines the
reeducation program in terms of the three-phase sequence introduced

3. Chris Argyris, "T-Groups for Organizational Effectiveness," *Harvard Business Review*, Vol. 42 (March, 1965) , p. 61.
4. *Ibid.*, pp. 61–63.

earlier: unfreezing and analysis of old behaviors, attitudes, and values; choice and practice of replacements, if appropriate; and refreezing of the new behaviors, attitudes, or values, should they lead to the desired consequences.[5] For example, Argyris argues, T-Groups can provide a direct experience of the true ineffectiveness of the pyramidal values. In that learning context, "power, control, and organizational influences are minimized" and the incompleteness of the old values becomes manifest. In an effective T-Group, moreover, a special culture develops that can facilitate experimentation with new values and behaviors. Since basic control of the learning experience is in the hands of the learners, Argyris also notes, the probability of resistance to learning is reduced and the probability of some internalization of any learning consequently increases. Argyris also provides data which establish that some transfer of learning to the worksite does occur.

b. Toward Basic Structural Change: Replacing Traditional Organizing Concepts

Other observers have extended Argyris's beachhead somewhat. They also propose to avoid the consequences of the pyramidal values, but this time by changing the basic concepts for organizing in which these values inhere. Bureaucracy is also the demon these observers seek to exorcise. Some bravely proclaim that its end has come,[6] more or less, while others see it as increasingly inappropriate under a wide variety of conditions to which today's organizations are routinely exposed. But all agree that the kind of consequences sketched by Argyris can in significant measure be laid on the doorstep of the bureaucratic model. Out it must go, consequently, root and branch.

Basically, the bureaucratic model is seen as a social invention whose time has come and, to greater or lesser degree, has gone. The bureaucratic model rests on propositions such as these five:

- a well-defined chain of command that vertically channels formal interaction
- a system of procedures and rules for dealing with all contingencies at work that reinforces the reporting insularity of each bureau
- a division of labor based upon specialization by major function or process that vertically fragments a flow of work
- promotion and selection based on technical competence, which is defined consistently with the first three items

---

5. *Ibid.*, pp. 63–73.
6. Warren Bennis, "Organizations of the Future," *Personnel Administration*, Vol. 30 (September, 1967).

- impersonality in relations between organization members and between them and their clients

It is no great simplification to tease out of these propositions a guiding metaphor and an overall bias. The guiding metaphor of the bureaucratic model is a precision clock. Once appropriately designed and machined, it would go on ticking away with awesome regularity. The overall bias is strongly elitist and authoritarian, moreover. "Only those higher in the hierarchy are to be trusted with judgment or discretion," Alvin Toffler concludes. "Officials at the top make the decisions; men at the bottom carry them out. One group represents the brains of the organization; the other, the hands."[7]

The strength of these propositions under one set of conditions has be-

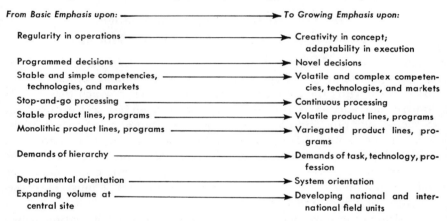

Figure 2. Two Sets of Emphases to Which Organizations Can Respond

From Basic Emphasis upon: ⟶ *To Growing Emphasis upon:*

Regularity in operations ⟶ Creativity in concept; adaptability in execution

Programmed decisions ⟶ Novel decisions

Stable and simple competencies, technologies, and markets ⟶ Volatile and complex competencies, technologies, and markets

Stop-and-go processing ⟶ Continuous processing

Stable product lines, programs ⟶ Volatile product lines, programs

Monolithic product lines, programs ⟶ Variegated product lines, programs

Demands of hierarchy ⟶ Demands of task, technology, profession

Departmental orientation ⟶ System orientation

Expanding volume at central site ⟶ Developing national and international field units

Source: Robert T. Golembiewski, "Organization Patterns of the Future," *Personnel Administration,* Vol. 32 (November, 1969), p. 11.

come their weakness under another set. Toffler put the point simply. The "typical bureaucratic arrangement is ideally suited to solving routine problems at a moderate pace," he noted. "But when things speed up, or the problems cease to be routine, chaos often breaks loose."[8]

Prevailing conditions have departed in major ways from the conditions built into the bureaucratic model. Things indeed have "speeded up," to make a complex story simple if not necessarily sweet. Figure 2 suggests some of the diverse senses in which the conclusion holds. Basically, instead of a precision watch, the guiding metaphor for many of today's organizations is a kaleidoscope. Contemporary organizations increas-

7. Alvin Toffler, *Future Shock* (New York: Random House, 1970), p. 125.
8. *Ibid.*, p. 125.

162

ingly have to respond to emphases like those in the right column, while the bureaucratic model is designed for the more stable and simple conditions implied by the emphases in the left column. Variability and change become the watchwords, and "project teams" or "task forces" come and go in bewildering profusion. The bureaucratic model awkwardly fits both the pace and the structure that are increasingly characteristic of organizational life. Rather than building permanent organizations, one observer notes acutely, we need to create "self-destroying organizations . . . lots of autonomous, semi-attached units which can be spun off, destroyed, sold bye-bye, when the need for them has disappeared."[9] Toffler notes that we need an "adhocracy" model to replace bureaucracy, consistent with the growing emphasis on temporary organizations versus permanent ones.

The specific form of the organizing concepts suitable for this adhocracy is still evolving, as Section A of Part III will especially show in detail,

Figure 3. Two Contrasting Managerial Systems

Emphases in Systems of Coercion-Compromise	Emphases in Systems of Collaboration-Consensus
■ Superordinate power used to control behavior, reinforced by suitable rewards and punishments	■ Control achieved through agreement on goals, reinforced by a feedback system that provides continuous feedback about results
■ Emphasis by leadership on authoritarian control of the compliant and weak, obeisance to more powerful, and compromise when contenders are equal in power	■ Emphasis by leadership on direct confrontation of differences and working through of any conflicts
■ Disguise or suppression of real feelings or reactions, especially when they refer to powerful figures	■ Public sharing of real feelings, reactions
■ Obedience to the attempts of superiors to influence	■ Openness to the attempts of others to exert influence, whatever their status
■ Authority/obedience used to cement organization relationships	■ Mutual confidence and trust used to cement organization relationships
■ Structure is power-based or hierarchy-oriented	■ Structure task-based or solution-oriented
■ Individual responsibility	■ Shared responsibility
■ One-to-one relationships between superior and subordinates	■ Multiple-group memberships with peers, superiors, and subordinates
■ Structure which is based on bureaucratic model and is intendedly stable over time	■ Structure which emerges out of problems faced as well as out of developing consensus among members is intendedly temporary or at least changeable

Source: Based on Herbert Shepard, "Changing Interpersonal and Intergroup Relationships in Organizations," in James G. March (ed.), Handbook of Organizations (Chicago: Rand McNally & Co., 1965), pp. 1128–31.

---

9. Donald A. Schon, quoted in *Commission on the Year 2000*, Vol. I (Cambridge, Mass.: American Academy of Arts and Sciences, 1965), p. 106.

but a preview is possible here. To use common catchwords, the new concepts will be "organic" rather than "mechanical," and they will emphasize "collaboration-consensus" more than "coercion-compromise." In somewhat more detail, even a few contrasts establish the social and emotional gulfs between traditional organizing concepts and those needed to respond to increasingly common contemporary demands. The contrasts are basically borrowed from Herbert Shepard's seminal contribution,[10] but the "translation" used in Figure 3 is free and may not be entirely faithful to the original.

5. SOME ALTERNATIVE OD DESIGNS: DIVERSE MEANS TO COMMON GOALS

While we wait on the development of the systems suitable for collaboration-consensus, an unenlightened organizational world whirls on, and OD specialists can either leap aboard to try to help, or they can pout. Short of the millenium, that is, numerous designs need to be developed that seek to approach the goals of the laboratory approach to OD, and they are both particularistic and comprehensive. The purpose here is dual: to provide some sense of the range of specific OD designs, and to suggest some general boundary conditions for applications of such designs. To summarize the basic intention of this subsection, OD designs exist for many purposes, but these designs are not applicable in all organizations under all conditions.

a. An OD Micro-Design: Four Characteristics Illustrated

A brief illustration will begin our approach to the diversity of OD designs. That illustration clearly reflects the major properties of OD designs: it is experiential; the emphasis is on process more than substance; the emphasis is also on increasing information, choices, and resources; and it is collaborative in several senses. The illustration is called a micro-design because it is intended to affect directly a narrow range of one group's activities.

The micro-design was developed for a certain committee whose members had major problems of trusting one another and had real reasons for their collective mistrust. Only a skeletal caricature is possible here, but some stage-setting is needed. The committee members were highly

---

10. Herbert Shepard, "Changing Interpersonal and Intergroup Relationships in Organizations," in James G. March (ed.), *Handbook of Organizations* (Chicago: Rand McNally & Co., 1965), pp. 1128–31.

competitive with one another in a win/lose sense, a situation cultivated by their superiors. The members also represented organization units that "played their cards close to their chest," and with a vengeance. A prime consequence was that committee members often were conflicted about what information to divulge to other committee members. When in doubt, they "clammed up." The dilemma was appreciated by all. The committee made significant decisions and recommendations, so valid communication was essential; but each committee member realized that some information could tip the hand of the unit he represented, which could put him and his colleagues at a disadvantage in their relationships with other organization units.

The demands on an OD design were direct: to increase feedback and disclosure under conditions of substantial lack of trust and high risk. Some vehicle was necessary to let committee members know if potentially significant information had been withheld from the decision-making process on a particular issue. Given such knowledge, they could appropriately hedge their recommendations or decisions, even if they were unsure what part of their data was withheld or was pure moonshine. Committee members unanimously felt that no fundamental changes were possible. The managerial style of their superiors—a kind of pure coercion-compromise model—was considered unchangeable. And the objective fact is that the committee members were and would remain highly competitive. The personal stakes were too high for them to risk a change, they felt. Three of the 12 committee members would be promoted in the next three to five years to the next level, with munificent benefits accruing to the winners. The losers expected to be expendable.

The micro-design was a simple one. Committee members designed several simple scales, and specified "critical values" for each scale. For example, committee members decided on a 1–9 scoring range for this scale:

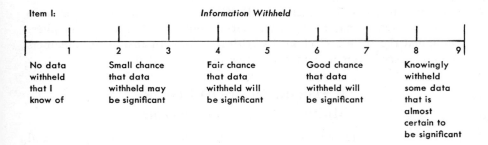

Item I: *Information Withheld*

| 1 | 2 | 3 | 4 | 5 | 6 | 7 | 8 | 9 |

| No data withheld that I know of | Small chance that data withheld may be significant | | Fair chance that data withheld will be significant | | Good chance that data withheld will be significant | | Knowingly withheld some data that is almost certain to be significant | |

Committee members decided that a mean score of 4.5 or greater signaled a "critical" condition in the committee's decision-making processes. Moreover, one 9 also was considered sufficient evidence of a critical condition, as were any two scores of 6 or greater.

The procedures guiding the use of this social invention were straightforward. The several scales were to be completed anonymously, immediately after each Thursday committee meeting, and mailed individually to a consultant who would tabulate the scores for each scale. If any scale "went critical," the consultant was empowered to call a special process conference for early Monday morning. There efforts would be made to surface whatever factors made the scores "go critical." Failing this, efforts were made to hedge or postpone any action taken at the meeting in question.

As an added feature, the consultant was empowered in the first year to call no more than two phony process conferences, to test whether committee members who were not playing the game could be "smoked out" by a convincing role-play by the consultant. This feature again signaled that committee members were willing to trust the consultant somewhat more than each other, but not very much more.

This micro-design can hardly be held up as the ideal OD effort, but it does reflect the major properties detailed above. Overall, the design's purpose was to get its members to share information, if at all possible, even if only to avoid the stress of an emergency process meeting which would upset schedules, draw attention, and so on. The design also provided a backup system should these primary intentions go unrealized. All in all, the design encouraged feedback in several ways, which OD designs should do.

The micro-design also meets the four properties that were introduced earlier as characteristic of OD designs. Specifically, the design is experiential in that it deals with interpersonal and intergroup phenomena and developed in ways consistent with the culture of the larger organization. The emphasis is on the "how," or processes of decision-making. The purpose is clearly to increase the information, choices, and resources available to committee members. Finally, the OD micro-design is truly collaborative in major senses. Of especial note is the fact that members designed the scale and chose its critical values. In this sense, members could succeed even as their committee processes failed.

b. The Range of OD Designs:
Multiple Varieties of the Genre

The micro-design above may be seen as anchoring the "special and limited purpose" end of a continuum of OD designs, which extends through comprehensive efforts to change large sociotechnical systems. Designs at each end of this continuum will get some attention, in turn.

All these designs seek in common to improve an organization's health, and they rest on the participants' willingness to seek to work more collaboratively. Building from that essential agreement, OD designs proceed by simultaneously:[11]

- *working with* the people who are affected by particular proposed changes in the organization
- *linking* to all those who can influence the outcome
- forming a tentative *general goal* which, by joint process, will convert to a specific group goal
- working on *changing the quality of relationships* from one in which the individual is conditioned to isolation, destructive competition, and interpersonal conflict ("I'm up—you're down") to one of collaboration and healthy competition ("we"). To bring about such a change, the manager must encourage direct and open communication and himself set an example
- building active *feedback* loops from all knowledgeable sources so that organization members can perceive the shape of events as realistically as possible and can monitor their organization's progress

Looked at from another perspective, OD designs also can cover the full range of organizationally-relevant elements, or they can apply to them selectively. To make the point conveniently, note the behavioral factors in social systems that are potential OD targets, as enumerated by Gordon Lippitt. The factors include:[12]

- goals and objectives
- norms and values of the system's culture
- structure and roles for task accomplishment and maintenance
- problem-solving processes
- power, authority, and influence issues
- perpetuating processes, such as recruitment or training
- the environment, both immediate and distant, as it bears on system performance
- communications process

OD applications comprehensively or selectively deal with all or any of these behavioral factors in social systems.

---

11. Jack K. Fordyce and Raymond Weil, *Managing with People* (Reading, Mass.: Addison-Wesley Publishing Co., 1971), p. 18.
12. Gordon L. Lippitt, *Organization Renewal* (New York: Appleton-Century-Crofts, 1969), p. 47.

Some Special and Limited-Purpose OD Designs

Figure 4 sketches a number of special and limited-purpose designs, more or less in the order in which they are likely to be resorted to in organizations. In common, the designs are intended to approach in action the goals and objectives stressed above. To this end, generally, the designs are run in the presence of skilled resource persons, who often are called change agents or interventionists. Beyond that, the designs differ widely in crucial particulars—the breadth of their purposes, the complexity of the phenomena likely to be encountered, the probable level of threat experienced by participants, and the skills required for successful coping by participants.

One differentiating element which is especially relevant indicates the approximate point at which participants should be given extended experience with the values, skills, and behaviors consistent with the laboratory approach. More or less, the first four designs in Figure 4 deal with the diagnosis of existing and limited situations. These designs are:

- Manager in a Consulting Pair
- Manager's Diagnostic Meeting
- Team Diagnostic Meeting
- Goal-Setting and Planning Groups

Skilled resource persons in such designs normally can provide gentle if necessary guidance consistent with the goals of the laboratory approach. This generalization holds even for rather large populations who are naïve about OD goals, values, and attitudes.

For the last three designs in Figure 4, particularly, the emphasis is more decisively on changing some existing and complex situation, as well as on diagnosing it. There is a quantum difference between the four designs named above and the following three:

- Third-Party Interventions
- Internal Team-Building
- Interface Team-Building

Substantial proportions of the learning populations, at least, must have appropriate values, attitudes, and behavioral skills in these last three kinds of designs. The first two sections of this volume define these appropriate values, attitudes, and behavioral skills. In their absence, the three designs immediately above are unlikely to be effective.

The three kinds of Interface Groups may be considered intermediate in complexity and in skills and attitudes required of participants. They can be ranked in terms of increasing threat and potential complexity, as below. The three kinds of Interface Groups pose somewhat more for-

168

Figure 4. Some OD Designs

■ *Manager in a Consulting Pair.* The parties are a manager and a resource person from outside the manager's immediate organization, with the manager and consultant developing a close and continuing relationship for the purpose of early sharing of problems and possible solutions.

■ *Manager's Diagnostic Meeting.* The learning group is the manager, an outside resource person, and some one or few resources with organizationwide responsibility, such as personnel managers.

The focus is on diagnosis of the manager's workteam, to consider the need for change or improvement under conditions of low threat to the manager.

■ *Team Diagnostic Meeting.* The learning group is an organizational family, a manager, and his immediate work group.

The diagnosis may center on specific tasks or problems, or it may have a summary quality, as by considering issues:
   a. What we do best
   b. What we do worst

■ *Goal-Setting and Planning Groups.* These may either be individual pairs of superiors-subordinates, or they may be individual family teams throughout the organization.

The focus is on systematic review of performance that leads to the setting of targets or goals, that are the products of mutual commitments. Progress toward the goals or plans will be mutually reviewed.

■ *Interface Groups.* The learning groups may be composed of different functional specialties, such as sales and engineering, labor and management, the managements of two organizations working through a merger, or organizational insiders and an outside group such as customers or clients.

As many as 100 or more persons may participate, usually meeting for a day or less, and the emphasis is on groups rather than individuals. These three factors limit the intensity of the design.

As Sherwood explains, such groups are "a problem-solving mechanism when problems are known to exist. An action-research format is used. The entire management group of an organization is brought together, problems and attitudes are collected and shared, priorities are established, commitments to action are made through setting targets and assigning task forces."*

Three types of interface groups are common:
   a. *Mirror Groups.* This design allows some inside group to get feedback from one or more key clientele groups to whom it relates, e.g., customers, suppliers, or inside users of the target group's services.

   This is a one-way confrontation. The target group sees itself mirrored, as it were, by the clientele group. The target group does not mirror back.

   The design can end with proposals to improve conditions, which usually are generated by mixed teams each having members from the target group and from the clientele groups. The mixed teams report back their suggestions to the total group.

   b. *Goal-Setting Interface Groups.* Representatives from several related groups of organization units meet to set goals for action or change, usually on quite specific issues.

   The basic work is typically done in mixed subgroups of five or six members representing each group or unit so as to facilitate cross-fertilization in the collection of information and the setting of goals.

   The subgroups report back to the total population of participants, and some known procedure is used to integrate the results. For example, a manager might take the results as inputs to guide his decision-making. Or a steering committee composed of one representative from each subgroup might prepare a composite report for all participants, or for some manager or group of managers.

   c. *Confrontation Groups.* Here two or more groups are brought together, such as black employees and white employees, to begin building a relationship or to repair a defective one. The groups share perceptions of how they see themselves and others, with the intent of surfacing issues, letting the groups know how they are perceived, and permitting groups to compare their own group concepts with perceptions of others.

   The intent of such a design is to "clear the air," to provide a realistic and open base on which to build relationships. Such a meeting typically concludes with an action phase: What can be done to do what needs to be done?

■ *Third-Party Interventions.* These OD interventions use a skilled third person to help in the diagnosis and resolution of difficult human problems between two individuals or two groups.

169

Figure 4—continued

The purpose is to provide an outside perspective that may be unavailable to the parties in difficulty, and to use the third person as a trusted agent to begin rebuilding relationships between the parties.

■ *Internal Team-Building.* The learning group consists typically of a manager and one or more levels of his immediate subordinates, up to a limit of 15 or so participants.

The focus is on work problems, and especially on their early identification and solution. The broad emphasis is on interpersonal, procedural, and organization blockages to effective functioning. The design is distinguished by depth of analysis, scrutiny of interpersonal relations, and focus on individuals.

Interpersonal relations in team-building can be variously improved, as by working on: (1) increased openness and owning of ideas and feelings; (2) heightened mutual trust, acceptance, and understanding of team members; or (3) changing patterns of communication.

Procedural and organizational blockages can receive major attention, as by adapting differentiated procedures for different tasks or by analyzing patterns of delegation to isolate and possibly eliminate their awkward consequences.

■ *Interface Team-Building.* Involves two or more groups, separate organization units, simultaneously dealing with the same kinds of issues that are encountered in internal team-building.

This design is extremely complicated and demanding, since it also deals with complex intergroup phenomena such as intergroup competition or the presence of two or more coequal authority figures.

*John J. Sherwood, *An Introduction to Organization Development,* Experimental Publication System. Washington, D.C.: American Psychological Association No. 11 (April, 1971), Ms. No. 396–1. Also reprinted in J. W. Pfeiffer and J. E. Jones (eds.), 1972 Annual Handbook for Group Facilitators (Iowa City, Iowa: University Associates Publishers, 1972).

midable challenges than the first three OD designs, more or less in this order:

■ Mirror Groups
■ Goal-Setting Interface Groups
■ Confrontation Groups

Although the conclusion is patent, it is no less significant. Certainly no later than immediately before or after the time an organization progresses to OD designs using Interface Groups, a dose of T-Group experience is recommended to provide some in-depth experience with the laboratory approach. "Sensitivity training may be viewed as basic training" for the latter three OD designs, at least, to quote Jack Fordyce and Raymond Weil, who made a similar distinction between OD designs.[13]

A Comprehensive OD Design

Without doubt the most comprehensive OD design is based on Robert Blake's Managerial Grid, whose format can be reviewed here briefly to reflect its inner logic.[14] Basically, Blake's educational program rests on

13. Fordyce and Weil, *op. cit.,* pp. 89–90.
14. For greater detail, see Robert R. Blake and Jane S. Mouton, *The Managerial Grid* (Houston, Tex.: Gulf Publishing Co., 1964).

170

an elaboration of the Grid described below, around which are built six overlapping phases of an OD program. The first two phases deal with managerial development, more specifically, and the latter four phases with organization development proper.

Phase I: Grid Seminars. The introduction to the Grid design for OD is a week-long seminar, spent either in stranger or cousin groups of small size. Cousin groups are members of the same total organization who generally have not worked with one another before and who will not do so immediately after the training. The heart of the experience includes a variety of team tasks, in which individual and group problem-solving styles are interpreted in terms of the "Grid." In one exercise, for example, each participant gets feedback from members of his team concerning their impressions of his managerial style. Using a 9×9 grid, whose axes are "Concern for People" and "Concern for Production," a participant may be described as a:

- 1,1 Manager, who has minimum concern for both people and production
- 1,9 Manager, who gives thoughtful attention to the needs of people and helps induce a comfortable, friendly, but slow-paced tempo at work
- 5,5 Manager, who trades off satisfactory morale for satisfactory output
- 9,1 Manager, who seeks high levels of efficiency in operations by arranging work so that human elements interfere in minimum degree
- 9,9 Manager, who seeks significant accomplishment at work through committed people, whose interdependence rests on relationships of trust and respect.

Two points require emphasis. First, Phase I is a kind of pump-primer and is not expected to produce immediate effects in organizations. Second, the Grid experience is a focused T-Group, in effect, and as such is clearly one species of the genus laboratory approach. Thus the values underlying the Grid are like those discussed above. But the T-Group and Grid Seminars are different while genetically related. "The strongest similarity comes in the face-to-face feedback experience," several observers note. "Even here, however, the Managerial Grid Seminars take a more structured approach by focusing on managerial styles rather than on personal behavior characteristics which may or may not be related to management."[15]

---

15. Robert R. Blake, Jane S. Mouton, Louis B. Barnes, and Larry E. Greiner, "Breakthrough in Organization Development," *Harvard Business Review*, Vol. 42 (November, 1964), p. 135.

Phase II: Team Development. This is the initial on-the-job extension of Phase I, in which each manager and his subordinates make use of Grid experience and vocabulary to explore managerial styles and operating practices. The thrust is to use 9,9 concepts at work and to develop a 9,9 style.

Phase III: Intergroup Development. The focus here is on extending 9,9 concepts and style beyond individual work groups. The goal is to move groups from win/lose competition to joint problem-solving, and complex subdesigns are tailored to individual situations in specific organizations.

Phase IV: Organizational Goal-Setting. The orientation here is to move toward areas that require commitment at many organization levels, as in cost control or labor-management relations. In contrast to earlier phases which use learning vehicles representing one or a few hierarchic levels, devices like the "diagonal slice" are used to develop special task forces composed of individuals representing several functions and several levels of organization.

Phase V: Goal Attainment. Given the problem areas isolated by the special task forces, other teams are set up throughout the organization to sharpen statements of problems, clarify goals, and assign responsibilities for necessary action.

Phase VI: Stabilization. This phase serves to reinforce changes made in earlier phases, as well as to evaluate and build on that experience so as to inhibit regression.

Flow Chart of a Typical OD Program

Whether OD programs are limited in purpose or comprehensive, to conclude this section on the range of learning designs, they tend to share a common developmental form. The flow chart in Figure 5 seeks to sketch a number of the prominent features of this common pattern of development. The flow chart is stylized, but it does depict the major generic activities in an OD program, as well as the sequence of these activities.

The flow chart in Figure 5 of a typical OD program should be self-explanatory, in the main, but several features deserve highlighting. *First,* the chart is deliberately open-ended. The intended symbolism suggests that there are only two organizational alternatives to pursuing a heightening developmental spiral like the one for individuals described in Section A, Part I. Those alternatives are: fixation at a specific level of development or, more likely, a regressive spiraling inward and downward that feeds on its own offal and pollutes the quality of life in organizations. The choice is between continuous renewal and two dismal alternatives.

172

Figure 5. A Flow Chart of a Typical OD Program.

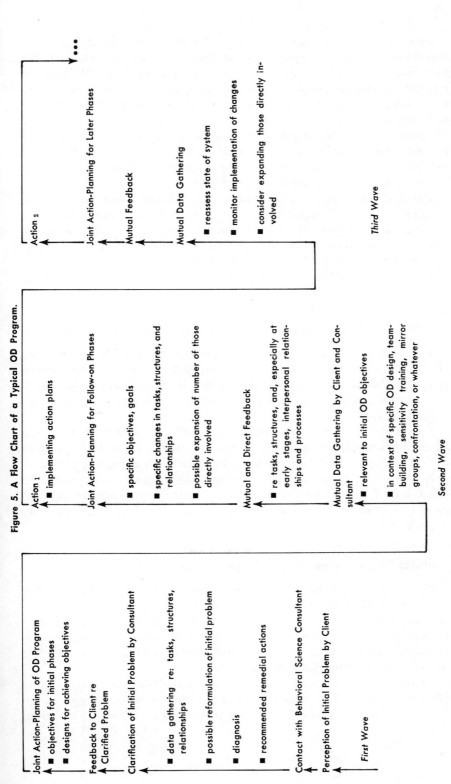

First Wave

Perception of Initial Problem by Client

Contact with Behavioral Science Consultant

Clarification of Initial Problem by Consultant
- data gathering re: tasks, structures, relationships
- possible reformulation of initial problem
- diagnosis
- recommended remedial actions

Feedback to Client re Clarified Problem

Joint Action-Planning of OD Program
- objectives for initial phases
- designs for achieving objectives

Second Wave

Mutual Data Gathering by Client and Consultant
- relevant to initial OD objectives
- in context of specific OD design, team-building, sensitivity training, mirror groups, confrontation, or whatever

Mutual and Direct Feedback
- re tasks, structures, and, especially at early stages, interpersonal relationships and processes

Joint Action-Planning for Follow-on Phases
- specific objectives, goals
- specific changes in tasks, structures, and relationships
- possible expansion of number of those directly involved

Action₁
- implementing action plans

Third Wave

Mutual Data Gathering
- reassess state of system
- monitor implementation of changes
- consider expanding those directly involved

Mutual Feedback

Joint Action-Planning for Later Phases

Action₂

Source: Patterned after the model of Wendell French, "Organization Development: Objectives, Assumptions and Strategies," *California Management Review*, Vol. 12 (November 2, 1968), esp. pp. 23–28.

Second, the various waves of a typical OD program commonly have two features. These are explicit in the flow chart but significant enough to warrant special emphasis. That is, succeeding waves of an OD program typically deepen the intensity of the design elements. Thus the interview-*cum*-feedback of the first wave is a less intense design than the team-building or sensitivity training that often come in the second wave. Moreover, succeeding waves of an OD program typically expand the number of organization members who are directly involved. These are not linear tendencies, however. As the circle of those involved expands to very large numbers, OD designs typically become less intense.

Third, the flow chart is moot on one significant point. Note that it "begins" with the perception of an initial problem by a client. This is a convenience only, patently. For example, the genesis of such perceptions can be in a stranger T-Group experience. That is, one or more organization members might be encouraged by such an experience to experiment with whether their worksite could be made more need-satisfying.

c. The Reach of OD Designs:
Some Practical and Theoretical Limits on Applications

The "range" of OD designs can be usefully distinguished from their "reach." There are numerous OD designs that are available for various purposes, that is, but those designs are not necessarily applicable in all organizations. The range of OD designs may not reach a specific organization, in short.

Two limits on the reach of OD designs will be emphasized. First, not all organizations are "culturally prepared" for the laboratory approach to OD. Second, even where the host organization is culturally prepared, only gross models are available for guiding organization change. In effect, both of these limits on the reach of OD designs demand high degrees of insight, sensitivity, and adaptability from those who intend to apply OD designs.

Cultural Preparedness of Host Organization

No available measuring instrument permits a judgment about whether or not a specific host organization is culturally prepared for the laboratory approach to OD, but such judgments always must be made. Fortunately, Nature seems to be quite benign in this case. OD designs seem applicable over a broad range of conditions in organizations with a diversity of missions, histories, and futures.

Knowledge of the broad applicability of OD designs in the generality of cases is comforting for some purposes, but relying on these benign boundaries is inadequate for at least three reasons. That is, conditions

174

do exist under which failure is more likely, and it is important for many purposes to know about those conditions. Moreover, specific designs may be more or less appropriate under various conditions. In addition, the conservation of energy encourages some sense of the limitations which could reduce the probability of failure in specific cases. At least initially, change efforts could be concentrated in organizations where the probability of success is high. As experience with specific OD designs accumulates, they could be extended to lower-probability cases.

In the sense of making even a little needed headway, then, four aspects of cultural preparedness will be introduced and illustrated. Overall, the underlying model is a curvilinear one. To explain, each aspect of cultural preparedness can be such that an OD effort is not indicated. Up to some unspecified point, increases in all four aspects of cultural preparedness will raise the probability of both the need and the success of an OD application. Beyond these unspecified points, the need for an OD effort continues to rise, but the probability of success begins to decrease.

First, to begin illustrating the pattern of curvilinearity and cultural preparedness, the laboratory approach to OD seems most applicable under conditions of substantial tension in a system, as a result of an organization's inefficiency, inability to adapt or change, or whatever. At very low levels of tension, as in a highly successful organization, the motivation for an OD effort is likely to be low, even if insightful souls correctly perceive the dark clouds behind the silver lining. Where tension in the system is "extremely high," and the quotation marks are appropriate in the absence of specific meaning, an OD effort may be sorely needed, but its probability of success will be low because the tension or threat is immobilizing. For example, it is in general better to begin an OD program after major reductions in personnel have been made, rather than while that sword is hanging over people's heads.

Second, the quality of interunit relations in an organization seems an important aspect of cultural preparedness. Given "good" interunit relations—low degrees of conflict or disruptive competition and high degrees of collaborative efficiency—an OD effort is not needed very much. Up to a substantial point, deterioration in the quality of interunit relations at once increases the need for an OD effort as well as the motivation to make it succeed. Beyond some unknown but very real point, the quality of life can deteriorate so much as to make OD efforts far more chancy, if not impossible.

Third, the legitimacy of focusing on interpersonal and intergroup relations constitutes an important aspect of an organization's cultural preparedness for an OD application based on the laboratory approach. Where this legitimacy is already high, the need for and impact of OD designs will be less great. Up to a significant point, decreases in the legitimacy of dealing with human relationships heighten the need for the

175

laboratory approach and increase the probability of its effectiveness. However, the legitimacy may be so low in the cases of enough organization members as to contra-indicate an OD effort. Such low legitimacy might be expressed as extreme resistance to "probing at my psyche" or abhorrence at "violations of my privacy."

Fourth, the resistance of key officials is a final contributor to cultural preparedness of a host organization. Again, despite the inability to be specific about what the words mean, "too much" resistance can be the death of OD programs. This is not only so in the trivial case that key officials can control resources, although that is a point of moment. Most people attach considerable legitimacy to an authority figure, even when that means giving him apparent support even when he does not see the writing on the organization walls. At the other extreme, there may seem no such thing as "too much" support from key officials. But too-enthusiastic support by key officials may be interpreted by other organization members as an effort to co-opt or manipulate them. Hence it is that many successful OD programs have a common developmental history, which can be thumbnailed here and will be detailed in Section C of Part II. Some middle-level member of an organization—often a staff man in personnel—gets interested in OD. He develops a relationship with some prestigious outside expert, while he also develops local support in his organization. At some point, while support is developing at lower levels, a presentation is made to executive levels, who often are known to be unaware or even hostile to OD. The overall progression is one of reverse co-optation, or perhaps manipulation from below.

A Model for OD Programs

In addition to such factors reducing an organization's cultural preparedness for OD designs, applications also are limited by the crude state of available models of organization change. The availability of sophisticated models patently would increase the probability that the appropriate OD design would be selected and that it would lead to the desired results.

The state of the art relating to models of organization change can be suggested by one illustration. As in the case of individual change in T-Groups, the most developed model for organization change is based on Lewin's tripartite model: unfreezing/change/refreezing. Gene W. Dalton studied a number of successful OD interventions[16] and found they could be interpreted in terms of this sequential process:

---

16. Gene W. Dalton, "Influence and Organizational Change," in Anant R. Negandhi and Joseph P. Schwitter (eds.), *Organizational Behavior Models* (Kent, Ohio: Comparative Administration Research Institute, 1970), pp. 77–104.

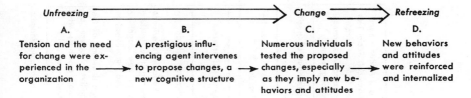

Unfreezing		Change	Refreezing
A.	**B.**	**C.**	**D.**
Tension and the need for change were experienced in the organization	A prestigious influencing agent intervenes to propose changes, a new cognitive structure	Numerous individuals tested the proposed changes, especially as they imply new behaviors and attitudes	New behaviors and attitudes were reinforced and internalized

Dalton also isolated four subprocesses, each of which is characterized in successful OD efforts by movement from one condition in the left column below to its paired condition in the right column. Specifically:

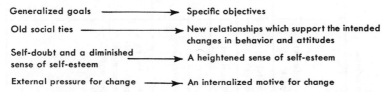

Generalized goals	→	Specific objectives
Old social ties	→	New relationships which support the intended changes in behavior and attitudes
Self-doubt and a diminished sense of self-esteem	→	A heightened sense of self-esteem
External pressure for change	→	An internalized motive for change

Dalton's combination of three sequences and four subprocesses generates a model of the influencing process in organizations, as in Figure 6, which accords quite well with several descriptions of successful programs of change in organizations. Specifically, the model begins with tension as an antecedent condition which chafes existing interpersonal and intergroup relationships and also lowers the self-esteem of organization members. The collective friction and individual concern about lowered self-esteem generates some leverage for change and can provide a prestigious influencing agent with an opportunity to intervene. The task is substantial. As Dalton notes: ". . . unless there is to be protracted resistance, someone must gain the acceptance and possible support of individuals not seeking change and even those who feel threatened by it."[17]

Internal influencing agents who seize such opportunities tend to act in a common way, the available descriptive literature suggests. That is, they tend to act in ways that seem at apparent odds. They provide an external impetus to change, often in the form of a statement of generalized objectives that have the effect of shaking or replacing prior social ties. These objectives constitute a "new cognitive structure," in effect, a new way of conceiving what is to be done and how it is to be done. That structure may be overt or implied, but it apparently should be generalized. Moreover, the influencing agent is perceived as acting in ways that enhance rather than depreciate the self-esteem of the individuals who are affected. This has the character of metaphysical jujitsu, and its dynamics are inadequately appreciated. But they have something of the quality of sincerely saying: "I know you can do better."

---

17. *Ibid.*, p. 84.

Figure 6. A Model of the Successful Change Process in Organizations.

Tension Experienced within the System	Intervention of a Prestigious Influencing Agent	Individuals Attempt to Implement the Proposed Changes	New Behavior and Attitudes Reinforced by Achievement, Social Ties and Internalized Values—Accompanied by Decreasing Dependence on Influencing Agent
	General Objectives established, new cognitive structure offered →	Growing specificity of objectives—establishment of subgoals →	Achievement and resetting of specific objectives
Tension ↑	Prior social ties interrupted or attenuated →	Formation of new alliances and relationships centering around new activities →	New social ties reinforce altered behavior and attitudes
Lowered Sense of Self-Esteem ↑	Esteem-building begun on basis of agent's attention and assurance →	Esteem-building based on task accomplishment →	Heightened sense of self-esteem
	External motive for change provided by influencing agent →	Improvisation and testing by experience of new cognitive structure induced by generalized objectives of influencing agent →	Internalized motive for change, resulting from: Verification through experience of the new cognitive structure Application of new cognitive structure and improvisation with it A psychological owning of the new cognitive structure by organization members who make it their own

Source: Adapted from Gene W. Dalton, "Influence and Organizational Change," p. 81, in Anant R. Negandhi and Joseph P. Schwitter (eds.), *Organizational Behavior Models* (Kent, Ohio: Comparative Administration Research Institute, 1970).

These ways of behaving that characterize successful internal managers of change can be illustrated briefly. Consider this description of a new plant manager's first meeting with all his supervisors. The manager, an observer tells us, described "a few basic goals" that he expected to reach, despite the fact that he had heard of Plant Y's bad reputation and had been warned that many of its personnel were not competent at their jobs. However, the manager expressed optimism, even if of the wait-and-see variety: "I am willing to prove that this is not so, and until shown otherwise, I personally have confidence in the group."[18]

This brief illustration supports rich speculation. The manager's expressed confidence might heighten self-esteem. The generalized objectives propounded by the influencing agent also might contribute to self-esteem, in the sense that they leave ample room for the contributions and influence of other organization members. This is particularly the case since successful change agents typically begin to actively listen to their subordinates and to react to them, which is some of the stuff of inducing heightened self-esteem via moving toward regenerative interaction sequences. At the very least, these generalized objectives provide a possible direction toward which enough organization members to make a difference might work in an effort to reestablish their self-esteem. In any case, Dalton concluded that:

> Interestingly, a movement toward greater self-esteem seems to be a facilitating factor not only in the establishment of new patterns of thought and action, but also in the unfreezing of old patterns. The abandonment of previous patterns of behavior and thought is easier when an individual is moving toward an increased sense of his own worth. The movement along his continuum is away from a sense of self-doubt toward a feeling of positive worth—from a feeling of partial inadequacy toward a confirmed sense of personal capacity. The increased sense of one's own potential is evident throughout this continuum, not merely at the end. This may seem a paradox, but the contradiction is more apparent than real.[19]

Beyond this point, Figure 6 should be self-explanatory, and that is at once its value and its limitation. Dalton's schema seems to adequately describe the major features of successful programs of change, and it awaits the expansions or modifications that will come with empirical testing.

---

18. Robert H. Guest, *Organizational Change* (Homewood, Ill.: Dorsey Press, 1962), p. 62.
19. Dalton, *op. cit.*, p. 93.

6. SOME ISSUES ABOUT CONSTRAINTS ON LABORATORY TECHNOLOGY: A MATTER OF DIFFERENCES IN HOST ORGANIZATIONS

Perhaps the major constraints on OD applications based on the laboratory approach inhere in differences between host organizations, and this subsection is intended to further sensitize the reader about this crucial point. Some groundwork has been laid. The previous subsection sketched some differences in the cultural preparedness of host organizations that reasonably could affect the success of OD applications. Moreover, that section also implies that available models of the change process in organizations have progressed only to the level of providing a general sense of broad sequences rather than a high-resolution motion picture of a dynamic process.

Two approaches to further sensitization about differences in host organizations will be taken here. First, several growth strategies of organizations will be isolated, for the purpose of suggesting how OD applications face different challenges in various organizations. Second, several distinguishing features of public organizations will be introduced, by way of detailing how various institutional environments imply constraints on OD applications.

a. Technological Constraints on Approaching OD Objectives: Growth Stages and Organization Missions as General Cases

Host organizations will differ in at least two major senses. These differences, which will affect both the need for OD programs and the probability of their success, derive from different stages of organizational growth[20] and from different organization missions.[21] The purpose here is to provide some perspective on these differences, as well as on their effects. The overall strategy is that recommended by Charles Perrow, who urges seeking many *theories* of organization rather than a *theory* of organization. He explains:

> We know enough about organizations now to recognize that most generalizations that are applicable to all organizations are too obvious, or too general, to be of much use for specific

---

20. Lippitt, *op. cit.*, esp. pp. 29–39, presents an alternative model for organizational growth that is more detailed than the model used here.
21. Charles Perrow, *Organizational Analysis: A Sociological View* (Belmont, Cal.: Wadsworth Publishing Co., 1970), p. 19.

predictions. This was not true in the past when there was less organizational knowledge, fewer complex organizations, and fewer organizational varieties.

The argument can be previewed briefly. Both stage of growth and organization mission are conceived as predisposing variables. That is to say, the need for an OD effort tends to increase for organizations at specific stages of growth and for organizations having certain kinds of missions. Some stages of growth and organizational missions may also serve as more impactful motivators of OD programs. OD efforts as here conceived can succeed when the predisposing variables are not favorable, however,[22] as several cases in point establish.[23]

Four Growth Stages

One set of Perrow's theories must deal with where organizations are as to level of development. It is not now clear what the eventually adequate concept of developmental levels will be. As a starter, however, organizations beyond some minimal size may be conceived as passing through at least four major stages of growth, which are more or less sequential but which can occur in various combinations. The four stages are:[24]

- *growth at some single site,* as by expansion of a plant, or restaurant, or whatever
- *growth by adding field units,* as when replicas of the original single site are developed at new geographical locations
- *growth by adding functions, or activities,* as when an organization begins to add internal resources that were previously supplied by outside sources because the organization was too small to economically justify them
- *growth by diversification,* as when organizations add product lines, goods, or services

Two points about these stages are critical. Even very large organizations can exist without exhausting early strategies for growth. Du Pont during World War I was already a monster corporation, for example, but

22. Proponents of the position that OD is appropriate only in a limited range of organizations often cite the research by Tom Burns and George M. Stalker, *Management of Innovation* (London: Tavistock Publications, 1961). A similar interpretation is possible of Joan Woodward, *Industrial Organization: Theory and Practice* (London: Oxford University Press, 1965).

23. Alfred D. Marrow, David G. Bowers, and Stanley Seashore (eds.), *Management by Participation* (New York: Harper & Row, Publishers, 1967), report one such successful application. See also Robert R. Blake, Jane S. Mouton, Richard L. Sloma, and Barbara Peek Loftin, "A Second Breakthrough in Organization Development," *California Management Review,* Vol. 11, No. 2 (1968), pp. 73–78.

24. Based on Alfred D. Chandler, Jr., *Strategy and Structure* (Cambridge, Mass.: M.I.T. Press, 1962), p. 42.

was still at the stage of growing by adding field units. Also, even apparently minor extensions of an organization's mission can have profound organizational consequences. Consider that a convenient way to enjoy the relative simplicity of early stages of growth is to have a homogeneous product line, such as producing a raw material. Some very large but essentially simple organizations have followed this strategy. When that mission is extended to (for example) fabricating as well as producing the raw material, however, quantum increases in complexity occur as new functions are added and as the product line burgeons. Careful analysis has demonstrated that for growth by diversification to be a successful strategy, for example, basic innovations in organization structure are necessary.[25] Essentially, the bureaucratic model becomes increasingly inappropriate as organizations progress through the four stages of growth. Hence major organizations which attempted significant growth by diversification—like Sears, General Motors, Du Pont and the like—experienced major failures until they innovated a new structural form. Additional perspective on this structural revolution will be provided in Section A of Part III.

The several growth stages imply different needs for OD interventions based on the laboratory approach. That is clear even at this point. Consider only the quantum increases in problems of communication that are characteristic of the stages for growth. Given expansion at a central site, problems of communication do increase. But experience suggests that even very large organizations at a single site can be monitored by very few individuals who do not miss much that goes on.[26] Communication and organizational problems rapidly increase when field units are added. For example, the classic issue of "dual supervision" implies both problems in clear communication and challenges for structural innovation. Instead of the relatively unambiguous superior-subordinate relations under the first strategy for growth, field management can find itself (as below) reacting both to the headquarters "line" (solid line) and to headquarters "staff" (broken lines). For a variety of reasons, the dual demands often are unavoidable, and they commonly generate major internal problems.[27] As new functions are added—the third strategy for growth—such internal problems increase additively. As new products or services are added, the potential for conflict, misunderstanding, and confusion probably increases multiplicatively or even exponentially.

25. Chandler, *op. cit.*, pp. 52–113, for example, provides detailed evidence of the structural innovations required in E. I. du Pont de Nemours & Co. See also Ernest Dale, *The Great Organizers* (New York: McGraw-Hill Book Co., 1960).
26. Henry Ford's huge River Rouge plant illustrates the point. Ford essentially ran a barony for many years, with heavy reliance on a small and personally loyal intelligence service.
27. Robert T. Golembiewski, *Organizing Men and Power* (Chicago: Rand McNally & Co., 1967), esp. pp. 31–116.

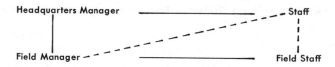

Several factors underlie this sharp increase in potential for trouble under the fourth stage of growth. Just a few will be listed. Obviously, the integrative burden increases sharply as an increasingly large number of functions have to be brought to bear at appropriate times on an increasingly large number of programs or products or services. Then, too, many of the functional specialists have more or less different training, backgrounds, interests, and perhaps even idioms and professional values. Certainly many such specialists operate under different pressures of time and consider themselves variously valuable or prestigeful in their organizations. Such differentiating factors can lead to divisiveness, the prevention and/or management of which is increasingly critical as organizations add functions or grow by diversification. Whether it is to be management or prevention of divisiveness, the need is common: to develop appropriate structures, policies, and procedures that will at least help avoid worse leading to worst.

The list could be extended much further, but the factors mentioned imply the increasing relevance of OD at later stages of growth. Broadly, later stages of growth imply major problems in communication and serious challenges for innovations in structure, policies, and procedures. The relationship of later stages of growth and the increasing need for OD should be clear. The prime goal of OD, of course, is to create open channels of feedback and disclosure. And the consequence of such open channels can be the development of structures and policies and procedures that are responsive to perceived needs.

Four Kinds of Organizational Missions

The ingenuity of man provides the only limit on distinguishing organizations in terms of the character of their basic missions, so only illustration is possible here. Perrow's approach is both simple and useful, distinguishing organizations in terms of their basic search processes and of the variety of problems or stimuli to which they must respond. Figure 7A generates four basic kinds of organizational missions, based on a rough twofold differentiation of each basic dimension. Examples of the four basic kinds of missions come to mind easily. A pin factory clearly would have a Routine Mission, just as the design of the C–5A transport would be a Nonroutine Mission.[28] And the fabrication of

---

28. For a classic distinction of Routine versus Nonroutine missions, consult the comparisons of firms in the cardboard carton versus plastic industries in Paul R.

Figure 7A. Two Dimensions Generating Four Classes of Organization Mission

	Low Variability of Problems	High Variability of Problems
Search Procedures Not Well Understood	CRAFT 1	NONROUTINE 2
Search Procedures Well Understood	4 ROUTINE	3 ENGINEERING

Source: Adapted from *Organizational Analysis* by Charles Perrow. Copyright 1970 by Wadsworth Publishing Company Inc. Reprinted by permission of the publisher, Brooks/Cole Publishing Company, Monterey, California.

aluminum stock for a variety of uses implies an Engineering Mission. These examples have a thing bias, of course, but similar distinctions can be made between people-changing organizations.[29] Figure 7B provides further illustrations of Perrow's approach to classifying organizations in terms of their basic missions, again for manufacturing only.

Organizations stand in need of OD interventions more or less in direct relationship to the degree that they approach a Nonroutine Mission, whether that approach is counterclockwise through Engineering or clockwise through Craftsmanship Missions. Essentially, that is, the bureaucratic model is best suited to Routine Missions of the four types of missions distinguished here. As an organization mix of missions begins to move toward the Nonroutine, however, problems in communication begin to increase under the organization structure consistent with the bureaucratic model, and increasingly troublesome outcomes tend to

---

Lawrence and Jay W. Lorsch, *Organization and Environment* (Homewood, Ill.: Richard D. Irwin, 1969).

29. Perrow, *op. cit.*, pp. 78–79.

Figure 7B. Some Examples of Four Kinds of Organizational Missions

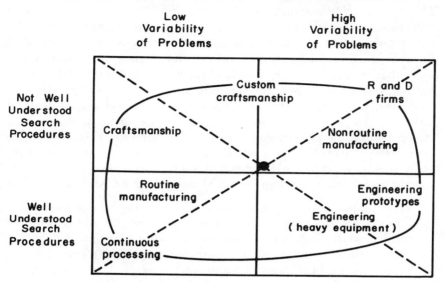

Source: Adapted from *Organizational Analysis* by Charles Perrow. Copyright 1970 by Wadsworth Publishing Company Inc. Reprinted by permission of the publisher, Brooks/Cole Publishing Company, Monterey, California.

proliferate. Perrow captures the essence of the challenges to both communication and orthodox structural arrangements in this description of Nonroutine Missions:

> . . . supervisors of production work closely with the technical people in the administration of production since the latter cannot call the shots for the former on the basis of routine information sent upstairs. Indeed, job descriptions may be such that it is difficult to distinguish the supervisory level from the technical level. Both groups are free to define situations as best they can. Therefore, both have considerable power with respect to such matters as resources and organizational strategies.
>
> This model resembles what others have called the organic as opposed to the mechanistic structure, or the professional or collegial as opposed to bureaucratic structure. This type of structure is probably efficient only for highly nonroutine organizations.[30]

Directly, the relevance of OD is implicit in the fact that Nonroutine Missions for organizations have increased spectacularly since World

---

30. From *Organizational Analysis: A Sociological View* by Charles Perrow, p. 81. Copyright 1970 by Wadsworth Publishing Company. Reprinted by permission of the publisher, Brooks/Cole Publishing Company, Monterey, California.

War II. Certainly, Nonroutine Missions are not the only ones that exist. About nonroutine organizations, Perrow notes: "There are few of these, even though they are quite visible and attractive to social scientists who see in them reflections of their academic institutions and values. Most firms fit into the quite routine cell."[31] But Perrow no doubt would agree that even firms clearly classifiable as having a Routine Mission, on balance, contain some or many subunits that have Nonroutine Missions. Moreover, most organizational environments are dynamic, at least at certain stages. Thus operations in any new power plant probably have major Nonroutine aspects, even though the mission can become Routine after a few years.[32] Finally, many or most organizations are being variously shaken today by major external forces that have profound nonroutine implications for their internal operation. As Argyris explains:

> Two major changes that are presently occurring in our society are (1) a break with traditional authority and (2) the growth of democratic ideology and accelerated rate of change. To the extent these observations are validated, mechanistic organizations will be in difficulty because they may no longer attract the youth that they will need to manage their organizations. Also, a society full of change may spill over to upset their stable equilibrium.[33]

In any case, there are plenty of opportunities for OD applications, and those opportunities without question are proliferating splendidly.

b. Institutional Environments as Constraints on Approaching OD Objectives: Public Agencies as a Special Case

The character of broad "institutional environments" also can pose significant constraints on the degree to which OD objectives are attainable. The essential point is commonplace: where you sit, as it were, helps determine what you see and how you interpret it. For example, Robert Blauner has argued that the technology of four industries—printing, textiles, chemicals, and automobiles—has had powerful and differentiating effects on the attitudes and behaviors of their employees.[34]

31. *Ibid.*, p. 81.
32. Floyd Mann, "Toward an Understanding of the Leadership Role in Formal Organizations," in Robert F. M. Dubin (ed.), *Leadership and Productivity* (San Francisco: Chandler Publishing Co., 1965), pp. 68–102.
33. Chris Argyris, *Innovation Theory and Method* (Reading, Mass.: Addison-Wesley Publishing Co., 1970), p. 87.
34. Robert Blauner, *Alienation and Freedom* (Chicago: University of Chicago Press, 1964).

186

Although the point applies broadly, the focus here is specific. The illustrative emphasis is on the "public" institutional environment, which has important commonalities with the "private" environment but must be distinguished from it in important particulars.[35] The motivation for this effort derives from several major propositions.

- Government agencies have begun experimenting with various OD approaches, if less bullishly so than business and service organizations.

- The public sector has a variety of distinctive features that provide special challenges to achieving typical OD objectives.

- These distinctive features have received inadequate attention in the literature and in the design of OD programs in public agencies.

- The public sector is of major, and growing, significance in determining the quality of life people experience in organizations. This is patently due to such factors as the rapid growth in public employment, in the scope of public activities, and so on. More specifically still, the present point refers to the declining status of public employ—especially at the federal level. Government was in many critical senses a model employer until World War II, when it began definitely to lose that leadership role.

- Applications of OD programs in public agencies probably will become more common. The need to tailor OD programs in public agencies more closely to the distinctive constraints of their environment should consequently increase, and perhaps sharply so.

A bold introduction is appropriate. Public agencies present some distinctive challenges to OD programs, as compared with business organizations where most experience with OD programs has been accumulated. The focus below is on one major question: What properties of public agencies, and especially those at the federal level, make it especially difficult to approach OD objectives? The following discussion provides a variety of perspectives on governmental OD programs and also summarizes experience from a number of OD efforts in public agencies at federal and local levels. Not all these agencies can be identified here, unfortunately, but the data base consists of seven cases.

Four properties of the public institutional environment particularly complicate achieving the common goals of OD programs. First, public agencies are characterized by multiple sets of authoritative decision makers which are deliberately built into the institutional framework of

---

35. For treatments emphasizing the commonalities and differences, see Frederick C. Mosher, *Democracy and the Public Service* (New York: Oxford University Press, 1968), esp. pp. 186–93; and Emmette S. Redford, *Democracy in the Administrative State* (New York: Oxford University Press, 1969).

our political and governmental system. Second, the public arena encompasses a bewildering diversity of interests, values, and reward/punishment structures, which often are mutually exclusive. Third, public agencies have command linkages that are characterized by major competing identifications, affiliations, and loyalties. Fourth, hierarchical linkages in public agencies can be weak at crucial spots, especially at the point where public executives are linked to operating managers.

These four properties of public agencies exist within a habit background, a set of rules of the game which variously exacerbate the constraints on approaching OD objectives that inhere in the four properties above. This habit background will be sketched under a fifth heading below, following brief discussions of the four properties of the institutional environment.[36]

Multiple Access to Multiple Authoritative Decision-Makers

As compared to even the largest of international businesses, the public environment in this country is characterized by what might be called, following David Truman, unusual opportunities for *multiple access to multiple authoritative decision makers*. Multiple access is, in intention if not always in effect, a major way of helping to assure that public business gets looked at from a variety of perspectives. Hence the purpose here is to look at the effects of multiple access, not to deprecate it. Figure 8 details some major points of multiple access relevant to OD programs in four interacting systems: the executive, legislative, special-interest, and mass-media systems.

Multiple access has its attractive features in beginning OD programs in public agencies. For example, one large OD program was inaugurated in an economical way: a top departmental career official sponsoring an OD program had developed a relation of deep trust with the chairman and the professional staff of a congressional appropriations subcommittee. That relation quickly, even mercurially, triumphed over lukewarm support or even opposition from the department head, the Bureau of the Budget, and the U.S. Civil Service Commission.

But multiple access can cut two ways. Funds for that very OD program "became unavailable" after its inception, despite strong if not uniform support from both career and political officers at the top levels. In short,

---

36. This section draws heavily on Robert T. Golembiewski, "Organization Development in Public Agencies: Perspectives on Theory and Practice," *Public Administration Review*, Vol. 29 (July, 1969), pp. 368–76. On the differentiating properties of the public sphere, see also Timothy W. Costello, "Change in Municipal Government," in F. Gerald Brown and Thomas P. Murphy (eds.), *Emerging Patterns in Urban Administration* (Lexington, Mass.: D. C. Heath & Co., 1970), pp. 13–32.

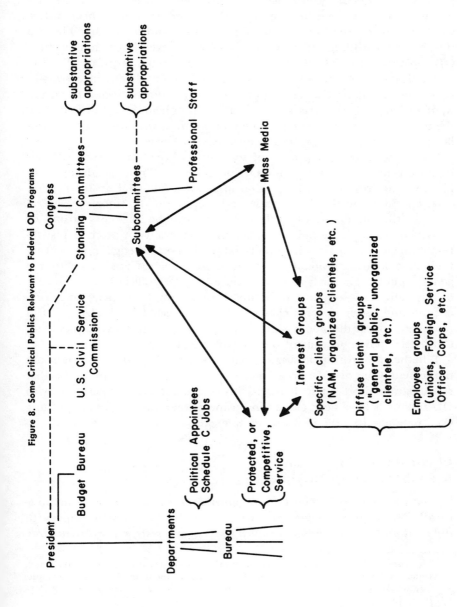

Figure 8. Some Critical Publics Relevant to Federal OD Programs

the successful counterattack was launched by agency personnel in the protected/competitive service, an interest group representing these employees, members of a concerned substantive committee of Congress that did not always see eye to eye with the appropriations subcommittee which authorized the funds for the OD program, and the media. The two themes of the counterattack were common to several reactions against OD programs of which I know. First, ordinary decency required allowing the dedicated civil servants who were affected to complete their careers in peace and in the traditional ways rather than being subjected to an unwanted program that was seen as having problematic value.[37] Second, the use of sensitivity training in the OD program was disparaged as violating the privacy of organization members, or worse.

Viewed from the perspective of top-level political and career officials intent on inaugurating a public OD program, the "iron quadrangle" in Figure 8 inspires substantial pessimism about a fair trial, in the general case. Specific conditions may raise or lower the odds, since the several links in the counterattacking forces above can be variously strong or weak. For example, a public agency may have a very positive institutional image, which gives its top officials an important edge in presenting their case to congressional committees, to the mass media, or to the general public. Similarly, top political and career officials can induce— or capitalize on—organized clientele opposition to policies and procedures and use it to force changes at the protected levels. Or political resources and professional skills may provide agency executives with substantial power to control their environment.[38]

Whether the iron quadrangle is more or less integral, the design and implementation of OD programs in public agencies have given that constellation short shrift. Perhaps this is because most experience with OD programs have been gained in business organizations, where nothing even remotely like the iron quadrangle exists.

Diverse Interests, Values, and Reward/Punishment Structures

Again as compared to business organizations, the public arena involves in all OD programs a greater variety of individuals and groups with *different and often mutually exclusive sets of interests, reward structures,*

---

37. The theme also appeared in mass-circulation news stories and editorials which argued against Project ACORD in the U.S. Department of State, for example. Stewart Alsop, "Let the Poor Old Foreign Service Alone," *Saturday Evening Post*, June, 1966, p. 14.
38. See, generally, Francis E. Rourke, *Bureaucracy, Politics, and Public Policy* (Boston: Little, Brown & Co., 1969).

190

and values. In the case outlined above, for example, the appropriations subcommittee was interested in improved operations and reduced costs. But the substantive subcommittee was concerned more with safeguarding agency programs and career personnel with which they had developed a strong identification. And never the twain did meet. Role conflicts between legislators and administrators also seem to have been significant. For example, one congressman explained his opposition to an OD program in these terms: "Improvement of efficiency is O.K., but messing with people's attitudes sounds subversive to my constituents." The agency's top administrators felt no such constituency pressures, and their view was that attitudes toward work had to be changed.

Such incongruencies of expectations, rewards, and values also occur in business organizations, of course, as in labor/management issues. In my experience, however, they occur there in less intense and exotic forms.

A conclusion need not be forced. All OD programs have to stress the development of viable interfaces, that is, relations between individuals or groups with different values and interests. This problem is enormously complicated in public agencies undertaking OD programs and has received little explicit attention in concept or in practice. For example, in no case that I know of has the development of an explicit interface between legislative and administrative interests been attempted as part of an OD program, apparently in part because of the constitutional separation of powers.

The failure to build such interfaces was a major contributor to the death of a major recent urban OD program. Department officers rejected the idea of attempting to build an explicit interface between two crucial legislative groups—a substantive subcommittee and an appropriations subcommittee—and the agency as part of an OD program. Tradition, jealousy over prerogatives, and separation of powers were blamed, and with good reason. But it also seemed that many department officials preferred things as they were. The lack of integration between the two subcommittees, perhaps, provided alternative routes of access to Congress and also gave department officials some room to operate. One suspects that these officials were unwilling to threaten this flexibility, even if the other payoffs were gilt-edged, which they are not in the early stages of any OD program.

Competing Identifications, Affiliations, and Loyalties

The line of command within public agencies, as compared to business and service organizations, is more likely to be characterized by *competing identifications, affiliations, and loyalties.* Again the difference is one of degree, but it approaches one of kind. Consider only one aspect of the integrity of command linkages common in business organizations. In them, typically, "management" is separated from "labor" only very far down the hierarchy, at or near the level of the first-line supervisor. Moreover, the common identification of all levels of management is often stressed. Management in business, moreover, commonly does not enjoy the kind of job security that can come from union contracts. One of the probable effects of such features is the more facile implementation of policy changes at all levels of business organization.

Hierarchy has its effects in public agencies as well as businesses, but the line of command seems less integral in the former. Thus a unique family of identifications alternative to the hierarchy exists at levels both low and high in public agencies, the apparent underlying motivation being to maximize the probability that evil will not occur, or at least will be found out. That is, the chain of command at the federal level is subject to strong fragmenting forces even up to the highest levels, where political and career strata blend into one another. For example, the ideal of a wall-to-wall civil service is approached closely in practice, and it provides a strong countervailing identification to the executive chain of command. Career officials are "out of politics," but their allegiance to programs may be so strong as to inhibit or even thwart executive direction.[39]

That the public institutional environment permits (indeed, encourages) a fragmenting of the management hierarchy at points well up into the higher levels may be illustrated in three ways. First, the "neutrality" of civil servants has been a major defensive issue in at least two federal OD programs in which I have participated, the OD efforts having been painted by many career people as sophisticated but lustful raids on a chaste protected service. Second, Congress is an old hand at creating countervailing identifications so as to enhance its control over administration,[40] for which the Constitution and tradition provide a solid rationale. Third, executive officials have also played the game of fragmenting the authority structure. Consider the presidential-inspired Federal Executive Boards. Basically, these Boards were intended to be a horizontal link between field units of federal agencies and a vertical link between the Presidency and top career field officialdom. The FEB's provided career field managers with a potential way to supplement or even bypass departmental reporting relations and thus to bypass both career employees and political appointees in their line of command. Indeed,

---

39. For a sensitive summary of the program commitments of career personnel, see John J. Corson and R. Shale Paul, *Men Near the Top* (Baltimore, Md.: Johns Hopkins Press, 1966), pp. 28–51.

40. Joseph P. Harris, *Congressional Control of Administration* (Washington, D.C.: Brookings Institution, 1964).

President Kennedy may have intended the FEBs as just such a bypass around "the feudal barons of the permanent government," whom he saw as frustrating his ambitions for change.[41]

A conclusion flows easily. Congress often encourages slack in the executive chain of command to facilitate its oversight of the President and his major appointees; and the executive as well as the protected service itself often use the same strategy. The integrity of the executive chain of command suffers. Although the consequences are mixed, public executives are limited in initiating[42] such things as OD programs. Witness the furor over the mere handful of Schedule C jobs removed from the protected service during Eisenhower's first term to permit greater executive leverage. Any corporation president would have an immensely broader field to act upon. The motivation to avoid "spoils politics" is recognized, but managerial rigidity is the other side of the coin. Herbert Kaufman concludes that although extensions of the civil service were intended to provide upper-level political administrators with capable help, the latter have often been driven to "pray for deliverance from their guardians."[43] So it has been in the case of a number of OD programs at the federal level.

Weak Linkages between Executives and Operating Managers

Exacerbating the point above, the *linkages between political and career levels* are weak as a consequence of numerous features of the public institutional environment. This slippage between managerial levels significantly complicates beginning and implementing OD programs and severely challenges the linkage of executive management with operating management.

The generalization concerning weak linkages in the managerial chain of command is meant to apply in four distinct senses. First, political and career levels often are weakly linked, due to the brief tenure of the former. Second, the job of linking the political leadership and the permanent bureaucracy must be handled by a tiny group of executives— political appointees and occupants of Schedule C jobs—who owe diverse

41. Arthur Schlesinger, *A Thousand Days* (Boston: Houghton Mifflin Co., 1965), p. 681.
42. President Truman expressed the point directly in contemplating the problems that General Eisenhower would experience as President Eisenhower, without the discipline and definite career patterns and established ways of doing things he knew in the military. "He'll sit here," Truman predicted, "and he'll say, 'Do this!' 'Do that!' *And nothing will happen.* Poor Ike—it won't be a bit like the Army. He'll find it very frustrating." Richard E. Neustadt, *Presidential Power* (New York: John Wiley & Sons, 1960), p. 9. His emphasis.
43. Herbert Kaufman, "The Rise of a New Politics," in Wallace S. Sayre (ed.), *The Federal Government Service* (Englewood Cliffs, N.J.: Prentice-Hall, 1965), p. 58.

allegiance to the chief executive.[44] Third, there is reason to suspect significant slippage between the top career officialdom and lower levels. For example, what lower-level careerists usually see as necessary protections of tenure, top career officials may perceive as cumbersome limitations on managerial flexibility. Fourth, the Presidency often weakens its own managerial linkages, as it seeks sometimes-irreconcilable political and administrative goals. Thus the unionization of public employees, which was legitimated by presidential executive order, certainly drew no opposition from labor unions. It may even have helped fill the campaign warchests of one of the national political parties, which thereby strengthened its image as the "working man's party." But one of the groups of federal employees to organize were inspectors in a regional office of the U.S. Civil Service Commission. Such inspectors would be seen as "management" in most business organizations, and their allegiance to the command structure would be zealously guarded.

OD programs consequently must face the issue of somehow interfacing political and career linkages which powerful forces—constitutional, political, and historic—tend to pull apart. Consider only one dilemma facing OD programs. The general rule of thumb is that OD programs should begin "at the top" of organizational hierarchies, or as close to the top as possible. The rationale is obvious: that is where the power usually is in business organizations. Respecting this rule of thumb in public agencies raises a multidimensional dilemma. Basically, "the top" in public agencies is more complex than in most businesses. Initiating an OD program at the level of the political leadership maximizes formal executive support, but it may also raise complex problems. Support from the political leadership is problematic for multiple reasons, including: frequent personnel changes at that level,[45] possible well-entrenched resistance from the permanent service, legislators who fear that any strengthening of the executive chain of command would only mean fewer points of access and sources of information for legislators, and employee associations that resist executive direction. Relying more on support from those in the protected/competitive service maximizes the chances of permanent support, and it may raise congressional and Civil Service Commission trust in the program. But this approach may en-

44. Dean E. Mann, "The Selection of Federal Political Executives," *American Political Science Review,* Vol. 58 (March, 1964) , pp. 81–99.
45. One ambitious OD program, for example, was unable to overcome the rumor that several political appointees were negotiating terms of private employment. Agency personnel were encourgaged in inaction, since rumor had it that these officials would "soon be riding their OD hobbyhorse" someplace else. These officials did leave. But all claim that the stories were seeded by career personnel who opposed the OD program and that it was only the intensity of such "dirty fighting" that encouraged the political appointees to seek private employment after the rumors began. In truth, probably a little bit of initiative on both sides existed.

courage executive resistance from such vantage points as the Office of Budget and Management or political appointees.

The OD specialist faces real dilemmas, then, in choosing the "top" of the hierarchy at which to direct his interventions. I have participated in change programs that have taken both approaches to seeking a power base, and they show only that avoiding Scylla seems to imply meeting Charybdis. The ideal is a triune appeal to political officialdom, the permanent service, and the hydra-like legislature as well, of course. But that is a demanding ideal indeed.

In summary, four properties of the institutional environment of public agencies complicate attaining the objectives of typical OD programs. Consider the objective of building trust among individuals and groups throughout the organization. Technically, viable interfaces should be created between political officials, the permanent bureaucracy, congressional committees and their staffs, and so on and on. Practically, this is a very tall order, especially because the critical publics tend to have mutually exclusive interests, values, and reward systems. Indeed, although it is easy to caricature the point, Congress has a definite interest in cultivating a certain level of distrust within and between government agencies so as to encourage a flow of information to legislators. This may seem a primitive approach but, in the absence of valid and reliable measures of performance, it may be a necessary one. No OD program in a business organization will face such an array of hurdles, that much is certain.

The Character of the Public Habit Background

The habit background of public agencies also implies serious obstacles to approaching OD objectives. Five aspects of this habit background are considered below by way of illustrating their impact on OD objectives. These aspects do not comprise an exclusive list, and they are conceived of only as general patterns and behaviors which give a definite flavor to the broad institutional environment sketched above. If one is in the CIA, in sharp contrast, a different habit background would apply.

Patterns of Delegation. Habit background is perhaps better illustrated than defined. First, in my experience, public officials tend to favor patterns of delegation that maximize their sources of information and minimize the control exercised by subordinates. Specifically, the goal is to have decisions brought to their level for action or review. The most common concrete concomitants of the tendency are functional specialization and a narrow span of control, one of whose major consequences is a large number of replicative levels of review.[46]

---

46. Before a reorganization inspired by an OD program in the Department of State, some review layers were so numerous that "it could take as long as six months

Layering of multiple levels of review is not unique to public administration. Indeed it inheres in generally accepted organization theory. But layering is supported in unusual degree by factors more or less unique to public agencies that have been powerful enough to substantially curtail innovation of ways to centralize policy and to decentralize operations in public administration.[47] And this even after two or three decades of experience in business had indicated at least the general need of such a strategy beyond some size and complexity thresholds that federal agencies had long since passed. Perhaps the most epochal devotion to centralization was evidenced by the U.S. Civil Service Commission, whose procedures so complicated and delayed some necessary hiring during World War II that at least one observer saw the Commission as the most dangerous enemy the Allies had.[48]

Such judgments may bring a smile, but they have a sardonic quality because the effects are clearly too much of a good thing under the wrong circumstances. For example, it might be said that the protection of the public interest requires centralized surveillance. The rationale is familiar. Political officials of short tenure often cannot rely on as much control over career rewards and punishments as is common in business organizations or in the military. The lack in many public agencies of even such crude measures of performance as profits no doubt also raises executive anxieties and encourages close supervision. However, the legislature will hold the political officials responsible. Consequently, political officials seek to maximize information sources and minimize the control exercisable by subordinates. This tendency is reinforced by law and tradition so that it permeates down the hierarchy throughout the permanent bureaucracy. The tendency is often referred to as "keeping short lines of command."

Keeping chains of command short implies constraints on approaching OD objectives in public organizations, based on my experience as well as the logic of the situation. Consider only two common OD objectives:

- to locate decision-making and problem-solving responsibilities as close to the information sources as possible

---

for an important problem to reach the Deputy Under Secretary. Now it takes an average of two days." Alfred J. Marrow, "Managerial Revolution in the State Department," *Personnel*, Vol. 43 (December, 1966), p. 13.

47. Structural innovation along these lines has been the major trend in large businesses over the past three or four decades. See Robert T. Golembiewski, *Men, Management, and Morality* (New York: McGraw-Hill Book Co., 1965), and *Organizing Men and Power* (Chicago: Rand McNally & Co., 1967). Strong pressures for just such innovation are now being widely felt in public administration. Aaron Wildavsky provides a case in point in his "Black Rebellion and White Reaction," *The Public Interest*, No. 11 (Spring, 1968), esp. pp. 9–12.

48. John Fisher, "Let's Go Back to the Spoils System," *Harper's Magazine*, Vol. 191 (October, 1945), pp. 360–68.

■ to increase self-control and self-direction for people within the organization.

To the degree that the rough distinction above is accurate, public agencies will experience difficulties in approaching these two objectives. The prevailing habit pattern in public agencies patently constitutes a tide to swim against in these two particulars, although there are outstanding exceptions to this generalization.[49]

Legal Habit. Second, and again only as a description of what exists, legal patterns make approaching OD objectives severely more difficult in public agencies than in business organizations.[50] The point applies in two major senses. Thus patterns of administrative delegation are often specified in minute detail in legislation, basically so as to facilitate oversight by the legislature. To be sure, we are a considerable distance beyond the first Morgan case, which seemed to argue that only administrative actions personally taken by, or under the direct supervision of, a department head were constitutionally defensible. But flexibility in delegation is still a major problem. Perhaps more important, a corpus of law and standard practice exists which also makes it difficult to achieve OD objectives. For example, considering only those employees on the General Schedule, salary and duties are tied to a position classification system whose underlying model emphasizes transdepartmental uniformity and compensation for individual work.[51]

This legal habit background complicates approaching OD values. Consider efforts to achieve the common OD objective of locating decision-making and problem-solving responsibilities as close to information sources as possible. This objective may run afoul of the possibility that relocating responsibilities in one agency is considered to have systemwide implications, with consequences that complicate the making of local adjustments. As one official noted of an OD effort in such straits: "I feel

---

49. Clara Penniman, "Reorganization of the Internal Revenue Service," *Public Administration Review*, Vol. 21 (Summer, 1961), pp. 121–30.

50. A very useful discussion of the antimanagerial thrust of much legislation is provided by Harris, *op. cit.* Some of these problems due to the separation of powers seem to be less intense in municipal governments. This conclusion is suggested by the results of several OD programs. See, for example, Chris Cherches and Richard E. Byrd, "Shared Management: An Innovation," *Minnesota Municipalities*, Vol. 56 (November, 1971), pp. 344–45, 360. This article summarizes an OD experience in a small town. Data from a large metropolitan government are summarized in Dick Heimovics, Robert J. Saunders, William B. Eddy, and F. Gerald Brown, "Results from an Ongoing Organization Development Program in a Public Agency" (Paper delivered at the Annual Meeting, American Society for Public Administration, April 19–21, 1971, Denver, Colorado).

   For a summary treatment, consult William B. Eddy and Robert J. Saunders, "Applied Behavioral Science in Urban Administrative/Political Systems," *Public Administration Review*, Vol. 27 (January, 1972), pp. 11–16.

51. Robert T. Golembiewski, "Civil Service and Managing Work," *American Political Science Review*, Vol. 56 (December, 1962), pp. 961–74.

like I have to raise the whole civil service by my bootstraps." Relatedly, a common OD objective seeks:

- to supplement the authority associated with role or status with the authority of knowledge and competence.

This objective is utopian to the degree that a pattern of delegation is specified in law, which is often the case. The same point applies to any rigidities due to the duties classification common in public agencies in the United States, and especially to the concepts for assigning authority and for organizing work which underlay the duties classification. Job enlargement begun as part of OD programs has run afoul of such rigidities, for example, even though some progress has been made (for example) in moving toward "rank in the man" as well as in the job.

At the bread-and-butter level, existing legal patterns also inhibit approaching OD objectives. Consider that a typical OD objective proposes:

- to develop a reward system which is sensitive to both the achievement of the organization's mission and its continued development.

Existing law and practice severely limit movement toward such a reward system. Thus rewards for exceptional performance—in money payments or in higher-than-normal GS levels for personnel in the civil service—are now possible, but they still are exceptional in practice. Equal pay for equal work, in sum, still practically means that exceptional work is not rewarded exceptionally. Management in business organizations typically has far greater control over reward systems, and especially at managerial levels. More of a problem, neither existing law nor practice promise much in way of support for various group compensation plans. Experiments in industry with such plans have yielded attractive results.[52]

Need for Security. Third, the need for security or even secrecy in public agencies is likely to be strong enough to inhibit approaching OD objectives. Military and defense agencies come to mind first, but they hardly exhaust the list. The "need for security" as used here can concern national security, it can be induced by a general anxiety born of a need to make significant decisions whose results will not be manifest for a very long time, or it can derive from felt needs for protection from such outside forces as a congressman with fire in his eyes.[53] The need can also be real, exaggerated, or even imagined in various combinations.

Consider one case, which reflects all of these components. Agency

---

52. Frederick G. Lesieur (ed.), *The Scanlon Plan* (New York: John Wiley & Sons, 1958).
53. Great needs for "security" as here broadly defined can rigidify an organization and curb the effectiveness of its members. To the point, see Chris Argyris, "Some Causes of Organizational Ineffectiveness within the Department of State," Center for International System Research, *Occasional Papers*, No. 2 (1967).

personnel were exposed to sensitivity training, one of whose major purposes is to increase skills in being open about both positive and negative emotions or reactions. The training staff provided several settings in which these intentions might be approached, one of which was a "park bench." During one week of sensitivity training, some time was set aside each evening for a meeting of all participants in a large room which was the locus of the "park bench." But agency personnel seldom used the arena, although there was a good deal of nervous laughter from the periphery of the "park." After some three abortive tries of an hour each, one participant approached me. "I see the point of the thing," he said, "but a park bench is all wrong." Suddenly, the dawn came. "Park benches" were seen as stereotypic sites for sexual assignations and/or for exchanging secrets with enemy agents. Without doubt, some participants thought the "park bench" a silly notion, and hence did not participate. For most participants, however, the symbolism was so compelling that they could not use the "park bench." Moreover, many agency personnel were so closed, distrustful, and fearing of taking a risk that they could not talk about their guiding symbolism, even if they were aware of it. Nor could they cope with the situation in ways other than by flight and pairing and (much later) by some diffuse fighting reactions.

This greater need for security cannot be measured specifically, to be sure, and all that may be said definitely is that to the degree this need exists so are OD objectives more difficult to reach. Consider only that it is commonly a major objective of an OD program:

- to create an open, problem-solving climate throughout the organization.

An open climate and a great need for security or for secrecy do not mix well.

Procedural Regularity and Caution. Fourth, for a variety of reasons, government personnel are rather more likely to stress procedural regularity and caution. Perhaps better said, even if agency personnel are convinced that certain heuristics provide solutions that are "good enough," this conviction may conflict with other (and especially congressional) needs for external control. For example, sample checking of vouchers was widely accepted as an efficient enough administrative approach in business long before relevant publics in Congress and the General Accounting Office recognized it as appropriate for their control purposes.

Good reasons support this bias toward procedural regularity and caution in public agencies, of course, and so much the worse for OD objectives. For example, the bias patently runs against the grain of perhaps the basic OD objective, which seeks:

- to help manage according to relevant objectives rather than according to "past practices" or according to objectives that do not make sense for one's area of responsibility.

The underlying rub, of course, is that a "past practice" making little or no sense administratively may seem an utter necessity from the legislative point of view. To be sure, the dictum "where you sit determines what you see" will always apply to all organizations. But the needs and identifications of administrators and legislators are likely to differ more than is the case for (let us say) the executives and middle managers of a business organization.

"Professional Manager." Fifth, the concept "professional manager" is less developed in the public than in the business arena, in rough but useful contrast. The relative incidence of business schools and schools of public administration suggests the conclusion,[54] as do the Jacksonian notions deep at the roots of our basic public personnel policies. For example, the "career system" notion has been a difficult one to develop in this country at the federal level. No small part of the difficulty derives from the value we place on an "open service" with lateral entry. Hence the tendency of our public personnel policies to emphasize hiring for a specific position rather than for long-run potential.

Derivations from these taproots have had profound impact. For example, to simplify a little, massive federal attention to training was long delayed by the wrigglesworthian legislative notion that, since the federal service was hiring people who already had the abilities to do the specific job for which they were hired, there was no need to spend money on training.[55] The relative attractiveness of public employment at the federal level, at least through World War II, provided the proverbial finger in the dike, but conditions changed much faster than did public policy. Instructively, also, the system of regional executive development centers manned by the U.S. Civil Service Commission began as late as 1964, and then only with a miniscule budget and against substantial congressional opposition. Roughly, business has a 10 to 20-year lead over government (except the military) in acting on the need for training. Not very long before, in contrast, the federal government was considered *the* model employer.

The relatively lesser stress on the "public professional manager" implies significant problems for approaching OD objectives. Thus one common OD proposes:

---

54. Revealingly, it was not until 1946 that Cornell developed the first two-year master of public administration program comparable to the MBA long given by schools of commerce or business administration.

55. Paul P. Van Riper, *History of the United States Civil Service* (Evanston, Ill.: Row, Peterson, 1958), pp. 429–34.

200

- to increase the sense of "ownership" of organization objectives throughout the work force.

No sharp contrast is appropriate. But a definite bias of public personnel policy limits such a sense of identification with, and commitment to, public agencies. If there is one thing most civil service reformers did not want, it was a public work force who "owned" the objectives of their agency. The only "owner" was the public; the model employee was a politically neutral technician who repressed his own values in return for guaranteed tenure. Only thus could an elite and unresponsive bureaucracy be avoided, according to a major theme shot through our public personnel policies and institutions.

Some Applications for Individuals in Organizations

Part II. Some Applications for Individuals in Organizations

A. INTERVENTIONS
AIMED AT INDIVIDUALS:
COMMON PROCESSES AND THEIR
CONSEQUENCES IN VARIOUS DESIGNS

Organizationally, this section of the volume and the next can be visualized as warp and woof, or as two overlays. The pervasive emphasis in both is on two basic processes of the laboratory approach. Both sections, in addition, review the impact of these processes in a variety of learning designs. These designs involve T-Groups, and also include three non–T-Group designs in work-related contexts dealing with demotions, dyadic interpersonal relations, and career planning.

1. FEEDBACK AND DISCLOSURE IN
THE LABORATORY APPROACH:
TWO CENTRAL PROCESSES IN
ALL LEARNING DESIGNS

This section begins with an emphasis on two central processes in the laboratory approach, feedback and disclosure. The overall conclusions are the same, whether feedback and disclosure are induced in a T-Group or in some other learning vehicle of the laboratory approach. Whatever happens in the laboratory approach, at whichever level of organization, has its immediate origins in feedback and disclosure supplied by individuals in interaction. Hence the critical nature of the two processes and the profound consequences of their properties as well as of the values or operating guidelines that underlay them. The T-Group, in short, is the matrix learning vehicle which provides the clearest picture of the power of feedback and disclosure. And this power, in turn, encourages attempts to generate those processes in non–T-Group designs. This section and the one following seek to cover both trails.

Feedback and disclosure may be distinguished crudely. The former refers to information—both verbal and nonverbal—we give another about how he appears or is reacted to by us; and disclosure involves revealing something about ourself to another. Not that the two come distinct in nature. Typically, indeed, every piece of feedback tells or implies to the Other something about the sending Self, and hence is commingled with self-disclosure. Similarly, disclosure often implies feedback from the Self to the Other, if only: "I believe you can be trusted with this information." The general notion here thus can be sketched as:

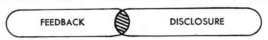

Moreover, the two processes also are subtly linked in another way: one typically triggers the other. Discussing the one, then, implies analysis of the other.

a. Toward Inducing More Helpful Feedback: Some Properties and Guidelines

Basically, the laboratory approach seeks to provide a broad range of learning designs that maximize the chances of effective feedback. Using the cybernetic analogy, feedback may be viewed as information concerning the efficacy of some data processor's adaptations to his environment. Thus a home furnace is linked with a temperature sensor so that the heating unit can approximate some desired temperature setting. If that feedback linkage does not function effectively, the furnace will reflect maladaptive behaviors. Individuals and organizations can similarly expect maladaptive responses if their feedback processes are inadequate. And the stakes are high, even incredibly high. As one source expresses the criticality of feedback to both sender and receiver: "Feedback, then, is a way of giving help; it is a corrective mechanism for the individual who wants to learn how well his behavior matches his intentions; and it is a means for establishing one's identity—for answering Who am I?"[1] Feedback, in sum, is central to the quality of life and living.

This description reflects a venerable theme in the behavioral sciences concerning the efficacy of providing an actor with information about the

---

1. NTL Institute for Applied Behavioral Science, "Feedback and the Helping Relationship," in Robert T. Golembiewski and Arthur Blumberg (eds.), *Sensitivity Training and the Laboratory Approach* (Itasca, Ill.: F. E. Peacock Publishers, 1971), p. 73.

adequacy of his responses. The more timely and accurate the feedback, the better the performance.[2] The usual rationale is uncomplicated. The acting individual has a prime goal of being competent, of making happen what he wants to have happen. Thus an individual is motivated to adjust when he learns that his behavior is perceived as differing from his core concept of himself, or when he learns that his responses to some stimuli are ineffective or maladaptive.[3] In fact, it is not too much to say that all of us deeply need such information to remain sane and human.

A viable feedback linkage depends upon the nature of both the input and the throughput, in the popular vernacular of systems theory. As for feedback viewed as input, human beings and large organizations are alike in that they are no better in adapting than their feedback is timely and validly reflects what exists. Hence, the critical significance of degenerative interaction sequences, and their pernicious self-heightening features. That is, an *existential* reason to distrust A often will generate an *anticipatory reaction* that A is not to be trusted. Hence B is likely to be less open, low trust in A is thereby reinforced, and the system cycles to a new and higher degenerative state. The crucial role of feedback is clearest in the T-Group, or a small unstructured group which is the basic learning vehicle of the laboratory approach. "How did I come across to you when I did that?" may be group member A's signal that he wants feedback. And other group members may respond by providing that evidence on which they have a monopoly, their own reactions, feelings, and attitudes. The essential products are profoundly simple. Participants see how difficult but rewarding it is to risk sharing their ideas or feelings; they experience how much they limit themselves and others by not being open; they demonstrate the prime importance to others of their ideas and feelings and reactions; and they gain skill and insight in giving and receiving feedback, as well as in reversing degenerative interaction systems.

Feedback also is usefully viewed as throughput. For human beings and organizations will be *no better* in adapting than their feedback is timely and valid. However, they can be *worse*. Like all servomechanisms, that is, men in organizations must be appropriately programmed to deal with as well as to provide feedback. As with the furnace, that is, the ideal is not providing it with just any feedback that is to be processed in just any way. How the feedback is given and how it is responded to—the

---

2. James N. Mosél, "How to Feed Back Performance Results to Trainees," *Training Directors Journal*, Vol. 12 (February, 1958), pp. 37–47; and R. Jack Weber, "Effects of Videotape Feedback on Task Group Behavior," *Proceedings*, Annual Convention, American Psychological Association, 1971, Vol. 6, pp. 499–500.
3. Kenneth J. Gergen, "Self Theory and the Process of Self-Observation," *Journal of Nervous and Mental Disease*, Vol. 148 (November 4, 1969), pp. 224–37.

style of the throughput—is patently of great significance. For immediate purposes, we consider only two throughputs: (1) some properties of helpful feedback and (2) some guidelines for giving and processing helpful feedback.

Some Properties of Helpful Feedback

Detailing the properties of helpful feedback—the kind of throughput desired in the laboratory approach—is an artichoke problem, a peeling off of layers of meaning. Six such levels are distinguished here, and even they are more suggestive than definitive. A large research literature exists,[4] and many designs for variously inducing feedback are available.[5] What will be done here is to stress the dominant central emphases in that research and practice, as they appear to the author.

Enhances Mutual Interpersonal Competence. At the most general level, first, helpful feedback has at least the properties noted below when viewed from the perspective of the Self sending the message. In helpful feedback: Self describes Other's *recent behavior* and its *impact on the Self,* while Self's message acknowledges Other's *right to change* (or not to change) as well as the *possibility* that the perceptions and reactions of Self are *unique.*

One can home in on helpful feedback from another angle. Feedback that will help both Self and Other in enhancing their mutual interpersonal competence has these major properties:[6]

- The information exchanged is minimally distorted, which requires that both Self and Other have a relatively high degree of self-awareness and self-acceptance.

- The information is relatively consistent and noncontradictory; consequently it does not pose (for example) ambiguities or double binds.

- The information is directly verifiable by Self and Other, which is to say that it should neither be interpretive nor based on inferred categories.

- The information is descriptive and minimally evaluative as to "good" versus "bad," etc.

---

4. Leland P. Bradford, Jack R. Gibb, and Kenneth D. Benne (eds.), *T-Group Theory and Laboratory Method* (New York: John Wiley & Sons, 1964), esp. pp. 130–31, 156–59, and 429–33.
5. For example, Gail E. Myers, *et al.,* "Effect of Feedback on Interpersonal Sensitivity in Laboratory Training Groups," *Journal of Applied Behavioral Science,* Vol. 5 (April, 1969), pp. 175–85.
6. Chris Argyris, "Conditions for Competence Acquisition and Therapy," *Journal of Applied Behavioral Science,* Vol. 4 (March, 1968), pp. 147–77.

- The information contributes to effective problem-solving, "effective" taken to mean that the solution does not generate other problems of equal or greater magnitude and that the solution enhances or at least maintains the viability of the problem-solving processes.

Each of these properties is, in effect, an artichoke in its own right.

Facilitates Autonomy. Second, perhaps the major property of helpful feedback is that it facilitates autonomy, increases the chances of learning accompanied by feelings of psychological success. In common, the notion implies that directiveness and dependency are to be minimized in the learning process and that collaboration and helping are to be maximized. As the autonomy of the learner is facilitated, goes the extended rationale, so is he likely to own the consequences of the learning experience or, to say much the same thing, so is he likely to feel in control of the learning and confident about transferring it to other situations. This thrust toward personal autonomy via community is patent in Leland Bradford's view of the centrality of feedback. "Each individual needs to get accurate information about the difference between what he is trying to do and how well he is doing it," he observed. "He needs to be able to use this information to correct or change his actions. *Then, basically, he is steering himself.*"[7]

Directly, that is, designs based on the laboratory approach seek to maximize psychological success so as to facilitate learner autonomy. Chris Argyris is especially insistent on the point, and he relentlessly follows that insistence to its logical consequences. He thus urges that all laboratory learning designs offer participants frequent opportunities to:[8]

- define their own learning goals
- develop their own approaches to meeting the goals
- relate both goals and approaches to central needs of participants
- choose a challenging level of aspiration that extends their present abilities but does not overwhelm them

The underlying notion is one of the growth-oriented person seeking self-enhancement and aid in more effective coping. That model person is not survival-oriented or deficiency-oriented, in Argyris's vocabulary.

Seeks a Special Level. Relatedly, a third property of helpful feedback in the laboratory approach is its seeking of a special track, or level. Globally, the focus is on preconscious or conscious processes, as is implicit in the emphasis above on information that can be verified directly by Self and Other. Feedback oriented toward eliciting the so-called un-

---

7. Leland P. Bradford, "A Fundamental of Education," *Adult Education,* Vol. 6 (April, 1952) , p. 85. My emphasis.
8. Argyris, *op. cit.,* pp. 153–54.

conscious processes is not a deliberate goal of the laboratory approach. Oppositely, indeed, unconscious processes often are approached via a second kind of information, information relying on inferred categories that can be validated only in terms of some theoretical or conceptual framework.[9] Compare two ideal responses to a long, evocatively rich description that invokes images of floating on dark and stormy waters, of a feeling of drowning with only impassive rocks looking on, and so on. Probing this imagery for unconscious materials would take one route. Thus the speaker might be asked to close his eyes, to again imagine his feeling of drowning, while taking special note of those "rocks." What feelings in him do they evoke? Does he sense anything familiar in them? The trend of the questions should be clear enough. They seek to explore the ontological roots of one interpretation of the images as reflecting a separation from fellowmen and, perhaps, as implying some precipitating rejection by a critical person earlier in life. In sharp contrast, an appropriate here-and-now response might be: "You confuse me when you use all that complex imagery. I have to struggle for meanings. It would help me if you would take one theme at a time, and relate it to how you're feeling and reacting now. Maybe I could help more then."

Insight is possible via the use of both kinds of information, but the appropriate learning situations are quite dissimilar. For example, Leonard Horwitz notes that: "Therapeutic and training groups emphasize two different methods of insight-giving: the training group depends more upon personal feedback from one's peers, while the therapy group depends largely on the therapist's interpretation of transference to him."[10] That is, at the level of basic T-Group design, reliance on directly verifiable information "encourages peer observation in the form of mutual evaluations in which each member has the opportunity of hearing a consensus opinion about his role in the group."[11] In contrast, reliance on information inferred from a conceptual scheme implies a unique role for the person most in touch with the conceptual scheme, i.e., the therapist. "Although various kinds of distortions, projections, and manipulations occur in the behavior of members toward each other," Horwitz notes of the basic orientation of common approaches to group psychotherapy, "the therapist uses these behavioral data in relation to the common tension toward him."[12] In sum, interpretation of the transference involving the therapist is the basic mechanism in group psychotherapy;

9. Alvan R. Feinstein, *Clinical Judgment* (Baltimore, Md.: Williams & Wilkins Co., 1967).
10. Leonard Horwitz, "Transference in Training Groups and Therapy Groups," in Golembiewski and Blumberg (eds.), *op. cit.*, p. 188. Originally published in *The International Journal of Group Psychotherapy*, Vol. 14 (1964), pp. 202–213.
11. *Ibid.*, p. 189.
12. *Ibid.*, p. 188.

feedback from peers is the dominant process in the laboratory approach. The distinction is certainly not absolute, but it is useful.

Feedback has a number of advantages in those insight-producing situations which are brief and whose goal is to make persons more aware of how they come across to others. Horwitz stresses three advantages. Feedback is likely to encompass a broader range of behaviors than the "group focal conflicts" stressed in group psychotherapy, and certainly the emphasis will not fixate on individual patterns of relating to the authority figure. In addition, feedback utilizes the greater social pressure implicit in its approach to insight. Group scapegoating must be guarded against. But a dominant or unanimous opinion coming from members of a group can make the individual uniquely aware of aspects of himself which he has heard about from others, but which he has been relatively free to discount as more-or-less random and perhaps even hostile, if consistent, observations. Finally, and crucially, emphasis on information that is directly verifiable is intended to avoid the profound regression that the therapist seeks to induce so as to surface unconscious conflicts that impair functioning. "The trainer [in the laboratory approach] is content to work with more superficial and more conscious layers of the personality than is the therapist,"[13] is the way Horwitz puts it.

Relies on a Contingent Process. The fourth property of helpful feedback involves a delicately contingent process. As C. Gratton Kemp observes: "Trainers agree that verbal feedback should await the development of mutual trust and a pattern of interchange and support from person to person. Some verbal feedback is laden with anxiety, and the skill needed to evaluate constructively is slow to develop."[14] In terms of degenerative systems, then, the foundations of helpful feedback are: sufficient increases in interpersonal trust, and sufficient reductions in risk. If achieved, these predisposing states will support increased openness and owning, and they will induce a readiness on the part of the sender and the receiver of the feedback. The sense of the two conditions is sketched in Figure 1.

The mini-models in Figure 1 do not imply that no feedback will occur in the cycle of mistrust.[15] Some harmful feedback can occur, but the far more probable condition is one of withholding or masking at least verbal feedback. Nature is kind in this regard, however. To the degree that a cycle of mistrust exists, so also is any expressed verbal or nonverbal feedback likely to be devalued, misinterpreted, or rejected as the effort of a stranger or enemy to hurt.

---

13. *Ibid.*, p. 190.
14. C. Gratton Kemp, *Perspectives on the Group Process* (Boston: Houghton Mifflin Co., 1970), p. 184.
15. Gordon L. Lippitt, *Organization Renewal* (New York: Appleton-Century-Crofts, 1969), p. 90.

Figure 1. Two Cycles for Characterizing Interpersonal Relationships

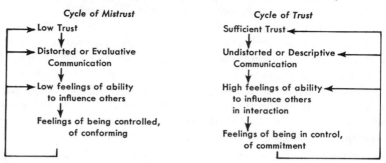

Source: Based on a model attributed to Dale Zand by Gordon L. Lippitt, *Organization Renewal* (New York: Appleton-Century-Crofts, 1969), p. 90.

Does Not Destroy Defenses. Derivatively, helpful feedback does not seek to assail and destroy a person's defenses. This fifth property denies the common myth, and it denounces what may even be the reality at times. The intent of the laboratory approach is to induce an analytical view of one's defenses, of how they help and hinder learning, of how they are variously functional or dysfunctional for the individual's goals. Change in the defenses may be appropriate, or it may not be. But it is cavalier to contemplate assailing and destroying a person's defenses, even if that were consistent with the laboratory approach's stress on autonomy and psychological success. That is, an individual's defenses exist for at least two significant reasons: they are conceptual systems that have proved at least modestly useful for him in the past, and they imply major values that help guide an individual's life.[16]

Rather than assailing or destroying defenses, in fact, the goal of the laboratory approach is to create a climate of trust that legitimates safely looking at one's defenses, in part through the eyes of others. Jack R. Gibb details the point in broad sweep when he rejects a "climate which induces defensiveness" for a "climate of supportive communications." He explains that the person who perceives or anticipates threat must devote an appreciable part of his energy to defending himself, which reduces the energy packet available for learning or change. The defensive person, Gibb notes, is too busy to be of much help to himself:

> . . . he thinks about how he appears to others, how he may be
> seen more favorably, how he may win, dominate, impress, or
> escape punishment, and/or how he may avoid or mitigate a
> perceived or anticipated attack. . . . The more "supportive"
> or defense reductive the climate the less the receiver reads into

16. Roger Harrison, "Defenses and the Need to Know," in Golembiewski and Blumberg (eds.), *op. cit.*, pp. 80–83.

the communication distorted loadings which arise from projections of his own anxieties, motives, and concerns. As defenses are reduced, the receivers become better able to concentrate on the structure, the content, and the cognitive meaning of the message.[17]

Gibb emphasizes a people process rather than a language process and stresses that fundamental improvements in communication consequently require improvements in interpersonal relationships. Gibb's approach to improving such relationships is to reduce the degree of defensiveness that commonly characterizes them. The challenge of improving communication thus becomes one of behaving in ways that reduce threat.

How is this challenge of reducing defensiveness to be met? Based on his study of recordings of numerous discussions, Gibb isolated two contrasting climates and six categories of behavior that are characteristic of each of them. The contrasting nature of these two climates can be suggested economically, although reference to the original piece is necessary to provide details. Defensive climates are characterized by evaluation, for example; and supportive climates emphasize description. Moreover, controlling behaviors are numerous in the former climates, while a problem-solving orientation characterizes the latter, and so on. Gibb stresses the tendency of these two classes of behaviors to increase and decrease defensiveness, respectively:

Defensive Climates Tend to Be Induced by	Supportive Climates Tend to Be Induced by
1. Evaluation	1. Description
2. Control	2. Problem orientation
3. Strategy	3. Spontaneity
4. Neutrality	4. Empathy
5. Superiority	5. Equality
6. Certainty	6. Provisionalism

The laboratory approach, in its essentials, is oriented toward developing learning designs that help demonstrate the significance of climate to communication, as well as the difficulty of inducing the appropriate climate. Significance is patent. Not only do defensive communicators send off contradictory and inconsistent value, motive, and affect cues, for example. Defensive recipients also distort what they perceive, Gibb explains. The difficulty of inducing supportive climates is also easy to establish. Gibb emphasizes the subtlety of shifting behaviors from evaluation to description, to illustrate the point. "Anyone who has attempted to train professionals to use information-seeking speech with neutral affect," Gibb explains, "appreciates how difficult it is to say even the simple, 'who did that?' without being seen as accusing."

17. Jack R. Gibb, "Defensive Communication," *Journal of Communication,* Vol. 11 (September, 1961), p. 144.

The common thrust of these considerations should be patent. Helpful feedback requires more respecting of defenses than it does assailing or destroying them. Witness the themes that feedback is far better solicited than imposed, that it should take into account the needs of the recipient as well as those of the giver of feedback, and that it should be minimally evaluative.[18] The latter prescription, for example, attempts directly to reduce "the probability of making the receiver defensive, thereby creating conditions favorable to an increase in accurate listening."[19] An assault on a person's defenses might be: "Stop that behavior, stupid." The laboratory approach advises: "When you behave that way, I have these reactions." The style does make a difference.

Is Most Effective in Group Situations. The sixth property of helpful feedback is that it is usually most impactful and helpful in a group situation. Patently, consistent feedback coming from many or all members of a group can be very powerful stuff. The group context also provides individuals with substantial security against getting bushwhacked by an unscrupulous fellow member or two. In addition, the group situation provides a wide range of resources. Thus some members may not like X in member A, but others may provide support for A or even report they find charming in A what others find repelling. These diverse resources can provide shelter from even intense feedback, while the individual determines his long-run course of action. Frederick Stroller describes both the short-run probabilities and the ideal in this regard:

> Most people either succumb completely to pressure or unequiv-
> ocally oppose it and it is only when they have had the opportu-
> nity to experience it clearly and see it through that they seem to
> have the option to deal with pressure in a more differentiated
> fashion—to pick and choose what they want to resist and what
> they want to accept; the free individual has the option to stand
> up against or go along with.[20]

And it is free individuals that the laboratory approach seeks to nourish: free in the essential senses of being in command of more of the information that permits them greater control in their interpersonal and intergroup relations.

Six Guidelines for Helpful Feedback

The properties above should demonstrate that the laboratory approach does not legitimate just any kind of feedback, and it is possible to get

---

18. NTL Institute for Applied Behavioral Science, *op. cit.,* p. 72.
19. Argyris, *op. cit.,* p. 157.
20. Frederick H. Stoller, "A Stage for Trust," in Arthur Burton (ed.), *Encounter* (San Francisco: Jossey-Bass, Inc., Publishers, 1969), p. 90.

quite a bit more specific about the kind of feedback that is considered ideal. This feedback is a composite. It is in part a skill that can be augmented by practice. In larger part, ideal feedback implies the acceptance of the values of the laboratory approach sketched in Sections A and B of Part I. Essentially, these values prescribe that the individual behave in ways that enhance his self-awareness and self-acceptance while also enhancing those of others, as situations change willy-nilly and responses have to be innovated.

The focus here is on these values, which are reflected in six guidelines for helpful feedback. The basic design of this section is straightforward. The guidelines for feedback will be listed below, and their application to a sample piece of feedback will be illustrated.

The reader might help make this section more experientially meaningful to himself by using the guidelines to judge his own skill level in providing feedback. Only simple preparations are necessary. The reader can prepare a piece of feedback that he would like to send to someone. Write it in prose, as you envision yourself saying it to the intended target. You can later measure your piece of feedback against the guidelines, after they have been described and illustrated.

Figure 2 details three value-loaded guidelines for helpful feedback, for a starter. These guidelines will be briefly described and illustrated.

Emphasis on the Here-and-Now. First, helpful feedback is based on a scratch-it-when-it-itches principle. As much as possible, feedback should refer to ongoing situations, to the here-and-now. The rationale is both practical and profound. As the here-and-now is emphasized, practically, so is it easier to deal with more-or-less immediately verifiable data, unclouded by recollections that differ or are dim. More profoundly, as the here-and-now is emphasized, so is it easier to avoid several kinds of inappropriate behaviors. Less likely, for example, is the kind of there-and-thening which has numerous possible explanations for everything and reasons for nothing. Less likely, also, is the amateur psychiatry that seeks ontological, there-and-then roots for behavior.

Emphasis on the Individual Act. The second guideline for helpful feedback is that it should emphasize individual acts, attitudes, or values, as opposed to the total person. The purpose is dual: to zero in on the specific phenomenon of concern, and to do so without unnecessarily raising the target's defenses or without denigrating him as a person. The difference in wording of feedback can be profound. Compare "I hate you" with "You hurt me when you didn't recognize me at the party," when the common stimulus is a perceived social snub. The underlying rationale for this guideline is elemental. A denigration of the total person is most likely to induce a flight response, or perhaps even fight. Neither of these responses is likely to achieve what helpful feedback requires: hearing the full import of the message by the target, and keeping defenses low enough, or porous enough, so that both target and sender can expend maximum energy in problem-solving, as opposed to facade maintenance.

Emphasis on Nonevaluative Feedback. The third guideline is far more complex and subtle. Helpful feedback should be nonevaluative and descriptive. This is meant in at least three more-or-less distinct senses. In the most elemental sense, feedback should be nonjudgmental. That is, it should be characterized by an absence of evaluations like "good" or "bad," especially as these evaluations refer to a total person.

Relatedly, effective feedback should be noninterpretive. Consider the husband who complains that the potatoes at dinner were hard. "Poor dear," his wife may respond by leaping to an interpretation, "had a hard day at the office, I see." Such interpretations imply serious problems.

Figure 2. Three Guidelines for Helpful Feedback

Guidelines for Helpful Feedback:

- emphasis on the here-and-now versus the there-and-then
- emphasis on the individual behavior, attitude, or value, versus the total person
- emphasis on feedback that is nonevaluative in at least three senses:
  a. it is nonjudgmental
  b. it is noninterpretive
  c. it reports the specific impact on the Self of Other's behavior, attitude, or value

Sample Feedback:

"George, you are a stereophonic SOB. And I know why. Your father rejected you as a child."

They often are a way of not hearing what the sender intends, or of devaluing it, for example. In addition, there is a good chance that the interpretation may be inaccurate. The husband above might retort: "I had a wonderful day at work, as a matter of fact. I repeat: the potatoes were hard." The subsequent dialogue might go several ways, none of them very promising. Finally, interpretations of many sorts deal with data that are not immediately observable, or that may even be validatable only against some theoretical schema. Back to the wife again, to illustrate. She might reply soothingly, recalling (she believes) some potent stuff on Momism from Home Econ 217, "Your Happy Home." "I know how difficult it is for you to be open with me, dear, given how you were dominated by that other woman in your life, your mother. Now just tell me all about how rough your day was. You can trust me, I'm not out to tie you to my apronstrings." And all that from some underdone potatoes.

Finally, feedback should be nonevaluative in the sense that it reports the feelings in Self induced by the Other's act, attitude, or value. As

216

the sender of the feedback is in touch with his reactions—as he is aware and accepting of himself—so are such reports descriptive rather than evaluative.

The rationale for this guideline has several components. A major one is the equivalent of the rule of best evidence. That is, the Self is the world's expert about such reactions, literally. Moreover, such reactions are vital to any Other intent on testing or improving his interpersonal competence. Other basically needs to know whether his actions are having the effects he intends, in short, and consequently has to touch base at least occasionally so that he can appropriately adjust his "experienced and anticipated competence," a notion introduced in Section A, Part I. Of great importance, also, this guideline reinforces an emphasis on the here-and-now, which is central in the laboratory approach.

The sample piece of feedback in Figure 2 helps illustrate these first three guidelines, if in a negative way. The reader can assume the basic responsibility for the effort. Note here only the skeleton of such an evaluation:

- The emphasis is basically on the there-and-then, e.g., in the alleged childhood of George.
- The emphasis is on George as a total person, who is an SOB from whatever angle one views him.
- The sample feedback:
  a. judges George as a total person (stereophonic SOB)
  b. interprets why George is the way he is (childhood experiences)
  c. fails to report the specific impact on the sender of George's unspecified acts, attitudes, or values, although the general tone clearly reflects George's negative impact on the sender

Guidelines 4, 5, and 6 for helpful feedback can be described and illustrated as complements to the first three, as shown in Figure 3.

Emphasis on Facilitating Change. The fourth guideline for effective feedback takes into account the fact that it typically is related to at least the possibility of change: doing something different; or doing more of something; or at least continuing to do something. As such, helpful feedback should have three attributes, following the basic Lewinian model of change. At the very least, a piece of feedback should encourage the target to look at some part of himself or his behavior. Two elements are involved: a specificity by the sender about what the sender is directing attention toward; and a receptivity by the target, which is often a function of the degree to which he perceives the immediate climate as helpful and supportive. The desired condition is described as "unfreezing," where the target feels secure enough to view some part of himself

217

and to evaluate its contribution to his interpersonal competence. The antigoal is typified by the tightly wound Don Knotts character. "Are you ner——," begins a question. "No!" the character replies before the question is finished. And we all laugh, with some compassion, knowing how hard it will be for that character to learn from his experience when he so quickly rejects even what is so obvious to all.

Moreover, feedback that facilitates change will imply or suggest replacement behaviors, attitudes, or values. Consider the anticase. "You say I disgust you," says one person. "I'd like to change that. Perhaps you could help by telling what there is about me that evokes such a strong reaction." The unhelpful response is: "I don't know. There's just something about you that rubs me the wrong way." Unless this unpromising dialogue goes much further, no change is a very solid bet.

Finally, on the issue of choice and change, helpful feedback will provide reinforcement for any new behaviors, attitudes, or values with which the target of feedback might experiment. At a minimum, this implies a willingness of others to respond openly concerning reactions to the new or intensified acts. Further, reinforcement implies openness to point up any backsliding, as well as social support for the effort and for any progress.

Emphasis on Psychological Safety. Helpful feedback will emphasize the psychological safety of the target of the feedback, a kind of contract about "trust in leveling" that binds both sender and target. For the sender, this fifth guideline implies feedback that is requested rather than forced and that meets the needs of the target as well as the sender. For the target, the guideline implies that he is in control of the feedback process and can indicate both when he wants more feedback and when he has had enough. As Gerard Egan notes of the ideal climate in T-Groups: "Each individual must feel that it is safe to expose his feelings, drop his defenses, and try out new ways of interacting."[21] The point also applies to non–T-Group learning environments, although they typically must suffer some dilution of learning because they are not so suited to developing the depth of psychological safety attainable in a T-Group.

Emphasis on Creating a Community. The sixth guideline is related to the fifth. Helpful feedback is more likely in the context of a community of learners or a society dedicated to mutual help. The T-Group is the prime example of such a learning-helping community. In its broad philosophical perspective, the goal is to create in a T-Group a true moral and ethical order, a basic agreement concerning fundamentals

21. Gerard Egan, *Encounter: Group Processes for Interpersonal Growth* (Belmont, Cal.: Wadsworth Publishing Co., 1970), p. 247.

that alone can permit individuals to differ and to be different without opting for isolation or scapegoating.

T-Groups are not always and everywhere appropriate or convenient, of course, and alternative designs might require that some resource person encourage or even supply adherence to the values of the laboratory approach.[22] Even in such a case, the use of group settings can be of great value. If nothing else, they can provide consensual validation. Moreover, group settings can contribute to the feelings of safety of the target of the feedback. Both features are implicit in such questions as: "That's how I see Fred. I wonder if others have a different perception of him?"

Figure 3. Three Additional Guidelines for Helpful Feedback

Guidelines for Helpful Feedback

- emphasis on facilitating change in three ways:
  a. by helping to "unfreeze" the old behavior, attitude, or value
  b. by suggesting replacements that may be tried
  c. by reinforcing any new behavior, attitude, or value
- emphasis on "trust in leveling," on psychological safety of target of feedback
- emphasis on creating and maintaining an "organic community"

Sample Feedback

"George, you are a stereophonic SOB. And I know why. Your father rejected you as a child."

The sample feedback in Figure 3 permits convenient illustration of these final three guidelines. Again, the reader can do much of the work. In outline, however, it may be helpful to note that in the sample piece of feedback:

- The emphasis does not facilitate change because:
  a. the target is not clear on what old behaviors, attitudes, or values might be changed
  b. the replacement behaviors are not clear, short of a return to the womb to start over again
  c. there is consequently no clear promised reinforcement of any changes; in fact, quite the contrary seems implied
- The emphasis is clearly not on the psychological safety of the target, even though presumably some needs of the sender are being met.

---

22. See, for example, the designs illustrated in Sections B, D, and F of Part II below, especially Subsections 3 and 4 under Section F.

219

- The emphasis is on a one-to-one relationship, and the "community" in that dyadic relationship seems oriented only indirectly toward helping and learning.

Alternative Forms of Feedback

The discussion above may seem to suggest that there is only one way to skin this particular cat, and that suggestion must be scotched. For example, feedback relevant to interpersonal or group situations can be provided in various ways, as by:

- listening to an audiotape of a conversation or problem-solving effort[23]
- providing summary statistics derived from questionnaires that were previously completed[24]
- watching a videotape playback of a conversation or group interaction[25]

Videotape feedback seems to have a broad range of especially attractive features. For example, videotape can preserve the many nonverbal cues that can be critical in communication.[26] Unlike interpersonal feedback, in addition, videotape allows the person direct access to his presentation of self, without the need to factor out of another person's reactions those induced by the presented self from those that the observing person projects. Videotape feedback can also be processed without an outside consultant, thus avoiding such issues as confidentiality of data, the attempt to schedule a happening for the consultant's benefit, and the danger of the outside consultant being seen as judgmental or evaluative or manipulative.

The data are hardly all in, but the available findings suggest that there are several viable media for providing effective feedback. Indeed, R. Jack Weber sees major advantages of videotape feedback for such purposes as OD programs and team development activities, as compared to stranger or family T-Groups. He notes:

---

23. Thomas J. Bouchard, "Personality, Problem-Solving Procedure, and Performance in Small Groups," *Journal of Applied Psychology Monograph*, Vol. 53 (1969), pp. 1–29.
24. Frank A. Heller, "Group Feedback Analysis: A Method of Field Research," *Psychological Bulletin*, Vol. 72 (August, 1969), pp. 108–17.
25. R. Jack Weber, "Repetitive Self-Observation and Changes in Interaction Behavior in Small Task Groups," mimeographed (Hanover, N.H.: Dartmouth College, 1972); and William N. Dehon, "Self-Confrontation via TV," *Training and Development Journal*, Vol. 21 (October, 1967), pp. 42–46.
26. Ray L. Birdwhistell, *Kinesics and Context* (Philadelphia: University of Pennsylvania Press, 1970).

Compared to [them], repetitive television-mediated self-observation is usable by ongoing task groups in an organizational setting, thus eliminating the encapsulation of training implicit in conventional residential laboratory designs. Moreover, videotape replay provides clear and non-evaluative feedback, facilitates personal diagnosis of social-emotional and task behavior at both the individual and the group level, and permits group members to use the raw data of their own experience to build theories and change behaviors or perceptions, or to ignore the entire experience. Finally, the types of behavior change reported above occurred without the intervention of an extra-group process consultant. Additionally the data suggest that substantial experimentation with new behavior will occur without attempting to direct member attention to selected individual and group process issues.[27]

b. Toward Inducing More Relevant Disclosure: Some Conditions for Productive Sharing

Disclosure has not received the attention accorded to feedback and, if some of our religious and social philosophers have a handhold on reality, the loss is great. Consider only two variations on the common theme. For Paul Tillich, Christ on the cross provides the model for man in daily life. The prime human quality is man's courage to be his real self in his relationships with others, as Christ had the courage to be himself even as it led to his own agony. For Tillich, then, self-disclosure is the act of primary meaning, without respect to the character of the disclosure.[28] From another perspective, O. Hobart Mowrer argues toward a theory of pathology based not on what the individual did but on his failure to disclose what he did, whether it was intentional or accidental. Consequently, guilt does not inhere in some act which transgresses moral or legal codes, but in the failure to disclose that act.[29] The underlying notion is that failure to disclose induces a press against the consciousness, a kind of massive unfinished business, which can generate neurotic conflicts.

The more or less immediate implications of these philosophic concepts are profound. H. M. Lynd seems to measure his statement of this pro-

27. Weber, *op. cit.*, pp. 17–18.
28. Paul Tillich, *The Courage to Be* (New Haven, Conn.: Yale University Press, 1952).
29. O. Hobart Mowrer, "Loss and Recovery of Community," in George M. Gazda (ed.), *Innovations in Group Psychotherapy* (Springfield, Ill.: Charles C. Thomas, Publisher, 1968), pp. 130–89. See also Mowrer, *The New Group Therapy* (Princeton, N.J.: D. Van Nostrand Co., 1964).

fundity: "a person who cannot love cannot reveal himself,"[30] and vice versa. As for the T-Group, Egan notes that all participants "must agree to make some efforts to reveal the person within to other members." He explains that this assumes that "responsible self-disclosure is a kind of royal road to community. This sharing of the human condition—in its sublimity, banality, and deformity—pulls people together."[31]

The specific focus here on disclosure has more modest purposes, three of which can be identified. *First*, disclosure is seen as a common quid pro quo for feedback, and hence it is of great importance. The model piece of disclosure of the laboratory approach, that is, often contains a clear or implied request for feedback. For example, this statement at once discloses and seeks feedback: "I'm very concerned with how you see me."

Second, more broadly, there seem to be major reasons why a person should disclose, perhaps even needs to disclose in some ultimate sense. Samuel A. Culbert notes of non–self-disclosure that "one general consequence does stand out." That consequence is "the added difficulty a non–self-disclosing person faces in obtaining information about the reality or objective aspects of relationships in which he participates."[32] A major consequence that is, indeed, one that is easily associated with such effects as the probable onset and severity of mental illness.

Third, concern here about self-disclosure is also motivated by the need to explicitly define "congruent" or "authentic" relationships as a two-way street. Specifically, some interpretations of "being congruent" or "being authentic" imply "letting it all hang out," whether in feedback or disclosure. This implies one-way authenticity or congruence, and perhaps even a narcissistic dead-end that makes impossible what it seeks to enhance. Overall, there are strong reasons for rejecting the conclusion that, because more disclosure can be a good thing, unlimited disclosure is consequently the very best thing.

William Dyer provides one perspective on the associated issues in his discussion of the dilemmas of "congruence," which Carl Rogers has defined as "an accurate matching of experiencing, . . . awareness, and communication." The simplest example for Rogers is the infant. "If he is experiencing hunger at the physiological and visceral level," Rogers illustrates, "then his awareness appears to match this experience and his communication is also congruent with his experience."[33] Increases in

---

30. H. M. Lynd, *On Shame and the Search for Identity* (New York: Science Editions, 1958), p. 241.
31. Egan, *op. cit.*, p. 193. Broadly, see Sidney M. Jourard, *Self-Disclosure* (New York: Wiley Interscience, 1971).
32. Samuel A. Culbert, "The Interpersonal Process of Self-Disclosure: It Takes Two to See One," in Golembiewski and Blumberg (eds.), *op. cit.*, p. 75.
33. Carl Rogers, *On Becoming a Person* (Boston: Houghton Mifflin Co., 1961), p. 308.

congruence, Rogers advises, will result in enhanced interpersonal relations.

Dyer acknowledges both the wisdom and the problems associated with congruence as a strategy.[34] Particularly as a countervalue to overcontrolled behavior imposed by restrictive societies or organizations, congruence within broad limits can be a tonic. There, he explains, "the problem for many people is not going 'too far' with congruency but dealing with over-controlled behavior." Dyer stresses the theme of congruence within limits, in the context of overexuberant extensions of Rogers's core insight. Does congruence, Dyer questions, "mean that it is all right for a person to behave in any way so long as it is consistent with his current state of awareness and experience?" Congruence, he observes, "in this direct and immediate sense has become a major value for some." Dyer reflects his own values about such an extension of Rogers's concept, values which are consistent with the laboratory approach detailed above. He explains:

> Being congruent is not the only value I hold. *I also value the rights of others.* My personal value system stands for trying to live a helpful life with others, to value a society based on mutual respect and acceptance. If I were to engage in behavior that might be "congruent" at the moment, it would also violate a great many other values that I deem important. I will not violate those just to be congruent.[35]

Argyris has developed a similar point forcefully.[36] He urges thinking of the related concept of authenticity as an interpersonal phenomenon rather than a personal state or characteristic. He conceives of human relationships as "the source of psychological life and human growth," especially in that such relationships can involve increasing awareness and acceptance of self and others. Authentic relationships are, in fact, those in which an individual enhances his awareness and acceptance of self and others, while he does so in ways that permit others to do the same. Consequently, for Argyris, it is no more possible to be authentic independent of others than it is possible to cooperate with yourself. A person's authenticity, then, will be a mutual function of his capacity to create authentic relations with others, as well as of their capacities to create authentic relationships with him. Epigrammatically, it is easy

---

34. William G. Dyer, "Congruence and Control," *Journal of Applied Behavioral Science,* Vol. 5 (April, 1969), pp. 161–73.
35. *Ibid.,* pp. 164–65.
36. Chris Argyris, *Interpersonal Competence and Organizational Effectiveness* (Homewood, Ill.: Dorsey Press, 1962), p. 21.

but ultimately futile to serve aces if there is no other player on the other side of the net. That is not how the game is played. So much more does the point apply to life.

One fine point is in order. Argyris specifically notes that he is speaking of what Culbert calls real–self-disclosure, as contrasted with non–self-disclosure. Non–self-disclosure is what I would be practicing if I announced breathlessly here that I had been a professional ballet dancer. Culbert draws a useful distinction. Clearly enough, failure to disclose makes it unlikely or impossible for a person to be accepted by others. Non–self-disclosure adds a major complexity to this position: it suggests the image of the person who cannot win for losing. Culbert concludes: "Receiving acceptance for nonself-data—by which one has tacitly agreed to be known—decreases the likelihood that real-self-data, to correct these misimpressions, will eventually be disclosed."[37]

Some Guidelines for Disclosure

It is only possible to be suggestive concerning the kinds of disclosure that seem better adopted to inducing increased awareness and acceptance by both Self and Other, so brevity is appropriate here. This is especially the case since Culbert, who will be relied on basically here, has recently summarized the available thought and research on disclosure. Six features of disclosure will be emphasized.

First, disclosure will be helpful as it is perceived as appropriate to the situation in which the disclosure is made. Patently, this guideline hardly constitutes a firm principle. Extreme examples are easy enough to handle, such as the high probability of the inappropriateness of the child in a theater who loudly discloses during a tender scene his intentions to use the restroom facilities. More difficult are cases in which prevailing norms do not sanction disclosure, but where the disclosure might still be appropriate. Consider a potential candidate for President who discloses he is an alcoholic, as recently happened. Judging "appropriateness" in this case depends clearly on one's personal values, on perceptions about what it takes to be President, and on how badly one wants to be President.

Second, the motivation seen as prompting a disclosure will be significant in determining its impact on the authenticity of the relationships existing between sender and receiver. Culbert stresses the perception by others of the congruence between what the discloser states or implies are his motives, and what motives the receivers attribute to him. He concludes: "To the extent that the communicator is seen as congruent, the receiver is likely to accept his participation at face value and to be open

---

37. Culbert, *op. cit.*, p. 76.

to the possibility of viewing his communications favorably."[38] In contrast, communications that are viewed as incongruent will tend to evoke guarded or defensive reactions, at least until the receiver can decide on a strategy that can protect his interests.

Third, timing will be critical in the impact of a piece of self-disclosure. *"Now* you tell us" suggests a disclosure that could have been made earlier.

Fourth, self-disclosure apparently has different effects, depending upon whether its orientation is toward the past, present, or future. Disclosures from the past can be significant, but they also can develop into complicated histories that critically depend on the perceptual filters of the person supplying the narrative. The appropriateness of past-tense disclosures to ongoing situations also may be unclear. Hence Egan notes that past-tense disclosures often are "history," or pseudo self-disclosure. He notes of "history" that:

> It is actuarial and analytic, and usually has a strong "there and then" flavor. It clicks off the facts of experience and even interpretations of this experience but leaves the person of the revealer relatively untouched; he is accounted for and analyzed, but unrevealed. The person relates many facts about himself, but the person within still remains unknown. History is often a long account. It is long and often steady because it fears interruption. Interruption might mean involvement, and a person engages in history to avoid, rather than invite, involvement.[39]

Disclosure about the future also can be meaningful, but resolution may flag and recollection may dim when the chips are down.

For such reasons, and especially to avoid the pitfalls of a there-and-then orientation, Culbert notes that most sensitivity training attributes key status to present-tense disclosure. He explains that "such disclosures typically have the highest interpersonal relevance, generate the greatest amount of feedback, and make for the greatest receptivity to the feedback of others." The conclusion is direct. "Hence, present-tense disclosures, all other things being equal," Culbert notes, "are believed to possess the highest potential for increased self-awareness and personal growth."[40]

Fifth, growth in awareness and acceptance of self and others seems to be a curvilinear function of self-disclosure. Some research[41] supports

---

38. *Ibid.,* p. 77. That is, the suspicion of gamesmanship is likely to induce gamesmanship in return.
39. From *Encounter: Group Processes for Interpersonal Growth* by Gerard Egan, pp. 234–35. Copyright 1970 by Wadsworth Publishing Company, Monterey, California.
40. Culbert, *op. cit.,* p. 78.
41. *Ibid.,* p. 75.

common sense[42] in this regard. Too much self-disclosure can be as destructive to interpersonal relationships as too little. The former overwhelms the other person, while the latter starves the relationship.

Effective self-disclosure, then, may be characterized as being uninhibitedly appropriate, and to the correct degree. In most cases, this poses no great problem, even given the lack of specific content of the terms "appropriate" and "correct." By and large, too little self-disclosure characterizes most interpersonal relationships. So "more" is a generally applicable prescription for self-disclosure. Questions of how much is too much are more complicated. As Culbert notes:

> The problem of too much disclosure is less clear-cut. What constitutes *too much,* under *what* circumstances, and by *whom* is a thoroughly complex issue. Appropriateness, motivation, timing, and tense all enter in. Moreover, what constitutes the *optimal* amount of self-disclosure is a no less complicated issue.[43]

Sixth, self-disclosure can be useless or perhaps even dangerous under certain conditions. Uselessness is Egan's basic concern, by far. He sees it as a probable outcome to the degree that self-disclosure is:[44]

- exhibitionistic rather than oriented toward establishing or deepening a relationship
- not responded to with support and acceptance by the receivers
- history, in the sense defined above
- first promised by someone who then reneges on the promise
- incomplete in a situation where completeness is required

More broadly, self-disclosure may even be threatening *sui generis,* and perhaps acutely so for some people. Egan observes: "Self-disclosure both crystalizes and, in a sense, reifies aspects of the self that a person would rather live with silently—however painful the living—than face."[45]

As with feedback, then, disclosure should be disciplined by the values of the laboratory approach and, as far as it is possible to do so, by the prior development of appropriate skills. Normally, however, there are major limits on how many situations can be predicted and prepared for ahead of time. Hence Argyris's emphasis on the importance of providing individuals, "along with the knowledge of any specific behavior, the basic skills needed to diagnose new situations effectively and those needed to develop cooperation with others involved to generate the com-

---

42. S. M. Jourard, *The Transparent Self* (Princeton, N.J.: D. Van Nostrand Co., 1964).
43. Culbert, *op cit.,* p. 79.
44. Egan, *op. cit.,* pp. 241–43.
45. Egan, *op. cit.,* p. 207.

petent behavior appropriate to the situation."[46] That is what the laboratory approach is about, whatever the specific learning design.

The need for guidance as to appropriate disclosure is uniformly pressing. Guidance is necessary for the trainer, where the existing evidence tentatively implies that both more[47] and less[48] self-disclosure by the trainer himself is useful in T-Groups. Guidance is also necessary for the full range of self-disclosure: to self-disclosure in the "real world," as well as to designs that attempt to induce disclosure in specific learning environments. One micro-design for stimulating disclosure which could be an exercise within a normal T-Group, for example, has participants list the three persons whom they trust the least in their group, or like the least, or whatever. At an extreme, entire experiences have been designed around the induction of disclosure, as in a Weekend of Rational Encounter whose learning segments are based on such directions from the leader as: "What member of this group would you like to tell off? Why? Tell him or her off, right now."[49] Choices between such designs imply major empirical and value questions whose complexity is in substantial part beyond our present grasp. General guidelines it must be, then.

2. PROVISIONAL COST/BENEFIT ANALYSIS FOR T-GROUPS: CRITICAL CONSEQUENCES OF THE MATRIX LEARNING VEHICLE

Existing opinions about the effects of T-Groups on individuals cover the huge range from the malevolently harmful to the pleasantly benign. Some see the T-Group as a cunning device that can brainwash all but the most wary;[50] and others see it as a variably pleasant experience essentially of the water-off-a-duck's-back variety. Other opinions tightly pack the space between these extreme positions.

---

46. Argyris, "Conditions for Competence Acquisition and Therapy," p. 222.
47. Samuel A. Culbert, "Trainer Self-Disclosure and Member Growth in Two T-Groups," *Journal of Applied Behavioral Science*, Vol. 4 (January, 1968), pp. 47–73.
48. Kenneth Goodall, "Casualty Lists from Group Encounters," *Psychology Today*, July, 1971, p. 28.
49. Albert Ellis, "A Weekend of Rational Encounter," in Burton (ed.), *op. cit.*, esp. pp. 112–16. The "feel wheel" is a less-extreme device. See Anthony L. Rose, Martin J. Thommes, Terry Van Orshoven, and Loyne A. Longfellow, "A Facilitator for Group Interaction in the Vicissitudes of Everyday Life," *Psychology Today*, Vol. 5 (May, 1972), pp. 45–53.
50. "Sensitivity Training," *Congressional Record*, U.S. House of Representatives, June 10, 1969, pp. H4666–79; Gary Allen, "Hate Therapy: Sensitivity Training for Planned Change," *American Opinion* (John Birch Society), January, 1968, p. 73; and John Steinbacher, *The Child Seducers* (Fullerton, Calif.: Educator Publications, Inc., 1971).

The purpose here is to chart a point of view on the relative balance of costs and benefits of T-Grouping. This point of view will be an amalgam of two emphases. The issue of the possible harmful effects of sensitivity training will be considered first. More extended attention will later be given to the broad range of effects attributable to T-Grouping. The focus throughout is on stranger T-Groups.

a. The Record of Harmful Effects: Myth/Reality of Psychological Damage

From the very first, the issue of psychological damage attributable to sensitivity training has been center stage.[51] Discussions often have been lively, although (or, perhaps, *because*) empirical data were in short supply. And separating myth from reality was usually not possible. Everybody had his own stock of anecdotal evidence, whether based on personal experience or on the real or alleged personal experiences of others. Verification was all but impossible.

The data have begun to come in, and they permit an optimistic if qualified judgment about the effects of T-Groups. Carl Rogers provides perspective on the judgment and several of its qualifiers in discussing a major potential risk involved in an intensive group experience. He notes:

> . . . the individual may become deeply involved in revealing himself and then be left with problems which are not worked through. There have been a number of reports of people who have felt, following an intensive group experience, that they must go to a therapist to work through the feelings which were opened up in the intensive experience of the workshop and were left unresolved. It is obvious that without knowing more about each individual situation it is difficult to say whether this is a negative outcome or a partially or entirely positive one. There are also very occasional accounts of an individual having a psychotic episode during or immediately following an intensive group experience. On the other side of the picture is the fact that individuals have also lived through what were clearly psychotic episodes, and lived through them very constructively, in the context of a basic encounter group. My own tentative clinical judgment would be that the more positively the group process proceeds the less likely it is that any individual would be psychologically damaged through membership in

51. George S. Odiorne, "The Trouble with Sensitivity Training," *Journal of the American Society of Training Directors,* Vol. 17 (October, 1963), pp. 9–20.

the group. It is obvious, however, that this is a serious issue and that much more needs to be known.[52]

Because the issues are serious and much more needs to be known, this section is a significant one. The basic assumption is that concern about psychological damage is appropriate in the case of every new learning technology. Moreover, this is a convenient time for stock-taking, given the recent availability of relevant data. Specifically, the following argument considers such factors, in turn:

- the acknowledged properties of T-Groups that can induce threat or anxiety
- the level of emotional arousal intended in T-Groups
- the available data relevant to the success of T-Group technology and trainers in achieving these intentions
- some conclusions concerning greater success in achieving T-Group intentions by creating realistic expectations in potential participants

Elements Inducing Anxiety or Threat in T-Groups

A variety of elements in typical T-Group designs do induce anxiety or threat. This conclusion holds in several senses, four of which are usefully distinguished. *First,* the T-Group itself in effect facilitates learning by the potential for anxiety or threat that inheres in the specific group situation. The essential features of the T-Group-*qua*-vehicle that imply such potential are well known and can be summarized as follows:

> Members of the [T-Group] are usually told that they can learn much about their own behavior, from continuous observation and analysis of experiences in the group. The trainer refuses to act as a discussion leader, but proposes to help group members to find ways of utilizing their experiences for learning.
>
> Essentially, a kind of social vacuum is produced. Leadership, agenda, procedures, expectations, usually pre-established by some authority, are blurred or missing. As tension produced by the vacuum mounts, members endeavor to supply the missing elements and their behavior output also mounts. Because the group has not developed ways of making decisions, suggestions for action are generally not accepted by the group. In fact, because of the tensions produced by the ambiguous situation, individuals have difficulty in even hearing the contributions of

---

52. Carl R. Rogers, *Carl Rogers on Encounter Groups* (New York: Harper & Row, Publishers, 1970), pp. 38–39.

others, let alone acting on them. Individuals, as the group endeavors to form some viable structure and organization, face situations and dilemmas they have not faced before, and so begin a process of testing, trying out, and testing again.[53]

Second, the T-Group context encourages a regression as individuals respond to the new social environment, usually by mobilizing their defenses until a greater predictability is attained. As Kenneth D. Benne notes: "A whole range of issues, once thought settled, were brought up for reevaluation in the T-Group context."[54] In effect, the individual initially may experience what Benne calls a "primitivization" of behavior as, for example, the individual finds he cannot rely on the status or formal authority that simplifies his life in the world outside the T-Group. The experience is enjoyable and within the tolerance of most participants. But all will experience some threat or anxiety as they essentially redefine their selves in interaction, and perhaps as they observe a primitivized or regressed Self which they find variably difficult to accept as their real Self.

Third, more sharply, the T-Group context implies an identity question for all members, and even an identity crisis for some few. That is, almost every individual has a self-concept, a definition of who he is that is protected by a number of defenses. Because the defenses help reduce anxiety via blunting threat to the self-concept, they become valued and resistant to change. The T-Group design tends to challenge this condition. As John P. Campbell and Marvin D. Dunnette explain: ". . . in the T-Group when an individual's usual mode of interacting is thwarted and his defense mechanisms are made a direct topic of conversation, considerable anxiety results. Such anxiety then constitutes a force for new learning because, if the group experience is a successful one, new methods of anxiety reduction will be learned."[55] In the process, however, the individual's identity is stressed. That is, people gain identity in their relations with other people and in differentiation from them, as well as from their position and function in a social system. The T-Group requires quick resolutions of new challenges to settled identities and, as Bradford notes, consequently raises some degree of identity crisis for every member. Leland Bradford concludes:

> In a situation with few boundaries and very little structure and
> direction, each person is uncertain as to what he is supposed to

53. Bradford, Gibb, and Benne (eds.), *op. cit.,* pp. 40–41.
54. Kenneth D. Benne, "From Polarization to Paradox," in Bradford, Gibb, and Benne (eds.), *op. cit.,* p. 237.
55. John P. Campbell and Marvin D. Dunnette, "Effectiveness of T-Group Experiences in Managerial Training and Development," *Psychological Bulletin,* Vol. 70 (August, 1968), p. 76.

do and, consequently who he is to be. Frequently, the identity stress generated in the T-Group motivates individuals to examine many more areas of their lives than the ones involved in the immediate situation.[56]

Patently, there is at least some threat or anxiety for all T-Group members in such questions about who they are and how they are perceived.

Fourth, and especially at the beginning of a T-Group, members experience a variety of stress situations that imply threat or anxiety. For example, the T-Group experience induces a heightened awareness of Self, one of whose threatening implications is that the individual may discover something about himself which is unacceptable to others and perhaps even to himself. Relatedly, this possibility may induce anxiety about the difficulty of change, should such a something become apparent. Or the individual may anticipate that he will be unable to change, in which case the anxiety or threat of being exposed to feedback is probably at a maximum.[57]

The Projective Hypothesis and Optimal Anxiety

The intent is to use these anxiety-provoking features of the T-Group design in quite a specific way and to a specific degree. The T-Group goal is to induce projection and regression, that is, and the intended degree is "moderate."

These two intended features of T-Grouping can be developed briefly. What may be called projective psychology implies that a person's psyche abhors an apparent vacuum. As a situation is ambiguous, so does the individual tend to project into it his own needs, desires, fears, and fantasies. The T-Group is intended to facilitate easy projection by individuals. These projections then become a basic source of data from which individuals can learn about themselves and others. Note the qualifier above that refers to "easy projection," which reflects a second major foundation of the T-Group technology. Specifically, the T-Group context is seen as ambiguous enough to induce sufficient anxiety to encourage learning. But that ambiguity and its resulting anxiety are not intended to be so great as to inhibit learning. Roy M. Whitman refers to "optimal anxiety" in this regard. He explains: "Too much anxiety is disintegrating to the organism. Too little anxiety makes a person unwilling to abandon his usual approach. The concept of optimal anxiety im-

---

56. Leland P. Bradford, "Membership and the Learning Process," in Bradford, Gibb, and Benne (eds.) , *op. cit.*, pp. 95–96.
57. Bernard Lubin and William B. Eddy, "The Laboratory Training Model," *International Journal of Group Psychotherapy*, Vol. 20 (July, 1970) , pp. 317–18.

plies discomfort somewhere between these extremes; some anxiety or discomfort is needed for change."[58]

Much the same is true of regression in the T-Group. Some regression facilitates looking at the mature Self, but extreme regression could be extremely discomforting to the person who might rightly feel he was "coming apart at the seams." The intent implies the techniques. Psychoanalysis implies deep regression, a plumbing of the unconscious. Hence reliance on the couch or on being gently supported in warm water, both of which are intended to induce major regression. Hence also "word association," which attempts to lull the conscious mind and thereby reveal the unconscious. T-Groups deal with conscious or preconscious materials, in contrast, and the stimuli to regression are correspondingly mild. Such stimuli include the legitimating of experimentation, of "trying things out." Hence also the significance in the T-Group of the emphasis on here-and-now feedback and disclosure.

A contrast may make the point more explicit. The ambiguity and threat in a T-Group come from objective dilemmas of creating an environment for learning, of each person finding a comfortable place in it, and so on. And however high the ambiguity and threat, they are at least potentially amenable to resolution by the participants. In contrast, both ambiguity and threat might be bogus, of greater intensity, and beyond member influence. For example, ambiguity and threat might be induced by a false report that a participant's family had been victims in a boating accident. Although no bodies had yet been recovered (the bogus report might continue), all were presumed drowned.

There are at least two classes of reasons why the second approach above to ambiguity and threat is very bad laboratory technique. The tactic violates the values underlying the laboratory approach, as they are sketched in Sections A and B of Part I. For example, the report is never-was versus here-and-now; it is a fabrication rather than authentic; and so on. Second, and relatedly, the tactic violates the notion of optimal anxiety, which is to say that it is unlikely to generate learning of the kind desired in the laboratory approach.[59] In sharp opposition to the use of maxi-threat in learning, for example, Gibb argues for the primacy of trust as a facilitator of learning in T-Groups. Gibb explains:

> A person learns to grow through his increasing acceptance of himself and others. Serving as the primary block to such ac-

---

58. Roy M. Whitman, "Psychodynamic Principles Underlying T-Group Processes," in Bradford, Gibb, and Benne (eds.), *op. cit.*, p. 313. The conclusion rests upon a prominent line of research, including Irving L. Janis and H. C. Milholland, Jr., "The Influence of Threat Appeals on Selective Learning of the Content of a Persuasive Communication," *Journal of Psychology*, Vol. 37 (1954), pp. 75–80.

59. For some purposes, such maxi-threat may be appropriate. See Office of Strategic Services Staff, *The Assessment of Men* (New York: Rinehart, 1948).

ceptance are the defensive feelings of fear and distrust that arise from the prevailing defensive climates in most cultures. In order to participate consciously in his own growth a person must learn to create for himself, in his dyadic and group relationships, defense-reductive climates that will continue to reduce his own fears and distrusts. . . .

The critical function of the T-Group is to augment this process of personal learning. The person learns to participate with others in creating a defense-reductive climate, becomes aware of the processes of such creation, and learns how to generalize these learnings to other dyadic and group situations. That is, he learns how to create the interpersonal situations which will help him to accept himself and others—to grow to help others grow.[60]

Some empirical research establishes that early trust among T-Group members does in fact significantly determine what degree of learning eventually takes place.[61] Early trust seems to be, in fact, the best predictor of the emergence of growthful outcomes from a T-Group.

At the level of intent, then, the T-Group may be described in terms of two vectors of opposed force. On the one hand, a certain amount of initial anxiety or threat is used to set the learning juices flowing. The ambiguity inherent in the T-Group design induces that initial anxiety or threat and encourages the possibility of change or, at least, of self-evaluation. On the other hand, the actual mobilization of this potential will depend in critical ways on the trust that members have or can develop in each other and in the learning situation.

Clearly, then, the T-Group goal is not simply and malevolently to increase the threat or anxiety until "someone cracks." Indeed, the values of the laboratory approach are oriented oppositely. Ideally, at least, the learner selects the level of anxiety or threat he can safely tolerate, with the values of owning and openness being the vehicles for continuously monitoring the fit between the individual and his learning environment. To do otherwise is to invite psychological failure for the learner, goes the rationale underlying the laboratory approach.

How High Is "Optimal Anxiety" in Practice?

But how high is this "optimal anxiety," really? Even assuming the benign nature of the intentions sketched above, many questions remain

---

60. Jack R. Gibb, "Climate for Trust Formation," in Bradford, Gibb, and Benne (eds.), op. cit., pp. 279–80.
61. Frank Friedlander, "The Primacy of Trust as a Facilitator of Further Group Accomplishment," Journal of Applied Behavioral Science, Vol. 6 (October, 1970), pp. 387–400.

unanswered. Consider just a few samples. Is the optimum so high as to pose a danger to a substantial proportion of potential participants? Moreover, even if that optimum is almost always tolerable, what is the probability that a guileless trainer or a relentless group can in an excess of zeal create major psychological trauma for their brothers and sisters?

A substantial body of opinion comes down hard on the real dangers of major psychological damage from T-Grouping. Such observers see the optimal anxiety in a T-Group as very high indeed, although the evidence offered usually is anecdotal and difficult to evaluate. "The critical statements assert that the level of emotional arousal . . . is extraordinarily high," Bernard Lubin and Marvin Zuckerman note, "and is likely to be psychologically damaging to participants. In these critical statements, however, no objective evidence has been presented."[62]

The available data do not permit unqualified judgments but, overall, they suggest an optimistic if mixed conclusion concerning the dangers of T-Grouping. Thus the data suggest that the available technology respecting the values of the laboratory approach tends to induce a level of emotional arousal that is well within the limits of the overwhelming proportion of potential learners. The closing session of a typical group-oriented laboratory illustrates the point. An observer reports in these terms on the last few minutes of such an experience, as the leader asks if anyone has anything to say:[63]

> All our faces seem softened. The effect is that the men look like boys. At length a voice:
> "I'll give you one word: Fan-tastic."
> (From the opposite side of the circle) "Wonderful."
> "Flyin' high."
> "Thank you."
> "I'll echo that: thank you."
> "Thank you."
> "Thank you."

However, the available data also suggests that T-Grouping can be a demanding experience, for some people, and especially under certain conditions. This dualism can be suggested by two articles appearing in the same issue of a prestigious journal. One article described the use of sensitivity training for medical students as having sanguine effects. Not

---

62. Bernard Lubin and Marvin Zuckerman, "Level of Emotional Arousal in Laboratory Training," *Journal of Applied Behavioral Science*, Vol. 5 (October, 1969), p. 484. For some critical reports, see "Yourself as Others See You," *Business Week*, March, 1963, p. 160; and L. A. Gottschalk, "Psychoanalytic Notes on T-Groups at the Human Relations Laboratory, Bethel, Maine," *Comparative Psychiatry*, Vol. 7 (1966), pp. 472–87.

63. Richard Todd, "Notes on Corporate Man," *Atlantic*, Vol. 228 (October, 1971), p. 86.

only did 73 freshman medical students complete the training without major incident, but the experience also was seen as providing major socioemotional support for them during that demanding first year of medical school. As one evidence, it was explained that psychiatric consultations during the school year following the introduction of the sensitivity training are "one-half those of last year and one-third those of each of the previous two years."[64] The other article, in stark contrast, reported this impressive array of symptons in one population of 32 T-Group participants:[65]

- one psychotic reaction
- one borderline acute psychotic withdrawal reaction
- four marked withdrawal reactions with lack of participation
- two severe depressive reactions with withdrawal
- two severe emotional breakdowns with acute anxiety, crying, and temporary departure
- one sadistic and exhibitionistic behavior pattern
- four mild anxiety or depressive reactions

Three sources of data provide more specific and rigorous support of the appropriateness of a mixed conclusion concerning the potential costs of T-Grouping: (1) mega-consequences of T-Grouping, (2) comparative stress levels in life situations, and (3) potential for, and causes of, psychological distress.

Mega-Consequences of T-Grouping. The low incidence of very serious negative reactions to T-Groups seems clear enough, despite differences and ambiguities in the definitions of "very serious." Consider the records of the NTL Institute for Applied Behavioral Science. Some 14,200 persons experienced a stranger T-Group under the Institute's auspices between 1947 and 1968. The T-Group was stressful enough to require 33 of the 14,200 to leave before the completion of the program.[66] Another large sample of T-Group participants had a "psychiatric casualty rate" of the same order of magnitude, about one half of 1 percent, "as measured by hospitalization, overt psychosis, or a need for psychiatric attention."[67] The experience with T-Grouping by YMCA professional staff is

64. James Cadden, Frederic F. Flash, Sara Blakeslee, and Randolph Charlton, Jr., "Growth in Medical Students through Group Process," *American Journal of Psychiatry*, Vol. 126 (November, 1969), pp. 862–67.
65. L. A. Gottschalk and E. M. Pattison, "Psychiatric Perspectives on T-Groups and the Lab Movement: An Overview," *American Journal of Psychiatry*, Vol. 126 (November, 1969), pp. 823–39. See also Gottschalk, "Psychoanalytic Notes on T Groups at Human Relations Laboratory," *Comparative Psychiatry*, Vol. 7 (December, 1966), pp. 472–87.
66. *NTL Institute News and Reports*, Vol. 3, No. 4, p. 1.
67. American Psychiatric Association, *Encounter Groups and Psychiatry* (Washington, D.C., April, 1970), p. 13.

consistent. There were some 1,200 participants, and a systematic effort to track down every "allegedly severe negative experience" found four such cases. The study directors added this important qualification, in addition:

> Even in those four cases, however, the experience as a whole was not completely negative. Data gathered from careful interviews with the principals themselves, their work supervisors, their sensitivity group trainers, other group participants, and, where applicable, with clinicians working with the principals, indicate that for three out of four persons thus involved the disruptive experience actually turned out to be helpful and is now appraised by them as being a valuable learning experience which has enhanced their effectiveness as individuals and as YMCA Directors. In the fourth case, although the individual does not evaluate the experience as being a positive one for him, he has not been incapacitated by the experience and is continuing to do an effective job in his position as a YMCA Director.[68]

Diverse significance can be attributed to even these large samples. For example, somewhere between two and three tenths of 1 percent of the two samples experienced serious negative reactions. Is that too high a price to pay? Opinions will vary, and for substantial reasons. A brief mention of the several bases for these contrasting opinions implies the complexity of the issue. *First,* in part, a judgment about whether the costs of T-Grouping are acceptable will depend on the histories of those who have experienced major emotional trauma in a T-Group, or as a clear consequence of T-Grouping. The early evidence suggests that, by an overwhelming proportion, the few cases of serious effects were experienced by persons with prior histories of serious emotional disturbances.[69] If this is the case, patently, the probability of serious trauma can be markedly reduced by a simple screening of participants.

Second, it is not clear what proportion of major emotional trauma associated with T-Groups would in any case have occurred as responses to more ordinary life situations had there been no experience in sensitivity training. Anecdotal evidence suggests that T-Groups can provide the proverbial straw for some participants, as by overstimulating or overloading the vulnerable person.[70] In these cases, T-Groups are among a wide

---

68. R. T. Batchelder and J. M. Hardy, *Using Sensitivity Training and the Laboratory Method* (New York: Association Press, 1968), pp. 83–84.
69. Julius E. Eitington, "Assessing Laboratory Training Using Psychology of Learning Concepts," *Training and Development Journal,* Vol. 25 (February, 1971), p. 4.
70. Irvin D. Yalom and Morton A. Lieberman, "A Study of Encounter Group Casualties," *Archives of General Psychiatry,* Vol. 25 (July, 1971), p. 25.

236

range of life situations from which the vulnerable person should be protected.

Third, for some people T-Groups literally have provided the only environment in which they could with safety and support determine how bizarre were their perceptions of the world around them. In such cases, one can hardly fault the T-Group technology for creating emotional disturbances, although it clearly helped surface them.

Fourth, the costs of T-Grouping will be influenced by other effects, which do not qualify as mega-consequences but which can be significant nonetheless. The two following points provide insight at this level.

Comparative Stress Levels in Life Situations. Recent efforts have been made to compare the peak stress in T-Groups with stress-levels experienced in other life situations. Preliminary data suggest that the highest level of emotional arousal in a T-Group approximates the level of stress experienced by college students prior to an examination.[71]

More refined analysis suggests other points of reference for ranking the peak stress in a T-Group relative to other life situations. For example, Kim Griffin and Kendall Bradley have used T-Group methods to *reduce* the anxiety of students of public speaking who experience "stage fright."[72] This implies a lower and more ameliorative level of anxiety in T-Groups than the stage-frighted person experiences in public-speaking situations. For another benchmark, two researchers compared participants in a group-oriented T-Group with subjects in perceptual isolation studies which restricted visual, auditory, and tactile sensations for periods of 6, 8, and 24 hours. The researchers used measures[73] of anxiety, depression, and hostility—three important negative affects—to estimate the stress levels in the four situations. The T-Group experience was very substantially less stressful by every criterion. Aggregatively, participants in the T-Groups scored significantly lower on the three measures than the subjects in all of the perceptual isolation studies, with the differences being far beyond usually accepted levels of statistical significance. Relatedly, about one third of the subjects in the isolation studies generated scores that can be considered unusually high by common statistical conventions.[74] No such scores were generated by T-Group participants, although some of them scored as high or higher than the 60 or so percent of the isolatees who did not score "unusually high."

71. Bernard Lubin and Alice W. Lubin, "Laboratory Training Stress Compared with College Examination Stress," *Journal of Applied Behavioral Science,* Vol. 7 (October, 1971) , pp. 502–507.

72. Kim Griffin and Kendall Bradley, "Group Counseling for Speech Anxiety," *Journal of Communication,* Vol. 19, No. 1 (1969) , pp. 22–29.

73. Marvin Zuckerman and Bernard Lubin, *Multiple Affect Adjective Check List: Manual* (San Diego, Cal.: Educational and Industrial Testing Service, 1965) .

74. T scores from the standardization sample were employed. See Lubin and Zuckerman, "Level of Emotional Arousal," pp. 485–88.

Potential for, and Causes of, Psychological Distress. Other data imply that a significant number of T-Group participants can expect to have a trying experience, if that is defined as "considerable and persistent psychological distress." So it is not appropriate to promise potential T-Group participants a rose garden. A major large-scale study indicates "a very appreciable casualty rate," some 16 out of 208 participants.[75] A substantial range of negative reactions qualified as "considerable and persistent psychological distress," but their order of magnitude is consistent with other data. In a very large population, for example, approximately 10–15 percent of T-Group participants felt concerned enough during their training to consult a counselor available to all participants. Their concerns centered around situational anxiety, depression, agitation, and insomnia,[76] all of which are associated with the unfreezing and self-analysis characteristic of T-Groups.

Several features of a recent comprehensive study[77] about psychological distress as a result of T-Grouping deserve highlighting, for at least two reasons. Thus the findings variously reinforce the efficacy of the values of the laboratory approach, as they are developed in this book. Moreover, the findings reflect the kind of comparative study which requires replication for various groups, learning designs, and so on. Four features of this research deserve note.

First, the style of a group's trainer was *the* crucial element in the production of casualties. Approximately 25 percent of the trainers had 45 percent of the casualties, with casualties covering a range from one member being "uncomfortable and anxious about his peripheral membership," his failure to be accepted being similar to rushing a fraternity and not making it, to individuals who had psychotic episodes during or shortly after their T-Group.[78] These high-risk trainers were called the "aggressive stimulators." Behaviorally, the aggressive stimulators:

- were very intrusive, challenging, and more authoritarian
- revealed much of themselves
- focused on the individual rather than on the group
- tended to measure the participants against the aspirations of the trainer, and to intensely care about it, as opposed to encouraging the individual to change (or not to change) in terms of the participant's own standards and potentials

Some descriptions of characteristic behavior and attitudes further imply the senses in which aggressive stimulators did not respect the values

75. Yalom and Lieberman, *op. cit.*, pp. 16–30. Goodall, *op. cit.*, presents a summary of the data.
76. American Psychiatric Association, *op. cit.*, p. 13.
77. Yalom and Lieberman, *op. cit.*, pp. 21, 26 and 29.
78. *Ibid.*, p. 24.

of the laboratory approach sketched above, especially in Sections A and B of Part I. Irvin Yalom and Morton Lieberman note that such trainers "appeared to operate on an immediate gratification system; they . . . demanded that their members change and change 'now.' " Moreover, such trainers seemed guided by a common assumption, or value: that "everyone in the group had the same needs and had to accomplish the same thing in the group." In addition, aggressive stimulators focused on the individual rather than the group. Finally, these trainers "asserted firm control and took over for the participants." These trainers, in effect, made the decision of what to work on, and at what pace. They "developed a hot-seat, no-escape-hatch format."[79]

Second, the casualties were usually attributed to two sources. First, the casualties tended to be attacked or rejected by a trainer, especially an aggressive stimulator. Second, casualties tended to be attacked or rejected by members of their T-Group. This was especially common in those T-Groups having trainers who seldom intervened and hence probably did not encourage enforcement of laboratory values.

Third, low-casualty rates were achieved in groups that tended to follow the values attributed to the laboratory approach. Such groups had two major features:

- a group climate of trust and acceptance, in whose creation the trainer played a major role
- a pace that was basically determined by the members, either in the presence of a trainer or in a group that was intentionally leaderless with the few structuring instructions being on audiotape

Fourth, the casualties-to-be had a number of distinguishing preexperience characteristics. In sum, the casualties-to-be had great needs, but they were poorly equipped to do what required doing. "Their needs were extreme," Yalom and Lieberman[80] note of one subgroup among the casualties, "and [these extreme needs] would have been an appropriate ticket of admission to any psychotherapy group."

Facts about those with these preexperience characteristics included:

- One quarter of the 16 eventual casualties had unrealistically high expectations about the experience, bordering on a hope for salvation.
- Five of the 16 eventual casualties had seen a psychotherapist beforehand, at least in a brief encounter, which was over three times the rate for noncasualties.

---

79. *Ibid.,* p. 26.
80. *Ibid.,* pp. 24, 28.

- The casualties tended to score lower on initial measures of self-esteem and to have less positive self-concepts before their learning experience.

Yalom and Lieberman conclude that the "entire picture is a consistent one." Casualties were more likely to come from "individuals with generally less favorable mental health with greater growth needs and higher anticipations for their group experience and yet who lacked self-esteem and the interpersonal skills to operate effectively in the group situation. . . ." The bind is clear. Such individuals come into a T-Group with very high hopes, but they may find that they induce very quickly in T-Groups the same unsatisfactory set of relationships that characterize their real-world relationships. Giddy optimism can quickly turn to black depression, as such individuals confront the harsh reality that there are no easy ways out and that their social and interpersonal skills are inadequate even in the comfortable confines of a T-Group. Yalom and Lieberman describe one such person. "He entered the group with relatively severe problems including strong homosexual conflicts. He had been lonely and isolated at college and entered the group, in part, to search for friends."

The data summarized above are too fragile to support hard-and-fast generalizations, but several major points constitute at least interesting foci for future analysis. First, the incidence of casualties seems directly related to extensions or violations of the values sketched in Sections A and B of Part I. For example, aggressive stimulator trainers can create failure experiences for individuals who have great expectations about their group experience but who also have an inadequate base of "experienced and anticipated competence," to allude to Hampden-Turner's model reviewed in Section A, Part I. Second, the data suggest the efficacy of the climate of mutual help and trust stressed above, as in the triggering of casualties by rejection of a member by trainer or group. Third, the data suggest that casualties-to-be have a fair-enough vision of the extensive help they really need.

Toward Generating Realistic Expectations

However one evaluates the results above, clearly, there is room to reduce the negative consequences of the T-Group experience. A number of factors converge on one conclusion: realistic expectations about the costs/benefits of any group experience will help reduce the casualties. As potential participants come to realize what T-Groups are and are not, so also should the proportion of negative experiences decrease for those for whom the additional T-Group anxiety was literally the straw that ruptured their coping capabilities. Three factors constitute a major start toward generating such realistic expectations.

First, participation in a T-Group may not be appropriate for individuals already feeling substantial threat or anxiety. T-Grouping can be a trying process, and may involve substantial anxiety for some participants while it seems well within the thresholds of the bulk of those in the studies referred to above. Note that most T-Group participants are adults with more-or-less settled and personally meaningful ways of coping. Hence the anxiety potential in the T-Group which, as Egan notes, "is a very soul-searching process. It requires the individual to introspect, to look at his own values and his own emotions, to ask himself whether and why he likes them, and whether he wishes to live the way he has."[81] There are two derivative questions. Thus, does an individual have the general ability to tolerate the anxiety in such introspection about his established ways of life? Moreover, is an individual contemplating a T-Group currently experiencing a major stress involving himself or some member of his family? If so, the T-Group may generate just enough anxiety to overwhelm his coping capabilities.

Second, participation in a stranger T-Group should be voluntary and noncoercive, both at inception and in process. Forcing participation in a stranger T-Group, patently, might propel an individual into a stressful situation with which he was not willing to cope and with which he was incapable of coping. If anything, noncoerciveness is even more appropriate during a T-Group. That is, the meaning of T-Group activity may vary significantly—even wildly—for its members, due either to earlier traumatic episodes[82] or to basic personality differences.[83] Hence the crucial status of the guideline that learning in the laboratory approach should proceed at the learner's pace. Illustratively, a situation that is duck soup for one person may be screamingly threatening to another person.[84] This is the inherent wisdom in the laboratory approach's stress on the individual's commitment to and owning of the learning, which factors increase the probability of learning under conditions of psychological success. The guidelines also reduce the probability that an individual will be coerced into learning situations that are too stressful for him, whether the coercion is by a trainer or by other group participants.

---

81. Egan, *op. cit.,* p. 47.
82. Steven L. Jaffee and Donald J. Scherl, "Acute Psychosis Precipitated by T-Group Experiences," *Archives of General Psychiatry,* Vol. 21 (October, 1969) , pp. 444–47.
83. Richard S. Lazarus, *Psychological Stress and the Coping Process* (New York: McGraw-Hill Book Co., 1966) , esp. pp. 120–49.
84. In one case, for example, an aggressive T-Group released two overwhelming memories in a participant, one dealing with a homosexual experience and the other with the participant's earlier unwillingness or inability to help his father. These memories apparently were easily accessible to the participant, and the T-Group experience released them. As Jaffee and Scherl, *op. cit.,* p. 447, note: "defenses may be lowered without compensating supportive mechanisms becoming available. This raises the risks of psychopathological reactions occurring."

Third, participation in a T-Group should be based on informed choice. Two kinds of information are especially helpful. Thus the T-Group is not intended for people who require, or believe they may require, something more than an augmenting of their interpersonal skills. There is some reason to believe, however, that the T-Group is seen by some participants as a replacement for long-term therapy.[85] Moreover, since anticipation is often worse than actual confrontation,[86] any information that will reduce threat or anxiety before the fact of T-Grouping may be very helpful. Particularly important in this regard are attempts to dispel any magical notions about the processes of T-Grouping, as via an openness concerning its anticipated consequences. There is no evidence that prior knowledge of T-Group techniques reduces their efficacy, in any case. If anything, in fact, such knowledge seems to encourage participants to get on with it in more purposeful fashion.[87]

b. The Difficulty of Establishing
Growth-Oriented Effects:
Factors Complicating Research on T-Groups

This topic intends to provide perspective on a final approach to the costs/benefits of T-Grouping. The focus is on the factors that complicate research of T-Group effects and that, consequently, bear directly on establishing the value of the technology.

A wide range of factors complicate the researching of T-Group phenomena, and the purpose here is to illustrate that broader range. Other conveniently available sources can be relied on to supplement the brief discussion here, as in establishing the methodological difficulties that obfuscate the interpretation of existing findings while they also bedevil the design of more satisfactory research.[88] The illustrative focus here is on only three factors complicating T-Group research: (1) the ambitions of sensitivity training (2) the assumptions made about applications of the T-Group technology, and (3) the complex interactions that must be accounted for by any elegant research on T-Groups.

---

85. Yalom and Lieberman, *op. cit.,* pp. 21, 26, and 28; and American Psychiatric Association, *op. cit.,* p. 7.
86. Lazarus, *op. cit.,* pp. 35–38.
87. Relatedly, see the discussion about systematic preparation of patients for psychotherapy in Egan, *op. cit.,* pp. 37–38.
88. See, especially, Campbell and Dunnette, *op. cit.,* pp. 73–105; Roger Harrison, "Problems in the Design and Interpretation of Research on Human Relations Training," in *Explorations in Human Relations Training and Research* (Washington, D.C.: National Training Laboratories, 1967).

Ambitions of T-Group Applications

The prime difficulties of research on T-Group effects inhere in the breadth and subtlety of the ambitions of the technology. In its broadest sweep, as Dunnette and Campbell note,[89] the laboratory approach seeks nothing less than "new patterns of individual and organizational behavior." Fulfilling this basic ambition requires meeting four especial needs. First, the T-Group must help persons develop enhanced analytic and diagnostic skills related to gathering data about interpersonal and intergroup problems. Second, very large numbers of people will have to become trained observers of themselves in interaction. This will require less self-centeredness and reduced defensiveness, as well as an expanded awareness and openness about the effects of the Self on Other. Third, greater willingness to surface and resolve conflict must be developed. Fourth, unprecedented motivation and skills to work collaboratively with others must also be developed. Both increases in individual skills and more effective problem-solving will depend on such collaborative effort.

There is broad agreement about the intended T-Group contributions to meeting these ambitions. Six intended contributions are most central. That is, T-Group training is intended to:[90]

- increase insight and awareness by Self about behavior in social contexts, by learning how others perceive and interpret behavior, as well as by gaining knowledge of why Self behaves differently in different social situations
- increase sensitivity to the behavior of Other, by becoming aware of the full range of verbal and nonverbal communicative stimuli as well as by developing the ability to infer correctly how Other is feeling or reacting
- increase awareness and understanding of processes that facilitate or inhibit the functioning of groups
- sharpen diagnostic skills relevant in social and interpersonal contexts
- augment behavioral skills so that an individual can intervene successfully in social and interpersonal contexts
- induce a continuing predisposition to analyze interpersonal relations to help Self and Other achieve more productive and satisfying outcomes.

---

89. Marvin D. Dunnette and John P. Campbell, "Laboratory Education: Impact on People and Organizations," *Industrial Relations,* Vol. 8 (October, 1968), p. 5.
90. *Ibid.,* pp. 6–7.

Assumptions of T-Group Applications

The task of early T-Group research is not merely to judge whether such outcomes generally occur, however. That would be relatively easy, even if it strains our existing research findings and technologies. The more difficult task is the development of a growing specificity about which outcomes occur under which conditions. This specificity about conditions is even further beyond our present capabilities. Some day, that is to say, a body of theory and experience may exist which will permit refined predictions about which specific outcomes can be confidently predicted in which specific T-Groups with which specific set of participants exposed to some specific design. But that day is not yet.

Several major assumptions about T-Grouping serve in the stead of such a sophisticated corpus of theory and experience, and no doubt will have to do for an indefinite period. At least seven major assumptions can be distinguished.[91] Their effects are both complex and subtle. Awareness of the assumptions can provide explanations of why expected effects do not occur, at their best. At their worst, the assumptions can provide rationalizations that provide reasons for everything and explanations for nothing. In perhaps the most basic sense, however, all of the assumptions come to pretty much the same point. They complicate the design and interpretation of research on T-Group effects. The assumptions are:

First, a feeling of psychological safety can be induced in many or all T-Group participants in a brief period of clock time, whether the participants are strangers or share a common history.

Second, every, or almost every, T-Group participant lacks interpersonal competence, which the person is motivated to remedy when it is psychologically safe enough to attempt to do so.

This assumption has both existential and motivational elements. Existentially, that is, everyone (or almost everyone), often enough to cause him concern or to be less competent than he desires, does not hear what is said, fails to communicate what he intends, has a distorted sense of how he is perceived by others, and so on. Motivationally, also, the assumption is that everyone wants to diminish the number and degree of such cases.

Third, under conditions of relative psychological safety, many or all members of a T-Group will be willing to enter into a mutual contract for learning. The contract has two main clauses. Participants should strive to be constructive as opposed to destructive; and they should provide honest feedback and self-disclosure to one another.

Fourth, the T-Group environment generates behaviors that all or most of its members consider to be significant aspects of themselves, either

---

91. Campbell and Dunnette, "Effectiveness of T-Group Experiences," p. 77.

244

actually or ideally. As this assumption is met, so do T-Group members come to take any learning seriously, to own it.

Fifth, despite their individual deficiencies in interpersonal competence, members of a T-Group collectively tend to pool wisdom and helpfulness, as opposed to compounding ignorance and vindictiveness. Consider feedback, for example. The assumption of maximizing assets and minimizing deficiencies implies multiple conditions. At least four conditions are involved:

- T-Group members collectively will come to observe more or less the same (real versus imagined) aspects of the same participant's behavior in meaningful interpersonal situations.
- They can articulate what they see and how they react to it.
- T-Group members can convey their messages in ways that are nonmalicious even if not massively helpful to the target of the feedback.
- What is observed and communicated will somehow involve a more-or-less-complete view of a significant aspect of the behaviors, attitudes, or values of the target of the feedback.

Sixth, despite their individual deficiencies in interpersonal competence, T-Group members collectively can provide the resources appropriate to the range of concerns likely to be encountered. Minimally, these resources include observational and communicative skills. They may also include warmth, or support, or skills in confronting versus skills of flight, depending on the specific directions a specific T-Group takes.

Seventh, a T-Group member's behavior is representative of what the individual is, or would like to be, outside of the T-Group environment. This implies the possibility of the transfer of learning from the T-Group context, as well as the motivation to do so. Without either this possibility or that motivation, the T-Group experience is at best temporary and at worst contraceptive.

The evidence indicates that these are safe-enough assumptions for the general run of T-Groups and their participants, but the assumptions still have troublesome consequences for research and its interpretation. Consider the motivation to perform research. The assumptions either hold, more or less, or no permanent learning occurs. Or perhaps some negative side-effects may develop. As this third class of effects is uncommon or is not very visible, so are the assumptions likely to go untested.

Similarly, the assumptions can confound the interpretation of existing research. Suppose individual A comes out of a T-Group with a lowered sense of self-esteem and trust for others. Did sensitivity training as a technology fail in that case? Or was it just that in one particular T-Group some crucial assumptions were not met? The faithful will lean toward the latter possibility; the critic toward the former. And neither will really know, usually.

Overall, as Campbell and Dunnette note, the validity of the assumptions is open to question "since they involve extremely complex processes with as yet only a very thin research context."[92] More specifically, we are only now beginning to develop the case literature which provides detailed insight into the kinds of conditions under which the assumptions are not likely to hold. Broadly, those antagonistic conditions may be defined as "extreme": extreme in the sense of massive and unmet needs, of conflicts of priorities and values great enough to generate rejection and alienation, and of insensitivity and inappropriateness far beyond the average. Consider the case of a white woman, who entered an encounter group carrying a sense of deep shame with which she had long struggled, as well as a deep need to be validated as a worthy person by others. She left the group feeling perhaps even greater shame and self-contempt. As she struggled to reveal herself to the group, that is, she succeeded only in having other group members reject her. As Yalom and Lieberman describe the situation, she could not win for losing.[93] The woman planned her agenda well in advance, and she deliberately disclosed a great deal about herself very early in the group. Her disclosure included the intimate details of her liaisons with black men, and also her deeply held racist feelings. And she forced these disclosures on a group of whites and blacks who were preoccupied with racial tensions. The intimacy of her disclosures and her insensitivity to the readiness of others overwhelmed her group, whose members were not ready for that degree of intimacy. Self-disclosure, as was shown above, implies demands on others for reciprocal disclosure. The demands in this case were too great. Other group members, Yalom and Lieberman conclude, "withdrew from her and regarded her as a problem, a sex maniac to whom they could not relate. This sequence of events was extremely noxious to her. . . ."

Interactions of T-Group Effects

Far more than by ambitions and assumptions, research on T-Groups is complicated by the myriad interactions that must be accounted for by any reasonably comprehensive theoretical network. Matthew Miles makes the general point in his very convincing summary of the difficulties facing the evaluation of any attempts to induce change. He notes:

---

92. *Ibid.*, p. 77.
93. Yalom and Lieberman, *op. cit.*, p. 24.

Research on any form of treatment is classsically difficult, unrewarding, and infrequent. When the product of a process is change in persons, the criterion problem is ordinarily a major one, whether the treatment occupies the domain of education, mental health, or social functioning. Goals are vaguely stated (partly because of ignorance and partly, it has been suggested, to protect the practitioner against charges of malpractice). Often, it is claimed that "real" change may not be assessable until long after the treatment has occurred. Even if goals are precisely and operationally defined, treatment programs themselves are usually hard to describe accurately enough for later replication. Furthermore, test-treatment interaction is quite likely; subjects are easily sensitized by pre-measures. Even more crudely, it is frequently difficult to locate anything like a meaningful control group, let alone establish its equivalence. Finally, numbers are usually small, and the treatment population is often biased through self-selection.

Thus it is not surprising that perhaps 95 percent of all treatment efforts go unstudied, and that even the 5 percent typically show serious defects in design, measurement, or data analysis stemming from insufficient attention to the problems alluded to above. And, methodological problems aside, most treatment studies have a central substantive weakness: being relatively atheoretical, they lead to no coherent additions to either science or practice. The variables presumed to explain the amounts of change in subjects are rarely specified, and change processes during treatment are hardly ever studied.[94]

A substantial catalog of additional difficulties provides detailed support for Miles's summary. This catalog is not exhaustive. But it does establish the awesome scope of establishing the interaction of T-Group effects; and the catalog also sketches the progress made thus far. Eight factors that complicate the design and execution of research, as well as its interpretation, are detailed.

First, adequate T-Group research must deal with a broad phenomenal range. This range includes: primary intrapsychic phenomena such as emotions, reactions, and feelings; attitudes and values which have both affective and intellectual components; and overt behaviors, which can be variously in-phase with emotional or intellectual states. The implied matrix of effects is a formidable one.

A sharp contrast is rather more than less appropriate. Thus far, re-

---

94. Quoted in Batchelder and Hardy, *op. cit.,* p. 40.

search has been focused on the first two phenomenal levels.[95] The major payoff of T-Grouping must eventually come via changes in behavior, however. The existing bias of research—however understandable or convenient—may be awkward. At the very least, that bias discourages the confrontation of a critical issue, the value of alternative models for change. Peter Lenrow, for example, contrasts two such models:

> One view proposes that if you want someone to change a generalized mode of behavior you should punish him when he engages in any of these behaviors and reward him (e.g., with approval and privileges) when he uses acceptable substitutes. The other view proposes that any important mode of behavior to be changed requires first changing the person's way of thinking and feeling about himself and his situations. Changes in the undesirable behaviors will then occur pretty much by themselves as the person tries to make his behavior consistent with the new attitudes.[96]

This theoretical issue has eminently practical aspects. For one thing, judging the success of T-Groups in inducing change will depend in critical ways on one's basic theory of change.

Second, T-Group effects must be considered in terms of individuals as well as averages or medians, but the typical research focus has been on whether a sensitivity training experience makes a difference for an entire T-Group. Exceptions to this generalization do exist,[97] but the overall state of the research literature is such that it may hide significant interactions between individual differences and specific training techniques. Individuals may so differ, for example, that most participants will profit from T-Grouping, some few will have achieved such a level of interpersonal competence that the T-Group experience had little impact, and perhaps even some others are harmed by it. Interactions between individual differences and training outcomes plague the design and interpretation of T-Group research.[98] Thus participants may differ in their initial level of some critical variable. There is no reason why

---

95. Clayton P. Alderfer and Thomas M. Lodahl, "A Quasi-Experiment on the Use of Experiential Methods in the Classroom," *Journal of Applied Behavioral Science,* Vol. 7 (January, 1971), p. 44.
96. Peter B. Lenrow, "A Framework for Planning Behavior Change in Juvenile Offenders," *Journal of Applied Behavioral Science,* Vol. 2 (July, 1966), pp. 290–91.
97. Yalom and Lieberman, *op. cit.,* and Warren G. Bennis, Richard Burke, Henry Cutter, Herbert Harrington, and Joyce Hoffman, "A Note on Some Problems of Measurement and Prediction in a Training Group," *Group Psychotherapy,* Vol. 10 (December, 1957), pp. 328–41.
98. Campbell and Dunnette, "Effectiveness of T-Group Experiences," p. 96.

similar learning outcomes should be experienced by individuals who enter a T-Group with such diverse attributes.[99]

Third, relatedly, research on T-Groups must discriminate intervening conditions as well as outcomes. The dominant focus has been on outcomes, however. For example, a typical design calls for pre- and post-training comparisons of the congruence of self-images with the self as perceived by others. Assume that the post-training score is greater, on the average. This is interesting information, but no more meaningful than if decreased scores had been observed, on balance. Specifically, confidence in any observed regularities increases only as it is consistent with intervening conditions. For example, increases in the congruence of self-image and the image held by others should be associated with high versus low differences in the feedback received by specific T-Group members. To merely note that increases in congruence occur in T-Groups is not very enlightening, if only because no increases can be expected under some conditions. However, few studies deal with such intervening conditions.[100]

Fourth, there is no necessary reason to expect similar outcomes from even two T-Groups, let alone from the diverse range of trainer styles that may be distinguished.[101] That is, learning designs differ markedly, and no adequate typology yet exists for classifying group experiences. Relatedly, trainer variations patently have major impact on participant learning.[102] But the research technology is not yet available to assess trainer style, which could then be treated as an independent or intervening variable that could be related to specific training outcomes.[103]

That a T-Group is not necessarily a T-Group poses clear problems for the design of research, and even more vexing ones for the interpretation of findings. For example, what does it mean if two studies show self-esteem is raised in one T-Group and lowered in another? Is it that the technology has no predictable effect on that variable? Or is it that the designs of the two T-Groups differed enough to generate the contrary outcomes, even though all other things were more-or-less equal?

---

99. For one case in point, see Eugene B. Nadler and Stephen L. Fink, "Impact of Laboratory Training on Sociopolitical Ideology," *Journal of Applied Behavioral Science,* Vol. 6 (January, 1970), esp. pp. 79, 86–87.

100. John R. P. French, Jr., John J. Sherwood, and David L. Bradford, "Change in Self-Identity in a Management Training Conference," *Journal of Applied Behavioral Science,* Vol. 2 (April, 1966), pp. 210–18.

101. Roger Harrison, "Research on Human Relations Training: Design and Interpretation," *Journal of Applied Behavioral Science,* Vol. 7 (January, 1971), pp. 79–80.

102. Yalom and Lieberman, *op. cit.;* and Samuel A. Culbert, "Trainer Self-Disclosure and Member Growth," pp. 47–73.

103. Lee G. Bolman, "The Effects of Variations in Educator Behavior on the Learning Process in Laboratory Human Relations Education" (Ph.D. diss., Yale University, 1968), and his "Some Effects of Trainers on Their T Groups," *Journal of Applied Behavioral Science,* Vol. 7 (May, 1971), pp. 309–26.

The issues involving T-Group outcomes are exceedingly subtle for another reason. On many dimensions, that is, no standardized learning outcome can be expected. The learning will depend on what the learners bring with them to the T-Group. As Douglas Bunker explains:

> A close look at some of the original data indicates that some subjects are perceived by their describers as having changed adaptively in the direction of an increase in assertive behavior and more willingness to take a stand; while other subjects are approvingly described as having decreased their aggressive behavior and become more sensitive to others' feelings. These findings indicate that in the training programs studied there is no standard learning outcome and no stereotyped ideal toward which conformity is induced.[104]

Fifth, T-Group research has relied heavily on self-reports by participants, which imply multiple methodological problems. For example, participants may merely create self-reports that they believe will satisfy the researcher.[105] Similarly, some data indicate that others may be better observers of a person's behavior than he is himself.[106]

Such possibilities patently make it difficult to interpret much T-Group research and also encourage the use of measures other than self-reports. For example, so-called unobtrusive measures[107] at once avoid issues of participant differences in perceptual accuracy and, even more important, they do not intrude into the flow of interaction. In any case, both self-reports and reports by others are necessary to establish the full range of T-Group effects.

Sixth, T-Group research must distinguish what may be called "interim effects" from "terminal effects." Little relevant research is available, however.[108]

---

104. Douglas R. Bunker, "Individual Applications of Laboratory Training," *Journal of Applied Behavioral Science,* Vol. 1 (April, 1965), p. 142.
105. Stanley Milgram, "Some Conditions of Obedience and Disobedience to Authority," *Human Relations,* Vol. 18 (1965), pp. 57–76, suggests the great lengths to which participants might go to please (obey) an authority figure like an experimenter.
106. Iain Mangham and Cary L. Cooper, "The Impact of T-Groups on Managerial Behavior," *Journal of Management Studies,* Vol. 6 (February, 1969), p. 56.
107. Eugene J. Webb, Donald T. Campbell, Richard D. Schwartz, and Lee Sechrest, *Unobtrusive Measures: Nonreactive Research in the Social Sciences* (Chicago: Rand McNally & Co., 1966).
108. Paul C. Buchanan, "Laboratory Training and Organization Development," *Administrative Science Quarterly,* Vol. 14 (September, 1969), p. 470. For a few exceptions, see George Psathas and Ronald Hardert, "Trainer Interventions and Normative Patterns in the T-Group," *Journal of Applied Behavioral Science,* Vol. 2 (April, 1966), pp. 149–69; Herbert A. Thelen and Watson Dickerman, "Stereotypes and Growth of Groups," *Educational Leadership,* Vol. 6 (February, 1949), pp. 309–16; Martin Lakin and Robert C. Carlson, "Participant Perception of Group Process in Group Sensitivity Training," *International Journal of Group*

A number of factors suggest this gap in research is significant. As Section A, Part I suggests, for example, there is real reason to believe that T-Group learning may occur in more-or-less distinct phases, such as unfreezing, change, and refreezing. Especially given the bias toward studying outcomes as opposed to intervening processes, the possibility of phaselike learning presents formidable barriers to the design and interpretation of T-Group research. As Roger Harrison notes:

> As yet no one knows how long the phases may be expected to last nor how to identify, in practice, the transition from one to another. What is clear, however, is that if this model is correct the phase a person is in makes a great deal of difference in the kind of changes we should look for as training outcomes. What we usually mean when we talk about [T-Group] outcomes is the "refrozen" stage, in which the individual has integrated and stabilized new patterns of cognition, perception, and behavior.[109]

The implications of the notion of stages or phases of development may be profound for the prediction of effects, as well as for the interpretation of the results of specific studies. For example, the findings of individual studies may speak more to the issue of when post-treatment effects were observed than to the efficacy of the T-Group technology. Interestingly, if not conclusively, a number of studies indicate an appreciable time lag between the end of a T-Group experience and the eventual appearance of several terminal learnings associated with the refrozen state.[110]

Seventh, a mature research literature on T-Group effects would encompass "internal" and "external" measures. Internal criteria are measures linked directly to the content and processes of the sensitivity training; external criteria are linked directly to performance in some contexts outside of the training environment.

Despite this coessentiality in understanding T-Group effects, internal criteria have received the bulk of the research attention.[111] This imbalance is awkward.

Eighth, T-Group research is characterized by problems in meeting accepted scientific standards for evaluating training outcomes. For example, many T-Group studies lack a "control" or "comparison" group,

Psychotherapy, Vol. 14 (January, 1964), pp. 116–22; Richard D. Mann, *Interpersonal Styles and Group Development* (New York: John Wiley & Sons, 1967); and Bernard Lubin and Marvin Zuckerman, "Affective and Perceptual Cognitive Patterns in Sensitivity Training Groups," *Psychological Reports,* Vol. 21 (1967), pp. 365–76.

109. Harrison, "Problems in the Design and Interpretation of Research," pp. 466–67.
110. Roger Harrison, "Cognitive Change and Participation in a Sensitivity Training Laboratory," *Journal of Consulting Psychology,* Vol. 30 (December, 1966), pp. 517–20.
111. Campbell and Dunnette, "Effectiveness of T-Group Experiences," p. 891.

which is a central element of scientific technology. As Dunnette and Campbell note:

> . . . measured changes shown by the trainees between pre- and post-training periods should be compared with changes, if any, occurring in a so-called control group of similar, but untrained persons. Using control groups is the only way to assure that changes observed in the experimental (or trainee) groups are actually the result of training procedures instead of possible artifactual effects—such as the mere passage of time, poor reliability of measures, Hawthorne effects, or other spurious components.[112]

Explaining the lack of control groups is an exercise in multiple possibilities. Several garden-variety factors contribute to this methodological vulnerability of most T-Group research. These factors include: the small numbers of participants in any single T-Group or collection of T-Groups exposed to the same training design and staff; the awkwardness or the impossibility of finding groups for purposes of comparison; the dominant early concern with developing the T-Group as a vehicle for helping; and the early emphasis on innovations that emotionally heighten the T-Group experience, as compared to the paucity of innovations that cognitively organize and comprehend the experience. Beyond these basics, many other factors contribute to the lack of control groups in T-Group research. Some argue that in-depth analysis of individual cases has a higher priority in early research, for example. Others note that such elements as control groups derive from physical science; such students also argue that the application of natural-science technology in the behavioral sciences can be self-defeating in complex ways.[113]

Whatever the reasons for the common lack of control groups, however, the prime consequence is clear and direct. The interpretation of the results of studies of T-Group effects is a chancy business in their absence.

c. The Record of Growth-Oriented Effects: A Selective Catalog of Common Effects in T-Groups

In the context of these major factors affecting the design and interpretation of the findings of T-Group research, this section reviews some common effects of the technology. Fortunately, this section can rely on

---

112. Dunnette and Campbell, "Laboratory Education," p. 8.
113. See, especially, Chris Argyris, "Issues in Evaluating Laboratory Education," *Industrial Relations,* Vol. 8 (October, 1968), pp. 28–40, and "Some Unintended Consequences of Rigorous Research," *Psychological Bulletin,* Vol. 70, No. 3 (1968), pp. 185–97.

major help.[114] T-Group research has been reviewed recently in at least eight major sources, and those reviews do multiple duty here. Thus the reviews permit unusual confidence in the broad thrust and details of the summary below, and they also permit brevity and selectivity here, as this section at once relies on and supplements the existing critical literature.

Overall, the evaluation of T-Group effects has a schizoid quality. Despite methodological problems and the difficulty of getting at many central research questions, most observers conclude with Paul Buchanan that on balance the "evidence rather clearly indicates that laboratory training has a predictable and significant impact on most participants. . . ."[115] On the other hand, agreement becomes more tentative on the crucial issue of what specific *and* lasting behavioral changes are generated by T-Groups. Dunnette is both a critical and a sympathetic commentator on this point. He notes:

> In spite of our disenchantment with the way studies have been done, we have concluded that T-Group training probably does induce behavioral changes in the back-home setting; however, any specification of the nature of these changes and their antecedents must be an article of faith rather than a conclusion based upon a firm foundation of empirical evidence.[116]

Something like a sense of tentative optimism characterizes this section, consequently. Some central tendencies are beginning to emerge from research on T-Group effects, that is, despite the huge potential for confounding both the design of studies and the interpretation of findings which was sketched above. The ambitions, assumptions, and interactions

---

114. For a convenient introduction to these effects, see Rogers, *Carl Rogers on Encounter Groups*, pp. 70–84. For several major summaries of the research literature, see Dorothy Stock, "A Survey of Research on T-Groups," in Leland P. Bradford, Jack R. Gibb, and Kenneth D. Benne (eds.), *T-Group Theory and Laboratory Method* (New York: John Wiley & Sons, 1964), pp. 395–441; Paul C. Buchanan, "Evaluating the Effectiveness of Laboratory Training in Industry," in *Explorations in Human Relations Training and Research*, No. 1 (Washington, D.C.: National Training Laboratories—National Education Association, 1965); Robert J. House, "T-Group Education and Leadership Effectiveness: A Review of the Literature and a Critical Evaluation," *Personnel Psychology*, Vol. 20 (Spring, 1967), pp. 1–32; Campbell and Dunnette, "Effectiveness of T-Group Experiences," pp. 73–105; Dunnette and Campbell, "Laboratory Education"; Buchanan, "Laboratory Training and Organization Development"; Mangham and Cooper, "The Impact of T-Groups on Managerial Behavior"; Cary L. Cooper and Iain L. Mangham, "T-Group Training Before and After," *Journal of Management Studies*, Vol. 7 (May, 1970), pp. 224–39; Jack R. Gibb, "The Effects of Human Relations Training," in A. E. Bergin and S. L. Garfield (eds.), *Handbook of Psychotherapy and Behavior Change* (New York: John Wiley & Sons, 1971); and Martin Lakin, *Interpersonal Encounter* (New York: McGraw-Hill Book Co., 1972), pp. 181–207.
115. Buchanan, "Evaluating the Effectiveness of Laboratory Training," p. 1.
116. Marvin D. Dunnette, "People Feeling: Joy, More Joy, and the 'Slough of Despond,'" *Journal of Applied Behavioral Science*, Vol. 5 (January, 1969), p. 29.

detailed above, on the face of it, would seem capable of masking even dominant effects. However, some patterns of T-Group effects seem marked enough to be discernible even among that myriad of factors that could mask any effects or that could cause T-Group effects to vary, willy-nilly. This suggests an emergence of dominant patterns from still-gross research designs.

Six conclusions summarize some major central tendencies that seem emergent in T-Group research.

Behavioral Change a Consequence

Behavioral change is a common consequence of participation in a T-Group experience, not only during the experience but also extending beyond it. At the anecdotal level, for example, numerous testimonials attest to the massive and dramatic impacts many participants attribute to T-Groups.[117] The bulk of these testimonials, at least, has to be impressive.

Several similarly designed studies[118] provide data consistent with these personal testimonials about the efficacy of T-Groups. Consider a simple example. Matthew B. Miles did a follow-up study of 34 school principals after they had a two-week experience in a T-Group.[119] He was interested in changes in job-related behaviors in the 8–10-month period following the training. The trained principals were compared with two untrained control groups, one nominated by the trained persons and a second which was chosen at random. All three groups completed an open-ended questionnaire soliciting information about behavioral changes on the job, and their self-reports were compared with descriptions provided by at least six of their colleagues. In terms of gross changes, the comparisons clearly favored the trained principals. In sum, the three groups had these significantly different proportions of change:

---

117. Batchelder and Hardy, *op. cit.,* pp. 53–69.
118. J. B. Boyd and J. D. Ellis, *Findings of Research into Senior Management Seminars* (Toronto, Canada: Personnel Research Department, The Hydro-Electric Power Commission of Ontario, 1962); Bunker, *op. cit.;* Matthew B. Miles, "Changes during and following Laboratory Training," *Journal of Applied Behavioral Science,* Vol. 1 (July, 1965), pp. 215–43; William J. Underwood, "Evaluation of a Laboratory Method of Training," *Journal of the American Society of Training Directors,* Vol. 19 (January, 1965), pp. 34–40; Douglas R. Bunker and Eric S. Knowles, "Comparison of Behavioral Changes Resulting from Human Relations Training Laboratories of Different Lengths," *Journal of Applied Behavioral Science,* Vol. 3 (October, 1967), pp. 505–23; Michael I. Valiquet, "Individual Change in a Management Development Program," *Journal of Applied Behavioral Science,* Vol. 4 (July, 1968), pp. 313–26; and David Moscow, "T-Group Training in the Netherlands," *Journal of Applied Behavioral Science,* Vol. 7 (July, 1971), esp. pp. 434–37.
119. Miles, *op. cit.,* esp. pp. 225–26.

Trained Group	Nominated Control Group	Random Control Group
73%	29%	17%

The specific changes tended to be of anticipated kinds. They included enhanced skills in communication, greater sensitivity to the needs of others, and greater awareness of and skills relevant to socioemotional processes as well as task.

The literature, on balance, supports Miles's findings. Some contrary research exists,[120] and even Miles's total findings are inconsistent.[121] But a variety of replicatory studies[122] validates the central thrust of the summary above. This balance of research led Iain Mangham and Cary Cooper to three conclusions:[123]

- Significantly more changes tend to be attributed to those who experienced a T-Group than to untrained comparison groups.
- Observers tend to agree about the kind and direction of these changes: "improved skills in diagnosing individual and group behavior, clear communication, greater tolerance and consideration, and greater action skill and flexibility."
- The changes tended to last for some substantial time after training, a year or so, beyond which time reports conflict about whether a learning fadeout tends to occur.

Such studies also impressed Robert J. House, who was taken by the lack of contradiction in six studies like the one briefly described and by their relative methodological sophistication. He concludes:

These findings take on special significance when one considers the rigor with which the studies were conducted. All of the studies employed control groups to discount the effects of factors other than the T-Group experience. All of the evidence is based on observations of the behavior of the participants in the actual job situation. No reliance is placed on participant response; rather, evidence is collected from those having frequent contact with the participant in his normal work activities. The source of the evidence is especially important because of

---

120. W. W. Wolfe, "A Study of a Laboratory Approach to In-Service Development Programmes for School Administrators and Supervisors" (Ph.D. diss., University of Texas, 1965).
121. Miles reported no change on several instruments on which changes might have been expected, the Ohio State Leader Description Questionnaire and the Group Participation Scale.
122. See Footnote 118 above; and D. A. Geitgey, "A Study of Some Effects of Sensitivity Training on the Performance of Students in Associate Degree Programs of Nursing Education" (Ph.D. diss., University of California at Los Angeles, 1966).
123. Mangham and Cooper, "The Impact of T-Groups on Managerial Behavior," p. 72.

the possibility of bias resulting from self descriptions of participants.[124]

A Vehicle for Learning

Some evidence suggests that the T-Group is an unusually powerful and perhaps unique vehicle for learning, that is, for inducing behavioral change. A variety of studies support this summary conclusion. For example, J. B. Boyd and J. D. Ellis compared two training experiences, one a T-Group and the other a lecture-discussion against a nontrained, matched control group.[125] Six weeks and six months after completion of the training, the authors interviewed five sources—the person's super-

Table 1. Summary Data concerning Impact of Two Training Technologies

	T-Group (N = 42)	Lecture-Discussion (N = 10)	Nontrained Controls (N = 12)
Number of observers reporting positive changes	153.5	29	24
Number of observers reporting negative changes	9.5	0	2
Net number of observers reporting positive changes	144	29	22
Number of observers reporting no change	61	27	39
Net percentage of observers reporting positive changes	70%	52%	36%

Source: Based on Iain Mangham and Cary L. Cooper, "The Impact of T-Groups on Managerial Behavior," *Journal of Management Studies*, Vol. 6 (February, 1969), p. 62.

visor, two peers, and two subordinates. The purpose was to determine whether participants had changed after the training and, if so, whether the changes persisted. Table 1 summarizes some comparative data from an analysis of interview data, which were consistent with results obtained at the same time from an objective measuring device, "Manager Behavior Description." The data in Table 1 favor the T-Group less than results reported by Argyris in a much more complicated comparative study of the same two approaches to training.[126]

The basis of the reported advantage of the T-Group technology seems clear enough. The heart of that technology is in small-group dy-

124. House, *op. cit.*, p. 450.
125. Boyd and Ellis, *op. cit.*
126. Chris Argyris, "Explorations in Interpersonal Competence—II," *Journal of Applied Behavioral Science*, Vol. 1 (July, 1965), pp. 255–69.

namics, in high levels of participation, involvement, and communication. As Mangham and Cooper conclude:

> . . . this unusually high degree of participation seems to have tremendous potential advantage over other training methods for producing real and lasting changes in attitudes and behavior. It is certainly true that most studies report few attitudinal or behavioral changes for participants who show *low* involvement in training activities. Potentially, therefore, laboratory education has the capacity to change participants, and both self-report and more objective measures confirm the *immediate* efficacy of the technique.[127]

No Change in Basic Personality Traits

The changes typically following T-Group experiences cannot be characterized as basic personality alteration. The available research seems clear on the point. Although shifts have been observed along broad dimensions tapped by projective techniques and standardized personality measures,[128] there is no evidence of change in basic personality traits.[129] For example, Harold Kassarjian used the I-O Social Preference Scale—which has proved useful in other research—to determine whether T-Grouping would change a fundamental orientation in participants—the predisposition to be inner-directed or other-directed. The I-O Scale revealed no short-run shifts one way or the other, when trained participants were compared to controls on two administrations of the scale before and after T-Group training. The design called for one T-Group session per week over some 15 weeks. Agreement also seems to exist about why such changes in personality traits or character structure should not be expected. As Kassarjian concludes: "to expect that a single training experience over a . . . 15 week period would create a measurable change in the basic underlying social character of a person that has taken twenty to forty years to instill, may well be too much to expect. . . ."[130]

127. Mangham and Cooper, "The Impact of T-Groups on Managerial Behavior," p. 54.
128. C. N. Zirnet and H. J. Fine, "Personality Changes with A Group Therapeutic Experience in a Human Relations Seminar," *Journal of Abnormal and Social Psychology*, Vol. 51 (July, 1955), pp. 68–73. See also Frederick J. Axelberd, "Effects of Growth Groups on Self Concept as Measured by the Tennessee Self Concept Scale" (Paper presented at National Convention, American Personnel and Guidance Association, New Orleans, La., 1970).
129. J. Kernan, "Laboratory Human Relations Training: Its Effect on the Personality of Supervisory Engineers" (Ph.D., diss., New York University, 1963).
130. Harold H. Kassarjian, "A Study of Riesman's Theory of Social Character," *Sociometry*, Vol. 25 (1962), pp. 213–20; and "Social Character and Sensitivity Training," *Journal of Applied Behavioral Science*, Vol. 1 (October, 1965), pp. 433–40.

Rather than expecting basic personality change as a result of T-Group training, to approach the present point from another perspective, a more realistic view contains at least three emphases. *First,* T-Group training encourages experimentation with new behaviors, attitudes, or values, or the greater activation of behaviors that are of relatively low incidence in a participant's normal life space. That experimentation may enlarge a participant's latent repertoire, as it were, without affecting his basic personality traits or orientations or even changing his behavior outside the T-Group. Moreover, the results of that experimentation or heightened activation in the T-Group might be extremely significant for the learner. The demonstrated *capacity* to quickly establish warm interpersonal relationships with strangers in a T-Group, for example, can be very important to some participants even if they henceforth do not change one whit their frequency of seeking or establishing such relationships after the T-Group. This is especially the case for those whose life situations are such that they have been more instrumentally oriented, and those who might even have begun to question their ability to develop strong affective ties. The potential for such effects in T-Groups is substantial for many participants. As Betty Meador notes of her research on developmental processes in a small population, "It is apparent that these individuals obtained a level of relating to each other not characteristic of ordinary life."[131]

Second, T-Group training seems to alter the distribution of the performance of old behaviors, attitudes, or values, with general increases in some behaviors and decreases in others. Thus a person might become somewhat more aware of his feelings and somewhat less distrustful of the motives of others. Such redistributions, or changes in the probability of occurrence, may or may not show up as major differences on narrow behavioral or attitudinal measures. In either case, however, they would not be likely to make much of a dent in measures of basic personality traits or orientations. A number of these narrower changes are reviewed briefly below.

Third, T-Group effects can be situation-specific. That is, new behaviors, attitudes, or values may be developed, and the incidence of the old may change substantially. But these changes will be reflected only in some situations. This seems to have been a major consequence of cousin T-Groups at Alcan:Canada, for example, where learning was transferred with some frequency to the trainee's family but less so to his worksite. The individual becomes a more complex and perhaps adaptive actor as his situation-specificity increases, but his basic personality traits or character patterns are not likely to be modified significantly. Indeed, the emerging view of stranger and cousin groups with respect to transfer

131. Betty Meador, "An Analysis of Process Movement in a Basic Encounter Group" (Ph.D. diss., U.S. International University, 1969).

of learning is that they are a kind of "I have been to the top of the mountain" experience. That is, the participant in a stranger or a cousin T-Group experience is exposed to an alternative set of values that he might possibly apply at nontraining sites, and he can also experiment in the T-Group with behaviors, attitudes, and values appropriate for that alternative social order. From this perspective, the stranger T-Group experience is basically relevant to only a part of the total change process. As Roger Harrison and Barry Oshry observe:

> Practitioners of laboratory training have been coming to see the residential T-Group laboratory as primarily an unfreezing experience rather than one which, by itself, induces permanent change in organizational behavior. Consultants have in the past few years been developing an increased respect for the influence of organizational norms and of the matrices of mutual expectations among work associates over behavior. These norms and mutual expectations seem to stabilize behavior against attempts at change. Increasingly, consultants are coming to see laboratories as producing an expanded awareness of alternatives in interpersonal relationships and perhaps an increased level of aspiration for their quality, but are not relying on the T-Group laboratory alone for lasting change in work relationships. Rather they are moving towards following-up such laboratory experiences with on-the-job training, preferably with so-called "family groups" where persons who work together explore the interpersonal processes of their relationships in a T-Group setting. In these experiences, the consequences of interpersonal relationships for day-to-day decision-making, supervision, communication, etc., can be explored in a realistic framework.[132]

In this view, the T-Group participant becomes more differentiated, latently, even though no changes in some nontraining loci may be observable. Basic personality change would tend to occur, in this view, only in the long run as nontraining loci became sufficiently accepting of the aspects of the Self that were differentiated by the T-Group experience.

Characteristic Specific Outcomes

Evidence implies that a family of more-or-less specific outcomes is characteristic of T-Group experiences. Four kinds of outcomes illustrate the broader range.

---

132. Roger Harrison and Barry I. Oshry, "The Impact of Laboratory Training on Organizational Behavior: Methodology and Results," mimeographed. Quoted in Batchelder and Hardy, *op. cit.*, pp. 46–47.

First, T-Group training is characterized by tendencies toward changes in a variety of attitudes or attributes relevant to interpersonal and intergroup relations. These changes include:

- increased acceptance of self[133]
- increased acceptance of others[134]
- increased sensitivity to and tolerance for differences in others[135]
- a greater openness and receptivity[136]
- enhanced open-mindedness, reduced dogmatism[137]

These effects imply a central tendency which is consistent with the goals of the laboratory approach, and their significance is enhanced by some research dealing with these effects integratively rather than as individual outcomes. For example, one study accepted Robert Kahn's challenge that: "The theory of T-Groups implies that reduction in prejudice should be one of the results of a general increase in sensitivity to the needs of others and insight into one's motives and behavior as it affects others. No research is available, however, to test this prediction."[138] Irwin Rubin focused on one aspect of Kahn's suggestion by investigating a two-phase proposition: that a T-Group experience would tend to increase a person's self-acceptance, and that increases in self-acceptance would have the effect of raising a person's acceptance of others.[139] Rubin's findings were generally positive. That is, self-acceptance increased for 23 of 38 T-Group participants in Rubin's sample. Six other participants did not change, and nine decreased in self-acceptance, as Rubin measured it. However, changes in acceptance of others seemed less flexible, almost as if there were a threshold effect before increases in self-acceptance would trigger increases in acceptance of others. Only those who increased their self-acceptance a great deal increased their accept-

---

133. Bunker, *op. cit.;* David R. Peters, "Identification and Personal Change in Laboratory Training Groups" (Ph.D. diss., Massachusetts Institute of Technology, 1966) ; and Irwin Rubin, "The Reduction of Prejudice through Laboratory Training," *Journal of Applied Behavioral Science,* Vol. 3 (January, 1967) , pp. 29–50.

134. Bunker, *op. cit.,* and Rubin, *op. cit.*

135. Cary L. Cooper, "T-Group Training and Self-Actualization," *Psychological Reports,* Vol. 28 (1971) , pp. 391–94.

136. Lawrence N. Solomon, Betty Berzon, and David P. Davis, "A Personal Growth Program for Self-Directed Groups," *Journal of Applied Behavioral Science,* Vol. 6 (December, 1970) , pp. 427–51; Bunker, *op. cit.,* pp. 142–43; and Argyris, "Explorations in Interpersonal Competence—II," pp. 259–61.

137. Franklyn S. Haiman, "Effects of Training in Group Processes on Open-Mindedness," *Journal of Communication,* Vol. 13 (December, 1963) , pp. 236–45; and Nadler and Fink, *op. cit.*
   For a study which did not find such effects, see Kernan, *op. cit.*

138. Robert Kahn, "Aspiration and Fulfillment: Themes for Studies of Group Relations" (unpublished MS, University of Michigan, 1963) , p. 14.

139. Rubin, *op. cit.*

ance of others. Neither modest nor negative changes in self-acceptance were associated with increased acceptance of others.

This central tendency has a softness at the edges, at least. Methodological concerns encourage further research, for example. Of especial concern is the possibility that other training technologies might have induced similar outcomes. As Cooper and Mangham conclude, then: "Further research using comparison groups, that is, groups trained by some other methods, should be encouraged to discount [this] possibility."[140]

Second, T-Group training tends to reduce extreme attitudes or behaviors. In some cases, this is a matter of rounding off some of the rough edges; in other cases, it is a matter of building up responses that occur too infrequently. For example, the talkative boor is likely to reduce his extreme behavior as a result of a T-Group experience and begin to talk more selectively, and the underparticipator is likely to be encouraged to increase his output by fellow T-Group members. Similarly, an unassertive person is likely to reduce that extreme behavior by becoming somewhat more assertive, and a domineering T-Group member is likely to get feedback that encourages moderation on his part. As Harrison concludes, this view of the T-Group as moderating attitudinal and behavioral extremes cuts two ways:

> [It sees] the T-Group as the place where sharp edges are rubbed off people. Alternatively, we may say that the T-Group is a place where each individual is encouraged to explore and express the latent and underdeveloped aspects of himself. From the standpoint of experimental design, these both come to much the same thing . . . it is noteworthy that there is not, to the author's knowledge, any study which has used this method which has failed to show significant results. The individual growth point of view seems to "fit" the laboratory training process very well.[141]

A substantial number of studies establish such an effect,[142] if with varying degrees of methodological elegance. Deviant findings also exist.[143] Although they are in a definite minority, truth may be theirs. P. B. Smith provides a particularly nice demonstration of the moderating powers of

140. Cooper and Mangham, "T-Group Training," p. 236.
141. Harrison, "Research on Human Relations Training," p. 78.
142. Peter B. Smith, "Attitude Changes Associated with Training in Human Relations," *British Journal of Social and Clinical Psychology,* Vol. 3 (June, 1964), pp. 104–13; William C. Schutz and Vernon L. Allen, "The Effects of a T-Group Laboratory on Interpersonal Behavior," *Journal of Applied Behavioral Science,* Vol. 2 (July, 1966), pp. 265–86; and Nadler and Fink, *op. cit.*
143. R. Meigniez, *Evaluation de Resultats de la Formation* (Paris: L'Association Francaise pour l'Accroissement de la Productivite, 1961).

the T-Group. He focused on attitudes toward affection and control in a population of 108 managers, before and after T-Group training, using six control groups. Although controls did not change, T-Group participants tended to decrease markedly the overall disparity between their own behavioral tendencies and the behaviors they desired from others. The largest decreases in disparity, consistently, were experienced by those participants who initially described themselves as treating others with high control and low affection, but who also described themselves as preferring behaviors from others that were low on control and high on affection.

Such findings about reductions in extreme behaviors or attitudes generate dual reactions. One reaction is very supportive of the T-Group technology. "These changes are consonant with the aims of the T-Group method," as Campbell and Dunnette conclude. But cautions are also appropriate. The same two authors stress several problems with interpreting much research of this genre:[144]

> There were no comparison groups, and the strong possibility that any one of a number of other human-relations training methods would produce similar results cannot be entirely discounted. Also, the items appeared to be geared to the stated goals and content of the training program. Thus, the "correct" answer was apparent to the respondent, and a positive response bias may have been elicited which would account for the results.

Third, T-Group training is characterized by complex and but dimly understood changes related to interpersonal perception. At least three varieties of research must be distinguished.

Measuring Skill in Interpersonal Perception. A major goal of the T-Group technology involves increased skill and accuracy in interpersonal perception, of seeing the Other for what he is. Research has not been able to establish specific and consistent effects of this kind, however. As Campbell and Dunnette conclude: ". . . the studies incorporating a measure of how well an individual can predict the attitudes and values of others before and after T-Group training have yielded largely negative results."[145] This conclusion must be balanced by at least two kinds of data. Thus some research has isolated a broad range of expected effects. Richard L. Burke and Warren G. Bennis summarize the results of one such study in these expansive terms:

> Members of T-Groups during the course of their training experience became more satisfied in their perception of self, moved their actual percepts in the direction of their ideal, be-

144. Campbell and Dunnette, "Effectiveness of T-Group Experiences in Managerial Training and Development," p. 94.
145. *Ibid.,* p. 91.

came, at least by certain measures, more congruent in their perception of others, and came to see others more as the other individuals see themselves. Results lend some support to the claims of human relations practitioners that participation in a training group can be beneficial in re-orienting perceptions of others, and that the training group, and the concept of total laboratory atmosphere, is a powerful medium of change.[146]

In addition, T-Group participants commonly report having experienced such effects.

Measuring Perception of Reality. Research suggests that major shifts tend to occur in how T-Group participants perceive reality after training, in their cognitive style, as compared to before. One approach, for example, requires two descriptions of some unresolved interpersonal problem at work, one pre-training and the second following it. The post-training descriptions reflect a perceptual pattern consistent with the goals of the laboratory approach, e.g., after training, participants see more clear connections between the satisfaction of interpersonal needs and problem solving.[147] The effects are not universal,[148] but they are dominant.

Measuring Clarity of Self-Perception. On balance, research does seem to indicate that the clarity of self-perception tends to increase as a result of T-Group training. For example, David Peters[149] reports a controlled study in which the discrepancy between a person's actual self and his ideal self decreased as a result of T-Group training. Basically, the changes in discrepancy resulted from changes, following training, in a person's perceptions of his actual self. This finding supports the thrust of a number of other studies.[150] However, it does not agree with the in-

---

146. Richard L. Burke and Warren G. Bennis, "Changes in Perception of Self and Others during Human Relations Training," *Human Relations,* Vol. 14 (February, 1961), pp. 165–82. For opposing results, see Suzanne M. Gassner, Jerome Gold, and Alvin M. Snadowsky, "Changes in the Phenomenal Field as a Result of Human Relations Training," *Journal of Psychology,* Vol. 58 (July, 1964), pp. 33–41.
147. A. G. P. Elliott, "An Experiment in Group Dynamics" (unpublished MS, Simon Engineering Ltd., 1958); Roger Harrison, "The Impact of the Laboratory on Perceptions of Others by the Experimental Group," in Chris Argyris, *Interpersonal Competence and Organizational Effectiveness,* pp. 261–71; Barry I. Oshry and Roger Harrison, "Transfer From Here-and-Now to There-and-Then: Changes in Organizational Problem Diagnosis Stemming from T-Group Training," *Journal of Applied Behavioral Science,* Vol. 2 (April, 1966), pp. 185–98; and Arthur Blumberg and Robert T. Golembiewski, "Laboratory Goal Attainment and the Problem Analysis Questionnaire," *Journal of Applied Behavioral Science,* Vol. 5 (October, 1969), pp. 597–600.
148. Buchanan, "Laboratory Training and Organization Development," p. 472.
149. David R. Peters, "Self-Ideal Congruence as a Function of Human Relations Training," *Journal of Psychology,* Vol. 64 (October, 1970), pp. 199–207.
150. Burke and Bennis, *op. cit.;* and Harry Grater, "Changes in Self and Other Attitudes in a Leadership Training Group," *Personnel and Guidance Journal,* Vol. 37 (March, 1959), pp. 493–96.

significant results of several studies[151] or with the mixed results of a major and well-controlled study.[152]

The research on interpersonal perception implies that the empirical world in this area is excruciatingly complicated. The particularistic bias of much T-Group research makes the worst of this complexity. For example, take for granted that a T-Group experience influences a participant's perception of an interpersonal problem. However, does this reflect a new interpersonal sensitivity; or merely that the participant has learned to talk a new game? Similarly, as Peters observes, it is too simple to assume that phenomenal changes in perception will have a direct relation to enhanced personal functioning.[153]

Fourth, T-Group training is characterized by improvement in a variety of interpersonal skills, such as listening, encouraging the participation of others, enhanced functional or role flexibility, and greater ability to relate in interdependent ways. An impressive array of studies supports this provisional conclusion,[154] albeit as a central tendency and not an inevitability of T-Group training. Boyd and Ellis suggest the range and relative incidence of changes in such interpersonal skills in this summary of their own research:

> One of the most frequently reported changes in behavior for the laboratory group was an increase in listening which accounts for about 12 percent of the reports. By listening is meant paying more attention to what other people are saying, being easier to communicate views to, and so on. Equally frequent is better understanding and better contribution in group situations such as meetings.[155]

Effects Dominant for Average T-Group Members

These effects may seem feeble from one point of view, but the effects are very dominant ones indeed from another. That is, the effects are typically reports of gross tendencies for the average T-Group member of assumedly similar T-Groups. Patently, however, there is no reason to expect that every T-Group or every member should experience the same

151. Bennis *et al., op. cit.*
152. Gassner, Gold, and Snadowsky, *op. cit.*
153. Peters, *op. cit.,* pp. 205–6.
154. Schutz and Allen, *op. cit.;* Bunker and Knowles, *op. cit.;* Geitgey, *op. cit.;* Richard A. Schmuck, "Helping Teachers Improve Classroom Group Processes," *Journal of Applied Behavioral Science,* Vol. 4 (October, 1968), pp. 401–35; and Jay Hall and Martha S. Williams, "Group Dynamics Training and Improved Decision Making," *Journal of Applied Behavioral Science,* Vol. 6 (January, 1970), pp. 39–68.
155. Boyd and Ellis, *op. cit.,* p. 6.

effects. Members and groups can be expected to differ in significant ways that tend to be unspecified in the existing literature. The general failure to specify such differences—or intervening variables—generally would tend to overwhelm or mask any relationships among T-Group effects. From this perspective, then, the central tendencies discussed above suggest that very prominent relationships do in fact exist among T-Group effects, and this prominence will become increasingly manifest as experience is gained about differentiating intervening conditions that are related to different effects.

Available evidence suggests the major role of intervening conditions in dealing with T-Group effects. Five illustrations must suffice.

First, evidence suggests that those persons learn or change most during a laboratory experience, within wide limits, whose attitudes, values, and skills are initially most discrepant from the values of the laboratory approach.[156]

The general failure to specify this intervening variable can have profound effects on the results and interpretations of T-Group research. For example, consider an extreme case in which all or many members of a T-Group had attitudes, values, and behavioral skills that were initially close to laboratory ideals. A T-Group experience might have little impact on such persons. Less extreme distributions of low-discrepancy members also could have major effects on aggregate results, as by keeping changes from reaching usually accepted levels of statistical significance.

Second, evidence suggests that a participant's involvement in a T-Group is a critical determinant of how much he learns or changes.[157] Typically, however, this important intervening linkage is not specified. Those low and high on involvement typically are lumped together in most research to determine, for example, whether the discrepancies between their actual self and ideal self have been reduced. This is ingenuous, even if convenient. For knowledge of actual self will no doubt be influenced by a participant's involvement in a T-Group and, relatedly, by the amount of feedback he receives.[158]

Again, the failure to specify variables that intervene between the T-Group experience and intended outcomes can pose major problems for evaluating research. Depending upon the various distributions of participants high or low on involvement or feedback, different predictions would be appropriate for various outcomes in different T-Groups. All but universally, such distributions are not specified in available research, which frame their hypotheses in terms of what should happen

156. Schutz and Allen, *op. cit.;* and Nadler and Fink, *op. cit.*
157. Bunker, *op. cit.,* p. 145.
158. French, Sherwood, and Bradford, *op. cit.*

in an idealized T-Group setting where all or most assumptions for learning are met. Alternative explanations, consequently, often are appropriate whether the findings of any specific study are expected or surprising.

Third, evidence suggests that T-Group learning depends upon group composition, with change or learning being most likely under two conditions. T-Groups should be so composed that each member can find substantial sources of support from fellow members with similar characteristics, and so composed that each member can also interact with a substantial proportion of fellow members who have contrasting characteristics.[159] The underlying model is one of balance. It seeks to avoid:[160]

- too much stress, which threatens or confuses the individual so that he is unable or unwilling to expose and test his normal interpersonal skills and values
- too much "success," where the individual's preferred skills and values are supported by most or all group members, which would discourage self-analysis and search for alternative skills or values
- inadequate alternative models against which the individual could compare his own skills or values and from which he might choose experimental alternatives to enlarge his skills or values
- inadequate socioemotional support for alternative behavior, as when most or all others want to keep the individual just as he and they are

Or to put it positively, as Harrison has done:

> To facilitate learning, then, we would provide situations in which participants would (1) be stressed by ambiguity and provoked or encouraged to use their preferred styles of perception and behavior to understand and control the interpersonal situation; (2) meet with a degree of failure in this attempt which would stimulate them to (3) search for and consider alternatives; and (4) find support for the exploration and experimentation with the alternatives.[161]

It is not yet certain which characteristics are most central for achieving contrast-*cum*-support, nor is it clear how these characteristics may be best measured. But the evidence suggests strongly that impactful T-Groups may with some facility be formed from individuals with contrasting "cognitive structures." For example, half a T-Group's mem-

---

159. Roger Harrison, "Group Composition Models for Laboratory Design," *Journal of Applied Behavioral Science,* Vol. 1 (October, 1965), pp. 409–32.
160. *Ibid.,* pp. 411–12.
161. *Ibid.,* p. 410.

bership might score high on the need to exercise power[162] or might have a marked tendency toward "concrete thinking."[163] The other half of that T-Group's membership might be composed of individuals with low needs for power or with a tendency toward "abstract thinking."

The research is slim, but that literature does suggest the value of the "balance" rationale sketched above for composition effects. Learning apparently is aided both by contrast in member characteristics and by availability of socioemotional support for all members. Thus heterogeneous versus homogeneous groups seem to induce greater behavioral change;[164] and T-Group learning has been related in subtle ways to the availability of socioemotional support for the learner.[165]

If this jostle/support—or "elaboration of opposites"[166]—approach seems reasonable enough, it is a rare T-Group indeed in which such composition effects are either known or deliberately used to form groups. Hence, again, the interpretation of research is made chancy. At least potentially, for example, members of groups which are "too much alike" could not be expected to learn or change as much as groups with contrasting memberships. Noncontrasting groups would tend to be resource-poor: poor in alternative behaviors, perspectives, stimuli, and so on.

Fourth, evidence suggests that T-Group learning is a function of individual differences. Of course, globally, the inappropriateness of T-Grouping for individuals with major inadequacies in managing stress or anxiety has long been appreciated.[167] Other studies have begun the more delicate task of establishing precise linkages of specific learning outcomes to specific individual differences,[168] as in the case of "work-oriented" versus "person-oriented" participants, or participants who vary on such qualities as their degree of dogmatism. Such work is suggestive of the reasonable impact of individual differences on learning, but it is not yet definitive about the specific patterns.

The influence of individual differences in learning and retention

---

162. Roger Harrison and Bernard Lubin, "Personal Style, Group Composition, and Learning," *Journal of Applied Behavioral Science,* Vol. 1 (July, 1965), pp. 286–94.
163. O. J. Harvey, *Experience, Structure, and Adaptability* (New York: Springer Publishing Co., 1966).
164. Harrison and Lubin, *op. cit.*
165. Yalom and Lieberman, *op. cit.*
166. James V. Clark and Samuel A. Culbert, "Mutually Therapeutic Perception and Self-Awareness in a T-Group," *Journal of Applied Behavioral Science,* Vol. 1 (April, 1965), pp. 180–94.
167. Harrison, "Group Composition Models for Laboratory Design," p. 410.
168. Fred I. Steele, "Personality and 'Laboratory Style,'" *Journal of Applied Behavioral Science,* Vol. 4 (January, 1968), pp. 25–46; Yalom and Lieberman, *op. cit.,* esp. pp. 26–28; and B. Meierhoefer, "The Open and Closed T-Group" (M.S. thesis, Memphis State University, 1970).

should come as no surprise,[169] but these effects commonly are not provided for in research on T-Groups. At times, this neglect reflects a kind of homogeneity hypothesis: that everyone in a T-Group "has the same needs and had to accomplish the same thing in the group."[170] Most often, the neglect has roots in pressing practical considerations. These include: the lack of convenient, valid, and reliable instruments for differentiating personality differences in participants, as well as the enormous problems of classifying T-Groups in terms of differences in their members' characteristics.

Whatever the reasons for the lack of specification of individual differences, however, the outcomes are likely to be the same. Existing relationships are likely to be hidden by confounding variables, and research findings will be difficult to interpret.

Fifth, evidence on the point is mixed, but on balance it appears that at least some learning from T-Groups is not immediately apparent. William Schutz and Vernon Allen, for example, gathered data re participant change at two points in time, two weeks after a T-Group and some six months later. The effects of the training took time to develop, perhaps two to four months.[171] On the other hand, some studies report significant changes that are almost instantaneous.[172]

Lack of knowledge about timing effects clearly complicates the interpretation of research. Consider the question of changes in "fundamental personality traits" as a result of T-Group training. The orthodox position is that such changes cannot really be expected, since it "may be just too much to expect in such a short-lived experience."[173] And so it may be, although the existing research is mixed.[174] It is also possible that research typically does not follow T-Group participants long enough to pick up any fundamental changes which might occur. Perhaps this stretches the point. At least, however, the interpretation of any study reporting no-change effects must be open to the possibility that the effects it sought merely took longer to mature than the period of observation, which is typically a brief one.

---

169. Ernest R. Hilgard, *Theories of Learning* (New York: Appleton-Century-Crofts, 1956), esp. pp. 486–87.
170. Yalom and Lieberman, *op. cit.,* p. 29.
171. Schutz and Allen, *op. cit.* See also J. L. Khanna, "A Discovery Learning Approach to Inservice Training" (Paper presented at Annual Meeting, American Psychological Association, San Francisco, September, 1968); and Jack R. Gibb and Lorraine M. Gibb, "Emergence Therapy," in George M. Gazda (ed.), *Innovations to Group Psychotherapy* (Springfield, Ill.: Charles C Thomas, Publisher, 1968), pp. 96–129.
172. Axelberd, *op. cit.;* and Paul W. Koziey, Joel O. Loken, and James A. Field, "T-Group Influence on Feelings of Alienation," *Journal of Applied Behavioral Science,* Vol. 7 (November, 1971), pp. 724–32.
173. Cooper and Mangham, "T-Group Training," p. 233.
174. *Ibid.,* pp. 233–35.

Permanence of Change in Members

Although T-Group training does commonly induce change in participants, research into the permanence of any changes and their transfer into other environments has yielded mixed results. On the one hand, dramatic illustrations exist which show that even substantial T-Group learning was not carried over into contexts beyond the initial learning environment.[175] On the other hand, studies establish that major transfer did occur and that much of the learning was retained over extended periods.[176]

It seems likely (but hardly certain) that the specification of intervening variables will help increase the consistency of the results reported about transfer and permanency of changes. Overall, we should no more expect that all or even most participants in any specific T-Group would transfer learning into other areas of their life space than we should expect all or many participants to experience the same learnings in more or less the same degree. What little research is available implies that transfer and permanence of learning are more likely under a variety of conditions that seem reasonable enough. Five such conditions suggest the broader range.

First, evidence suggests that transfer of T-Group learning into other contexts is a direct function of the learner's status in that context. To the degree that a person can influence or control an environment, goes the reasonable rationale, so also is he likely to transfer T-Group learning into it. For example, Miles found that high rates of transfer of learning into schools by administrators following a T-Group experience were achieved by participants who had:[177]

- high security, as measured by length of tenure
- high power, as measured by the number of persons supervised
- high autonomy vis-à-vis immediate superiors, as measured by the length of time between required reports

Second, evidence suggests that transfer of T-Group learning into other contexts is more likely if the design of the experience includes an emphasis on application of the training to back-home situations.[178] *Mirabile mirabilibus.* There is little of the earth-shaking in this point.

Third, evidence suggests that the transfer of T-Group learning will depend upon the properties of the context into which it is to be intro-

---

175. Chris Argyris, "T-Groups for Organizational Effectiveness," *Harvard Business Review,* Vol. 42 (March, 1964), p. 71.
176. See also footnote 114 above for some appropriate sources.
177. Miles, *op. cit.,* p. 219.
178. Bunker and Knowles, *op. cit.,* pp. 520–21.

duced. There is no easy way to measure the differences, but transfer is less likely as the culture of the proposed context differs from the values of the laboratory approach. William J. Underwood suggests why this is the case. A number of T-Group trainees in his firm were seen as having changed, but some of them in ways that were interpreted as decreasing their organizational effectiveness. He explains:

> The experimental subjects were reported to show decreased effectiveness in the personal category in a substantial number of reports. An analysis of these changes reveals a heavy emotional loading in the nature of the change. It is speculated that these subjects were venting emotion to a greater degree than usual and to the observers, *operating in a culture which devalues such expression,* this behavior yielded a negative evaluation.[179]

Just such negative reinforcement reduces the probability of transfer to a host organization that is not culturally prepared.

Fourth, evidence suggests that fadeout of transfer of T-Group learning is not so much a matter of lost capacity as it is of suppression. The mobilization of negative reinforcement in an organization encourages the suppression. The evidence is anecdotal, but convincing. Argyris observed such an effect about 10 months after T-Group training,[180] with ex-participants still exercising their retained capacity for openness, but mostly with other ex-participants!

Fifth, evidence suggests that transfer is a direct function of the participant's involvement in the T-Group, of the amount and quality of feedback he receives as well of his reactions to it.[181] Also, for example, the duration of a T-Group experience was directly related to the probability of subsequent transfer of learning.[182] Greater duration permits enhanced opportunities for involvement and feedback, as well as for direct attention to transfer.

The view that the degree of participant involvement affects both the extent of learning in a T-Group and its subsequent transfer seems reasonable enough. However, few studies provide even such information. The consequence is a familiar one: the results of studies of the transfer of T-Group learning are difficult to interpret and evaluate. Existing studies tend to take the global form: of X participants in a T-Group, Y made

---

179. Underwood, *op. cit.,* p. 37. Reprinted by special permission from the January, 1965 issue of the *Training and Development Journal.* Copyright 1965 by the American Society for Training and Development.
180. Argyris, "T-Groups for Organizational Effectiveness," p. 71.
181. French, Sherwood, and Bradford, *op. cit.;* and Miles, *op. cit.,* p. 215.
182. Bunker and Knowles, *op. cit.* But note that T-Group time limits have received very little rigorous attention, as is stressed by Gottschalk and Pattison, *op. cit.,* p. 836.

changes in some back-home context after their training, which persisted for such-and-such a time.

3. TOWARD MORE SATISFYING RESEARCH ON T-GROUP EFFECTS: SOME GUIDELINES

The brief review above should support at least two conclusions. First, there seems no question that some significant and powerful things take place within T-Groups. Second, the research literature is in major need of early upgrading.

Several guidelines for this upgrading seem patent, to rely on the outline of Campbell and Dunnette. As they note, given the equivocal nature of much of the research, "one might properly speculate on how research should proceed if one is to gain a better understanding of what the effects of T-Group training are."[183] They offer six informed "shoulds."

First, greater attention should be given to specifying the precise behavioral outcomes that are expected from a T-Group experience, as well as the conditions under which these outcomes will be especially strong or weak. This is to say that a third generation of T-Group research is necessary. Many first-generation studies used a wide array of outcome measures to detect whatever changes might occur.[184] A second generation of T-Group research has tended to be more precise in specifying the direction of expected outcomes. A third generation of research must extend this tendency to specify outcomes, and it must also identify with increasing precision the conditions that intervene between training and specific outcomes.

Second, more measures of differences between T-Group participants should be incorporated into third-generation research. Much existing research assumes that all (or almost all) persons will experience similar training effects at the same pace. This expectation is simply not consistent with the differences between people that have been clearly established in other areas.

Third, more attention should be given to the interaction between T-Group outcomes and the properties of external contexts into which any learning might be transferred. These external contexts include families, schools, and organizations.

Fourth, the outcomes of T-Group training should be compared in detail with the effects of other training methods, including other designs

---

183. Campbell and Dunnette, "Effectiveness of T-Group Experiences," p. 99.
184. Cooper and Mangham, "T-Group Training," p. 224, stress the early incidence of such research.

based on the laboratory approach. Several such designs are discussed in subsequent chapters, and they might be able to achieve some T-Group effects without running some of the risks associated with T-Grouping.

Fifth, the various elements in the T-Group technology should be understood more fully. For example, attention might be devoted to reducing the chanciness of feedback and disclosure processes in T-Groups, as by rationalization of the processes[185] or by instrumentation.[186] Similarly, major attention needs to be given to the trainer's role. Thus recent research associates some trainer styles with psychological casualties in T-Groups,[187] and research on those styles consequently cannot be as skimpy in the future as it has been in the past. It might even prove possible to eliminate trainers in whole or part, as in "leaderless T-Groups,"[188] or by the use of participant analysis of videotape playback.[189] Such designs might achieve many or all of the effects associated with T-Groups, but with less stress for participants.[190]

Sixth, greater attention should be directed toward establishing the linkages between changes induced by T-Groups and enhanced participant effectiveness in various contexts into which learning might be transferred. Numerous personal testimonials lay claim to such increases in effectiveness,[191] but these are of first-generation sophistication only. A second generation of research has used work colleagues to confirm or disconfirm self-reports of changes, and usefully so. A third generation of research should extend this beachhead and also seek to relate specific training effects to such other measures of effectiveness as production, turnover, absenteeism, and so on.

185. Ellis, *op. cit.*
186. Philip G. Hanson, Paul Rothaus, Dale L. Johnson, and Francis A. Lyle, "Autonomous Groups in Human Relations Training for Psychiatric Patients," *Journal of Applied Behavioral Science,* Vol. 2 (July, 1966), pp. 305–24; and Avis Manno Brenner, "Self-Directed T Groups for Elementary Teachers: Impetus for Innovation," *Journal of Applied Behavioral Science,* Vol. 7 (May, 1971), pp. 327–41.
187. Yalom and Lieberman, *op. cit.*
188. Hanson, *et. al., op. cit.*
189. Dehon, *op. cit.*
190. Yalom and Lieberman, *op. cit.,* esp. pp. 21–22.
191. Batchelder and Hardy, *op. cit.,* pp. 53–65.

B. INTERVENTIONS AIMED AT INDIVIDUALS: TOWARD APPLYING LABORATORY VALUES TO JOB AND CAREER

The catalog of complaints against the laboratory approach is long. To sample only: it is mawkish at precisely the time we need hard-nosed realism; it foolishly attempts to substitute group consensus for individual initiative; and it creates an illusion of emotional comfort in costly groups that perversely work to envelop themselves in an artificial and temporary environment when the life-and-death issues are everywhere around us with an immediacy that cannot ever be shut out. Malcolm McNair[1] put this line of criticism as directly as anyone, although his target was broader than sensitivity training. He charges that too much "emphasis on human relations encourages people to feel sorry for themselves, makes it easier for them to slough off responsibility, to find excuses for failure, to act like children." The themes McNair would like to see more emphasized are: will power, self-control, personal responsibility, analysis, judgment, and decision-making. More and more, however, McNair sees a world "in danger of wallowing in self-pity and infantilism." He illustrates:

When somebody falls down on the job or does not behave in accordance with accepted codes, we look into his psychological background for factors that may be used as excuses. In these respects the cult of human relations is but part and parcel of

1. Malcolm P. McNair, "What Price Human Relations?" *Harvard Business Review,* Vol. 35 (March, 1957), pp. 15–22.

the sloppy sentimentalism characterizing the world today . . .
undue preoccupation with human relations saps individual responsibility, leads us not to think about the job any more and
about getting it done but only about people and their relations. . . .

There are some real challenges, and perhaps some deep anger, in Mc-
Nair's words.

Four themes in this section of the volume attempt to show how spin-
offs from the laboratory approach can be all that McNair would like
them to be. This section describes designs based on the laboratory approach that face difficult and real issues for what they are, emphasize
the role of individual initiative, and cope with critical issues that must
be worked through to decision and implementation. The four subsections below deal, in turn, with:

- demoted managers striving to make a decent adjustment to new
  jobs with less pay and status
- pairs of individuals confronting problems that have impaired their
  effectiveness at work
- individuals beginning to face the critical questions of what they
  would like to do, and can do, with the rest of their work lives
- an organized search seeking early identification of those persons
  with managerial potential which has dual goals: to isolate individuals with the qualities of self-control, judgment, and so on
  that McNair cherishes; and to reduce the probability that talent
  will variously get overlooked in large organizations.

4. INDIVIDUAL ADAPTATION TO
ON-JOB TRAUMA:
THE CASE OF THE 13 DEMOTEES

This subsection describes how one design consistent with the laboratory approach can be helpful for a new kind of OJT,[2] on-the-job trauma.
This kind of OJT assumes an especial significance in today's organizations, where rapid change implies a growing prominence of trauma as
a part of work, trauma generated by reorganization, reassignments, demotions, upgrading some programs and downgrading others, the obsolescing of even newly acquired skills or knowledge, and so on. Not only
will there be more such trauma than ever before, but adaptations to
them must at once be more rapid and more effective than before.

The pace of change has accelerated so much that clock time can no

---

2. The familiar usage of OJT is shorthand for on-job training.

longer be relied on as the healer of all things. Clock time was never all that effective, to begin. Moreover, in today's organizations, the game often will be over before the effects of clock time can take effect. At the same time, it is both morally and practically awkward to neglect the consequences of often unavoidable urgency.

There is only one way out of this dilemma. Ways must be found to accelerate healing effects in psychological time, as it were. This section suggests one such approach to engaging much psychological time in a few hours of clock time.

Within its broad focus on man in organizations, this section has two central themes, both of which are relevant to applications of the behavioral sciences in "real-life situations." First, considerable psychological trauma can be generated by events such as the demotions reported on here. Second, substantial evidence suggests that a learning design based on the laboratory approach can significantly moderate such trauma. Methodological problems inhibit assigning all observed effects to the learning design. But the presumptive evidence is strong that this action design is one way to apply in organizations the massive forces often observed in sensitivity training groups, one way to apply *in vivo* the values that commonly guide the development of the miniature societies that are T-Groups. The action design, in sum, seems to accelerate effects in psychological time that would occur (if at all) only during far longer periods of clock time.

a. Integrating Disrupted Work Patterns: An Action Design for a Critical Intervention

The purpose here is to detail one application of the laboratory approach, one example of a broad family of critical interventions at work. The focus is on the demotion of 13 field sales managers, many of whom were senior employees. The basic intent of the intervention was to help ease the inevitable stresses on the demotees. These stresses inhered in diverse personal adaptations required of demotees as they changed jobs, schedules, and routines, and as they modified levels of aspiration and perhaps self-concepts. Stresses also inhered in the need to develop viable work relations between the demotee and his new manager, who formerly had been a peer. The demotions also meant major reductions in salary for most of the men, so the trauma that the demotees were expected to experience could have a major economic component.

The intervention had both personal and organizational aspects. For the demoted men themselves, the intent was to ease what was probably a major and even painful emotional experience for all of the men, and one that was economically costly for most demotees. For the organization, the intent was to preserve its valued human resources. Although they were demoted, the men's past efforts and their anticipated future contributions were perceived as significant enough to warrant risking a difficult transition. Except for management's confidence in the laboratory approach, indeed, it is probable that the men in question would have been released. Demotions are uncommon, because of the problems they imply.

The intent of the intervention also can be suggested by two crude equations.[3] Equation A sketches the grim consequences to be avoided.

$$\text{Eq. A:} \left(\begin{array}{c} \text{Imaginings} \\ \text{triggered} \\ \text{by demotion} \end{array} + \begin{array}{c} \text{Relative} \\ \text{aloneness} \end{array} + \begin{array}{c} \text{Relative} \\ \text{helplessness} \end{array} \right) = \begin{array}{c} \text{Initial} \\ \text{increases} \\ \text{in} \end{array} \left\{ \begin{array}{l} \text{anxiety} \\ \text{depression} \\ \text{hostility} \end{array} \right.$$

It proposes that the imaginings or speculations induced by the demotions, given the aloneness of the field situation and the helplessness to do anything but resign, would generate immediate increases in anxiety, depression, and hostility. Such effects probably would not serve the individual, nor would they help in making necessary adjustments at work. In contrast, Equation B proposes to confront the imaginings induced by the demotions with the sharing of resources in a community setting that hopefully will increase a demotee's sense of mastery over the consequences of his demotion.

$$\text{Eq. B:} \left(\begin{array}{c} \text{Imaginings} \\ \text{triggered} \\ \text{by demotion} \end{array} + \text{Community} + \text{Mastery} \right) = \begin{array}{c} \text{Effective} \\ \text{coping, or} \\ \text{early reductions} \\ \text{in initial} \end{array} \left\{ \begin{array}{l} \text{anxiety} \\ \text{depression} \\ \text{hostility} \end{array} \right.$$

The action design for this critical intervention is based on the laboratory approach. Perhaps the term "action design" is dramatic, but we wish to distinguish the design from sensitivity training in several major senses. To illustrate these differences only, the design in this case deals with a very real problem; the target concerns are rooted firmly in specific organizational relationships, although the focus may extend beyond the worksite; and the thrust is toward a working resolution of major concerns that have long-run implications rather than toward dealing with reactions and feelings in a temporary group. Although they differ in important particulars, however, this action design and sensitivity training are viewed as *species* within the *genus* laboratory approach, consistent with the usage throughout this book.

The Demoted Population

As part of a broader reduction in force, 13 regional managers from the marketing department of a major firm were given two choices: ac-

---

3. Richard M. Jones, *Fantasy and Feeling in Education* (New York: New York University Press, 1968), p. 77.

cepting demotion to senior salesmen, or terminating. Table 1 presents some descriptive data about the men and their eventual choices and implies that they were a heterogeneous lot. Consistently, although most of the demotees would suffer a major reduction in salary, reductions would range from less than $1,000 to approximately four times that amount for the demotees with most seniority.

Several forces in tension influenced the decisions of the 13 men. In favor of choosing termination were such factors as the generous separation allowances available to those with seniority affected by reductions in force. To suggest the countervailing forces, the job market was tight, the company was considered a good employer, and market conditions required cutting as deeply as the 13 managers, all of whom were satisfactory performers.

Table 1. Selected Data about Demotees

Demotee	Age	Years with Company	Years as Regional Sales Manager	Decision to Accept Demotion
1	36	12	1	No
2	35	10	5	No
3	40	7	6 mos.	Yes
4	39	9	7 mos.	Yes
5	51	23	16	Yes
6	33	5	10 mos.	Yes
7	43	12	5	Yes
8	44	17	7	Yes
9	43	12	5	Yes
10	35	11	8 mos.	Yes
11	55	24	17	Yes
12	35	10	2 yrs. 6 mos.	Yes
13	50	13	10	Yes

All but two of the managers accepted the demotion and, as Table 2 shows, were given an early work assignment intended to facilitate their making the required adaptations as effectively and quickly as possible. The demotees knew that the "integrative experience" had been discussed with, and approved by, several managerial levels in the marketing department. In addition, almost all of the demotees and all of their superiors had long-standing relations of trust with the four consultants who variously participated in the development and implementation of this action design.[4]

4. This section draws heavily on Robert T. Golembiewski, Stokes B. Carrigan, Walter R. Mead, Robert Munzenrider, and Arthur Blumberg, "Toward Building New Work Relationships: An Action Design for a Critical Intervention," *Journal of Applied Behavioral Science* (in press).

For an application of the laboratory approach in the case of individuals who have

Table 2. The Timing of the Action Design

Day 1	Day 2	Day 6	Day 7	Day 45
13 managers informed of choices:	Decision required:	Three major activities:	Two major activities:	Demotees and superiors respond to MAACL:*
■ demotion to salesman ■ termination	■ 11 managers accept demotion	■ demotees and superiors respond to MAACL:* pretest	■ demotees meet individually with their new superiors	■ test of persistence of changes
If demotion accepted, an early work assignment would involve reporting to a midwestern city for an "integrative experience" along with their new superiors		■ demotees spend balance of day in discussion ■ superiors have briefing meeting	■ demotees and superiors respond to MAACL:* posttest	

* Multiple Affect Adjective Check List.

Five Broad Purposes

Five broad goals of the critical intervention may be distinguished. *First,* the action design was intended to build on the values of the laboratory approach. The company had invested in a major way in a program of organization development, in which a voluntary offsite sensitivity training experience for organizational peers was a major early learning vehicle.[5] Eighteen of the 22 participants—the 11 demotees and their immediate supervisors—had such a learning experience earlier. The other 4 men had their sensitivity training postponed only by the major reduction-in-force at issue here. Moreover, 19 of the men had been involved in various "team development" activities that attempted to extend the initial offsite training directly into organization activities. Commonly, the thrust of such OD activities was toward helping organization members in two ways: to build a specific set of norms or values into their workaday relations; and to aid in the development of attitudes and behavioral skills appropriate to those norms. By way of review, two sets of values consistent with the laboratory approach were considered most relevant:

just lost their jobs, see George F. J. Lehner, "From Job Loss to Career Innovation" (Paper delivered at NTL Conference on New Technology in Organization Development, New York, October 8–9, 1971).
5. For the basic design, see Robert T. Golembiewski and Arthur Blumberg, "Sensitivity Training in Cousin Groups: A Confrontation Design," *Training and Development Journal,* Vol. 23 (August, 1969), pp. 18–23.

Meta-Values of Laboratory Approach:[6]	Organization Values Consistent with Laboratory Approach:[7]

■ an attitude of inquiry reflecting (among others):
  a. a hypothetical spirit
  b. experimentalism
	■ full and free communication

	■ reliance on open confrontation in managing conflict, as opposed to using coercion or compromise
■ expanded consciousness and recognition of choice	

■ a collaborative concept of authority, having as two core elements:
  a. a spirit of collaboration
  b. open resolution of conflict via a problem-solving orientation
	■ influence based on competence rather than on personal whim or formal power

	■ expression of emotional as well as task-oriented behavior
■ an emphasis on mutual helping relationships as the best way to express man's interdependency with man, to express man's basic social nature and connectedness	■ acceptance of conflict between the individual and his organization, to be coped with willingly, openly, and rationally
■ an emphasis on authenticity in interpersonal relations, a high value on expressing feelings and their effects	

As the first four sections of this book detail, these norms or values are meant in the sense of ideals to be strived for, as individuals become increasingly convinced that it is safe to do so, and as they learn by experience whether they can meet their own needs by following the norms.

The challenge posed by the demotions was simply to apply the norms of the laboratory approach in a specific case that was personally and organizationally meaningful. Significantly, the specific case is complex and subtle. Demotions involve difficult transitions, in emotions, in work routines, and in relations. In the case of most of the present demotees, as was noted, major salary cuts also could require economic adjustments.

Second, the purpose was to begin developing integrative linkages at the earliest possible time after the demotion announcements. The special

6. Adapted from Edgar H. Schein and Warren G. Bennis, *Personal and Organizational Change through Group Methods* (New York: John Wiley & Sons, 1965), pp. 30–35; and Leland B. Bradford, Jack R. Gibb, and Kenneth D. Benne (eds.), *T-Group Theory and Laboratory Method* (New York: John Wiley & Sons, 1964), pp. 10–12.
7. Philip E. Slater and Warren G. Bennis, "Democracy Is Inevitable," *Harvard Business Review*, Vol. 42 (March, 1964), pp. 51–59.

characteristics of the field situation encouraged prompt action. For example, typically, the field salesman might spend perhaps 9 out of 10 working days on his own, which creates special problems for supervisors as well as for the salesman who might want or need help. The focus of the derivative two-day design was on common personal or interpersonal data. On the first day, these data included the reactions of the demotee, his concerns about attending regional sales meetings as a peer rather than as a manager of salesmen, etc. On the second day, the focus was on supervisory relations between the 11 pairs of men who had been peers, the demoted one of whom would sometimes have substantially more seniority than his new superior.

Third, the intent was to provide a specific action arena in which feelings could be expressed *and* worked through, if possible. The working symbolism was the cauterization of the wound, not pleasant but preferable to the possible or probable alternatives. The antigoals were obsessiveness, and the postponement of a required facing-up to new work demands that would probably loom larger with the passage of time.

Fourth, the goal was to provide diverse support to the demotees at a critical time. This support was to come from demoted peers, superiors, and the employing organization. The common theme was: "We want this to work for you as much as possible, and not against you." At the most elemental level, most managers perceived that the expense of the integrative experience itself was a signal measure of "the organization's" concern and support.

The vicious cycle to be avoided can be sketched. Depression was an expected result of the demotions, for example, especially for the more senior men. Unless carefully managed, depression can work against the man. The consequences of believing "the organization is against me" can be both subtle and profound, especially for the field salesman. Incoming cues and messages might be misinterpreted, and outgoing projections of self might trigger unintended consequences. More broadly, Ari Kiev traces an unattractive catalog of the "manifestations of depressions," which include

> diminished incentive, interest, morale, and ability to concentrate, feelings of alienation, inability to assume responsibility or to follow a routine, diminished ability of self-expression, self-assertiveness and decreased pride, irritation with interference, feelings of being unappreciated or worthlessness. . . . [The] psychophysiological concomitants of early depression . . . include insomnia, loss of appetite, excessive worrying, indigestion, and decline in energy.[8]

---

8. Ari Kiev, "Crisis Intervention in Industry" (Paper delivered at Annual Meeting, New York State Society of Industrial Medicine, Occupational Psychiatry Group, December 10, 1969), p. 2.

Fifth, the integrative experience was intended to provide early readings about possible adaptive difficulties, readings for managers, the demotees, and the training staff. Efforts were made to legitimate early contacts from both supervisors and demotees if future help were necessary.

b. Characteristics of the Action Design:
Toward New Status and New Relationships

A simple learning design was developed to meet these multiple goals. The constant target was adaptation to the new status, which implied the development of new work relationships. In terms of time, roughly 50 percent was spent with the demotees working together and 50 percent with the demotees individually attempting to work through issues of concern with their new supervisors.

The first design component brought the demotees together for discussion of their concerns, problems, and needs. Approximately four hours were devoted to this exploration, with two resource persons available. The formal afternoon session was kept deliberately short, although it provided the model for several informal sessions in the evening. The announced design intent was to help prepare the demotees for the next day's sessions with their individual managers concerning work relations. This action thrust sought to harness emotional energies to organization purposes rather than to diffuse them through ventilation.

The role of resource persons in seeking to harness emotional energies rather than diffuse them was a mixed one. In capsule, the resource persons sought to direct attention to "content" as well as to "process," whereas the trainer's role in sensitivity training emphasized the latter. Although the distinction is not an easy one to make briefly, as Section C of Part I should amply have established, the notions refer to an emphasis on *what is done* and on the *way things are done,* respectively. In some detail, the model for interventions was an insight ⟶ action model, with the emphasis clearly on the action. Illustratively, assume that individual A was sending signals of fear and anger concerning some technical aspect of his new job. The resource persons sought to intervene at a process level as in a T-Group, with the goals of making A aware of those signals and of putting him in touch with the inducing emotions, if possible. The seven old T-Group hands among the demotees were very active in this regard, also. The capstone intervention here tended to be associated with the readiness of A to raise the concern and the associated feelings with his new manager, with whom he would meet the next day. The action thrust is patent. Moreover, the technical content at issue also would be explored. Sometimes the resolution was easy, as in clarifying a misunderstanding or a misinterpretation. When the resolution was difficult, interventions by the resource persons tended to be questions with an action thrust. What does individual A prefer?

281

What are the other alternative strategies? What role can or should his new manager play in the matter, especially in the meeting between the two that was scheduled for the next day?

More specifically, the developmental sequence built into the first day of the design began with personal reactions to the demotions and then trended toward a growing emphasis on the problems the demotees perceived as relevant in developing the required new work relationships. The following list provides some flavor of the main themes dealt with:

- comparing experiences, especially about the diverse ways in which various relevant organization policies were applied to their individual cases
- encouraging expression of anxiety or hostility about the demotions themselves or about the associated processes or their style, timing, etc.
- surfacing and testing suspicion of management, as in the concern that another personnel purge was imminent
- isolating and, as far as possible, working through demotees' concerns about authority and dependence, as in the complaint that the demotees did not see themselves being treated as adults, or that they were men enough to take the demotions without the integrative experience
- dealing with a variety of issues on work relations—e.g., explaining demotions to clients or other salesmen—so as to develop strategies and norms that would reduce the probability of either avoiding the matters or awkwardly handling them in the field
- identifying relevant others with whom interaction had been stressful or with whom it might prove to be so, the emphasis being on strategies for handling such interaction

Surely success varied from case to case, but the intention of the resource persons was constant. That intention, in sum, was to: facilitate expression of feelings and reactions; help reveal the diversity of the demotees' experiences and coping strategies; and work toward a successful adaptation to the demands of the new job. More broadly, the resource persons were not advocates of management actions; nor were they neuters without emotional response to the sometimes tragicomic dynamics of the demotions. But they were committed to helping the demotees face their demotions as clearly and realistically as possible. Hence demotees might decide to accept termination after the integrative experience. None of the men did so, but the option was announced to the men, after top-level management's agreement had been secured.

282

It is not possible to convey the diversity of the products of this first design component, but two themes provide a useful substantive summary. The first is that almost all demotees emphasized the positive meaning of the integrative experience, whatever its specific outcomes. The design implied to them their value to the organization and reflected a continuing effort to provide resources which would help them do the job. From this perspective, the design had substantial value as a sign that efforts to act on the norms of the laboratory approach would be made even under conditions of substantial stress, which no doubt provide the best test of managerial intentions. This positive evaluation was variously shared by all the supervisors. One of the demotees took a different approach. He resented the integrative experience as "hand-holding" and "coddling."

The second theme is that the first component of the learning design emphasized some common elements among the demotees, as well as some differentiating factors. The training staff saw both the commonality and differentiation as being reality-based, and their conscious strategy was to avoid at all costs a strained display of ardent but feigned homogeneity or good fellowship among the demotees.

The elements of commonality that emerged in discussion among the demotees were expected ones. They include: the impact of the demotion on the self; experiences with important referents such as wives, colleagues, or salesmen from other firms; and concerns about taking on the salesman's job, about "picking up the bag again" to cover a sales territory, about participating in sales meetings, and so on.

The differentiating elements were harder for the men to openly identify, but they were no less clearly reality-based. For example, the demotees included both long-service employees and recent managerial appointees. Reasonably, on balance, the younger men could be expected to feel more optimism about being repromoted at some future date. The prognosis for the longer-service men was far less bright, realistically, and they generally if sometimes grudgingly acknowledged the point. Relatedly, some men professed shock at being confronted with the choice of demotion or termination. Others maintained they had more-or-less expected some action, because of falling demand in the industry, or performance problems, or both. A few even expressed pleasure that the action was not as severe for them as it had been for those of their colleagues who were released outright.

The second component of the integrative experience took two approaches to extending demotee concerns into action, via the development of new working relations between the managers and their new subordinates. In the first approach, the managers met for some two hours to discuss the design for the next day and their role in it. The meeting's initial tone was a kind of gallows humor, which the training staff interpreted as understandable anxiety among the managers about their role. This initial tone quickly dissipated into the theme of making the transitions as easy as possible for all concerned. The basic thrust was to empathize with how the demotees were feeling and to channel those feelings toward making the most successful adaptation possible.

The second was that each demotee spent approximately three hours of the second day of the design with his manager, one-on-one. The resource persons sat in on some of the dyads, as time permitted, and especially the dyads with senior demotees. The major concerns involving these dyads were:

- the building of early supervisory relations, as in mutual pledges to work harmoniously together, which was easy enough in some cases because some of the demotees were able to choose their new managers as they exercised various options to relocate
- technical problems such as going over sales territories, etc.
- developing strategies by which the manager and man could be mutually helpful, as in discussing ways to moderate the formation of cliques that the demotions could encourage
- isolating likely problems and cementing a contract to agree to meet any such problems mutually and early

Some dyads concentrated on one of these concerns, while others gave attention to several themes.

c. Measuring Intended Effects of the Design: Anxiety, Depression, and Hostility as Target Variables

The effects of the action design for helping integrate disrupted work patterns were judged by changes in the Multiple Affect Adjective Check List (MAACL) developed by Marvin Zuckerman and Bernard Lubin. MAACL, a brief instrument for tapping the psychological aspects of emotion, conceives of affect not as a trait but as a state. That is, a time referent is specified for the respondent, who reacts as he feels "today" or "now" as opposed to how he feels "generally" or "occasionally." The researchers explain that MAACL

> was designed to fill the need for a self-administered test which would provide valid measures of three of the clinically relevant negative affects: anxiety, depression, and hostility. No attempt was made to measure positive affects but some of the evidence indicates that the scales are bipolar, and that low scores on the full scales will indicate states of positive affect.[9]

9. Marvin Zuckerman and Bernard Lubin, *Manual for the Multiple Affect Adjective Check List* (San Diego, Cal.: Educational and Industrial Testing Service, 1965), p. 3. Reproduced with permission.

Its authors place MAACL "in a research phase and . . . not yet recommended for routine applied use," but accumulating evidence suggests its value,[10] at least as a measure of generalized negative affect. In an early study, for example, the validity of the test was suggested by significant increases in the Anxiety scores of students just prior to an examination, as expected. Similar changes in the Depression and Hostility scales were induced by administering a classroom examination a week earlier than announced. An extensive bibliography provides detailed reinforcement of these illustrations of validity.[11]

The expectations in this case were direct. The demotees were expected to have high initial scores on Anxiety, Depression, and Hostility, the three target variables, which a successful intervention would reduce significantly in a post-treatment administration of MAACL. Lower initial scores were expected for the managers, and the post-treatment administration was not expected to reveal any major shifts in scores, except perhaps on Anxiety. This expectation is based on the assumption that the managers, who had to develop new relations with their former peers, might be somewhat anxious initially about their role in the learning design. This anxiety was expected to fall as the design unfolded, and especially as it proved useful.

The design's intent was not only to provide topical relief via temporary reductions in the target variables, however, but also to induce persisting reductions. Consequently, a third follow-up administration of MAACL was administered by mail approximately a month after the planned intervention. The purpose was to develop data about the persistence of any before/after changes. A potent training intervention was expected to preserve over time any reductions in anxiety, depression, and hostility induced by the demotions, in the face of the relative isolation and threat of the field situation.

Respondents were given code numbers that permitted comparing the before/after responses of specific individuals.[12] One of the 22 subjects did not respond to the third administration. Hence the number of subjects varies in the several statistical tests reported on below.

d. Some Major Effects of the Design: Sharp and Persisting Reductions in All Target Variables

The design had the major intended effects, which can be characterized by six themes. *First,* as expected, the demotees initially generated

---

10. *Ibid.,* pp. 6–16.
11. Marvin Zuckerman and Bernard Lubin, *Bibliography for the Multiple Affect Adjective Check List* (San Diego, Cal.: Educational and Industrial Testing Service, 1970) , 8 pages.
12. Note that on the third administration, researchers made an assignment decision in one questionable case. Statistically, it turns out, the assignment affects the results in trifling ways only.

high scores on all three MAACL scales. That the demotions were traumatic can be demonstrated in several ways. For example, the demotees initially scored higher than the managers on all three MAACL scales, the differences being statistically significant far beyond the .005 level. To a similar point, Lubin and Zuckerman tell us that a transformed "score of 70 is generally accepted as the point beyond which scores on a psychometric instrument are considered to be unusually high, as that point represents a score higher than that achieved by 98 per cent of the standardization sample."[13] Two of the 33 transformed scores for demotees on the three scales reach that level on the initial administration, but an

Table 3. Overall Effects of Intervention on Three MAACL Administrations

| | Mean Scale Scores, by Administrations of MAACL | | | t-test Values for Paired Administrations | | |
	1	2	3	1 vs. 2	1 vs. 3	2 vs. 3
Demotees						
Anxiety	9.8	7.5	6.5	2.59**	2.74**	2.14*
Depression	17.8	14.8	13.6	2.88***	2.65**	1.09
Hostility	9.5	7.2	7.2	2.90***	1.98**	0.15
Managers						
Anxiety	6.3	5.3	4.6	1.24*	1.83*	0.83
Depression	9.8	9.5	9.5	0.23	0.38	0
Hostility	5.1	5.3	5.7	− .30	− .87	− .62

   * indicates .05 level of statistical significance.
  ** indicates .025 level of statistical significance.
 *** indicates .01 level of statistical significance.

additional eight men have transformed scores of 60 or above on the pretest. In sum, the demotees reacted strongly to the demotion, but their MAACL scores were not "unusually high."

Second, the data meet all expectations concerning changes attributable to the training intervention. Specifically, as Table 3 shows, demotees reported statistically significant decreases on all three scales on the second administration of the MAACL, and these sharp and sudden reductions were at least maintained through the third administration. As Table 3 also shows, indeed, a comparison of the Anxiety scores on administrations 2 versus 3 shows a statistically significant reduction following the earlier major reductions.

The major and sudden reductions in MAACL scores between the first

---

13. Bernard Lubin and Marvin Zuckerman, "Levels of Emotional Arousal in Laboratory Training," *Journal of Applied Behavioral Science,* Vol. 5 (October, 1969), p. 488.

two administrations imply the potency of the brief training intervention. The conclusion is reinforced by the lack of evidence that respondents become adapted to the MAACL items in responding to successive administrations. What is not known is how long these initially high levels would have been maintained in the absence of the training intervention.

Third, the scores of the managers showed a significant change only for Anxiety. That reduction is most easily attributed to a successful intervention, a building down from a realistic prior concern about what the integrative experience would demand of the supervisor. Interestingly, scores on the Hostility scale increased for the managers, although not significantly so. This may reflect a reasonable reaction against the action design, or against the training staff, whose clear bias was to help the demoted men rather than the managers. The moderate increase in Hostility scores suggests a neglect of supervisory needs, in sum, which subsequent design variations should recognize.

Fourth, a variety of analytical approaches establishes that the design had quite uniform effects for all demotees, regardless of their other differences. An analysis of variance—reported in Table 4 only for the demotees—supports the point in one way. An analysis of variance for the managers yielded the same pattern.

There are other ways to demonstrate the dominance of treatment effects. For example, a correlation analysis investigated the effects of four variables describing individual demoted managers: age; years with company; years as regional manager; and loss of salary involved in the demotion. The four individual variables were highly and positively intercorrelated. Indeed, their intercorrelation matrix contains these five very high values: .7309, .7430, .8593, and .9545, all of which attain at least the .01 level of statistical significance. However, in only 1 case in 72 does any one of these four variables correlate significantly with any of 18 measures of outcomes: the nine absolute scores of Anxiety, Depression, and Hostility in each of the three administrations; and the nine measures of relative change on the three MAACL scales which compare scores on the three administrations, taken by pairs. Consider "salary loss," for example. Not one of its 18 correlation coefficients with the various outcome variables attains the .05 level of statistical significance, ±.60 by two–tailed test. In fact, only 3 of the 18 coefficients reach ±.40, while 9 coefficients fall in the interval +.199 through −.199.

Such data support the dominance of treatment effects. No attempt was made to deal with partials in the correlation analysis, given the small N. In fact, such partialling probably would indicate even more attenuated covariation than that implied by the low coefficients reviewed in the paragraph immediately above.

Fifth, the effects on individuals also establish the efficacy of the training design. Two perspectives on the data provide evidence. A crude com-

Table 4. Analysis of Variance of Three Administrations of MAACL, by Scales

Sources of Variance	Anxiety Scores				Depression Scores				Hostility Scores			
	df	SS	MS	F-ratio	df	SS	MS	F-ratio	df	SS	MS	F-ratio
Subjects	9	58.87	6.54	1.36	9	127.4	14.16	1.07	9	46.87	5.21	0.94
Treatment	2	150.53	75.26	15.67*	2	599.37	299.68	27.67*	2	293.47	146.73	26.64*
Residual	18	86.47	4.80		18	237.93	13.22		18	99.13	5.51	
Total	29	295.87			29	964.70			29	439.46		

* designates the .001 level of statistical significance, or beyond.

parison of the first and second MAACL administrations reveals that of the 33 comparisons—11 demotees on three MAACL scales—26 were reductions in scores and 3 were no-changes. No demotee had an increased score on more than one scale, in addition. Looked at from another point of view, the data show only a single demotee who has even one score significantly greater than the mean of any scale on the first administration. Using a more demanding convention, the demotees can be divided as:

- three men, all of whose scores in the third MAACL administration were "major decreases," that is, they scored at least one standard deviation less than the means on each of the three scales on the first administration
- three men who had major decreases on two MAACL scales and a more modest reduction on the third scale
- one man who had a major decrease on one MAACL scale and more modest reductions on the other scales
- two men who experienced no reduction of greater than a standard deviation on any scale
- one man who had a "major increase" on the third administration of one standard deviation greater than the initial mean on one MAACL scale and who was at or near the initial means on all three scales
- one man who had a major increase on one MAACL scale plus a major reduction on another and who was substantially above the initial means

Sixth, postexperience interview and questionnaire responses from the demotees and several levels of supervision underscore the value of the experience. Many of the details cannot be revealed, since they tend to identify specific individuals. But the responses all but universally acknowledge the positive impact of the design. Similarly, the betting odds beforehand were that major problems could be expected with perhaps half of the demotees in the transition. Significantly, but not conclusively, all 11 demotees were still on the job some six months later, and the adaptations of 10 of the men were rated by their managers as "in great shape" or "more than adequate" on a 20-point scale running through "adequate," "somewhat inadequate," and "critically inadequate."

e. Impetus to Applications of the Laboratory Approach: The Real, if Restrained, Promise in the Results

The application of a learning design based on the laboratory approach, then, seems to have induced the intended consequences. Conservatively, the intervention seems to have quickly reversed emotional states that could have generated consequences troublesome for the individual and the organization. Specifically, scores on Anxiety, Depression, and Hostility scales were reduced significantly for a small population of demoted field supervisors, following the learning experience. These reductions were maintained or augmented in a third administration of the measuring instrument, spaced in time far enough after the intervention to test persistence.

Note also that it seems likely that the present learning design profited from earlier work in the host organization to develop norms, attitudes, and behaviors consistent with the laboratory approach. No concrete proof exists, but the training staff feels strongly that the observed effects derive in some substantial part from the earlier work in sensitivity training groups, as that training influenced individual behavior and as it helped develop appropriate attitudes and norms in the host organization. At least in the absence of very compelling (and presently unavailable) evidence, this design may not be applicable in organizations as a first-generation effort.

Methodological inelegancies prohibit uniquely attributing the effects to the learning design, but the presumptive evidence is strong. For example, the initial reductions cannot easily be attributed to the passage of time. The interval between the first and second MAACL administrations was a brief one, and the demotees had patently developed and sustained high scores on the three marker variables in the five or six days intervening between the demotion notices and the integrative experience. It is of course possible that the observed changes were artifacts of the design. But it does not seem likely that, for example, the announcement of the integrative experience alone triggered the high MAACL scores, which naturally dropped when that experience proved benign. Post-interviews with the demotees largely scotch this explanation, although some minor "anticipation effect" no doubt existed.

In other senses, however, more substantial reservations must hedge attributing the observed results to the learning design. For example, was the real magic in this case in the process analysis and the values of the laboratory approach? Or did some or all of the potency derive from the very act of bringing the men together, a kind of Hawthorne token that management really cared, and no matter about the specific learning design? Similarly, it is not known how long the initial levels of anxiety, depression, and hostility would have persisted if nature had been allowed to run its course.

Only a fool or a very wise man could definitely answer the latter questions. The issues are incredibly complex. This pilot study suggests one promising extension of the laboratory approach into large organizations and urges the comparative analysis of other designs that can safely be added to the kit of the change agent.

290

5. COPING BY PAIRS WITH ON-JOB TRAUMA: THE CHARACTER AND CONSEQUENCES OF THIRD-PARTY CONSULTATION

Two opposed forces are at the heart of organizational life: conflicts that separate many people; and interdependencies at work or in life that for good or ill require that many of the very same people integrate their efforts as smoothly as possible. This section deals with the central dilemma inherent in these forces-in-opposition, from the perspective of a spin-off technology from the laboratory approach that seems useful for helping resolve or manage that dilemma. Hence the dual focus here on the character and consequences of third-party consultation, one of the growing family of more-or-less distinct learning technologies developed from the matrix vehicle of the laboratory approach, the T-Group.

a. On-Job Trauma between Pairs as an Organizational Given: Some Conceptual Distinctions and Their Reality Base

If there were an organizational book of Genesis, it no doubt would start with these words: "From the beginning, there was interpersonal conflict; and technological development begat increasingly more interpersonal conflict." In fact, formal organizations are in an important sense vehicles for coping with diverse and often-opposed interests and desires,[14] which puts them in the interpersonal conflict business in a big way. The extent of this involvement is suggested in Richard E. Walton's definition of the term: "Interpersonal conflict is defined broadly to include both (a) personal disagreements over substantive issues, such as differences over organizational structures, policies, and practices, and (b) interpersonal antagonisms, that is, the more personal and emotional differences which arise between interdependent human beings."[15]

Moreover, the two general bases of interpersonal conflict—substantive and emotional—can develop in diverse ways. For example:[16]

> ▪ A recurrent conflict between two managers was based on a misunderstanding of motives, with one manager having persistently seen the other as seeking to take over his job.

---

14. Herbert Kaufman, "Organization Theory and Political Theory," *American Political Science Review*, Vol. 58 (March, 1964), pp. 5–14.
15. Richard E. Walton, *Interpersonal Peacemaking: Confrontations and Third-Party Consultation* (Reading, Mass.: Addison-Wesley Publishing Co., 1969), p. 2.
16. *Ibid.*, p. 6.

- Two organization members got into a mutually destructive conflict, due to contrasting personal styles and contradictory definitions of their work roles.
- Two managers who were directly competing for the same job pursued their mutually exclusive goals with such abandon as to support the cause of Self by undercutting Other.

Powerful forces imply that such interpersonal conflicts will be at least a constant feature of life in organizations, if not an increasing one. The catalog of such inducing forces is impressive. *First,* as Section A, Part III especially will show, today's organizations are characterized by escalating interdependencies—between units of the same organization;[17] between units of different organizations linked as major contractors and subcontractors; and between organizations and government as a coparticipant, or buyer, regulator, or even competitor,[18] not to mention the bewildering combinations of all these relationships and more besides. There seems no imminent relief from these massive forces toward multiple interdependencies.

Second, interpersonal conflict also has a variety of advantageous features, so that there would be important reasons to preserve it even if it could be eliminated. Given that it is easy to overdo any useful thing, for example, a certain amount of interpersonal conflict can encourage a sharpening of job descriptions or definitions of work roles. Such clarification in turn could make it easier to establish responsibility for performance. Again, without being able to say what is really meant in unambiguous terms, "a certain amount" of interpersonal conflict might serve to bring out the best in people at work. This is the sense of the "friendly competition" for which football coaches often say they strive.

Third, however, there are very good reasons to suspect that interpersonal conflict in all organizations often goes beyond the "certain amount" which can be a good thing. To begin with a conclusion, multiple forces act so as to discourage the early raising of interpersonal conflicts, with the consequence that any organization is likely to have a substantial backlog of unfinished business to which additions are continually made. If nothing else, this backlog can serve to create a state of readiness that can be escalated into interpersonal conflict by apparently minor episodes.

Consider only three forces that impede the resolution of unfinished business deriving from interpersonal conflict in organizations. A variety of inhibitors to raising interpersonal issues, especially of the emotional

---

17. Leonard R. Sayles, *Managerial Behavior* (New York: McGraw-Hill Book Co., 1964) , pp. 58–82.
18. Don K. Price, *The Scientific Estate* (Cambridge, Mass.: Harvard University Press, 1967) .

kind, tends to exist in all organizations. In the terminology of Section D, Part I, to illustrate, these inhibitions are likely to increase as the pyramidal values are accepted. Relatedly, conservation of energy may dictate avoiding some interpersonal conflicts. This may be a short-run saving, of course, that turns out to have major long-run costs. But the plain fact is that many interpersonal issues are set aside in any organization in the rush of other immediate business. Finally, there are risks in surfacing interpersonal conflict in all organizations. If nothing else, surfacing a perceived conflict requires that at least two parties be willing to disclose or reveal themselves, and there can be a risk in such disclosure. Elementally, for example, disclosure by one party of a perceived conflict may be greeted with a denial by the other party that he or she feels any conflict at all. As a general rule, in addition, the risk is greatest where interpersonal conflict is most pronounced. Consequently, explicit raising of interpersonal conflict is least likely precisely where it is most necessary.

b. Third-Party Consultation: A Learning Design for Aiding Conflictful Pairs

A wide variety of interventions have been developed to either resolve or manage interpersonal conflict, however it gets triggered. Three more-or-less traditional models can be distinguished. Thus the work can be restructured or reorganized to make variously sure that the parties in conflict do not interact with one another, or the jobs of the individuals might be changed so as to reduce or eliminate the previous interdependency.[19] Alternatively, a legal-judicial model might be followed. Here the resolution or control of the conflict depends on determining what are the applicable rules and precedents and somehow adjudicating the difference between the contending parties.[20] Or one might follow a bargaining model, where the resolution will be influenced by issues of equity but only as they are significantly mediated by the relative power potential of the parties in dispute.[21] Of course, combinations of these three basic strategies also are possible.

A more-or-less distinct strategy has recently begun to emerge for

---

19. The classic catalog of such strategies to affect the flow of interaction is provided by William F. Whyte, "The Social Structure of the Restaurant," *American Journal of Sociology,* Vol. 54 (January, 1949), pp. 302–10.
20. The labor mediator often stresses this strategy, especially in the quasi adjudication of grievances and disputes. See Ann Douglas, *Industrial Peacemaking* (New York: Columbia University Press, 1962).
21. This model tends to be characteristic of international relations, but note that the relative power potential of a country can vary with many conditions other than its wealth or armed might. See Oran Young, *The Intermediaries: Third Parties in International Crises* (Princeton, N.J.: Princeton University Press, 1967).

resolving or controlling interpersonal conflict, what Walton calls "social science analysis and intervention."[22] This strategy, in partial contrast to the three models above, "would take into account many additional facets of the social system and would attempt to find a resolution to the dispute consistent with the objective of preserving or changing the social system, or certain of its characteristics."

Third-party consultation is one kind of social science analysis and intervention applicable in organizations which recently has been spun off from the laboratory approach, largely through the efforts of Richard Walton.[23] Basically, the approach calls for a confrontation between two parties in interpersonal conflict, in the presence of a qualified facilitator who seeks to help the parties move toward resolution or control of their differences. Often, the confrontation à trois takes place after the consultant has interviewed both parties. Third-party consultations have diverse intended effects, which may be illustrated by the results of the technique's application to the three examples of interpersonal conflict introduced earlier. The results cover the range from resolution of the issues in conflict, to managing or controlling some of the consequences of issues that remained unresolved:[24]

- A recurrent conflict between two managers was based on a misunderstanding of motives, with one manager having persistently seen the other as seeking to take over his job.

   Third-Party consultation convinced the parties that there was a discrepancy between perceived intention and actual intention, and they developed a new understanding which eliminated that discrepancy.

- Two organization members got into a mutually destructive conflict, due to contrasting personal styles and contradictory definitions of their work roles.

   Third-party consultation permitted the individuals to explore these differences. No changes were made in personal styles, but the emotional conflict was reduced and the definitions of work roles were modified to reduce the contradictions.

- Two managers who were directly competing for the same job pursued their mutually exclusive goals with such abandon as to support the cause of Self by undercutting Other.

22. Walton, op. cit., pp. 12–13.
23. Richard E. Walton, "Third Party Roles in Interdepartmental Conflict," Industrial Relations, Vol. 7 (October, 1967), pp. 29–43; "Interpersonal Confrontation and Basic Third Party Functions: A Case Study," Journal of Applied Behavioral Science, Vol. 4 (July, 1968), pp. 327–44; and Interpersonal Peacemaking.
   For other behavioral applications of the third-party notion, see Virginia Satir, Conjoint Family Therapy (Palo Alto, Cal.: Behavior Books, 1964).
24. Walton, Interpersonal Peacemaking, pp. 6, 15–70.

The third-party consultation helped the antagonists reach an agreement that outlawed certain destructive tactics, in the sense of an interpersonal treaty of nonaggression in certain areas.

The more specific character of third-party consultation can be circumscribed in terms of four elements. *First,* the technique is a confronting one which seeks to reverse degenerative systems of interaction between two specific individuals, to use the vocabulary defined in Sections A and B of Part I. The involved parties, in sum, take responsibility for their conflict and for working toward its resolution or management. More comprehensively, Walton explains that:[25]

> Interpersonal confrontation involves clarification and exploration of the issues in conflict, the nature and strength of the underlying needs or forces involved, and the types of current feelings generated by the conflict itself.
>
> If well managed, the confrontation is a method: for achieving greater understanding of the nature of the basic issues and the strength of the principals' respective interests in these issues; for achieving common diagnostic understanding of the triggering events, tactics and consequences of their conflict and how they tend to proliferate symptomatic issues; for discovering or inventing control possibilities and/or possible resolutions.

Second, the third party serves two basic functions in his role as helping the pair to confront their conflict in constructive ways. Thus he serves as a form of process consultant in observing the interacting pair, in the several senses defined in Section C, Part I. The consultant attempts to reflect a process orientation in his own interventions, and he also seeks to encourage the pair to increasingly respect the same values in their interactions in the learning situation as a prelude to later self-maintenance of their interaction at work. In sum, this means (to use Edgar Schein's definition again) that the consultant attempts to generate "a set of activities . . . which help the client to perceive, understand, and act upon process events which occur in the client's environment."[26] In this role, the consultant may:[27]

- regulate interaction between the pairs, as by terminating a discussion that is repetitive or counterproductive
- suggest items for discussion between the pair

---

25. *Interpersonal Peacemaking: Confrontations and Third Party Consultation* (Reading, Mass.: Addison-Wesley Publishing Co., 1969), p. 95. Quoted by permission.
26. Edgar H. Schein, *Process Consultation* (Reading, Mass.: Addison-Wesley Publishing Co., 1969), p. 9.
27. Walton, *Interpersonal Peacemaking*, pp. 122–29.

- constantly summarize what he understands has been said or projected nonverbally by the principals, so as to clarify and perhaps even redefine issues, with the goal of increasing the consensus about what all three participants understand as the sense of ongoing communication and, hence, of increasing the credibility and reliability attributed to the communicative signs being exchanged
- encourage feedback between the principals, and between the principals and himself
- make observations about the processes that exist between the pair in conflict, and perhaps himself and them
- diagnose the sources of conflict
- prescribe techniques that may facilitate discussion
- suggest ways to resolve or manage the conflict

In perhaps his most crucial role, the consultant serves to encourage adherence to the values and goals of the laboratory approach, as they are sketched in Sections A and B, Part I. He is a gatekeeper for laboratory values, in short. These values relate especially to openness, willingness to risk interpersonally and to experiment, owning the conflict as well as the emotions associated with it, and acceptance of the responsibility for the consequences of the confrontation. This is not usually as difficult as it appears, because the principals often have had a T-Group experience before they begin a third-party consultation and the two parties identify their consultant with the laboratory approach. In many cases, indeed, the consultant has been the T-Group trainer of one or both principals. The effects are central to the success of third-party consultation. As one source explains: ". . . because of the nature of the third party's professional identity and the clients' prior experience with persons in the profession, his presence by itself tended to provide emotional support and reinvoke some of the behavioral norms which were instrumental to the conflict confrontation and resolution process."[28]

This description suggests one approach to influencing the four variables in a degenerative interaction sequence. Third-party consultation seems to have dual effects. It places primacy on heightening trust through reliance on the consultant so as to induce increases in owning and openness; and it also decreases the risk of experimenting. The goal is to reverse degenerative interaction systems, or to engage regenerative systems.

Third, since interpersonal conflicts tend to be cyclical, a major task of the third-party consultation is to isolate those factors which trigger the conflict as well as those which dampen it. Such information can serve one of two purposes. An elemental strategy for managing conflict would

---

28. Walton, "Interpersonal Confrontation and Basic Third Party Functions," p. 327.

straightforwardly seek to minimize the occurrence of trigger events and to maximize the dampeners. Beyond that, knowledge of the specific triggers and dampeners may spotlight the causal issues which must be dealt with by any real resolution of the conflict.

Fourth, a variety of conditions seems to be necessary for a productive third-party consultation. These conditions may be sampled here briefly, since a fuller treatment with illustrations is conveniently available.[29] The conditions often can be influenced markedly by the consultant. They include:

- Mutual and synchronized positive motivation by both principals seems a prerequisite, apparently in that it is a measure of willingness to invest in the confrontation and to own its consequences, both of which no doubt are powerful factors predisposing toward a successful experience.

- Some balance in the power of principals in the learning situation seems important, which the consultant can help supply by interventions that help both parties get air time or that draw attention to the domination by one of the pair. The usefulness of balance seems related to reduced defensiveness or resistance on the part of a principal with lower objective power. E.g., the subordinate in a manager/employee pair might feel that he "will lose every time" in the learning situation as well as outside of it, in the absence of efforts by the consultant to achieve some relative balance of power or influence.

- Of critical importance is the appropriate pacing of the two basic phases characteristic of third-party consultation, differentiation and integration. These may occur several times, especially when a complex string of issues is involved.
  a. *Differentiation* often is time-consuming, as each party develops his own sense of the conflict, elaborates other differences between the two parties, and ventilates feelings and reactions toward the other. The level of tension is likely to be high.
  b. *Integration* often can occur in brief if important episodes, as in stressing the commonalities between the pair, expressing a new respect or even a mutual warmth, and moving toward commonly accepted solutions that manage or resolve the interpersonal conflict.

- An intermediate tension level seems useful for learning in third-party confrontations. Low levels of tension imply low motivation; and very high levels of tension apparently bind principals in ways that confound and complicate the learning situation.

29. Walton, *Interpersonal Peacemaking,* pp. 94–115.

No research literature exists that establishes the unqualified value of third-party consultation, or even the conditions under which success is probable. But the presumptive case is strong, supported as it is by some systematic research and by developing practice in a variety of organizational, institutional, and family settings, as well as by the logic of the laboratory approach developed above. Indeed, even when the goals of a specific third-party consultation are not achieved, real progress may have been made. As Walton concludes:

> when participants candidly express and accurately represent themselves to each other, they increase the authenticity of their mutual relationships and individually experience a sense of enhanced personal integrity. The very fact of having invested personal energy in a relationship usually increases their respective commitments to improve the relationship, provided there is some small basis for encouragement. Even when there is no emotional reconciliation, if the parties are able to explicitly or implicitly arrive at better coping techniques, they tend to feel more control over their interpersonal environment and less controlled by it.[30]

Whatever the case, Walton points to a number of researchable propositions with which the next developmental stage in third-party consultation must deal.

6. INDIVIDUAL ASSESSMENT OF
A LIFE'S WORK:
TOWARD CAREER PLANNING
AS A PREOCCUPATION

One of the many ongoing mini-revolutions in organizations involves "career planning." Its emergence along with OD programs based on the laboratory approach is certainly not an accidental thing.[31] This conclusion applies in at least two senses. Career-planning designs, which often are based on the laboratory approach, have attempted to extend T-Group values and dynamics into a critical, practical setting. Given the values toward interpersonal confrontation and openness of the laboratory approach, it is in retrospect a natural development that the same values

30. Walton, *Interpersonal Peacemaking: Confrontations and Third Party Consultation,* (Reading, Mass.: Addison-Wesley Publishing Co., 1969) , p. 95.
31. Many facts establish the linkage. For example, Herbert A. Shepard has been a major contributor to career planning as he was also to OD applications based on the laboratory approach.

would be applied to the critical work zone of a person's life space. To level with one's self about career, epigrammatically, certainly is consistent with levelling with others in interpersonal relations.

In a broader context, the new reemphasis on career planning is also understandable, perhaps predictable. A caricature might be useful. In days gone by, when one hired a "hand" it was of little consequence where the rest of him was as long as that "hand" kept moving appropriately. Today, and for many operators as well as managers, it makes a great deal of difference where the total woman or man is, in complex physical, social, and emotional space. Many organization roles today demand so much of their incumbents that serious consequences increasingly occur if the individual is not "all there." For the individual, the costs may be psychic ones of staying in a need-depriving job, of acting a role that has lost its attractiveness. For the organization, the costs might be decreased innovation or productivity, opportunities that are neglected, or a quality of life with the zest sucked from it. Even more futuristically, we can perhaps anticipate the time when the pace of technological change and knowledge accumulation is so great, and perhaps life so long, that it will be necessary to plan two or three careers in addition to planning for an extended retirement. We see some of the effects already, as in military personnel who retire after 20 years and then seek advanced degrees to prepare for a second career of teaching, or some such. Mothers with grown children constitute a far larger potential for similar second careers.

Hence it is both practical and charitable that increasing organizational attention should be directed at career planning. For this design confronts the critical issue of whether a person's work is providing him what he really wants and needs, and vice versa. If work is not need-satisfying enough, it is to the advantage of both the person and the organization that the fact be recognized early and that plans be made to do something to change the situation.

a. Some General Features of Career Planning: Costs/Benefits of Stimulating Continuous Review

There are many possible kinds of career planning, and some elementary distinctions will be useful. Thus approaches to career planning variously emphasize "can do" and "will do" issues.[32] The former deal with specific skills or knowledge, and the latter involve motivation. Relatedly, approaches to career planning differ in their concern with the psychometric measurement of skills or attitudes as a basis for career

---

32. The distinction is made by Bernard Haldane and is reflected in his "Managerial Excellence Kit" (Washington, D.C.: Bernard Haldane Associates, 1968).

planning.[33] Various approaches also differ in their concern about validation of effects, although little research is available about the consequences of career-planning activities.[34]

Despite these and other distinctions, the general flavor of career-planning activities can be suggested by the introduction to an in-house seminar lasting two full days which is given in Figure 1. The participant gets these orienting cues at the very start.

Such a career-planning seminar has dual purposes. It seeks to induce values and attitudes in participants that encourage more-or-less continu-

Figure 1. Introduction to Career-Planning Seminar

CAREER-PLANNING SEMINAR

The purpose of this seminar is to help you set personal career goals and plan how to attain them. This will be done by assessing and defining your present skills and strengths more precisely.

Many people in large organizations like this one have come into the company with a vague goal of "being successful." This meant moving "up" in the organization, making more money, having an office instead of a work space, supervising others, etc. The assumption was that good performance and appropriate behavior would be rewarded with increased status and money.

The trouble with this "success formula" is that it never asks the question, "What do *you* really want to *do*?" Instead of the job being rewarding in itself, many of us see it only as a *means* to get other rewards—newer, bigger cars, better furnished homes, more pleasant vacations, and a college education for our children.

People find work more meaningful and rewarding when they can relate it to their personal career goals. Unfortunately, many people have difficulty defining career goals.

In this two-day seminar you will

- Define who *you* are in terms of your aptitudes, skills, and strengths
- Define what *you* mean by success
- Define where *you* want to go
- Plan how *you* will get there

Source: Career-planning seminar designed and developed by Walter R. Mead, Corporate Personnel, Smith, Kline and French Laboratories, 1971.

ous review of career progress and individual needs. There are many possible focal questions. Is my career development so satisfying that I can really let myself get into my work? If so, fine. Or do I continuously hold back my efforts because I wonder: Is all this effort getting me what I really want? If not, the questions are legion. What needs are being frustrated in my present job? And why? And what skills do I need to develop in order to avoid the need-depriving consequences of my present job and career prospects? The antigoal is dying on the vine, which is both individually tragic and organizationally wasteful. The hope of career planning is that the tragedy and the waste can be avoided or at least

---

33. For a career-planning program that uses attitudinal measures heavily, see Behavioral Science Center, Sterling Institute, *Achievement Motivation: A Seminar for Managers*, July, 1970.
34. For one evidence of the impact of a Haldane program, see *U.S. Employment Service Review*, December, 1965, p. 15.

reduced if the appropriate issues are confronted throughout a man's career, early as well as late.

Career planning can also have an especial value at a variety of critical points in a work life.[35] Some of these critical points occur in every work life at more or less predictable times:

- You, like many men in their forties, start to raise fundamental questions about how you wish to spend the second half of your life.

Other critical career points are difficult or impossible to program. Some examples include:

- You find an attractive job opportunity has become open, but it will require relocation of your family.
- You are a fairly senior technical man and are considering whether you should apply for a managerial position and whether you would accept one if it were offered.
- You have acquired a specialty which technological advance is making increasingly obsolescent. Do you hang on until the bitter end? Or do you seek to develop a new specialty as early as you can?
- You have come to doubt the value of what had been a life's calling, as in leaving business for the clergy or in leaving the celibate clergy to marry and raise a family.

Some Issues for Organizations

Whether viewed as continuous review or as applied to an immediate situation, career planning raises significant cost/benefit questions. Consider some typical costs from the organization's point of view. Thus career planning is dangerous in organizations that will in principle hold people in jobs that are need-depriving, or in jobs to which individuals are not committed. No value is placed on this organization strategy, for there are circumstances such as a just war which might justify it. The narrower point here, rather, is that a career-planning program that really works will encourage at least some people to try something new, either in the organization or outside of it. In a sense, the organization with a real career-planning program sanctions learning that will encourage some people to leave their present jobs, or even the organization. And these departures will not always be the persons for whom management would be pleased to host a going-away party, on short notice. Such sanctioning requires a major commitment by the host organization, and

---

35. See Jack K. Fordyce and Raymond Weil, *Managing with People* (Reading, Mass.: Addison-Wesley Publishing Co., 1971), pp. 132–33.

certainly one that is inappropriate where the emphasis is to be on career planning "for the good of the organization."

Career planning also would become a hollow effort if it is seen as an indirect way of getting rid of people or of molding them to some master plan for their own destiny of which they are not yet enlightened enough to be aware. The real tests are who gets invited to participate in career-planning activities, and whether the organization can develop a tradition of responding helpfully to even awkward products of career planning. If many clear organizational losers get invited, for example, the program may quickly develop a reputation as a kind of preparatory training for a separation anxiety. If only organizationally-convenient career programs get acted on, similarly, invitees will no doubt become reticent about undertaking any real self-analysis. "The organization" will provide direction in its own good time.

Moreover, career planning can raise issues for individuals and the organization that might be better avoided unless a real commitment to following-through exists. From the individual's point of view, disquieting questions may be raised that require time and patience to explore. Organizationally, career-planning programs may indicate that specific policies, procedures, or structures create impossible situations for people. Career development thus must be tied to the possibility of meaningful change in the organization. If the individual must adapt to a given organization—becoming the kind of peg the organization requires—a career-planning program is not likely to be productive. In fact, it may be bitterly resented. The individual probably will feel that he has sold his soul to the company store in this case; he is not likely to feel that he is directing and charting his own future in the ways that career planning intends.

In addition, organizations must face the issue of the advisability of worrying about whether one has the right job, as opposed to worrying about how to perform more effectively in the job one has. There is no single best response to such a concern. Different conditions will make different responses reasonable. In an economy of rapidly obsolescing skills, the priority often will be on whether a person is in the right job. For yesterday's training and experience will not necessarily suffice for today's job demands.

Finally, career plans are no better than their implementation. And here's a major rub. For an individual might plan, but implementation commonly requires the help of others, such as supervisors, and resources not controlled by the individual. Moreover, some career plans might require that the plans of others be modified, new strategies be developed, and so on. If career planning is viewed basically as a way of easing people out of the organization, in sum, it is a very involved and treacherous way of doing it because so many interlocking factors are involved.

Some Benefits for Individuals

The benefits for the individual can cover a broad range, although no real research literature exists that provides unchallengeable guidance. But at least three desirable outcomes seem generally implicit in programs of career planning. *First,* the individual may feel a new sense of control over his life as he struggles to determine whether his present course is the one he really desires. Even if no change results, the individual may feel a new commitment and dedication to a career pathway that he has analyzed and come to accept at a deeper level in his own way and time.

Second, and relatedly, the individual may come to feel a new sense of responsibility for where he is in his career. This is certainly the case if he decides to take some new direction as a result of career planning. An enhanced sense of personal responsibility is also likely even if the individual continues as before, after a hard look at career planning. As with the laboratory approach, the goals are to increase the degrees to which individuals can own their career choices, feel commitment to them, and have the sense and reality of having some control over what happens in their work lives.

The strategy of career planning is a transparent one, then, in these first two particulars. To choose is the ultimate human act, and to feel responsible for a choice is to announce ownership and commitment. Career planning attempts to create the conditions where greater opportunities exist for responsible choice, conditions that permit persons to affirm their existence in part of their lifespace. In essence, then, career planning is oriented toward a new quality of life in organizations.

Third, conscious weighing of "musts" and "likes" with personal skills and abilities in career planning can put the individual in a more realistic attitude. Does he or she really need a certain source of satisfaction at work? Or is it more a matter of that source being an attractive but unessential feature? And does the person either have the skills to achieve his musts, or can he somehow reasonably expect to gain them? Or is he just engaged in wishful thinking? These are critical questions that a career-planning program seeks to have each participant confront, as he widens his base of realistically appraised factors relevant to career planning.

b. A Sample Design[36] for Openers: A Career-Planning Seminar

Figure 2 sketches the outline of a career-planning seminar based on the laboratory approach, an opening experience that is intended to encourage

---

36. The seminar was developed by Walter R. Mead, Corporate Personnel, Smith, Kline and French Laboratories, 1971.

Figure 2. Design for a Career-Planning Seminar

Duration (minutes)	Description of Activity	Purpose of Design Element
?	1. Premeeting work. Each participant prepares a list of six "most satisfying achievements since leaving high school" and describes in writing specifically what he did. The list is to be brought to the first meeting of the Career-Planning Seminar.	1a. to start the individual thinking about what things he finds valuable and satisfying 1b. to start the individual thinking about his positive skills and abilities reflected in these achievements.
90	2. Groups of six individuals briefly introduce themselves, and then in turn: ■ Each individual describes and briefly discusses his first most satisfying achievement. ■ Other individuals jot down the skills and abilities seen as relevant in that achievement. ■ Each individual in turn describes the second most satisfying achievement, then the third, etc. ■ Notes about skills and abilities reflected in these other achievements are taken. ■ Each of the six persons in the Seminar ends up with five sets of notes about his skills and abilities, one set from each of the other five participants who heard each of his achievements described.	2a. to provide a positive start to self-analysis 2b. to provide each individual with lists of his positive skills and abilities as perceived by others 2c. to provide each individual with some gentle feedback concerning what others perceive as his strengths which he might later use to make his career plans as realistic as possible
35–40	3. Each individual prepares a list of how five specific individuals who know him well would describe him, with the instructions this time calling for both positive and negative features: ■ Participants prepare descriptions of "Me as Seen by Others." ■ Participants in turn share these descriptions by reading them aloud.	3a. to introduce gently the individual's negative features 3b. to provide some reality testing of these negative features by other participants, based on their probably limited acquaintance
5 5 15 5 15	4. The focus is on the various roles that participants assume in their work lives and at home. The subelements of the design variously expand on this theme: ■ In a deliberately brief period of time, participants prepare as long a list as they can of roles they play. ■ Participants in turn share their lists of roles. Each participant adds to his own list as he hears roles shared by others that are reasonably applicable to himself. ■ Each participant then distinguishes two lists: a. roles that are most satisfying b. roles that are least satisfying ■ Taking only the list of least-satisfying roles, each participant deals with two critical questions: a. What do I dislike about the least-satisfying roles?	4a. to remind participants of the variety of roles they play, and of their diverse reactions to them 4b. to encourage participants to think of specific factors in roles that induce dislike or dissatisfaction 4c. to raise motivational issues with participants, to help determine whether there is any way of avoiding the performance of disliked/dissatisfying roles 4d. to heighten the sense of personal choice and individual responsibility by choosing to accept certain roles and to reject others

304

Figure 2—continued

b. Why do I continue to fulfill these least-liked roles?

60–75 ■ Participants share as much about answers to these two critical questions as they wish.

60–75 5. The focus is on "success patterns," dealing at greater depth with the six most satisfying achievements introduced in items 1 and 2 above:
■ Each achievement is rated in terms of 10 possible satisfactions, each of which is to be listed as a "major" or "minor" factor in each achievement.
■ A scoring system helps the individual to discern if there is an underlying consistency in which particular combinations of satisfactions define personal "achievement" or "success."
■ Based on these combinations, the individual develops "My Definition of Success" in writing.
■ The results are shared with the group of six, especially the definitions of success.

5a. to encourage the individual to think about what he needs to succeed or achieve, in terms of specific satisfactions relevant to Self
5b. to search for patterns in personally defined clusters of satisfactions
5c. to develop a written definition of "success" against which to measure current job roles, etc.

60–90 6. A "fantasy experience" concludes the design for the first day, with the focus on three things each participant would like to have done with his career:
■ Each participant draws three pictures representing these three unfulfilled desires.
■ The admonition is to draw a picture, not a projective image.
■ The pictures can be shared.

6a. to end the day with an ostensibly light exercise

6b. to induce some minor regression that may reveal insights controlled under other circumstances

30–45 7. Deliberately, the design begins to deal with more difficult issues:
■ Each participant describes Self in detail in writing, in the third person.
■ The third-person descriptions are read to the other participants, who react.

7a. to encourage the participant to be an observer of Self, to facilitate personal analysis by adapting an observational perspective of the Self
7b. to provide some measure of how realistic the person is in assessing his own qualities, in observing the Self

60–75 8. While preceding design elements were intended to sharpen insights, the focus here is directly on the present or future job, as well as on action steps to make it meet the individual's needs and values:
■ Each participant drafts an ideal future job description that would meet his needs
■ each participant must detail the specifics of what resources he has or requires in order to fill that ideal job description, e.g.:
   a. credentials
   b. information
   c. skills
   d. contacts
These products are not shared.

8a. to encourage participants to develop their plans to fit their needs and values
8b. to encourage participants to match their resources, job preferences, and values with specific career plans
8c. to reinforce the critical notion that, beyond a certain point, career planning rests on individual decisions and initiatives

Figure 2—continued

90–120	9. All participants are told that they cannot change their jobs, short of major and unexpected developments, and hence must improve their present jobs: ■ Each participant designs five initial steps for a job-improvement plan. ■ Each individual has one hour to begin or complete as many of the five initial steps as he can. ■ Six participants reassemble to share reactions to their efforts to implement their job-improvement plans.	9a. to encourage participants into an action mode, as a complement to the earlier analytical mode 9b. to provide an experience with the possibilities for improving a job environment 9c. to give the participant a sense of control over his environment and a feeling of individual responsibility for increasing the need-satisfying potential of his work
30–40	10. Each participant prepares a list of "Excuses for Inaction" and shares it by reading it to other participants, who discuss each list.	10a. to warn participants of the seductive quality of "excuses" or "reasons" for not acting after the Seminar 10b. to emphasize, from a negative perspective, that failure to act is often a self-imposed restriction and a lost opportunity to exercise initiative 10c. to reinforce any developing norms or values toward future action/planning re careers of participants
15	11. Wrap-Up and Evaluation.	

organization members to give continuing attention to their own development. Participation is voluntary. Basically, the design can speak for itself, since it is quite transparent in intent, as the column "Purpose of Design Element" in Figure 2 should establish. The internal logic of the design also should be clear enough. For example, it begins with less threatening subelements and escalates to those that can be quite threatening. Note also that the transitions between subelements of the design are not treated here. Runs of the design have been conducted by a resource person, as well as by taped instructions that participants cue up and respond to on their own. For most purposes so far checked, one approach seems as useful as the other.

Note here in addition to the description in Figure 2 that the design respects the values of the laboratory approach and has the properties attributed to OD designs. The reader can test out for himself the design's congruence with the laboratory values in Sections A and B of Part I.

That the career-planning design has the five major properties of an OD design can be briefly established here. *First,* the career-planning design is experiential in a variety of senses. This is perhaps most dramatically the case in design subelement 9, which provides direct experience with career planning by instructing participants to take some initial steps toward improving their existing job situation. More broadly, the total design is rooted in the individual's experiences of achieving or failing, in his own standards or criteria of success or failure.

Second, the design for career planning reflects a dominant emphasis on the how versus the what. The design attempts to touch a number of the key elements in any career plan, in quite specific ways. For example, the individual totes up his assets and liabilities, and then seeks confirmation from others that he has done an objective job of it. The what of career planning is the individual's responsibility, in fact as well as by intent of the design. Indeed, as was noted, career planning that emphasizes the what is likely to be perceived as manipulative and as narrowing the zone of individual freedom. These are antigoals in career planning.

Third, the career-planning design seeks to increase the valid information available, to add to the choices perceived as potentially open, and to add resources relevant to decisions about career planning. The various ways in which the design thus augments the individual's resources should be more-or-less clear from the description and purposes in Figure 2.

Fourth, the design in Figure 2 seeks a true collaboration between participants that reinforces their sense of individual responsibility and initiative. The fine line is between seeking increases in information or choices or insight from others and avoiding possible dilution of an individual's initiative and responsibility to act after he has searched his environment. Hence the basic design progression in Figure 2. The design initially emphasizes feedback and inputs from others, as each participant sharpens his own sense of career planning. Then, design elements 8 and 9 in Figure 2 shift the emphasis to individual planning and action. Finally, design element 10 returns to the group locus for what can be done better there than by separate individuals: to share ideas, stimulate further probing, and provide reinforcement as well as emotional support for additional efforts toward career planning in the future.

Fifth, the career-planning design has a variety of relational thrusts. Thus it seeks to develop simultaneous payoffs for individuals and for their organization, based on the belief that any need-depriving situation is in the long run, at least, a breeder of unattractive consequences for both. Moreover, the design seeks to relate individuals as helpers in a common effort, as that is appropriate. And it also strives to make a more difficult connection. That is, at some point, each individual best serves himself as well as others by turning inward on his own resources to take responsibility for actions or decisions. The theme is paradoxical: assertion of self through others. Specifically, inputs from others usually are necessary to help a person reach a decision or take an action. But each person must assert his difference from others if he is to lay any claim to control of his environment, perhaps even if he is to affirm his very existence. He must own the decisions or actions. That is, he must take initiative in and responsibility for those actions or decisions.

7. ORGANIZATIONAL IDENTIFICATION OF INDIVIDUAL POTENTIAL: THE ASSESSMENT-CENTER STRATEGY

The laboratory approach also appears in various guises in other efforts to deal with individuals in organizations, as in the burgeoning tendency to use assessment centers to evaluate individual potential for new responsibilities. Briefly, the assessment-center concept seeks to identify individuals with characteristics considered to be indicators of anticipated success in a specific position or level of management. The approach is especially favored for the early identification of potential for first-level supervision, that is, at the point the individual transitions from a functional or technical specialty to a job with integrative managerial responsibilities.

The assessment-center concept has its immediate developmental roots in the multiple-assessment procedures which can be traced to the period of World War II. The typical concern then was to determine which individuals had the potential to be effective spies, or military officers, or whatever, quickly and in large numbers.[37] Recognition of broader applications came quickly.[38] The basic approach is a simple one: Increases in predictive and explanatory power, relevant to estimating potential to perform effectively in some capacity, are sought via several independent assessment techniques. That is, multiple assessment would use such approaches to testing for potential for effective performance as:

- personality testing, as in the use of projective tests
- paper-and-pencil testing for specific abilities or skills, as for verbal facility

---

37. OSS Assessment Staff, *Assessment of Men* (New York: Rinehart, 1948), gives credit for the emphasis to German psychologists seeking those with potential as military officers.

38. The advantages of multiple-assessment procedures are detailed by John C. Flanagan, "Some Considerations in the Development of Situational Tests," *Personnel Psychology*, Vol. 7 (Winter, 1964), pp. 461–64.

That efforts to capitalize on such advantages came thick and fast is patent in the fact that there have been at least 50 articles and reports published in the past five years about the assessment-center strategy, many of which have penetrated the general management literature. See "Where They Make Believe They're the Boss," *Business Week*, August 28, 1971, pp. 34–35; Robert C. Albrook, "How to Spot Executives Early," *Fortune*, Vol. 78 (July, 1968), pp. 106–11; William C. Byham, "Assessment Centers for Spotting Future Managers," *Harvard Business Review*, Vol. 48 (July, 1970), pp. 150–60 and John J. McConnell and Treadway C. Parker, "An Assessment Center Program for Multi-Organizational Use," *Training and Development Journal*, Vol. 26 (March, 1972), pp. 6–15.

- situational testing, as in exercises or simulations that are analogs of the situations that the assessed person will face in performing the task in question

Situational testing constituted the major breakthrough in multiple assessment, in at least three major senses. Paramountly, situational testing has the clearest obvious relevance for estimating performance on the target task. Relatedly, studies tend to show, at the least, that situational tests make "a substantial and unique contribution to the prediction of management success."[39] Moreover, many studies indicate that situational tests are not only useful but tend to be the most useful of the three types of assessment procedures. Paper-and-pencil tests of ability tend to be of intermediate value, and personality tests of least value, in assessing potential. As Douglas W. Bray and Donald L. Grant conclude:

> Justification of the high cost of the [approach] can be obtained from the finding that the assessment ratings [based on situational tests] account for more of the variance in the progress criterion than do the simpler pencil-and-paper ability tests, or, for that matter than does any single method used.[40]

The focus below will be on situational testing, which is at least a major element in all assessment centers and constitutes the heart of many of them.

a. Three Generic Features of the Strategy

There are three central features of the assessment-center strategy. *First,* assessment centers deal with a number of individuals at the same time, say 12 or so persons who are exposed to a design of variable length, depending usually on the level of management in relationship to which they are being assessed. Figure 3 outlines such a typical design, typical in that it includes individual, group, and interview experiences keyed to the target position or level.[41]

Broadly, the intent is that the design components induce behaviors

---

39. Herbert B. Wollowick and W. J. McNamara, "Relationship of the Components of an Assessment Center to Management Success," *Journal of Applied Psychology,* Vol. 53 (October, 1969), p. 352.
40. Douglas W. Bray and Donald L. Grant, "The Assessment Center in the Measurement of Potential for Business Management," *Psychological Monographs,* Vol. 80, No. 17, Whole No. 625 (1966), p. 24. See also J. R. Hinrichs, "Comparisons of 'Real Life' Assessments of Management Potential with Situational Exercises, Paper-and-Pencil Ability Tests, and Personality Inventories," *Journal of Applied Psychology,* Vol. 53 (October, 1969), pp. 425–32.
41. For other designs, see Bray and Grant, *op. cit.;* and J. M. Greenwood and W. J. McNamara, "Interrater Reliability in Situational Tests," *Journal of Applied Psychology,* Vol. 51 (June, 1967), pp. 226–32.

Figure 3. Situational Exercises and Simulations in an Assessment-Center Design

Day 1

- *Management Game.* Four-man teams seek to form different kinds of conglomerates by bartering companies. Each team sets its own acquisition objectives and policies and must organize to meet them.

- *Background Interview.* A 90-minute interview is conducted by an assessor.

- *Individual Fact-Finding and Decision-Making.* Each participant is told to imagine himself a division manager who has the immediate problem of reviewing a rejected request for funds to continue a research project. The research director appeals the decision of the previous manager to his successor. The participant gets a brief description of the situation and is given 15 minutes to ask questions that will provide additional data. He then must make a decision, deliver it orally, and be prepared to defend his decision under challenge from a member of the assessment panel.

Day 2

- *In-Basket Exercise.* The participant is told he has been suddenly promoted to a first-level supervisory position and is given a simulated in-basket left by his predecessor. The participant is to deal with the contents, as by scheduling and planning, delegating, making decisions, answering questions, and so on.

  An assessor reviews the results of the completed effort and conducts an hour interview with the man to gain insight into his strategies, thought processes, awareness of problems, and the like.

- *Assigned Role in Leaderless Group.* Each participant is instructed that he is a member of a compensation committee which will meet to allocate $8,000 in salary increases among six supervisors and managers from different departments.

  Each participant represents a different department and is instructed to do the best he can for the employee from his department.

  Participants and assessors rate the performance of members of the committee.

- *Individual Analysis and Presentation, Followed by Group Decision-Making.* Participants are each instructed to act as a consultant to an executive who faces two problems: a division that consistently loses money, and alternate plans for corporate expansion.

  Participants are given data about the company, from which they are to recommend courses of action.

  Each participant presents his recommendations in a 7-minute oral presentation.

  Following the presentations, participants form a group that is instructed to develop a single set of recommendations.

Days 3 and 4

- Assessment panel meets to share their observations, as well as to evaluate each participant as to: overall potential; each specific trait or attribute seen as relevant to the job; and training or development needs.

Source: William C. Byham, "The Assessment Center as an Aid in Management Development," *Training Directors Journal,* Vol. 25 (December, 1971), p. 19.

and skills relevant to effective performance on the task. The task is formidable,[42] although its magnitude will only be suggested here. Clearly, for example, this intent implies a careful analysis of the task, of the demands it makes on the individual as well as the skills it requires of him. Clearly, also, this intent implies a range of knowledge about which specific exercises or simulations are appropriate to test for potential to

---

42. For a comprehensive treatment, see George G. Stern, Morris I. Stein, and Benjamin S. Bloom, *Methods in Personality Assessment* (Glencoe, Ill.: Free Press, 1956), esp. pp. 35–56; and Donald E. Super and John O. Crites, *Appraising Vocational Fitness* (New York: Harper & Row, Publishers, 1962), esp. pp. 29–55.

perform specific tasks, how many such exercises provide the best assessment of potential, and so on and on.

Second, the assessors are a panel of people familiar with the demands of the position or organization level. Each panel includes perhaps four to six members, who are usually "line" personnel from one or two organization levels above that of the target against which individual skills and attitudes are being assessed. The assessors normally do not have a direct supervisory relationship with those being assessed. Individuals on such panels tend to serve only episodically. In such a large organization as A.T.&T., however, assessors serve a six-month tour of duty.

The assessment panel typically operates at two evaluative levels. Assessors often make some overall rating of participants such as: Does Participant A have the potential to be promoted to middle-management levels in the next 5 to 10 years? In addition, assessors typically rate each participant on a number of more-or-less discrete qualities. In one case, for example, assessors rated each participant on these 12 traits: (1) Aggressiveness, (2) Persuasive or Selling Ability, (3) Oral Communications, (4) Planning and Organization, (5) Self-Confidence, (6) Resistance to Stress, (7) Written Communications, (8) Energy Level, (9) Decision-Making, (10) Interpersonal Contact, (11) Administrative Ability, and (12) Risk Taking.[43]

This dual evaluation is the heart of the assessment center. Assessment will be effective in uncovering potential for future growth as several conditions are simultaneously met. These conditions include: the specification of characteristics significant for performance on some task or at some organization level; defining those characteristics in behavioral terms; setting up exercises or simulations that highlight the strengths or weaknesses of specific individuals in behaving so as to meet the demands of the task; and training members of assessment panels to perceive and interpret that behavior correctly.

The assessing panel's major responsibility is to develop a report on each individual.[44] As Figure 3 indicates, the panel typically spends a day or so writing up reports concerning the performance of the participants on the interview as well as in the group and individual experiences or simulations. Typically, the reports are considered one part of each assessee's total record when he is later considered for promotion or a new job. In much early experience with assessment centers, however, the re-

43. Hinrichs, *op. cit.,* p. 427. The qualities to be rated vary from position to position and from one assessment center to another for the same position. For another list of qualities to be rated, see John H. McConnell, "The Assessment Center: A Flexible Program for Supervisors," *Personnel,* Vol. 48 (September, 1971), pp. 36–37.

44. For a sample, see William C. Byham, "The Assessment Center as an Aid in Management Development," *Training Directors Journal,* Vol. 25 (December, 1971), pp. 20–21.

ports were put in a restricted file, while the assessed individuals went on their diverse organizational ways. Various measures of organizational performance later are compared with the assessment record, so as to estimate the validity of the assessment procedures while seeking to avoid the contamination of managerial action with the assessment reports.

Third, assessment centers blend two sets of critical activities: assessment (or evaluation), and development (or training). For those assessed, the dual point should be patent. Thus a typical goal of the assessment report is to suggest remedial or broadening experiences to meet inadequacies surfaced in the performance of individuals on design exercises or simulations. Relatedly, for those assessed, each design component can at once facilitate assessing an individual while it provides him with training opportunities. For example, the In-Basket[45] component of the illustrative design in Figure 3 has both potentials. Not incidentally, the assessed individual is likely to be very interested in improving his performance during his stay at the assessment center and hence may be "unfrozen" in the sense defined in Sections A and B of Part I. In such a state, the individual is unusually and perhaps uniquely open to training inputs.

Assessment centers also provide training and development opportunities for members of the assessing panel as they go about evaluating the skills and attitudes of others, which point may not be so obvious. Assessors receive some prior and intensive training which, in combination with the actual experience of participating in specific runs of assessment designs, can be a powerful stimulus to their own development. For example, the development of assessors can be enhanced in senses such as:[46]

- improved interviewing and listening skills
- enhanced skills relevant to observing behavior
- increased understanding of group dynamics and leadership styles
- new insights as to why specific individuals behave as they do
- strengthening management skills via working with and observing various design components, such as In-Baskets, case studies, or simulations
- broadening the range of their repertoire of responses to management problems
- establishing and sharpening standards in terms of which to evaluate performance

---

45. The In-Basket is a training technique which uses 10–20 letters, memos, transcripts of phone calls, etc., to test an individual's ability to organize work, handle complexity and uncertainty, and so on. The trainee is instructed to act as the holder of a job, the features of which are usually specified, who has to deal with the pending business in his in-basket.
46. Byham, "The Assessment Center as an Aid in Management Development," p. 12.

- developing a more precise vocabulary with which to describe behavior or group dynamics

So compelling have such training advantages for assessors been to some wielders of power in organizations, indeed, that they have deliberately increased the ratio of assessors to participants so as to expose more of the former to the training opportunities implicit in the assessment-center approach.

b. Some Points of Articulation with the Laboratory Approach

The assessment-center strategy can variously rely upon and reflect facets of the laboratory approach. The clearest kinship is in their common experiential thrust. Thus Robert Albrook explains that assessment centers basically deal with "observing how executive candidates perform in management games that often achieve startling realism." That realism derives from the experiential and job-related nature of the assessment design. He explains:

> These techniques are powerful because they measure actual behavior in a standardized fashion. They do not depend upon a candidate's self-assessment as to whether, for example, he "likes people"—the approach often taken in ordinary interviewing or psychological testing. Nor do they depend upon the sometimes suspect "reference" from a friend, teacher, or former employer . . . The games provide a live demonstration of such factors in a realistic setting.[47]

Three points establish other specific points of articulation between assessment centers and the laboratory approach. *First,* a process orientation is at the heart of the assessment-center concept. This is patently true for the assessors, who focus on behavior, leadership, and group dynamics that are seen as relevant for performance in the specific position or level of organization which is the standard for assessment. Simulations or exercises like those in Figure 3 provide the context for such a process orientation. And they also provide a measure of how the participants can bring to bear a variety of skills, such as financial management, planning, etc. Since process and content issues are ineluctably mixed in assessment centers, a premium is placed on the skill of the assessment panel in being aware of both. Various learning designs based on the laboratory approach, including T-Groups, can help sharpen assessor competence in identifying and managing process issues.

Assessment centers also commonly induce a strong process orientation

47. Albrook, *op. cit.,* p. 106.

in participants, whether by intent or merely in the nature of the design. Thus William Byham notes that "a 'T-Group' atmosphere is often created to increase self-learning." Interestingly, also, the job-boundedness of assessment-center designs may provide a safeguard against the negative effects of sensitivity training discussed in Section A, Part II. Byham notes relevantly that: "Conditions . . . are sufficiently well-controlled . . . that none of the negative effects which have occasionally characterized the T-Group session have been noted. . . ."[48]

Even if attempts are not made to create a T-Group-like environment of low defensiveness and high disclosure, a strong process orientation will very likely characterize assessment experiences. If nothing else, participants are understandably concerned about how and why things happen as they do in the simulations and exercises, as well as about how they can improve their interpersonal and technical competence in achieving what they intend to accomplish. Many assessment centers accentuate this natural tendency, in a variety of ways. Typically, participants rate themselves and others on total performance as well as on such process-related dimensions as leadership, ideas contributed, and so on. Such data gathering encourages a process orientation, of course. More elaborately, participants as part of the design also often:[49]

- analyze and discuss their performance in exercises or interviews as they watch videotape replays
- engage in critiques of their performance in discussion groups led by outside resource persons
- meet in small groups of participants to share their responses and strategies in specific exercises or simulations, to have their reasoning tested by others, and to enlarge their repertoire of possible administrative responses by listening to others explain their approaches

Second, feedback to participants is emphasized in assessment centers. Because the focus is on feedback related to performance on the tasks or exercises, it consequently has technical as well as interpersonal emphases.

The quantity and character of the feedback processes vary broadly in different assessment programs. The amount of feedback will vary in proportion to the level of the assessment target, for example, as will the formality of the feedback processes. Thus the approaches to process orientation above will create many opportunities for feedback, and some assessment centers go much further, especially for higher-level positions. As Byham observes:

Higher-level participants get much more information than lower-level participants. Career counseling and planning discus-

48. Byham, "Assessment Centers for Spotting Future Managers," p. 152.
49. Byham, "The Assessment Center as an Aid in Management Development," p. 12.

sions are often combined with assessor feedback for higher-level participants. Most feedback interviewing ends in a written commitment to action on the part of the participant and sometimes the organization.[50]

Whether for high-level or low-level participants, however, the use of feedback in assessment centers has a two-way relevance to the laboratory approach. Thus various discussions above (especially in Section A, Part II) have a direct relevance for the assessment-center strategy. In effect, moreover, the exercises and simulations in an assessment-center design constitute a context for limiting and focusing feedback on performance-related issues. This probably intensifies the relevance of the feedback and makes it more difficult to avoid. In a T-Group, in contrast, a feedback may be more diffuse and not so life-relevant. The assessment-center concept in this sense is a significant model for other applications of the laboratory approach.

Third, the values guiding the specific assessment centers seem to be critical. If the values emphasize a helping relationship and the primacy of the needs of the participants, that is one thing, even given the potential for difficulty in the effort. Other values could trend in radically different directions, as toward the creation of organizational look-alikes patterned after some monolithic grand design. Such value sets would induce more repression than psychological owning of any learning. By way of an overview, William Byham and Regina Pentecost implicitly and briefly highlight the potential for both open learning and covert manipulation in assessment centers. "Carefully designed exercises can subtly change candidates' attitudes during assessment," they note.[51] Hence the centrality to the assessment-center concept of the normative issues raised in Part I above.

c. Some Attractions of Assessment Centers and Qualifications Thereof

Although a creation of the past few years only, the assessment-center strategy has spread widely. At least 100 businesses now employ the approach, we are told,[52] and a number of government agencies have also begun to experiment with the strategy.[53] This subsection will sketch the broad attractions of assessment centers that seem to explain their burgeoning popularity. Five factors below suggest the fuller rationale. Several

---

50. *Ibid.,* p. 12.
51. William C. Byham and Regina Pentecost, "The Assessment Center: Identifying Tomorrow's Managers," *Personnel,* Vol. 47 (September, 1970), p. 23.
52. *Ibid.,* p. 10. For bibliographies of various programs, see *ibid.,* pp. 21–22; and Hinrichs, *op. cit.,* p. 432.
53. Tennessee Valley Authority, *TVA's Experiment in the Assessment of Managerial Potential* (Knoxville, Tenn., n.d.).

critical qualifications are stressed to keep those attractions somewhat in perspective.

First, the growing scale of the assessment problem has forced experimentation with new approaches. In A.T.&T. alone, for example, 70,000 candidates for first-level supervisory positions have been assessed in recent years. The assessment load has roots in industrial and population growth, clearly enough. In addition, the dramatic recent decline in the size of the critical 35–45 age group[54] places a special premium on the early identification of those with managerial potential, so that they may get suitable developmental experiences. The decline reflects the lack of Depression-era babies and the low birth rates of 1930–40.

Second, traditional methods of assessment apparently have left much to be desired, at least as far as many organizations are concerned. The intent of assessment centers is to help do better what must and will be done, in one fashion or another. The goal is to provide an additional, and hopefully a well-informed, source of information to help guide evaluation and promotion decisions. Perhaps the archetypal block to evaluation or promotion is the lower-level functionary who defensively devotes himself to assuring a hard time for any young employee who is better trained, or whatever, than he. Or perhaps the motivation is an inadequate concept of the managerial job.

Hence perhaps the key potential weakness of some assessment-center plans is that they rely on nomination of participants by their immediate supervisors. As Byham delicately observes: "Some high potential employees may never be nominated because qualities of aggressiveness, curiosity and intelligence that might make a person successful at higher levels of management are not always appreciated by lower-level supervision."[55] This may be especially probable today, given the relative flood of unprecedentedly trained youngsters in many fields with skills beyond those of persons only a few years senior to them. Consequently, a number of organizations have resorted to self-nomination as a bypass around obstructive supervisors. And the voluntarism of self-nomination probably also would help intensify the training and development aspects of assessment centers.

Third, several validation studies support the effectiveness of assessment centers for identifying both organizational winners and losers.[56] Significantly, also, these studies usually indicate the superiority of the center concept over such approaches as supervisory appraisals or paper-and-pencil tests.[57] For example, one study is especially convincing about

---

54. David Nadler, *The NOW Employee* (Houston, Tex.: Gulf Publishing Co., 1971), pp. 4–5.
55. Byham, "The Assessment Center as an Aid in Management Development," p. 16.
56. Bray and Grant, *op. cit.*
57. Hinrichs, *op. cit.*

the former point.[58] It dealt with 123 college-trained new hires and 144 noncollege individuals who were already first-line supervisors. After assessment, by design, the results were locked away. Eight years later, independent measures of progress of the 267 participants were made. The study had a variety of emphases. Most strikingly, however, the assessment panel correctly identified 95 percent of those who did not attain promotion to middle management.

A mixed conclusion seems appropriate. The assessment-center concept is still in a developmental stage, and a specific assessment effort is no better than the clarity with which job-relevant behaviors and skills are defined, induced by the design, and perceived accurately by assessors. Research does suggest just those things tend to happen, more rather than less, but the magic is clearly not in the concept but in its implementation. The point is particularly appropriate should a bandwagon aspect develop and should adoptions of the concept be attempted without the careful tailoring of assessment designs to specific jobs in specific organizations. The temptation to seek such shortcuts is great, but the penalties seem severe.

Fourth, the typical assessment-center design seems to deal with performance-relevant factors, although care is necessary to assure that its exercises and simulations do in fact elicit behaviors, skills, and attitudes appropriate to the target job or organization level. The value of the emphasis on performance is perhaps greatest in the case of assessing minority and female employees.[59] Many paper-and-pencil tests, that is to say, discriminate against the culturally deprived. Moreover, the relevance of such tests to performance at work often has been obscure or indirect. Recent court decisions—such as *Griggs et al.* v. *Duke Power*—encourage special care that selection and appraisal standards and procedures be job-relevant.[60] The content of exercises and simulations in assessment-center designs can provide such job relevance.

Fifth, the use of assessor panels has variously aided acceptance of the assessment-center concept, especially via greater understanding of its strengths and weaknesses. Use of line managers as assessors, for example, has eased acceptance of the concept by other managers and by the participants as well. Greater involvement in the assessment program goes hand in hand with greater understanding, which Byham considers an "extremely important result." He cites the contrasting illustration of psychological testing, on whose results managers typically overrely or underrely. Byham explains that managers "have difficulty determining the correct

58. Bray and Grant, *op. cit.,* esp. p. 18.
59. Douglas W. Bray, "The Assessment Center: Opportunities for Women," *Personnel,* Vol. 48 (September, 1971), pp. 30–34.
60. William C. Byham and Morton E. Spitzer, "Personnel Testing: The Law and Its Implications," *Personnel,* Vol. 48 (September, 1971), pp. 8–19.

emphasis because they are not familiar with the tests, tester or intent of the program." Assessment-center reports can be misused for similar reasons, of course, but the probability seems lower because of the participation of line managers in developing specific assessment designs as well as in assessing itself. "When a manager who has been an assessor gets the assessment report," Byham concludes, "he knows the basis for the observations and judgments and can more accurately weigh them against data on job performance and other available information."[61]

---

61. Byham, "The Assessment Center as an Aid in Management Development," p. 13.

C. INTERVENTIONS
AIMED AT GROUPS:
SOME DEVELOPMENTAL TRENDS
AND A CASE STUDY

This section and the next have two straightforward goals. First, major developmental trends in applications of the laboratory approach to groups will be sketched. "Group" here refers generally to aggregates of 20 persons or so at the largest which directly interact and share an immediate psychological identification. The focus here is on groups such as a small work unit in a formal organization, as opposed to categoric groups.

These developmental trends in the history of OD applications to groups provide the background for subsequent subsections of this section and all of Section D below. The material to follow etches detail into selected areas of the developmental background by describing a variety of OD applications in specific groups. Illustrations will provide a counterpoint for the description of general trends.

1. GROUP CHANGE VIA LABORATORY METHODS:
SOME OVERALL TENDENCIES

The laboratory approach went to school on the experience of other behavioral science approaches to groups, to use the golfer's idiom, and the results were mixed. The emphasis on the T-Group was the product of the initial phase of this parallel development, but the virtues of

319

Phase I were also its major liabilities. Crudely but revealingly, Phase I maximized the impact of the initial laboratory learning experience, almost always in a stranger T-Group. The cost was the probable loss of transfer of learning from the training environment. To be sure, the loss was not invariant. The probable loss was less pronounced in transfers into close relationships like the family, and the loss was more pronounced in attempted transfers into organizations. Phase II emphasizes transfer of learning, at the risk of reduced impact of the initial learning experience.

a. Laboratory and Other Behavioral Science Approaches to Groups: A Case of Parallel Development, Phase I

The value and impact of the T-Group as a vehicle for learning clearly is implied in the developmental history of other behavioral science approaches to the group. Three chronological stages of that history are especially relevant for establishing the point. To begin, early observers dating back to at least Aristotle[1] and through at least Le Bon[2] were impressed by a common observation that the behavior, attitudes, and beliefs of individuals are rooted basically in interpersonal and intergroup relations. Aristotle saw nobility in man's social nature, and Le Bon saw his groupiness as the source of much mischief. Whether for base purposes or noble, however, one generalization underlies ever such disparate notions as Aristotle's and Le Bon's: groups are a major source of influence over their members' behavior, attitudes, and beliefs.

In this elemental sense, the group is a *medium of control*. It is a major context in which people develop their concepts of who they are, or, to say almost the same thing, of how they relate to others. Hence the compelling character of T-Group dynamics.

The emphasis on the T-Group effectively derives from two conceptual extensions of the basic observation that groups influence behavior.[3] One developmental notion was a product of the 1930s and 1940s, basically. Its core insight was direct. If groups can influence or control behavior, attitudes, and beliefs—goes this core insight—then it is expedient to think of the group as a *target of change*. A variety of theoretical and applied work leaped at the challenge of gaining the leverage inherent in a group's influence over its members so as to change either individual

---

1. Aristotle defined man as a "social animal," and a splendid one, in his *Politics*.
2. Gustave Le Bon, *The Crowd* (16th impression; London: T. F. Unwin, 1926).
3. The following argument was suggested by Dorwin Cartwright, "Achieving Change in People: Some Applications of Group Dynamics Theory," *Human Relations,* Vol. 4 (October, 1951), pp. 381–92.

or group behavior. Thus group contexts were used to induce mothers to regularly feed orange juice to their babies, to encourage industrial workers to raise output, or to get housewives to use uncommon cuts of meat so as to ease wartime shortages.

This first conceptual extension of the basic group insight generated considerable research and applied activity, usually called "group dynamics."[4] Several derivative statements of basic relationships—or principles of group dynamics—resulted from this interest, and they have had a wide impact. Illustratively, the following principles have been applied in a broad range of teaching, healing, and work contexts:

- The greater the attractiveness of a group for its members, the greater the influence it can exert over its members, and the more widely shared are a group's norms by its members.
- The greater the attractiveness of a group for its members, the greater the resistance to changes in behavior, attitudes, or beliefs which deviate from group norms.
- The greater the prestige of an individual among group members, the greater the influence he can exert.

There is one particular weak link in attempts to apply such principles of group dynamics, especially in industrial or administrative situations. Encouraging the development of groups does make available an enormous potential for the control of behavior, but there is no guarantee that groups will "do the right thing" as far as formal authorities are concerned. For example, if workers view their group as attractive on social grounds, that group will not necessarily be a useful medium for changing attitudes about output levels in the way that management desires. A more attractive group might only be able to better mobilize its resources to resist management, in fact.[5]

Consequently, it became increasingly clear that other principles of group dynamics were necessary to predict whether, and in what direction, a group's influence would be applied in specific cases. Some significant other principles illustrate the broader field.

- The greater the sense of belonging to a common group that is shared by those people who are exerting influence for a change and those who are to be changed, the more probable is acceptance of the influence.

---

4. Robert T. Golembiewski, *The Small Group* (Chicago: University of Chicago Press, 1962) , esp. pp. 8–33.
5. Full realization of this fact came slow and hard. Arnold Tannenbaum and Stanley Seashore, *Some Changing Conceptions and Approaches to the Study of Persons in Organizations* (Ann Arbor, Mich.: Institute for Social Research, University of Michigan, n.d.) .

- The more relevant are specific behaviors, attitudes, or values to the bases for attraction of members to a group, the greater the influence a group can exert over these behaviors, attitudes, or values.

Such principles imply a second and profound conceptual development of the primal observation that groups influence behavior. Directly, much of the resistance inherent in the use of the group as a target of change could be avoided by using the group as the *agent of change.*

The radical implications of the concept of a group as the agent of change were reflected in a number of behavioral science approaches, such as the treatment of delinquents, but those implications were nowhere so clearly realized as in the T-Group. Within very wide limits, in fact and by intention, members of a T-Group can determine their own destiny as a temporary social system. T-Group members early "begin to focus upon their relationship to each other, the problems of intimacy and closeness," one observer notes, "and learn from this emphasis on peer relationships about their characteristic modes of interaction."[6]

The great scope for self-determination in a T-Group enhances the probability of undiluted group influence. Crudely, the T-Group needs to apply fewer of its resources to resisting outside authority and more of them to the learning or influence process. The experience with T-Groups consequently reflects the effect of several other major principles of group dynamics:

- The greater the shared perception by group members of the need for a change, the more the pressure for change that will originate within the group, and the greater the influence that will be exerted over members.
- The more widely information about plans for change and about their consequences is shared among group members, the greater is member commitment to the change and to its implementation.
- The strains deriving from change in one sector of a group will produce systemic strains in other sectors, which can be reduced by negating the change or by readjusting the several sectors of a group.

Perhaps *the* source of power of the T-Group, then, lies in the degree to which the group itself is used as the agent of change.

The concept of the group as the agent of change encouraged two basic uses of the T-Group. The first historic use involved small populations of participants in stranger T-Groups, and the power of the T-Group was linked to two goals. Thus the T-Group was seen as an especially convenient and valuable context for quickly generating fundamental group

---

6. Leonard Horwitz, "Transference in Training Groups and Therapy Groups," *International Journal of Group Psychotherapy*, Vol. 14 (November 1, 1964), p. 208.

processes, research concerning which could add to basic knowledge in important ways.[7] Moreover, and consistent with the cognitive thrust implied in this first goal, the T-Group was linked with in-depth conceptual understanding of group processes by participants, as well as with practice and mastery of specific "basic skills,"[8] in about equal measure. These biases were massively reinforced. Significantly, participants in these early T-Groups tended to be members of the various "helping" professions or occupations: teachers, industrial trainers and personnel officials, pastors and clerics, youth workers, staff from service and charitable organizations, counselors and clinicians, and so on. These early populations clearly had strong needs to understand their experience, to develop instrumental skills consistent with it, and to evaluate the experience in terms of the institutions or professions or occupations which they tended to represent.

The power of the T-Group as an agent of change also generated a second Phase I usage. That is, the T-Group was used for large numbers of participants in stranger experiences for the broad purpose of confronting the self-in-relation. This second usage went through a succession of more-or-less distinct progressive forms, as developed in Section B of Part I. Overall, the T-Group experience was more intense and impactful. Simply, learning designs focused far more on affect and emotion, and far less on understanding or specific skill practice. Significantly, also, participants increasingly tended to come with different motivations, and apparently with more intense needs. Thus participants increasingly sought to alleviate feelings of alienation or loneliness, for example, and many anticipated or even demanded the experience of an "emotional high."[9] These participants tended to have high expectations about the T-Group experience, and these expectations emphasized personal impact as opposed to professional or occupational application, to risk a simplification that is meant only in a relative sense.

The two Phase I usages of the T-Group had consequences that differed in more than trivial ways. For example, rapid increases in the number of applicants for training and the intensity of learning designs in the second usage raised major practical issues. These included: questions of

---

7. Dorothy Stock and Herbert Thelen, *Emotional Dynamics and Group Culture* (Washington, D.C.: National Training Laboratories, 1958).
8. The T-Group was originally called a "basic skill-training" group, in fact. See the revealing history in Kenneth D. Benne, "History of the T-Group in the Laboratory Setting," in Leland P. Bradford, Jack R. Gibb, and Kenneth D. Benne (eds.), *T-Group Theory and Laboratory Method* (New York: John Wiley & Sons, 1964), pp. 87–113.
9. Martin Lakin, "Some Ethical Issues in Sensitivity Training," *American Psychologist*, Vol. 24 (October, 1969), pp. 923–28; and Max Pages, "Bethel Culture, 1969: Impressions of an Immigrant," *Journal of Applied Behavioral Science*, Vol. 7 (May, 1971), pp. 267–84.

the qualifications of the burgeoning number of trainers who responded to the growing demand; the matter of criteria for admission to training; and the difficulty of follow-up on cases of unexpected reactions among trainees. In contrast, the first T-Group usage raised such issues in diluted form only. The then-small coterie of trainers, for example, could rely on face-to-face interaction as the basic control. Major ethical issues permeate these practical concerns, patently.

Both the practical and ethical issues of the second Phase I usage of the T-Group are heightened by various mutant forms of training, such as the broad class of encounters described in Section B, Part I. Illustratively,

- The centrality of the trainer in many mutant forms of T-Grouping heightens the issue of his ethical responsibility for outcomes, as opposed to the emphasis in the orthodox T-Group on participant initiation and commitment versus trainer direction.

- The motivation of many recent participants is far more cathartic than cognitive, more expressive than intellective, and the intensity of the emotionality is thus more likely to pose major problems for some participants while outstripping the ameliorative potential of the time-bounded experience.

- The trainer may use direct or subtle methods to induce emotional expressiveness that subverts the basic quality of a T-Group as a member-based society of mutual learners.

- The participation of greater numbers of psychologically disturbed seems to have been encouraged by this common cathartic or expressive quality, which apparent trend raises the intensity of ethical issues about who should be admitted to T-Groups, about the realism of expectations about training outcomes, etc.

These two uses of the T-Group as an agent of change rest on several commonalities, while they differ profoundly in the ways just sketched. The critical commonalities include the basic notion that optimal (or perhaps, maximal) openness will occur only where T-Group participants feel psychologically safe. The stranger T-Group encourages this sense of safety in several critical senses:

- It meets for an extended period on a "cultural island."

- Its members will probably never meet again, which reduces or eliminates one major source of threat.

- Its culture is intentionally different from the back-home world, more supportive and less evaluative.

- It is a temporary system, and hence encourages a relative abandon by members to express themselves and experiment in ways they probably would not risk in more permanent systems.

b. Applications of Laboratory Approach to Groups: A Case of Parallel Development, Phase II

The two Phase I uses of the T-Group were at once consistent with the developmental history of other behavioral science approaches to groups, while they were also profoundly at odds with it. The point is easy to overstate or oversimplify, but it is worth making nonetheless. Basically, Phase I's emphasis on the stranger T-Group as a vehicle implied a trade-off of transfer of learning for initial impact of the T-Group experience.

The evidence underlying this crucial conclusion may be sketched in terms of four propositions. *First,* the purpose of the laboratory approach is clearly not to change individual behavior per se. Dorothy Stock and Herbert Thelen note that the usual presumption is that the changes in behavior "will lead to increased effectiveness in the back-home situation. . . ."[10] This presumption often was neglected, for diverse reasons, as the following points help demonstrate.

Second, the early research literature generated mixed results concerning the persistence of changes induced in stranger T-Groups, as well as about their contribution to increased effectiveness in various back-home situations.[11] Such findings demonstrated that transfer of learning into real-time contexts was more subtle than Phase I implied in its assumption that learning in one context would be more-or-less directly transferred to most or all areas of a person's life. Hence the more impactful his experience in a stranger T-Group, went the rationale, the greater the positive effects on his total group and personal relationships. This rationale was at least too facile.

Third, early concern increased that stranger experiences with no planned back-home design loops might actually create problems for learners. The concern was that mischief might result, in rough proportion to the initial impact on the individual. This was a case of losing proportionately with winning and was far more serious than simple fade-out, or decay, of learning. As Warren G. Bennis, Kenneth D. Benne, and Robert Chin cautioned in 1962: "Isolating the individual from his organizational context, his normative structure which rewards him and represents a significant reference group makes no sense. In fact, if it sets up countervailing norms and expectations, it may be deleterious to both the organization and to the individual."[12]

Fourth, the mixed results in the research literature increasingly were interpreted as establishing the need "to be concerned with altering both

---

10. Stock and Thelen, *op. cit.,* p. 244.
11. Floyd C. Mann, "Studying and Creating Change," in Warren G. Bennis, Kenneth D. Benne, and Robert Chin (eds.), *The Planning of Change* (New York: Holt, Rinehart, & Winston, 1962), pp. 605–15.
12. Bennis, Benne, and Chin (eds.), *op. cit.,* p. 620.

the forces within an individual and the forces in the organizational situation surrounding the individual."[13] As Floyd C. Mann concluded his summary of a number of human relations training efforts:[14]

> At best, these studies suggest that this type of training has little or no general effect. . . . Training which does not take the trainee's regular social environment into account will probably have little chance of modifying behavior. It may very well be that human relations—as a procedure for initiating social change—is most successful when it is designed to remold the whole system of role relationships. . . .

The implied shift in focus is critical. The focus was on the individual in his permanent social settings rather than in temporary learning groups.

Hence Phase II of the parallel development of the laboratory approach and other behavioral sciences. Directly, Phase II seeks designs that attempt to convert various natural-state groups into agents of change. Increasingly, the initial experience with laboratory values was in the family group, at work or wherever. This was a great leap forward. "It was learning to *reject* T-Group stranger-type labs," Robert Blake noted, "that permitted OD to come into focus."[15] The tradeoff is clear. Phase II proposes to compensate for any losses in impact of the initial learning experience with the more direct application in relevant contexts of whatever learning does occur.

c. The Growing Emphasis on Team Development: Toward a Phase II Application of the Laboratory Approach to Groups

"Team development" is the most current exemplar of Phase II applications of the laboratory approach to groups. Basically, it seeks to build analogs of T-Group processes and dynamics into ongoing groups. Sometimes this is accomplished by the direct use of T-Groups. Most often, however, the vehicle is an emphasis on "process analysis," which derives in important ways from the T-Group. As Section C, Part I establishes, you can take process orientation out of the T-Group. But you cannot take the T-Group out of the process orientation, in at least two senses. Thus the T-Group is at once a major contributor to the development of the science/art of process observation, as well as a uniquely useful con-

---

13. Mann, *op. cit.*, p. 612.
14. *Ibid.*, p. 608.
15. Quoted in Wendell French, "A Definition and History of Organization Development" (Paper presented at NTL Conference on New Technology in Organization Development, New York, October 8–9, 1971), p. 11.

text in which individuals can sharpen and develop skills in process observation.

Specifics about team development[16] can be detailed under five heads.

Units of Composition

The approach to team development assumes that small task groups or teams of 5 to 20 members—such as the manager and the first level or two of his subordinates—are the basic units of organization. "Individual learning and personal change do occur in OD programs," Richard Beckhard notes, "but as fallout—these are not the *primary* goals or intentions."[17] The overall organization is seen as a complex clustering of such teams. Consequently, when changes in the behavior, attitudes, or values of individuals are necessary, the norms and culture of several variously inclusive teams at several levels of organization might also have to be changed.

Analysis of Experience

Team development designs variously use experience-based learning. That is, analysis of existing team activities and relationships is intended to lead to a plan of action for influencing future team activities or relationships. Three general steps consequently are involved in all team-development designs, which otherwise can vary widely in their details. The general steps are:

- collection of information about team activities or relationships
- feedback of this information to the team
- action-planning by the team, based on the feedback and reactions to it

Beckhard calls this team-development approach an action-research model of intervention.[18]

As Kipling observed earlier in another context, there are at least 39 ways to structure a team-development experience, and every one of them

---

16. For efforts to describe the characteristics of team development, see such sources as Newton Margulies and Anthony P. Raia, "People in Organizations: A Case for Team Training," *Training and Development Journal*, Vol. 22 (August, 1968), pp. 2–11; and Gordon L. Lippitt, "Team Building for Matrix Organizations," in Gordon L. Lippitt, Leslie E. This, and Robert G. Bidwell, Jr., *Optimizing Human Resources* (Reading, Mass.: Addison-Wesley Publishing Co., 1971), pp. 158–70. A case study of a team-development experience is provided by Iain L. Mangham, J. Hayes, and Cary L. Cooper, "Developing Executive Relationships," *Interpersonal Development*, Vol. 1 (1970), pp. 110–27.
17. Richard Beckhard, *Strategies of Organization Development* (Reading, Mass.: Addison-Wesley Publishing Co., 1969), p. 16.
18. *Ibid.*, pp. 16, 27–28.

can be right under various circumstances. In fact, the following selected designs have all helped move a team-development experience through the three steps above:

- A sophisticated and open team might periodically meet to work toward action-planning based on answers to these questions: How are we doing? And why? How can we do better?

- An outside resource person could interview members of the team, for the purpose of reporting back his aggregate impressions of their responses to such questions: How can we improve the efficiency and effectiveness of this team?[19]

- A team might collect information and get feedback by arranging a "mirror design," as when a service group asks a marketing unit how it is perceived by this important customer, with the intent of using the feedback for action-planning by the service group.

- A team can choose a T-Group experience[20] to generate data and provide feedback about internal interpersonal relationships, with the goal of using that data to improve communication and decision-making.

- A team could decide on a variety of development programs specialized in by consulting firms, such as that based on Blake's Managerial Grid.[21]

- Two or more teams could agree to engage in a confrontation session,[22] in which each provides information and feedback about how it perceives the other. This feedback can then become the basis for action-planning by each team or by both together.

Normally, these designs are scheduled for perhaps two to five days at a neutral site. Not uncommonly, work teams will schedule a team-development activity at intervals of 6 to 12 months.

Differentiated Focus of Activities

The focus of team-development activities can be variegated. The full range will be suggested here in two ways, both of which emphasize what every effective team should or must do. From one perspective, each team must develop a viable and necessarily dynamic balance between at least five sets of simultaneous demands, as Figure 1 suggests. In broad concept, neglect of any one of these demands will have a long-run impact on

---

19. For an example, see Subsection 3 of Section D below.
20. For an example, see Subsection 4 of Section D below.
21. Robert R. Blake and Jane Mouton, *Corporate Excellence through Grid Organization Development* (Houston, Tex.: Gulf Publishing Co., 1968).
22. For an example, see Subsections 3 and 4 of Section F below.

Figure 1. Five Levels of Demands That Teams Must Balance

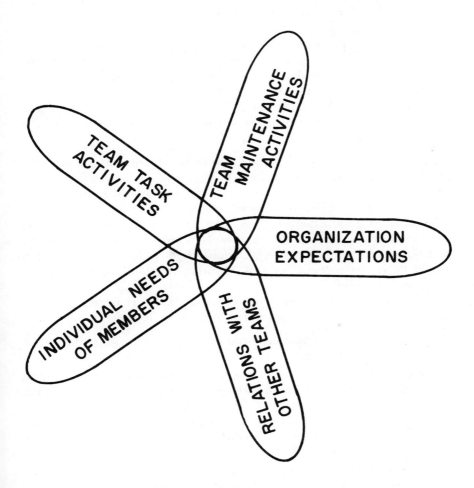

the others and, consequently, on team effectiveness. Hence the need for periodic fine tuning, if not gross adjustment, of the allocations of resources made by a team to the several demands.

To develop the sense of Figure 1 somewhat, team-development activities can focus on the crucial balancing of two external demands. They are:

- *organization expectations* about team performance, which may be expressed in terms of production standards, acceptable levels of quality, broad policies and procedures, etc.

- *relations with other groups,* which can be critical in at least three general cases:
  a. where two or more teams work simultaneously on subsystems of some project or product which must be integrated
  b. when two or more teams perform sequential steps on some project or product, so that the work pace and quality of one team is either dependent upon and/or directly influences another team or teams
  c. where two or more teams are related as seller/buyer or producer/consumer of some service, as in typical line-staff relationships

The challenges in integrating these two levels of demands are multiple and should be more-or-less obvious. For example, organization expectations about productivity might force two interdependent teams into win/lose competitive situations, as when each blames the other for lower-than-expected production. In the vernacular, successfully "throwing dead cats" by one team into the backyards of other teams might help the first team meet organization expectations about productivity. The gain would be at the potential cost of polluting relationships between the two teams, however.

Each team must also seek a balance of three internal demands with the two external ones sketched above. The prime internal demands are:

- the *group task,* whose short-run demands may be so compelling as to be overwhelming
- *group maintenance,* which refers to the management of what team members do *"to* and *with* each other" as they work on the common task, for a team "needs to have a growing awareness of itself . . . , of its constantly changing network of interactions and relationships, and of the need to maintain within itself relationships appropriate to the task."[23]
- *individual needs* of team members, which variously influence and relate to how a team does its work, and whose relative satisfaction crucially determines the individual's involvement and commitment to his team

The integrative challenges posed by these internal demands are classic, and they can influence the ways in which the external demands are managed. Consider the case of the blindly ambitious head of a team whose individual need is so great that he neglects all group-maintenance activities so as to complete some task in order to exceed organization expectations. He gets promoted just as his team's effectiveness begins to

---

23. Gordon L. Lippitt, *Organization Renewal* (New York: Appleton-Century-Crofts, 1969), p. 102.

deteriorate, which leaves his successor with major internal and external problems. And the newly promoted man might even uncharitably note of his successor's problems that one could hardly expect two managerial paragons in a row in that most-demanding position.

Hence the common focus of team-development activities is on managing the complex interfaces of multiple internal and external demands. The task is especially subtle because at least several major logics operate, and they often conflict. The logics are those associated with: hierarchy or authority, bargaining between individuals or groups, and socioemotional adjustment.

From a second and related perspective, the thrusts of team-development activities can be suggested in terms of what "teamwork" requires. Team development often centers around balancing such components of teamwork, to rely basically on Gordon L. Lippitt, as:[24]

- an understanding of, and commitment to, common goals
- the integration of resources of as wide as possible a range of team members, so as to use their contributions and also to increase their owning of and commitment to a team's goals or products
- the ability and willingness to analyze and review team processes, so as to prevent the accumulation of unfinished business and to improve team effectiveness
- trust and openness in communication and relationships
- a strong sense of belonging by its members

Team-development activities commonly seek to realize these "shoulds" of teamwork. More demanding, team development also must deal with potential and painful conflicts in such "shoulds." Thus a strong sense of belonging to a team can become dysfunctional, as when the team's mission changes or is curtailed while team members seek to protect their comfortable relationships.

Intergroup Aspects

Team-development designs might involve intergroup aspects. The significance of the point defies all but the most extravagant exaggeration. Patently, organizations generate numerous needs for smooth intergroup relationships. Moreover, the probability is high that these linkages will prove as troublesome as they are significant. Section A of Part III develops the point in detail. Note here only, then, that at least three common aspects of intergroup relations could be targets of development designs. Thus destructive competition between two or more groups might

---

24. *Ibid.*, p. 107–13.

be the target of a team-development experience. Or improvement in communication might be the goal. Finally, trust and confidence between groups whose efforts must be integrated is often lacking and could motivate an intergroup design.

Importance of Start-up

Team-development activities are particularly important at start-up. Thus team development is especially applicable in cases such as these: a new organization unit is being formed, such as a new project group; key members of an existing team are to be replaced, as via a program of job rotation; or an ad hoc committee or task force must quickly confront and complete a task, after which it will disband. The examples imply that, as Beckhard notes,[25] organizational start-ups tend to have common characteristics which make team-development activities particularly useful.[26] To embellish on his basic list of these characteristics, start-ups typically involve several features that require early owning up to and quick resolution. These features are:

- substantial confusion about roles and relationships
- fairly clear understanding of immediate goals but lack of clarity about provisions to be made for longer-run operations, which cumulatively encourage a strong desire to get on with the task and yet a concern that precedents will be set unreflectively, which can mean trouble over the long run
- fixation on the immediate task, which often means that group maintenance activities will receive inadequate attention and individual needs will be neglected[27]
- a challenge to team members which will induce superior technical effort, but which may also have serious consequences for personal or family life[28] and which in any case probably will generate an intensity in work relationships that requires careful monitoring

25. Beckhard, *op. cit.*, pp. 28–29.
26. Roger Harrison, "Effective Organization for Startup," mimeographed, Boston, Mass., Development Research Associates, Inc., July 8, 1970. See also Fred Fosmire, Caroline Keutzer, and Richard Diller, "Starting up a New Senior High School," in Richard A. Schmuck and Matthew B. Miles, *Organization Development in Schools* (Palo Alto, Cal.: National Press Books, 1971), pp. 87–112.
27. The point is strikingly suggested by changes in supervisory styles in power plants from start-up onward observed by Floyd C. Mann and L. Richard Hoffman, *Automation and the Worker: Social Change in Power Plants* (New York: Holt, Rinehart, and Winston, 1960). See also Mann, "Toward an Understanding of the Leadership Role in Formal Organization," in Robert F. M. Dubin (ed.), *Leadership and Productivity* (San Francisco: Chandler Publishing Co., 1965), pp. 68–103.
28. The phenomenon is especially marked in aerospace project teams, which no doubt illustrate an increasingly significant organizational form. For a broad perspective, see Philip Slater and Warren G. Bennis, *The Temporary Society* (New York: Harper & Row, Publishers, 1968); and Alvin Toffler, *Future Shock* (New York: Random House, 1970), esp. pp. 119–20.

From diverse perspectives, then, start-ups can generate major challenges for team-development activities.

2. A SHORT-CUT APPLICATION OF THE LABORATORY APPROACH: NOT REALLY CHANGING A GROUP'S NORMS/CLIMATE

That the developmental lessons about applications of the laboratory approach to groups were learned the hard way can be suggested in some richness by a case study, which serves a number of purposes. The case study introduces a variety of common features and issues of OD efforts. Moreover, it implies the limitations of adherence to the form of the laboratory approach or of professions of support for the values and norms introduced in Sections C and D of Part I, which can be so much lip service. The substance of the laboratory approach involves the building of the social relationships and attitudes that can provide the continuing support needed to build the values of the laboratory approach into organizations, and to keep them there. Finally, the case study will provide an arena for some process analysis of an executive team's interaction. This process analysis will help illustrate the kinds of issues that normally get raised in team-development experiences.

Organization USA, a public agency, provides an illustration for making the multiple points of this subsection. The mini-history is dated by a decade or so and consequently reflects a charming naiveté about organizational change, knowledge about which has been so enormously expanded of late. Indeed, we now know so much about organizational change that efforts like the one below are not likely to be attempted, thereby forfeiting the developmental opportunities inherent even in humble OD efforts.

a. Characteristic Features and Accidentals: An OD Start-up in Organization USA

Although when a laboratory program starts or who starts it are problematic in essential senses, more certainty is possible about the conditions that are congenial to start-up of an OD effort. Organization USA typifies the usual case. Briefly, the OD effort in Organization USA rested on a number of congenial conditions. Five such conditions deserve especial note:

- a Mr. Inside, an agency employee who was enthusiastic about the laboratory approach and was allowed by his immediate superior to gather information about its applications, but who also was

333

grimly convinced that his superior was only interested in "keeping me quiet by letting me do a little spadework"

- The linkage of Mr. Inside with the author, who was used as a prestigious-other in helping gain the attention of superiors and as a risk-taker when organization members felt unable to move or felt unsafe about trying
- nurturing support by members of Mr. Inside's immediate staff which bubbled up to a common superior who had requisite authority to sanction an extensive program
- a proximate facilitating background, which in Organization USA's case involved such components as: an organization of thousands of employees, doing its present tasks with a high reliability but with an essential death sentence facing its present mission and role, under a general managerial style unsuited for a creative start-up, with general agreement that appreciable budgetary "fat" had been accumulated, and with turnover among the "better" employees that was considered too high
- numerous disturbing signs that the organization could make adaptations only with great difficulty, including sharp departmental fragmentation and a growing "don't rock the boat" atmosphere throughout the organization

As in many similar cases, the OD effort in Organization USA also had an immediate precipitating incident. It occurred during a meeting of the author with Mr. Inside's immediate superior, Mr. Headman. The meeting ostensibly was a spontaneous courtesy to a visiting fireman, but actually was prearranged by Mr. Inside with the fervent hope that it might "help get something started." Mr. Headman managed a large staff organization which served various headquarters executives. Moreover, Mr. Headman was closely linked to the head of Organization USA, whom we shall call Mr. Top Man. Mr. Headman was a key official in several senses, in sum. Mr. Headman had just begun to expound that much behavior is accidental and unplanned and idiosyncratic, and hence even the idea of applying behavioral sciences in organizations was foreign to him, especially since he was an engineer by profession. Just then, chance intervened in the person of an agitated subordinate requesting information about a work assignment. After settling the matter to his own satisfaction, Mr. Headman pleasantly turned to inquire: "Now just how were you saying that you have helped executives with that consulting pitch of yours?" The answer shot back. "Why, I try to help executives and their subordinates to recognize and avoid what happened to the man who just left."

The executive reacted angrily, and only an appeal to his scientific background calmed him. He agreed to "run a test" on my observation, by seeking out and confronting the subordinate. Finding the subordinate proved something of a problem but, once found, his distraught condition was patent. And his reactions suggested the source of substantial organizational costs and communicative difficulties. That an outsider recognized the situation particularly impressed Mr. Headman, or perhaps it especially distressed him.

b. "Some Organizational Commandments": Guidelines for Interaction in STAFF

Mr. Headman took quick steps to help assure that he would never again so bind employees that they withheld even overpowering issues. Unprecedentedly, he took the next day off. Immediately on returning to work, he summoned Mr. Inside and gave him a mandate. "Write me up some organizational commandments that will help open communication channels between me and people on the STAFF," he said. "I want to publicly acknowledge and practice them, to encourage others on my staff to do the same. We'll have a STAFF meeting when you are done and I have accepted your effort."

Note that, most of the time, reference here will be to an 11-man group composed of Mr. Headman and his immediate subordinates. For convenience, they will be called the STAFF, or members of the STAFF. Each STAFF member, in turn, headed up a work group of variable size.

Mr. Inside was able to respond quickly. Within two days, guidelines for Project USA were developed for and approved by Mr. Headman. The guidelines are reproduced in Figure 2. Only a three-man committee, Mr. Headman, and this writer knew of the work.

That matters moved so swiftly surprised many later, but speed in this case rested on some solid preliminary work. Mr. Inside, that is, had been doing his homework well. He had closely studied a firm with whose

Figure 2. Six-Point Credo, an Early Step in Organization USA toward a Program of Laboratory Development

I believe that every member of the STAFF is an important person and is a contributing member of a team made up of different and valuable professional skills. We, you and I working together, can individually achieve highest productivity and reward by developing in our interpersonal relations an atmosphere of openness and trust by understanding and using these guidelines:

1. Value criticism as a compliment and a privilege—give and accept it.
2. Keep communications open and patiently hear the other person out before responding.
3. Recognize that defensiveness blunts communications and impedes understanding—don't put the other person on the defensive.
4. Cooperate, don't compete, with your work partners—volunteer and ask for help.
5. State your feelings openly in response to an assignment.
6. In problem solving, confront the problem and the person directly—get conflicts into the open.

MR. HEADMAN

experience he could at once shape and support his desire for an OD program based on the laboratory approach in Organization USA. This business firm, which will be called Organization A, was well known and highly respected in Organization USA. Mr. Inside had even prepared a presentation script which was duplicated in quantity in the hope that Mr. Inside could gain an audience with Mr. Top Man and/or with his top-line aides.

c. Toward the Laboratory Approach
via Prestigeful Association:
Hitchhiking on the Experience of Organization A

With the guidelines completed and approved, Mr. Inside turned his attention to the presentation concerning Organization A he was preparing for the top STAFF officials. That presentation had been scheduled for some time, and Mr. Inside's preparation for it was cut short by the unanticipated work on the guidelines. Mr. Inside wanted to get the guidelines done first, even though he assumed that Mr. Headman would keep the guidelines "in his hippocket," at least for a while.

The actual presentation to STAFF officials who met in Mr. Headman's office stressed one dominant theme. Organization A and Organization USA shared so many surface similarities that even obstinate opponents would have to gingerly avoid the argument that the laboratory approach "can't work here." Organization A had apparently met its challenges with considerable success and gave the laboratory approach much of the credit. Organization A, in sum, had confronted many problems analogous to those facing Organization USA:

- developing from a one-customer to a multiple-customer organization
- developing from a producer into an innovator
- evolving from a narrow to a broad product line
- shifting from producing a product for which there is a market increasingly toward developing both market and product
- blending an "old" management team that had established the organization with "new" and numerous officials having radically different social backgrounds, skills, and experiences
- stressing the new organizational importance of managerial functions, long considered secondary to technical and scientific skills, the stress being a response particularly to the need to develop new and constantly changing sets of missions and roles
- reinforcing the importance and legitimacy of central planning and

direction, which had been considered largely as obstacles by technical-scientific personnel and which had been more or less contemptuously assigned to "nonscientific types"

- opening up a wide variety of communication channels—up, down, and across traditional lines—to facilitate massive organization change and adaptation, whereas a high degree of departmental balkanization had existed and was tolerated when the organizational tasks were accepted from outside rather than innovated from within

Mr. Inside dealt from strength in this presentation, in several senses. *First,* officials in Organization A were both known to and respected by members of the STAFF, and the success of the firm was beyond casual refutation. Both factors inhibited easy challenge to Mr. Inside's summary of the experience of Organization A with their program of change and career development based on the laboratory approach. The managers of this "fast-paced organization" after three years of experimentation, members of the STAFF were told, credit the program with giving them "a new perspective on their management responsibilities, a new appreciation of the capabilities of their subordinates, a new facility in the exchange of information, and an atmosphere in which hard work is not only fascinating but fun." More specifically, employment in Organization A rose nearly 90 percent during a five-year period, while sales tripled. Moreover, professional turnover decreased from 20 percent—somewhat under the average for Organization A's industry—to a startling low of some 7 percent. Carefully, however, Mr. Inside noted that "he did not imply" that Organization A's progress resulted "solely from the career development program." At the same time, he noted, "it does appear that the program had a substantial impact on the success of the company."

Second, the experience of Organization A reflected a total program for a mass clientele. Its experience was thus particularly salient for members of the STAFF, who saw their own training problems framed in the same terms. Thus Organization A's total program emphasized training both in the gamut of technical skills and in interpersonal and group skills. Interpersonal and group skills were to be developed essentially in four stages:

- assimilation of new organization members, a period lasting as much as five days per employee, which orients the employee to the firm and to his specific department and job
- pre–T-Group introduction to career development in Organization A via literature, films, and lectures
- voluntary participation in cousin T-groups at or near the worksite which were composed of individuals at approximately the same organization levels who did not usually work together

337

- participation in team development at or near the worksite in family groups composed of individuals who did work together, whether or not the individual had chosen to attempt to augment his interpersonal and group skills in a cousin T-Group

Third, members of Mr. Headman's STAFF recognized a central similarity between the two organizations, the orientation toward conflict. The prime consultant to Organization A highlighted the centrality of conflict. He noted in a working paper intended for management in Organization A that conflict was usually managed in terms of one of two alternative strategies:

> The alternatives seem to be *avoiding it* (being passive, ignoring it, rationalizing it, seeing the issues as someone else's business) versus *fighting* (being aggressive, insubordinate, dictatorial, competitive, etc.) . In Organization A there is a good deal of reluctance about being dictatorial (or otherwise aggressive) . Looking downward, it is felt that arbitrary or dictatorial action will destroy morale and lead to the loss of highly valued technical people. Hence the passive alternative is often selected. A third constructive but more difficult alternative exists. Confronting involves getting the conflict out into the open, helping the parties to analyze the situation, getting feelings expressed so they can be separated from the real issue (if there is one) , and assisting in the search for an integrative solution.

Members of STAFF—long aware of their need to preserve a good image —made a direct transfer. "All we will have to do," admitted one STAFF member who was not overly friendly to Organization USA's attempt at laboratory work, "is change a few titles and Organization A's history comes very close to home."

Fourth, despite the similarities between the two organizations, no effort was made to simply import the program of Organization A. Quite the opposite was the case, indeed. There existed—the members of Mr. Headman's STAFF were told—no "book answers." "Experimentation, innovation, and continuous feedback from all those in Organization USA had to characterize a successful" Project USA, Mr. Inside stressed over and over. Gone, consequently, was the critics' opportunity to gain a cheap victory by stressing the unique needs and problems of Organization USA. Mr. Inside recommended an approach rather than provided answers, in short.

d. A Positive Reaction and a Surprise: A Proposal to Shortcut a Developmental Sequence

The discussion which followed Mr. Inside's presentation was positive, revealing of the closedness of STAFF interaction, and surprising in that

Mr. Headman at Mr. Inside's invitation chose to spring the guidelines on STAFF officials. In sum, the spontaneous proposal was to adopt the values consistent with the laboratory approach without going through the process of developing supportive attitudes and behavioral skills by experiential learning, as in T-Groups.

The discussion of the presentation of the history of the OD program in Organization A began in revealing ways. Four major themes stand out. *First,* consider this sequence:

> MR. HEADMAN: I would like to ask for your comments to this presentation.
>
> MR. P: I would like to say something about one point that struck me. The first time it came up, I didn't understand it until a little further down when [Mr. Inside] said criticism is the highest compliment. Then later on he said it is far more constructive to confront [and so on for another hundred words.] Confrontation is something that we are sadly lacking here. . . . At most of our major meetings, there seems to be quite a reluctance to confront or to critique in public.
>
> MR. HEADMAN: Charlie, how do you feel about this?
>
> CHARLIE: I thought it was a real good pitch. . . .

This brief sequence reflects much of the reality of Organization A. That Mr. P is not considered powerful or perhaps even meaningful seems patent in Mr. Headman's abject brushing aside of his contribution, for example, and patency mirrors reality. Mr. P's burying of his reaction at the tag end of an avalanche of words implies the same point, and particularly in an environment given verbally to staccato bursts of a few sentences. That Charlie is considered powerful also is suggested in Mr. Headman's overriding concern about his reaction. Indeed, although Charlie is Mr. Headman's subordinate, the former has open and long-standing access to the latter's superior.

Second, and significantly, only desultory conversation intervened between Charlie's opinion and Mr. Headman's surprise revelation of the six-point credo. That is to say, the six points of the credo urging openness in communication were neither conceived nor introduced in an open way, paradoxically but revealingly, and this created some ironic and surprised reactions. If nothing else, the approach reduced the likelihood that members of the STAFF would accept the six points as their own. They experienced a sense of juicy irony, even if they did not feel railroaded. Charlie, as it were, set and sprung his own trap in this sequence:

> CHARLIE: After studying the program in Organization A, what is your feeling about local application?
>
> MR. INSIDE: Excellent!

CHARLIE: What is the chance of it?

MR. INSIDE: I think it is willing to start in this room right now if Mr. Headman wants to make his proclamation, which is behind the curtain up there. May I trot it out? The enthusiasm seems to be here.

Only then was it revealed that a committee of three—including Mr. Inside—had some days before developed the "guidelines that we might use in the STAFF, which Mr. Headman might announce, and over a period of 60 to 90 days, all of us might look at it and try to apply it as we go. Mr. Headman saw it the other morning and this is now his proclamation." As far as can be determined, it seems that the visual containing the six points was placed in the meeting room by Mr. Inside on the outside chance that Mr. Headman would choose to mention it. Caught up in the spirit of the moment, Mr. Inside spontaneously precipitated that mention. Or so he says.

In sum, the guidelines were conceived and announced like many programs in Organization USA: covert if not clandestine preparation by peers; private selling to a superior; opportune disclosure to other peers, with no question that the program was that of their common superior and that it could admit little or no modification; and with the supporting admonition that somebody else—and preferably a prestigious somebody—might act if the proposal were rejected. The last point was of particular significance to the STAFF. For getting there first was as paramount a consideration for them as it is in many staff units. Given the felt need to increase the prestige of the STAFF, indeed, the need to get there first may have been particularly intense. The point was made massively by Mr. Headman, who observed that Mr. Inside also was to give his presentation about Organization A to other line units in Organization USA. Mr. Headman noted that time might be a-wastin':

> . . . you know Mr. Inside gave this presentation to line manager X and his top people, and that they kept him for a long discussion after. . . . They were pleased, I was told, and I didn't believe it. Because that is not the way I judge X and his group. That was the last organization unit, I thought, that ever would listen to something like this.

Given the lack of suspense about who favored what, Mr. Headman put this question directly to the STAFF very early in the discussion following Mr. Inside's presentation: "Are we ready to adopt this set of principles as an internal experiment for our internal relationships for, say a period of three months to give it a try?" How matters stood was crystal clear. "If these weren't adopted," asked one staff member, "could we get an equivalent set of principles which would be recognized by all that would be identifiable? I know, as an individual character, I surely do not respond and react as everyone else in here." Responded Mr. Headman: "I feel as a group we could not work with many individual charters. . . . If we want to make group progress, we would have to agree on a joint set of objectives." The credo, in short, was indeed "the proclamation" of Mr. Headman.

That proclamation was accepted, in the form of a general commitment "to adopt this set of principles as an internal experiment for our internal relationships for a period of two months to give it a try . . ." The arrangements were reasonable, if modest. For the summer vacation season was perhaps 90 days away, and new projects soon getting underway would complete the job of scattering members of the STAFF to the four winds. Moreover, Mr. Inside was acutely aware of his impending departure, and concluded that something small he got started would have a better chance of life than something more grandiose which "never got off my drawing board."

Third, the discussion following the presentation also massively demonstrates that STAFF members were neither motivated to evaluate their own processes nor skilled in doing so. Consider one attempt by Mr. P, who had been silent since his initial response to Mr. Headman was brushed aside. The door was opened by Mr. Headman himself, who ironically noted late in the meeting that: "If a man does not display respect for other individuals, his ability and judgment have no real place in the group. He is not a contributing factor." But that point apparently did not relate to Mr. Headman or Mr. P. Consider the lack of skill and sensitivity that met Mr. P's relatively direct statement that: "One thing that might generally cover the whole list, you might say, is the privilege of openness without fear of recrimination. Openness really is one word that covers all the items put together." Mr. P got his usual treatment, with one minor exception. These interactions immediately followed, to support the point. The observations and interpretations about process in parentheses are mine.

> MR. T (with overt disregard of the personal and emotional tone of Mr. P's statement) : You have a code of ethics in engineering. You look at the six points and they become a code of ethics really.
> MR. HEADMAN (further shutting out Mr. P) : Now, you wanted to make a comment on one of the other points, Stan.
> STAN (opening the door again) : I am going to ask for an interpretation from several people to get some idea of what people in here think about ". . . defensiveness blunts communications and impedes understanding—don't put the other person on the defensive."

341

MR. P (responding to the overture, although it was not overtly directed to him) : I have found in practically any presentation or meeting that, if anything is done that tends to get a guy's fear up a little bit and he goes on the defensive, it usually stops the meeting as far as getting anything productive is concerned. You put a guy on the defensive in anything, you have stopped progress right then and there.

MR. W (neglecting the patent probability that P is speaking about himself) : Isn't this somewhat relative?

. . . . .

STAN: Respect is what Mr. Headman was talking about.

MR. HEADMAN: Let me try this—I feel a little differently about it. . . .

That the issue of Mr. P's self-esteem—and other issues equally powerful—were not worked on is partially a function of limited time, but it also reflected the lack of skilled resources within the STAFF or available to it. Mr. Inside had experienced a dose of laboratory training, but he was necessarily preoccupied with getting a program in motion. An outside consultant or trainer, because of his relative independence of the client organization, could particularly encourage looking at issues related to group and personal functioning. No such resource was available, largely because there was no alternative in Organization A. Consider the reaction to my repeated recommendation that an organizational change agent—an employee of the organization but insulated from it in some way, as by being on detached duty from the National Training Laboratories—be hired. This was generally regarded as an impossibility in Organization USA. Its department of personnel could exercise little control in technical recruiting, I was told, but what they could control they did. "Change agents" seemed definitely controllable. Mr. Inside explained the resort to guidelines in terms consistent with both interpretations:

> What we are trying to do here is, without the expenditure of all the time that Organization A did, all the consultants . . . and all the basic laboratory training that the people had; try to gather from their experience some values which we think would help the STAFF in its work role.

Fourth, that the STAFF was furiously piling unfinished business in front of itself also is suggested by the way in which overtures to confrontation were made and responded to. Those few offers were made tentatively, gingerly evaded in substance, and reacted to generally in

342

terms of flight or fight. Consider only this sequence, originally directed at Charlie during a discussion of "competition":

> MR. INSIDE: Yes, well let's have a specific example: you, Charlie and I have a functional conflict: where does the technical system pick up and where does the management system start? It is a never-never land. But instead of us fighting with one another, we should be able to get together and agree on a workable division or a phasing point in that relationship.
> MR. HEADMAN: You would almost say bring that out, consider it a conflict and approach it by bringing it out into the open.
> MR. INSIDE: Yes, that would be much better than letting it fester.

No one went beyond "almost saying to bring out" the very real source of conflict which Mr. Inside offered to confront, however, and some did their best to suppress that offer. That is, on the one hand, flight occurred in this case as it did in all (most) other cases during the meeting because no one accepted the offer to confront, and particularly not Charlie. But suppressing a response to an offer to confront an issue apparently did not remove it from consciousness. Fight sequences typically followed such abortive overtures, that is to say, and this was certainly true in the present case.

Charlie's fight reaction in the case above closely followed Mr. Inside's offer to confront, to support the summary conclusion above. Significantly, after some very brief elliptical comments following the offer, Charlie announced: "Now to get back to the point I raised in the very beginning." Charlie not only signaled that he was not about to respond to Mr. Inside's invitation to confront. He went on to raise these two issues: Are the guidelines of Project USA really those of the STAFF? And if they are, do not those guidelines constitute a clear and direct criticism of the operations of the STAFF?

Charlie raised two central issues. For example, Mr. Inside was soon scheduled to leave Organization USA and—you guessed it—Charlie was to take over his responsibilities! In one sense, then, Charlie might have been asking how the STAFF could make it easier for him to implement a program in which he had had no direct formative role. "I was looking for a way to get on board," he later told me, "and especially because Mr. Top Man had given me a mandate in taking over Mr. Inside's job that heavily emphasized the use of electronic data processing and had little to say about people processing." Consistently, Charlie at times took pains to underscore that he was not being critical in raising these issues. But he got little help. "You see," he noted, "I just cannot cover this point

without somebody getting the feeling I am being critical about the list—
I am not." The ensuing "Laughter" noted in the transcript of the
meeting suggests the lack of help Charlie received in getting on board.

Organizational life being as complex as it is, Charlie was not mono-
lithically concerned with getting on board. The broader range of underlying issues that he touched on is implicit in the potential traps of the
argumentative web that Charlie seems to have been concerned to spin.
Consider but one perspective that Charlie emphasized. If the guidelines
were developed specifically for Organization USA, he noted, "that means
that back behind these six statements, somebody had recognized certain
weaknesses in the management of the STAFF." The implicit trap here
was the prevailing organizational norm that dirty laundry could hardly
be washed in public, and particularly staff laundry, even if the laundry
was dirty only by implication. Initially, therefore, Charlie worked to get
Mr. Headman or Mr. Inside to admit that "in some of these areas we
do a really good job." Both skirted the potential trap gingerly. But the
transcript also clearly reflects their dual discomfiture. On the one hand,
they could be interpreted as being roundly critical of the STAFF if they
merely stated the guidelines. This might be a damaging admission in the
inevitable scuffles for scarce resources with line officials who were powerful and already predisposed to believe the worst. On the other hand, the
STAFF could undercut the rationale for the guidelines if they agreed
that "in some of these areas we do a really good job."

Charlie was not about to risk forcing the issue, given Mr. Headman's
initial commitment to the guidelines, but he at least gained some am-
munition for a later showdown. For example, Charlie established that the
six guidelines were not in fact developed specifically for Organization
USA. He thus gained some potential debater's points for later challenges. This potential source of leverage emerges from this sequence:

> CHARLIE: . . . if a guy walked into this room who had never
> seen the STAFF and he sat down and you said, "Here is a list
> of six things we are concentrating on," and he would read the
> list, he would say, "this list tells me a lot about the STAFF."
> MR. HEADMAN: If he is a smart man, he doesn't need to read
> the list. I understand this to be an extract from Organiza-
> tion A.
> MR. INSIDE: It came from there, not from the STAFF.
> CHARLIE: This is then a verbatim extract from Organization A?
> MR. INSIDE: No, not a verbatim—no.
> CHARLIE: I thought this grew from three statements to thirty,
> and then was cut to six, as was explained earlier.
> MR. HEADMAN: That is right, in the wordings.
> MR. Q: We on the committee appointed by Mr. Headman to

develop the guidelines only heard this pitch one time, like you did. Then we sat down and talked and no one took any notes. . . . it was interesting to me that the points in the presentation about Organization A's experience almost shaped the thoughts in the guidelines.

Whatever the mechanics, the implied state of organizational dynamics was clear to Charlie. "I am not critical of the guidelines," he explained again. But the process of their development did little to encourage his support. "I just think," he noted, "that this step is very instructive about the way Mr. Headman talks to us and the way we talk to each other. I think there is a personal message here—for us all to learn." And there this overture to confront remained.

As his just-quoted comments suggest, Charlie worked at multiple levels. Here he was open and willing to risk; in other cases, his position is unclear. For example, the discussion about local applicability of the six-point credo might provide Charlie with a way of owning the guidelines, although they had been sprung on him without warning. Mr. Q, one of the members of Mr. Headman's covert committee, observed that his perspective in drawing the guidelines "was absolutely not" the STAFF. This dialogue followed:

CHARLIE: Your perspective was in any organization?
MR. Q: Right, the world. I do not know about Mr. Inside. He has been in the STAFF discipline so long, it would occur to me that his perspective might have been somewhat in this area.
CHARLIE: His perspective is Organization A.

No one contradicted this apparent approach to coping with Mr. Inside. Moreover, whether or not Mr. Inside felt he was in the process of being written out of Organization USA, Charlie's comments apparently did shackle him temporarily. Mr. Inside did not speak again although the meeting lasted 15 to 20 additional minutes, during which Mr. Headman and Charlie discussed how they might present the program to their superiors.

In sum, although tentativeness is in order concerning the longer-run implications of the meeting, there is no question that some promising opportunities to build relations, to confront issues, and to support openness went aglimmering. For example, no one explored or reinforced Mr. Headman's openness in raising the issue that immediately precipitated the guidelines. It was patently a piece of unfinished business for Mr. Headman. Thus he explained:

You see, I was in the dark. I didn't have the faintest idea of his reaction. I had no intention whatsoever to hurt his feelings in any fashion—had no reason to believe I had done so, yet this was the case. So I want to say as always to all you people, I want you to speak up. If you have a point to make, I want you—I expect you—to make the point. I want to know your opinions. In this particular case, I was grossly surprised. The situation, all in all, is really deplorable.

With no one able to note that Mr. Headman had done more or less the same thing to Mr. P just moments before, or that he had done the same thing to others, Mr. Headman was free to let himself off very easily. "I regret any bad feeling about such a situation developing," he noted, *"and the whole thing was caused by the fact that this guy would not give me his opinions."* Cognitive learning, they all say, is far removed from skill in practice. Note particularly that Mr. P was the very person whose reaction triggered Mr. Headman to commission the guidelines.

e. Feedback at $T = 60$ Days: Consequences and Limitations of Shortcuts

All OD programs based on the laboratory approach face a vital challenge: to test for commitment at all stages of development. The relevant design in this case was a simple feedback model, based on interview-*cum*-feedback. Some 60 days after the decision to experiment with the guidelines, Mr. Inside conducted semistructured interviews with all members of the STAFF who had attended the natal meeting. The results were to be fed back to Mr. Headman, but in a summary way designed to insure anonymity. The rationale is transparent, to provide feedback to Mr. Headman under relatively safe conditions for him, and particularly for his subordinates. Feedback becomes increasingly direct as trust and skill grow, to state the underlying generalization.

The design for testing the initial commitment of members of the STAFF yielded mixed data, unsurprisingly. A direct summary is appropriate. The feedback design highlighted some of the pitfalls facing any laboratory program of organization development; and the design especially emphasized the fragility of the bases for commitment to the six-point credo. The interview responses can be classified under the following five heads, which correspond to the major sections of the semistructured interview schedule used by Mr. Inside:

- participants' reactions to the "openness meeting"
- attempts made to act on the six points among the immediate associates of each of the members of the STAFF
- reactions to the impact upon working relations of the six-point credo within the STAFF

346

- effects of the credo on the full range of work relations, up, down, and across the organization
- any experimentation based on the six points

Participant's Reactions to "Openness Meeting"

The passage of 60 days did little to dim the memory of the initial meeting about the guidelines. Indeed, common references to "the openness meeting" implies it had taken on a kind of epochal quality. Judgments ranged from "good meeting," through "beneficial," and were definitely skewed toward "one of the best we have had." The uniformly positive tone may be illustrated easily. "We need to sit down and talk like that," one interviewee concluded. "We need this openness. I like it."

These positive reactions to the meeting seem to have at least three bases. *First,* the initial meeting helped legitimate looking at issues of concern that were previously not admissible to open discussion. As one executive noted, the meeting "served to reinforce in a probably more understandable way the feeling that there is not the most desirable rapport between all our people in the STAFF." Another variation of the point suggested that a new kind of interaction contract had been drafted and tentatively signed, in fact. "People seemed to promise," one STAFF member noted, "that they would be more candid." This promise implied a better working tomorrow. The sense of "writing of a new contract" is a common one in laboratory programs. Publicly raising previously unfinished business—even if everyone privately was aware of the business—has the effect of establishing a tentative commonality and of implying the need for mutual work. The form is typically elemental: "Let us agree only to look at the processes of our interaction." This commitment is crucial, but it does not seem to ask too much.

Second, three STAFF members stressed the potential for establishing new and more satisfactory work relations with Mr. Headman. Thus one executive noted of the meeting that much more was accomplished than he thought possible. He traced the effect directly to the refreshingly new style that encouraged him and others to get to their points with fewer of the usual obscurantisms and with less communal defensiveness. And at least one member of the STAFF had no difficulty in isolating the cause. Mr. Headman modelled the new behaviors, and others tended to adopt them. For this individual, the meeting "demonstrated that Mr. Headman is developing the ability to be free in front of his people." Others came to a similar point, but only after being startled. Mr. Headman's agreeing with the six-point credo, one executive reported, "surprised me more than anything he has ever done before."

Again, the effect is a common one. If the superior in an organization models open behaviors even a little, the resulting openness among subordinates is often startlingly greater. Highly dependent subordinates do as their boss tells them, in effect. And less-dependent subordinates are pleased to do as they desired all along. Small inputs of openness, in sum, may trigger large outputs. Nature is usually less generous about its returns on other inputs.

Third, a few individuals saw the beginnings of an increased reliance on internalization of work objectives by subordinates, as opposed to mere compliance with objectives imposed on them. Psychologically, the difference is immense. As employees internalize work objectives as their own, for example, enforcement is simplified. For the employee himself does much of the enforcing. In the case of compliance, enforcement helps establish an I/they distinction with resist/enforce characteristics. Moreover, the new style suggests a greater emphasis on command by "do as I do," as opposed to command by "do as I say." One member of the STAFF made both points in explaining that "openness is a good idea." "The program should be sold, not enforced," he observed. "The top STAFF must embrace the six points more than the office chiefs."

This third component underlying the positive reaction to the initial openness meeting—a kind of do unto yourselves as you would have others do unto you—implies an important curb on the exploitative use of laboratory programs of organization change. Directly, subordinates can be "manipulated" only as superiors agree that the same kind of "manipulation" applies to them. Specifically, that is, if superiors desire open upward communication by subordinates, the contract implies that both superiors and subordinates agree to analyze their processes of interaction. And superiors contract to hear and work through issues other than those that are of perceived relevance to themselves. The consequences can be profound. The contract sharply reduces the probability of manipulation of the one-way variety. Neatly, the agreement to analyze interaction processes encourages reciprocal influence.

Extensions to Immediate Staffs

Despite the positive tone of their reactions, STAFF members were clearly cautious about extending their early commitment to the guidelines to their immediate staffs. Overall, interviewees had little to say about their own follow-up, which may say it all. Specific reactions covered the range from denials of the need to follow up with immediate staff, all the way to admissions that nothing specific was done. "I talk straight to all my people," went one denial, "and they talk straight to me." Another noted: "I did not talk with my secretary or people." Still another went some distance, but not very far. He reported: "No staff follow-up. Gave my secretary six points to read. She said, 'Do you think they mean it?' I said an attempt is being made to adopt it."

This is not to say that no action with immediate staff took place. Most of the STAFF members, that is, arranged to have their immediate staff sit in on presentations by Mr. Inside about the experience of Organization A with its laboratory program of change and development. And two STAFF members talked with their people, one individually and one in a one-hour "open session" in which they discussed the presentation "in general, and the six points in particular."

Impact on Total STAFF

Observers were quite divided in their estimate of the impact of the guidelines on the operations of the total STAFF organization. Two thirds of the respondents did witness some degree of improvement in internal relations. But most of the same two thirds also revealed very real doubts. Some respondents—one of them the central Charlie—indicated they felt no change and/or perceived actual resistance to the trial period with the six-point credo.

The shadings of negative reactions to the trial period will be illustrated first. The negative range extends from pale reliance on the six-point credo all the way to firm reactions that it made no difference. Thus one executive allowed only that: "They are mentioned from time to time, but I don't know that we have practiced the six points." To a similar point, another respondent opined that "people do use openness as a crutch when they want to make a statement to their boss. It's some kind of catalytic." One central member of the STAFF left even less room for optimism. "No change," he concluded. "Not the faintest change when compared with the promise of the first meeting. Maybe it has helped, but I don't see it."

Most members of the STAFF reported more positive change, if with important variations. Thus one respondent reported a "definite improvement" in internal STAFF relations. Another varied the general theme. "I believe things are a little bit different," he concluded. "Maybe it's because I want to believe it." But desire in this case did not overwhelm the senses. "STAFF meetings were a little bit different for a while," he continued, "but now they are back in the old rut."

By far the most significant difference among these positive reactors concerned their feelings about the commitment of Mr. Headman. On the one hand, some respondents saw both conviction in, and practice of, the six points by their chief. Mr. Headman "has put his heart into this a little" went one variation theme. It received support in these terms:

> There are more open discussions than previously, both horizontally and vertically. Mr. Headman has made a real sincere attempt to buy it. He tries to hear people out more, he is more

open. On one occasion I saw him have a try at confronting, but he didn't go all the way.

Other members of the STAFF saw Mr. Headman's position on the six points as clearly but more pessimistically. The evidence they perceived had strong contradictory strains. Thus one executive noted: "People tend to express their opinions more freely to one another, but not to Mr. Headman." Others were quick to supply explanations of why this was the case. "I dread to go into his office," one respondent explained, "because he thinks I can never do anything right." Another executive observed: "The big question still is: What does Mr. Headman understand and mean by the six points? It is hard to keep communications open with Mr. Headman. He's always throwing up his hands and saying, 'that's all, I don't have the time.'"

Reactions cover the full range, then. Some respondents could be euphoric; and others could downgrade what they saw as "a new fad that will pass." For those for whom the attractions and repulsions were more mixed, the situation was more difficult. One member of the STAFF reflected this greater difficulty in his summary of feelings about the trial period:

> My observations can best be understood against the time period before the last 60 days. Many times in the last four years, I wanted to get up and walk out of a staff meeting. I asked myself what am I doing here with all these strangers. Now, after all these years for fleeting moments, I feel a little more at home since fellows are more free in their discussions. I am starting to talk to Mr. Headman, and starting to be blunt since he opened the door. Staff meetings have become more open. . . . That makes a big difference. Mr. Headman can't relax on the job. He knows how to work but he doesn't know how to deal with people unless it's about work. He doesn't understand that his way isn't the only way to present a set of facts. His knowledge and wisdom are always a help, but his words don't fit my mouth. I should have a freedom of choice for what words, what colors, what charts.

This concern about the real and lasting commitment of superordinates is both understandable and common in laboratory programs. For good reason in many cases, organization authorities are focal points of speculation and concern. Any change in an authority's behavior consequently can raise anxieties and doubts. Moreover, given a long list of items that could be attended to, subordinates can be pardoned for even acute concern over whether "the boss *really* means it this time." With their characteristic open-endedness, laboratory programs of organizational change

350

are prone to trigger such concerns and their public expression. Paradoxically, therefore, up to a considerable point the raising of such concerns is a sign of the early acceptance of the laboratory approach by participants. Were participants more suspicious, they would remain silent.

The Broader Environment

STAFF members were of one mind in assessing the impact of the trial period on the broader sets of organizational relations in which they were involved. "No effect"; "No measurable change"; "No significant effect": these typify the evaluations of the early effects of the guidelines.

Multiple reasons for this lack of broad impact exist, no doubt, but several respondents expressed a notable hesitance to even try. "If we do practice the six points and in fact get into the habit of doing it," one member of the STAFF noted, "we will therefore by nature start to do it in dealing with people who haven't had the privilege of looking at this sort of thing and we will start to get shot at quite rapidly. . . . We will get a worse reputation than we already have." That is, the six points ran directly counter to the prevailing organization culture in Organization USA.

Any Experimentation

The full impact of any laboratory program of organization change is seen most clearly in terms of greater tendencies to experiment. Few conscious attempts to do so at $T = 60$ days were reported. Experimentation involves the performance of new behaviors, often behaviors that have been openly discussed, publicly recommended to the actor by others, and consciously practiced with individuals committed to the success of the total process. In such a way, an individual is reinforced at all stages from intention to change through practicing the appropriate behaviors, and this by individuals he trusts. The importance of reinforcement in any change can hardly be overestimated.

That even a few conscious attempts to experiment were reported at $T = 60$ days is hopeful, given that a solid foundation of trust must preexist. There were some signs of a softening of the system, for example, by superior and subordinates. Thus one STAFF member acknowledged one experiment with the new tolerance level of Mr. Headman, even if he fell into it "not knowingly." He explained:

> One day in my office, another man and myself were preparing a letter for Mr. Headman with a short delivery date. Mr. Headman continued to contribute ideas on what it should contain and I listened as long as I could. Then I said, "Please get out so we can start the letter." He did.

351

A few tentative experimental episodes do not make an open organization, to be sure, but it is only by countless similar episodes that openness will be tested and reinforced.

f. "We Have No Common Tie Mentally": A Basis for Further Development?

Even with this mixed record, no one (at least publicly) wanted to even suggest giving up the ghost on the guidelines. Indeed, some of the verbal rationales offered in support of its continuation suggest that members of the STAFF were developing an increasing awareness of the broader usefulness of their initial OD effort. One excerpt particularly suggests this growing perception of the broader value of the program. "If people cannot identify themselves as one activity," one member reported, "there is no mutual respect. We have no common tie mentally. Openness can be this common tie. . . . Openness could serve to provoke a rapport between people so that they could respond, tolerate, and be productive."

Whether such reactions could serve as a basis for further development was problematic at the time, but several encouraging signs appeared. *First,* concern about the processes of extending the guidelines suggested some learning contrary to usual norms in Organization USA. "Let's not pound this thing," some noted. "It is good. Don't get it ridiculed." Specific ways of reducing the probability that Project USA would get "pounded"—"oversold," that is, or forced on others and then left to die because of their reactions against being forced to do the unforceable— also were suggested. Organization USA needed someone "who is going to pursue the guidelines as a duty and with conviction. The program will take three years to catch on." Nor were members of the STAFF neglectful of what role this "someone" should play, and where. He was to be an internal change agent who would be more free to take risks than others with continuing program responsibilities. And as for where he would be located, that was easy. "Don't attach him to Mr. Headman," one respondent warned. He continued: "He would be too tightly held— not enough freedom. Mr. Headman gives packaging assignments, not problem-solving assignments, and is more prone to solve the problem than help his subordinates solve it."

Second, most members of the executive staff had come to the apparent conclusion that their interpersonal and group skills required upgrading. Thus eight of the STAFF indicated varying desires to participate in a stranger T-Group. These expressions ranged from "give my right arm to go" to more moderate statements of interest. Two respondents had reservations. Thus one noted that T-groups are "too open for some people— me."

Third, general agreement was reached that a series of periodic meetings should be held. As one STAFF member explained: "At these meetings, we sit together as a group of people—not chiefs. . . . These meetings could answer the question, 'Do we all have the same understanding in what we are trying to do?' " The suggestion was heeded. Propitiously for the life chances of an OD program in Organization USA, Mr. Headman supported the suggestion and scheduled such a meeting very soon after the reactions abstracted here were fed back to him in summary form.

That a meeting was scheduled implies points both moot and probable. Thus Mr. Headman's rationale may only be guessed at. He may again have been surprised by the tone of the reactions as well as by how much of relevance was being withheld from him by members of the STAFF. And perhaps he again responded by trying to create the conditions that might change matters. Whatever the rationale, however, one point seems probable. The system was showing some signs of increased openness.

g. The Beginnings of OD in Organization USA in Retrospect: Some Common Features and Issues

Retrospectively, the nascent OD effort in Organization USA highlights a number of features and issues characteristic of most and perhaps even all similar programs. These features and issues can be briefly listed here, to serve as a kind of checklist of the common cross-pressures that affected this OD program and will affect most others. A number of positive motive forces get initial attention:

- As is typically the case, the OD effort was in critical senses the product of the integration of the interests of a lower-level insider and the needs of a line official with responsibility for a substantial organization unit and with some autonomy in its management.
- As is often the case, the responsible line official had a "conversion experience," some precipitating episode that highlighted the inadequacies or awkward consequences of the manager's style which he is motivated to avoid.
- Typically, the build up of a variety of organization pressures precedes an OD effort. These pressures signal that traditional ways of coping or doing business will become increasingly awkward, and the wise manager takes early heed.
- The "good experiences" of an organization with comparable characteristics often supply major motivation for an OD effort.

These forces predisposing an OD effort in Organization USA were opposed by a number of counterforces that can be anticipated in most similar programs. Several major counterforces deserve special note:

- Explicitly recognizing the need for a change in group climate is made difficult by the dilemmas raised thereby, as in the political inadvisability in some organizations of owning up to any "defect" for fear that it will be used against the unit in bargaining situations or in contributing to an "unfavorable climate of opinion" that may work against the unit.

- All OD programs test and usually challenge existing power relationships, and all group members tend to resist disturbing any balance of power which favors them.
- Personal ambitions can provide a highly volatile component to OD programs, and these ambitions can be those of the persons "pushing" an OD program, as well as those who have a vested interest in the status quo.
- Especially in groups with a history of authoritarian management, requests to be open and trusting are likely to be viewed with varying degrees of incredulity and even deep suspicion.
- The responsible line official—conversion experience and all—often is conflicted about how much openness he wants, from whom, and about what. This conflict can reinforce incredulity or suspicion.

Organization USA also points up the significance of the cement or glue that can bond together such forces and counterforces. That cement is blended of the values, attitudes, and behavioral skills associated with the laboratory approach. Intentions or edicts are not likely to supply the required social and emotional bonding. Various learning designs derived from the laboratory approach—whether in T-group formation or in other designs—are intended to help supply that "common mental tie" whose lack in Organization USA was noted above.

D. INTERVENTIONS
AIMED AT GROUPS:
THREE BASIC APPROACHES TO CHANGE

The emphasis here is on dealing with small groups in OD programs, the target being conceived as a small number of individuals who share some common identity and who are interested in looking at their internal processes. A president and his team of immediate subordinates could constitute such a small group, as could the coaching staff of a professional football team. The historical emphasis in OD work has been to start with the single highest-level group possible—such as a board of directors or an executive team—and work down the hierarchy. But OD work is possible with groups at all levels, and OD interventions aimed at groups can be so designed as to deal with a number of similar units in parallel programs.

Many approaches are possible in OD applications to small groups, but only three will receive explicit attention here. The three illustrative applications in Subsections 3, 4, and 5 below, in turn, highlight: interviews with members of some small group by a consultant or a change agent who will feed back his findings to the host group; use of T-Groups to induce systemic change in the properties of small groups; and structural changes that encourage behavior consistent with laboratory values.

3. THE CHANGE AGENT AS MIRROR REFLECTING LABORATORY VALUES: A STANDARD DESIGN FOR OPENERS

The classic OD design[1] for initiating the analysis of a small group's processes is interview-*cum*-feedback by a consultant or change agent. In effect, the consultant or change agent serves as a mirror, reflecting back the image projected to him by some group. The design is economical in some important ways, as in the sense that only the change agent requires initial skills and values consistent with the laboratory approach. Group members thus can have a quick and easy experience of what things would be like if they took the time themselves to enhance such skills and values and if they behaved congruently with them. What nature gives, however, she tends to take. Viewed from another perspective, that is, the economy of the design can leave group members in a difficult position. Thus group members may be left unprepared to deal with the issues opened by the consultant. Members also might be so dependent on the change agent or so defensive at being mirrored in ways they cannot accept that their own learning is inhibited.

The interview-*cum*-feedback design is now a standard one for OD openers, viewed in two basic senses. The design is a gentle one for a group intent only on surveying or auditing its own processes. "How are we functioning?" is the guiding question. Or it can be an opener for extended programs of change in a group's processes, with the interview-*cum*-feedback feature serving as an introduction to the use of T-Groups for the development of attitudes and skills consistent with the laboratory approach. These attitudes and skills, goes the argument, will help a group to analyze its own processes and also to change them, if members consider that appropriate. "How can we change our processes to get more of what we want?" is the basic question underlying this second use of the interview-*cum*-feedback design.

a. A Typical Interview-*cum*-Feedback:[2] An Organizational Locus and a Design

There are diverse varieties of this classic design, and it is far easier to illustrate one than it is to describe them all. Consider a simple example

---

1. Chris Argyris, *Interpersonal Competence and Organizational Effectiveness* (Homewood, Ill.: Dorsey Press, 1962), pp. 57–132.
2. This author has used this design five times with several groups of university administrators. The case study reported here is typical. Some details have been altered to preserve anonymity.

   For another version of the design and a supporting rationale, see Jerry B. Harvey and D. Richard Albertson, "Neurotic Organizations: Symptoms, Causes, and Treatment" (Paper presented at NTL Conference on New Technology in Organization Development, New York, October 8–9, 1971).

developed for the top executive group of a major state university. That example reflects how the specific organizational locus affects the details of the design, while the generic features of the design still come through.

The executive group in question—the university president and his six immediate subordinates—was unique in several senses, as are all such groups. Five features should establish their uniqueness. *First,* the president was relatively new in his job, which was a major step upward from his previous responsibilities. The reasons for his managerial style are problematic: perhaps he was feeling his way, or he simply might have preferred it that way, or perhaps external demands on his time were so great that they could not be diplomatically avoided. But the character of his managerial style is pronounced and definite. The president exercised his prerogatives with a very gentle hand, and his initial role was sharply limited.

Second, several new members had been recently brought together on the president's executive team. The normal processes of adaptation were no doubt still working themselves out at the time of the OD intervention.

Third, major jurisdictional issues stressed relationships in the executive group. These disputes may have been caused by personal conflicts among the president's subordinates, as some maintain. In any case, the consequences of the jurisdictional issues certainly strained the relationships between several members of the executive group.

Fourth, these jurisdictional and personal issues had a special edge because they occurred during a period of consolidation, following an unprecedented decade of budget increase upon increase upon increase. Priorities became a very real issue. Various interest groups among students, faculty, and legislators encouraged their particular champions in the executive group to get the best of suddenly scarcer resources. The stakes were major ones. To a substantial degree, radically different interests and priorities would be served by the several different policy positions that leading members of the executive group were known to support. Such encouragement no doubt exacerbated the potential for conflict inherent in the jurisdictional issues caused by new members of the executive group who challenged the prior decision-making coalition.

Fifth, diverse images of the executive group held by various relevant publics were made known to the author. The president saw his executive group as deliberately getting its ducks in a row, under very difficult conditions. The common stereotype among administrators one or two levels removed from the top provided a stark contrast. The public meetings of the executive group were perceived as pleasant enough, but the popular concept of the executive group was not uniformly flattering. The characterization was that of a hard-working group which spent enormous amounts of time in wheel-spinning, in dealing with minutiae, and in laboriously redoing the work of each other and of their subordinates. And all this fiddling was going on while, figuratively speaking, the university Rome was at least threatened by fire if it was not already burning merrily away.

The author was introduced into this organizational context by influentials who were concerned about this public/private contrast in images. The influentials persuaded the president to raise the question of a "socioemotional audit" with his executive group, following a simple design. The author would privately interview each executive and report back to the group his findings in ways that would preserve the anonymity of his sources. Some reading material was provided, should the president or his executives like an idea of the kinds of issues that could be raised by the design. Two points were stressed. The design was only an introductory experience in moving toward a more open organization. Moreover, the design was offered with the reservation that it often was better not to start such process analysis unless a real possibility of following through existed. The design was not suited to diddling, in short, nor was it a delaying tactic to relieve some of the heat that the executive group might be feeling.

What could lay beyond this initial approach interested the president. Two sequential steps were described as possible follow-ons to the interviews-*cum*-feedback. If the executives decided some improvement in their interpersonal or intergroup processes was indicated by the feedback, the author could sit in on their meetings as a process observer, schedules permitting. The consultant's purpose would be to raise here-and-now issues related to the group's intergroup and interpersonal relations, so as to improve problem-solving effectiveness. Still further down the track, the executives might decide that T-Group training would be an appropriate way of developing their process-analysis skills.

The president two or three weeks later reported the agreement of his executive group to experience the design, and that decision was implemented quickly. Interviews of at least 90 minutes were scheduled, with the added notion that more time often was useful and that executives might helpfully clear their calendars for a longer period if that were at all possible. Follow-up interviews thus could be avoided. The average interview ran somewhat under two and one-half hours.

The interviews were broadly standardized, and also sought to explore specific targets of opportunity. Stereotypically, each interview opened in the same way. The consultant briefly made six points:

- Any management group can improve its operations.
- Effectiveness of such groups is important, if only as preparation for stress situations such as student disturbances.
- Review of interpersonal and intergroup processes is one way to improve operations.
- The interviews were an initial approach to surveying group processes.

- Summary data from the interviews would be fed back to the total group, as far as it was possible to do so and protect anonymity.
- The executive group might decide to look at their processes in more depth later, based on their positive reaction to the consultant's feedback session.

The interviews themselves all touched some common bases, as they were guided by the same general outline. At a minimum, and in this order, respondents were asked to:

- Sketch the major challenges that they felt top management would have to face in the immediate future.
- Rate the quality of their functioning as an executive team (especially in their weekly meetings, which typically lasted several hours and might last all working day), from several perspectives:

  a. Respondent's Rating

  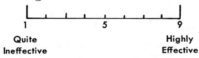

  b. Respondent's Estimate of the Average Rating of Other Executives

  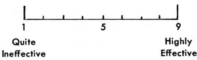

  c. Respondent's List of Specific Executives with Highest and Lowest Ratings
- Discuss the special strengths of the executive group in their meetings.
- Discuss the special weaknesses of the executive group in their meetings.

  If the points were not spontaneously raised, the respondent was asked to comment on at least these three characteristics of their group processes:

  a. the openness of executives with one another, in public sessions and in private
  b. problem-solving effectiveness in group meetings, as in dealing with the real problems, coming to timely decisions, and so on
  c. the ways in which conflicts were resolved
- Discuss the clarity of role definitions and lines of authority in the internal relationships of the executive group.
- Discuss the president's managerial style, as it influenced group meetings and the relationships between executives.

359

b. Some General Properties of the Design:
The Change Agent as Helpful/Expendable

What features of interview-*cum*-feedback encourage groups to devote their time to the design? It is not hard to tick off reasons for rejecting such a design. The pressures of time, and incredulity that an outsider can gain much perspective in a brief series of interviews, illustrate the broad range of negative motivators.

What is there on the positive side? Each situation has its own idiosyncratic motivators, but some general motivators also usually encourage having a go at such a design. There are four such common motivators. *First,* concern about interpersonal and intergroup processes is common, even (perhaps, especially) in effectively functioning groups. The common theme goes something like this: "We're audited financially, aren't we?" This is likely to be a special concern at higher levels of organization, where interpersonal and intergroup relationships tend to dominate. Technical and mechanical issues tend to grow in importance as one descends the hierarchy.

Second, concern about socioemotional processes can be especially intense under two conditions. Crudely, much data may be in the Hidden and Blind Areas of the Jo-Hari Window of several or all members of a group. Members may be unwilling to raise such issues because of the perceived risk, or they may simply lack the skills or persistence necessary to work through the issues they clearly perceive. Similarly, but more potentially ticklish, one or two group members may have a major blind spot. For example, the blind spot may concern the impact of a managerial style on relationships between subordinates of which the manager is blissfully unaware. Others may perceive this but, especially if the person is (let us say) the president, his subordinates may balk at raising the issue. In either of these two cases, group members may overtly or secretly hope that the change agent can help either surface the hidden data or illuminate the blind spots.

Third, the consultant-as-mirror might variously enrich a group's appreciation of its own processes. At a minimum, the consultant might only confirm that of which every member is already aware. This may seem a small blessing, but some things cannot be confirmed too often lest people come to doubt their reality. A little more ambitiously, the change agent's intervention may encourage later attention by group members to process issues. This would contribute to greater self-maintenance of regenerative communication systems, even if the specific feedback by the consultant is not particularly helpful or enlightening. More expansively, the consultant may induce the release of hidden data or perceive the significance of factors which group members undervalue. In some cases, the change agent also may be able to put the proverbial two and two together, and here he can really earn his salt.

I recall one such two-and-two case, which has a simple-simon quality, but only in retrospect. The author was reviewing the processes of a certain agency largely supported by a massive gift from one donor. The agency head gave me only one ground rule. There was to be no mention of additional funding, either to the donor or to his staff. The donor was bitterly unhappy with the lack of progress, I was informed, and any request for needed funding should only follow some real accomplishment. The director reflected more of his inner conflicts than of reality. The donor's first comments were of the order: "I don't see how they can make it without more of my money." Neither could I, and we spent most of our time in working through the two realistic alternatives: termination of the project, or additional funding. Among other things, the donor interpreted the failure to request more funding as a sign that agency personnel were tired of being financially dependent on the donor, if they were not in fact rejecting her as a person. I reported that I had no such evidence, in fact ample evidence to the contrary. She left undecided, but my report to the director stressed above all the lack of realism of his decision to avoid the issue of additional funding.

Fourth, the interview-*cum*-feedback design is a safe one for the participants, if it can be harrowing for the change agent. Potentially delicate issues can be brushed aside, for example, with varying degrees of delicacy. Hence: "It is unfair to expect that consultant could have really tuned in to how we do things here, given the short time he could devote to us. You know, sometimes we really ought to set aside the time necessary to do the job well." Legion are the other devices by which a group can avoid hearing what is being communicated by the consultant in feedback sessions. Or having heard all too clearly what was reported, group members can engage in animated and artful discussions which subtly avoid what the "mirror" is reflecting back to them. One assumes from such behavior signals that at least some group members are unhappy about what they see reflected in that mirror held up to them by the consultant.

c. Some Specifics of One Interview-*cum*-Feedback: An Executive Group Being Mirrored

One hour had been set aside for the feedback session to the executive group described above, and the meeting began pleasantly enough with the high hopes for learning expressed by the president. The consultant introduced his feedback in terms of the notion of a degenerative communication system introduced earlier, which was greeted with knowing nods as accurately describing the state of affairs among other groups of university executives. The consultant also noted that the feedback session could be quite short. Despite the variations on a theme that could be detailed, in short, a dominant pattern emerged from all interviews. And this pattern could be conveyed via a simple illustration. Several more complex ways of making the same point had been prepared, the consultant concluded, and the executive group could later decide whether it wished to go into them. But it would in no sense be necessary to do so.

As the simple illustration was developed, the pleasant tone of the feedback session changed appreciably. Apparently, the executives interpreted the presentation as implying that their interaction system had major degenerative properties. Whatever the case, the presentation developed two aspects of a single theme:

- On almost all issues, the executive group contained two or more subgroups with significantly different perceptions, expectations, and evaluations concerning their interpersonal and intergroup relations.

- More significantly, on almost all issues, the executives were either unclear or mistaken about the perceptions, expectations, and evaluations of their fellow executives concerning interpersonal and intergroup relations.

The two points were illustrated by detailing how the executives responded to rating their effectiveness as a group in meetings, on a low/high scale running from 1 through 9. Some highlights may be sketched, with uncommunicated but interesting data being presented in parentheses:

- There were two clusters of scores about group effectiveness, especially at meetings: 2–4 and 7–8.

- Almost without exception, each executive's rating for self was 2–4, while his estimate of the average ratings of his fellow executives was 7–8.

  (The one exception was the president, whose self-rating was 7 and who was unwilling to guess the ratings of the others "because I just don't know." This datum was not communicated.)

- The executives guessed poorly as to which of their fellows rated the executive group highest/lowest on effectiveness: in fact, over half of the executives made at least one maximum error, e.g., guessing that executive A was the lowest rater of the group's effectiveness whereas in fact he reported the highest obtained by consultants in the interviews.

  (There is much food for thought in this one. Were executives merely unaware? Or had they conveyed a false impression to their colleagues, while being straight with the consultant? Or had they been putting on the consultant, while they were four-square with their colleagues? These questions were not raised explicitly. More food for thought: the president correctly picked the executive who scored his group the lowest on effectiveness, but his guess about

362

the highest scorer was far off. The assumed-highest scorer was in fact next-to-lowest.)

- One executive refused to give a single rating, but he did provide three ratings for effectiveness of the executives as a group, and especially in their meetings:
  a. to learn what's going on: 7
  b. to get at basic problems: 2–3
  c. to create a sense of cooperation or team identity: 4

Presenting this illustration took only a few minutes of clock time, almost as long as the silence that followed the consultant's request for reactions! The logjam was broken by a brief statement from the elder statesman of the group. "Damn," he said, "you heard everything I told you, and most of the stuff I was thinking." ("That saved you," I was told later by one of the executives in a private review of "the" meeting. "Two or three of us, including me, were ready to sandbag you at the first opportunity." I agreed.)

The exchanges flew thick and fast for awhile, and then the request: "Well, what else do you have for us?" That established the pattern for a meeting that ran three hours beyond the originally scheduled time. We went back to similar wells six times in all, each time being a replica of the other. The consultant would summarize data on one point; the usual silence would follow, as if the group were catching its breath; someone would confirm that there seemed substantial-enough reality reflected in the summary; and discussion would follow. These major topics were considered, in this order:

- major challenges facing the executive group
- various formal-role definitions that influenced the group's interpersonal and intergroup relations
- contrasting personal and analytical styles of the several executives
- the ways of dealing with conflict in the executive group
- the role of the president and its impact on interpersonal and intergroup relations

Several recommendations were made for follow-on, but these were not implemented in the form presented. The executive group did take a three-day "retreat" to work on their relationships, but they decided against using a process observer when I proved to be unavailable. My schedule was a factor in the unavailability but I did observe that, given the probable punitiveness of my feedback session, establishing a long-run relationship with the executives might be subtle and trying. But I would be pleased to do an interview-*cum*-feedback session some 12 or 18 months later to provide some kind of check on any developmental changes in the group's processes.

The retreat was held, and the president and most of the other executives have gone out of their way to emphasize its value and especially that of the feedback session. "It got us down to elementals with one another," reads one letter. Another letter tickles me: "We have started to waffle with one another 3 or 4 times in meetings since you were last here. And then someone would say: 'If we keep this up, Big Bob will come get us.' That always breaks us up, and gets us leveling again." That breaks me up, too, but it leaves me unsatisfied and questioning. Perhaps someday I will conduct that audit to get direct perspective on how much the demanding values of the laboratory approach have taken root from a simple OD design.

d. Forces Encouraging Openness: Why and How Such Survey Feedback Designs Seem to Work

Despite the simplicity of the interview-*cum*-feedback design illustrated above, it can generate complex dynamics. Figure 1 outlines some of the design's motivating properties. That figure applies not only to the design illustrated above, but also to the broader family of "survey feedback" designs for OD. That family covers a range of designs: from those using an open-ended interview schedule such as the one above, which leaves substantial room for consultant's interpretation and organization of the data; to forced-choice questionnaires which are designed by the team being surveyed, whose members also interpret the raw data. The range of designs has diverse advantages and disadvantages. For example, the consultant-oriented designs at once take advantage of his potential skills, while they probably also tend to make it somewhat difficult for the team being mirrored to own the feedback, or even to accept it and hear it without some initial defensiveness. Available research does not yet permit assigning specific weights to the various mixes of advantages and disadvantages.

Figure 1 should be self-explanatory, in the main. Following the lead of Charles T. McElvaney and Matthew B. Miles, it distinguishes three components of survey feedback designs. All such designs clearly deal with data, with immediate consequences like those listed in Figure 1. Relatedly, survey feedback designs also involve a variety of meetings of the target unit, at least to hear and respond to the feedback but perhaps also to help plan the interview schedule, interpret raw data, etc. These meetings in themselves can have positive effects on team development, as the list of five items in Figure 1 suggests. Finally, all survey feedback designs variously seek to build more of a process analysis into teams, as that orientation is described in Section C of Part I.

364

Figure 1. Idealized Schema of Survey Feedback Design Components and Consequences

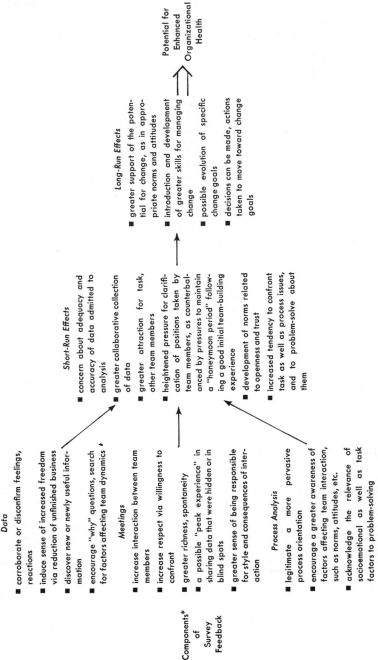

*Following Charles T. McElvaney and Matthew B. Miles, "Using Survey Feedback and Consultation," in Richard A. Schmuck and Matthew B. Miles (eds.), *Organization Development in Schools* (Palo Alto, Cal.: National Press Books, 1971), pp. 116–17.

Beyond these three basic components of survey feedback designs, several effects tend to occur. Figure 1 details some short-run effects, as well as those with longer lead times. The research in this area is sparse and mixed.[3] Hence these effects can hardly be anticipated in every case; and hence Figure 1 is labeled an "idealized schema."

4. APPLICATIONS OF
LABORATORY VALUES VIA T-GROUPS:
TOWARD CHANGE ALONG BASIC DIMENSIONS

The literature also contains models for more deliberate efforts to build laboratory values into small groups. Frank Friedlander's training-reseach effort is one of the most impressive examples of what can be done.[4] Friedlander's work uses family groups exposed to what he calls "organizational training laboratories" in an intended effort to overcome the perceived shortcomings of the initial resort to stranger experiences. As Friedlander explains:

> . . . these training sessions deal with the intact work group as an integrated system into which is introduced procedural and interpersonal change, rather than with a collection of strangers representing different organizations—or unrelated components of the same organization.
>
> .   .   .   .   .
>
> The organizational training laboratory is directed at helping the individual bridge the hazardous, yet critical transition from his trainee role to the "real life" role of his back-home environment, and at preventing dissipation of the training effects. Since much of the discussion centers upon the relevant work problems which the group actually faces, and since the members of the

---

3. Charles T. McElvaney and Matthew B. Miles, "Using Survey Feedback and Consultation," in Schmuck and Miles (eds.), *op. cit.*, esp. pp. 129–30, detail the results of one administration of the design which was disappointing to them. Support for the position sketched above can be found in such sources as: Stuart M. Klein, Allen I. Kraut, and Alan Wolfson, "Employee Reactions to Attitude Survey Feedback: A Study of the Impact of Structure and Process," *Administrative Science Quarterly*, Vol. 16 (December, 1971), pp. 497–514; and Clayton P. Alderfer and Ray Ferris, "Understanding the Impact of Survey Feedback" (unpublished MS, Yale University, 1971).

4. Frank Friedlander, "The Impact of Organizational Training Laboratories upon the Effectiveness and Interaction of Ongoing Work Groups," *Personnel Psychology*, Vol. 20 (Autumn, 1970), pp. 289–307. See also his "Performance and Interactional Dimensions of Organizational Work Groups," *Journal of Applied Psychology*, Vol. 50, No. 3 (1966), pp. 257–65.
   For a generically similar design applied in schools, see Richard A. Schmuck and Matthew B. Miles (eds.), *Organization Development in Schools* (Palo Alto, Cal.: National Press Books, 1971), esp. pp. 51–69.

training group are also the members of the organizational work group, ideally there is a perfect consolidation of the training and organizational membership roles. The back-home and the here-and-now are one and the same.

. . . . .

Research emphasis is not only upon behavioral change in the individual, but also upon change of the individual within his organizational context, and changes in the organizational context or organic system of which the individual is one interacting part.[5]

Friedlander's research is thus an example of the third-generation effort described in Section C of Part II. The group itself is the target for change as well as the medium in which change occurs.

a. Toward Improving Effectiveness and Interaction of Ongoing Work Groups: One Training and Research Design

Working within one of the armed services' largest research and development facilities, Friedlander reports a training-research program involving 12 work groups with 91 total members. The focus was internal, on each group's interpersonal and intergroup processes, as opposed to an emphasis on external relationships with other groups. Although several groups at a number of hierarchical levels were involved, the design was (to use the vocabulary of the electrician) parallel rather than serial.

A few other features of the training-research effort will aid the review of results below. The groups represented four hierarchical levels, had from 5 to 15 members, and met regularly once or twice a week for a variety of purposes. Such groups might, for example, discuss and resolve problems, disseminate information, or plan for the future. The training goal was to improve their effectiveness and interaction via organizational training laboratories. Friedlander describes the training design briefly:

The nature of this training quite naturally varies among groups in some ways. In general, however, the laboratory sessions last approximately four to five days and are attended by *all* members of a particular work group. The purposes of the sessions generally are (a) to identify problems facing the work-group system and the reasons for their existence, (b) to invent possible solutions to the problems in the form of needed system changes, and (c) to plan implementation of these solutions through regu-

---

5. Friedlander, "The Impact of Organizational Training Laboratories," p. 291.

lar and newly-constructed channels. Within this problem-solving context, the group explores numerous inadequacies in interpersonal and intergroup processes which directly or indirectly influence the total work system.[6]

Straightforwardly, this describes an application of the laboratory approach in the context of a group history evolved during work experiences over an extended period. The learning situation consequently is structured in major senses, as compared, for example, to a normal sensitivity training group. The values, attitudes, and behavioral skills consistent with the laboratory approach—as described in the first four sections of this book—are adapted to the context provided by past work experiences.

Friedlander's research design inspires unusual confidence. He exposed four task groups to an organizational training laboratory. He also gained the collaboration of eight additional task groups that he considered "comparison groups,"[7] which would permit judgments of some definiteness about the impact of the laboratories on the experimental groups. The basic measure of the impact of the training experience was the Group Behavior Inventory, or GBI, which was developed specifically to test the effects of Friedlander's OD effort based on the laboratory approach. The underlying motivation was to develop a set of dimensions capable of describing *the* central group phenomena. Suitable changes along these dimensions were conceptualized as improving a group's effectiveness and its internal interaction. The only data came from self-reports. No independent measures of outcomes of the training were available.

Some further details about the Group Behavior Inventory will circumscribe its development and use. The Inventory is a paper-and-pencil test for self-reports of a group's properties by members of the group. The GBI was developed by factor analysis of a large number of items describing aspects of group phenomena. As refined, the GBI includes six major dimensions, each tapped by a number of separate items. The dimensions may be described in these terms:

6. Friedlander, "The Impact of Organizational Training Laboratories," p. 290. See also his "Performance and Interactional Dimensions of Organizational Work Groups," pp. 258–59.
7. Friedlander, "The Impact of Organizational Training Laboratories," p. 294, aptly observes: "The term 'comparison group,' rather than the experimental psychologist's term 'control group' is used throughout this paper since there is virtually nothing controlled in these eight groups. While it is true that they did not participate in a planned training experience, it is also likely that many events occurred in the eight groups during this period which had a positive or negative impact upon characteristics relevant to this study. Perhaps the term 'control group,' as used by the field-researcher, is a soothing misnomer which tends to gloss over a myriad of variables that might otherwise be quite relevant."

I. *Group Effectiveness:* This dimension describes group effectiveness in solving problems and in formulating policy through a creative, realistic team effort.
II. *Approach to vs. Withdrawal from Leader:* At the positive pole of this dimension are groups in which members can establish an unconstrained and comfortable relationship with their leader—the leader is approachable.
III. *Mutual Influence:* This dimension describes groups in which members see themselves and others as having influence with other group members and the leader.
IV. *Personal Involvement and Participation:* Individuals who want, expect, and achieve active participation in group meetings are described by this dimension.
V. *Intragroup Trust vs. Intragroup Competitiveness:* At the positive pole, this dimension depicts a group in which the members hold trust and confidence in each other.
VI. *General Evaluation of Meetings:* This dimension is a measure of a generalized feeling about the meetings of one's group as good, valuable, strong, pleasant, or as bad, worthless, weak, unpleasant.[8]

The intended effects of the OD design were direct. By hypothesis, increases in (for example) Mutual Influence were expected to result from the organizational training laboratories, and these increases were in turn expected to be one of the necessary conditions for improving a group's competence to deal with interpersonal and intergroup issues.

The GBI was administered to the 12 groups in the study, following this schedule:

	Administration I	Administration II
Training Groups	Day 1	approx. Day 181
Comparison Groups	Day 1	6 months after training

b. "Complexity of the Training Impact":
Some Consequences of Organizational Training Laboratories

After careful analysis of responses to the GBI, Friedlander concluded that: "These results, in general, point to the complexity of the training impact upon group members."[9] Without presuming to redo his careful analysis, several points can serve to summarize the complexity to which Friedlander referred.

---

8. *Ibid.,* p. 295.
9. *Ibid.,* p. 299.

First, consistent with the literature, a potent application of the laboratory approach was expected to induce changes in many or all six GBI dimensions. For example, common consequences attributed to the laboratory approach are increased mutual influence (GBI Dimension III), heightened involvement and participation by members (IV), and increased intragroup trust among group members (V). And certainly the laboratory approach seeks to make group meetings more productive (VI), as well as to increase the sense of overall group effectiveness (I). The question of rapport with a formal leader (II) is more complicated. The openness characteristic of the laboratory approach can by hypothesis be expected to help develop rapport between a formal leader and his work group and to increase the level of comfort in interaction. However, different consequences can be envisioned. For example, that very openness also can deprive formal leaders of some of the crutches provided by status and office, thereby making them more vulnerable and exposing that they are in reality "not much without the uniform" of office and status. The effectiveness of particular applications of the laboratory approach, in combination with the ability of all group members to "unfreeze" and change, if appropriate, would determine whether the formal leader would be more approachable (II).

Second, in general, the organizational training laboratories did have major impact on responses to the GBI, as judged by average group responses as well as by the responses of individuals. Specifically, the Training Groups changed significantly more in expected directions on three of the GBI dimensions: (I) Group Effectiveness, (III) Mutual Influence, and (IV) Personal Involvement. On two of the three other dimensions, the pattern is similar. Training Groups also improve their other GBI scores in the direction consistent with the laboratory approach, but the changes do not attain statistical significance. Only Leader Approachability (II) goes against this grain, with a modest reduction in the Training Groups and a major one in the Comparison Groups.

Third, it seems likely that this summary of changes in the Training Groups understates the impact of the organization training laboratory. Table 1 presents some data which strongly suggest that conclusion. The higher the GBI score in that table, the closer the approach to the values of the laboratory approach.

A progressive argument in three stages is necessary to reflect the fuller impact of the training design. The section "Before Project" in Table 1 indicates that the Comparison Groups initially had a higher level of interpersonal competence than the Training Groups on five of the six GBI dimensions. Three of these five differences attain usually accepted levels of statistical significance. One interpretation is that the less-competent groups in effect "turned themselves in" for training, since participation in the laboratories was voluntary. Whatever the interpretation,

370

Table 1. Mean Raw Scores on Six GBI Dimensions Before and After Training-Research Project

Group Dimensions	Before Project			After Project			Change	
	Training Groups	Comparison Groups	Differences in Training vs. Comparison Groups	Training Groups	Comparison Groups	Differences in Training vs. Comparison Groups	Training Groups	Comparison Groups
I. Group Effectiveness	2.08	2.35	−.27*	2.41	2.38	.03	.23*	−.07
II. Leader Approachability	2.46	2.78	−.32*	2.37	2.62	−.25	−.09	−.16**
III. Mutual Influence	2.44	2.40	.04	2.61	2.37	.24*	.17*	−.03
IV. Personal Involvement	2.53	2.57	−.04	2.68	2.51	.17	.15*	−.06
V. Intragroup Trust	2.13	2.58	−.45**	2.25	2.45	−.20	.12	−.13
VI. Evaluation of Meetings	2.04	2.13	−.09	2.08	2.02	.06	.04	−.11

* designates a difference statistically significant at .05 level.
** designates a difference statistically significant at .01 level.
Source: Frank Friedlander, "The Impact of Organizational Training Laboratories upon the Effectiveness and Interaction of Ongoing Work Groups," Personnel Psychology, Vol. 20 (Autumn, 1967), p. 302.

however, these data imply that Training and Comparison Groups differ in a fundamental way that probably would understate the impact of the laboratory training on the former.

The section "After Project," to take another step in developing the argument, shows that the Training Groups essentially turned the pre-laboratory situation around. Training Groups now appear as more inter-personally competent on four of the six GBI dimensions, with one difference attaining statistical significance.

The section "Changes" provides a final perspective on the impact of the training design. Notice that the Training Groups have changed on five of the six GBI dimensions toward the values of the laboratory approach. Leader Approachability (II) is the sole exception. Three of these changes (GBI Dimensions I, III, and IV) attain usually accepted levels of statistical significance. In contrast, Comparison Groups move uniformly lower on after versus before GBI scores, which is consistent with movement away from the values of the laboratory approach. One of those differences attains statistical significance.

This extended discussion of Table 1 can be brought to a direct conclusion. Not only did Training Groups change in ways consistent with a closer approach to laboratory values, but they did so while Comparison Groups were changing markedly in the opposite direction. The general sense is that of the training design swimming upstream against worsening conditions in the parent organization. This view of the results implies a potent training design.

c. A Conclusion and Some Concerns: Cost/Benefit Ratios and Group-Level Interventions

Data like those above suggest that, within limits, it is possible to design group-level interventions based on the laboratory approach that will have the desired effects. Five sets of these limits are relevant to the illustration above. *First,* not every individual or every grouping of individuals will respond similarly to such training interventions. In the case above, enough individuals and groups responded as expected to generate statistically significant differences. But aggregate analysis is only a start. Too little is known about deviant cases, the individuals or groups for whom the experience does not "take" or for whom even hurtful consequences occur.

Second, the conclusion above of the efficacy of the training design assumes the usefulness of the measuring instrument. Only many replications of the training-research design will establish that usefulness. Since at least some questions can be entertained about the validity and reliability of any measuring instrument, a tentativeness is appropriate when interpreting results such as those above. An awkward measuring instrument can, in any single study, either mask relations that are really there or isolate regularities that are only apparent. It is not clear which of these it is in the present case, for the real relationships may be more marked than they appear above. Alternatively only random relationships may exist.

Third, and relatedly, the study above would profit from a test of outcome variables other than those provided by self-reports, and short of "general effectiveness" or "productivity" measures. Unobtrusive measures of the middle range are ideal, such as measures of changes in interaction patterns following training that can be rated from tape recordings in terms of detailed classification schemes.[10] If nothing else, this makes compliant self-reporting more difficult. Some have charged that self-reports can tell more about how much respondents like the experimenter than about what the stimulus situation really was.

Reliance on unobtrusive measures of the middle range avoids two dangerous positions that are easy enough to fall into. One position essentially argues that changes such as those in the GBI cited above are morally desirable ends in themselves, no matter what their other consequences. The other extreme position urges that changes in interpersonal and intergroup competence such as those apparently measured by GBI will directly lead to improved performance, as conventionally defined in terms of higher productivity or lower turnover. The first position is mindless of several factors, one of which is that science is nothing if it is not an expanding network of multiple cross-checks. Without a passion for such multiple cross-checks, an approach runs the risk of rigidifying into an ideology to be protected rather than evolving into a growing network of relations to be expanded. The second position is too simplistic, because complex intervening variables no doubt must be specified in linkages of interpersonal competence and such outcome variables as productivity.[11]

Fourth, formulations like Friedlander's avoid the complexities of phase analysis, perhaps at the expense of understanding. For example, Friedlander does not distinguish phases in which various variables become critical, but Figure 1 suggests one model of two flows of effects over time. Without some pump-priming level of trust, the model implies, the processes of approaching the values of the laboratory approach do not

---

10. Chris Argyris specifically designed one classification system for this purpose. See his "Explorations in Interpersonal Competence," *Journal of Applied Behavioral Science,* Vol. 1 (July, 1965), pp. 255–69.
11. This was the outcome of the efforts to link satisfaction and productivity, and there is no reason to expect linkages of competence and productivity to be any different. For example, an interpersonally competent individual should be able to develop better relations with others, which could permit higher productivity. But he might also be better able to keep his output low while he preserves his superior's good graces.

begin.[12] That level either exists when training begins, or it must be induced. Some ongoing groups have achieved that level; and it appears that some ad hoc groups quickly decide that high trust is appropriate. Model I in Figure 2 covers these two cases. Other ongoing groups have not achieved that requisite level, and it appears that some ad hoc groups quickly decide that low trust is appropriate. These cases are detailed by Model II in Figure 2. Here the initial strategy is a delicate building of shared influence and personal involvement to help generate a requisite level of trust. The going is difficult. In Model II, until the cycle is somehow broken, every issue eventually ends up in a demonstration that the

Figure 2. Two Models for Engaging Dimensions of Friedlander's "Group Behavior Inventory"

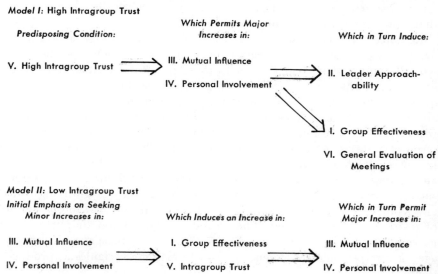

Model I: High Intragroup Trust

	Which Permits Major	
Predisposing Condition:	Increases in:	Which in Turn Induce:

V. High Intragroup Trust → III. Mutual Influence

IV. Personal Involvement → II. Leader Approachability

I. Group Effectiveness

VI. General Evaluation of Meetings

Model II: Low Intragroup Trust

Initial Emphasis on Seeking Minor Increases in:	Which Induces an Increase in:	Which in Turn Permit Major Increases in:

III. Mutual Influence

IV. Personal Involvement → I. Group Effectiveness

V. Intragroup Trust → III. Mutual Influence

IV. Personal Involvement

trust level is not adequate to support work toward changes consistent with the laboratory approach.

It requires only a little imagination to explain results like Friedlander's, or anyone else's, by assuming various combinations of high-trust and low-trust groups as they enter training. Suffice it here to note that different developmental phases for groups can be conceived of, and that groups can truly enlarge their competence even if they achieve only relatively low plateaus of learning. The point is the same in both cases.

12. The primacy of preexisting trust is suggested by several studies. See, for example, Frank Friedlander, "The Primacy of Trust as a Facilitator of Further Group Accomplishment," *Journal of Applied Behavioral Science*, Vol. 6 (October, 1970), pp. 387–400.

Any attempt to measure several groups by the same simple standard of progress, or of change, involves an oversimplification. Unfortunately, not enough is yet known to avoid this convenient oversimplification.

Fifth, working with individual groups, whether as singles or several in a parallel design, can induce significant problems. Changing a group's internal processes can cause relational problems with other groups which have not experienced a similar learning experience, in short. There are two conditions that minimize such an effect: when the group is somehow singular or self-contained, as a management team in a field location in a decentralized organization; or when the group is at or toward the top of its particular hierarchy. This wheels-within-wheels effect is suggested by the Friedlander data, especially in the singular inability of the organization training laboratories to increase Leader Approachability. Hypothetically, the group leaders may have patterned their behavior after a powerful oganization figure, and this model remained unchanged while they perceived demands from group members to modify their own leadership style. This cross-pressure hypothesis could account for Friedlander's major deviant finding.

5. APPLICATIONS THAT BACK INTO LABORATORY VALUES: TOWARD CHANGE IN CLIMATE THROUGH STRUCTURAL VARIATION

This subsection briefly changes the usual order of things in the discussions above by dealing with interaction as the dependent variable, as it were. That is, the focus is on two applications to structural change that seem capable of inducing behavior consistent with the laboratory approach. These two applications can be said to back into laboratory values. The first application is quite specific to a particular situation, involving the collaborative development of a job description. The second application, which can be generalized to a wide variety of work situations, involves the structuring of work so as to induce a range of desired behaviors.

a. One Variation on the Theme of Collaborative Authority: Writing a Job Description for Self or a Superior

One OD design based on a collaborative concept of authority in the writing of a job description was inspired by a specific problem. The position in question had caused trouble for over a decade. As one sign, the average tenure in the position over the previous 12 years had been 11 months, followed in all cases by the incumbent being demoted or leaving the company. The position had developed quite a reputation, which is not difficult to understand. There was, however, no dearth of fresh candidates for it. Substantial financial rewards encouraged people to try their hand at riding this particular tiger, and the position provided enough visibility in the industry that other outside major opportunities could reasonably be expected. By this time, the position had become an inside joke in the industry, and anything more than a year's tenure was considered a sign of a successful performance.

Sketch of an Organizational Problem

The basic difficulty faced by incumbents lay in their being in the middle between headquarters and field units. Over historical time, the field units had been virtually autonomous, with all hands drawing major satisfaction from the fact that operations "ran themselves" as if an invisible hand were at work. After 20 to 30 years, it became necessary for headquarters to intervene in field affairs, but that necessity was not sufficient to motivate cooperation by the field. Rather than remaining pleasantly self-managing entities, the field units more and more became "baronies that go their own way as if there were no corporate interests distinct from their own." Headquarters responded by creating an integrative executive position between the field units and the responsible corporate official. Although (or perhaps because) the corporate official had not been able to "clip the wings" of the field units, their heads felt demoted by the insertion of the integrative executive between them and their previous superior. Moreover, that integrative executive initially and thereafter was seen as a "headquarter's man," even though he invariably was selected from field personnel. The field units struggled to preserve their prerogatives, and jurisdictional disputes became the order of the day. Sooner rather than later, the test of power would come, and whoever happened to be the integrative executive at that moment was the consistent loser. Headquarters wanted more influence over the field, but not at the expense of creating morale problems among the field personnel in what clearly was a seller's labor market.

One of the first official duties of a newly promoted corporate official was to remove another occupant of the integrative executive position— he had lasted only nine months—and this act apparently was followed by a major resolution to slow down the revolving door somewhat. The new corporate official had in mind three willing candidates for the position, all from among the six field officials who would be directly supervised by the new integrative executive. And the corporate official had a goal: to keep the incumbent in office at least 18 months.

376

Design Based on a Collaborative Concept of Authority

This writer was asked to develop a design to meet the corporate official's goal, and he took a direct approach. The job description for the integrative executive's position was to be rewritten by the six field managers, three of whom were candidates for the position and all of whom would be affected in one direct way or another by the outcome. In addition, as one factor in his choice of the integrative executive, the corporate official would periodically observe the six field men as they developed the job description.[13] Two consultants would be available throughout the design, both of whom were known to all the field men and to the corporate official. The process observers' goal was to help each of the men show to his own best advantage.

The corporate official accepted the design, after brief consideration. Three days were quickly set aside for it, with the corporate official risking the commitment to the basic job description that would emerge. That commitment, however, did not mean that the corporate official would not raise questions or would fail to reflect his feelings and reactions. He did specify a few features of the job description he considered desirable, although he was not adamant about any of them. Moreover, the corporate official could envision circumstances under which he would veto some job descriptions. Basically, however, he made a major commitment to a collaborative exercise of authority.

The rationale of the design is more or less straightforward. Five features are most prominent. *First,* the design emphasized the induction of empathy for the holder of the position for which the new job description was to be written, and such consideration was an expected result of "taking the role of the other."[14] At least three of the field men, in fact, were candidates for the job of that Other for whom they were writing a job description. For them, the exercise was very real. Commonly, the field men would evaluate a portion of the job description in such terms: "Now if you were in that slot, and situation X arose, how would you react to it, given element Y in the job description?"

---

13. For a more detailed OD design for personnel selection based on the laboratory approach, see Donald C. King, "Selecting Personnel for a Systems 4 Organization" (Paper presented at NTL Conference on New Technology in Organization Development, New York, October 8–9, 1971).

14. For some relevant theory, see Ralph H. Turner, "Role-Taking, Role Standpoint, and Reference Group Behavior," *American Journal of Sociology,* Vol. 61 (January, 1956), pp. 318–21, 326. For an application, see R. Fred Ferguson, "Field Experiments: Preparation for the Changing Police Role," mimeographed, undated.

For an OD use of the role approach similar to the description above, see Roger Harrison, "Role Negotiation: A Tough-Minded Approach to Team Development," in W. Warner Burke and Harvey A. Hornstein (eds.), *The Social Technology of Organization Development* (Washington, D.C.: NTL Learning Resources Corporation, 1972).

Second, the design hoped to simulate some of the cross-pressure situations that the integrative executive would later face. "So this is how it feels to be in between," was a typical reflection that the design at times had such an effect. Problem-situations were talked through in terms of the provisions of alternative job descriptions, with the goals of anticipating difficulties and of developing some sense of how they might be managed.

Third, the design hoped to increase the sense of owning of the job description by all field personnel, as well as by the eventual choice for the integrative executive. The associated theme is, more or less: You made your bed, now . . . etc., etc.

Fourth, the design intended to reduce the potential for jurisdictional conflicts, which had been so divisive over the previous decade. Such reduction could come in two ways: by clarifying what the likely jurisdictional issues would be, at a minimum, given various job descriptions; and by seeking to resolve these jurisdictional issues, by anticipating them both formally in the job description and behaviorally in working toward the creation of norms and attitudes that could be applied outside the learning situation to the resolution of jurisdictional issues that might develop later.

Fifth, the design sought to introduce another reality element into the choice of the new integrative executive. The promotion choice would be based in some part, then, on public performance on a common task. That is, if X could not work effectively with the others in the learning situation, this would be an important datum that should be considered in making the eventual choice. As it developed, indeed, the three-day design showed one field official in such a good light that the corporate official felt it necessary to reshuffle his rankings in a major way. His initial first choice still got the promotion, however.

Did the Design Work?

There is no simple evaluation of this design. The corporate official found it easy to live with the job description, even though he would have written it much differently. Moreover, the corporate official's goal was met, and that eminently satisfied him. At last reckoning, the new integrative executive had been in office for 28 months. How much of that tenure can be attributed to the design is moot, of course. Only one point is not debatable. The design was a grueling one for all concerned. The participants drifted away quickly when the job description was completed and after the choice for the new integrative executive was announced. "I slunk home to stick my head in the sand," one participant announced. "I bled through every pore for the guy who was to fill that job description. And I wasn't even a candidate!"

b. Organizing Work in Human Terms:
Toward Motivation through Work Itself

Most OD effort has focused on interaction patterns, and only very secondarily on organization structure. In large part, this reflects the strong bias of major OD practitioners to apply the laboratory approach at the highest organization levels, where the quality of interaction is extremely important and structural constraints are minimized. Relatedly, many OD applications have been in host organizations whose technology is interaction-centered, e.g., marketing organizations, welfare or service agencies, and so on.

This primary emphasis on interaction versus structure is an awkward one, however, given the philosophic grounding of the laboratory approach. That is, the laboratory approach is conceptually centered on the simultaneous satisfaction of human needs and organization demands, and it is system-oriented. If the satisfaction of human needs in any particular case can be attained by affecting only patterns of interaction, consequently, so be it. But if the system for analysis is technology-rich, or if the satisfaction of human needs is mediated in significant ways by organization structure or task configurations—both of which are often the case[15]—applications of the laboratory approach must emphasize structure. Otherwise, those applications will be false to the logic of the approach. Hence OD applications based on the laboratory approach should be interaction-centered or structure-oriented, or both, as the specific situation requires.

A Concept for Need-Satisfying Work

There are relatively few OD applications based on the laboratory approach which are structure-oriented,[16] but the nature of the tie-in seems clear enough. For example, early work with Frederick Herzberg's concept of motivation[17] has been promising, despite the fact that important methodological questions have been raised about its underlying two-

---

15. This has been a dominant theme of much research over the past two or three decades, of course. For one approach, see Newton Margulies, "Organizational Culture and Psychological Growth," *Journal of Applied Behavioral Science*, Vol. 5 (October, 1969), pp. 491–508.

16. The most prominent application of the laboratory approach to a structured work environment is provided by Alfred D. Marrow, David G. Bowers, and Stanley Seashore, *Management by Participation* (New York: Harper & Row, Publishers, 1967). But little attention is given to the specific linkages of the socioemotional and technical systems. More or less, the laboratory approach was used to reduce resistance to the technical changes, it appears.

17. Frederick Herzberg, *et al.*, *The Motivation to Work* (New York: John Wiley & Sons, 1959); and Herzberg, *Work and the Nature of Man* (Cleveland, Ohio: World Publishing Co., 1966).

factor model.[18] Basically, Herzberg's approach stresses that man's needs at work are met essentially by the nature of his work. The major *motivators* that can be built into work are:[19]

- the actual achievement of the employee
- the objective recognition that the employee attains for his achievement, which must be distinguished from the "recognition" accorded as a public relations gesture
- increased responsibility assigned to the employee because of his performance
- increased opportunities to grow in knowledge about a task and in capability to perform it
- increased chance for advancement to a higher order of task

Another class of factors, *maintenance* or *hygiene* factors, is also distinguished by Herzberg. These factors can prevent trouble, as it were, but they do not eliminate its causes. Some hygiene factors are:

- company policies and administration
- the technical or interpersonal quality of supervision
- working conditions
- salaries, wages and benefits, which can sometimes but not usually be classified as motivators because they are indicators of success

Roughly, the presence of motivators in work can raise the ceiling for effort; the presence of hygiene factors provides a floor that will prevent motivation from falling to dangerously low levels. Looked at from another perspective, attractive hygiene factors can encourage an employee to do enough to stay in the system. The presence of motivators, in sharp contrast, can motivate an individual to approach his best effort at work.

"Green-lighting:" A Vehicle for the Concept

The concept for change is implemented in ways that reflect the experience reviewed in Section C above—a group is used as the agent of change. Robert N. Ford at A.T.&T. used "natural families" of super-

---

18. For example, factor-analytic studies show that much covariation in data batches can be accounted for by Motivator and Hygiene clusters of variables. But the same research indicates that the two-factor model requires modification. Robert B. Ewen, Charles L. Hulin, Patricia Cain Smith, and Edwin A. Locke, "An Empirical Test of the Herzberg Two-Factor Theory," *Journal of Applied Psychology*, Vol. 50 (November 6, 1966), pp. 544–50; and Charles L. Hulin and Patricia A. Smith, "An Empirical Investigation of Two Implications of the Two-Factor Theory of Job Satisfaction," *Journal of Applied Psychology*, Vol. 51, No. 5 (1967), pp. 396–402.
19. See Robert N. Ford, *Motivation through the Work Itself* (New York: American Management Association, 1969), pp. 23–26.

visors in a creative way. A concept for structuring jobs is explained to the supervisors, who then develop the specific plan for implementing the concept in "green-lighting" (or brainstorming) sessions that are facilitated but not directed by an outside resource person. Ford does not give great detail about these sessions.[20] But they clearly have two goals: to make use of the operating information possessed by the supervisors and to encourage their ownership of the job enrichment program, as it applies to their specific organization units.

Comparisons of Ford's use of groups to the T-Group concept need not be forced. In common, trainers in both groups attempt to get their members to accept a guiding concept, or set of values. In common, also, resources within the group are given very wide latitude in acting consistently with that concept or those values. In both kinds of groups, finally, members may reject the guiding concept or values. When that happens neither group "takes off," in the terminology common to Ford and to T-Group aficionados.

An Experiment with a Specific Job

Ford spearheaded several efforts to build motivation into work in low-level tasks or jobs, and these tended to be successful. About the concept of providing satisfaction of human needs at work, Ford explained: "The theory is quite clear on one point. You can't motivate people from outside [themselves] for long. But you can give them a chance to succeed and to improve at tasks that challenge them. Then they will develop their own drives toward tasks."[21] Toward this end, it is necessary to:

- load the task with true work motivators
- remove the dissatisfiers, the inadequate hygiene factors
- remember that good hygiene factors will not compensate for a boring job

A.T.&T. experimented with a substantial number of jobs. Overall, these had been work-simplified to the point that they were need-depriving. Work simplification might have reduced the training burden, in sum, but it often created problems of morale and motivation. A.T.&T. was particularly concerned with one reflection of these problems— turnover that often reached epidemic proportions.[22] This turnover increasingly came to be seen as a consequence of the need-depriving ways in which work was structured.

---

20. *Ibid.*, pp. 153–58.
21. *Ibid.*, p. 25.
22. *Ibid.*, pp. 13–15.

Figure 3. Initial Motivator-Poor Organization of Work of Correspondents

Work Group
Responding ⟶ Verification ⟶ Supervisor ⟶ Mail Room
to Complaint   Unit
Letters

Source: Based on Robert N. Ford, *Motivation through the Work Itself* (New York: American Management Association, 1969), pp. 23–26.

Consider the flow of work illustrated in Figure 3.[23] Members of the work group were college trained and responded to a wide variety of letters, some of which raised complicated issues. Their workflow was motivator-poor, in numerous senses:

- Verifiers checked every proposed response, which set narrow limits on the responsibility of the members of the work group.

- Employees responding to complaint letters felt little sense of achievement, because both verifiers and the supervisor often changed a response without informing the employee.

- The employee had no regular way of learning how well he had done, although he might get some "negative recognition" in responses changed by verifiers or supervisor.

- At least for many months, responses by new employees were signed by verifiers or the supervisor, which diluted the responsibility an employee could feel for performance.

- Few opportunities to grow in task knowledge or for promotion based on performance were available.

Various levels of supervision became involved in making this job of responding to complaint letters richer in motivators. Their guide was to increase the "vertical loading" of work, enlarging or rearranging a job so as to make it more challenging. "Horizontal loading," in contrast, adds task elements to a job without making it more challenging, as by enlarging the brain surgeon's job by assigning him the clean-up duties as well. Vertical loading of a job attempts to follow guidelines such as those in Table 2.

The reorganized workflow of the job of responding to complaint letters variously reflects these guidelines. Basically, respondents were

---

23. This account is synthesized from *ibid.*, pp. 26–41. Also see William W. Dettelback and Philip Kraft, "Organization Change through Job Enrichment," *Training and Development Journal,* Vol. 25 (August, 1971), pp. 2–7.

   Similar and earlier efforts toward greater need-satisfaction through job design had developed independent of Herzberg's major distinction between Motivators and Hygiene factors. See especially Louis E. Davis, "Job Design and Productivity," *Personnel,* Vol. 33 (March, 1957), esp. pp. 419–27, and "The Design of Jobs," *Industrial Relations,* Vol. 6, No. 1 (1966), pp. 21–45.

Table 2. Enriching the Work of Correspondents by Adding Motivators

Method of Loading	*Motivators Involved*
1. Removing some controls without removing responsibility	1. Responsibility; personal achievement
2. Increasing the accountability of individuals for their own work	2. Responsibility; recognition
3. Giving a person a whole natural unit of work	3. Responsibility; achievement; recognition
4. Giving a person greater job freedom, or additional authority	4. Responsibility; achievement; recognition
5. Making periodic reports available directly to the employee rather than to the supervisor	5. Internal recognition
6. Introducing new and more difficult tasks into the job	6. Growth and learning
7. Assigning specialized tasks to employees to help them become expert	7. Responsibility; growth; advancement

Source: Based on Robert N. Ford, *Motivation through the Work Itself* (New York: American Management Association, 1969), p. 24.

given greater opportunities to gain recognition for their efforts, as well as to be responsible for them. Figure 4 suggests how these goals were approached. The simple changes in the job were designed to variously add motivators so as to permit greater satisfaction of individual needs and, hence, to induce lower turnover and higher quality. Existing levels of output were to be maintained.

The efficacy of restructuring work in Figure 4 involves broad philosophic

Figure 4. Restructured Motivator-Rich Organization of Work of Correspondents

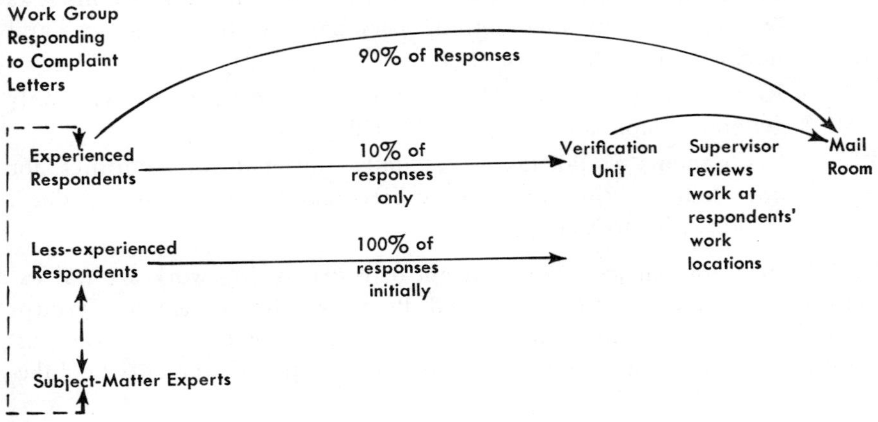

Source: Based on Robert N. Ford, *Motivation through the Work Itself* (New York: American Management Association, 1969), pp. 24–26.

issues as well as detailed steps. The opposed philosophic persuasion argues that work is not, cannot, and (apparently) should not be a central concern for the overwhelming bulk of people, and often proposes that attention consequently ought to be given to such factors as job security rather than to job design.[24] The approach in Figure 4 maintains that work can be made less need-depriving and, consequently, more central in the scheme of things for more people. At a normative level, it also implies that work should be made less need-depriving, if at all possible, if only because of humanistic concerns and because what work a person does is critical in his self-concept. To blot out 32 or 40 hours a week of life as noncentral is too high a price to pay, in this view, and paid it will have to be for the foreseeable future.

Ford's approach to reducing those costs is to enrich the flow of work. In the specific case of the respondents to complaint letters, such methods were:

- Individual respondents were given full responsibility for responses.
- Subject-matter specialists were chosen within the work group to provide immediate advice.
- The rate of verification was related to experience of respondent.
- The freedom of respondents was increased, as by reducing the degree of overhead supervision.
- The supervisor became less another review level and more a facilitator, as responses were routed directly from verifiers to the mail room, with the supervisor now conducting sample reviews at individual work locations and counseling individual respondents.
- Respondents were variously encouraged to own their responses, as by signing their own letters, personalizing the responses, and having responsibility for them.
- Responsibility for pace of work was left to respondents, with only general admonitions about a "full day's work."
- Respondents could take personally initiated opportunities for growth by seeking advice of subject-matter experts and, indeed, could aspire to that position.

The two approaches to the concept of restructuring work are not exclusive, but they tend to be polarized. Perhaps different reference groups play a role. For example, "management" tends to be excited by the possibilities of building motivators into work; "unions" tend to be luke-

---

24. The most recent argument of this genre is provided by Mitchell Fein, *Motivation for Work*, Monograph No. 4, American Institute of Industrial Engineers (New York, 1971).

warm, at best. Alternatively, job security tends to interest "unions" far more than "management."

The cumulative impact of such factors in the case of correspondents was to induce major changes in the climate of interpersonal and intergroup relations, to judge from the verbal reports. Cooperation increased; relationships seemed to be less "phony" and more leavened by the realities of performance; and an atmosphere of freedom-*cum*-accountability prevailed, with greater self-control and self-initiative by employees and less pressure from supervisors. Overall, the spirit was one of greater responsibility for a task, greater freedom in performing it, and greater initiative in seeking help when wanted.[25]

Some Quantitative Results

The factors above suggest that the new vertically loaded job was more need-satisfying for individuals. Specifically, only one respondent resigned because of her dislike of the new responsibilities. Moreover, the verifiers —who lost some of their previous power—apparently did not prove troublesome in the transition.

But what of organization demands? A.T.&T. was primarily interested in reduced turnover and increased quality of service to the customer. Data from the case sketched above, as well as from others, suggest that simultaneous satisfaction of individual needs and organization demands did occur. The richness of data can only be sampled here. Although no specific figures are given, Ford notes that turnover for the Experimental Group "was greatly reduced during the period of the study," while turnover in a Control Group remained at previous levels.

Quality of service in the Experimental Group also increased sharply, as Figure 5 shows. Three points amplify this conclusion. *First,* the index of the Experimental Group is initially lower than that of a Control Group, both in February and in April, when the study began. But the index for the Experimental Group reaches a substantially higher level six months later, after an initial dip. This initial dip in the index of the Experimental Group is attributed to the learning required by the vertical loading of jobs.

Second, a sharp decay is evident in the Customer Service Index, for both Experimental and Control Groups, in the months preceding the study. Hence management's major concern.

Third, an upward trend also occurs in the index for the Control Group during the period of the study. Managers of the Controls variously attempted to raise quality. They succeeded, at least in the short run, for Figure 5 reflects an ongoing improvement in quality independ-

---

25. Ford, *op. cit.,* pp. 31–41.

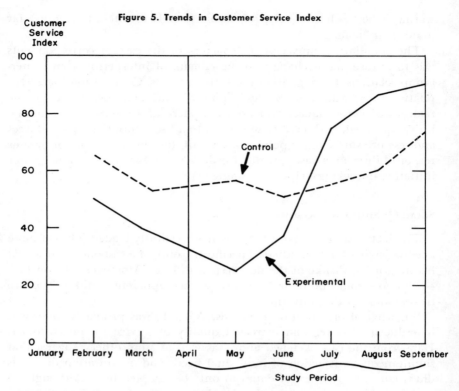

Figure 5. Trends in Customer Service Index

Source: Robert N. Ford, *Motivation through the Work Itself* (New York: American Management Association, 1969), p. 33.

ent of the job-loading program. That is, there are two ways to skin this particular cat, at least in the short run, even though one way seems to be more rewarding. Moreover, it is not known whether the techniques used in the Control Group to raise quality had any adverse long-run consequences.

386

E. INTERVENTIONS AIMED AT
COMPLEX ORGANIZATIONS:
CHANGING PATTERNS OF
INTERPERSONAL
AND INTERGROUP RELATIONS

As in most innovative efforts, early applications of the laboratory approach in complex organizations were preoccupied with reinventing the wheel. This is no criticism of anyone or anything, not even of the logic of incremental advance that is reasonable and perhaps even unavoidable in the early development of any technology. It is simply stating the fact that the early developmental history of OD efforts based on the laboratory approach has come out very much like the experience of similar behavioral science applications. Hence the characterization of that development as a reinventing of the wheel, certainly for a different vehicle used for different purposes, but a recognizable wheel nonetheless.

This section of the volume and the one following seek to characterize the developmental history of OD applications based on the laboratory approach. Section E provides a kind of fore-and-aft perspective. Subsection 1 briefly sketches some highlights of the developmental history of OD applications. The emphasis is on the premises from which early applications tended to start, as well as on those premises that underlie recent OD efforts based on the laboratory approach. Subsection 2 details two major OD efforts that consciously seek to build on that history. The goal of both efforts is comprehensive change in an organization's climate or style, which will induce or reinforce behavioral and attitudinal changes by individuals that are consistent with the laboratory approach.

Section F to follow will focus on the design and consequences of a number of more restricted OD efforts which also were mindful of the developmental history of applications of the laboratory approach in complex organizations.

1. ORGANIZATION CHANGE VIA LABORATORY APPROACH: SOME OVERALL TENDENCIES

In the broadest possible summary, the history of organization change via the laboratory approach can be characterized by two themes. First, the early emphasis was on changes in the attitudes, values, and behaviors of individuals who—after their numbers reached some critical mass— could later begin inducing changes in their organization. The general model was:

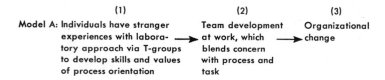

Second, the contemporary emphasis more directly seeks changes at the organization level, so as to build upon as well as to facilitate individual change. It not only gets to organization applications, in short, it begins with them. This contemporary emphasis may be generalized as:

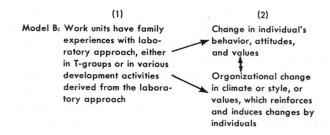

This section variously looks at this shift in emphasis about what is cart and what is horse. The choice of one basic intervention strategy or the other is a critical one, not that one is necessarily better but in the sense that each basic strategy implies its own internal logic.

388

a. A Horseback History of Behavioral Science Applications in Organizations: A Case of Delayed Learning from Experience

As it turns out, organization applications of the laboratory approach could well have gone to school on the experience of other behavioral science applications. Consider the striking case of a two-week training program to increase certain specific attributes and skills for foremen at International Harvester Company. The case goes back to the mid-1940s. Initially, changes in attitudes of individual foremen occurred in the expected direction, but soon the power of back-home organization relations showed its awesome impact. No sooner had the foremen returned to work than changes due to training not only began to decay, but they actually reversed. So great was the reversal, in fact, that after a short period back at work the trained foremen actually scored lower on the target variables than a control group of foremen who had experienced no training. The only trained foremen who retained their increases, significantly, worked for superiors who themselves scored high on the target attitudes. As Gene W. Dalton concludes:

> The other foremen [whose superiors did not place a high value on consideration] returned to a pattern very close to that of their chief. Daily interaction completely negated the effect of the training program. The foremen's ties had been interrupted only during the two week training period. Then they returned to a situation where the most significant relationship was with their own supervisors. No continuing new relationships had been established which would act to confirm and reinforce any attitude changes begun in the training program.[1]

More or less, experience with other behavioral science applications in other organizations ran to a similar pattern.[2]

Such earlier experience with other behavioral science applications did not guide initial organizational applications based on the laboratory approach, however. For a variety of reasons, Model A became the usual guiding concept, although several factors inhibited follow-through into organizational change. In part, unrealistic expectations or even naïveté about the ease of transfer into organizations of the commonly potent

---

1. Gene W. Dalton, "Influence and Organizational Change," in Anant R. Negandhi and Joseph P. Schwitter (eds.), *Organizational Behavior Models* (Kent, Ohio: Comparative Administration Research Institute, 1970), p. 90.
2. Arnold Tannenbaum and Stanley Seashore, "Some Changing Conceptions and Approaches to the Study of Persons in Organizations," mimeographed. (Ann Arbor, Mich.: University of Michigan, Institute for Social Research, n.d.).

learning gained in stranger T-groups explains this inhibited follow-through. Moreover, the general popularity of stranger T-group experiences, plus a shortage of skilled trainers, no doubt contributed to a lack of concentrated attention on the problems of the transfer into organizations of any learning gained in stranger experiences.

It was not long before organizational applications of the laboratory approach began to point up some central problems with its leading concept, whatever the reasons supporting it. Six themes reflect these inadequacies. *First,* Model A above rests heavily on the sanguine effects of personal insight on organization systems. Experience clearly demonstrated that personal insight and organization change are not necessarily linked, however. Specifically, personal insight does imply some control over intellectual and emotional aspects of some issue. But one can have insight by the yard, with little or no control over the strategic variables necessary for organization change. As Warren Bennis notes:

> . . . It is not obvious that insight leads to sophistication in rearranging social systems or in making strategic organizational interventions. It seems therefore that the insight strategy . . . is a questionable strategy. If anything, applied social science depends on the policy makers controlling the relevant variables. Insight provides these as far as personal manipulation goes, but it is doubtful that it can lead directly to external manipulations of social systems.[3]

Alexander Winn adds important counterpoint to Bennis's position in the question: ". . . how can one transfer the climate of trust, of emotional support and acceptance for what one is, from [a T-Group] into a wider [organization] [that] more frequently than not, shares different values, different beliefs, norms, and expectations?"[4] Insight would not suffice, clearly enough.

Second, the relevance to the worksite of material discussed in stranger T-Group experiences was not always clear and direct. For example, a here-and-now conflict in a stranger T-Group might provide insight and perspective for individual A about a role conflict he had back at the shop. Linkage with the worksite is the critical act, however. Stranger experiences cannot immediately make that linkage, and they had a spotty track record in inducing such linkages after the training. The point has even deeply penetrated the popular literature. For example, Sheldon Davis pungently reacts to the lack of follow-up at work on stranger laboratory experiences:

3. Warren G. Bennis, "A New Role for the Behavioral Sciences: Effecting Organizational Change," *Administrative Science Quarterly*, Vol. 8 (September, 1963), p. 138.
4. Alexander Winn, "Social Change in Industry: From Insight to Implementation," *Journal of Applied Behavioral Science*, Vol. 2 (April, 1966), p. 78.

Say a man has a good experience. He comes back to the job full of new values—and sits down in the same crummy atmosphere he left a week before. He may be changed, but his environment isn't. How can he practice confrontation with a boss and a secretary and colleagues who don't even know what it's all about? In a few weeks he's either completely dazed or has reverted, in self-defense, to the old ways.[5]

The same effect seems common even for cousin T-Groups.

Third, indeed, experience suggested that a stranger experience might even complicate the subsequent reraising of such an issue at the worksite, which is the only place it can be resolved. This point applies in several senses. The stranger experience might only dissipate feelings or reactions that could have motivated action at the worksite. Hence these potential motivators might be ventilated in a context where the underlying problem may be explorable, but where it is definitely not resolvable. Relatedly, stranger experiences might only deepen despair about constructive action at work, as individual A experiences how much his here-and-now reactions are determined by the there-and-then issue, which might become bigger than life in the absence of a direct opportunity to work on it.

Fourth, a stranger experience lacks a critical reality of all back-home organizations, the authority structure. At the very least, this deprives participants of a learning experience that is highly relevant in all organizations[6] and, indeed, in all of life. Moreover, many changes that individuals might make as a result of a T-Group experience sooner or later have to be tested with organizational authorities, who can have considerable influence on the individual's career and advancement. At their worst, finally, some normal T-Group processes might generate unintended consequences in the absence of the elemental reality of the authority structure to which the member of an organization will return. Consider "unfreezing" in the typical T-Group, which is facilitated (as Bernard Bass describes it) "by removing the familiar props and customary social mechanisms, by violating the expectations of trainees, and by

---

5. Davis is quoted in John Poppy, "New Era in Industry: It's OK to Cry in the Office," *Look,* July 9, 1968, p. 65.

K. Bamforth, "T-Group Methods within A Company," in G. Whitaker (ed.), *ATM Occasional Papers,* Vol. 2 (Oxford, England: Basil Blackwell, 1965), reports a similar effect in T-Groups composed of "diagonal slices" of an organization. That is, their members represented different hierarchical levels but included no immediate superiors or subordinates. The effect encouraged Bamforth to discontinue direct use of T-Groups.

6. Sharon Lieder and Newton Margulies, "A Sensitivity Training Design for Organizational Development," *Social Change,* Vol. 1, No. 1 (1971), p. 6; and Robert T. Golembiewski and Arthur Blumberg, "Training and Relational Learning," *Training and Development Journal,* Vol. 21 (November, 1967), pp. 35–43.

creating an ambiguous, unstructured situation for them of unclear goals and minimum cues."[7] Bass is concerned that this aspect of the T-Group technology might generate serious consequences in some cases, while it facilitates learning in others. For example, this aspect of the technology might foster feelings among some trainees which reflect Bakunin's broadside that: "All exercise of authority perverts and all submissiveness to authority humiliates." Bass worries that:

> . . . it may be that some laboratory participants lose their confidence to use authority which may be needed in the future for organizational reasons. This may be neither the intent of the program nor a logical outcome, but it may occur just the same. At the same time, there may be a correspondingly reduced acceptance of submissive behavior that may be necessary at times for the interests of good organization. In short, the "destruction" of the customary authority structure in the T-Group in order to promote exploration and change in the individual participants, coupled with an emphasis on the values of democracy and consensus, may produce, in some participants at least, sufficient antiauthoritarian leadership attitudes to reduce their contributions to the organization at times when such directive leadership is required.[8]

Fifth, greater appreciation was developed of the complexity of the linkages between a stranger T-Group experience and increased effectiveness of individuals as they later readopted specific organization roles. In part, this complexity derives from the fact that various tasks tend to imply their own specific demands.[9] There could be no guarantee that enhanced individual mental health and maturity will meet all such demands, accumulating experience showed.[10] Consequently, as Bass concludes, training people "to be better diagnosticians with greater tolerance and social awareness" is perhaps necessary but not sufficient for organization development.[11]

Sixth, stranger experiences by definition do not provide the continu-

---

7. Bernard M. Bass, "The Anarchist Movement and the T-Group," *Journal of Applied Behavioral Science,* Vol. 3 (April, 1967), p. 215.
8. *Ibid.,* pp. 215–16.
9. At a trivial level, see Robert T. Golembiewski, *The Small Group* (Chicago: University of Chicago Press, 1962), esp. pp. 201–4, for a discussion of task effects.
10. To choose an extreme example, see William J. Goode and Irving Fowler, "Incentive Factors in a Low Morale Plant," *American Sociological Review,* Vol. 14 (October, 1949), pp. 618–24. In the organization described there, it is reasonable to conclude, poor mental health was more appropriate for organizational success.
11. For one case where T-Group training was not sufficient for organizational success, see Samuel D. Deep, Bernard M. Bass, and James A. Vaughn, "Some Effects on Business Gaming of Previous Quasi-T-Group Affiliations," *Journal of Applied Psychology,* Vol. 51 (No. 5, 1967), pp. 426–31.

ous reinforcement that is at least useful and perhaps necessary to transfer individual learning into organization contexts. Indeed, some frustration may set in as individuals fail to gain reinforcement at work. Consequently, they might have to "negatively relearn" in order to get back in phase with organization norms. This is psychically herniating.

Some Effects on OD Designs

Such factors encouraged important shifts in opinion about OD designs. At the very least, the factors emphasized the need to develop ways to translate stranger experiences into organization contexts, if Model A were followed. Such factors also motivated OD applications based on Model B.

The specific effects on OD designs induced by these shifts are complex. Four effects will illustrate the broader range. *First,* in the most simple sense, more realistic expectations developed about the impact of T-Groups on managerial behavior. Thus Ernest G. Miller concluded that organization climate is critical to general changes in member behavior. "Few if any evaluative studies of T-Group training," he explains, "can be expected to show notable and continuing impact upon managerial behavior *unless* that training is linked to a continuing program of team building or organizational development."[12] Paul Buchanan provides valuable detailed perspective on the growing conclusion that an effective work team does not automatically develop just because most or all of its members participated in a stranger or cousin T-Group.[13] Specifically, Buchanan stresses the gap between the kinds of learning characteristic of such experiences and organization performance. Typical learnings of stranger or cousin T-Groups include:[14]

- reduced extreme behavior: persons who originally reflected many dominant behaviors reduce their incidence, while individuals originally high on submissive behaviors become more assertive
- increased openness, awareness, and tolerance concerning differences in behaviors and values
- increased operational skills, such as more effective listening and greater empathic abilities
- an enhanced sense of the importance of emotional factors in relations at work

12. Ernest G. Miller, "The Impact of T-Groups on Managerial Behavior," *Public Administration Review,* Vol. 30 (May, 1970), p. 297.
13. Paul C. Buchanan, "Sensitivity, or Laboratory Training, in Industry," *Sociological Inquiry,* Vol. 41 (Spring, 1971), p. 219.
14. Paul C. Buchanan, "Laboratory Training and Organization Development," *Administrative Science Quarterly,* Vol. 14 (September, 1969), pp. 466–80.

Buchanan notes that such learning is consistent with the goals of the laboratory approach but still falls short of engaging major organizational changes. He concludes that: "it is easy to see that such changes, even if of great magnitude and even if attained by a sizeable proportion of the members of an organization . . . , would not, without further planned improvement effort, be likely to result in major changes in the functioning of the organization."[15]

Multiple morals are implied in this new realism. To illustrate, one can begin an OD program following Model A, if that seems appropriate in a specific case. But one must always be aware of the fact that any persisting changes from a stranger experience will require reinforcement at work. Moreover, some of these changes may directly conflict with back-home organizational norms or structure. This can create some nasty conflict situations. Indeed, if no possibility exists for changes in the host organization, T-Group training in cousin and even in stranger groups is at least questionable.

Second, early results of OD efforts encouraged a shift in attention from individual skills to changes in organizational values or attitudes. This may seem a minor shift, but it is actually critical. That is, if the focus is on changes in individual skills, the intense stranger experience is the preferred vehicle, and the more intense, the better. If the focus is on changes in organizational values and attitudes, the learning thrust is toward:[16]

- a new "view of the possible" for guiding interpersonal and intergroup relations at work, with the values of the laboratory approach generating an ideal which can be compared by organization members as to its need-gratification potential with the actual relations in their organization
- an enhanced sense of collaboration among organization members that derives from sharing the values and norms of the laboratory approach, of membership in a common social order
- improving trust, respect, and communication among members of the organization
- a reduced sense of individual needs as inevitably opposed to "the organization"

The more appropriate vehicle for such learning is a family experience, whether in a T-Group or in some learning design consistent with the laboratory approach. Some sparse empirical research consistently supports the greater effectiveness and appropriateness of such family experi-

---

15. Buchanan, "Sensitivity, or Laboratory Training, in Industry," p. 219.
16. Adapted from *ibid.,* p. 221.

ences when the goal is organizational change.[17] Moreover, even when family groups are employed, effectiveness seems to vary with the extensiveness of pretraining and posttraining activities.[18] This implies the reasonable need by participants to feel a part of a long-run program as a condition of their fuller commitment to working toward a change in organizational values and climate.

In the theoretical rationale underlying the focus on values, as opposed to skills, change in values is clearly an effort in education, or reeducation, which helps distinguish the laboratory approach from therapy, as it is conventionally understood. Moreover, values are seen as strategic in inducing appropriate skills, but the reverse probably is not the case. "The development of valid values will tend to lead automatically to the development of proper skills," Chris Argyris observes about the point. "Skills follow values; values rarely follow skills."[19] Finally, the emphasis on values provides a systematic and common frame of reference for individuals and groups which can have self-reinforcing consequences. The goal, as James Clark notes, is the creation of social orders at work, of "effective sociotechnical systems which support the kind of human encounters in which there is greater likelihood that people's authentic beings will be expressed in relation to one another and their work."[20] Once established, the dynamics of enhanced authenticity have self-heightening effects. Robert Tannenbaum and Sheldon Davis explain that:

> In order to achieve a movement toward authenticity, focus must be placed on developing the whole person and in doing this in an organic way. . . . In time, [these] become values in and of themselves. And as people become less demotivated and move toward authenticity, they clearly demonstrate that they have the ability to be creative about organizational matters, and this too becomes a value shared within the organization. As these values are introduced, and people move towards them in an organization, this movement in and of itself contains many forces that make for change and opens up new possibilities.[21]

17. Robert B. Morton and A. Wight, "A Critical Incidents Evaluation of an Organizational Training Laboratory," mimeographed (Sacramento, Cal.: Aerojet General Corporation, Personnel Department, 1964) ; and Reed M. Powell and John F. Stinson, "The Worth of Laboratory Training," *Business Horizons*, Vol. 14 (August, 1971) , pp. 87–95.
18. Frank Friedlander, "A Comparative Study of Consulting Processes and Group Development," *Journal of Applied Behavioral Science*, Vol. 4 (October, 1968) , pp. 377–99.
19. Chris Argyris, *Interpersonal Competence and Organizational Effectiveness* (Homewood, Ill.: Dorsey Press, 1962) , p. 135.
20. James J. Clark, "Task Group Therapy," mimeographed, p. 11.
21. Robert Tannenbaum and Sheldon A. Davis, "Values, Men, and Organizations," *Industrial Management Review*, Vol. 10 (Winter, 1969) , pp. 67–83.

Third, a direct and radical effect of early OD experiences encouraged OD designs based on Model B. Witness the position of Jack and Lorraine Gibb. "The group experience is more powerful and permanent if it is imbedded in significant organizational life," they conclude. "Training in a natural team is far more powerful than training in the heterogeneous groups that are common in group therapy and sensitivity training."[22]

Fourth, the designs of OD programs have begun diversely to cope with the inadequacies summarized above. The designs vary along two dimensions: use of T-Groups, or reliance on analogous processes only; and initial emphasis in OD programs on interaction patterns or on structure. Some of these designs utilize T-Groups directly; others dispense with the T-Group and concentrate on interpersonal and intergroup processes via a variety of other designs that derive from the T-Group, which is the matrix learning vehicle of the laboratory approach. Relatedly, some of the designs initially seek to change patterns of interaction, while others first seek structural change and then try to induce or reinforce behaviors, attitudes, or values consistent with that structure. Several examples suggest the range of such designs:[23]

- Designs of stranger experiences following Model A induce organizationally relevant processes and issues, as by simulations, task groups, or intergroup competitions.
- Designs of stranger experiences following Model A involve T-Groups in quasi-organizational activities, as in planning aspects of their own experience or in developing a special-purpose organization[24] where process and content issues must be dealt with simultaneously.
- Designs of stranger or cousin experiences following Model A facilitate later organizational transfer of learning, as by an initial focus on managerial styles in Blake's Phase I, which provides a relatively direct base for subsequent work in family groups.[25]
- Designs of learning experiences blend Models A and B by combining aspects of stranger and family experiences: e.g., time is divided during a training period between work in T-Groups composed of individuals from different organizations which deal with

22. Jack R. Gibb and Lorraine M. Gibb, "Role Freedom in a TORI Group," in Arthur Burton (ed.), *Encounter* (San Francisco: Jossey-Bass, Inc., Publishers, 1969), p. 47.
23. Bass, "The Anarchist Movement and the T-Group," pp. 222–25, provides the model for the catalog that follows.
24. Richard E. Byrd, "Training in a Non-Group," *Journal of Humanistic Psychology,* Vol. 7 (1967), pp. 18–27.
25. Robert R. Blake and Jane S. Mouton, *The Managerial Grid* (Houston, Tex.: Gulf Publishing Co., 1964).

here-and-now interpersonal and intergroup processes, and in homogeneous family units which deal with common back-home issues.[26]

- Designs of family experiences following Model B concentrate on team-development activities re work issues, rather than on T-Groups, the consultant's role being to gradually introduce concerns relating to interpersonal and intergroup processes.[27]
- Designs of either family or stranger experiences use simulations of a business game, each play of which is followed by a detailed review led by professional trainers who deal with content issues as well as with process analysis,[28] but not in a T-Group context.
- Designs for family groups attempt to induce processes associated with the laboratory approach, as by increasing feedback in a family group, but without resort to a T-Group.[29]
- Designs for family groups emphasize structural change consistent with the laboratory approach; and behavior, attitudes, and values consistent with that structure can then be induced and/or reinforced by various OD designs, some using T-Groups while others emphasize analogous processes only.[30]

b. Rationale for the Learning Lag in OD Applications: Some Issues of Theory and Practice

It was not perversity that led advocates of the laboratory approach to rediscover painfully what had been learned in other applications of the behavioral sciences in organizations, of course. Major conceptual and practical concerns influenced, perhaps even dictated, the direction that the laboratory approach would initially take in complex organizations.

The conceptual considerations that directed early OD applications based on the laboratory approach can be illustrated in two ways, one that is unquestionable and a second that is somewhat speculative. Consider voluntarism, which ranks high in the pantheon of values of the laboratory approach. Stranger experiences maximize voluntarism, which was

---

26. Robert B. Morton and Bernard M. Bass, "The Organizational Training Laboratory," *Training Directors Journal,* Vol. 18 (October, 1964), pp. 2–18.
27. Bamforth, *op. cit.*
28. Alan B. Wagner, "The Use of Process Analysis in Business Decision Games," *Journal of Applied Behavioral Science,* Vol. 1 (October, 1965), pp. 387–408.
29. Robert T. Golembiewski and Arthur Blumberg, "Confrontation as a Training Design in Complex Organizations," *Journal of Applied Behavioral Science,* Vol. 3 (December, 1967), pp. 525–47; and Matthew B. Miles, Paula Holzman Calder, Harvey A. Hornstein, Daniel M. Callahan, and R. Steven Schivaro, "Data Feedback and Organizational Change in a School System" (Paper presented at Annual Meeting, American Sociological Association, August 29, 1966).
30. See Section D, Subsection 5.

seen as crucial in inducing several desired learning outcomes. Thus it was seen as reducing resistance to change and defensiveness, while it facilitated unfreezing as well as the learner's psychological owning of the consequences of the learning experience. These are important considerations in any learning situation, and they cannot be casually jeopardized. In contrast, family experiences patently had to contend with the question of how much (if any) voluntarism could be sacrificed without perverting the essence of the laboratory approach. As proponents of the laboratory approach were feeling their early way, consequently, stranger experiences it tended to be.

The conceptual bind over voluntarism had its practical sides also. Opponents of the laboratory approach, whatever their motives, patently had a powerful weapon in a strict interpretation of voluntarism. Winn clearly reflects the point in this summary of his own early experience in Alcan:Canada:

> There is no problem with regard to securing as many as 200 or more participants from its managerial and professional ranks for the many [stranger] two-week laboratories organized every year. The participants come voluntarily, and most of the personnel look forward with a great deal of anticipation to this experience. The situation changes drastically, however, when it comes to filling the places for a family or intergroup laboratory. Voluntarism decreases markedly, and resistances reappear in strength. It is all right to play "the behavior-change game" away from subordinates or peers or work companions, but it is not quite the same to play this "forbidden game" at one's work. It is too threatening.[31]

As is common, then, convenience reinforced an apparent principle. The early bind should be apparent. For example, Winn advises that major efforts to allay anxieties, to publicize the value of family experiences, and so on, were necessary to encourage worksite applications. Patently, however, such efforts in large part rest on prior resolution of the issues they are intended to solve. Hence it is understandable that emphasis on family experiences did not emerge early, full-blown.

It is also understandable that the T-Group and the formal organization would initially be seen as so different as to be antithetical. Certainly, such an initial concept was encouraged by a distinguished theoretical tradition in the social sciences. This tradition stemmed from the seminal distinction of *Gemeinschaft* from *Gesellschaft*,[32] and was contradicted only in small if variable part by major contemporary theoreticians or

---

31. Winn, *op. cit.*, p. 181.
32. Ferdinand Tonnies, *Fundamental Concepts of Sociology* (New York: American Book Co., 1940), pp. 18–28.

philosophers.[33] Indeed, at least some contemporary commentators see the acceptance of the basic antithesis between primary groups (such as T-Groups) and secondary groups (like bureaucracies) as being a still-basic article of social theory.[34]

Hence organizational applications of laboratory learning may have been initially viewed as something akin to developing the container for a universal solvent. The reasonable result was a concentration on stranger T-Group experiences that, whatever else, were patently impactful. Given the seductive quality of the leading ideas of any time, however, it would be remarkable if proponents of the laboratory approach could have unambiguously and definitively dissociated themselves from the leading ideas of their own time and disciplinary traditions, even if they wanted to do so.[35] To be sure, this argument is speculative.

That early OD applications based on the laboratory approach emphasized Model A and thus had to relearn the experience of other organizational applications of the behavioral sciences also can be traced to a practical issue nested in conceptual problems. In a real sense, the early OD years can be seen as a necessary gestation period for the development of change agents or interventionists skilled in the laboratory approach and in organizational analysis. This gestation involved at least several related elements: the development of an interventionist's role, which implied a sense of the organizational issues to be faced as well as of the style in which they were to be responded to; and the availability of an increasingly refined technology appropriate to those issues and that style. Figure 1 adds some of the required detail to the unfolding role of the interventionist. The figure reflects some of the emerging sense of the basic issues he faces, and it also suggests the style with which those issues will be dealt. Figure 1 should be self-explanatory. It has taken a number of the preceding sections and will take most of the succeeding ones to sketch some sense of the range of designs available to the interventionist.

---

33. Talcott Parsons, "The Social Structure of the Family," in Ruth N. Anshen (ed.), *The Family: Its Function and Destiny* (New York: Harper & Row, Publishers, 1959), pp. 260–63.

34. Eugene Litwak and Henry J. Meyer, "A Balance Theory of Coordination between Bureaucratic Organizations and Community Primary Groups," *Administrative Science Quarterly*, Vol. 11 (June, 1966), pp. 31–32.

35. For example, Chris Argyris's critique of traditional organization theory in *Personality and Organization* (New York: Harper and Row, Publishers, 1957), was widely interpreted as reinforcing the basic incompatibility between primary and secondary groups, even as he was careful to stress that alternative structures in secondary groups differed profoundly in their potential for satisfying human needs. Even if Argyris were clear as to the differences between his own and the traditional position, then, other scholars persisted in interpreting his work in traditional terms. Hence the incredible staying power of any leading ideas that are normally quite simple but profoundly pervasive.

Some summary conclusions are possible here, then, even though much of the burden of proof remains. Figure 1 should suggest some of the reasons why organizational translations of initial stranger experiences came slowly, given the difficulties of the role of the organization interventionist. Figure 1 also suggests a critical circularity. As the interventionist's role took on added definition, so also did it become more likely that OD applications based on the laboratory approach would be attempted. As the range and diversity of designs available to him consequently grew, moreover, so also did the probability increase that OD

Figure 1. A Schema of the Interventionist's World

Primary Tasks of Interventionist:

■ to help client system generate valid information

■ to help client use information for making more informed and responsible free choices

■ to help client generate information and make free choices in ways that enhance the internal commitment by client

■ to help client, in general, to:
  a. select goals with minimal defensiveness
  b. define approaches to achieve goals
  c. relate choices of goals and approaches to central needs
  d. build challenging but attainable level of aspiration into choices

Qualities Needed by Interventionist:

■ confidence in his own philosophy of intervention and its derivative strategies

■ ability to perceive reality accurately, especially under stress

■ ability to perceive and accept client's attacks and mistrust, and willingness to encourage client's expression of them

■ capacity to use stressful situations as learning opportunities for self and client

Conditions Faced by Interventionist:

■ a high degree of discrepancy and ambiguity:
  a. between his views and those of client about causes of problems
  b. between his views and those of client about design of effective systems
  c. between consultant's own ideals and his behavior

■ marginal membership in the client system, which is at once a source of a consultant's value and a problem for him

■ mistrust by clients, as reflected in their misperception of consultant's motives or misunderstanding of his communication

■ minimal feedback from client about his effectiveness

Possible Dysfunctional Adaptations by Interventionist:

■ increase in defensive behavior, and a decrease in the use of appropriate coping behaviors

■ high needs for inclusion in the client system; or, alternately, to engage with the client system on a limited technical or scientific basis only

■ unrealistic level of expectation, a compulsion for "impact" or "success"

■ high needs for confirmation or disconfirmation by client

Source: Based on Chris Argyris, *Intervention Theory and Method* (Reading, Mass.: Addison-Wesley, 1970), pp. 128–76.

applications based on the laboratory approach would be carried through to some form of organizational transfer, whether Model A or Model B guided the effort. As someone once noted, complexity has a great future, what with everything being contingent on everything else.

c. Present Status of Organization Applications of Laboratory Approach: The Base for an Applied Behavioral Science

Developments in OD applications were motivated by success as well as adversity, whether these developments facilitated follow through on the initial stranger experiences of Model A, or whether they generated designs based on Model B. The focus above was on various inadequacies that stimulated change and development. Six positive developmental forces will be outlined below by way of establishing the existing base of success experiences that supported future applications of the laboratory approach in organizations.

First, and especially in the past few years, major organizational showcases have highlighted the potential of the laboratory approach, in business and in government. Some of these showcase applications were basically *wunderkinder* whose virtues spread early by personal contact among cognoscenti and later even engaged the interest of the mass media.[36] Other examples had a more definite research thrust[37] and added significant counterpoint to more pragmatic claims about the possibility of a more humane and effective organizational life based on the laboratory approach. Moreover, some of these applications followed Model A

---

36. TRW Systems is perhaps the best example. See Sheldon A. David, "Organic Problem-Solving Method of Organizational Change," *Journal of Applied Behavioral Science,* Vol. 3 (January, 1967), pp. 3–21. See also a set of brief Harvard case studies describing the OD program at TRW and its roots in the laboratory approach, in Gene W. Dalton, Paul R. Lawrence, and Larry E. Greiner (eds.), *Organizational Change and Development* (Homewood, Ill.: Irwin-Dorsey, 1970), pp. 114–53.

Popular attention to TRW's efforts came through such vehicles as John Poppy's "New Era in Industry: It's OK to Cry in the Office," pp. 64–76.

37. Cyril Sofer, *The Organization from Within* (New York: Quadrangle Books, 1961); Robert R. Blake, Jane S. Mouton, Louis B. Barnes, and Larry E. Greiner, "Breakthrough in Organization Development," *Harvard Business Review,* Vol. 42 (November, 1964), pp. 133–35; Robert R. Blake, Jane S. Mouton, Richard L. Sloma, and Barbara Peek Loftin, "A Second Breakthrough In Organization Development," *California Management Review,* Vol. 11 (No. 2, 1968), pp. 73–78; Alfred J. Marrow, David G. Bowers, and Sheldon S. Zalkind, "The Impact of an Organizational Development Program on Perceptions of Interpersonal, Group, and Organization Functioning," *Journal of Applied Behavioral Science,* Vol. 5 (July, 1969), pp. 393–410; Alfred J. Marrow, David G. Bowers, and Stanley E. Seashore, *Management by Participation* (New York: Harper & Row, Publishers, 1967); and Richard A. Schmuck and Matthew B. Miles (eds.), *Organization Development in Schools* (Palo Alto, Cal.: National Press Books, 1971).

and developed designs to encourage the transfer of any initial learning into organization contexts,[38] while other applications were seminal efforts to innovate Model B approaches.[39]

Second, the applications tended to establish that T-Group effects were not of a "magic mountain" variety, attainable only on narrowly defined cultural islands. Basically, as the number of applications increased, so did the number and range of OD designs. The appreciation of which designs were more appropriate for which broad types of situations also increased correspondingly. Some of these innovative designs utilized family T-Groups in novel ways with positive results, for example. An experience at Non-Linear Systems is illustrative. An entire work unit was exposed to sensitivity training as an initial experience, with no apparent loss in potency and with important advantages. These advantages included:[40]

- Presence of superiors reduces participants' fantasies about tales being carried to the boss by the trainer or fellow participants.

- Reinforcement of any new behaviors resulting from the training is easier, and any learning can be more-or-less immediately applied to the job.

- Interpersonal relationships and communication among participants are improved on the job because of reductions in the mass and multiple ignorance about true feelings and reactions that are characteristic even among work colleagues of long standing.

- There is a conscious discipline operating in family groups. They focus on improved interpersonal relationships and communications that are relevant at work, rather than on the generalized personal development of individual participants. This eases the task of translating any learning in job-oriented terms and provides

---

38. Project ACORD in the U.S. Department of State used an initial "cousin" experience following Model A, for example, and helped develop such approaches to organizational transfer of learning as third-party consultation, which is described in Section D, Part I. See also Richard Beckhard, "An Organizational Improvement Program in a Decentralized Organization," *Journal of Applied Behavioral Science,* Vol. 2 (January, 1966), pp. 3–26; and Beckhard and Dale G. Lake, "Short- and Long-Range Effects of a Team Development Effort," pp. 421–39, in Harvey A. Hornstein, Barbara Benedict Bunker, W. Warner Burke, Marion Gindes, and Roy J. Lewicki (eds.), *Social Intervention: A Behavioral Science Approach* (New York: The Free Press, 1971).

39. Arthur H. Kuriloff and Stuart Atkins, "T-Group for a Work Team," *Journal of Applied Behavioral Science,* Vol. 2 (January, 1966), p. 63. They note that: "Superiors and subordinates together attended the [T-Group] sessions. This has not been usual. . . ."

See also Alton C. Bartlett, "Changing Behavior as a Means to Increased Efficiency," *Journal of Applied Behavioral Science,* Vol. 3 (July, 1967), pp. 381–403.

40. Kuriloff and Atkins, *op. cit.,* p. 64.

more-or-less common criteria for data introducible into the training session.

Other innovative designs are spin-offs from the matrix learning vehicle of the laboratory approach, or they induce analogs of T-Group processes which do not involve sensitivity training as such. Their common import is that the laboratory approach can generate a large number of designs for affecting behaviors, attitudes, and values, whether in T-Groups or in other learning contexts.

Third, such applications reinforced the critical role of transfer. Two general approaches were taken. Thus family experiences were used to initiate OD efforts, following Model B, so as to facilitate transfer by making the work unit the training unit. Other applications followed Model A, but transfer of learning from stranger experiences was easier for several reasons. Thus the need to reinforce any individual learning by corresponding changes in organizational climate and/or structure—as by team-development activities, or some such—was more appreciated. In addition, the reported success of several showcase applications provided greater motivation for organization activities that followed after the initial stranger training experience. Finally, the issue of voluntarism eased somewhat. In part, this resulted from a better job of meeting participant anxieties, as well as from positive reports about personal and organizational consequences of the newly available showcase applications. In part, also, voluntarism was less salient because of the availability of various non–T-Group designs for OD starters that implied fewer demands of participants, who could then test their readiness for participation in stranger or family T-Group experiences. A common rule of thumb was that no organization should force its employees into a T-Group experience. When family units underwent team-development experiences, however, participation was a condition of continued employment.

Fourth, a number of the showcase applications at least implied that changes induced by successful OD efforts based on the laboratory approach persisted over extended periods. This eliminated many cheap victories possible before the results of such longitudinal studies were available. The granddaddy of all longitudinal studies covers a period of some eight years, in fact. Major changes were reported in before/after comparisons covering the first few years of the OD effort.[41] Approximately six years later, although the results were "somewhat mixed and with a few contrary elements," a research team reported that the "organization, far from reverting to its prior condition, has during recent years made additional progress toward the organizational goals envisioned by the owners and managers in 1962, and envisioned as well by superiors

41. Marrow, Bowers, and Seashore, *op. cit.*

and production employees at a somewhat later time." The two principal investigators concluded, somewhat facetiously, that:

> We confess a brief regret that there was not an opposite outcome, for we are rather better equipped with ideas about organizational stability and regression than we are with ideas about organizational change and continuing development. For example, before the data became available, we were prepared to make some remarks about the "Hawthorne effect"—about the superficiality and transient quality of organizational and behavioral changes induced under conditions of external attention and pressure; but it boggles the mind to think of a "Hawthorne effect" persisting for over eight years among people half of whom were not on the scene at the time of the original change. Similarly, we were prepared to make wise remarks about cultural forces, habits, and the natural predilection of managers for nonparticipative methods; these we thought would half explain a reversion to the prevailing conditions in organizations. We were prepared to assert that in the absence of contrary environmental forces, external influences, and purposive continuing change efforts of a vigorous kind, an organization would migrate back to some more primitive form of organizational life.[42]

That the principal investigators did not have to say such things constituted major organizational news that reinforced previous hopes, hunches, and fragmentary data.

Fifth, the showcase applications stressed the value of a "system orientation." That is, it might be appropriate to begin working to change patterns of interaction by T-Group methods as a starter in a specific case, but any OD program sooner rather than later should seek "mutually reinforcing change actions across the psychological, organizational, and technological domains." As two researchers summarize a basic thrust of their own breakthrough OD effort:

> A central idea was to make structural changes in the organization that matched the work system and did not violate reasonable assumptions about the values and motives of individual members. . . . The idea of systematic consistency is surely an elementary one, no more than common sense—a habit of thought for those who have learned to view the factory as a total system in which all elements are interdependent. The interdependence of elements tends to preserve, to enhance, and to

42. Stanley E. Seashore and David G. Bowers, "Durability of Organizational Change," *American Psychologist,* Vol. 25 (January, 1970), p. 232.

"lock in" the central characteristics of the system and thus to prevent retrogression.[43]

This system orientation helped scotch the earlier unrealism about the T-Group as a kind of one-shot "magic bullet" that would cure many organizational ills. Some such notion can be attributed with varying degrees of directness to many early Model A approaches to OD.

Sixth, some of the showcase OD applications began to show a major interest in variables other than the quality of life and interaction patterns. Perhaps the prime example is the parallel research study of an OD application of Blake's Managerial Grid,[44] whose phases are described in Section D, Part I. Basically, the Grid seeks to induce a specific style of management, building from a concern with individuals and working on successively larger groupings as the training proceeds. The results of that training-research effort have been reviewed very positively in the popular managerial literature, and for good reason. The research effort was comprehensive and touched on many variables of central concern to both students and managers of complex organizations. Hence the positive reactions. For example, one summary article stresses these results of that seminal OD application:

> . . . The firm experienced a considerable increase in profits and a decrease in costs. The researchers attributed 56% of the profit to increase in noncontrollable factors, 31% to a reduction in manpower, and 13% (amounting to several million dollars) to improved operating procedures and higher productivity per man-hour. The increase in productivity per employee was achieved without increased investment in plant and equipment. Other criterion changes cited were an increased frequency of meetings, increased transfers within the plant and to other parts of the organization, a higher frequency of promotion for young line managers as opposed to staff men with more tenure, and a greater degree of success in solving organizational problems.[45]

43. *Ibid.,* p. 233.
44. Blake *et al., op. cit.* General support for the expected effects of Phase I is provided, for example, by M. Beer and S. W. Kleinsath, "The Effects of the Managerial Grid Lab on Organizational and Leadership Dimensions" (Paper presented at the Annual Meeting, American Psychological Association, Washington, D.C., September, 1967).
45. Julius E. Eitington, "Assessing Laboratory Training Using Psychology of Learning Concepts," *Training and Development Journal,* Vol. 25 (February, 1971), p. 15. Reprinted by special permission. Copyright 1971 by the American Society for Training and Development.
    Note that other studies do not replicate some of these effects, both at earlier or later phases of Grid training. See Peter B. Smith and Trudie F. Honour, "The Impact of Phase I Managerial Grid Training," *Journal of Management Studies,*

Such results imply multiple attractions, especially for the researcher who sees the manipulation of a relatively specific intervening variable (managerial style) and its association with outcome variables (such as profits and costs) as a start toward developing a complex model of the relationships affected by OD programs.

Other showcase applications also are sufficient to whet the appetites of those with major organizational responsibilities, although the linkages in them between intervening variables and organizational outcomes have not been traced so directly. Beckhard summarized the results of one such OD program. He stressed a dramatic improvement in profits in the year following the OD program, for example, which came in the face of stabilized profits in the industry. Beckhard also stressed evidences of improved interpersonal and intergroup relations, such as very low turnover in an industry characterized by high mobility. In addition, he noted various increases in the effectiveness of performance in most units, such as reduced costs as a function of sales. To be sure, Beckhard did not attribute all of these changes entirely to the OD educational effort. But he also urged that the OD program "has made a significant contribution through developing attitudes of commitment to company objectives, a shared value of concern for costs, and a measurable increase in operating efficiency of almost all units."[46]

In summary, the combined effect of such positive forces was to encourage numerous training-research programs that seek to establish in comprehensive practical and theoretical detail the conditions and consequences of specific OD designs. The early developmental history of the laboratory approach to OD, in short, was that promising.

2. TWO DIRECT APPLICATIONS OF THE LABORATORY APPROACH: CHANGING ORGANIZATION CLIMATE

The designs and results of two OD efforts to change the organization "climate" or "style" of several sales units in a business organization illustrate an attempt to apply, in an ongoing organization, the developmental lessons just sketched. The illustration has two thrusts: it should establish that quite a bit is known about which OD training designs tend to lead to which consequences, and it demonstrates that we often

Vol. 6 (October, 1969), esp. pp. 319–22; and S. R. Maxwell and Martin G. Evans, "An Evaluation of Organizational Development: Three Phases of the Managerial Grid," mimeographed (working paper, School of Business, University of Toronto, July, 1971).

46. Beckhard, op. cit., pp. 23–24.

know better than we can do, because of lack of resources or because of the intransigence of specific practical situations.

The common OD learning design, was derived from the laboratory approach and sought to create a specific kind of social order as well as to provide experience with appropriate skills and attitudes. The first OD effort—a pilot study—dealt with 16 managers who supervised the national sales of a well-known personal-consumption product. The men represented three hierarchical levels and had 80 salesmen in the field reporting to them. Sales were in excess of $40 million during 1968. In the second OD effort, a replication of the training design, more managers at more hierarchical levels were involved. The common goal in both studies was change in "climate" which, following George H. Litwin and Robert A. Stringer, Jr., may be defined as "a set of measurable properties of the work environment, perceived directly or indirectly by the people who live and work in this environment and assumed to influence their motivation and behavior."[47]

By way of introductory summary, a one-week learning experience helped induce significant changes in self-reports by managers about the climate of interpersonal and intergroup relations in their organizations. The bulk of the learning time was spent in sensitivity training groups, which were intended to prepare subordinates for a confrontation with their superiors concerning the needs of both as they were variously met by their unit's interpersonal and intergroup climate. The entire managerial populations were exposed to the learning design, so that there were no control groups. Consequently, the changes in self-reports can only be tentatively attributed to the experimental design rather than to random factors or the passage of time.

The motivation for this coverage of the two OD efforts is direct. Programs of planned change in organization style have received increasing attention from both researchers[48] and practitioners,[49] but serious gaps exist in knowledge about appropriate learning designs as well as about their consequences.[50] Both aspects of the problem are explored here.

The first six subsections below deal with the pilot study; a seventh sub-

47. George H. Litwin and Robert A. Stringer, Jr., *Motivation and Organizational Climate* (Boston: Harvard Graduate School of Business Administration, 1968) .
48. Robert T. Golembiewski and Stokes B. Carrigan, "Planned Change in Organization Style Based on the Laboratory Approach," *Administrative Science Quarterly* Vol. 15 (March, 1970) , pp. 79–93, and "The Persistence of Laboratory-Induced Changes in Organization Styles," *Administrative Science Quarterly,* Vol. 15 (September, 1970) , pp. 330–40.
49. Edgar H. Schein and Warren G. Bennis, *Personal and Organization Change through Group Methods* (New York: John Wiley & Sons, 1965) .
50. Donald T. Campbell, "From Description to Experimentation: Interpreting Trends as Quasi-Experiments," pp. 212–42, in Chester W. Harris (ed.) , *Problems in Measuring Change* (Madison: University of Wisconsin Press, 1963) .

section describes a replication of the learning design in a more complex organization.

a. Objectives of the Planned Change: Broad Values and Instrumental Goals

Overall, the normative thrust of the laboratory approach to OD seeks to create a specific kind of social order and provides experience with the skills and attitudes appropriate to that order. The typical learning design has three emphases, whose basic thrust is to use some temporary environment to generate learning which can be applied at the worksite. First, members of an organization discover, by experience in a learning design, that certain norms or values can guide interpersonal and intergroup relations while helping meet important personal and organizational needs. The norms or values underlying typical OD efforts were dealt with in Sections C and D of Part I, especially. Second, members gain experience with attitudes and behavioral skills necessary to approach these norms. Third, a substantial cadre of organizational members becomes convinced that laboratory norms should guide behavior in organizations and also that the members can provide or develop attitudes and behavioral skills appropriate to those norms.

Initial experience with these norms and with their associated attitudes and behavioral skills may be gained in a variety of temporary learning environments. The sensitivity training group, or T-Group—a small number of people with the common goal of learning about one another from one another within a framework of values for guiding interpersonal and intergroup relations—is a particularly useful vehicle for inducing such learning. Experience with appropriate norms and skills can also be gained in other learning contexts, however, such as Managerial Grid training.

The various temporary learning environments derived from the laboratory approach commonly attempt to provide a model for interpersonal and intergroup relations, for application first within small learning groups and later in large organizations. That model emphasizes increasing trust and decreasing risk among the participants. The specific goal is to permit the individual to relax his attachment to his old values and behavioral skills, at least enough to experiment with and evaluate new ones. In this sense, the design considered here was a very safe one. Its focus was narrowly on managerially relevant dynamics, as opposed to a total life style; participants were not strangers on a cultural island; totally new relations did not need to be developed among participants; and so on.

The crucial issue in OD programs is the transfer into large organizations of the initial experience with laboratory norms, attitudes, and be-

408

havioral skills that typically has been gained in small groups. The practical difficulties of transfer are great, but compelling reasons support the attempt. Sections C and D of Part I, which detailed these reasons, also emphasized one guiding belief of OD applications based on the laboratory approach. In the long run, the satisfaction and productivity of members will be greatest when individual and organization needs are both met.

More specifically, the pilot study had three short-run and three long-run goals. They were a combination of operating needs (as perceived by the managers who comprised the experimental population) and of consultant strategies[51] intended to meet these needs. The consultants had long-standing experience with the parent organization from which the managers came, and mutual trust was at a high level from the first phases of the program. Acceptance of the consultants as external change agents was both easy and rapid.

Short-run Goals

The paramount short-run goal was to integrate a new management team at the top three levels of a national field-sales organization (Figure 2). Within the year preceding the program, there had been personnel changes at all three management levels, including a new national sales manager, a divisional sales manager, and three regional sales managers. The goal was to develop effective and adaptive top-to-bottom and bottom-to-top relations among all three managerial levels in the experimental unit.

As a second goal, horizontal linkages were to be developed between divisional managers, and especially between regional managers. The regional managers had been spending about 60 percent of their time in direct selling but would rapidly transition to perhaps 90 percent of their time in managerial work, coincident with the introduction of a radically different product line. Changes in both roles and product required complex and unparalleled cooperative and innovative effort. The underlying concept of the planned change was the creation of three interlocking teams, as in Rensis Likert's notion of the linking pin.[52] This concept required building a sense of team identification within hierarchical levels, as well as between them. The concept also explicitly rejected the common strategy of building cohesiveness in each of the divisional units by inducing win/lose competition between them.

A third goal of the planned change was to help confront and resolve

---

51. This and the next two subsections derive basically from Golembiewski and Carrigan, "Planned Change in Organization Style," pp. 80–91.
52. Rensis Likert, *New Patterns of Management* (New York: McGraw-Hill Book Co., 1961).

Figure 2. Proposed Linkages within Experimental Unit

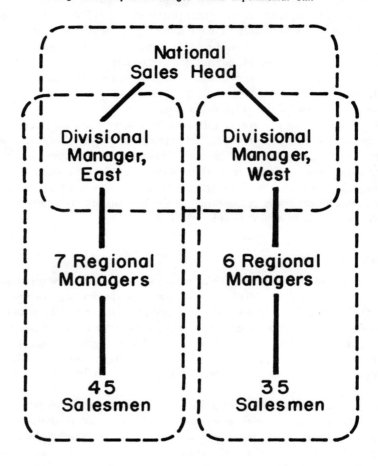

some nagging problems of personal style and organization history. Specifically, the new national sales head was widely seen as so aggressive and punishing that his subordinates were afraid of him. The regional managers feared that their interests would not be accurately represented to him and/or that the head would dominate the divisional managers. The divisional managers themselves had similar concerns. Consequently, upward communication was inhibited at the very time it was most vital. Furthermore, common opinion held that the regional managers had been poorly and even harshly managed over an extended period. The sales head and the two divisional managers individually were anxious to make changes, but they were concerned that almost any change would be interpreted by their subordinates as callous or vengeful, or worse. Finally, several of the regional managers had been involved in the organizational scuffling for the two top jobs, either as competitors or as supporters of competitors. Consequently, relations between peers were stressful when goodwill and trust were greatly needed.

Long-run Goals

The first long-run goal of the program was to increase the congruence between the behaviors that the prevailing organization style demanded and the behaviors that the managers preferred. For example, all of the managers feared that the existing relations in the experimental unit required substantial mistrust and secrecy, while the managers themselves preferred to be more trusting and open. Directly, the purpose was to increase the degree that individual needs could be met while organization demands were dealt with.

A second long-run goal was to inhibit a threatened and feared decrease in the congruence of individual needs and organization demands. Roughly, the goal was movement toward an open, adaptive, and problem-solving system; the antigoal was a closed, coercive, and hierarchy-serving system. The experimental unit initially was perceived by the consultants as somewhere between these polar extremes. The unit was widely perceived as threatening to move significantly in the closed direction under the new managers.

The third goal of the program was to experiment with a bottom-up approach to organization development, instead of the more typical top-down approach. Change agents usually direct their interventions toward the top of the organization hierarchy, or as near to it as possible, for good reasons. However, this top-down strategy often produces resistance at lower levels, and it certainly limits points of access by external change agents. In any case, the present goal was to gain knowledge and experience about organizational conditions and learning designs that facilitate change at the middle levels of a large organization.

The basic learning design attempted to meet two imperatives: managers were encouraged to consider a change in the style of their interpersonal and intergroup relations, but they were continually alerted to the constraints on what they and their immediate superiors could reasonably influence. Consequently, the learning design featured a number of decision points explicitly intended to test commitment by various levels of management to the unfolding program. The consequence to be avoided was a feeling by any of the managers that they had been manipulated into a position they found uncomfortable, but from which they could not gracefully escape. In positive terms, the overall objective was a feeling of psychological success among the managers: a sense of personally owning the change program, as opposed to a sense of the program being imposed upon them.

411

b. A Sketch of the Learning Design:
Sensitivity Training in OD Programs

The learning design relied on the laboratory approach in a variety of ways. Thus the design emphasized the use of T-Groups, which provided the initial experience with, and developed skills and attitudes appropriate for, values to guide interpersonal and intergroup relations that differ from the pyramidal values commonly accepted by members of large organizations. Moreover, the design attempted to suggest how laboratory values and dynamics could be built into more complex organizations, as by improving feedback processes in large units. The design also attempted to motivate organization members to evolve a set of values that would reinforce and encourage building analogs of laboratory dynamics into their work units.

Within the context of a specific learning design,[53] the pilot study's OD program based on the laboratory approach had five specific features. *First,* the final decision to adopt the approach was reached through planned stages. The national sales head and divisional managers individually had stranger or cousin sensitivity training experiences to give them some basis for deciding whether or not to authorize an OD program based on the laboratory approach. All three managers were attracted to the approach, based on their own independent reactions and those of 65 other members of their parent organization who had had T-Group experiences in other company programs. In addition, the regional managers were given an opportunity to express their reactions to a program based on the laboratory approach, in the form of a discussion of a descriptive article about T-Groups. Any strong resistance by the regional managers would at least have delayed the program. Both the three top managers and the consultants were careful not to overload the already tense relations between managerial levels. The regional managers agreed to participate, and the program began.

Second, the initial phase of the learning design was a T-Group experience for the regional managers at which the consultants served as trainers. This initial phase lasted four and one-half days, at a resort site. The overall goal was to improve interpersonal and intergroup relations in the organization, not necessarily to enhance personal growth or to provide an emotionally moving experience. This structured the experience in significant ways. For example, the focus limited both the topics and the emotional depth of discussion, as compared with T-Groups composed of strangers. The regional managers were told that the T-Group was preparation for the day and a half following it, when they could confront the two divisional managers with their concerns about interpersonal and intergroup relations in the experimental unit. The

---

53. Robert T. Golembiewski and Arthur Blumberg, "Sensitivity Training in Cousin Groups," *Training and Development Journal,* Vol. 23 (December, 1969), pp. 18–23.

words "could confront" were emphasized. The consultants had only arranged with the two division managers that they be available on short notice, should their presence seem appropriate, and this arrangement was shared with the regional managers as a first piece of business in their T-Group. The regional managers quickly and correctly perceived it as an escape hatch, should a confrontation with superiors seem too risky to them or inappropriate to the consultants.

Building toward the possible confrontation with superiors as a climax, the regional managers were encouraged to explore their feelings and reactions, both about the organization and the T-Group experience. The discussion shifted between emphasis on here-and-now dynamics triggered in the T-Group and there-and-then episodes involving organizational issues. The consultants used that discussion to help the regional managers become more aware of their feelings and reactions and to attach these reactions more precisely to the stimuli that induced them. Such sensitivity was seen as crucial preparation for the possible confrontation with the divisional managers, when a premium would be put on how and why the regional managers were reacting and feeling. The regional managers tested how rewarding openness was in their T-Group and consciously weighed the openness they were willing to risk in the confrontation with the two divisional managers. In addition, the T-Group provided experience with attitudes and skills that would facilitate the confrontation between superior and subordinate. The discussion permitted a cross-validation of concerns and reactions about organization relations, so that each regional manager would know as clearly as possible what his colleagues were thinking and feeling. Again the purpose was to facilitate the subsequent confrontation. For example, consensual validation among the managers about the real issues would reduce the risk to individual regional managers of confronting their superiors.

Third, the regional managers proved eager for the confrontation. During the confrontation phase, they met either as two divisions, each with their superior, or as a joint group with both divisional managers present. Only minimal structuring cues were provided for the regional managers. They were given a half day to decide whether to hold the confrontation and to plan it. The confrontation was described by the consultants as an opportunity for the regional managers to test the degree to which the national sales head and the two divisional managers really wanted an open, problem-solving system. The risks to the division managers received careful attention. From the start, the design stressed the risks implied in the confrontation, lest any manager should unconsciously adopt too crusading a spirit. Indeed, the motto for the training experience was based on the history of another group of Crusaders: "More went than came back." Instructions also underscored the need to concentrate on issues that were within the competence of superiors or that could be influenced by them.

The two divisional managers presented a more difficult problem. Their anxiety levels were high; they were very conscious of being outnumbered; and they did not know what they might expect from their subordinates. The consultants attempted to work through such concerns with them in a briefing session immediately before the confrontation. The briefing was facilitated by the fact that the consultants had been the trainers in the T-Groups previously attended by the two divisional managers. The divisional managers were instructed only to try to understand any feedback offered by the regional managers, to explore both ideas and feelings with as little defensiveness as possible, and to try to do so without projecting an attitude of "catharsis is good for them." The consultants were available during the confrontation, to provide support and to reinforce adherence to the norms of the laboratory approach.

Fourth, following the confrontation, the divisional managers met individually with the National Sales head to clarify their own relations, in part in response to the confrontation. This phase was preplanned and announced to the regional managers as a possibility in the introductory session of the training design.

Fifth, process observers—who were trained company employees—attended subsequent meetings at worksites of managers at all three levels. Their position as observers symbolized the transfer of the guardianship of the laboratory values from outside consultants to agents of the organization. Process observation was intended to reinforce laboratory values in action settings, both by the presence of the observer and through his interventions, which encouraged looking at the socioemotional processes of the meeting as well as its content. The goal was to preclude the initial off-site training experience being seen as unique and perhaps precious, but remote from the workaday world.

The flow of the learning design may be summarized as follows. Overall, the learning design sought both to initiate attitudinal and behavioral change in a temporary learning environment and to transfer that change into the organization. The T-Group experiences were meant to relax old attitudes about interpersonal and intergroup relations. The confrontation provided an opportunity to practice new attitudes and behaviors under actual conditions, as well as to test the risk involved for all. And process observers at subsequent work meetings of the regional managers reinforced the new behavioral skills and attitudes in organizational settings.

c. Measuring Progress toward Planned Change: "Profile of Organizational Characteristics"

Progress toward planned change in the organization style of the sales unit was measured in the pilot study by self-reported changes in the 48

414

items of Likert's Profile of Organizational Characteristics.[54] Six properties of the Profile and its application require emphasis. *First,* each item is represented by a 20-point scale anchored by four descriptions, as illustrated in Figure 3.

Second, Likert distinguishes the four major intervals as different systems of organization, with the Participative Group system being most consistent with the laboratory approach. Therefore, scores on the 48 Profile items can provide estimates of the degrees to which the style of an organization approaches the norms of the laboratory approach.

Third, responses were uniformly coded so that scores ran from 1 for the extreme Exploitative-Authoritative rating to 20 for the extreme Par

Figure 3. Representative Item from Likert's Profile

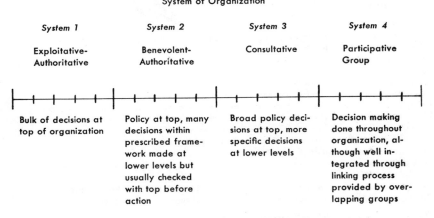

Item 33: At what level in the organization are decisions formally made?

ticipative Group rating. The Likert scales vary in direction, so as to inhibit a response set. However, all discussion below is based on the uniform coding of responses, irrespective of the scale direction of items.

Fourth, each Profile item was rated twice: as *Ideal,* or as respondents felt their organization unit should be, and also as *Now,* or as respondents actually saw their organization unit to be. All responses were sent directly to the senior consultant at his university address, with guarantees that only aggregate data would be reported. Responses from individual managers were identified by name, which made possible matched comparisons of the responses of each manager.

Fifth, the Profile taps a range of processes that determine an organiza

54. Rensis Likert, *The Human Organization* (New York: McGraw-Hill Book Co., 1967).

Figure 4. Individual Items from Likert's "Profile of Organizational Characteristics"

Leadership

1. Extent to which superiors have confidence and trust in subordinates
2. Extent to which subordinates, in turn, have confidence and trust in superiors
3. Extent to which superiors display supportive behavior toward others
4. Extent to which superiors behave so that subordinates feel free to discuss important things about their jobs with their immediate superior
5. Extent to which immediate superior in solving job problems generally tries to get subordinates' ideas and opinions and make constructive use of them

Character of Motivational Forces

6. Underlying motives tapped
7. Manner in which motives are used
8. Kinds of attitudes developed toward organization and its goals
9. Extent to which motivational forces conflict with or reinforce one another
10. Amount of responsibility felt by each member of organization for achieving organization's goals
11. Attitudes toward other members of the organization
12. Satisfaction derived

Character of Communication Process

13. Amount of interaction and communication aimed at achieving organization's objectives
14. Direction of information flow
15. Where downward communication initiated
16. Extent to which superiors willingly share information
17. Extent to which communications are accepted by subordinates
18. Adequacy of upward communication via line organization
19. Subordinates' feeling of responsibility for initiating accurate upward communication
20. Forces leading to accurate or distorted upward information
21. Accuracy of upward communication via line organization
22. Need for supplementary upward communication system
23. Sideward communications, their adequacy and accuracy
24. Psychological closeness of superiors to subordinates (i.e., friendliness between superiors and subordinates)
25. How well does superior know and understand problems faced by subordinates?
26. How accurate are the perceptions by superiors and subordinates of each other?

Character of Interaction-Influence Process

27. Amount and character of interaction
28. Amount of cooperative teamwork present
29. Extent to which subordinates can influence the goals, methods, and activity of their units and departments, as seen by superiors
30. Extent to which subordinates can influence the goals, methods, and activity of their units and departments, as seen by subordinates
31. Amount of actual influence which superiors can exercise over the goals, activity, and methods of their units and departments
32. Extent to which an effective structure exists enabling one part of organization to exert influence upon other parts

Character of Decision-Making Process

33. At what level in the organization are decisions formally made?
34. How adequate and accurate is the information available for decision making at the place where decisions are made?
35. To what extent are decision makers aware of problems, particularly those at lower levels in the organization?
36. Extent to which technical and professional knowledge is used in decision making
37. Are decisions made at the best level in the organization as far as availability of the most adequate information bearing on the decision?
38. Does the decision-making process help to create the necessary motivations in those persons who have to carry out the decisions?

416

39. To what extent are subordinates involved in decisions related to their work?
40. Is decision making based on man-to-man or group pattern of operation? Does it encourage teamwork?

Character of Goal Setting or Ordering
41. Manner in which goal setting or ordering is usually done
42. To what extent do the different hierarchical levels tend to strive for high performance goals?
43. Are there forces to accept, resist, or reject goals?

Character of Control Process
44. At what hierarchical levels in organization is there major or primary concern with the performance of the control function?
45. How accurate are the measurements and information used to guide and perform the control function, and to what extent do forces exist in the organization to distort and falsify this information?
46. Extent to which the review and control functions are concentrated
47. Extent to which there is an informal organization present and supporting or opposing goals of formal organization
48. Extent to which control data (e.g., accounting, productivity, cost, etc.) are used for self-guidance or group problem-solving by managers and non-supervisory employees, or used by superiors in a punitive, policing manner

tion's style. They are: (1) leadership, (2) character of motivational forces, (3) character of communication process, (4) character of inter-action-influence process, (5) character of decision-making process, (6) character of goal-setting or ordering, and (7) character of control process. The complete list of Profile items is given in Figure 4, although to conserve space the four statements that anchor each 20-point scale for each item are not specified.

Sixth, respondents were instructed to think of the experimental unit as a whole in making their ratings. The data treated here are the self-reports by the regional managers.

The Profile can serve both descriptive and predictive uses. Descriptively, responses to the Profile items could have been used to estimate the initial climate of the experimental unit. Ideal scores before the learning experience were expected to cluster in the System 4 area, and most Now scores were expected to fall between Systems 2 and 3. Administration of the Profile before the learning experience could have helped judge the cultural preparedness of the system for the laboratory approach. For example, a System 1 organization is probably not a likely host for an OD program based on the laboratory approach. In the present case, the consultants relied on their intuition and knowledge of the parent organization when making the moral judgment to recommend the laboratory approach.

Likert's Profile also can be used predictively. The goals of the OD effort were defined in terms of anticipated changes in scores on the Profile between two administrations of the questionnaire, given a successful learning design. Test 1 came early in the week of training, and test 2

417

followed four months later. If the learning design had the intended effects, comparisons of the two tests should have supported the following five expectations:

- *Expectation 1.* The original state of interpersonal and intergroup relations in the sales unit would fall significantly short of the expectations of participants; i.e., Ideal 1 scores would be significantly greater[55] than Now 1 scores.

- *Expectation 2.* The intervention would raise participants' expectations about how need-gratifying their organization could be expected to be; i.e., Ideal 2 scores would be significantly greater than Ideal 1 scores.

- *Expectation 3.* The intervention would significantly change the organization style in the direction that participants preferred; i.e., Now 2 scores would be significantly greater than Now 1 scores.

- *Expectation 4.* A successful intervention need not eliminate the differences between the existing interpersonal and intergroup climate and the expectations of organization members; i.e., Ideal 2 scores still might differ significantly from Now 2 scores.

- *Expectation 5.* Although a successful intervention need not eliminate them, the differences between scores of the existing climate and scores of the preferred climate should at least remain constant, if not decrease, so as to avoid differences that might become so large as to be demotivating; i.e., at a minimum (Ideal 2–Now 2) differences would be no larger than (Ideal 1–Now 1) differences.

It was not possible—given the nature of the organization and the small managerial population—to employ a control group in the research design. Two points provide detail about this major limitation. The entire managerial population was exposed to the experimental treatment. This was due to the small number of managers in the experimental unit, and it also was convenient because of features of the learning design that argued against exposing only a part of this small number of managers to the laboratory.[56] Relatedly, the use as a control of a matched group of

---

55. Note that an "increase" or "decrease" in a Likert score is to be understood as a change toward or away from the System 4 portion of the Likert Profile, which is built around four basic organizational "systems" or "types": (1) Exploitative-Authoritative, (2) Benevolent-Authoritative, (3) Consultative, and (4) Participative Group. The closer the organization approaches the Participative Group segment of the continuum, the more open its climate is considered to be. Each item of the Profile is scored from 1 to 20, with 20 being the extreme score of the Participative Group system of organization. The pilot-study learning design was intended to induce changes in interpersonal and intergroup relations that trend toward System 4.

56. See Golembiewski and Blumberg, "Sensitivity Training in Cousin Groups."

managers at similar levels from throughout the organization was considered inappropriate. The experimental unit was unique in many senses: it was adding a radically different product line; it had experienced a major managerial succession; and its history had a strong and distinctive pattern.

d. Some Results of Planned Intervention: Toward the Participative Group System

Despite the lack of control groups, the responses on two administrations of the Likert Profile in the pilot study implied that significant changes in the climate of the experimental unit occurred in the four-month interval after the learning experience. In general, these changes in self-reports implied that managers were more free to behave at work in ways they preferred and that the managers' work climate became more what they wished it to be. Table 1 suggests the massive nature of these changes, although in a gross way.

Table 1. Comparison of Scores on Two Tests of the Profile

System	Test 1		Test 2	
	Ideal	Now	Ideal	Now
Exploitative-Authoritative	0	0	0	0
Benevolent-Authoritative	0	1	0	0
Consultative	3	41	1	18
Participative Group	45	6	47	30

The specific changes in self-reports can be suggested by an interpretive summary of the effects on the 48 Profile items, as judged by two administrations some four months apart. The data will be reviewed in terms of the five expectations about changes introduced above.

Expectation 1

There was initial major incongruence between the needs of the managers and the organization style that they reported as existing before the planned intervention. Ideal 1 was greater than Now 1 in all 48 cases, and 43 of these differences reached the .05 level of statistical significance, or better. This provided impressive support for Expectation 1. For example, for item 1, the data showed that participants desired significantly more trust and confidence than the organization style encouraged.

419

Expectation 2

The results strongly implied that the intervention helped significantly change what the participants expected of their organization. The changes from Ideal 1 to Ideal 2 scores were positive in 42 of 48 cases, with 19 of these reaching the .05 level or better. None of the six negative changes approached usually accepted levels of significance. This change in Ideal scores is important because the heightened expectations could be expected to induce motivational forces to change the organization style so as to reduce the discrepancy between Ideal and Now scores. Such an effect could be expected, except where the gap between Ideal and Now scores was so great as to induce pessimism or even despair.

Expectation 3

The data supported Expectation 3 and its imputation of motivational force to increases in Ideal scores. That is, comparison of Now 2 scores with Now 1 scores demonstrated that the participants' descriptions of the experimental unit reflected movement toward an organization style consistent with the laboratory approach. N_2 was greater than N_1 in 47 of the 48 comparisons, with 28 reaching the .05 level of significance, or better. An additional 10 cases approached the .05 level. This impressive statistical record implies the massive and consistent impact of the learning design on the managers.

With both Ideal scores and Now scores increasing in the interval between tests, the question arises as to whether changes in organization style ran fast enough to stand still, as it were, relative to the heightened expectations implied by increasing Ideal scores. The danger is that the learning design merely increased the gap between Ideal and Now scores. Up to a point, such a gap has the motivational properties associated with a demanding but still attainable level of aspiration. However, the gap could grow so great as to create doubts that the level of aspiration is attainable. Such gaps would probably curb efforts to attain the goals and would have demotivating properties. Tentativeness is appropriate here, however, given that little is known about the optimum discrepancy for inducing maximum learning, as the last section of Section B, Part I, should have established.

Expectations 4 and 5 attempt to take such issues into account. They are meant as boundary conditions for defining a successful learning design. However, Expectation 5 provides that the I–N gaps should at least not be increased substantially by the learning design. The point of this boundary condition is a conservative one: to avoid increasing I–N gaps beyond that unknown point at which they become demotivating. This is a strict criterion of the success of the learning design.

420

Expectation 4

The learning design did not eliminate *I–N* differences, which meets our permissive Expectation 4. Considering only the second test, I_2 was greater than N_2 in all 48 cases, and 47 of these cases reached at least the .05 level of statistical significance. This pattern is similar to that generated by comparisons of Ideal scores and Now scores for test 1.

There is no easy interpretation of what these gaps in Ideal versus Now scores mean. That significant differences between Ideal and Now scores still existed on the second Likert administration does not mean that nothing happened as a result of the training design. How to evaluate what the data do mean is a problem, however. Certainly, also, the patterns of Ideal and Now scores imply one danger of OD programs. The learning design apparently created rising expectations, and these increased expectations will decrease the alternatives available to management. Should future changes in organization style move toward systems that are closed, coercive, and hierarchy-serving, the increased Ideal scores imply a heightened resistance by managers. An organization development program based on the laboratory approach, in this sense, seems to set a tiger lose in the streets.

Expectation 5

The gaps between Ideal and Now scores were reduced, even though those gaps are still significant. This meets Expectation 5 for a successful change. Since Ideal scores are almost always greater than Now scores, $(I_2 - N_2) - (I_1 - N_1)$ should be negative if there were a decrease in the gap between Ideal and Now scores. This is indeed the case: 36 of the relevant 48 comparisons were negative. Although only 8 of these negative values reached the .05 level, an additional 15 cases closely approached that level, and 2 others showed no difference. Less than one case in five reflected an increased gap between Ideal and Now scores, relatedly, and not one of these positive changes approached usually accepted levels of significance.

The OD effort in the pilot study did not merely raise aspirations about what the organization climate should be, then, thereby making the gap between Ideal and Now scores so great as to produce pessimism. Ideal scores did increase, but basic changes in organization style were also encouraged by the learning design.

e. Attributing the Results to the Design: Some Methodological Cautions

The pilot-study learning design to change organization style may seem in general to have generated the intended effects, but the results also

421

imply some significant issues to which no definitive response can yet be given. For example, the lack of a control group and the reliance on self-reports make the interpretation of results somewhat chancy. Once these points are acknowledged, counterclaims are appropriate. Thus it does not seem probable that the changes observed reflect only environmental changes or the mere passage of time, rather than the impact of the learning design. Basically, the changes in self-reports were contrary to the history of the experimental unit, as well as to the previous styles of the national sales head and the divisional managers. Indeed, organization members tended to agree that time alone would not have induced movements on the Likert dimensions like those observed. Furthermore, the changes in self-reports were marked and consistent with the broad theory underlying the laboratory method. These considerations only suggest the potency of the training design. At a minimum, however, they do urge further research dealing with organizational applications of the laboratory approach.

In the absence of replicatory studies, in addition, a kind of Hawthorne effect may be said to explain the results. That is, changes in self-reports might be due not so much to the training design as to the attention given the regional managers by consultants and top management. No one can conclusively reject a Hawthorne effect in this case. The general consistency of the results with the theory underlying the training design argues against a Hawthorne effect determining the results, but only replications of the training design could test this objection. More seriously, the results below may not reflect actual behavioral change. Trainees may have learned the kinds of behavior that the consultants valued, and they may have dutifully reported appropriate changes in their self-reports as cooperative subjects in an experiment often do.[57] Yet the climate of their organization might not have changed at all. Similarly, change in self-reports may be due in part to the practice gained in responding twice to the Likert form[58] or to reliability problems with the instrument.

The possibility that the changes reported below do not reflect actual behavioral changes must be taken especially seriously, even though a plausible countercase can be built. Substantial anecdotal evidence suggests that extensive behavioral change did take place. In addition, rating each Likert dimension as Ideal and Now was an attempt to force respondents to distinguish between wish fulfillment and reality. Various

---

57. Stanley Milgram, "Some Conditions of Obedience and Disobedience to Authority," *Human Relations,* Vol. 18 (February, 1965), pp. 57–76.
58. V. R. Cane and A. W. Haim, "The Effects of Repeated Testing: III," *Quarterly Journal of Experimental Psychology,* Vol. 2, pp. 182–95. For a review of the inadequacies of self-reports versus observations of actual behavior, see Martin Lakin, *Interpersonal Encounter* (New York: McGraw-Hill Book Co., 1972), pp. 197–99.

technical details—such as spacing the two administrations of the Likert Profile four months apart and varying the direction of scales for individual Likert items to prevent a response set—at least made it more probable that respondents would base their reports on actual behavior. However, the research reported here did not deal directly with behavioral change, and the possibility of a subtle kind of wish fulfillment cannot be rejected.

The most basic reservation about attributing the observed effects to the learning experiences lies in the research design, however, which Donald T. Campbell called a one-group, pretest, posttest design.[59] Schematically, the design is O_1 X, O_2, where O is an observation and X is the experimental treatment. The O_1, X, O_2 design does not eliminate hypotheses alternative to the X in explaining any observed effects. For example, history may exert uncontrolled effects. That is, an observed change between O_1 and O_2 may be due not to the experimenter's X but to some other common events experienced by most or all of the experimental population. Alternatively, any change may be attributed to some ongoing maturational processes, such as normal developmental phases. Or an observed change may reflect practice effects of responding twice to the same measuring instrument, or such statistical artifacts as the probably incomplete correlation between the two test administrations, even if conditions were static.

Some of the problems with the O_1, X, O_2 design can be illustrated in Figure 5, Case 1. For example, the initial results showed increases in the dependent variable, indicated by the line segment BC. The interpretation of the increase is ambiguous, however. Other observations might reveal a curve like ABCD, for example, in which case the line segment BC could be more plausibly attributed to long-run maturational effects than to the X. Or other observations might generate a curve like EFBCGH, where BC might be more reasonably attributed to common historical events at B and G rather than to the experimenter's X. Or BC might only reflect test-retest effects, such as improvements on IQ tests due to a previous trial or the incomplete correlation between two administrations measuring a dependent variable that did not change.

The time-series design permits more definite interpretations. This design may be generalized as O_n, X, O_{n+1}, O_{n+2}, O_{n+3}, O_{n+4}, . . . , where O_n represents more than one pretreatment administration of the test instrument. Given a time-series design, the line segments GABCD in Figure 5, Case 2, can be explained plausibly as effects of the experimental treatment. That is, the design sharply reduces the probability that the observed effects are due to history, maturation, or to test-retest. Campbell

59. Donald T. Campbell, "From Description to Experimentation," in Chester W. Harris (ed.), *Problems of Measuring Change* (Madison; University of Wisconsin Press, 1963), pp. 212–42.

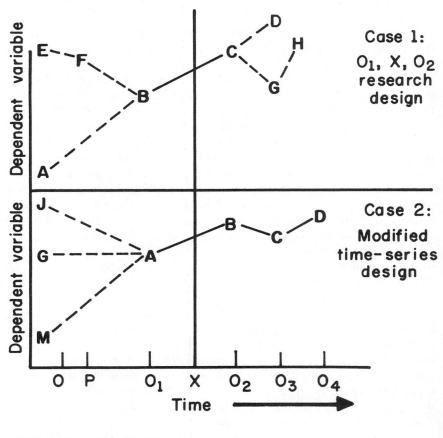

Figure 5. Comparison of an O_1, X, O_2 Research Design with Modified Time-Series Design

Note: _____ = actual data.
  _ _ _ = hypothetical data.
  O_p = any observations prior to O_1.

evaluated the time-series design in careful terms, concluding that it "is one of the frequent research designs of the biological and physical sciences. While to date appropriate and successful applications may be lacking in the social sciences, the design should probably, nonetheless, be granted a position of semi-respectability."[60]

The advantages seen by Campbell can be illustrated by considering a modified time-series design, which is the design underlying the test of the persistence in the changes observed in the pilot study. That per-

<hr>

60. Campbell, *op. cit.*, p. 230.

sistence will be discussed below. Here note that a modified time-series design may be described as O_1, X, O_2, O_3, O_4, which provides for an experimental treatment preceded by a single pretest and followed by multiple posttests. The line segments ABCD in Figure 5, case 2, represent the changes in Likert Profile scores observed over time. Since the design has only a single pretreatment observation, O_1, to begin, results represented by ABCD in Figure 5, case 2, cannot be ascribed only to the experimental treatment. Maturational effects might provide an alternative explanation of the results, for example. That is, some hypothetical observation, O_p, might yield a dependent variable score, M, and maturational effects are implied in the line segments MABCD. Similarly, another observation might generate a score at J, in which case JABCD might reasonably be said to reflect some common historical event between J and B, as opposed to the X.

Although inferior to the time-series design and certainly to the control-group design, the modified time-series design does have significant advantages over O_1, X, O_2. Test-retest effects are minimized. Moreover, a maturational explanation is less credible, if only because the analyst must explain the peaking of the maturational processes coincident with the posttreatment observations. Common historical events still remain an alternative explanation of observed effects, the plausibility of which can only be eliminated by some form of control-group design. These alternative explanations may be devalued by the researchers' intimate knowledge of the situation, as well as by the reports of participants. But they nonetheless remain as possible explanations of observed effects.

Finally, even granting that the organizational style of the experimental unit was changed in ways that are more satisfying to its members, have the effectiveness and efficiency of the experimental unit been increased? There are no data to answer this question, largely because the missions and roles of the experimental unit have changed rapidly. Participants report more involvement and satisfaction at work; and they generally agree that the style will enhance their total performance in the long run. In addition, sound theoretical reasons urge that high output will coexist with high satisfaction of interpersonal and intergroup needs. But such considerations stop far short of demonstrating that the present change had favorable consequences on output variables.[61]

These methodological cautions are significant ones, and there is no way that they can be dismissed. Two approaches to reducing the credibility of the cautions do exist, however. First, the changes were tested

---

61. A few such demonstrations do exist. See Louis B. Barnes and Larry E. Greiner, "Breakthrough in Organization Development," *Harvard Business Review*, Vol. 22 (November, 1964), pp. 139–65; and Alfred D. Marrow, Stanley Seashore, and David G. Bowers, *Management by Participation* (New York: Harper & Row, Publishers, 1967).

for persistence over time. Any marked persistence, of course, strongly urges the conclusion that the observed changes are more than artifacts or random variations. Second, the learning design was used in a more complex organization. If that replication were to generate a pattern of results similar to that sketched above, of course, the impact of the methodological cautions would be reduced sharply. The following sections deal with these two approaches to reducing the credibility of the methodological cautions discussed above.

f. Persistence of the Observed Changes:[62] Reducing the Credibility of the Cautions

Two administrations of the Likert Profile in the pilot study beyond those reported above made substantially more plausible the hypothesis that pervasive changes in the climate of a multilevel organization unit were induced by a training design based on the laboratory approach. The two additional observations reduced the plausibility of attributing observed effects to maturational processes, common historical events, or practice effects in responding to the Likert profile. This approximate schedule was followed, where O = observations using the Likert profile and X = experimental treatment:

Event	O_1	X	O_2	O_3	O_4
Day	1	8–15	135	345	525

The schedule reflected convenience, realism, and necessity. The last two administrations of the Likert Profile were simply convenient, given the managers' other obligations. The four-month interval between O_1 and O_2 was an attempt to be realistic. The managers involved were part of a headquarters-field complex, and researchers felt considerable elapsed time was necessary to test whether various aspects of the climate of the organization had really changed. Where face-to-face contacts are more frequent, less time between pretreatment and posttreatment administrations probably would suffice to capture any changes. Observations necessarily ceased after 525 days because a major reorganization was impending.

Any marked persistence of the changes in climate beyond O_2 would be noteworthy, even though the persistence could not absolutely be attributed to the training design. The broad environment at best remained stable, overall, and probably worsened so as to stress interpersonal and intergroup relations. For example, the organization unit and especially its parent company faced a variety of serious problems, which worsened

---

62. This section draws from Golembiewski and Carrigan, "The Persistence of Laboratory-Induced Changes in Organization Styles."

during the period of observation. Interunit collaboration became an unprecedented concern, largely because the experimental unit had spotty success in developing the complex interfaces with various line and staff units required to market its new products. These broad systematic issues were counterbalanced to some unknown extent. Between observations 2 and 3, the experimental unit had successfully introduced a new product line which looked favorable, despite many problems. Moreover, a reclassification study raised the managers' job to the next higher class between observations 3 and 4, in response to the escalating complexities associated with marketing the new product line.

Any persistence of changes in organization climate would also be noteworthy because the original learning experience was only mildly reinforced. Consultants had recommended a booster learning experience of two or three days, to be held approximately one year after the experimental treatment, but the recommendation could not be acted upon. Beyond that time, no further interventions were recommended, because of a reorganization that was to increase the size of the experimental unit by about 20 percent. However, a brief data feedback session was held shortly after O_3, when summary data from the first two administrations were shared and discussed. Consultants considered this feedback session a mild reinforcer, but the data reviewed below do show a general pattern of regression at O_3 and recovery at O_4 to O_2 levels, more or less. This implies that even the brief feedback session did serve as a reinforcer.

The observed changes can be summarized from four major perspectives to test the pervasiveness of changes in the interpersonal and intergroup styles in the host organization. Note that, because of reassignments toward the end of the experimental period, two regional managers in the original batch of 12 managers did not provide data throughout the full period. The data reported here for the first two administrations of the Likert Profile thus differ slightly from the data reported above. All observed changes are described uniformly and conveniently as having moved toward or away from the values underlying the laboratory approach.

Preferred Interpersonal and Intergroup Relations

Managerial self-reports on the Likert Profile about preferred interpersonal and intergroup relations changed in predicted ways, as the first six rows in Table 2 show, and the changes became more pronounced over the full period of observation. That is, 43 of the 48 comparisons of I_1 and I_2 scores are in the predicted direction, with 21 reaching the .05 level. Some regression occurred between observations 2 and 3, as row 4 in Table 2 shows. However, judging from rows 2 through 6, that regression was arrested and sharply reversed. As one evidence of that re-

Table 2. Changes in Ideal and Now Scores over Four Observations

Comparisons of Tests	Changes toward Laboratory Model			Changes away from Laboratory Model	
	Significant beyond .05 Level	Not Significant	No Change	Not Significant	Significant beyond .05 Level
Ideal scores					
I_2 versus I_1	21	22	0	5	0
I_3 versus I_1	12	29	1	6	0
I_4 versus I_1	24	19	3	2	0
I_3 versus I_2	1	17	3	24	3
I_4 versus I_2	4	21	3	17	3
I_4 versus I_3	6	24	6	10	2
Now scores					
N_2 versus N_1	27	19	0	2	0
N_3 versus N_1	15	27	1	5	0
N_4 versus N_1	17	21	3	7	0
N_3 versus N_2	0	11	1	32	4
N_4 versus N_2	0	8	0	35	5
N_4 versus N_3	2	17	1	22	6

versal, twice as many I_4 as I_3 scores were greater than I_1 scores, at usually accepted levels of statistical significance.

The first six rows of Table 2 permit a direct conclusion. Organization members seemed to increase their expectations about the satisfaction of needs that their interpersonal and intergroup relations at work should provide. This effect was an expected consequence of the training design.

Actual Organization Climate

Managerial self-reports about existing interpersonal and intergroup relations not only changed significantly and in predicted ways following the experimental treatment, but these changes also were substantially preserved over the full observational period. Row 7 in Table 2 shows that changes in the predicted direction for the Now scores occurred on 46 of the 48 items between observations 1 and 2 using Likert's Profile, with nearly 6 out of 10 of these differences reaching statistical significance. Rows 8 and 9 imply that these changes in Now scores stabilized at a high level, although some regression did occur. Thus N_4 scores are still greater than N_1 scores in 38 cases, nearly half of which reach the .05 level. Rows 10 through 12 in Table 2 also demonstrate that regression did occur after observation 2. But comparison of rows 10 and 12 suggests that this regression was arrested between observations 3 and 4, even though it was not entirely reversed.

Trends in Preferred versus Actual Scores

Managers initially perceived a significant disparity between their own ideals and their perceptions of the actual interpersonal and intergroup climate in their unit, and these significant disparities persisted throughout all four administrations of the Likert Profile. Specifically, Ideal scores were larger than Now scores in all 192 cases, with the definite trend being toward more statistically significant differences over time. The following data support both points:

	I_1 v. N_1	I_2 v. N_2	I_3 v. N_3	I_4 v. N_4
Larger and significant statistically	41	46	47	48
Larger but not significant	7	2	1	0

I–N Differences

A successful training design was not expected to eliminate $I-N$ differences, but the initial expectation was that the $I-N$ gaps probably would be reduced somewhat by a successful learning design. No change would have been acceptable. Maintaining or reducing $I-N$ gaps constitutes a strict test of the capacity of the learning design to help induce persisting changes of the kind desired. The test is severe at least in the sense that both Ideal and Now scores could change markedly, with an increase in the size of the $I-N$ gaps, and this might even be a desirable outcome because such increases probably are to some extent motivating. Moreover, one could not easily deny the change-inducing properties of the learning design in such a case. But such a case would violate the conservative limiting condition here that derives from ignorance about when $I-N$ gaps grow so large as to be demotivating.

Overall, the data indicate that the learning design did not violate the strict limiting condition. Managerial self-reports indicate a trend toward smaller differences between I and N scores, as Table 3 shows, although some decay occurred toward the end of the 525-day period of observation. Because of the way the comparisons are defined, negative entries in Table 3 reflect a closer fit between perceived climate and managerial ideals, comparing later administrations of the Likert Profile with earlier ones. The table indicates that 36 of the 48 $I-N$ gaps are smaller in O_2 than in O_1, as row 1 shows. This implies a closer approach of existing organizational relations to the ideal conditions defined by the managers. The third and fourth administrations reflect some decay of this data trend, as rows 4 and 5 show. At their worst in row 3, however, only 21 of

Table 3. Comparisons of Four Observations

Comparisons of Differences Between Now and Ideal Scores	Greater Difference in Later Administration		No Difference	Smaller Difference in Later Administration	
	Significant at .05 Level	Not Significant		Not Significant	Significant at .05 Level
(I_2-N_2) v. (I_1-N_1)	0	12	0	27	9
(I_3-N_3) v. (I_1-N_1)	0	19	0	25	4
(I_4-N_4) v. (I_1-N_1)	2	19	3	22	2
(I_3-N_3) v. (I_2-N_2)	0	40	0	8	0
(I_4-N_4) v. (I_2-N_2)	10	32	1	5	0
(I_4-N_4) v. (I_3-N_3)	8	26	2	12	0

the 48 scores in a later administration show a greater I–N gap than in the first administration.

Words such as "decay" and "worst" cannot be taken literally in interpreting such differences. All that can be said is that the data do not violate the limiting condition set by researchers, which is intentionally conservative. Other research can test whether a "big bang" approach is a more useful guide for programs of organizational change, for which learning designs should try to induce the largest possible I–N gaps.[63] The core theoretical issues were introduced in the Subsection 6 of Section B, Part I, which discusses three alternative models of change.

Toward a More Forceful Conclusion

Despite the inadequacies of the research design, the evidence strongly indicates that the training design helped induce and sustain major changes in a large number of measures of the style of a small organization unit. The presumed self-reinforcing linkages can be sketched in these crude but useful terms:

- A learning design based on the laboratory approach provides off-site experience with a set of behaviors, attitudes, and skills.
- This experience encourages participants in their work setting to either:
  a. adopt new patterns of behavior suggested by their off-site experience
  b. reorder the frequencies of performing old behaviors already in the repertoires of participants, increasing those behaviors that are consistent with laboratory ideals and decreasing the incidence of inconsistent behaviors.

---

63. Saul D. Alinsky, "The War on Poverty: Political Pornography," *Journal of Social Issues*, Vol. 21 (January, 1965), pp. 41–47.

- The derivative behavioral changes help to modify:
  a. the old organization climate for interpersonal and intergroup relations
  b. the norms supporting the old climate.

This overall conclusion implies several lines of research, four of which merit emphasis. *First,* follow-up research should involve greater attention to measures of behavioral change, especially non-obtrusive measures. In contrast, present measures have relied on self-reports that are probably reactive. The very processes of measuring may change what is being measured. Or respondents may have become questionnaire-bright, returning to the experimenter what he seemed to want. The effect has been commonly observed, even when what the experimenter wanted intentionally placed subjects in conflictful situations.[64]

Second, research is necessary to specify the conditions under which the learning design can be expected to generate desired effects. The questions involved come easily. When is an organization culturally prepared for the laboratory approach? Do organizations differ enough so that the laboratory approach is tailor-made for one system of management, as measured by the Likert Profile, but not another? And so on. Research answers will come only grudgingly.

Third, the results above suggest the usefulness of the Likert Profile for assessing change in organization climate, but closer analysis is required. In one preliminary study, it proved useful to distinguish two batches of items in the Likert Profile, "process" items and those concerned with "outcomes."[65] The degree of interpersonal trust was a process item, for example, and the perceived adequacy of information in the organization was an outcome item. Significantly, different clusters of results were obtained when the 48 Likert items were thus distinguished. A related approach to closer analysis of the Likert Profile items addressed itself to the classic empirical issue. That is, to what extent do the Likert items isolate dimensions of organizational reality as opposed to being mere variables? A factor analysis of the data now being gathered from a large managerial population, for example, may provide insights into this classic issue.

Fourth, and paramountly, the usefulness of the basic training design must be tested in larger and more complex units of organization. As replications yield a pattern of results similar to that sketched above, so will the usefulness of this design for a laboratory approach to OD be made explicit.

---

64. Milgram, *op. cit.*
65. Robert T. Golembiewski, "Organizational Properties and Managerial Learning: Testing Alternative Models of Attitudinal Change," *Journal of the Academy of Management,* Vol. 13 (March, 1970), pp. 15–41.

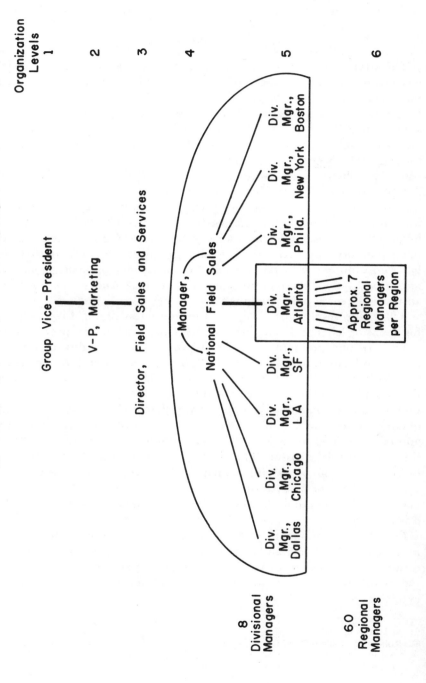

Figure 6. Complex Organization Involved in the Training Design

Organization Levels

1

2

3

4

5

6

Group Vice-President

V-P, Marketing

Director, Field Sales and Services

Manager, National Field Sales

Div. Mgr., Dallas

Div. Mgr., Chicago

Div. Mgr., LA

Div. Mgr., SF

Div. Mgr., Atlanta

Div. Mgr., Phila.

Div. Mgr., New York

Div. Mgr., Boston

Approx. 7 Regional Managers per Region

8 Divisional Managers

60 Regional Managers

432

g. A Replication of the Basic Learning Design:[66]
A Further and Major Reduction in Caution

The data above encouraged another OD effort to change the climate of a more complex organization with six hierarchical levels. Figure 6 sketches that complex organization. The thrust of this second OD effort was directed at the lower three hierarchical levels, and all systematic data about change were provided by the regional and divisional managers. The complex organization whose climate was to be changed was identified as National Field Sales. The basic underlying concept was the creation of interlocking teams, as in the pilot study.

Extending the Pilot Study

The replication of the learning design in a more complex organization extended the pilot study in five major senses. *First,* the replication constituted a demanding test of the design's usefulness in changing interpersonal and intergroup climates. Briefly, the target units in this study were "stability-oriented" or even "survival-oriented." Their members were grimly conscious of, and often pessimistic about, the rougher organizational days ahead. Table 4 contrasts the essential differences of these stability-oriented target units with the target units in the pilot study, which were "growth-oriented."

Table 4. Characteristics of Two Contrasting Types of Organization Units

Growth-Oriented Units	Stability-Oriented Units
1. Have short organizational histories.	1. Have several decades of organizational history.
2. Exercise marked flexibility in policies and procedures.	2. Exercise considerable rigidity in policies and procedures.
3. Have product lines that are new in markets that are sharply expanding.	3. Have aging or aged product lines in markets that are mature and perhaps declining.
4. Profit opportunities are attractive.	4. Profit opportunities are still good but declining, perhaps precipitously so.
5. Expect substantial growth, with expanding opportunities for promotion.	5. Substantial reductions in personnel will occur, hopefully by attrition only, with few and diminishing opportunities for promotion.
6. Are of apparently growing present and future importance to parent corporation.	6. Are traditionally the source of corporate leadership, but units probably will play lesser role in corporation of the future.
7. Look forward to continued growth.	7. Hope for stability or even a gentle decline.

66. Based on Robert T. Golembiewski, Robert Munzenrider, Stokes B. Carrigan, Arthur Blumberg, and Walter R. Mead, "Changing Climate in a Complex Organization: Interactions between a Learning Design and an Environment," *Journal of the Academy of Management,* Vol. 14 (December, 1971), pp. 465–81.

The stability-oriented units were expected to be more difficult change targets than the units in the pilot study. That is, the learning design could encourage authentic, caring, open, and trusting relations in the stability-oriented units. But the harsh environment would induce powerful forces in opposition. For example, the growth-oriented units grew by some 25 percent in the most recent 18-month period. For the stability-seeking units, the basic hope during the same period was that unavoidable personnel reductions could be achieved by normal attrition.

The basic differences between the two kinds of units implied a reasonable definition of success for this effort at planned change. The basic pattern of change here was expected to be the same as in the pilot study, but less massive changes were expected.

Second, this research dealt directly with three hierarchical levels and involved three additional levels at various stages in the training design. The pilot study, on the other hand, emphasized two hierarchical levels and involved a third level less directly. The present intention is direct. Laboratory approaches to OD must deal with the transfer into complex organizations of learning gained in small units. This research faced that crucial issue more directly than did the pilot study.

Third, the research design underlying the pilot study contained a number of inelegancies and weaknesses, which could be overcome to some degree. For example, the basic research design of this effort was a modified time series, which admits less interpretive ambiguity than the design in the pilot study.

Fourth, this research dealt directly with the reinforcement in broad systems of learning developed in subsystematic groups. Such reinforcement is at the heart of the application of the laboratory approach in complex organizations, but the small managerial N and the widely-spaced observations in the pilot study neither permitted nor required much attention to this critical process.

Fifth, this research tested the replicability of the common training design by using different staffs at different sites. The training design in the pilot study was monitored by a single pair of consultants at one site during a single week. Five different pairs of four consultants monitored the common training design in this research, at five different locations during a three-month interval. This feature permitted an estimate of the degree to which any observed effects can be attributed to the training design, as opposed to the styles of the trainers or the time of training.

Schedule of Training

The training design followed the hierarchy, building upon sensitivity training experiences for organization peers. Levels 1–4 in Figure 6 had

434

laboratory experiences over an extended period. Managers at level 5, the divisional managers, were exposed to sensitivity training during days 15–20 of the schedule. The common design emphasized values and skills appropriate for enhancing the quality of feedback in the organization, with the prime goal of improving communication within and between hierarchical levels. All regional managers, level 6 in Figure 6, subsequently had a similar experience, at one of four separate sites. The managers at levels 5 and 6 provided the data for this study, which assessed the impact of the training design on organizational climate as measured by six administrations of Likert's Profile of Organizational Characteristics, Form S.

The initial learning in T-Groups was tested in confrontation between hierarchical levels, as in the pilot study. In Replication II (see p. 438), for example, two groups of regional managers were the trainees at site B. They had a week-long T-Group followed by nearly two days of confrontations between the regional managers, their two divisional managers, and the manager of National Field Sales. The details of the confrontations were arranged by the trainees, within a common framework, and there were as many patterns as there were cases. Interpersonal and intergroup relations were discussed in a wide variety of formations—sometimes in pairs of individuals, sometimes in pairs of groups, sometimes with several overhead managers present at the same time, and sometimes with only one overhead manager present. The problem dictated the learning formation, as limited by the risk/reward ratio perceived by the managers.

Reinforcing Systematic Changes

Consultants anticipated that the impact of the training design would be vitiated because the training was done in small units at multiple sites over an extended period. Directly, the target was systematic change in values, attitudes, and behaviors. But the training was accomplished in nine subsystematic units at five locations. Hence the need to apply any learning gained by individuals in subsystematic groupings at the level of the total system of National Field Sales. The Reinforcement Session scheduled for days 200–202 in the training design (see p. 438) sought to facilitate such systemwide application.

The rationale for the Reinforcement Session is direct. From a technical standpoint, the necessity of scheduling a number of separate training periods at several sites sets limits on behavioral contagion, or on resonance, in which one's experiences are amplified or heightened because they are clearly shared by many or all relevant others. Some contagion was achieved in the present case by pairing the groups of regional managers,

435

but there was little direct sharing of experiences between the four pairs of regional groups, or between the regional groups and the group of divisional managers.

In a primal sense, then, the Reinforcement Session was intended to provide a community forum to test two crucial aspects of the training design. That is, the session would test the degree of commitment to new attitudes or values that had been developed by individuals in subsystemic units and that could provide guidance for interpersonal and intergroup relations at work. Moreover, the Reinforcement Session also would provide an arena to test the degree to which the actual behaviors of peers and organizational superiors were consistent with laboratory attitudes or values.

The Reinforcement Session had five major planned stages, extending over some two days. They are:

- a public opening session with top management, which proved an unexpected learning opportunity when a regional manager drew attention to an ongoing violation of laboratory norms by top management, resulting in eventual agreement that "this live example shows how difficult what we are trying to do is, despite our best intentions."

- a brief public overview of the overall changes in managers' responses on five administrations of the Likert Profile

- an extensive private review by each of the eight groups of regional managers and by the group of divisional managers of their individual records on each of the Likert Profile items, using summary data reported on large charts which were the private property of the individual groups (the divisional managers first met to discuss their record *qua* group, and later met with their individual groups of regional managers)

- a public report by each of the eight groups of regional managers, which used "force-field analysis" as a conceptual device for focusing on:
  a. the specific forces which over the past 245 days had permitted their regional group to more closely approach the values of the laboratory approach
  b. the specific forces that were yet to be overcome or that might never be overcome

- a brief closing session in which the manager of National Field Sales underscored his strong support of the change program and pledged resources to organization units or individuals who would be interested in specific extensions of the training design for their own purposes.

436

The four consultants perceived major risks in the Reinforcement Session, especially in the last two stages which, at their worst, could have been a saccharine experience. But the logic of the laboratory approach was followed.

Properties of the Research Design

This analysis of an OD program to change the climate of a complex organization can be characterized by five elements. *First,* the observations of change constituted a time-series design without a constant control group. For example, the design for the Dallas group of regional managers may be generalized as $O_1 O_2 X O_3 O_4 O_5 O_6$, where O = Observation and X = Training Intervention. For a variety of reasons, and especially because of the success of the pilot study, management rejected a placebo experience for part of the managerial population. The cost is clear. Basically, any effects observed in a time series may be explainable in terms of hypotheses alternative to the experimental treatment.[67]

The basic research strategy here of replication, as opposed to a strategy of emphasizing experimental controls, has complex roots. In part, the strategy rests on convenience or necessity, as in the general difficulty of providing for controls in field studies, or as in the specific case of top management's rejection of a placebo experience for part of the managerial population. In part, also, the rationale reflects the difficult issues associated with "control groups" or "matched groups" in research about organizational change.[68] Basically, however, the present rationale inheres in the first-generation character of this inquiry. Replications like this one hopefully will generate a need for more precise prediction in another generation of studies, whose goal is the specification of intervening variables and whose product is an expanding theoretical network.

Second, the staggered training design did generate a diminishing quasi-control group, which still had not been exposed to the training experienced by an enlarging experimental population. For example, until day 50 a distinction can be made in the total managerial population:

- Experimental group: Divisional managers
- Quasi-control group: All regional managers

Between days 50 and 65, the experimental group expanded and the quasi-control group lost approximately half its population. The training replications concluded at day 110.

The practical need to stagger training experiences has mixed consequences. To some degree, this feature augments the power of the time-

---

67. Campbell, *op. cit.*
68. Chris Argyris, "Issues in Evaluating Laboratory Education," *Industrial Relations,* Vol. 8 (October, 1968) , pp. 28–40.

series design and helps make less credible explanations of observed effects in terms of hypotheses alternative to the experimental treatment. The major disadvantage of the staggered training design is also clear. Any observed effects will be interactive consequences of at least common design, different consulting team, and time of training. To some degree, of course, these effects can be statistically isolated.

Third, the observational schedule called for six closely spaced administrations of the Likert Profile of Organizational Characteristics, Form S. Form S contains 18 items, each of which is rated twice on each administration:

- as *Now,* or where the respondent perceived that National Field Sales organization actually was on each of the 18 items
- as *Ideal,* or where the respondent desired that National Field Sales organization ideally be on each of the 18 items

The constant reference was the systematic set of interpersonal and intergroup relations in National Field Sales.

The approximate schedule for the six administrations of the Likert Profile, plus the various training activities, was:

Day 1	Observation I
Days 15–22	Training Replication I
Day 45	Observation II
Days 50–60	Training Replication II
Day 80	Observation III
Days 90–110	Training Replication III
Day 140	Observation IV
Day 200	Observation V
Days 200–202	Reinforcement Session
Day 245	Observation VI

The pilot study scheduled administrations of another version of the Profile at approximately four-month intervals and consequently was not sensitive to short-run changes. The closely spaced administrations of the present research were designed to permit getting some idea of the timing of changes in interpersonal and intergroup climate in a geographically dispersed population of managers.

Fourth, individual respondents were identified only as members of divisional or regional units. Anonymity was considered crucial by management, which is one sign of the perceived pretraining climate. Anonymous responses required the use of statistical techniques which made significant demands on the data. Identification of individual respondents would have permitted comparisons of changes over time by more straightforward techniques.

Fifth, due to a reorganization and a serious managerial illness, only six of the original nine organization units were available for the duration of the training design.[69] Separate experiences were designed for the units so affected, but they will not be discussed here. The data analyzed below came from six divisional managers and 37 regional managers, the total universe of managers during the full experimental period.

Basically, this research may be located at the "natural history" stage of empirical inquiry,[70] whose products are more-or-less qualitative classifications of factors that more or less seem to occur together. Specifically, the gross focus is on whether a specific training design tends to induce similar and expected effects in six teams of managers. This is necessary preparation for deductively formulated theories that may follow. But the present research pays a price in significant conceptual and operational lacunae in its approach. For example, the research design looks at one input (training design) and one kind of output (changes in responses to Likert Profile items). This focus neglects some potentially significant intervening variables, such as differences in the individual managers and their life histories, which could significantly influence reactions to the training experience.

Data Analysis

Data generated by six administrations of the Likert Profile indicate that systematic and expected changes took place in the organization units involved in the study. The data relate to two basic questions. First, did any systematic changes take place in organization climate? Second, can these changes be meaningfully said to result from the training design? The data imply that both questions should be answered affirmatively.

Five specific expectations about the impact of the training design on climate were tested. The first expectation tested the proposition that any observed effects were due to the training design rather than to independent and ongoing organizational processes. The latter four expectations were based on the results of the pilot study. Overall, similar effects on Now and Ideal scores were expected. Specifically, the expectations were:

- *Expectation 1.* Self-reports on the Likert Profile would tend to remain the same or decrease[71] for all organization units in observa-

---

69. Two of the missing units, Los Angeles and San Francisco, were reorganized into a single unit about midway in the study, a change due to errors in long-run forecasts about markets and triggered by a set of unexpected opportunities. A separate program of organization development, also based on the laboratory approach, was inaugurated for the newly created unit. The third unit, Boston, was excluded because its regional manager had to be replaced due to a serious turn in a long-term coronary condition, after an extended period of waiting for an expected recovery.
70. F. S. C. Northrop, *The Logic of the Sciences and the Humanities* (New York: Macmillan Co., 1948).
71. See footnote 55.

tions before they are exposed to the initial training experience. These cases may be considered a quasi-control population of decreasing size over time.

Statistically significant changes were not anticipated, but they should be associated with decreases if they are observed.

- *Expectation 2.* Self-reports on the Likert Profile would tend to increase for all organization units in managerial responses immediately following the initial training experience. These cases may be considered as an experimental population of increasing size over time.

- *Expectation 3.* Self-reports on the Likert Profile, on balance, would show mild regression in the second and succeeding observations after the initial training experience. This mild regression, a kind of postlearning slump, showed clearly in earlier studies.

  Statistically significant changes were not anticipated, but they should be associated with decreases in Likert scores if they are observed.

- *Expectation 4.* Managerial self-reports on the Likert Profile would tend to increase for all organization units after the common Reinforcement Session.

- *Expectation 5.* The divisional managers would tend to show a more positive pattern of changes on their Likert self-reports than the regional managers. The underlying rationale is that the divisional managers, who are few in number and who spend more time together, would be in a better position to test top-level commitment to change, as well as actual behavioral change. Divisional managers also would be more able to validate one another's perceptions of intended and actual changes than would the more numerous and geographically dispersed regional managers.

  Statistically significant changes were not expected, but they should be associated with larger scores for divisional managers if they are observed.

Table 5 begins the task of establishing that the expected pattern of changes did occur. This table presents a rough picture of posttreatment trends by considering the mean scores on the 18 items. The conventions are direct: X indicates the timing of the three replications of the initial training design, and R designates the common Reinforcement Session. Based on the pilot study, Expectations 2 and 4 above indicate that the training design should generate increases in Profile scores at 24 points, two for each unit on both Now and Ideal scores. These points are: after versus before the initial training intervention (X) for each unit on Now and Ideal scores; and after versus before the Reinforcement Session (R) for each unit on Now and Ideal scores.

Observations—Now Scores

		1		2		3		4	5		6
	1	12.6	X	13.4		13.9		13.7	13.6	R	14.9
	2	11.5	QC	10.3	X	11.4		11.5	10.3	R	12.0
Organization	3	13.0	QC	12.2	X	13.0		13.0	12.6	R	13.6
Units	4	12.4	QC	11.7	QC	11.2	X	12.2	12.6	R	12.3
	5	12.5	QC	11.8	QC	12.1	X	12.0	9.8	R	12.7
	6	13.3	QC	11.9	QC	10.5	X	13.7	13.9	R	14.5

Observations—Ideal Scores

		1		2		3		4	5		6
	1	15.9	X	16.9		17.9		17.2	17.2	R	17.9
	2	17.6	QC	17.7	X	17.8		18.1	17.9	R	18.5
Organization	3	17.0	QC	16.7	X	17.7		17.5	18.1	R	17.7
Units	4	17.0	QC	17.2	QC	16.9	X	17.4	18.0	R	17.7
	5	16.2	QC	15.7	QC	16.3	X	16.3	14.9	R	16.8
	6	16.7	QC	16.4	QC	16.8	X	17.5	17.6	R	17.6

Note: X = Initial training intervention.
QC = Quasi controls.
R = Reinforcement Session.

Table 5 shows that the expected increases in Profile scores did follow the training intervention and the Reinforcement Session in 18 of 24 cases. The pattern of increases is more marked for Now scores, where 10 of the 12 cases met expectations. For the Ideal scores, there were eight increases and two ties in the 12 cases. The data thus suggest that increases in Ideal scores are triggered by anticipation of the training design, while increases in Now scores follow it.

The magnitude of the changes in Table 5 is patently small, but the gross data do not permit a direct interpretation. Basically, Observation 1 does not provide a reliable base line against which to judge change. Indeed, considerable evidence suggests that early responses to the Likert Profile were consciously doctored by managers "to make the boss look good." Consistently, note that in seven of the eight cases labeled QC in Table 5, Now scores decrease in self-reports from managers in units which had not yet experienced the training intervention. There are at least two possible interpretations of this pattern: that managers were no longer inflating scores to protect themselves or their managers; or that interpersonal and intergroup relations were worsening over time. In either case, early responses are not an adequate base line against which to judge the extent of the observed changes. Only one thing is clear. The observed changes in Profile scores bucked long-run trends underway in the organization that were independent of the training design.

In any case, the data in Table 5 seem to be generated by nonrandom forces working in the expected direction, which implies the power of the OD design to induce the intended effects. Page's L supports this conclusion. This statistic tests for linear trends in ordered data. Here, the statistic tests whether the scores on the second observation are greater than those on the first, whether the scores on the third are greater than on the second observation, and so on, against the null hypothesis that the data contain no systematic pattern of differences. In the present case, the values of Page's L for both Now and Ideal scores reject the null hypothesis. For Now scores, the probability that the changes in Table 5 are random is less than .01; the value of Page's L for Ideal scores surpasses the .001 level.[72]

The values of Page's L also provide support for Expectations 2 and 4. In fact, the statistic no doubt understates the actual trend. That is, major positive changes for all organization units were not anticipated until all units had had their training experience, a condition which would first exist at O_4. Only the division managers should show increases in Profile scores beginning with O_2, to put the point otherwise. Patently, the changes in Profile scores after the training intervention and the Reinforcement Session were great enough to overbalance the fact that the staggered training design was not extended to all organization units until midway in the observational schedule.

An analysis of item-by-item changes is necessary to demonstrate that the intended effects actually did occur, and that demonstration must be involved. The data come from a large table with 3,240 cells, 18 Likert items $\times$ 6 units $\times$ 2 kinds of Likert scores $\times$ 15 paired-comparisons of observations 1–6. That table is not reproduced here, for obvious reasons, but its major trends will be spotlighted. Duncan's Multiple-Range test provides a standard against which to judge the magnitude of the differences, even though it is a very conservative indicator of statistical significance for present purposes.[73]

Expectation 1. The data indicate that self-reports on the Likert Profile items remained constant or decreased for all organization units in self-reports from managers before their exposure to the initial training ex-

---

72. E. G. Page, "Ordered Hypotheses for Multiple Treatments: A Significance Test for Ordered Ranks," *Journal of the American Statistical Association*, Vol. 58 (1963), pp. 216–24. For a brief discussion of the technique, see R. J. Senter, *Analyses of Data: Introductory Statistics for the Behavioral Sciences* (Glenview, Ill.: Scott, Foresman & Co., 1969), pp. 369–89.

The computed value of Page's L for these data are 488 for the Now scores and 533 for the Ideals. Minimum values of L for significance at the .01 and .001 level are, respectively, 486 and 499.

Page's L is most efficient with data in which no tied scores are present across ranks. Accordingly, computations were carried out to the second decimal in order to establish absolute rankings. When ties are present, the value of L increases appreciably.

73. Senter, *op. cit.*, pp. 281–92.

442

perience. In summary, over 74 percent of the Now scores show a decrease or no change in score for the quasi controls, comparing O_1 to all other Likert scores obtained from managers before they underwent their training experience. If only "large changes" are considered, the case is even clearer. Arbitrarily, a large increase (decrease) is defined as a change $\geqq +1.0$ or $\leqq -1.0$ on a mean Profile score. Only 21 of 198 paired comparisons show large increases on the Likert scores for the quasi controls. The data also show 109 large decreases, in contrast. Two of the decreases achieved the .05 level, by the Duncan's Multiple-Range test, while none of the increases in Profile scores did so. For Ideal scores, the distribution is approximately 50/50, with no statistically significant differences. This pattern suggests that Ideal scores had a greater tendency to increase in anticipation of the training experience, while Now scores strongly tended to decrease until after that experience.

If anything, then, interpersonal and intergroup relations were stable and probably worsening in the six organization units, as measured by the Likert Profile. This supports Expectation 1 above, whether the climate was actually worsening or whether managers simply were more realistic in describing the climate of National Field Sales. Consequently, any increases in Likert scores cannot easily be attributed to ongoing maturational processes or historical events independent of the training design. The training design probably had to buck a substantial trend, in fact.

Expectation 2. The data reflect a strong overall tendency for Likert scores to increase for all managers in the observation immediately following their exposure to the training design, and that pattern was especially dominant if one deviant organization unit is excepted. This strong tendency implies the usefulness of the training design, even in the harsh business environment in which the six units existed.

Supporting data may be sampled. For the Now scores, 82 percent of the paired comparisons showed increases in Profile scores in the observation immediately following the training intervention. In addition, over half of the decreases or no-changes occurred in unit 5. For the Ideal scores, the pattern was similar but a little less marked: 70 percent of the comparisons showed increases after exposure to the training experience. Unit 5 was again deviant, accounting for nearly 40 percent of the decreases or no-changes in Profile scores.

Again, the patterning of change is more consistent than its magnitude is great. For example, only 8 of the 216 relevant cases attain statistical significance, as determined by Duncan's Multiple-Range test.

Expectation 3. Self-reports on the Likert Profile showed a definite tendency to regress in the observations following the one immediately after the initial training experience. Like the decreases in the pilot study, these regressions typically did not attain usually accepted levels of statistical significance. The data generated in the replication study are consistent with the pilot study and also support Expectation 3. Specifically:

Now Scores	Ideal Scores
51 of 108 changes were negative, comparing the second observation after the experimental treatment with the preceding one	34 of 108 changes were negative, comparing the second observation after the experimental treatment with the preceding one

Only two of the decreases achieve statistical significance, as measured by Duncan's Multiple-Range test. No increase achieved the .05 level.

The direction of the changes, then, supports Expectation 3 above. However, the magnitude of the changes is such that they cannot unqualifiedly be attributed to nonrandom causes.

The regression erodes only part of the increases in Profile scores following the initial training experience, as in the pilot study. The generalization holds for all organization units, and especially so if unit 5 is again recognized as a deviant case. Comparisons of O_5 to the various observations immediately preceding the initial training experience for the various units help establish the point. Approximately 70 percent of the 216 relevant comparisons still show greater scores for O_5 although only 12 of the increases attain the .05 level on Duncan's Multiple-Range test. If unit 5 is removed, the cases showing greater scores on O_5 than on the observation immediately preceding the initial training intervention increase to exactly 80 percent of the total cases. Differences between Now and Ideal scores are minor.

This regression suggests a kind of postlearning slump, or two steps forward and one step back. The regression occurs, roughly, as some but not all of the learning is being consolidated or applied. The underlying notion is one of building plateaus as bases for further learning, a kind of consolidating of gains and of equilibrating expectations to reality.

Expectation 4. The common Reinforcement Session had the anticipated effect of increasing Profile scores, on balance, which supports Expectation 4. The pattern is especially marked for the Now scores. Nearly 80 percent of these scores show greater Profile scores for O_6 than for O_5. However, approximately one in seven of the increases are less than 1.0 changes on the 20-point Likert Profile, and only two of the increases achieve the .05 level on the Duncan test.

The Reinforcement Session had less of an impact on the Ideal scores. Specifically, about 65 percent of the Ideal scores are greater for O_6 and O_5, and only three increases in 216 cases reach the .05 level. The data for Ideal scores further urge the notion that they tend to increase early in the change program, even in anticipation of the training design. Consistently, one third of the increases after the Reinforcement Session

444

amount to changes of less than 1.0 on Likert scores. The image is one of rising expectations about desired interpersonal and intergroup relations, followed by actual changes in those relations. This effect was not observable in the pilot study, due to the extended periods between observations.

Another way of looking at the effects of the Reinforcement Session is to estimate the changes that occurred between early observations and O_6. Compare observations 2 and 6, for example. Nearly 88 percent of the Profile scores increase over that interval, although only 12 of 216 increases attain the .05 level, as determined by Duncan's Multiple-Range test. No decreases attain the .05 level.

Expectation 5. The divisional managers show a somewhat more positive pattern of changes on the Likert Profile than the five groups of their subordinate regional managers. There are many ways of suggesting the point. For example, the divisional managers clearly met two major expectations in more cases than the regionals. In sum:

	Divisional Managers	Regional Managers
Increases in Profile scores after X	92%	77%
Increases in Profile scores after R	100%	73%

Expectation 5 rests basically on greater opportunities for testing and validation open to the divisional managers concerning, for example, the benign intentions of the manager of National Field Sales. The pictures in the heads of the regional managers—whether based on experience or fantasy—were assumed to be more resistant to change over the 245-day period of observation. If nothing else, the divisional managers were in a better position to test their trust in the manager's sincerity and conviction about changing the climate in National Field Sales. They could directly observe evolving changes in the manager's values and behaviors, since they had numerous contacts with him in the period surrounding the training. Consequently, divisional managers would be more likely to modify their values and behavior earlier and more markedly than their subordinates, the regional managers. For the regional managers, their initial testing for change was basically confined to the brief confrontations programmed into the training design. This limited the regional managers in both testing and developing trust in the manager's motives. In addition, the confrontations were difficult arenas in which the manager attempted to reflect authenticity and openness, and his success varied greatly from case to case. Consistent with the data above, for example, his performance with unit 5 was by far the most inadequate, by mutual agreement of all parties.

Conclusion

Two conclusions are implicit in the data above. The first is that the training design did not lead to any major unexpected consequences. The pattern of change was anticipated, even in substantial detail in some cases. Even in a more complex organization in a harsh business environment, that is, the training design seems capable of helping induce major changes in the patterns of interpersonal and intergroup relations, both existing and desired.

The second conclusion is that the magnitude of the changes in this case is not as great as in the pilot study, but no easy conclusions seem appropriate. For example, the explanation that the training design "did not work" does not clearly apply in this case. Even including unit 5, indeed, the design had regular if not massive effects. This regularity is difficult to dismiss. On the other hand, the magnitude of changes is such that one must stress the qualifications that statistically random variation might explain the changes in Profile scores, as an alternative to explaining the consistent pattern of results as a consequence of the training design.

Some reasons for the smaller changes seem obvious enough. Patently, the results may provide more evidence that complex systems are more resistant to change than simpler ones. Or it may be that changes in complex systems simply require more time to work themselves out, a possibility that will be tested by another administration of the Likert Profile approximately one year after the last administration reported here. Alternatively, the training design in the present case may somehow have been less impactful. Very likely, in addition, environmental differences may have been crucial intervening variables. The pilot study dealt with units that had a bullish future. They had major problems, but they were relatively pleasant problems associated with expanding markets and growing staff and major promotion possibilities. The units in the present study faced a more uncertain future, perhaps even a dismal one. Significant personnel reductions were a real threat, traditional product lines no longer had the magic of yesteryear, and the bloom was definitely off the rose in terms of near-term potential, both in the organization and in the industry. At best, they were involved in a holding action. Reasonably, the units in the present study would generally constitute a more difficult target for a program of organization change.

Given these working explanations, indeed, one can persuasively argue that the smallish magnitudes of change in the replication are only apparent, because interpersonal and intergroup relations were so severely stressed during the period of training and observation. The smallish increases observed in Likert scores, in this view, must be considered in the context of major decreases that could have occurred in the absence

446

of the OD program. Even breaking even may be quite a feat under some circumstances, epigrammatically.

These working explanations are an optimistic approach to the smallish magnitudes of change in this study. One might alternatively argue, for example, that the larger size of National Field Sales or its greater number of hierarchical levels basically explains the fact that the training design generated the same pattern but smaller magnitudes of change than the pilot study. To the extent that size and hierarchical levels do explain the results here, the prognosis for programs of planned organizational change is less favorable. For large size and numerous hierarchical levels have to be successfully incorporated in any approach to planned change that has pretensions of dealing with major organizational realities.

The basic thrust of this study also deserves direct statement. The gross aim of the statistical analysis here is to expose patterns inherent in the data. A variety of straightforward comparisons were made above, usually with techniques of modest power which did not imply conditions that overpower the data. The underlying concern was that some statistical techniques might obscure or altogether miss patterns in the data rather than highlight them. For example, separate analyses of variance were run on the data, and the results support the pattern of results sketched above. Those results are not reported here due to their complexity, and also because the technique imposed conditions which the data did not always meet.

The concern about not overpowering the data with techniques derives from the properties of the measuring instrument used as well as exigencies of the research design. Data collected with the Likert Profile instrument are ordinal at best, which implies some indeterminacy in the use (or misuse) of parametric tests such as analysis of variance and Duncan's Multiple-Range test. Moreover, the Likert scale is attenuated at its top end. This leads to a clustering of scores, particularly Ideal scores, as an artifact of the measuring instrument. An additional problem is encountered in the short version of the Likert Profile, Form S, used here. No effort is made to control for response set on Form S. Use of the short form was dictated here, however, by the expectation of respondent fatigue over repeated administrations. The problems created by this tradeoff are serious and are aggravated even more by the requirement of anonymity imposed on the research. This condition made it impossible to check in any systematic manner for possible autocorrelation effects across administrations.

While such problems are serious, they are not considered overpowering. Such problems are to be expected in an essentially natural-history inquiry such as this. The need now is to devise both more rigorous research designs and more sensitive measuring instruments with which to monitor subsequent replications of the training design.

F. INTERVENTIONS AIMED AT COMPLEX ORGANIZATIONS: FACILITATING CRUCIAL LINKAGES AND COORDINATION

This section provides particularistic counterpoint to the wholistic emphasis in the preceding section. Section E above was concerned with OD applications in complex organizations that sought sweeping changes in the climate or style of interpersonal and intergroup relations. The focus here is on the linking and coordination of the subunits of complex organizations, with the specific focus on three central perspectives. Conveniently, if simplistically, these perspectives may be labeled: (1) command relationships, which are "vertical"; (2) relationships between peers in separate organization units, which are "horizontal" and can be collaborative or antagonistic; and (3) relationships between two or more separate organization units that must be merged, which relationships consequently must become "integrative."

Initial stress will be on the *vertical ties* that link all organizations. Specifically, the focal question is: How can the laboratory approach help engage feedback processes between a superior and his subordinates in a complex organization? The lily of this point defies gilding. Up-and-down communication linkages are crucial ones in the effectiveness of any organization. Such linkages may be reciprocally open, or they may be variously closed. The focus below is on two OD designs that seek to minimize the latter and to maximize the former condition. Which condition exists makes for profound differences in the quality and effectiveness of an organization. The OD designs seeking vertical linkages illustrate one approach with ad hoc, temporary groups, in Subsection 3 below. Subsection 4 illustrates a second approach with permanent work groups, on a mass scale.

Horizontal linkages between units of an organization also are critical. Thus Subsection 5 details the design and typical consequences of one OD design which seeks to improve these linkages. The OD vehicle is called the confrontation design. Horizontal linkages have been neglected in the literature,[1] and more's the pity. To be sure, superior-subordinate or command relationships are important in determining what happens in organizations. But lateral relationships between peers—whether collaborative or antagonistic—often are critical determinants of the effectiveness and of the quality of life in complex organizations.[2] Hence the emphasis in Subsection 5.

Units of complex organizations increasingly face ticklish issues of integration or disintegration as various mergers or unmergers succeed one another. The exigencies of technological, social, and product change are massively compelling, especially given the common strategy of creating unity in one social unit by differentiating it from other units in ways that complicate merger or even collaboration. For example, Communist China clearly uses the symbol of "war-mongering U.S.A." as a device for inducing home-front Chinese loyalties, as well as for rationalizations of deprivations felt by the citizenry. Various American groups similarly use the symbol of "atheistic Communism." What may be effective internally, to make the obvious point, can create problems in the relations between the countries.

Hence, Subsection 6 below deals with a subject that is as old as mankind, and as current as tomorrow's cold-war maneuver. The theme is the integration without which complex organizations could not exist, let alone societies.

3. ENGAGING FEEDBACK PROCESSES IN LARGE ORGANIZATIONS: AD HOC GROUPS COMMUNICATE UP THE HIERARCHY

The primal linkage in organizations is vertical, between one hierarchical level and another level with broader responsibilities. Indeed, without viable vertical linkages, not even modest-sized organizations could exist for very long. Moreover, despite devices for reducing the social distance

---

1. Henry A. Landsberger, "The Horizontal Dimension in Bureaucracy," *Administrative Science Quarterly*, Vol. 6 (December, 1961), pp. 299–332.
2. Leonard R. Sayles, *Managerial Behavior* (New York: McGraw-Hill Book Co., 1964), esp. pp. 58–82.

between hierarchical levels—such as decentralized patterns of delegation, power-sharing, and the like—hierarchical levels there will be. And the quality of upward communication will remain a critical factor in an organization's effectiveness.

The illustration below deals with one OD design for engaging feedback processes in large organizations,[3] under inhospitable circumstances. It will move from description of the organizational context in which the OD design was introduced to discussion of the nature of the design and its consequences. The illustration will conclude with a rationale that helps explain the effectiveness of the simple design.

a. The Organizational Context:
A Degenerative System between Hierarchical Levels

The organizational context into which the OD design to induce upward feedback· was introduced was a classic example of a degenerative system. The major factors contributing to this condition may be sketched briefly. *First,* the parent organization was beset by a variety of massive problems that called into serious question what it had traditionally done and how that was to be done in the future. The "what" and the "how" might even be unrecognizably changed in a short period of time.

Second, the prime consequence was a massive holding action. From lower levels, it appeared to be inaction born of indecisiveness and unwillingness to "bite the bullet." To those at the executive levels, the holding action was unavoidable as necessary data were being gathered, as options were being analyzed, and so on.

Third, the overall organizational climate was characterized by rumors and secrecy, in reciprocal sequences. That is, rumors flourished in the absence of clear statements of where the organization was going. And secrecy characterized executive deliberations, because news of even the most tentative possible option would sweep through the organization as the day's infallible pronouncement. This suggests an organizational equivalent of the classic double bind.

Fourth, a mutual despair clearly set in. Those at lower levels of organization often concluded that management decision-making did not inspire confidence. Those at upper levels emphasized the lack of impulse control

---

3. For other similar designs, see Matthew B. Miles *et al.,* "Data Feedback and Organizational Change in a School System," mimeographed (Paper presented at Annual Meeting, American Sociological Association, August 29, 1966) ; and John L. Aiteen, "Notes on Employee Surveys as O.D. Stimulants," mimeographed (Midland, Mich.: Dow Chemical Co., n.d.) .

For an insightful analysis of how degenerative interaction systems can develop in large organizations, and how the laboratory approach can help moderate or reverse them, see Jerry B. Harvey and D. Richard Albertson, "Neurotic Organizations: Symptoms, Causes and Treatment, Parts I and II," *Personnel Journal,* Vol. 50 (September, 1971) , pp. 694–99 and (October, 1971) , pp. 770–77.

of those subordinate to them, and their lack of comprehension of the complex issues that needed deliberate thrashing-out.

Fifth, major personnel reductions-in-force traumatized the organization. A major reduction in 1969 was widely regarded as the purge to end all purges. The usual explanations about "trimming the fat" and "tightening the belt" were common, and they may have induced some over-confidence among the survivors. The unexpected other shoe fell about a year after the first reduction-in-force and cut very deeply. The organization was shaken, especially by such cruel binds; it appeared that "The organization is asking for more loyalty from its employees, but it seems to feel little loyalty to its employees."

Middle managers felt particularly whipsawed through it all. They had to absorb the reasonable concerns of their employees, but they received little of substance from the executive levels, many basic choices still being under analysis. The managers were truly in the middle, above the lower levels and outside the confidences of the executive suite.

b. A New Division Manager:
Toward Reestablishing Viable Vertical Linkages

In the aftermath of the second reduction-in-force, a new Division Manager appointed from outside the organization set as one of his major priorities the reestablishment of solid communication links with his middle managers. At the initiative of an OD specialist, the Division Manager authorized a simple feedback design, to dramatize his intentions as well as to begin massive upward communication. The design involved all middle managers—approximately 60 of them—meeting in five-man groups composed of the widest possible range of functions or activities. Their charge was simple. They were to prepare reports for the division manager, of no specified form, but touching at least on:

- what they liked about their division and company
- what they disliked, or what they were concerned about

The groups attended two scheduled meetings and continued to meet on their own initiative afterwards. The Division Manager then would meet with each of the ad hoc groups to discuss their reports, share information, clarify ambiguities, and so on.

One Illustrative Report

The basic intention was to reverse a degenerative sequence, and the ad hoc groups had to decide on the specific level of openness which they felt was risky enough. The reports covered a broad range, some with dazzle and some cautiously. One group, for example, described its feelings

451

Figure 1. Feedback Report Induced by OD Design

CONFIDENTIAL

January 22, 1971

Memo To: Division Manager

From: Messrs. A, B, C, D, and E

Subject: Division Feedback Exercise

Attached is an outline of our discussions during last week's feedback session and subsequent meetings. We appreciate the opportunity to bring these matters to your attention.

DIVISION FEEDBACK EXERCISE

Positive Signs

We sense stronger leadership at the top, and have guarded optimism that the Division Manager will develop a strong team.

We have seen examples of greater decisiveness; greater willingness to take positive action after reasonable evaluation of pertinent facts and opinions (programs L and Z).

Division must have a more articulate voice to express its viewpoint to top management. Recent events (A, B, C, and D are samples) are promising examples of what we'd like to see more of.

The strong commitment to management by objectives (MBO), while the implementation will be painful at times, should get us results in the long run.

Concerns	Recommendations

Planning and Priorities

1. Top management should have better appreciation/feeling for what is reasonable and/or realistic when making requests for action or initiating work projects. Since top management tends to deal in more abstract, philosophical problems, we feel they lose sight, from time to time, of nuts and bolts of how things are done on the firing line.

   As part of this, we feel top management should do a better, more thorough, job of setting priorities before those below devote a lot of time and effort to assignments. Project P cited as example where great deal of effort was expended before learning project impossible from legal standpoint.

1. Top management should develop greater knowledge/appreciation of complexities of their areas of responsibility. Also they should not always assume attitude their people can do anything and/or surmount all odds. But, middle management should say no or be more forceful in advising superiors of unrealistic requests.

2. Great deal of concern expressed for where we're going and how we're going to get there. Considerable reservations (or lack of faith) in some recent and/or planned ventures implemented as stop-gap measures; for example:
   a. Product A—question $ payoff in view of eroding market potential.
   b. Product B—extremely time-consuming effort that will probably lose money.
   c. Product C—turned out to be a real detraction from earnings.

   Also related to this, some in group expressed concern over whether top management is giving enough time to serious introspection in developing long-range plans. For example, can we really compete in market Z when our plant costs are so high?

2. Feel major problem with this area of concern involves a lack of communications from top management on what's behind these projects in terms of decision-making process, alternatives, and financial risks. Perhaps if people knew more about these matters, they'd have more confidence in getting various ventures underway.

3. We are concerned about the arbitrary and uncoordinated manner in which cost-reduction programs are being implemented. Some of the steps taken indicate top management has no confidence in the ability of middle

3. Undoubtedly, many of the changes will result in significant reductions in our operating cost and therefore are needed. However, when the changes are strung out consecutively, each one seems only to put another nail in the

Figure 1—continued

management to operate efficiently within budget guidelines.

One example of uncoordinated planning was a series of cost-reduction steps taken within the past 18 months. There were significant layoffs in 1969 and again in 1970. A month later new policy was issued revising downward the timing and amount of salary increases of remaining employees. Cost-reduction programs were imposed arbitrarily without regard to the impact they would have on daily operations. Severance policies were modified a month ago to eliminate "windfalls."

Airline travel policies are currently being revised. Wasn't tourist air travel tried before, and rejected because of insignificant savings? Management should explain what each policy change means in terms of savings and report this information honestly.

4. We are concerned that the current profit center approach of charging for services can work against positive benefits. We suspect that Subsidiaries M and O probably are not taking advantage of services in other areas of the company because they cannot afford the cost. For the budget people, this probably seems proper, but if the spin-off operations become less efficient because of this, it can only work to the disadvantage of the corporation.

Human Resources

5. Workloads have increased to the point where there is some concern with our ability to get the job done in the best possible manner.

Time and priority pressures are causing managers to sacrifice attention to the kind of supervisory (and development of subordinate) duties they feel are necessary. This situation can have detrimental effects on:
   a. morale
   b. efficiency
   c. development of adequate back-up talent

6. We do not see any evidence, other than occasional lip service, of an overt managerial development program at division or corporate level. Such programs would seem important to:
   a. progress of individuals
   b. development of the strongest possible organization
   c. promotion from within

coffin. It would be much better to plan the necessary changes and make them simultaneously, so the employees could concentrate on what needs to be done to improve our future rather than worry about what further jobs, benefits, and privileges will be lost.

In the case of cost-reduction programs or travel policy changes, we would appreciate the opportunity to participate in finding solutions to the problems rather than merely accepting a dictated alternative. This would give us a sense of "ownership" in the decision and more commitment to its successful implementation.

4. Don't let "budgets" (particularly where fixed overhead costs are involved) influence what is and should be done. Something between a no-charge system and total charging where even a discussion is entered on the charge sheet could surely be worked out.

5. While we recognize that all workloads will and should be heavier than in the past, we must:
   a. minimize unnecessary or unrealistic projects
   b. have earlier dropping of projects that have little chance for real success
   c. be satisfied with less information for decision-making.

Must give recognition to the need for supervisory/managerial requirements in priority setting.

Should also give managers more input in judging value of assignments and allow more questioning of priorities. Trade-offs and alternatives are as important to priority setting as to budgeting.

6. Design and undertake, with input from middle management, specific development programs.

453

Figure 1—continued

7. A lack of credibility has long existed in some corporate communications. This credibility gap has been widened recently in communications re salary policy changes, severance pay and insurance policy, the establishment and discontinuance of the cost-reduction study.

7. Don't sugar coat the message. Don't assume managers are unable to see through specious arguments or explanations. The cure for this problem is obvious; we need management to communicate with us honestly and frankly so that reductions in staff, benefits, and programs can be put in perspective, particularly with respect to the anticipated results.

8. On Division matters it is evident that the flow of communications down varies from one department to another.

8. Make a greater effort to insure prompt and simultaneous downward flow of information. The distribution of the '71 Marketing Operating Plan, while it carries certain risks, is, in balance, a very positive step forward in communication.

of being a mushroom: "kept in the dark, up to their neck in fertilizer, and waiting to be canned." Quite revealing, that metaphor. The example in Figure 1 represents the more extensive, studied, and open of these reports. Brief or descriptive labels have been substituted for names of products, projects, or references that have no meaning to the outside reader. Otherwise, the report appears as it was submitted.

c. Forces Encouraging Openness: Why Such Simple OD Designs Can Succeed

A number of factors help explain why such open reports as that in Figure 1 were generated by a simple OD design. Seven factors seem most relevant. *First,* all middle managers in this case had been exposed to a sensitivity training experience in the year or two preceding their involvement in this OD feedback design. The OD design, indeed, was presented as an organizational extension of that initial training, as an opportunity to put into practice the values, attitudes, and behavioral skills that had been worked on in T-Groups. The assumption is that this earlier training experience contributed to the preparation of reports.

Second, in cases such as the one above, the OD feedback design amounts to taking the cork out of the communication bottle. The very act of requesting feedback thus may generate a gushing forth of repressed material. Indeed, the factor of catharsis may be so dominant that the products of such designs, once expressed, may seem to be more pointed than is appropriate. Once the concerns are ventilated, in sum, they can be set in a more realistic perspective.

Third, as in cases like the present one, there may be a tendency to give a new authority figure a chance to prove himself. If he makes a point of asking for feedback and commits many hours of time to the task, the initial bias probably is to assume that the request means what it says.

This is particularly probable when, as in this case, middle managers wanted to hear just such a request.

Fourth, group consensus may help give expression to items that individuals might feel inhibited about revealing. Often, such feedback designs make organization members aware of how many things they do share. Such reinforcement of observations, or whatever, is very potent stuff indeed.[4] The potential loss is the failure to report the off-beat or deviant notion that could be significant. Many of the reports in this case indicated minority opinions, which is a healthy sign.

Fifth, anonymity may help generate openness, although that particular sword cuts several ways. In this case, anonymity for individuals was possible. But the group clearly owned its report and had to be willing to discuss it face-to-face with the Division Manager. This feature may have smoothed some of the edges of some reports, but the manager preferred not to deal with totally anonymous feedback.

Sixth, the competition between groups can be a force encouraging openness, up to a point. Beyond some indeterminate point, that competition could help generate reports with a quality of "Can you top this?" This quality may be false to reality.

Seventh, action is no doubt the major motivator of openness in such OD feedback designs. Initially, the *hope* of action may be enough. Beyond that, only the *expectation* of action is likely to be a motivator. Feedback without action is likely to be perceived as manipulative, or worse. Indeed, if no action is anticipated in response to feedback, it hardly matters whether the feedback is open or accurate. Hence the Division Manager was careful to act on the feedback reports wherever he could, to initiate studies where necessary, and to explain lack of action where he had no other choice. For the new Manager was serious about reestablishing viable vertical communication linkages between himself and middle managers.

4. BUILDING FEEDBACK PROCESSES INTO LARGE ORGANIZATIONS: TEAM DEVELOPMENT ON A MASS SCALE

Both the risk and the reward of OD efforts escalate when the target is permanent work groups. Successes, and failures, will tend to live far beyond the OD intervention. The focus below is on one such high risk/ reward design and some of its consequences. The design immediately involved some 400 managers and salesmen who staffed 33 geographic marketing units. Thus the design not only dealt with permanent groups,

---

4. Robert T. Golembiewski, *The Small Group* (Chicago: University of Chicago Press, 1962), esp. pp. 9–26 and 46–56.

but with substantial numbers of them. Indeed, the design may be unique in this respect.

a. The Immediate Past History:
When Stability-Oriented Became Survival-Oriented

The 400 participants in the design had not long before experienced a major trauma. Market conditions required a cutback of some 20 percent in the national field-sales force, and the 400 were the survivors. Section E above reports some earlier, substantial OD work with the divisional and regional managers of this salesforce some 18 months before the ax fell so decisively and cut so deeply. The managers were described as stability-oriented in Section E, and their hope was that the inevitable reduction in force would be accomplished by normal attrition. It was not to be. Not only did market conditions fail to improve, but turnover among salesmen and managers reached all-time lows, due to the worsening national economy. Stability-oriented became survival-oriented, in short.

In addition, other major changes had occurred at a number of critical points. Most relevant, a new head of marketing had been appointed shortly after the cutback in personnel, and he had two distinguishing characteristics. First, he was not widely known to the field-sales force, although he had some years previously worked for the firm. Second, he had resigned from the very marketing division he now headed. The circumstances of his resignation are relevant. He cut his blooming relationship in a strong and widely circulated letter. The marketing division was on a collision course with reality, his letter announced. He emphasized, among other factors, that: officials were essentially avoiding a number of tough decisions forced by market conditions, communications were worsening, and a growing make-believe atmosphere was inhibiting a flexible response to a rapidly changing marketplace. Necessary action was avoided by a "paralysis of analysis" and vain hopes for a better day. Three years later he was back, in command this time.

b. Some Goals and a Design:
Toward a Regenerative System

The situation in the marketing division was a delicate one, which could easily become worse. And the approach to it was direct. The goals were basically two:

- to begin *team*-development activities for the 33 regional sales groups and to face problems as they were, as openly and directly as possible

456

- to begin to develop a new climate for the total field-sales organization, consistent with these basic thrusts of the new marketing head:
  a. to "tell it like it is," from all levels
  b. to avoid "promising rose gardens" to stimulate sales-force morale in bogus or unrealistic ways
  c. to develop open communication linkages—up, down, and across the marketing organization—to increase the validity and reliability of information available in the system for the hard decisions that still had to be made

In terms of the vocabulary introduced earlier, the overall goal was at least to build toward a more regenerative marketing system, if indeed the goal was not to reverse a degenerative system that was worsening, and fast. The fear was patent: that the trauma of the reduction-in-force would freeze salesmen into protective behavioral patterns that would increase the chances of maladaptive responses to the changes and challenges in products and markets that were still needed, and which the national sales meeting would help introduce. Failure to meet those changes and challenges effectively would have profound organizational and personal consequences.

The learning design was clean in its structure, if ponderous in execution. A national sales meeting was called, the first in the firm's recent history. The sequence of the learning flow, with an approximate balance of time and emphasis, can be sketched as:

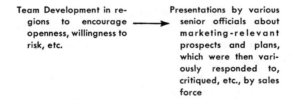

Whenever possible, the basic strategy was to induce action or decision in relation to issues as they came up. The point of it was a sense of marketing newly on the move. At times, it was possible to respond on the spot. For example, perhaps most of the surviving salesmen were interested in manpower planning estimates for the next year. Put otherwise, they were interested in whether still another cutback was planned. Traditionally, the estimates were highly confidential. This time salesmen were told how many average salesmen positions had been budgeted. This was not only a direct and correct answer. As with many anxieties, the anticipation was more enervating than the reality.[5] Given even low projections about

5. Richard S. Lazarus, *Psychological Stress and the Coping Process* (New York: McGraw-Hill Book Co., 1966), pp. 35–38.

normal turnover, indeed, the budgeted figure implied that some new hiring probably would be needed some months down the track. In many other cases, of course, action was not possible. Alternatively, then, ongoing deliberations were described and, whenever possible, likely dates for decision or action were shared.

The public theme of the regional team-development design was on feedback, in stereo, as it were. Over two days, the regional units gave and received feedback about:

- managerial tasks and styles,[6] as preferred by the men and as practiced by their regional managers
- functional roles,[7] as they were present or absent in each of the regions
- individual needs[8] of each regional member, as these were satisfied or frustrated in regional interaction
- properties of each region as an organization unit[9]
- skills in giving and receiving feedback[10]

The design of each learning unit was generically similar: brief cognitive inputs were used to help men organize their own experiences as members of a regional team, with the goals of seeing themselves and others more clearly and of beginning to build more effective and satisfying relations. In the case of functional roles, for example, a resource person sketched the differences between three kinds of roles and described their relevance to team-functioning. The roles were: Task-Oriented, Group Maintenance, and Self-Oriented. Then each participant was requested individually to look at himself and his colleagues in terms of their roles in the regional unit, noting which specific individuals tended to fill which roles. Each participant used a special form which listed numerous examples of the three basic roles. Subsequently, region members could share and discuss their role identifications, as they

---

6. A case study involved the selection for promotion of a manager from a list of possibles. This task had the projective quality of encouraging participants to surface and analyze their criteria for assessing a manager's style and performance, first in the case study and for later application to their own flesh-and-blood manager.

7. The traditional distinctions were made. See Robert T. Golembiewski and Arthur Blumberg (eds.), *Sensitivity Training and the Laboratory Approach* (Itasca, Ill.: F. E. Peacock Publishers, Inc., 1970), pp. 141–56.

8. Schutz's FIRO–B Model of needs was used, but participants used only verbal guidelines to rate their own needs, as opposed to the available questionnaires. See William C. Schutz, *FIRO–B* (New York: Holt, Rinehart & Winston, 1958).

9. Participants analyzed data from 6 items of the Likert Profile, which they had previously completed and which had been scored for them. Note that none of this data is reported in Table 1.

10. The basic design followed the guidelines for feedback in Section A of Part II, Subsection 1a. A few samples were analyzed by a resource person, but the basic focus was on pieces of feedback previously written up by participants as part of the subdesign. These were further analyzed in the regions as individuals felt free to share their feedback items and to analyze them in terms of the guidelines.

wished. Most wished to do so, and discussions tended to be lively and animated. Each learning unit closed similarly, also. The format for summarizing and transitioning was this, roughly:

> You have had a couple of hours to look at the various roles people play in your region. Some things you have seen no doubt please you, and some concern you. It is our philosophy that it is best to have both kinds of things out in the open, as much as you feel safe in doing so. We hope that sense of safety grows, not only in your region but in your dealings with your bosses and the people who work for you.
>
> Later, as you know, you will have a chance here to test that sense of safety outside your region, as you meet with various corporate officials.
>
> Remember, your management has agreed to provide the resources, should you wish to do more later than we have been able to do here with the notion of roles.
>
> Now, there's another notion in the behavioral sciences that may help in developing the kind of open and collaborative system that can help make work more meaningful and satisfying. . . .

Several details complete this rough sketch of the design. First, members of each of the 33 regions sat at separate circular tables in a large ballroom. Sometimes they would be in "general session," as when getting a cognitive input to focus their team-development activities. At other times, each region would focus on its internal processes. Second, six resource persons moved between the groups when they were in the latter mode, clarifying or whatever. Third, the resource persons had been the T-Group trainers for a number of the participants, including at least all of the 33 regional managers. Some prior relationships of trust existed, then. These were no doubt critical contributors to the acceptance of the design. Fourth, each regional manager had previously met in longer and more intense team-development situations with his superior, the division manager (Section E). The regional managers were to do only what their superiors had done perhaps 12 to 18 months before. There was some reasonable concern among regional managers before the present experience, but it was of low intensity. If the concern had been high in even several managers, the design would have been modified.

c. Two Days of Team Development on a Mass Scale: Three Kinds of Consequences

Three varieties of data imply the substantial impact of this brief design for team development in a large population. The sequence

459

clearly "pulled the cork" from many salesmen, for the following several days of presentations were responded to with considerable directness and force. In contrast, the developing motto in the field had been: "The silent way is the safe way—you may be next!" The new marketing head was especially pleased by the extra sessions the salesmen felt were necessary to clarify a wide range of points with their headquarters superordinates. The degree of involvement of the majority of the salesmen is implicit in the fact that it was their recreation and sleep time they were investing to get the answers they wanted. At the impressionistic level, then, the meeting was a clear success, both as to team development and in the sessions that followed.[11]

Two administrations of a 24-item version of the Likert Profile (introduced in Section E) provided extensive data which support these impressions. The administrations were spaced by some four months, with the training intervention coming midway between them. Some 329 salesmen responded, both times. The salesmen were asked to describe their own regions, as much as that was possible.

Table 1 presents summary data suggesting the pervasiveness of the effects of the design. The table summarizes changes in the 33 regional means on the 24 Likert items.[12] Specifically, about 72 percent of the changes in mean scores were in the predicted direction. Viewed from another perspective, 4 of the 33 regions accounted for somewhat more than 33 percent of the negative scores. And two of those four regions at least approached breaking even in terms of scores toward or away from the laboratory values defined by System 4 of the Likert Profile.

A word is necessary in explaining what is meant by the term "predicted direction" of change in this case. Consultants had designed for specific effects whose desirability the salesmen themselves had overwhelmingly reflected in their Ideal responses to each item on the first administration of the Likert Profile. The Now scores on the Likert Profile items, in short, were to change in the direction of the Ideal scores. Consultants generated the design predicted to help the salesmen move in the direction they preferred.

A final batch of data suggests there is a cutting edge to such team-development designs. Such designs induce rising expectations about what work should provide and, hypothetically, those expectations in turn create one or both of two outcomes: greater demand for need satisfaction, and a sharp negative reaction if those needs are not met. In the present case, for example, salesmen were asked to describe their regions in terms

---

11. Some 40 percent of the regions have opted for some follow-on, as of this writing.
12. There is food for design thought in the magnitude of these changes, as compared with the lesser changes of the stability-oriented division managers reported in Section A, Part III.

Table 1. Some Summary Data, by Regional Means, Reflecting the Impact on Regional Climate of a Mass Team-Development Design

Region	Changes in the Direction of Laboratory Approach			Changes away from the Direction of Laboratory Approach	
	Values Statistically Significant	Values Not Statistically Significant	No Changes	Values Not Statistically Significant	Values Statistically Significant
1	2	18	0	4	0
2	4	10	0	8	2
3	3	16	0	5	0
4	4	16	0	4	0
5	11	13	0	0	0
6	3	14	0	6	1
7	10	12	1	1	0
8	4	18	1	1	0
9	2	11	2	9	0
10	0	10	0	14	0
11	2	14	1	7	0
12	1	18	1	4	0
13	5	17	0	2	0
14	2	13	0	9	0
15	9	14	0	1	0
16	6	13	1	4	0
17	1	20	1	2	0
18	2	16	0	6	0
19	4	12	1	7	0
20	0	2	0	15	7
21	4	19	0	1	0
22	1	21	1	1	0
23	5	10	0	9	0
24	1	6	0	15	2
25	5	18	0	1	0
26	0	17	2	5	0
27	4	17	0	3	0
28	8	16	0	0	0
29	5	11	0	8	0
30	5	7	1	9	2
31	3	12	1	8	0
32	0	6	1	13	4
33	4	12	0	8	0
	120	449	15	190	18

of four of Halpin's[13] scales, each of which is tapped by several questionnaire items. The scales are:

- *Disengagement* describes a group which is "going through the motions," a group that is not "in gear" as far as its task is concerned.

13. See Andrew W. Halpin and Don B. Croft, *The Organizational Climate of Schools* (Chicago: Midwest Administration Center, 1963).

- *Hindrance* refers to members' feeling that management burdens them with duties and requirements that are deemed busywork and that management does not facilitate their work.
- *Esprit* refers to members' feeling that their social needs are being satisfied and also that they are enjoying a sense of task accomplishment.
- *Intimacy* refers to members' enjoyment of friendly social relationships during work, a need satisfaction that may be independent of task accomplishment.

Unlike the Likert items, which respondents were instructed to apply to their own regions, the Halpin items tended to relate to the broader managerial system. This was especially the case for the Disengagement and Hindrance items, but Esprit is also affected.

The summary in Table 2 implies that development of more favorable

Table 2. Some Results of a Mass Team-Development Design

	Disengagement (10 items)	Hindrance (5 items)	Esprit (9 items)	Intimacy (6 items)
Relationship of Postintervention Scores to Preintervention Scores	Higher in seven cases, two of which reached the .05 level	Higher in all five cases, two of which reached the .05 level	Higher in six cases, one of which reached the .05 level	Higher in three cases, one of which reached the .05 level
	Lower in three cases, none of which reached the .05 level	—	Lower in three cases, none of which reached the .05 level	Lower in three cases, none of which reached the .05 level

Note: The data summarized here are for 289 salesmen whose before and after scores were compared item by item. Mean scores for all salesmen on each item are compared.

relationships at the regional level does not necessarily carry over to other levels.[14] Moreover, the higher scores on Disengagement and Hindrance items suggest a potential challenge for both management and the sales force. Specifically, changes in the Likert Profile items suggest some major improvement in the climate of relationships within the regions. But the data from the Halpin Disengagement and Hindrance scales especially imply that there is considerable work to be done in improving the actual

14. Supporting data also were provided by responses to Litwin's climate scale, the theoretical background of which is described in George H. Litwin and Robert A. Stringer, Jr., *Motivation and Organizational Climate* (Boston: Division of Research, Graduate School of Business, Harvard University, 1968), esp. pp. 66–92.

462

quality of work so as to more fully engage the energies made available by the changes in the openness of the regional climates induced via the team-development design.

5. IMPROVING INTERGROUP RELATIONS IN LARGE ORGANIZATIONS:[15] CONFRONTATION DESIGN AS A SPIN-OFF OF THE LABORATORY APPROACH

The thrust of this subsection is toward the complex issues involved in applications of the laboratory approach in organizations that attempt to selectively engage T-Group dynamics in learning situations that do not employ T-Groups. The focus is on horizontal linkages at more or less the same hierarchic level of organization units whose contributions have to be integrated smoothly into common flows of work. Some sense of the complexity and significance of the focus is implied by the typical properties of intergroup relations when they take on a win/lose character.[16] Briefly,

- The cohesiveness of the involved groups increases sharply.

- The closing of ranks tends to smother dispute or differences within

---

15. This section draws heavily from Robert T. Golembiewski and Arthur Blumberg, "The Laboratory Approach to Organization Change: Confrontation Design," *Journal of the Academy of Management,* Vol. 11 (June, 1968), pp. 199–210.
   For a more detailed technical report, see Robert T. Golembiewski and Arthur Blumberg, "Confrontation as a Training Design in Complex Organizations: Attitudinal Changes in A Diversified Population of Managers," *Journal of Applied Behavioral Science,* Vol. 3 (December, 1967), pp. 525–47. See also Golembiewski and Blumberg, "Training and Relational Learning," *Training and Development Journal,* Vol. 21 (November, 1967), pp. 35–42.
   Other similar designs are described by Robert R. Blake, Jane S. Mouton, and Richard L. Sloma, "The Union-Management Laboratory: Strategy for Resolving Intergroup Conflict," *Journal of Applied Behavioral Science,* Vol. 1 (January, 1965), pp. 25–57; and Richard Beckhard, "The Confrontation Meeting," *Harvard Business Review,* Vol. 45 (March, 1967), pp. 149–55.
   The generic design also has been applied in a variety of nonorganizational situations, such as police/community and Arab/Israel relations. See Martin Lakin, J. Lomranz, and Morton Lieberman, "Arab and Jew in Israel: A Case Study in a Human Relations Approach to Conflict," Middle East Area Studies, Series No. 1 (June, 1969), American Academic Association for Peace in the Middle East; and R. L. Bell, S. E. Cleveland, P. G. Hanson, and W. E. O'Connell, "Small Group Dialogue and Discussion: An Approach to Police-Community Relationships," *Journal of Criminal Law, Criminology, and Police Science,* Vol. 60 (June, 1969).
16. Robert R. Blake, Herbert A. Shepard, and Jane S. Mouton, *Managing Intergroup Conflict in Industry* (Houston, Tex.: Gulf Publishing Co., 1968), esp. pp. 1–49. See also John A. Seiler, "Diagnosing Interdepartmental Conflict," *Harvard Business Review,* Vol. 41 (September, 1963), pp. 121–32. Useful conceptual elaboration is provided by Louis R. Pondy, "Organizational Conflict: Concepts and Models," *Administrative Science Quarterly,* Vol. 12 (September, 1967), pp. 296–320.

groups that could have led to a reexamination and enrichment of initial positions.

- A centralization of leadership and power tends to occur, which may be functional for the crisis situation but can imply longer-run internal problems when the intergroup competition is settled.

- Selective perceptions and evaluations begin to flourish: our group is all good: theirs is all bad.

- Negative stereotypes about Other develop:
  a. Motives of Other become suspect.
  b. Intellectual distortions about Other grow.
  c. Commonalities are minimized and differences are exaggerated.
  d. Stereotypes trigger feelings which may be incongruent with objective realities but which nonetheless reinforce stereotypes.

- Comprehension of the position of Other is reduced.

- The capacity for mutual empathy is impaired.

There is plenty of scope for OD in these dynamics of degenerating interaction sequences. Moreover, such sequences are easy to fall into, as when a formal head is tempted to use the strategy to reinforce his own position or to increase the morale of members of his organization unit.

Within the context of such typical intergroup dynamics, the present position has two facets. For some purposes, T-Group designs are not the only or even the best vehicles for OD efforts at the intergroup level. Moreover, alternative designs can be developed which at once exploit the learning potential associated with T-Groups while they avoid many of their major drawbacks in large organizations.

T-Groups are seen here as an ideal learning environment that need not or cannot be duplicated in many ways in the "real world" of organizations. Thus the intense interaction characteristic of T-Groups cannot (and, perhaps, should not) be generated in some organizations. At the same time, knowledge of T-Group dynamics can generate spin-offs of applied techniques useful in complex organizations.

The usefulness of seeking analogical spin-offs of T-Group dynamics suitable for complex organizations will be illustrated by describing the properties and consequences of the confrontation design. The focus is on a program of change in a large business organization, the overall purpose of which is to improve relations between several middle-managerial levels and functions. Specifically, this subsection summarizes some of the attitudinal changes experienced by a diversified group of middle managers from the marketing area of a large firm who participated in the design. Similar results have been obtained in public agencies as well as in other business organizations.

464

a. The Focus of the Confrontation Design:
Interpersonal and Organizational Paralysis

A wide range of problems exists to which the T-Group and its analogs may be applied usefully. Consider only the notion of degenerative interaction systems introduced earlier. A hypothetical but typical sequence of worsening relations between individuals A and B in an organization takes such a general form:

- A does not *own* up to his attitudes or feelings toward B.
- B, in turn, is less likely to be *open* with A.
- A and B, consequently, experience a diminishing mutual *trust* as the number of unresolved issues between them increases.
- A degenerative, self-heightening process can be set in motion as:
  a. A and B feel a diminished interpersonal competence, that is, as they experience an increased *risk* of recognizing and acknowledging their attitudes and feelings, as their processes for decision-making become increasingly burdened by unfinished business, and as A and B consequently become less effective in isolating and resolving substantive problems.
  b. A and B consequently feel diminished *psychological success* in solving problems that remain solved without creating other problems.
  c. A and B become more *dependent* on their superiors, with lessened openness and owning being associated with (for example) informing on peers or with "don't rock the boat" attitudes.

Such degenerative systems can grow to encompass the relations between organization units as well as between individuals. It is not dramatic to refer to such situations as "paralysis." The fear of doing the wrong thing tends to inhibit doing anything, especially the important things.

Now if A has a typical initial experience in a stranger or cousin T-Group, he very probably will gain valuable insights and skills in sensing and reversing such degenerative sequences in his relations with some C within the laboratory context. Thus A's self-esteem may be enhanced when he proves to himself he really can establish meaningful and authentic relations with C in a T-Group. Or A may sharpen his sensitivity to the early stages of degenerating communication sequences as well as augment his skill in dealing with them effectively. The other possibilities are numerous.

However, A faces many problems in attempting to transfer such new or augmented skills into his organization. He might reason: "If I could only get organization member B in a T-Group, he would see the light just as C and I did." The "if" is often a big one. Thus there are some things a T-Group can do poorly or not at all, when such degenerative experiences occur in organizations. For example, A's efforts to recreate in his organization the supportive environment typical of T-Groups may be frustrated for a variety of reasons. Typically, that is, degenerative communication sequences in organizations involve large numbers of people, diversely organized into units often having long histories of rivalry that might inhibit the intimacy and sharing characteristic of a T-Group, and each performing myriad day-to-day jobs that must be done. In contrast, stranger T-Groups typically involve only a dozen people or so with no past history, who will predictably go their largely separate ways after training and who have no task in the interim but learning about each other from one another. Or finally, some powerful organization figures might argue that the desirable consequences of a family laboratory experience are outweighed by the risks involved. T-Groups can range broadly, after all, and a man in that context thus might say things harmful to his career that had no relevance to his work. A similar revelation in a stranger T-Group would involve far less career risk, in contrast.

b. Seven Features of the Confrontation Design: An Organizational Analog of the T-Group

The confrontation design meets the issue of transfer head on. The learning vehicle *is* the organization unit, in short. That is, the design attempts to capitalize on basic laboratory dynamics while doing what the T-Group in large organizations can sometimes do weakly or not at all.

Confrontation designs share an intent with organizational applications of sensitivity training, but the two differ in critical ways. Although confrontation designs can vary widely in specifics, seven core features particularly distinguish them from learning designs using T-Groups. *First,* confrontation designs involve as participants individuals who are hierarchically and/or functionally involved in some common flow of work. The attitudinal changes reported here concern four levels of the same marketing organization and some nine of its component activities. Immediately, then, the confrontation design seeks learning that has direct on-the-job applications. In contrast, applications of sensitivity training in organizations often provide for an initial experience in stranger groups composed of individuals who do not know one another, or in cousin groups of individuals from the same organization who do not work together. Only after such a first experience, if then, is relational learning typically attempted in family groups.

Second, confrontation designs involve two or more organizational entities whose members have real and unresolved issues with one another, e.g., labor and management. In this case, the focus was on the relations between various headquarters activities and supervisors of a field-sales force. Confrontations are highly structured and content-oriented, in this sense; T-Groups are not.

Third, confrontation designs involve the mutual development of images as a basis for attempting to highlight unresolved issues. In this case, five Basic Learning Aggregates were instructed to individually choose Relevant Others, that is, any organization positions or units with which more effective relations were considered necessary to do an effective job. For each of these Relevant Others, participants were instructed to develop Three-Dimensional Images based on these questions:

- How do we see ourselves in relation to the Relevant Other?
- How does the Relevant Other see us?
- How do we see the Relevant Other?

The 3–D Images were to be written on large sheets of newsprint. Each Learning Aggregate prepared its 3–D Image in isolation.

The 3–D Image, in effect, instructs participants to engage processes of both feedback and disclosure. But both processes are far more limited and controlled than in a T-Group, by intention. Thus both feedback and disclosure are written, and hence more deliberate, in 3–D designs. Moreover, the 3–D Image focuses on organizational groups, not individuals; and items in 3–D Images are tested in advance before they are communicated, by individuals who have a common organizational stake in what gets communicated.

The learning design in this case was complicated by a variety of factors. For example, only four of the five Basic Learning Aggregates were formal units of organization; the fifth was a categoric group composed of specialists from various headquarters's units. Moreover, even the four formal organization units were but recently established. Such factors probably reduced the potency of the design. In general, we expect the confrontation experience to be more potent as each Basic Learning Aggregate is not merely a categoric group, that is, as its members share social norms and mutually identify.[17] To the degree that a Basic Learning Aggregate possesses such qualities of real "groupiness," so should they be able to consensually validate and reinforce the learning of each group member.

Fourth, confrontation designs provide for sharing 3–D Images. This confronting via images is the first step toward mutually working through any relational problems. In this case, consultants scheduled blocks of

17. For a detailed analysis of such group properties, see Robert T. Golembiewski, *The Small Group,* pp. 9–26.

time during which willing Relevant Others confront one another. A consultant was present at each confrontation.

Fifth, confrontation designs assume that significant organizational problems often are caused by blockages in communication. Confrontations "free up" people to "level" in communicating and thus set the stage for authentic interaction and effective problem-solving. Some objective dilemmas, such as a critical lack of money, cannot be resolved by confrontation designs, of course. In such cases, the ideal outcomes are greater clarity in communicating about the dilemmas and greater willingness to collaborate in doing as much as conditions permit.

Sixth, confrontations are short-cycle affairs. The confrontation design about which data will be reported here, for example, took some 12 scheduled hours. In contrast, a typical stranger experience in sensitivity training lasts two weeks.

Seventh, confrontation designs are seen as springboards for organizational action. Since such a design is typically brief, however, real limits exist as to what can be accomplished. Participants were instructed to do only two things: to try to understand the 3–D Images communicated to them, and to seek some areas of agreement where mutually beneficial accommodations might be made. In addition, Core Groups were set up following the confrontations to work on specific organizational issues. These Core Groups were formed as a terminal training activity, some work was begun in the groups, and plans were made for future meetings.

In sum, the learning in confrontation designs does not have to be transferred or made relational. It *is* relational.

c. One Application of a Confrontation Design: Selected Initial Effects

The initial effects of one application of the confrontation design will be illustrated in two ways. First, the representative 3–D Image in Figure 2 reveals that participants did not trifle with the design. The figure reflects many unresolved issues, some of which were surprises and none of which had been admitted to public dialog between the parties.

Further, providing more rigorous support of the efficacy of the confrontation is an involved matter. Our primary data concern before or after attitudinal changes. They were derived from a questionnaire administered before and immediately after the experience.[18] Only impressionistic data about behavioral changes are available, but they are consistent with the pattern of attitudinal changes that seem due to the confrontation.

---

18. For details, see Golembiewski and Blumberg, "Confrontation as a Training Design in Complex Organizations," pp. 529–36.

Figure 2. Sample 3-D Image by Regional Sales Group I with the Promotion Department as the Relevant Other

A. *How Members of Regional Sales Group I See Themselves in Relation to Promotion Department:*
1. Circumvented
2. Manipulated
3. Receiving benefits of their efforts
4. Nonparticipating (relatively)
5. Defensive
6. Used
7. Productive
8. Instrument of their success
9. Have never taken us into their confidence in admitting that a promotion "bombed"
10. The field would like to help but must be a two-way street

B. *How Members of Regional Sales Group I Feel Promotion Department Sees Them:*
1. Insensitive to corporate needs
2. Noncommunicative upwards, as holding back ideas and suggestions
3. Productive in field-sales work
4. Naive about the promotion side of business
5. Unappreciative of promotion efforts
6. Lacking understanding about their sales objectives
7. Belligerent
8. Overly independent operators
9. Not qualified to evaluate the promotions sent to us
10. Honest in opinions

C. *How Members of Regional Sales Group I Characterize Promotion Department:*
1. Autocratic
2. Productive
3. Unappreciative of field efforts
4. Competent with "things" but not "people"
5. Industrious
6. Inflexible
7. Unrealistic
8. Naive
9. Progressive in promotion philosophy and programs
10. Overly competitive within own department
11. Plagiarists who take field ideas but do not always give credit

Expectations about intended changes in attitudes were not simple. For example, four of the organization units about which data were gathered were represented at the confrontation by either one participant or none at all. No definite pattern of changes in attitudes toward these four targets was expected, consequently. For crude purposes, they are control groups. And two of the remaining five units or positions— representing some 15 percent of the sample—were perceived by the consultants as creating substantial new business during the design. Before the data were processed, then, the consultants distinguished three types of units or positions about which data were gathered and made three different predictions concerning them. The consultants distinguished:

I. Units which were deeply involved in the design, toward which the most favorable shifts in attitudes were expected, as measured by pre- and postconfrontation administrations of the questionnaire.

II. Units which had little or token representation in the design, toward which only a slight drift toward more favorable attitudes due to a halo effect was anticipated.

III. Units which had created substantial new business during the design, toward which the least favorable shifts in attitudes were expected. Basically, two units did not participate fully in the confrontation. For example, one produced only a Two-Dimensional Image, its members refusing to describe how they saw themselves.

In addition, three types of Criteria-Questions or Items were distinguished a priori. For each of these, different predictions seemed appropriate. The three types of questions were:

A. *Volitional Criteria-Questions,* 11 items which tapped attitudes considered relatively easy to change (e.g., How much do you want to collaborate with Unit Z?) or attitudes deemed particularly sensitive to the confrontation design (e.g., How much information have you received from Unit X?).

B. *Objective Criteria-Questions,* 10 items which tapped attitudes that could hardly be changed positively on the basis of the confrontation design, but which might very well drift negatively as people felt more free to be open about their attitudes toward self and others (e.g., What is the level of productivity of Unit Z?).

C. *Combined Criteria-Questions,* composed of 11 Volitional and 10 Objective Criteria-Questions, on which a general drift toward favorable changes in attitudes was expected.

These expectations may be summarized in a 3 × 3 matrix, as in Table 3. Interpretively, pre- and postconfrontation administrations of the questionnaire were expected to reveal that the most favorable[19] shifts in attitudes would be reported towards the Deeply Involved organization units on the Volitional items. On the Objective items, the expectation was that attitudes toward all organization units would tend to change negatively, and most sharply for the Unfinished Business units.

---

19. The terms "favorable" and "unfavorable" are convenient shorthand only. On the Volitional Criteria-Questions, attitudinal changes reporting an enhanced willingness to collaborate are "favorable;" on Objective items, attitudinal changes reporting a lower degree of perceived productivity are "unfavorable." On both kinds of items, the directions of scales were varied on the questionnaire to inhibit the development of response sets. However, the data were uniformly processed so that favorable changes are scored (+) and unfavorable changes are scored (−).

Table 3. Expected Shifts in Attitudes Due to Confrontation Design, by Type of Organization Unit and Kind of Attitude

		Types of Units		
		I. Deeply Involved	II. Under-represented	III. Unfinished Business
	A. Volitional	Most favorable shifts in attitudes	Moderately favorable shifts in attitudes	Least favorable shifts in attitudes
Types of Criteria-Questions	B. Objective	Least unfavorable shifts in attitudes	Moderately unfavorable shifts in attitudes	Most unfavorable shifts in attitudes
	C. Combined	Strong favorable shifts in attitudes	Slight favorable shifts in attitudes	Least favorable shifts in attitudes

The pattern of attitudinal changes above was not only expected, it was intended. Designing for "negative" or "unfavorable" shifts in attitudes on the Objective Criteria-Questions may seem perverse, but it is not. Basically, the learning design was a dilemma/invention model that captures much of the essence of the dynamics of T-Groups. Let us simplify grievously. The consultants concluded that members of the host organization had entered into a mutual defense pact expressed, for example, in terms of unrealistically high but mutual public estimates of performance. Illustratively, organization norms prescribed vigorous applause following a presentation, no matter how bad the performance. Lack of openness, in short, served to obscure basic organization dilemmas. The confrontation design attempts to induce the public recognition of such dilemmas via greater openness and risk-taking, by explicitly dealing with the reality perceived by organization members. Hence negative changes in attitudes on the Objective Criteria-Questions do not signal a dangerous deterioration of morale. Rather, such changes establish that dilemmas requiring attention have been acknowledged. During a confrontation, organization members are encouraged to activate the "dilemma" part of the dilemma/invention learning model, as by seeing themselves and others as less productive than they were willing to admit previously. At the same time, however, the confrontation design encourages organization members to work harder on the "invention" aspects of the learning model. That is, the design is intended to favorably change the attitudes of organization members on the Volitional Criteria-Questions,

471

toward a greater desire to cooperate in coping with organizational dilemmas.

The matter may be summarized briefly. In its basic intent, the confrontation design proposes to raise to public attention unacknowledged but real dilemmas in an organization that must be dealt with. The confrontation design also intends to induce greater commitment and effort toward developing inventions capable of minimizing or eliminating the dilemmas, as in the Core Groups built into the confrontation design or in the back-home situation. These two intentions are realized, in turn,

Table 4. Summary Data concerning Attitudinal Changes toward Nine Units of Organization, Based on Pre- and Postconfrontation Administrations of Questionnaire

			Types of Organization Units or Positions		
			I. Deeply Involved	II. Under-represented	III. Unfinished Business
Types of Criteria Questions	A. Volitional	Ratio ± Changes	14.00 (28/2)	2.33 (28/12)	1.86 (13/7)
		Ratio ± Statistically Significant Changes	Infinity (14/0)	4.45 (9/2)	1.67 (5/3)
	B. Objective	Ratio ± Changes	.65 (13/20)	.42 (13/31)	.38 (6/16)
		Ratio ± Statistically Significant Changes	.25 (1/4)	0 (0/10)	.18 (2/11)
	C. Combined	Ratio ± Changes	1.86 (41/22)	.95 (41/43)	.83 (19/23)
		Ratio ± Statistically Significant Changes	3.75 (15/4)	.82 (9/11)	.58 (11/19)

Note: Numbers in parentheses indicate the raw number of positive/negative changes.

as participants accept norms for giving and receiving feedback consistent with the laboratory approach.

Table 4 establishes that these complex expectations were generally supported by attitudinal changes in the host population. The ratios in Table 4 are derived from changes in before/after attitudes of all participants toward each of nine target positions or units of organization, including their own. A ratio greater than 1.0 indicates that favorable changes in attitudes outnumbered unfavorable changes; a ratio less than 1.0 indicates that negative or unfavorable changes in attitudes were more numerous.

Sampling the data in Table 4 reveals, for example, that Deeply Involved units attracted the most favorable shifts in attitudes, as expected. Favorable changes in attitudes toward those units at a minimum were 14 times more likely than unfavorable changes. The other two types of units, in contrast, experienced approximately a 2:1 ratio of positive/ negative changes. All three types of units, within a narrow range, experienced unfavorable attitudinal shifts on Objective items. Roughly, unfavorable attitudinal changes outnumbered favorable changes by 2–5 to 1. The negative trend was anticipated. As anticipated, also, the data do not even suggest wholesale rejection. Thus the Deeply-Involved units were the targets of roughly the same proportion of favorable/unfavorable changes on the Objective Criteria-Questions as the New Business units. In addition, although the data are not reported here, individuals describing their own unit saw themselves just as "unfavorably" on the Objective Criteria-Questions after the confrontation as did others describing them. So the drift toward negative changes was not an "us good guys" and "those bad guys" phenomenon.

As the summary in Table 4 suggests, then, a confrontation design imbedded in the context of a complex organization induced some of the same kinds of dynamics that are characteristic of T-Groups. The sharp favorable drift in attitudes on the Volitional Criteria-Questions implies that the confrontation attitudinally prepared people to improve relations that were not critically bad but that were of growing concern. At the same time, as the data on the Objective Criteria-Questions suggest, participants tended to describe their reality in somewhat sharper negative terms.

Two capsule characterizations seem appropriate. After the confrontation, first, individuals seemed more willing to undertake a task that they saw as more demanding than they had thought. This describes an orientation that is conducive to effective learning and change.

Without making too much of such data, second and more broadly, the summary data in Table 4 suggest the antithesis of a degenerative communication process. In the following particulars, that is, the data suggest an alleviation of the processes leading to interpersonal and organizational paralysis:

- A as a member of an organization unit was encouraged by the confrontation design to own up to his feelings and attitudes concerning B and/or his unit via developing a 3–D image.
- B as a member of an organization unit, in turn, was encouraged to be open in developing a 3–D Image.
- Both A and B experienced a growing mutual trust as the amount of unfinished business between them was reduced by the confrontation design, especially as it provided that A and B share their 3–D Images of each other and/or of each other's organization units.

473

- A healthy, self-correcting process can be set in motion as:
    a. A and B as members of organization units feel an increased interpersonal competence, that is, as they experience a lessened perceived risk of recognizing and acknowledging their attitudes and feelings, their processes for decision making are less burdened, and A and B can be more effective in problem-solving.
    b. A and B consequently feel greater psychological success by mutually solving problems that stay solved without creating other problems.
    c. A and B become less dependent on formal superiors and hence need concern themselves less with "tattling" or "not making waves."

d. Some In-Process Conclusions: Qualifications about Initial Effects

Although data support the efficacy of one spin-off of sensitivity training, four points must be stressed by way of qualification. *First,* the data trends in Table 4 probably understate the power of the confrontation design. Briefly, the learning situation was very complex in the present case, closure often was not possible when confrontations were held, and some mutually desired confrontations were not held because of lack of time. More favorable attitudinal changes should show up in cases where there are fewer loose ends.

Second, however, a variety of research is necessary to establish the specific conditions under which various consequences might be expected from applications of confrontation designs. For example, the results above strongly suggest one application was useful in modifying the attitudes of organization members. In turn, these attitudinal changes reasonably could be expected to facilitate behavioral changes that would (for example) improve degenerative communication sequences. No direct evidence about behavioral change is presented here, however, although various soft data strongly imply behavioral changes. For example, the history of the Core Groups was characterized by an excess of zeal, if anything. Specifically, some Core Groups attempted to engage in problem-solving in areas beyond their jurisdiction, against which consultants had strongly cautioned and advised. Predictably, superiors in the broader control system restrained some of the Core Groups. That superiors did so, of course, suggests that the attitudinal changes summarized above did induce behavioral changes in at least some participants.

Third, the confrontation design seems widely applicable and safe, but some potential host organizations may not be culturally prepared for it. No doubt, most culturally unprepared organizations would be aware enough to avoid soliciting such an experience. But consultants still face a real responsibility of judging the preparedness of the host organizations and its personnel to profit from what is for most organizations a novel vehicle for exerting influence.

Should the consultant misjudge an organization's preparedness, however, the most probable damage is the loss of a useful opportunity for development. That is, the confrontation design includes a wide array of safety features. For example, the present design provided that only mutually willing Relevant Others would confront each other. Avoiding a confrontation perceived as dangerous or unprofitable would not be difficult, then. And members of most organizations are very likely to avoid explosive situations. In addition, confrontation designs include a massive safety factor, the large number of points at which participants must make collaborative judgments about the degree of openness they are willing to risk. For example, the groups used in confrontation designs give each individual a range of resources which can advise against or support various statements in a 3–D Image. Elements of a 3–D Image are offered neither without conscious risk-taking, in short, nor without testing for commitment. And that is intended by the design. For we can really learn only as we risk and make real commitments.

Safeguards also inhibit taking the easy ways out of avoiding a confrontation or weaseling in the preparation of images. That is, any group developing a 3–D Image will be alert to the design property that watering down their image so as to guarantee safety may invite ridicule as their image is compared unfavorably to images developed by others. The derivative tension is very real, and it seems to result in a kind of escalation of truthfulness in which the relative merits of openness and closedness are very consciously weighed. As it should be, then, a major share of the responsibility for the success or failure of a confrontation design rests with members of the host organization. They are, after all, the ones who basically must live with the results.

Fourth, no particular skills are required of participants in a confrontation design, but skilled consultants should be provided each time images are actually shared. Such a resource person can intervene if things go badly; and he can always serve to encourage behavior that respects laboratory values, as well as to model for other participants the greater openness which is the goal of the confrontation design. Far more likely, however, his particular usefulness lies in encouraging participants to confront each other at deeper levels when he suspects some varnishing of the truth is taking place. Our original expectation was that consultants could intervene if (for example) a Basic Learning Aggregate began roughly confronting a "weak" individual. The only individuals confronted, however, were the top organizational officials. It was a matter of first things first, in short. The top officials required no aid, although consultants did intervene to point up what seemed to them defensive reactions by these officials during the sharing of the images.

A Technical Note

Note that different effects may have resulted if a "fishbowl" or "group-observing-group" vehicle had been used in the confrontation. A fishbowl formation would have had each group observing every other group in the *act of preparing its 3–D Image*. In the present case, participants saw the product of each other's processes and had to mostly infer those underlying processes. As Robert R. Blake notes in another connection, the fishbowl highlights some critical data. He explains:

> The fishbowl permits each group to see the other group members working together. . . . This permits the second group to observe group culture, tradition, power relations, and esprit . . . , to say nothing of hearing the content discussed. The same is true when the second group gets in the fishbowl. What this means is that critical aspects of behavior, usually unrevealed . . . , are brought into view. . . . The *image production and exchange* approach . . . obscures social process.[20]

Essentially, then, the present vehicle limits, and deliberately so, the degree to which one group gets acquainted with another.

Several generalizations seem to apply. Thus the fishbowl is likely to be a more potent vehicle, for good or ill, although the required comparative research is not available. For example, the fishbowl raises questions about who goes first, it may induce public competitiveness in the image production, and so on. In addition, the fishbowl is most appropriate when two groups are involved.[21] This is a major limitation, this author guesses, given the probable reinforcing effects of a community forum when (let us say) five units are involved. Finally, the issue of fishbowl vs. separate preparation suggests the detailed comparative work that as yet remains undone in the laboratory approach to OD.

e. Persistence of Initial Attitudinal Changes:[22] Potency of the Confrontation Design

Data were intentionally gathered over an extended period to test some of these qualifications about the effects of the confrontation design. Specifically, the standard questionnaire exploring attitudes about inter-departmental relations was administered three times to help establish

---

20. Robert R. Blake, "The Uses of the Past," *Journal of Applied Behavioral Science,* Vol. 7 (October, 1971), pp. 519–20.
21. Michael Blansfield, Robert R. Blake, and Jane S. Mouton, "The Merger Laboratory," *Training Directors Journal,* Vol. 18 (May, 1964), pp. 2–10, for example, deal with a case where $N = 2$.
22. This section draws heavily from Robert T. Golembiewski and Arthur Blumberg, "Persistence of Attitudinal Changes Induced by a Confrontation Design," *Journal of the Academy of Management,* Vol. 12 (September, 1969), pp. 309–18.

whether the observed attitudinal changes persisted over time. Administrations I and II were five days apart; Administration III followed by some seven months. All comparisons below involve Administration II versus Administration III and are based on questionnaire responses of 45 managers at several levels in subunits of the marketing division of a large corporation.

Any marked persistence of attitudinal changes suggests the usefulness of the confrontation design as one technique in the repertoire of organizational change agents. Since no planned reinforcement of the effects of the confrontation experience was attempted by managers or consultants during the interval between Administrations II and III, any persistence of effects implies the potency of the design.

Intervening Divisional History

The target organization experienced rough times in the seven-month period between Administrations II and III. This intervening history makes particularly noteworthy any substantial persistence of attitudinal change. Six interacting elements suggest the fuller range of forces operating on the marketing division in which the research was conducted.

First, a significant government action was taken against one major product. This was a double blow. The anticipated loss in sales would have significant effects on division performance. Moreover, the government action sharply limited promotion efforts on other products as well, and promotional skills were the division's major strength. Morale among the field-sales force was hit especially hard, and headquarters-field relations were sorely tested.

Second, division dependence on a few old products, on which patents had lapsed or were soon to run out, was highlighted by the government action.

Third, division sales and profits fell by nearly 20 percent in the seven months following the confrontation. This effect had multiple causes. Government action against a big product took its toll, as did sudden changes in buying habits of large customers. In part, the profit picture also reflected overstocked inventories of many buyers. The division traditionally promised ambitious profits to corporate, and delivered. The usual reward was substantial autonomy from corporate oversight. As sales and profits tumbled, corporate interventions escalated. The net effect was to stress headquarters-field relationships in critical regards. For example, the field salesforce felt the impact of corporate interventions as unresponsive to their requests for decisions or for policy clarification, as limitations on their sales approaches, as obstructions at just the time that increased sales argued for relaxation of normal policies and practices.

477

Fourth, sharp budget cuts were made in several departments to help achieve the profit target for the current year. Such cuts were widely perceived at lower levels as "Band-Aids." The "real answer" would acknowledge the lack of realism in profits promised to corporate, and would continue spending at planned levels. The danger of the budget-cutting was clear to many: unwise cuts in necessary expenditures might create a long-run lowering of sales and profits out of what many observers saw only as a short-term (if sharp and painful) dip. Budget-cutting it was, however. Crucial interdepartmental issues were raised as some budgets were cut sharply and others hardly at all.

Fifth, corporate policies toward the division seemed to change abruptly. Generally, division interests were not seen as getting forceful expression at corporate levels. The overall divisional effect was to give more attention to protecting the "big No. 1," one's department and/or one's job. The potential for interdepartmental conflict zoomed upwards, with the paradoxical effect of encouraging greater corporate oversight when what existed was already considered too much. The reasons for corporate involvement in division affairs are complex, but they all derived from a basic trend: the division posed increasing problems and contributed less and less to corporate profit. The specific reasons for increased corporate involvement in division affairs are complex. Some were long-run trends, while others were rooted in recent unexpected events. But they all came to a sharp focus during the seven-month period. The division was becoming a smaller and smaller part of the new acquisition-minded corporation. And the government action against a major product put the frosting on the cake.

Sixth, several significant personnel actions reduced responsibilities and salaries of key division employees. The derivative tensions exacerbated an already delicate situation.

Minimal Expectations about Persistence

Since all major factors did not remain more or less the same in the 7-month interval between Administrations II and III, the persistence of the effects of the confrontation design on managerial attitudes about interdepartmental relations is difficult to judge. The unanswerable questions are numerous. What negative effects on interunit rivalries and on managerial attitudes might be reasonably expected as a result of the events intervening between Administrations II and III? And would these effects have had even more impact if there never had been a confrontation experience? Or less?

The effect of time on the attitudinal changes induced by the confrontation design cannot be strictly isolated, therefore, but some insight is possible. In this spirit, for Volitional Criteria-Questions or Items only, one simple and conservative decision rule is proposed to judge the persistence over time of attitudinal changes induced by a confrontation design.

- *Decision Rule I:* The confrontation design can claim to have affected persisting attitudinal changes if comparisons of Administration III vs. II show that statistically significant negative changes occur on the Volitional Items in only a minority of cases.

Decision Rule I is reasonable, perhaps even rigorous. The sketch of the division's history implies massive impetus toward worsening interdepartmental relations and, as Table 5 shows, considerable potential existed for downward readjustments in attitudes. That is, comparing Administration II to Administration I, positive changes were observed on a total of 90 percent of the Volitional Items referring to deeply involved units or positions.[23] And 46 percent of all changes were positive and statistically significant. The effects are less marked but still substantial for the two other classes of organization units or positions. Any major decay rate over time in attitudinal changes induced by the confrontation design, then, can reasonably be inferred only from major

Table 5. Percentage Summary of Changes in Attitudes, Volitional Items Only, Administration II versus I

	Three Classes of Organization Units Which Were Targets of Attitudes		
Volitional Items	Three Deeply Involved Units ($N_1 = 30$)	Four Under-represented Units ($N_2 = 40$)	Two New Business Units ($N_3 = 20$)
Positive Statistically Significant Changes	46.3%	45.0%	25.0%
Positive Statistically Insignificant Changes	43.7	10.0	37.5
No Changes	3.3	15.0	2.5
Negative Statistically Insignificant Changes	6.7	25.0	20.0
Negative Statistically Significant Changes	0.0	5.0	15.0
	100.0%	100.0%	100.0%

Note: The percentages above are based on ratings by 45 managers of each of nine units on 10 Volitional Items. The total data base, then, includes 4,050 ratings. Ninety tests of significance were run on the differences between the means of each of the 10 items for each of the nine positions or units. The percentages are based on these ninety tests of significance. Hence $N_1 + N_2 + N_3 = 90$.

23. Recall that data were gathered about three classes of organization units or positions. "Underrepresented" units or positions had only one or no representatives at the experience, and no major changes in attitudes toward them were expected. "New Business" groups were those whose performance in the confrontation design was such as to raise new issues that were not resolved. Note also that one Underrepresented organization unit was dropped from Administration III. Originally, some of its members were scheduled to participate, but this did not prove possible.

statistically significant negative changes in attitudes, Administration III versus Administration II.

For the Objective Items, any prediction about managerial attitudes concerning interdepartmental relations must take into account major cross-pressures. On the one hand, *ceteris paribus*, the dilemma/invention model underlying the confrontation design implies the development over time of more favorable attitudes on the Objective Items. Roughly, that is, the rationale of the confrontation design may be sketched in these terms:

- Poor and deteriorating interdepartmental relations were seen by consultants, but organization members were cautious about voicing their concerns, even in private. Their motivation was complex: they feared risking disclosure; they sensed they might not get support; they fantasized openness would only make matters seriously and irremediably worse; etc. By hypothesis, this accounted for the relatively favorable responses on Administration I to the Objective Items.

- The confrontation design induced the public disclosure of data about interdepartmental relations that indicated widespread concern.

- The public sharing freed individuals to be more negative on the Objective Items in Administration II than in Administration I. Table 6 shows that the anticipated negative trend did occur between Administrations I and II, although it is not as marked as the positive trend in Table 5.

Table 6. Percentage Summary of Changes in Attitudes, Objective Items Only, Administration II versus I

| Objective Items | Three Classes of Organization Units Which Were Targets of Attitudes | | |
	Three Deeply Involved Units $(N_1 = 44)$	Four Under-represented Units $(N_2 = 33)$	Two New Business Units $(N_3 = 22)$
Positive Statistically Significant Changes	3.0%	0.0%	9.1%
Positive Statistically Insignificant Changes	21.2	15.9	13.7
No Changes	15.2	13.6	4.5
Negative Statistically Insignificant Changes	48.5	47.8	27.2
Negative Statistically Significant Changes	12.1	22.7	45.5
	100.0%	100.0%	100.0%

Note: The percentages above are based on ratings by 45 managers of each of nine units on 11 Objective Items. The total data base, then, includes 4,455 ratings. Ninety-nine tests of significance were run on the differences between the means of each of the 10 items for each of the nine positions or units. The percentages are based on these 99 tests of significance. Hence $N_1 + N_2 + N_3 = 99$.

- The new realism about poor and worsening conditions constituted an organizational dilemma which induced pressures toward resolution in many organization members.

- By hypothesis, organization members invented an approach to resolve that dilemma. They changed their attitudes on the Volitional Items in ways that indicated greater need and willingness to improve interdepartmental relations.

- By hypothesis, improved Volitional attitudes should over time tend to improve Objective attitudes about interdepartmental relations.

The organizational history intervening between Administrations II and III also induced powerful forces tending to worsen attitudes about interdepartmental relations, however. For example, cutting budgets so as to meet profit targets was well designed to intensify interdepartmental win/lose competition. These powerful forces should encourage worsened attitudes on Objective Items, which (among other foci) inquired into:

- the degree to which various organization units had built stable and effective work relations with other units

- the degree to which various organization units made help available

- the degree to which conflict was worked through openly and effectively

Such forces in opposition made prediction very chancy. Again, repeating the theme introduced in Subsection 6 of Section B, Part I, dealing with models of change, the basic question is the optimum discrepancy that will facilitate learning, or change. Specifically, is there some deterioration of scores on Objective Items that is so great as to be dysfunctional? All that can be said here is that, hypothetically, attitudes about Objective Items can be linked in at least two ways (as in Figure 3) to changes in attitudes concerning the willingness to improve interdepart-

Figure 3. Two Alternative Effects of Decreases in Scores on Objective Items

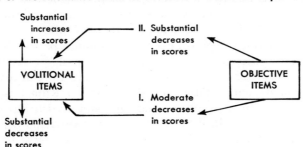

mental relations, as measured by Volitional Items on the standard questionnaire. The confrontation design encourages more realistic attitudes on the Objective Items dealing with interdepartmental relations, but, in the context of the helping relations emphasized by the design, this in turn motivates greater desire to improve the existing state of affairs. However, attitudes on Objective Items could fall to dangerously low levels, especially under the impetus of broad environmental forces and without the buffering of the helping quality built into the confrontation design. A runaway-train effect of the confrontation design would severely limit its usefulness.

The seven months of organizational history permit a fortuitous test of two basic questions about the confrontation design. First, do the more open and critical attitudes it induced make an organization especially vulnerable to massive environmental forces such as those described above, which will occur now and again in every organization? If so, applications of the confrontation design would be potentially dangerous. Second, and alternatively, is there any evidence that the improvements in Volitional Item attitudes also induced by the confrontation design have the opposite effect of making an organization more effective in coping with such massive environmental forces as those described above?

Given these massive imponderables, a standstill criterion is proposed here for estimating the efficacy of the confrontation design.

- *Decision Rule II:* The dilemma/invention model will be supported if Administration III of the standard questionnaire reveals no major negative trends on Objective items when compared to Administration II.

Operationally, "no major negative trends" is defined as an approximate balance of positive and negative changes on Objective Items, comparing Administration III with Administration II.

Tests of Minimal Expectations

A test of Decision Rule I strongly implies that the confrontation design had useful effects in the seven-month period between Administrations II and III of the standard questionnaire. That is, on the Volitional Items, the substantial improvements in attitudes following a confrontation experience tended to persist over a seven-month period. In this sense, the confrontation design seemed to provide a cushion against massive environmental forces; it did not amplify them. Specifically, Table 7 provides summary data establishing that Decision Rule I is met. Only one attitudinal change in 10 was negative and statistically significant, overall, comparing Administration III with II. Nearly 60 percent of the additional cases also are negative, but these changes were usually small

Table 7. Percentage Summary of Changes in Attitudes, Volitional Items Only, Administration III versus II

Volitional Items	Three Deeply Involved Units ($N_1 = 30$)	Three Under-represented Units ($N_2 = 30$)	Two New Business Units ($N_3 = 20$)	Weighted Average
	Three Classes of Organization Units Which Were Targets of Attitudes			
Positive Statistically Significant Changes	0.0%	0.0%	0.0%	0.0%
Positive Statistically Insignificant Changes	13.3	20.0	20.0	17.5
No Changes	13.3	10.0	5.0	11.2
Negative Statistically Insignificant Changes	56.7	53.3	70.0	58.8
Negative Statistically Significant Changes	16.7	16.7	5.0	12.5
	100.0%	100.0%	100.0%	100.0%

Note: The percentages above are based on ratings by 45 managers of each of eight units on 10 Volitional Items. The total data base, then, includes 3,600 ratings. Eighty tests of significance were run on the differences between the means of each of the 10 items for each of the nine positions or units. The percentages are based on these 80 tests of significance. Hence $N_1 + N_2 + N_3 = 80$.

and can confidently be attributed to random variations in the data.

The powerful impact of the brief confrontation experience on volitional attitudes also can be suggested by comparing Tables 5 and 7. For example, there were over three times as many positive statistically significant entries in Table 5 as there were negative statistically significant ones in Table 7. This suggests, of course, that the improvements in attitudes about interdepartmental relations induced on Volitional Items by a brief confrontation design were substantially preserved despite seven months of harrowing organization history and whatever decay rate there is in the effects of a confrontation design over time. Of course, such comparisons are only suggestive, but they imply modest decay over time of changes in Volitional Items induced by a confrontation design.

The summary data in Table 8 meet Decision Rule II, and they suggest that a runaway-train effect did not occur. The negative drift in Objective Items induced by the confrontation did not set the stage for an uncontrollable snowballing of negative attitudes unleashed by the divisional history intervening between Administrations II and III of the standard questionnaire. More broadly, the data suggest that the confrontation design set in motion dynamics that increase an organization's ability to cope with a hostile environment. One third of the attitudinal changes between the two administrations are negative and statistically significant, to be sure. But more than a third of the changes trend positively or do not change. Another third trend negatively but do not reach usually accepted levels of statistical significance. Given that massive environmental forces encouraged a major worsening of the relationships between

Table 8. Percentage Summary of Changes in Attitudes, Objective Items Only, Administration III versus II

Objective Items	Three Classes of Units Which Were Targets of Attitudes			
	Three Deeply Involved Units ($N_1 = 30$)	Three Under-represented Units ($N_2 = 33$)	Two New Business Units ($N_3 = 22$)	Weighted Average
Positive Statistically Significant Changes	3.0%	6.0%	9.1%	5.7%
Positive Statistically Insignificant Changes	15.2	27.3	22.7	21.7
No Changes	5.0	6.0	18.2	7.9
Negative Statistically Insignificant Changes	33.3	30.3	18.2	28.4
Negative Statistically Significant Changes	43.5	30.3	31.8	36.3
	100.0%	99.9%	100.0%	100.0%

Note: The percentages above are based on ratings by 45 managers of each of nine units on 11 Objective Items. The total data base, then, includes 4,455 ratings. Eighty-eight tests of significance were run on the differences between the means of each of the 10 items for each of the nine positions or units. The percentages are based on these 88 tests of significance. Hence $N_1 + N_2 + N_3 = 88$.

organization units, this record does not suggest a runaway-train effect.

Substantial evidence, in sum, supports the persistence over time of the attitudinal effects of a confrontation design, despite the uncertainties involved. This persistence suggests the value of further applications of the design and research associated with those applications.

6. TOWARD INTEGRATING SUBUNITS THROUGH CONFRONTATION:[24] IT TAKES TWO TO MAKE ONE

Applied behavioral scientists spend most of their time working on problems that pertain to a single group or organization. The common concerns include communication, problem-solving, organizational structure, interpersonal relations, and so forth. The purpose here is to highlight a related but different problem area: that which develops when two organizations join forces to create one functioning unit.

There is a small but growing body of literature,[25] predominantly from the business world, that is concerned with organization mergers and

24. This section is taken largely from Arthur Blumberg and William Wiener, "One from Two: A Behavioral Science Design for Merging Organizations," mimeographed. A number of stylistic and organizing changes have been made. Their report has been published in the *Journal of Applied Behavioral Science*, Vol. 7 (January, 1971), pp. 87–102.

See also Blansfield, Blake, and Mouton, *op. cit.*

25. See, for example, the publication *Mergers and Acquisitions* published by Mergers and Acquisitions, Inc., 1725 K St., N.W., Washington, D.C.

emphasizes financial effects. In a survey of factors that may lead to the success or failure of mergers, to cite a rare exception, John Kitching focuses on matters of management and organization, albeit not in great detail.[26] He indicates, for example, the necessity of having competent "managers of change" and of setting up clear reporting relationships in the newly formed organizational structure. Kitching's data also indicated that in 81 percent of the merger "failures" reported, reporting relationships were unclear and there was a tendency to change them often.

From the point of view of behavioral scientists, the financial and economic components of mergers are part of a total mix of problems that focus on such things as expectations about norm development, role change, leadership style, decision-making processes, and goal orientation. It is with such factors that this subsection is concerned. The format is that of a case study of a merger. It also suggests another specific use of the confrontation design just described, extending the technique into an area of considerable practical concern.

a. The Situation Inducing the Merger Design: A State of Preparedness and Wonderful Serendipity

The development of this focus on the dynamics of a merger was serendipitous. The unexpected beginning was at a two-day training session on consultation skills for 23 members of two geographically separated but contiguous units of a private voluntary community organization. The participants comprised the total professional staff of the two organizations, which also included the usual array of supporting activities. These units, though both part of a large national organization, had no formal or reporting relationships with each other. They might meet at professional, regional, or national conferences, but for all practical purposes they were separate. Each had its own governing board, did its own fund-raising, and developed its own programs.

These two organizations offered field consultation and guidance services to local constituent units within their respective geographic areas. One very important structural and functional difference did exist between the two. The larger of the units, hereafter called organization A, also provided direct program services to communities where no local constituent units were in operation, in addition to providing field consultation. In effect, then, the larger organization performed both line and staff operations, in contrast to the other, whose function was limited, for the most part, to staff activities.

It became evident to the consultant shortly after the training session had started that though the exercise was going well, the enhancing of

---

26. John Kitching, "Why Do Mergers Miscarry?" *Harvard Business Review*, Vol. 4 (November–December, 1967), pp. 84–101.

consultation skills was not uppermost in the minds of the participants. Discussion revealed that the underlying issue was that the national organization had recently decided that in the interests of program and resource utilization, the two organizational units would be merged into one. The date of the final merger was scheduled for a year later. To complicate matters, no decision had been made about who would be the new executive of the merged organization. It could conceivably be the current executive of either organization, or neither.

The hidden agenda items, then, were very powerful. They involved job tenure, working relations, leadership, program development, and a host of other personal and organizational issues. The matter of consultation skills was of lower priority than the merger, the participants agreed. At the consultant's spontaneous suggestion, they also agreed to engage with each other in activities that might lead toward the resolution of the problems that had developed, and to successful problem-solving that could aid in the creation of one productive unit from two.

It seemed abundantly clear that the first need of these two groups was to free their intergroup communications so that they would be able to talk with each other in meaningful terms about the coming merger. The practical question was: What is there about our two existing organizations that will aid our work together, and what will hinder us? In other words, the initial part of the total change effort was devoted to collecting data about the manner in which each group perceived itself and the other. Based on the results and analysis of this effort, the two organizations and the consultant would be in a position to plan further.

The consultant engaged the two groups in a 3–D confrontation exercise, as described above. Given the manageable size of the group, even if other instruments were at hand, this probably would have been the right decision. The exercise is simple, and has training as well as data-collection potential. It involves individuals or groups that focus their attention on three questions: How do we see and describe ourselves? How do we see and describe the other organization? How do we think members of the other organization see and describe us? After lists of answers to these questions are developed by the respective parties to the confrontation, they are shared with each other publicly. In the sharing session, the ground rules are that elaborating questions may be asked, people may analyze their own data and that of the other, but they should try not to react defensively. In other words, the confrontation exercise should form a basis for problem-solving, not conflict. Figure 4 details the 3–D Images produced by the two organization units.

Two major points are obvious from even a cursory scanning of Figure 4. These are:

- The prospective merger would have to join two organizations which, though having similar goal orientations, were quite different in a number of very important ways.

486

Organization A

I. Perception of Ourselves

1. Project- and task-oriented
2. Three staffs with separate functions (fragmented)
   a. services to local units
   b. district services
   c. governmental services
3. Individual empire builders
4. Reluctance to recognize merit and skill of each other
5. Don't know why one does what he does and how he feels
6. Style of work is 'block'
7. Not cohesive
8. Don't level—withdrawal from confrontation
9. Some change—now provide local unit service (was district-oriented and operators of activities)
10. Fast pick-up on board decisions and tasks
11. Staff participation in policy formulation

II. Our Perception of B

1. Issue-oriented—take stands and let it be known
2. Crusaders
3. Aggressive toward organizational goals and objectives
4. Sensitive to needs of each other
5. Swinging staff
6. Total unit knows where they stand and look to them for direction.

III. Our Estimation of How B Perceives Us

1. Cautious-status quo keeper
2. Building individual empires
3. "Country boys"—not cosmopolitan
4. Part of establishment viewed as unit with no shining stars (or rabble rousers)
5. Older—set in their ways
6. Resist change

Organization B

I. Perception of Ourselves

1. High degree of leveling with each other
2. Enjoy catharsis
3. Gutsy group—willing to take risks
4. Not task-oriented
5. Like to develop own agenda
6. Flexible
7. Free to change
8. Diversified internal resources
9. Proud bastards—we're glad we're humble
10. Innovative
11. High trust—open—brainstormers

II. Our Perception of A

1. Conservative on issues/race/money/politics
2. Task-oriented
3. Not together
4. Up tight
5. Lack openness with each other/others
6. Tradition-bound
7. Unwillingness to take risks. Scared? Of what?
8. Desire to be cooperative
9. Solid—dependable—safe

III. Our Estimation of How A Perceives Us

1. Way out—extremists
2. Controversial
3. Bunch of individualists
4. Quick triggers
5. Vocal
6. Swinging staff
7. Going too far—too fast
8. Bunch of proud bastards
9. Threatening but possibly explosive enough to carry them to new "things"
10. Insensitive to their kinds of work problems

■ The differences in the organizations were known to each other. That is, the manner in which each organization described itself tended to be congruent with the way it was described by the other. In addition, the estimates that each organization made of how the other would describe them were, in general, accurate.

487

With an eye toward the merger, some major issues clearly would have to be handled. *First,* organization A saw itself as task or project-oriented, while organization B's description implied that if concern was devoted to process issues, task and project accomplishment would flow naturally. This situation is reminiscent of T-Group dynamics where very frequently the initial conflict that develops is between those group members who wish to focus on some sort of task and those whose orientation is toward process.

Second, it appeared there were qualitative differences in the nature of the interpersonal and group communications that took place within each organization. Organization A's self-picture included nonleveling and avoiding confrontation. Feelings were not shared, which reasonably could lead to a fair amount of energy being expended in trying to find out just what the other person was really saying. The quality of the communications in organization B was different. The impression conveyed is that a good bit of leveling occurred, members reflected high trust, and the system was quite open.

Third, perhaps underlying the difference between the two organizations, and contributing generically to the problems that the two groups might meet when they joined forces, were attitudes about authority. One gets the feeling that organization A's members tended to be dependently oriented. The authority orientation of organization B seemed to be more independent with, possibly, a liberal sprinkling of counterdependency.

By engaging in the confrontation exercise, then, two developments took place that would play a major role in helping the organizations plan for their joint future. Data had been collected which, from the point of view of the consultant, indicated organizational problem areas that would have to be dealt with if the merger were to take place effectively. Moreover, the data were shared publicly by the two groups in a nondefensive manner. In other words, this public sharing was the beginning, hopefully, of the development of a norm for the merged organization that would encourage and maintain an openness of communication about organizational and interpersonal matters.

Finally, in regard to the confrontation exercise, it was obvious that though there were no statements of "We're better than you are" in the 3–D Images, one is left with a distinct impression of value differences between Organizations A and B—in which B had the edge. These impressions were reinforced at the time by inquiries made to the consultant by Organization A concerning his availability for some further training. Such overtures were not received from Organization B. There was some talk about the latter having engaged in a staff-development program that included sensitivity training. It was almost as though members of Organization B were saying about A, "They've got their problems to work out. Let's get together again when they've worked them through."

488

b. Enlarging the Data Base:
Independent Data to Confirm the 3-D Images

At this point, no agreement existed about going forward with any training for merger. But one point was clear. From the consultant's viewpoint, the data collected from the confrontation session constituted an inadequate base for any deliberative strategies for change. This meant, of course, that there was a need for the collection of additional data that would help diagnose more clearly the differences between the two organizations and that also could provide a better base from which to induce movement. The point was this: the data obtained from the confrontation design were interesting, but useful only for a limited purpose. What would be needed, if future consultant-client contact developed, would be a way of helping the two organizational groups formulate workable behavioral guidelines for their new organization to which all could commit themselves. It was also critically important that these guidelines be based on rational inquiry and deliberation as well as feelings. This latter point derives from the notion that questions about and conflicts of emotionality are crucial in opening a system and catalyzing it into action. But to base the action solely on emotional data is hardly a defensible posture to take when planning for change.

In addition to the practical problem of change, the consultant was curious about these two organizations from an academic viewpoint. The confrontation data indicated glaring differences between A and B. How would these differences show up in some sort of quantitative measure? From a diagnostic point of view, were there elements of each organization's character where little or no incongruence existed? What factors could conceivably account for the differences that had been observed and, in all probability, would be observed if additional data were to be collected?

In order to help answer both the operational and academic questions, permission was received to administer the Likert Profile of Organization Characteristics[27] and FIRO–B[28] to all members of each organization. Likert's Profile was chosen because it permits a measurement of the organizational characteristics as they are currently seen by the members and also solicits an ideal image of the organization. It was felt that the latter point would be of particular importance if the two organizations did agree to work and train together prior to the merger. In a sense, the measures of the ideal image of their organization could provide goals around which forces could be mobilized to create and agree upon behavioral norms that might induce goal attainment.

---

27. Rensis Likert, *The Human Organization* (New York: McGraw-Hill Book Co., 1967).
28. Schutz, *op. cit.*

As noted in previous sections, Likert's instrument is based on the idea of characterizing the management system of an organization in terms of seven organizational processes. Form J–2 of the instrument was used. It contains 18 items, each of which is rated on a 20-point scale. There are four major subdivisions of each scale. Each is described in some detail and corresponds to Likert's notion of management systems—System 1, Authoritative-Exploitative; System 2, Benevolent-Authoritative; System 3, Consultative; and System 4, Participative Group. Respondents are asked to rate each item according to the manner in which they *Now* see their organization, and also according to the *Ideal* they prefer for their organization. The results may be reported in either tabular or profile form.

The use of FIRO–B as another means to collect potentially important data was, frankly, more of a fishing expedition than it was based on any theoretically derived hypothesis. Given the differences that had developed, FIRO–B data were desired by the consultant in response to curiosity. Could it be that the organizational differences were related to differences of the interpersonal need structures of the members? FIRO–B, essentially, taps three kinds of need situations:

- inclusion
- affection
- control

Some of the data obtained with these two instruments is summarized below in the discussion of Tables 9 and 10.

c. The Pre-Merger Design: A Two-Phase Model

Given the opportunity to collect formal data, the strategy of the consultant became clarified. It included, at the discretion of the client systems, two additional meetings: one with Organization A which would be an attempt to help that group open its internal communications, and one in which both A and B would get together for a data-feedback and planning session. The consultant's services were requested for these meetings, and they were held.

The meeting with Organization A was a two-and-one-half-day affair. It was not a T-Group. Rather, the session focused on what might be termed "organizational garbage." That is, the attempt was to clear out the clutter of unresolved issues and confusions that appeared to have developed over a period of years. The issues dealt with seemed not to focus on matters of personality but on questions of policy clarification, more precise implications of organizational decisions that had been made, and issues of role conflict and ambiguity.

490

One very important decision was made during the meeting. Members of Organization A whose function was to offer direct program services, in contrast to the field consultative function, decided that their best interests would not be served by being part of the merger. They opted out, which was within their prerogative. This decision meant that future planning and deliberation concerning the merger would involve only those members of the two organizations who would conceivably be part of the new consolidated organization. Some eight members of each organization were thus excluded.

It appeared to the consultant that the most valuable result of the session with the members of Organization A was that their internal communications system seemed to have been opened. People said things that had been on their minds for a long time. No one had been punished. A good bit of behavioral feedback, though not here-and-now oriented, had been given and, more importantly, received. It was apparently the first time that this group had met in order to have a look at themselves, and from the comments of the participants, the effort had been well worthwhile. They had achieved a start on the road that might enable them to communicate with Organization B members on a level that both groups desired.

There was a side effect to the meeting which, though not related to its substance, was critical to the success of the merger program. Some sense emerged as to where the merger program might go. Indeed, it was at the close of this meeting that the consultant was asked specifically if he had time available to meet with both organizations in order to help them examine the data and make plans concerning the development of norms and operating procedures of the consolidated unit. The meeting was scheduled. Time conflicts permitted only a one-day session which would be held during a four-day meeting of the two organizations.

The design for the session was simple. Its two phases were feedback and action. As conceived by the consultant, the design would involve a brief review of the history of the problem, the presentation of the results of the data collection, and the convening of subgroup task forces around particular issues that arose from the data analysis. The job of the task forces would be to analyze the issues in depth and then propose a set of operational guidelines that would, hopefully, constitute the functional and procedural norms of the merged group.

Feedback re Characteristics of Two Organizations

The data were presented to the two organizations by use of a typical Likert Profile. Because of the length and complexity of the Profile, it is presented here in summary form, rather than item by item. No meaning is lost in this convenient substitution.

A comparison of Tables 9 and 10 indicates that there are marked differences in the two organizations as far as their Now scores are concerned. Organization A is clearly a System 3 or Consultative unit, while the mean Now scores for B are all within System 4, Participative Group. The Ideal scores for both organizations are System 4. In sum, A's mem-

Table 9. Profile of Organization A

Organizational Characteristics	Mean— Now Scores	S.D.	Mean— Ideal Scores	S.D.	T	Level of Significance
Leadership processes	11.53	3.9	17.16	4.6	3.83	.01
Motivational forces	11.94	3.2	17.16	4.6	3.97	.01
Communications processes	12.53	3.8	17.23	4.6	3.57	.015
Interaction-influence processes	12.27	4.3	17.99	4.7	3.96	.01
Decision-making processes	12.52	4.6	17.05	4.9	3.18	.025
Goal-setting processes	11.13	3.3	17.21	4.7	4.58	.01
Control processes	12.37	4.3	16.83	5.2	3.44	.02

Table 10. Profile of Organization B

Organizational Characteristics	Mean— Now Scores	S.D.	Mean— Ideal Scores	S.D.	T	Level of Significance
Leadership processes	17.29	3.1	17.87	2.8	1.79	N.S.
Motivational forces	15.87	3.5	16.87	3.7	2.00	N.S.
Communications processes	17.91	1.1	18.78	1.1	2.15	N.S.
Interaction-influence processes	18.18	1.3	18.99	1.0	1.77	N.S.
Decision-making processes	17.74	1.5	18.34	1.4	1.64	N.S.
Goal-setting processes	17.21	1.8	18.15	1.6	1.62	N.S.
Control processes	16.79	1.4	17.62	1.4	1.97	N.S.

bers would like their organization to be at the level at which organization B apparently was already operating. This latter point was, of course, central to the future program activities. In effect, the Ideal scores also indicated the operating norms that would be necessary for the merged organization to develop and maintain, if conflict were to be minimized and productivity enhanced.

Tables 9 and 10 are also consistent with the 3–D Images developed in

492

the confrontation exercise in which both organizations participated. That is, the systematic data obtained from the administration of Likert's Profile tends to confirm the sense of the confrontation results. It is possible that the confrontation exercise itself could be structured somewhat differently so that more focused data could be obtained, thus providing a quick measure of organizational or group characteristics.

The results of administration of FIRO–B revealed no differences between A and B members concerning questions of interpersonal compatibility or levels of interpersonal needs. Whatever the reasons for the differences between the two organizations, they seemed not to be related to interpersonal needs or compatibility, at least in the way these are measured by the FIRO–B instrument.

Planning Organizational Norms by Task Force

After the data were presented, task forces were formed by asking people to volunteer to work on proposals about those organizational issues in which they were most interested. The idea was that each task force would bring back to the total group its recommendations concerning operating norms that would, hopefully, induce a System 4 orientation into the merged organization. The group would react to the proposals, which would then be refined into document form. The final document described a management style preferred by members of the recently merged region. The document was addressed:

- to those suggesting candidates for the executive post
- to those making the decision on the executive post
- to those candidates for the executive post who wish to examine how the staff could work best to achieve a high level of productivity

In a sense, then, the two organizations had combined to "tell it like it is," both to those who would be making decisions about the new executive and to potential applicants for the position. The staff members involved were saying, in effect: "These are the organizational conditions under which we see ourselves working most productively. It would be to the best interests of our organization and us if our needs and desires regarding these conditions were congruent with those of the new executive." The substance of the final document is given in Figure 5.

Though the executives of A and B were present at the meeting at which the basics of the document were formulated, neither signed the document. Their reasoning was that this was a staff matter. Moreover, both might be candidates for the position in question.

493

Figure 5. A Preferred Management Style for a Newly Merged Region

The C Region Staff agreed upon the way in which the staff members can work best to achieve a high level of productivity.

There is consensus by the staff on:

1. decision-making processes
2. processes which would motivate us
3. goal-setting processes
4. type of leadership for this management system

We would like to share these characteristics of our Regional Staff Team with you.

Decision-Making Processes

Our staff feels that decision making in an open participative atmosphere is a staff competency of high priority. If a member of the C Region Staff, including the Executive, is in need of data for making a decision, the process would call:

1. For him to state to the staff the locus of the decision-making, i.e., an individual staff man, the Executive, the Regional Staff, other.
2. For the issue requiring a decision to be identified.
3. For all available data to be put on the table.
4. For a thorough testing of all opinions.
5. For choices to be clearly stated.
6. For the final decision and the reasons for the decision to be shared quickly with the staff.

The C Region Staff feels it important that each staff man be supported with an agreed-upon decision-making process which he may confidently exercise while in the field. We expect a supportive stance of our action by the Executive and our Staff Associates. One process would require answers to the following questions:

1. Has the problem been identified?
2. Have sufficient data been collected?
3. What are the options?
4. What is the decision?

In our relationships to all decision-making which affects this staff, an open initiative-consultative approach would be exercised by staff members. Therefore, we see our staff affecting decision-making at all levels through our interactional process with other Regional Staffs, Headquarters staffs, local staffs, or others.

Processes Which Motivate us

Running throughout our work together is our unanimous feeling that we are motivated to our highest level of productivity through participative management exercised at the optimum.

We believe that the processes of "Management by Objective" provide the best vehicle for achieving organizational objectives.

An open communication system of vertical and horizontal dimensions is essential to motivation as we demonstrate our initiative-consultative functions.

We are motivated by a continuing process of evaluation of our individual and staff work.

We believe that our motivation to be highly productive is correlated to the trust level experienced by the staff members, including the Executive.

Goal Setting

We believe it to be our management responsibility to have a process which sets goals by involving all staff affected by work related to achieving those goals.

We make use of a linkage system with other units (headquarters, local, other) to participate in establishing goals which affect us.

Likewise, the use of the consultative method in setting our own goals has consistently involved others beyond our Regional Staff.

Leadership Processes

We are in agreement that there are some essential guidelines for a leadership style for this staff team.

This team produces best with a participative leader who provides the following:

1. A generous amount of participation from fellow staff members in his style of leadership.

494

Figure 5—continued

2. A wide-open gut-level system of vertical and horizontal communication.
3. A sharing of leadership through the group in the planning and execution of overall responsibilities.
4. An open access to the power structure of the organization (lay and staff).
5. A management of the agreed-upon processes developed by the staff.

In our interpersonal staff relations we agreed that we would work best with an Executive who supports a supervisor-supervisee role which calls for mutually agreed-upon goals for the supervisee with his supervisor to be shared with the staff.

Job segments and the standards of performance, the elements of job accountability for each staff man, should be fully tested with the entire staff, including those job segments and standards of performance expected of the Executive.

Conclusion

In conclusion, this document is a description of how the C Region Staff agrees it could work best to achieve a high level of productivity. It is not intended to describe the functions of our work but to relate how we see ourselves working effectively toward the achievement of those functions accepted by this Regional Staff as appropriate to the Movement.

You may well find this information to be useful to you in achieving your stated task.

Epilogue

The executive of Organization A became the executive of the newly merged organization. Organization B's executive accepted a comparable position as director of another merged unit in a different section of the country. Informal discussion with the new executive of Organization C and some of his associates indicated that they viewed the process of planning for the merger as having been very effective. In their words, they were "off and running" and felt they were quite a bit ahead of the other organizational units that had merged through one process or another. Perhaps the most important thing that had occurred is that the staff developed, through the whole process, what seems to be a more articulated sense of their own power and trust in each other.

d. A Model for Mergers?:
Some Differences and Basic Similarities

The situation we have described does not bear a one-to-one relationship to merger conditions that exist in the world of business and industry. For example, though there was a parent unit involved and its influence was felt, this was not a case of one organization "taking over" another. Rather, the present merger created one supra-organization from two equals. In addition, though financial matters were important, because the organizational goals were oriented toward service and not profits or enlarged share of the market, the eventual success of the merger cannot be measured in usual business terms. Finally, the units in question were rather small ones and no doubt avoided major issues involved in larger-scale mergers.

495

Nevertheless, the events that have been discussed bear enough similarity on a process level to the broader picture so that some tentative statements may be made concerning the human problems of mergers and the potential resolution of these problems.

First, inherent in any merger situation is the substantial potential for tension and distrust among those individuals whose positions and function will potentially be most affected. Even if assurances about job tenure are given, the tensions will derive from questions of ambiguity about role and reporting relationships. This suggests, immediately, the necessity for an open acknowledgement of the tension-creating situation. Conditions must be created where people can talk about their concerns and have them listened to and understood.

Second, mergers mean change. It is not honest to say that "business as usual" will be the order of the day. There will be changes in procedures, operating norms, reporting relationships, and management styles, among others. The confrontation design, or some modification of it, could be helpful in laying the groundwork for such changes to proceed in a productive fashion. As well as providing a substantive input into the situation, the confrontation design can help create the openness that will be required as the merger process develops.

Third, some operational and quantifiable means of pinpointing specific organizational differences needs to be employed if those primarily involved in the merger are to be given the opportunity to examine organizational differences in a deliberate and intelligent fashion. It is not enough to acknowledge that differences exist and "we will take care of them as we go along." The utilization of Likert's Profile of Organizational Characteristics in the present case was very helpful.

Fourth, despite the small size of the units involved in this merger, the case provides real analogs relevant to merger teams dealing with far larger entities. Merger teams typically run to no more than 10 or so to a side, roughly the present size. Probably the major difference between this merger and one involving larger organizations is the effect of numerous levels. The present case involved only two levels, headquarters and the two field units. Larger mergers require integration between more hierarchical levels, and perhaps also between such categoric groups as labor and management which may be involved at each level.

Fifth, perhaps the most critical point of all in the present case, and probably in all mergers, is the need to obtain the collaborative involvement of those individuals whose jobs will be most directly affected by the merger. By this involvement around both the process and substantive issues of the merger it may be possible for people to feel a sense of ownership of the commitment to the new organization.

Sixth, in some merger designs, it might be important to use a fishbowl

496

or group-observing-group[29] formation. This is likely to be the case, especially, where the members of the two units are strangers to one another and where observing the processes of each group by the other could provide very rich data and insights. In this case, although the 3–D Images were developed by the individual groups in isolation, little was probably lost. The point-by-point correspondences of the 3–D Images, for example, suggest that the members of both groups had a detailed knowledge of one another. A group-observing-group design could help generate similar data for relative stranger groups.

29. Blake, *op. cit.*, pp. 519–20.

Some
Sense of
Future
Challenges

Part III. Some Sense of Future Challenges

A. PATTERNS FOR THE FUTURE:[1]
TOWARD THE ADAPTIVE ORGANIZATION

This section has several purposes which call for early spotlighting. The basic purpose is to provide a structural emphasis that is too little in evidence in many treatments of the laboratory approach to OD.[2] This neglect has several facets. First, the laboratory approach often has been applied at high levels of organization, where interaction is far more important than organization structure or job design. The neglect of the latter topics in the OD literature is, in this sense, natural and convenient enough. Second, convenience has often been preened into a law of nature, which neglects the practical and theoretical leverage inherent in structural change.[3] Third, OD efforts tend to assume that changes in attitudes must precede structural change. Substantial evidence suggests, however, that in a broad range of cases prior structural change not only can induce attitudinal change but is in fact essential to it.[4]

Hence this section directs attention to the major propositions that structural-technical arrangements tend to induce specific patterns of interaction and that, consequently, permanent behavioral change often will depend on structural-technical change. The present approach is

1. This chapter draws heavily on Robert T. Golembiewski, "Patterns of the Future: What They Mean to Personnel Administration," *Personnel Administration*, Vol. 32 (December, 1969), pp. 8–24.
2. The neglect is forcefully noted by Wallace Wohlking, "Management Training: Where Has It Gone Wrong?" *Training and Development Journal*, Vol. 25 (December, 1971), pp. 2–8. For a major exception to the usual neglect, see Gordon Lippitt, *Organizational Renewal* (New York: Appleton-Century-Crofts, 1969).
3. The potency of structural change is stressed by Eliott Chapple and Leonard R. Sayles, *The Measure of Management* (New York: Macmillan Co., 1971).
4. Chester A. Insko, *Theories of Attitude Change* (New York: Appleton-Century-Crofts, 1967), pp. 345–58.

through two alternative structural models applicable at all organization levels. These models can help guide OD applications based on the laboratory model, when structural versus interactional issues are more dominant.

1. A FRAMEWORK FOR ANALYSIS: PERSPECTIVES ON ORGANIZATION STRUCTURE

The framework for the following analysis requires bold statement, since that analysis often goes against the grain of common ways of dealing with organization structure. Two emphases will provide that statement. The first details the basic flow of the argument; and the second emphasis deals with two broad managerial conceptualizations that are profoundly important for organization structure.

a. The Basic Flow of Analysis:
Four Themes

Four themes can be identified in the essential flow of this analysis of organization structure. *First,* it would be perverse (and perhaps even worse) to persistently seek to modify behavior and interaction while the inducing structural arrangements remain untouched. The perversity would be greatest at lower levels of organization. This is where the clearest structural-technical constraints tend to be and, of huge significance, the lower hierarchical levels are home to the bulk of organization women and men. Chris Argyris made the point well in noting two relatively distinct challenges:[5]

- The lower one goes down the chain of command, the more the job and the work environment control the individual's behavior. Consequently, the more important it becomes to change the psycho-socio-technical environment. These include changes in technology, job design, incentive systems, budgeting, salary systems, and training activities.
- The higher one goes up the chain of command, the more the individual has control over his work environment and the more important it becomes to change the interpersonal environment. Its main features are trust, confidence, openness, nonconformity, as well as rivalry or defensiveness within the organization. Changes in such interpersonal features can support policy changes, in turn, as toward decentralization.

---

5. Chris Argyris, *Interpersonal Competence and Organizational Effectiveness* (Homewood, Ill.: Dorsey Press, 1962) , pp. 2–3.

The point may be put another way. OD applications high in the chain of command will tend to involve more straightforward uses of the laboratory approach to facilitate interaction and to improve group processes. Applications at lower levels often will involve intertwined structural and technological elements, and the early emphasis in OD programs at those levels might even be on such elements.

Second, all patterns for organizing work reflect and rest upon a set of ideas, ideas that deal in complex ways with what the world of work is and how it should be. One cannot be far wrong in calling each of these sets of ideas a "world view." For these sets of ideas deal with *the* basic issues: the nature of man, as well as the character and the quality of the authoritative relations that are appropriate for man. Two such world views are distinguished below. One is consistent with the laboratory approach; the other is not.

Third, the two world views will be related to specific alternative ways for structuring work. These alternative structural approaches are dealt with in generalized terms, but they apply at both high and low levels in all organizations.

Fourth, personnel administration will be the specific managerial function on which the impact of the two world views, as well as of the alternative models for organizing work generated by these world views, will be illustrated. The decision is not capricious. The rationale supporting the choice of personnel administration is direct. Applying the laboratory approach to OD will require basic changes in the dominant managerial world view, as well as in the prevailing way of structuring work. And for good or ill, much of the impetus for such changes must derive from the function generally identified as "personnel administration." Hence the choice here.

b. Two Contrasting World Views:
Push Theory vs. Pull Theory

Two contrasting world views about organizing work today occupy center stage in thought about management. For convenience, they are called the push theory and the pull theory. In the push theory, the employee scrambles and innovates and burns the midnight oil to avoid possible and perhaps inevitable harsh outcomes. In one version of this view, men work hard because it is morally bad to do otherwise. The properties of this view are like those of McGregor's Theory X, or 9,1 on Blake's Managerial Grid.

William H. Whyte's *The Organization Man*[6] illustrates the managerial push theory and laments its demise. Gone are the old stimuli to heroic

6. William H. Whyte, *The Organization Man* (Garden City, N.Y.: Doubleday Anchor Books, 1957).

effort such as survival-of-the-fittest training programs that tested a man's desire and skills or broke him. In their place, Whyte saw manifold nicely-nicelies such as longish training programs that effectively closed the school of hard knocks. In Whyte's view, organization men were whistling their way through the dark, hand in hand, neglecting harsh realities for which they were less and less prepared. Given the push theory, no harshness, no progress.

In the managerial pull theory, the focus is more on what you are reaching toward than on what you are seeking to avoid. In it, the employee also scrambles and innovates and burns the midnight oil. However, work is so need-satisfying that it elicits massive employee efforts. The goal is dual: doing the job better, and doing it in ways that permit unprecedented personal freedom in organizations. Indeed, this view almost says that *it is only through greater personal freedom* that a better job can be accomplished. Organization life is demanding in this view, but it does promise fulfillment at work. Warren Bennis articulates both emphases clearly:

> I think that the future I describe is not necessarily a "happy" one. Coping with rapid change, living in temporary work systems—all augur social strains and psychological tensions . . .
>
> In these new organizations of the future, participants will be called upon to use their minds more than at any other time in history. Fantasy, imagination, and creativity will be legitimate in ways that today seem strange. Social structures will no longer be instruments of psychic repression but will increasingly promote play and freedom on behalf of curiosity and thought.[7]

The underlying theme is patent. Contemporary organizations tend to place greater demands on their members. Consequently, organizations must provide greater potential for need-satisfaction. The managerial pull theory seeks to integrate personal needs and organizational demands.[8] In essence, the underlying rationale—consistent with the discussion in Sections C and D of Part I—proposes that:

- Many individuals find little satisfaction in their work, and this is a major deprivation for them personally as well as for their organization.

- Many or all individuals will be more productive as they exercise greater control over their work, and as work permits satisfaction of a broadening range of needs.

---

7. Warren G. Bennis, "Beyond Bureaucracy," *Trans-Action*, Vol. 2 (July–August, 1965), p. 35.
8. See especially Chris Argyris, *Integrating the Individual and the Organization* (New York: John Wiley & Sons, 1964).

504

- Organizations increasingly need superior output from more and more of their employees, and technological and skill requirements are such that these contributions must be elicited more than forced. Consequently, expenditures to redesign jobs and work relations and to change managerial styles or techniques are reasonable; indeed, in the longer run they are probably necessary.

2. THE NEAR-TERM PROSPECTS:
A MIXED EMPHASIS

It seems clear that personnel administration will have to be consciously concerned with both managerial theories. That the prospects for the immediate future imply a mixed emphasis may be established economically.

The pull theory seems destined to get increasing attention, if we

Figure 1. Some Technological Trends Influencing Today's Organizations

From Basic Emphasis upon:	To Growing Emphasis upon:
Regularity in operations	Creativity in concept; adaptability in execution
Programmed decisions	Novel decisions
Stable and simple competencies, technologies, and market	Volatile and complex competencies, technologies, and markets
Stop-and-go processing	Continuous processing
Stable product lines, programs	Volatile product lines, programs
Monolithic product lines, programs	Variegated product lines, programs
Demands of hierarchy	Demands of task, technology, profession
Departmental orientation	System orientation
Expanding volume at central site	Developing national and international field units

project today's trends a decade or so ahead. Specifically, the pull theory becomes increasingly appropriate as organizations move rightward in Figure 1, and such movement seems very probable. The reader can supply the full rationale for the relevance of the pull theory under the conditions sketched in the right column. To illustrate, you can order someone to obey when work or decisions are programmed. Ordering someone to be creative is quite another matter.

The organizational world will not soon be stood on its head, however. As was the case in the past, the personnel administration of the future no doubt will also give significant attention to structure and policies consistent with the push theory. Briefly, technological requirements influence which structure and managerial techniques are likely to be successful, and not all organizations will or even can move sharply rightward on the dimensions above. Certainly, at least different technologies and markets will move rightward at different times and places. Thus today's plastics industry reflects the characteristics in the right column, but the cardboard carton industry does not. As compelling new evidence suggests, opposite managerial styles can be effective in these two industries.[9] Roughly, the push theory is more appropriate to the technology and market of the cardboard carton industry than to the plastics industry. To the degree that technologies and markets like the carton industry will continue to exist, then, so also will personnel administration have to give attention to structure and policies consistent with the push-theory.

The point is not that the pull theory is inferior to the push-theory under some conditions. Rather, the position is a practical one. Man is a satisficing animal. Under conditions like those on the left in Figure 1, the push theory is likely to be less challenged than by the opposite set of conditions. The immediate pressure for change is likely to be low, as a consequence, and traditional patterns for organizing work are likely to persist.

3. THE LONG-TERM PROSPECTS: TOWARD THE PULL THEORY THROUGH FOUR POLARITIES

Since the managerial pull theory seems congenial to the technology of the future, our focus narrows. We live in a transitional period, and the following analysis extends what is already happening into a reasonably coherent view of what the future implies for personnel administration. The effort is somewhat speculative, but it is grounded in today's major organizational trends, from which it extrapolates somewhat.

a. Some Polarities: A Developmental Model in Four Variables

Probable changes in organizational patterns consistent with the pull theory can be described in terms of four polarities. Different times and technologies give different emphases to each. The four polarities are:

---

9. Paul R. Lawrence and Jay W. Lorsch, *Organization and Environment* (Boston: Harvard Graduate School of Business Administration, 1967). See also Alexander Winn, "Reflections on T-Group Strategy and the Role of Change Agent in Organization Development," *Journal of Applied Behavioral Science*, Vol. 2 (April, 1966), esp. pp. 6–8.

- differentiation/integration
- repression/wriggle room, or freedom to act
- stability/newness
- function/flow of work

These four polarities imply a common assumption as well as variegated structures for work. Short of anarchy, there is no real choice of structure or no structure. The emphases placed on these four polarities, however, significantly influence the kind of structure that does develop in organizations. A wide range of alternative organization patterns is possible.

Four points establish how organization structures are sensitive to variations in these polarities. *First,* any organizing pattern reflects relative emphases on differentiation/integration. Following Paul R. Lawrence and Jay W. Lorsch, "differentiation" can be defined in terms of the development among the several units of an organization of "different formal reporting relationships, different criteria for rewards, and different control procedures." In sum, differentiation is defined in terms of "the difference in cognitive and emotional orientation among managers in different functional departments." Integration refers to "the quality of the state of collaboration that exists among departments that are required to achieve unity of effort by the demands of the environment."[10]

Organization patterns of the near future will no doubt increasingly emphasize integration. Early organizational experience tended to reflect integration, as in the crafts. Over the first half of this century, however, the emphasis shifted to the differentiation of functions and skills. Thus bureaucracy dominated this phase of organization history, and that concept is rooted in differentiation. The concept "bureaucracy" includes:

- a well-defined chain of command that vertically channels formal interaction
- a system of procedures and rules for dealing with all contingencies at work, which reinforces the reporting insularity of each bureau
- a division of labor based upon specialization by major function or process that vertically fragments a flow of work
- promotion and selection based on technical competence defined consistently with the first three points above
- impersonality in relations between organization members and between them and their clients

More recently, integration has received increasing emphasis. The "system approach" and the computer are the major contemporary technical ex-

---

10. Lawrence and Lorsch, *op. cit.,* pp. 10–11.

pressions of this integrative thrust. Behaviorally, integration implies meeting both human needs and technical demands at work.

Second, a basic consequence of any pattern for organizing is its relative emphasis on repression and "wriggle room." Every structure intentionally limits behavior, that is, but some do so significantly more than others. No technical definitions seem necessary here, for "surplus repression" is commonly seen as a major product of bureaucracy. Increasingly, an emerging integrative emphasis seeks an organizational climate having the minimal constraints consistent with quality performance. This is the essence of the contemporary stress on management by objectives, or on A.T.&T.'s vertical loading of jobs described in Section D, Part II. Similarly, the popularity of sensitivity training reflects massive concern about such costs of repression as withheld effort or information.

There is no mistaking the root cause of today's deemphasis on repression. Contemporary organizations reflect a growing need for an organic and evolving integration, as opposed to a mechanical structuring. The consequences are profound. In short, adherence to a mechanical system can be enforced, but commitment to an organic integration can only be elicited and encouraged. Put another way, the integrity of a stable and simple technology may be safeguarded by culling deviants. But changing and complex technologies require the careful husbanding of selected kinds of innovation or adaptability in a widening range of employees. Hence the growing importance of wriggle room, or freedom to act.

The change in emphasis on repression/wriggle room may be characterized broadly, and with essential accuracy. The bureaucratic spirit is oriented toward developing a system to guard against man at his worst, to preclude error or venality. Flows of work are differentiated as functions or positions or motions, and surplus repression is the glue used to pull them together. The integrative spirit, on the other hand, is oriented toward creating an environment in which man can approach his productive best. Hence the emphasis on wriggle room, on learning how and when individuals can more often meet their own needs while contributing more effectively to a total flow of work with which they identify their interests.

There are costs whether the thrust is integrative or fragmenting, of course, and the purpose here is not to obscure this elemental datum. The costs of the bureaucratic logic are repression and narrowed developmental opportunities; and the costs of freedom to act may be calculated in terms of lessened control over behavior, or of more complex decision-making processes which hopefully facilitate the implementing of decisions. Thus the argument is not that integration is a facile panacea. Rather, the point here is that more and more technological developments require that we cope with the costs of the integrative model.

508

Third, the relative emphasis on stability/newness also has profound implications for organization structures. The acceleration of newness has been described in many places, even if one cannot feel it in his bones. Hence the bare notice here that all but overwhelming newness is a trademark of our times and that it is poorly served by bureaucratic properties. In sum, the bureaucratic model better serves the trends listed in the left column of Figure 1 than it meets those listed on the right.

Fourth, different emphases on the three polarities above imply different organization structures built around functions and flows of work, respectively. Illustrating this conclusion requires a major input.

b. Two Generalized Organizations:
Structural Embodiments of Opposed Polarities

Demonstrating that different emphases on the polarities above will generate different organization structures is straightforward,[11] if involved. Take an easy case, to begin: the organization of three activities, A, B, and C, which when combined yield some product or service. Figure 2 presents the skeletal structure consistent with these four emphases: differentiation, repression, stability, and flow of work.

The ways in which the two structures reflect extreme emphases on the four polarities can be suggested briefly. For example, Figure 2 essentially puts the same or similar activities together in its basic units of organization. That is, the model builds on departments *differentiated* by kinds of activities, usually called "functions" at high levels of organization and "processes" at lower levels. Relatedly, the narrow span of control is well designed to facilitate surplus repression in the details of operation. That is, the structure encourages centralization of decision-making at the level of M_{ABC}, who alone can make reasonable decisions about the flow of work, $A + B + C$. Hence he alone controls a "managerial unit." Finally, the model presumes a *stable* state. The underlying model is that of a mechanical meshing of parts rather than of a dynamic flow of work.

Figure 3 presents an alternative structure that is consistent with the principal adaptations that have been made to the ongoing organizational revolution. These adaptive arrangements include: decentralization, project management, matrix overlays, independent profit centers, management by objectives, autonomous teams, and numerous other variations on the theme.

As the Figure 3 model suggests, these adaptations in common stress integration, wriggle room, change, and flow of work. The compound con-

---

11. A detailed comparison of these models is provided in Robert T. Golembiewski, *Men, Management, and Morality* (New York: McGraw-Hill Book Co., 1965). For corroborative evidence, see Chapple and Sayles, *op. cit.;* and Eric Trist *et al., Organizational Choice* (London: Tavistock Institute, 1962).

Figure 2. A Structure Consistent with the Push Theory and the Values of Bureaucracy: Emphasis on Differentiation, Repression, Stability, and Function

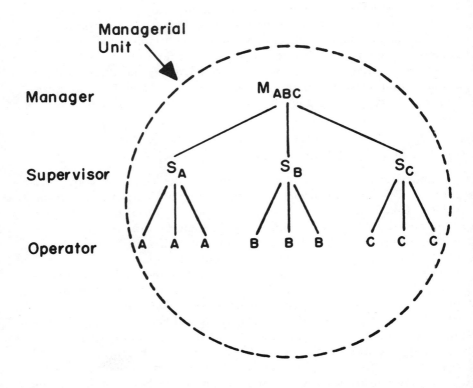

Underlying Properties

Authority is a vertical, or hierarchical, relation.

Departments are organized around the same or similar activities, called "functions" at high levels of organization and "processes" at low levels; that is, "like" activities are put together.

Only a relatively small number of people should report directly to any superior.

clusion will only be illustrated here. To begin, the unorthodox model organizes around *integrative* departments, that is, it groups together activities that are related in a total flow of work. This integrative thrust at the departmental level also can be extended to the operators, as through job rotation and job enlargement. In addition, the model seeks the *minimum control* that is consistent with end-item quality and quantity. The multiple opportunities for self-discipline and self-control built into the model, for example, reduce the need for external repression in tying individual needs to organizational goals. The key factors are teams

510

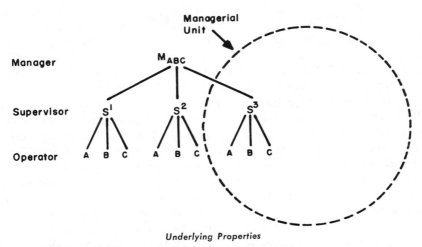

**Figure 3. An Alternative Structure:
Emphasis on Integration, Wriggle Room, Change, and Flow of Work**

Underlying Properties

Authoritative relations occur up, down, and across the organization, and all these vectors should be directed to similar goals by an effective structure.

Departmentation reflects the flow of work; that is, related activities are put together whether they are "like" or "unlike."

A relatively large number of people may report to any superior, given a structure that facilitates measuring performance.

which control a flow of work whose performance is easily and meaningfully comparable.

Implicitly, the role of higher management changes profoundly in a Figure 3 structure. The emphasis is on developing and monitoring measures of performance, and on responding to exceptions as that is necessary by training, by redefining policies, or by disciplinary action. Higher management in Figure 2 is far more in the fire-fighting business and is more oriented toward enforcing than eliciting.

Moreover, Figure 3 variously facilitates adapting to *change* and to *growth*. For example, Figure 2 structures tend to grow tall very quickly, with consequent increases in reaction time, in communication costs, and so on. The limited span of control is the major culprit. Figure 3 structures are much less growth-sensitive and can remain relatively flat even with manifold increases in size. For example, it would be possible to double the number of members in a Figure 3 structure while retaining its three hierarchical levels. Doubling the size of a Figure 2 structure would necessitate the creation of an additional supervisory layer.

Finally, Figure 3 structures departmentalize around *flows of work* as opposed to functions. Each S now controls a managerial unit.

511

The two structures are ideal types in that they are analytical extremes. In practice, they can be approached only in degree, often in complex mixtures. But approaches to one ideal model or the other will tend to generate significantly different consequences. The vertical loading of work described in Section D, Part II, for example, illustrates the movement from a Figure 2 job to a Figure 3 job at the operator's level. This movement implied major changes in the role of the manager as well as a freer work environment which emphasized self-control.[12]

A second example helps develop the fullness of the point and also illustrates the ideal association of interactional and structural emphases in an OD program based on the laboratory approach. The example comes from the early experience in the U.S. Department of State with Project ACORD, or Action for Organization Development. The OD program had two basic interacting elements: sensitivity training in cousin groups to help build appropriate values in the organization and to provide experience with necessary attitudes and values, and restructuring of work to approach laboratory values, when that was necessary. Figure 3 was the basic model guiding this structural change, and a Figure 2 model had basically inspired the existing structures which often required change. For example, a prevailing organizational feature was long chains of command, following a Figure 2 model, with many layers of review. A prime consequence was interminable decision-making times, even when what may be called a paralysis of analysis did not preclude timely action. A sensitivity training experience was intended to help prepare organization members to face such challenges. Beyond that, the structural emphasis in Project ACORD can be described in this summary way:

> As it were, structural reorganization was at once facilitated by this preparatory building of relations; and reorganization also raised the probability that these new relations would persist. Not surprisingly, one of the early emphases in Project ACORD was the creation of autonomous "program managers" who managed "activities that formed a coherent unit" and who reported directly to the Deputy Undersecretary of State for Administration.[13] The early experience seems very favorable. For example, one individual now reports directly to the Deputy Undersecretary. Prior to the reorganization, this towering chain of command loomed above him: Division Head, Office Director, Deputy Director of Personnel, Director of Personnel, Deputy

12. Robert N. Ford, *Motivation through the Work Itself* (New York: American Management Association, 1969).
13. Alfred J. Marrow, "Managerial Revolution in the State Department," *Personnel*, Vol. 43 (November–December, 1966), pp. 6–7.

512

Assistant Secretary for Administration, Assistant Secretary for Administration, and Deputy Undersecretary.[14]

A technology facilitating behavioral change, in short, undergirded a basic restructuring of work in this case. Note that it is convenient and even necessary to reverse that direction. At times, structural change might induce behavioral change.

c. Structural Forms and the Laboratory Approach: Linkages as Seen via Degenerative Interaction Systems

If the examples above seem to suggest that the laboratory approach to OD is more complementary with the structure in Figure 3 than Figure 2, that suggestion is intended. This section and the ones to follow will seek to establish the broad dimensions of the greater complementarity of the laboratory approach and a Figure 3 structure. Applications of the laboratory approach also are useful in a Figure 2 structure, especially in providing a palliative for the interpersonal and intergroup difficulties that tend to be induced by that kind of structure.

There is a gentle way of reflecting the greater complementarity of the laboratory approach to OD and a Figure 3 structure which simultaneously highlights the value of the laboratory approach even where a Figure 2 structure does not, and perhaps cannot, exist. Recall the notion of a degenerative interaction system, which involves a self-heightening model of four variables:

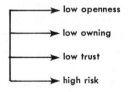

Such degenerative sequences are at once one of the prime targets for change of applications of the laboratory approach, one of the common products of a Figure 2 structure, and a major impediment to change-overs from Figure 2 to Figure 3 structures. Evidence also suggests that Figure 3 structures tend to induce forces that reverse degenerative sequences, as well as to reinforce regenerative sequences.[15]

Conveniently, a mini-argument sketches the fuller sense in which Figure 2 structures can encourage degenerative sequences. Consider only that $A + B + C$ generate some product or discrete subassembly and con-

14. Robert T. Golembiewski, *Organizing Men and Power: Patterns of Behavior and Line-Staff Models* (Chicago: Rand McNally & Co., 1967) , p. 153.
15. Golembiewski, *Organizing Men and Power*, pp. 60–267.

sequently must collaborate. But individual supervisors are responsible only for A or B or C, and thus tend to be drawn into zero-sum competitive games which fragment that which requires integration. For example, the very act of departmentalizing in a Figure 2 structure around like or similar activities encourages we/they dynamics. Illustratively, there are many reasons why A's will tend to identify in vertical cliques—reasons such as promotions, pay increases, etc. And organization dilemmas often make the worst of these reasonable identifications.[16] Thus S_A and an S_B could get involved in a question over the allocation of some costs in dispute, and any resulting socioemotional disturbance would at once be reinforced by the fragmentation inherent in a Figure 2 approach to departmentation, and it will also contribute to that fragmentation.

The common consequences of such fragmenting tendencies in a Figure 2 structure are reduced openness and owning between (for example) the units headed by S_A and S_B, which could lead to chronically low trust and paralyzingly high risk. The probabilities of such an outcome are increased by the problems of assessing validly and reliably the relative contributions to performance of A, B, and C, which issue plagues Figure 2 structures. The classic question is: How many A's are equal to how many B's? Appropriate standards are difficult to set and perhaps even harder to change, while they also involve major elements of arbitrariness. This combination encourages disputes, because all parties can rightly claim much virtue for their positions.

Moreover, M_{ABC} in a Figure 2 structure may have a vested if paradoxical interest in reinforcing such degenerative sequences. Assume his interest in avoiding low output. Note also that low output can be preserved tactfully only by the close cooperation of the three supervisors and their units. A certain measure of degenerative interaction between the Figure 2 units might seem a reasonable enough price to pay to avoid such an unwanted collaboration.

From many perspectives, then, Figure 2 structures often imply a high risk of trusting, of being open, and of owning one's ideas and feelings with those who are involved in the same flow of work.

Figure 3 structures trend oppositely. In a pure Figure 3 structure, performance of the units headed by S_1, S_2, and S_3 may be meaningfully com-

---

16. Leonard R. Sayles, *Managerial Behavior* (New York: McGraw-Hill Book Co., 1964), esp. pp. 58–82. Specifically, the relevance of regenerative systems increases, as does the scope and complexity of the task. Leonard R. Sayles and Margaret Chandler, *Managing Large Systems* (New York: Harper & Row, Publishers, 1971) p. 26, provide incisive illustration: ". . . in very large programs with long lead times incremental decisions must be made before the results of prior decisions are known. Step 4 depends on what happens in Step 3, but it may be necessary to begin 4 without knowing the results of 3." Low openness and trust in such a case could be catastrophic, patently, however more bearable it is in simple Figure 2 organizations.

pared, and at least some important elements such as productivity levels can be changed by the independent efforts of any individual work unit. This massive datum induces attractive relationships between $A + B + C$ in each of the three supervisory units. The structure encourages integration of what needs to be integrated, the several activities and persons necessary to produce some product or service. If A and B in S_1 are not open with one another, to bowdlerize the point, it could effect their mutual performance and consequently might come out of their combined hides.

Tersely, it is risky in a Figure 3 structure not to be open, not to own, and not to trust those in the same flow of work.

Several factors reinforce this tendency toward regenerative systems, where they are really needed. We/they relationships no doubt will exist in a Figure 3 structure between the units headed by S_1, S_2, and S_3, but relationships between those units are not critical to performance, except where massive antagonism between the units exists. In Figure 2 structures, in contrast, the probable we/they relationships are also the ones that should be integrative. It is by just such central tendencies that Figure 3 structures induce more attractive consequences than Figure 2 structures.

Relatedly, no tolerably acute M_{ABC} would be tempted to induce degenerative relationships within one of the supervisory units. Since valid and reliable measures of performance will be more available, M_{ABC} can rely more on self-control than on prodding, can concentrate on facilitating performance rather than on generating information by setting one unit against another.

d. Structural Forms and Their Consequences: Some Major Comparisons

The discussion above suggests that the major structural types based on the two alternative managerial views generate consequences that can differ profoundly. Table 1 at once consolidates, builds upon, and extends these differences between the two structural types. The table has been adapted somewhat for present purposes, but it is faithful to the existing research literature or to reasonable inferences where that literature is lacking. It stands on its own, especially since the preceding particularistic comparisons should provide a model for the comprehensive effort in the table.

Note that each structural form diversely gives as well as takes, that each has advantages and disadvantages. The critical issue then becomes one of choosing the structure which best meets the set of actual operating conditions, and the relevant challenge involves preparing to cope with the more-or-less inevitable problems generated by the structure that is

**Table 1. Comparisons of the Consequences of Two Structural Types,
Using Selected Properties of Performance**

Selected Properties	Figure 2 Structure: Functional Model	Figure 3 Structure: Flow-of-Work Model
1. Information Overload	1a. Tends toward information overload at level of integrative managers like M_{ABC}	1a^1. Reduces information overload at level of managers like M_{ABC}
	1b. Lengthens the social and psychological distances between the points at which messages originate, at which decisions are made, and at which actions will be taken	1b^1. Shortens the distance between points at which messages originate, at which decisions are made, and at which actions will be taken
	1c. Decreases the probability that messages will get through, at least without distortion	1c^1. Increases the probability that messages will get through, and with minimal distortion
	1d. Decreases likelihood that messages will be acted on	1d^1. Increases likelihood that messages will be acted on
2. Response Time	2a. Increases response time, due to longer communication chains	2a^1. Reduces response time, due to shorter chains
	2b. Prone to responses that are too little, too late, and to a paralysis of analysis.	2b^1. Increases the probability of timely awareness/response to rapidly changing conditions
	2c. Prone to errors of omission, to failure to communicate and/or to act	
3. Management Review	3a. Tends to refer decisions to higher management for prior review	3a^1. Tends to make decisions at lower levels, with later review at higher levels
	3b. Decreases likelihood of errors of commission at lower levels	3b^1. Increases likelihood of errors of commission at lower levels
	3c. Subjects decisions to considered judgment at various levels	3c^1. Decreases likelihood that decisions will benefit from top-level perspective
4. Decision Locus	4a. Centralizes decision-making	4a^1. Decentralizes decision-making
	4b. Decisions may suffer from lack of detailed and up-to-date information about operating situation	4b^1. Decisions may suffer in that they are so responsive to specific operating situation
5. Mutual Influence	5a. Reduces mutual influence across functional lines	5a^1. Increases and legitimates mutual influence across functional lines
	5b. Requires either informal bargaining or cumbersome up-over-and-down linkages of separate hierarchical chains of command that are integrated only far above the operating level	5b^1. Functions are integrated near the operating level via identification with a common flow of work
6. Competition/ Collaboration	6a. Encourages intergroup competition between functions	6a^1. Encourages collaboration between functions in same flow of work
	6b. Encourages we/they attitudes that fragment flow of work or, alternatively, a "mind your own business and we'll mind ours" attitude that isolates functions	6b^1. Encourages "we" attitudes that integrate contributors to a flow of work and that induce helping relationships between the several functions

516

Table 1—continued

Selected Properties	Figure 2 Structure: Functional Model	Figure 3 Structure: Flow-of-Work Model
	6c. Encourages blaming of other functions for problems	6c[1]. May induce some competition between units monitoring different flows of work
		6d[1]. Reduces blaming of other functions for problems
7. Dependence/ Independence	7a. Encourages dependence on higher authority and unwillingness to act without specific authorization	7a[1]. Encourages aggressiveness and independence of higher authority, plus an eagerness to act without specific authorization
	7b. Gives higher management a sense of significance and of being in control	7b[1]. May isolate higher management from the action
	7c. Equilibrates higher management's authority and responsibility	7c[1]. May lessen the sense of control by higher management

Source: Adapted from Roger Harrison, "Effective Organization for Startup," mimeographed (Cambridge, Mass.: Development Research Associates, Inc., July 8, 1970), p. 14.

chosen. Referring back to Figure 1 in this section, for example, the conditions in the right column impose demands that mate well with the features of Figure 3 structures. Similarly, referring back to Section D of Part I, Figure 3 structures would be more responsive to the needs of organizations whose basic strategy for growth is diversification, as well as responsive to problems faced in organizations whose missions can be described as Nonroutine.

Most broadly, Figure 3 structures seem appropriate at start-up time, even for organizations which are involved with relatively primitive strategies for growth and for organizations whose missions are basically Routine or Engineering. Specifically, start-up usually places a premium on quick responses to novel situations, innovative problem-solving, creative and spontaneous mixes of skills appropriate to meet the demands of the situation irrespective of rank or lines of authority, and so on. These factors suggest the right column in Figure 1 above and imply the value of a Figure 3 structure. After the shakedown period, however, the need may shift to regularity in operations, programmed decisions, and other properties in the left column in Figure 1. A Figure 2 structure might then become more appropriate.[17] Roger Harrison contrasts the differences between start-up and steady-state operations in these revealing terms:

17. Floyd C. Mann and Richard Hoffman, *Automation and the Worker: A Study of Social Change in Power Plants* (New York: Holt, Rinehart, & Winston, 1960).

A startup organization has a radically different climate from those operating under normal conditions. The best way of capturing the flavor of these differences is to consider the startup operation as a "wartime" battle situation, compared with normal "peacetime" conditions. . . .

The time pressure, the crisis decision-making amid grave responsibilities, the difficulties of communication, the stress on individuals, the fluidity and lack of structure of the organization are all typical of combat situations.

. . . During normal operations . . . most organizations value *efficiency* and *economy*. This leads, for example, to rules for the use and procurement of materials and manpower which are oriented towards *conservation* and *control*. During startup . . . the appropriate priorities are *delivery* and *performance* because of the greatly increased cost of having materials and services too little and too late. A degree of inefficiency and waste must be tolerated in favor of effectiveness. The costs of the wastage are frequently small compared to the costs of delay in startup.[18]

4. TOWARD THE PULL THEORY:
SOME CHALLENGES TO
PERSONNEL ADMINISTRATION

Various emphases on each of the polarities not only variously trend toward the push theory or the pull theory, but the emphases also imply major challenges for personnel administration. This interaction will be illustrated, if only briefly, to sketch the implications of the laboratory approach to OD for the development of this major function of management.

a. Differentiation/Integration:
Toward Uniting without Fragmenting

At least three major challenges for personnel administration are involved in shifting emphasis from differentiation toward integration. As used here, "personnel administration" usually refers to both the staff personnel job as well as to those personnel aspects for which a line manager is responsible. Basically, the interest here is in "what" needs to be done, rather than in "who" will do it. "Who" questions do get some attention, however.

---

18. Roger Harrison, "Effective Organization for Startup," mimeographed (Cambridge, Mass.: Development Research Associates, Inc., July 8, 1970), pp. 3, 5.

518

Developing Strategies for Motivation and Collaboration

First, new strategies must be developed for motivating individuals and groups while facilitating interpersonal and intergroup collaboration. Inducing win-lose competition between individuals and groups has been the standby strategy, and it does have its attractions. Triggering rivalry or conflict is easy; keeping it within bounds often is difficult. Moreover, the competitive strategy can engage substantial energies. In addition, much line and staff experience has been accumulated about "cattle prod" activities useful for inducing rivalry or win/lose competition.

The disadvantages of win/lose competition loom increasingly significant,[19] particularly in organizations with structures like that in Figure 2. Overall, technological demands increasingly require fluid collaboration between functions or processes. However, great potential for conflict and rivalry is built into Figure 2 structures.

The awkward effects of Figure 2 structures in this regard are particularly marked in industries like aerospace, but these effects are clear enough even in organizations with more Routine Missions. For example, the work of departments in a Figure 2 structure is not directly comparable, which often precludes reliable and nonarbitrary measures of performance. Each department provides only a partial contribution to a variety of flows of work, which implies major problems in factoring out departmental successes and failures. Because of this complexity, one department may win only as another department loses, e.g., in a cost-accounting allocation.

Structures like that in Figure 3 require that S perform a managerially integrative role, in contrast. S can take a generalist role in fact as well as intent, in that he can and indeed must make reasonable decisions about a total flow of work. These integrative features of Figure 3 structures have numerous advantages. Because the basic units of organization below M_{ABC} are autonomous and control an entire flow of work, for example, reliable and nonarbitrary measurement of performance is relatively simple. In addition, the basic unit of organization includes the full sequence of operations. Effort and performance are more likely to be congruent, as a consequence. Moreover, the wins of one department do not preclude wins by others. Even the competition in Figure 3 structures has integrative tendencies, in sum.

The issue of the broader usefulness of the laboratory approach has a "heads I win, tails you lose" quality about it, in addition. Behaviors and

---

19. To extend the argument, win/lose competition also is less useful at an interfirm or internation level. The magnitude of many projects requires exquisite coordination between "competing" firms, for example. And I have heard a major aerospace official say that, whatever the political issues between us, acute practical considerations require advanced cooperation between American and foreign firms as well as governments to cope with various projects in space, transportation, and so on.

values consistent with the laboratory approach are critical in managing a Figure 3 structure, and especially in changing over to such a structure. Specifically, Figure 3 structures basically permit decentralized patterns of delegation. And as Argyris observes:

> For decentralization to work, open superior-subordinate relationships are required, where trust is high, where conformity, fear, dependence are low, where experimentation and risk taking are prominent. These qualities cannot be issued, ordered, or even delegated. . . .
>
> The need is to find ways to uncover, to unfreeze these values wherever they exist. There is also a need to find ways to help man increase and strengthen these values because, lying dormant for years, they have tended to become weak, soft, and seemingly not very effective—especially in the tense, action-packed world of industrial life.[20]

There are also cases in which a Figure 3 structure may not exist or cannot even be approached. But even there high priority may be appropriate for the development of strategies based on the laboratory approach that facilitate interpersonal and intergroup collaboration. For example, interdepartmental conflicts and rivalries encouraged by Figure 2 structures may be ameliorated by improving the processes of interpersonal and group interaction. Consider the chief executive of a Figure 2 organization who spotlighted the divisive forces induced by the traditional structure in these words:

> The trouble with ABC is that nobody aside from me ever gives one damn about the overall goals of this place. They're all seeing the world through the lenses of their departmental biases. What we need around here are people who wear the ABC hat, not the engineering hat or the sales hat or the production hat.[21]

This complaint inspired the development of the ABC Hats, a group representing several functions and hierarchical levels that filled the integrative gaps resulting from a Figure 2 structure. Organizational applications of sensitivity training seek similar integration via improved interpersonal and group relations.[22]

Improving interpersonal and intergroup relations in a Figure 2 structure implies an uphill struggle all the way. Whatever improvement in

---

20. Argyris, *Interpersonal Competence and Organizational Effectiveness*, p. 4.
21. Warren G. Bennis, "Organizations of the Future," *Personnel Administration*, Vol. 30 (September, 1967) , p. 16.
22. For an analog of sensitivity training that shows promise, see Part II, Section F, Subsection 5.

communication results from sensitivity training or from a team-building experience, the structure will tend to keep on generating conflict and rivalry. Consequently, booster shots are necessary. Indeed, some organizations have evolved a change-agent role to provide just such a continuing stimulus to effective interaction between individuals and groups. Providing change-agent services, and particularly organizing for them, will generate major problems for personnel administration.

Developing an Integrative Role

Personnel administration must also give massive attention to developing a viable integrative role. Consider two possible approaches: some integrative role may be grafted to the basic functional structure in Figure 2; or integrative teams may become the basic units of departmentation, as in Figure 3. Both cases present problems. The second case is more attractive in concept, but for most organizations it would mean a major and perhaps difficult OD effort.

Consequently, integrative roles in organizations tend to be superimposed on a Figure 2 structure, as by establishing an interdepartmental coordinating committee or a project manager. Both are integrative overlays designed to counteract the fragmenting tendencies of the traditional structure of departments organized by functions or processes. To illustrate, the project manager develops a temporary integrative team to do some specific job, making requests for personnel as necessary from the functional departments. Team members then respond to two authoritative sources: to their more-or-less temporary project manager, and to the head of the functional department to which they will return when the project is complete. The resulting multiple lines of authority are sometimes called a "matrix overlay."

Integrative arrangements superimposed on a traditional structure can help reduce the conflict and rivalry characteristic of a Figure 2 structure, but they are tricky.[23] Thus questions of multiple authority may vex personnel administration. Or power may remain in the permanent functional departments, and this can make life difficult for integrative agents such as project managers or interdepartmental coordinating committees. In both cases, in addition, what is to be done with a project manager when his project is terminated? The experience in the aerospace industry does not suggest any easy ways out. Making conscious arrangements for an integrative role, then, implies serious problems for personnel administration.

---

23. Richard M. Hodgetts, "Leadership Techniques in the Project Organization," *Journal of the Academy of Management*, Vol. 11 (June, 1968), pp. 211–20; and Gordon L. Lippitt, "Team Building for Matrix Organizations," in Gordon L. Lippitt, Leslie E. This, and Robert G. Bidwell, Jr., *Optimizing Human Resources* (Reading, Mass.: Addison-Wesley Publishing Co., 1971), pp. 158–70.

Developing Values of Unity

Shared values that encourage organizational unity must be developed and broadly accepted. Otherwise, a significant shift of emphasis toward integration is unlikely. Prevailing organizational values—the "values of bureaucracy"—are hierarchy-serving in that they reinforce superior-subordinate relations. But they do so only at the expense of inhibiting the development of socioemotional ties that can integrate individuals or groups performing different functions in different departments in a Figure 2 structure. Since today's organizations increasingly must be integrative, and since they increasingly must stress dynamic knowledge gathering because they are truth-requiring, the values of bureaucracy will increasingly generate troublesome consequences.

The specific alternative to the values of bureaucracy is not yet clear. However, the following climate of beliefs suggests at least a first-generation response to the knowledge-gathering and truth-requiring demands of today's technology:[24]

- full and free communication, regardless of rank or power
- reliance on confronting processes in dealing with conflict, as opposed to coercion or compromise
- basing influence on technical competence and knowledge, as opposed to personal whim or hierarchical status
- an atmosphere that easily admits emotional expression as well as task-oriented behavior
- acceptance of conflict between the individual and the organization which is to be coped with openly

Getting acceptance of such values in principle, and working toward them in practice, should constitute a major near-future challenge for personnel administration.

b. Repression/Wriggle Room: Toward Satisfying Needs without Sacrificing Work

Two issues involved in the shift of emphasis toward wriggle room deserve special attention because they pose major problems for personnel administration. One issue involves tailoring both organization structure and interaction processes so as to meet human needs at work. The second issue deals with values and representational vehicles capable of supporting such changes in structure and interaction processes.

One major approach toward emphasizing wriggle room involves shaping organizations to fit people in the design of tasks and structure. His-

---

24. Warren G. Bennis, *Changing Organizations* (New York: McGraw-Hill Book Co., 1966), pp. 15–16.

torically, people were fitted to the organization. Many observers have argued the merits of tailoring tasks to man,[25] as through job enlargement, so we note only two major derivative demands on personnel administration. In the federal government, especially, classification experts still far outnumber specialists in job design. A traditional personnel specialty, especially in the federal government, needs to be reoriented if more wriggle room is the goal. Moreover, job enlargement is easier in a Figure 3 structure. Since a Figure 2 structure is what most organizations have, the implied challenge to personnel administration is the development of a potent OD specialty.

Relatedly, interaction processes can also usefully be tailored to man. Argyris has posited needs of man that are seen as typically frustrated in large organizations, especially in organizations patterned after Figure 2.[26] The pyramidal values discussed in Section D, Part I are clearly at home in a Figure 2 structure. Building satisfying interaction processes into organizations is a gargantuan task, and only scarcely begun. Thus some change agents attempt to use sensitivity training in family groups to try to improve relationships in an organization, which may raise major issues with traditional ways of organizing and managing. Others argue that building need-satisfying interaction into organizations is hopelessly utopian. Many variations exist between those anchor positions.

However matters evolve, the face of personnel administration is certain to change substantially. That much is clear from these broad values of the laboratory approach that imply what is often seen as lacking in organizations:

- an attitude of inquiry, reflecting a hypothetical spirit and an emphasis on experimentation
- an expanded awareness on the part of organization members, with a corresponding sense of a broader choice of alternatives for action
- an undergirding system of norms that stresses collaboration, as well as a problem-solving orientation to conflict
- an emphasis on the helping relationship as a major way to concretely express man's interdependence with man

Changes in tasks and interaction processes must be supported by appropriate values and representational vehicles. As an example, greater managerial concern for due process and sharing of influence seems necessary. Either the pull theory or the push theory can guide how the two are approached—since due process and influence-sharing will receive major attention, for good or ill—and the choice is a matter of real

---

25. David S. Brown, "Shaping the Organization to Fit People," *Management of Personnel Quarterly*, Vol. 5 (Summer, 1966), pp. 12–16. See also Section D, Part II, Subsection 5b.
26. Chris Argyris, *Personality and Organization* (New York: Harper & Row, Publishers, 1957), especially pp. 49–53.

consequence. That is, influence-sharing or due process can be granted with top management support in sensitive dialog with employees whose needs and capabilities are diversely evolving; or at a polar extreme, they can be wrested away by employees after heated battle with a boulwareian management. The pull theory recommends the former, of course.

No doubt much of the near-future resolution of issues involving due process and influence-sharing will be in familiar terms: employee unionization, more-or-less grudging management assent, and more-or-less successful efforts at rapprochement. Increasingly, however, the resolution will involve the breaking of new and uncertain ground. At least at managerial levels in many organizations, for example, determined efforts are underway to develop new and enhanced representational vehicles, encompassing "tell all" dinners, management councils, and God knows what. Only the brave fool would try to guess the product of this maelstrom, or even whether we can avoid a kind of organizational totalitarianism born of ineptness or unwillingness in developing appropriate values and vehicles. That personnel administration vitally depends on the outcome of the search for viable approaches to power-sharing and to organizational due process seems undeniable, in any case.

c. Stability/Newness:
Toward Change through Structure

Any shift in today's organizations toward newness implies at least two major challenges to personnel administration. First, the "change function" must be given greater priority, with such attendant challenges as better equipping people to tolerate ambiguity. We have only clues as to how to cope successfully with such an increased priority, both as to mechanics and organization. But the trends are there for everyone to see in the rapid evolution of project or task-force management whose structures are intentionally temporary, unlike the bureaucratic structure of Figure 2. For example, the project organization for the C–5A transport had a planned five-year life, involved tens of thousands of employees, 6,000 separate companies, and astronomical volumes of all manner of resources. "What we see here is nothing less than the creation of a disposable division," Toffler observes, "the organizational equivalent of paper dresses or throw-away tissues."[27]

In order to implement an increased priority for change, at the very least, an appropriate reward system is necessary. Existing reward systems usually are keyed to how much one produces, however, or how long one has been a producer. Neither bias facilitates change; both biases are at best irrelevant to change, if they are not inimical to it. Likely reinforcers of change imply a host of problems. I have in mind one labor agreement

---

27. Alvin Toffler, *Future Shock* (New York: Random House, 1970), pp. 119–20.

that rewards employees for their willingness to be continually retrained, as opposed to rewarding them for their productivity or for their seniority. Such arrangements imply very significant labor/management issues, with which we have precious little experience. One thing is clear, however. Much of the heart of traditional personnel administration—as in the general run of classification and pay plans—poorly suits arrangements designed to facilitate change. Nothing better could be expected of these products of our bureaucratic phase.

Organizationally, increased emphasis on change also poses real problems for personnel administration. The issues are most sharply joined in the evolving role of the change agent which is devoted to facilitating change and inducing appropriate interpersonal and intergroup climates for change. Where is the change agent to be located? Who is to be the change agent?

Working answers to such questions have tended to be unsatisfactory. Relying on external change agents such as consultants has some real advantages, but this places the change agent outside the organization's authority-and-reward structure and may compromise his effectiveness. Relying on internal change agents ties them into the system, but this cuts both ways. If things got rough for them, staff men who became change agents might be motivated to become a kind of nondirective and even gentle but nonetheless efficient gestapo in the pursuit of their own interests.[28] Embody the change-agent role in a staff man or unit, and that implies all of the problems that have plagued line-staff relations. Relying on change agents in the "line" provides no surefire alternative. If the line manager becomes the change agent, you avoid many ticklish authority problems but you run the risk of placing reliance for change in an individual who may be overbusy with day-to-day problems. Moreover, there is no guarantee that line officials will have the appropriate skills or training, or even the interest.

Managing the change-agent role, in sum, implies one grand job for personnel administration, conceived in its broad sense as an amalgam of line and staff responsibilities.

The second challenge is the shifting emphasis to newness, which implies a growing need to quickly develop and disband both large and small work units. The point clearly applies to the teams formed in project management, for example. Moreover, the need to revitalize today's organizations so as to prepare them for adapting to tomorrow's markets or programs also raises questions about managing temporary social systems.

Managing temporary social systems presents a formidable task in at

---

28. The temptation is great where such change agents use sensitivity training sessions, for example, during which much data about individuals and groups may be divulged. A similar problem faces such professionals as psychiatrists employed by organizations.

least two major ways. Such management requires that people develop a kind of instant but still intense commitment. This is difficult, but seemingly unavoidable. Complex systems often permit no alternative to the technical and social compatibility of team members. In addition, organization members will need to learn how to experience the loss of one temporary social system in ways that do not inhibit their commitment to future systems.

We are gaining some experience with effective management of temporary social systems, as via team development, or team building. The approach uses learning analogs derived from the laboratory approach, whose purest form is the sensitivity training group. For example, such team-building has proved useful in one multiplant firm using periodic rotation of management teams.[29] Plant technology of this firm is based on continuous processing and delicate integration of activities. The planned transfers typically caused a variety of dislocations that registered as decreases in productivity and employee satisfaction. Roughly, the typical relearning dip in several plants of this firm lasted six months. Moreover, as the plant technology became more integrated, that break-in period seemed to lengthen. Now, three- or four-day team-building experiences are provided early in the life of each new team. The relearning dip has been halved.

Less is known about disbanding a temporary social system in ways that do not inhibit the commitment of its members to future systems. Work with sensitivity training suggests that such separation anxiety can be effectively managed. However, socioemotional debriefing is still uncommon.

Experience with both terminating as well as creating temporary social systems seems worth developing. Consider aerospace firms, which typify what many organizations are increasingly becoming. One prominent feature in the aerospace industry is the socioemotional turmoil associated with developing, and more particularly with terminating, project teams. Members of teams gear themselves up to unflinching commitment, working long and hard. When the project is concluded, emotional depression often sets in, marital difficulties seem unusually common and severe, and so on. Both research and popular news magazines have painted an alarming picture of this new problem, which we can expect to become increasingly common.[30]

Managing temporary social systems also implies two major technical

---

29. Team-building has also been utilized on a mass scale by such firms as Alcan and TRW. See Alexander Winn, "The Laboratory Approach to Organization Development: A Tentative Model of Planned Change" (Paper presented at the Annual Conference, British Psychological Conference, Oxford, England, September, 1968).
30. Warren G. Bennis and Philip E. Slater, *The Temporary Society* (New York: Harper & Row, Publishers, 1968).

issues. One issue involves structural arrangements that encourage quick group identification and that also permit reinforcement by reward systems keyed to meaningful measures of performance. These dual goals are within reach. That is, both identification and the measurement of performance will be facilitated as organizations move toward Figure 3 structures. The point is of crucial significance. Indeed, Figure 3 structures offer a way out of nagging organizational problems. Thus managing the change-agent role might be handled effectively through team effort by members of a small integrative managerial unit, with members jointly responsible for the change-agent role. Team effort also could provide a basis for redefining line-staff relations, as is urged below. Consequently, such structural change must occupy much of the effort of personnel administration over the near future.

Figure 3 structures also permit convenient changes in incentive systems and philosophy. In one Figure 2 structure, for example, a very complex system of different wage rates for specific jobs required an elaborate supervisory and clerical apparatus for wage administration. Under a Figure 3 structure, a simpler system was possible. Management negotiated a base price tied to output with a producing team that controlled the entire flow of work, and the unit handled the internal distribution of its income.[31] That is, group incentives in a Figure 3 structure can help integrate a total flow of work and reinforce the allegiances encouraged by that structure. Supervision is consequently simplified. Compensation systems in Figure 2 structures, in contrast, tend to fragment flows of work and to complicate supervision.

A second major technical issue in managing temporary social systems concerns position classification. Figure 3 structures, and the temporary teams within them, encourage classification plans that place rank in the man rather than the job. On this score, the federal public service can expect special problems in managing temporary social systems. Although recent policies permit some recognition of the impact of the man on the job, the federal approach to classification emphasizes rank in position.

d. Function/Flow of Work:
Toward Departmentation That Unifies

Basic structural change that shifts emphasis from particularistic to integrative departmentation, from functions to the flow of work, will make it easier to respond effectively to the challenges facing personnel administration, but that change will be difficult. The root need is the development of a solid core of OD specialists who can maintain real

---

31. P. G. Herbst, *Autonomous Group Functioning* (London: Tavistock Publications, 1962).

momentum in long-run programs of change. Ideally, perhaps, every manager should be his own OD specialist. Practically, the OD function often will become a personnel specialty.

Redefined line-staff relations are necessary if personnel officials are to operate effectively in an OD role, it is important to note. Redefinition is necessary because OD means change, change in basic attitudes and values and ways of organizing work. Hence the inappropriateness of the traditional concept of staff as outside the chain of command, as advisory, and as organizationally inferior to the line.

Structural arrangements for a suitable redefinition of line-staff relations also seem clear, in general. A Figure 3 structure, for example, could provide a common organizational home for both a line manager and a staff personnel man. Their shared responsibility for the success of a total managerial unit would encourage a team effort, rather than line versus staff tension. The approach gets much support, from experience,[32] from theoretical analysis,[33] and from initial empirical research.[34] In contrast, Figure 2 structures are organized around separate functions or processes. This encourages fragmentation of line from staff and differentiation between line and staff.

Realistically, OD specialists can anticipate a formidable task. The difficulty is multidimensional. Even assuming the development of a core of OD specialists, three specific reorientations in outlook seem necessary. They will only be sketched. *First,* an emphasis on flow of work as opposed to functions will require a bottom-up approach to organizing work and to locating services. The first point need not be emphasized, but the location of services has been given less attention. Given a top-down approach, services tend to drift upward in the typical hierarchy. For example, staff probably would report to M_{ABC} in Figure 2, even though many of their inputs might be made at the level of S_4 or below.

A bottom-up approach would generate a different pattern. The point may be illustrated briefly. Typically, an overhead staff unit would both design and monitor patterns of work motions. In one large electronics firm, however, "time and methods" have been handled differently. Employees are themselves instructed in the basics of motion analysis by a very small overhead staff. These employees then design and monitor their own work-motion patterns.

Such bottom-up approaches as the example above imply multiple problems for personnel administration. Thus they may raise troublesome

---

32. Robert R. Blake and Jane Srygley Mouton, *Corporate Excellence through Grid Organizational Development* (Houston: Gulf Publishing Co., 1968), Appendix II.
33. Golembiewski, *Organizing Men and Power.*
34. Philip J. Browne, "Organizational Images: An Exploratory-Descriptive Study" (Ph.D. diss., University of Oregon, 1971); and Robert T. Golembiewski, "Personality and Organization Structure: Staff Models and Behavioral Problems" *Journal of the Academy of Management,* Vol. 9 (September, 1967), pp. 217–32.

status questions for both M_{ABC} and the men who report to him. Moreover, suitable work environments for such approaches must have one or both of two characteristics: employee efforts must be measurable, easily and validly; or the employees must be motivated to apply the principles of motion analysis. These are major problems, but they are less troublesome than the problems of enforcement and evasion likely under a top-down approach to motion analysis. For example, Figure 3 structures can help significantly to reduce problems of both measuring and motivating performance.[35]

Second, shifting emphasis to the flow of work requires a new line-staff concept. I have dealt with the matter at length elsewhere at the analytic level, and fragmentary research has proved very encouraging.[36] Note here only the multiple mischief of conceiving staff as a glorified prosthetic device, as a kind of enlargement of the senses of M_{ABC} in Figure 2. Such a notion does encourage centralized identification. Moreover, a centralized location always will be necessary for some staff, at least some of the time. Often too much is made of a good thing, however, with obvious costs in increased managerial complexity, heightened line-staff conflict, long communication chains, and a general rigidifying of relations at work.

Third, greater emphasis on the flow of work will require basic value reorientations in wide segments of the population. This resocialization of adults will require both defusing and infusing of values, as it were. As some intriguing research demonstrates, at least middle-class children seem to be acquainted with the essentials of a Figure 2 structure as early in life as the third or fourth grade.[37] This suggests the extent of the value-defusing that will be required and implies a major training burden that extends far beyond the workplace into the value-generating processes of the socialization of children.

There seems a solid base on which to infuse values more appropriate for Figure 3 structures, however. Thus many observers explain the fascination with McGregor's Theory X, Theory Y formulation in terms of a broad managerial desire to increase the congruence between their personal values and the presently legitimate organization values. The former values tend toward Theory Y; but the latter are Theory X-ish, decidedly. In addition, some evidence shows that managers in larger and technologically sophisticated firms are more likely to reflect Theory Y attitudes.[38] This suggests that contemporary technological demands will

35. Golembiewski, *Organizing Men and Power,* pp. 90–110 and 154–73.
36. Robert T. Golembiewski, "Personality and Organization Structure," pp. 211–30.
37. Herbert G. Wilcox has accumulated evidence of this socialization effect with an interesting research design. "The Culture Trait of Hierarchy in Middle Class Children," *Public Administration Review,* Vol. 28 (May, 1968), pp. 222–35.
38. Mason Haire, E. E. Ghiselli, and Lyman W. Porter, "Cultural Patterns in the Role of the Manager," *Industrial Relations,* Vol. 2 (February, 1963), pp. 95–118.

supply push/pull forces that will help change values such as those under-lying a Figure 2 structure.

5. THE NEW PERSONNEL ADMINISTRATION: SOME GENERALIZATIONS AND EMPHASES

Perhaps more than in most cases, the temptation here to make too much of too little must be resisted. However, at least three generalizations may be drawn regarding the challenges facing the staff personnel man:

- To the degree that the developmental trends sketched above do in fact become reality, so will personnel administration experience profound challenges.
- To the extent that specialists in personnel respond to those challenges, so will these specialists be able to ride the tiger of our ongoing organizational revolution.
- If personnel specialists do not make the required adaptations, someone else will try.

Five major emphases will characterize successful approaches by specialists in personnel, if the analysis above catches much of the flavor of the current ferment in organization thought.

First, and most broadly, reorienting the basic concept of personnel administration is in order. Crudely, the reorientation must emphasize training and organization development more than orthodox approaches to position classification, compensation, and incentives. Roughly, the reorientation is away from a punitive approach and toward a participative and, hopefully, a rewarding approach. Such a reorientation is fortunately underway in many areas, albeit in wildly diverse degrees.

Second, specialists in personnel administration must transcend the limitations of the traditional staff role as an appendage for human needs tacked on to an immutable technical structure for work, or staff conceived of as outside the lines of command. A basic redefinition of line-staff relations is in order. Basically, a training or OD role for personnel implies broad involvement in the go-go of the organization. A Figure 3 structure aids in developing line-staff relations necessary to permit such involvement.

Third, specialists in personnel administration must gain support for their new effort, but in an interdependent mode. That is, personnel specialists must avoid the temptation of forcing OD programs down the line, after having gained top-level backing by subtly or grossly playing the informant's role. Such things do happen,[39] and they are the death of

---

39. See Melville Dalton, *Men at Work* (New York: John Wiley & Sons, 1959), esp. pp. 18–109.

OD programs. This more-or-less standard staff strategy illustrates a dependent mode of promoting an OD program, much more consistent with the push theory than the pull theory.

Fourth, the processes within personnel departments will have to be analogs of the processes desired in the broader organization. If integrative teams are seen as the answer to the organization's ills, for example, personnel specialists must demonstrate their willingness and ability to develop such integrative teams, and to participate in them.[40] The Figure 3 teams in question have a very special character, which Leonard Sayles and Margaret Chandler incisively capture. Their manager, we are told, ". . . must create a system that will make . . . the organizations it embraces and the people in them . . . do what is needed in a system that is *self-forcing* (for excellence) and *self-enforcing.*"[41] There is no room in such a model for behavior often attributed to "staff," then. At the very least, this means that members of such teams will have trust, backed by experience, that their openness will not return to haunt them in the form of tales carried upward in the organization.

Fifth, personnel specialists will need fine skills in managing dependence and hostility as they broaden their role. It is a mature relation, indeed, in which help is given and accepted, period. When the issue is the change of long-standing patterns of behavior, both dependence on the helper and hostility toward him will become more prevalent. Both dependence and hostility will have to be confronted willingly and openly, which only means that everyone must be more heroic and emotionally healthy than sometimes is the case.

---

40. For one such approach, see Max R. Goodson and Warren O. Hagstrom, "Using Teams of Change Agents," in Richard A. Schmuck and Matthew B. Miles (eds.), *Organization Development in Schools* (Palo Alto, Cal.: National Press Books, 1971), pp. 155–84.
41. Sayles and Chandler, *op. cit.,* p. 104.

B. KALEIDOSCOPES
OF THE FUTURE:
CHANGING ORDERS AT WORK,
AT PLAY, IN LIFE

Each age builds its own monuments that survive to please, or bewilder, or infuriate the ages that succeed it. While this is no place to write a history of Western civilization, a few details may suggest the fuller sense of the point. The Cathedral of Chartres reflects the guiding spirit of an earlier age, for example, just as surely as the Empire State Building is the apotheosis of an age from which we are beginning to emerge. Nor is it an accident that writers of the recent past have rhapsodized about Cathedrals of Commerce. For that's where it has been, in recent times and in critical senses, just as it was when Gregorian hosannas filled other cathedrals in an earlier time.

Although one age proclaimed God and the other Mammon, their similarities are profound. For example, there are clear parallels between the righteous burning of heretics at the stake in one age and John D. Rockefeller's confidence that his Standard Oil trust was "merely a survival of the fittest." The common purpose was to cull the deviant. Thus Rockefeller went on to explain that: "The American Beauty rose can be produced in the splendor and fragrance which bring cheer to its beholder only by sacrificing the early buds which grow up around it. This is not an evil tendency in business. It is merely the working-out of a law of nature and a law of God."[1] Cardinal Bellarmine could not have put it any better, although he might have changed some of the symbols and

1. Quoted in Merle Curti, *The Growth of American Thought* (New York: Harper & Bros., 1951), p. 638.

532

terminology. Similarly, both ages also were committed to centralizing as well as ordering. "The truth is," one philosopher of the late 19th century noted with a moral force appropriate to pre-Reformation Christendom, "that the social order is fixed by laws of nature precisely analogous to those of the physical order. The most that man can do . . . by his ignorance and conceit [is] to mar the operation of the social laws."[2] Both ages built as if there were to be no age to succeed them, moreover, or perhaps they built massively so that no age could even contemplate taking their place. And both ages were elitist in thrust, even if the heroes of one got their meaningful contacts through burning bushes while the heroes of the other relied on calls from their brokers or tax men.

What is a fitting monument for us to leave to our posterity? An important part of the answer lies in the fact that modern man is likely to attach this condition to the question: if either monument or posterity there will be. That condition would not even have occurred to observers from most other ages.

What is this age's monument? Its character is more-or-less clear, on balance. A huge kaleidoscope seems appropriate: colorful, ever-changing, with recognizable bits and pieces reorganized in a bewildering number of arrays, attractive to the eye but inducing only an emotional commitment appropriate to the probability that another pattern no doubt will soon develop, and it will be at once as attractive and as impermanent. Epigrammatically, this is an age of relationships more than of relatives, of Now rather than of past or future, whose basic constant is that all relationships and values and institutions will be stressed, at work or play or in life.

Our kaleidoscopic present and future imply major challenges for organization development, or OD, as they put increasingly large numbers of us in enervating double binds. More commitment and skill will be required to do society's work, for example. But just as those psychic investments increase, so will the useful life of the skills tend to diminish. It will be a case of more and more for less and less, as it were, which is not always a sign of a good bargain.

1. SOME CHARACTERISTICS OF THE FUTURISTIC KALEIDOSCOPE: A PROFILE OF THE POSSIBLE AND, PERHAPS, OF THE PROBABLE

Specifically, the kaleidoscopic future includes at least five characteristics that have some reasonable chance of influencing—both quantitatively

2. Quoted in Richard Hofstadter, *Social Darwinism in American Thought* (Philadelphia: University of Pennsylvania Press, 1944), p. 31.

and qualitatively—the work, or play, or life of the future. These characteristics include four in the category of "probably will occur" and one "can occur." The one case of "can occur" implies that a significant role still exists for future choices by influential actors which can go in several directions. The cases of "probably will occur" are seen as being more predetermined by massive forces long since set moving.

Diversity of Groupings

The future will be characterized by a growing diversity of groupings, often temporary and sometimes spontaneous, that will be in diverse stages of starting-up or shutting-down. And these various systems—in various stages of coming and being and going—must be delicately and effectively interfaced, and without the discipline inherent in the fact that more permanent units would be around for an indefinite period and hence must be dealt with, keeping that in mind. The sense of it is truly revolutionary: the emphasis will be increasingly on isolating and solving problems and less on building power bases to influence or determine survival. Organization members will not suddenly become angels, of course. But their options probably will narrow, unless man's organizations are to collapse of their own weighty irrelevance. Harsh realities will be gaining fast, on both the organizational quick and certainly on the dead. It will be necessary to do far better organizationally even to stand still, in short.

Some sense of the future is already apparent in organizations, and similar if more exotic developments seem probable. Consider today's hotel industry. New and more-or-less permanent management teams are being constantly developed to manage new properties. The industry also makes use of many intendedly temporary systems, such as teams which are constituted to design a new hotel and to supervise its building and furnishing. Moreover, the intentionally temporary and more-or-less permanent systems also overlap in time, as in the final phases of construction and in various preopening activities.[3] The vision of tomorrow's organizations is dimmer, of course, but seers with good track records see bewilderingly more of the same, or else. For example, Warren E. Avis sees tomorrow's executives routinely working with a wide range of groups and interests, some abiding and some temporary, some in house and many others out of house, on a huge front of issues. As he explains:

> Chief executives today are being asked to form opinions and take actions affecting dozens of issues. They find they are involved whether they want to be involved or not. . . .

3. Richard Beckhard, "An Organization Improvement Program in a Decentralized Organization," *Journal of Applied Behavioral Science*, Vol. 2 (January, 1966), p. 19. See also Robert A. Luke, Jr., "Temporary Task Forces: A Humanistic Problem Solving Method" (Paper presented at NTL Conference on New Technology in Organization Development, New York, October 8–9, 1971).

Few chief executives try to revert to controlling the community. Many try to remain uninvolved. A few . . . have begun to actively seek out ways in which they can work with the community in solving its problems. ˊ

This is the direction of the future. By 1980, the chief executive of every corporation will routinely be working with committees made up of people from each group involved in a problem area to help identify and define the problem and to work out a solution, or there will not be any corporations or chief executives as we know them today. They will be under total governmental control.[4]

Fundamental Behavioral Changes

The future will increasingly require fundamental behavioral and attitudinal changes, which implies that change will increasingly involve deepseated emotional attachments and identifications. Figure 1 suggests the fuller sense of this point. By implication, futuristic change will be at once more potentially traumatic and rewarding, for the individual and for the multiple systems in which he functions.

This age is not the first that has experienced traumatic change, of course, but it is the first to do so under unique conditions. Thus there will be less of that universal balm—time—to ease the impact of change. Moreover, unprecedentedly larger numbers of people have diverse ways of hamstringing systems that do not meet their needs. A variety of collective approaches has been tried and found effective: strikes, marches, voting campaigns, nonviolent resistance, and so on. Individual decisions or actions also can have profound effects. A careless employee might help kill a stream or harbor with a flood of crude oil; or a determined electronics wizard might raise merry hell with our telephonic or data-processing systems.

Changes in Style of Effort

The future will be characterized by both subtle and gross changes in the style in which collective effort will be motivated, reflecting changes in the very bases of authority. This process has been underway for some time now, even in such arch-bureaucracies as the military,[5] but it will probably accelerate rapidly in the future.

---

4. Warren E. Avis, "Decision by Consensus," in T. J. Atchison and J. V. Ghorpade (eds.), *Proceedings*, Annual Meeting, Academy of Management, Atlanta, Ga., August 23–26, 1970.
5. Morris Janowitz, "Changing Patterns of Organizational Authority," *Administrative Science Quarterly*, Vol. 3 (March, 1959), pp. 473–93.

Figure 1. Targets of Change, Illustrative Methods, and Their Cognitive/Emotional Mix

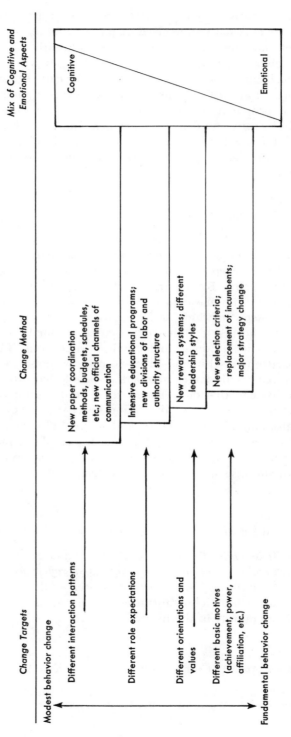

Source: Paul R. Lawrence and Jay W. Lorsch, *Developing Organizations: Diagnosis and Action* (Reading, Mass.: Addison-Wesley Publishing Co., 1969), p. 87.

Consider only two ways of homing-in on this point. First, there are several possible approaches by which A can induce what he considers appropriate behavior in B, and profound organizational consequences inhere in probably accelerating shifts in the approaches that will be utilized. The point unfolds simply, if laboriously. Following Warren Bennis, A might rely on the following strategies for inducing desired behavior in B:[6]

- *legitimate authority or traditional power,* which is power that stems from legal-historical traditions as they are embodied in institutional norms and practices
- *coercive power,* which is the ability of A to reward and/or punish B
- *expert power,* or the power that is associated with A's knowledge of, and ability to cope with, his job or specialty
- *referent or identification power,* or the power that inheres in a situation where A either personally, or as a surrogate for some broader aggregate, represents a role model or ego ideal for B, someone or something that B seeks to identify with and from which B seeks acceptance
- *value power,* or the influence that A gains because B accepts, or is attracted by, the values of A

These forms come mixed in nature, of course. Thus some coercive power inheres in legitimate authority, but A might have more coercive power than his formal organizational peers if he were also the chief executive's son.

A speculation and an implication complete the point. The speculation: the future is likely to see increasing emphasis on the third, fourth, and fifth approaches, as well as decreasing emphasis on the first and second. Some see a new coercion resulting from today's general deterioration of legitimate authority, oppositely, and so it may be. But that is not the present guess. The patent implication? Life in organizations will become increasingly tentative and problematic: complex and shifting authoritative relationships will become more common and delicate; individual responsibility will grow more fugitive still; and there will be a growing sense of the need for untidy organizational "happenings" that will further erode the sense of precise structure associated with the spirit of bureaucracy.

Second, probable changes in the motivation of collective effort can also be illustrated in terms of changes in strategies for social change. Conveniently, three prime strategies serve to suggest the point. That is, social

6. Warren G. Bennis, *Changing Organizations* (New York: McGraw-Hill Book Co., 1966), p. 168.

change involving A and B might be strategically approached as a problem in:[7]

- *power,* in which A variously seeks to bias outcomes in his favor, as by:
  a. making B more dependent on A
  b. threatening B with "harm, loss, inconvenience, or embarrassment"
  c. confusing B as to A's needs or preferences as to outcomes, etc.
- *attitudinal change,* in which A seeks to induce desired attitudinal change in B, as:
  a. when A takes the initiative to minimize the actual perceived differences between the goals of A and B, the characteristics of A and B, etc.
  b. when A takes the initiative to increase the actual or perceived mutual attractiveness of A$\longleftrightarrow$B
  c. when A takes the initiative to minimize the actual or perceived threat of A $\longrightarrow$ B, playing down actual or perceived differences in legitimate authority, etc.
- *problem-solving,* in which the potential exists that arrangements can be developed such that both A and B can gain or at least not suffer loss, or such that either A or B can gain but not at the expense of the other, as:
  a. when A and B isolate and acknowledge actual differences in their goals, recognize where commonality does not exist or is not possible, and seek solutions that accommodate those differences
  b. when A and B isolate and acknowledge the bases of mutual attractiveness and unattractiveness, where it is not possible or is not considered desirable to change the latter, and seek solutions that accommodate the differences
  c. when A and B isolate and acknowledge differences in legitimate authority, skills, etc., and seek solutions that accommodate the differences

The short of it is that the future will likely see more of the second and, especially, the third strategies. The past has seen more of the power strategy than is likely to be the case in the future.

Figure 2 helps elaborate on this critical point in several senses. It details sets of tactics that are suited to the two extreme strategies above, Power and Problem-solving. Figure 2 also serves a number of other uses.

---

7. Richard E. Walton, "Two Strategies of Social Change and Their Dilemmas," *Journal of Applied Behavioral Science,* Vol. 1 (April, 1965), pp. 167–77.

Figure 2. Some Basic Strategies for Change and Associated Tactics

Power	Attitudinal Change	Problem-Solving
Superficial Attachment to Laboratory Values	Pervasive Attachment to Laboratory Values	

TACTICS OF CONFLICT (SELECTED)	TACTICS OF COLLABORATION (SELECTED)
■ Behavior is purposeful in pursuing own goals.	■ Behavior is purposeful in pursuing common goals.
■ Secrecy.	■ Openness.
■ Accurate personal understanding of own needs, but they are publicly disguised or misrepresented. The purpose is to keep Other from knowing what Self really wants most, so that Other will not know how much Self is willing to give up to get it.	■ Accurate personal understanding of own needs, and they are publicly represented as such. The purpose is to allow Other to know exactly what Self wants in order to facilitate realistic and efficient problem-solving.
■ Unpredictable, mixed strategies, utilizing the element of surprise.	■ Predictable; while flexible behavior is appropriate, it is not designed to take other party by surprise.
■ Threats and bluffs are common.	■ Threats or bluffs are avoided.
■ Distortions of judgments and perceptions by both Self and Other are seen as functional in aggregating power at the expense of the Other.	■ Distortions of judgments and perceptions by either Self or Other are seen as dysfunctional in problem-solving.
■ Search behavior is devoted to finding ways of appearing to be committed to a position.	■ Search behavior is devoted to finding solutions to problems, utilizing logical and innovative processes.
■ Success is often enhanced by forming bad stereotypes of the Other, by ignoring the Other's logic, by demeaning competence, and by increasing the level of hostility. These tactics strengthen in-group loyalty, and also are intended to convince Other that Self means business.	■ Success demands that stereotypes be dropped, that ideas be given consideration on their merit regardless of sources, and that hostility not be induced deliberately. In fact, positive feelings about Self and Other are both a common cause and an effect of this approach to collective effort.
■ Pathological extreme is when Self assumes that everything that prevents Other from reaching Other's goal must facilitate Self's own movement toward his goal. Goals of the Self thus appear to negate the attainment of goals by the Other.	■ Pathological extreme is when Self assumes that whatever is good for Other is necessarily good for Self. Cannot distinguish own identity from Other. Will not take responsibility for Self.

Source: Based on Richard E. Walton, "How to Choose between Strategies of Conflict and Collaboration," in Robert T. Golembiewski and Arthur Blumberg, eds., *Sensitivity Training and the Laboratory Approach* (Itasca, Ill.: F. E. Peacock Publishers, Inc., 1970), pp. 336–37.

For example, notice that Power and Problem-solving are conceived as overlapping in part. The intent is to emphasize a strong developmental tendency. That is, in the normal development of decreasing reliance on the Power strategy, authority figures often have been attracted to the huge potential for behavioral control implied by the laboratory approach, particularly as reflected in the T-Group. Not uncommonly, then, early

OD programs emphasize the Attitudinal Change strategy, based on what is called "superficial attachment to laboratory values" in Figure 2. Power figures, in effect, were seeking ways to change attitudes so as to gain from organization members various inputs perceived as necessary by the power figures. These inputs include: greater openness in communicating, enhanced commitment to work, and so on. The *quid pro quo* for this one-way attitudinal change also was common. The power figures would expose themselves to public criticism, they might agree to admit a broader range of interests in decision-making, they would seek to reduce at least the overt evidence of the tactics of conflict listed above, and they would play down their legitimate authority and especially their coercive power.

The balance sketched above commonly is unstable, if it is not condescending or grossly manipulative, in the absence of what is referred to in Figure 2 as "pervasive attachment to laboratory values." Two perspectives illustrate the point: a bird's-eye view of the worm, as it were, and a worm's-eye view of the bird. From one perspective, the power wielders in an organization might view their subordinates as childlike, as fixatedly making up for past repressions by exaggerated displays of their new freedom, as in a phase that will hopefully pass but which seems to go on and on. However, superordinates will be reluctant to publicly expose their unflattering assessment lest it be perceived as a reappearance of coercive power. Superordinates might become overcontrolled as a consequence, acting in veiled and indirect ways. Hence superordinates can activate aspects of the Power strategy even as they doggedly seek to avoid the hint of them. The situation is no better from the subordinates' point of view. For example, some subordinates might be anxious to extend their new powers to Problem-Solving, which multilateral contract may be more than superordinates had bargained for in moving toward the Attitudinal Change strategy. This might encourage some subordinates in their own stead to activate some aspects of the Power strategy.

Opportunities for Personal Growth

The future can be characterized by unparalleled opportunities for personal expression and growth at work, as well as in other organized situations. Jack and Lorraine Gibb present a revealing picture of how this potential might become manifest. Basically, they view collective action from four perspectives: climate, or membership; data flow, or decision-making; goal formation, or productivity; and control, or organization. Table 1 sketches some of the specific dimensions along which change is possible.

Note that this futuristic projection is a "can occur" rather than a "will occur." Significant human choices will determine whether this new freedom will in fact occur. As of now, the actual outcome is in real doubt.

540

Table 1. Some Dimensions of Growth for Individuals in Group Situations

Critical Aspects of Growth	Growth Is Movement from:	Growth Is Movement toward:
Climate (Membership)	Fear-distrust: ■ role-role relations ■ defending against ■ evaluating ■ formalizing ■ rewarding, punishing	Trust-acceptance: ■ person-person relations ■ engaging with ■ allowing, enjoying ■ informalizing ■ expressing feelings
Data flow (Decision making)	Distance-facade: ■ withdrawal ■ strategy, gamesmanship ■ politeness, propriety ■ masking, camouflage ■ presenting ideal self	Openness-intimacy: ■ confrontation, fighting ■ open influence ■ directness, candor ■ unmasking, showing ■ presenting real self
Goal formation (Productivity)	Persuasion-competition: ■ teaching, modeling ■ correcting, remedying ■ goal imposition ■ advice-giving ■ persuading, counseling	Realization-search: ■ learning, searching ■ growing, becoming ■ self-determination ■ exploring, seeking ■ problem-solving
Control (Organization)	Dependence-dominance: ■ patterning ■ standardizing performance ■ controlling ■ static form ■ control by rules	Interdependence-emergence: ■ innovation, play ■ emerging norms ■ fluid form ■ interdependence ■ absence of rules

Source: Jack R. Gibb and Lorraine M. Gibb, "Role Freedom in a TORI Group," in Arthur Burton, ed., *Encounter* (San Francisco: Jossey-Bass, Inc., Publishers, 1969), p. 44.

Experimentation with Forms of Organization

The future probably will hold major experimentation with forms of organization, in work, politics, family life, play, and so on. Of course, a recent burst of such experimentation has been underway in recent years.[8] Examples include: communes; innovative organizations for political activity, both old style and new; and aggregations for various mixed economic, social, and political purposes. The future seems to hold much more of the same.

This experimentation does not seem chimerical and reasonably implies the failure of existing institutions and values in significant numbers of cases. There is no guarantee that experimentation will be for the better, of course, but some hope is appropriate. Consider the kibbutzim in

8. For example, see Lewis Yablonsky, *The Hippie Trip* (New York: Pegasus, 1968).

541

Israel, which have at least survived under difficult circumstances. The kibbutzim are monitored by democratic means, with kibbutzim in the number of 40 or 50 also being units within a representative system of similar communities. One observer concludes that the sense of community achieved in the small kibbutz helps integrate the individual into larger systems. The 230 communities of the kibbutz federation involving some 90,000 persons have no problems of violence, delinquency, crime, or unemployment, we are told. And psychotic breakdowns are said to be unusual events. Moreover, productivity on the kibbutzim is higher than on Israeli private farms.[9]

2. FORCES INDUCING
THE FUTURE AS KALEIDOSCOPE:
SOME DOMINANT ENVIRONMENTAL FEATURES

The profile sketched above rests on a variety of dominant environmental features. These features are seen as neither in the "can occur" nor in the "probably will occur" category, to distinguish them from the two kinds of elements in the futuristic if probabilitistic profile above. The dominant environmental features are seen as already extant, as significant aspects of today's world in all cases and as having been so for a substantial time in most cases. Six of these dominant environmental features will be highlighted here.

a. Accelerated Change/Intensified Coping:
Futuristic Social Siamese Twins

If only in the sense of repeating what everyone knows so that its truth cannot be forgotten, the future no doubt will bring even more accelerated change. Rather than a breathing spell from the last two or three decades, in short, more of the same it will be. The derivative need is for unparalleled coping, by unprecedentedly large numbers of people, on an ever-broadening front which typically involves complex blends of technical/mechanical and social/behavioral issues.

This first dominant environmental feature has implications for a broad range of life situations, many of them profound. Bennis was one of the first to try his hand at predicting the shape of these implications in large-scale organizations. His characterization serves to illustrate the range of impacts on the broader family of life situations. Bennis notes:

---

9. Naphtali Golomb, "Managing without Sanctions or Rewards," *Management of Personnel Quarterly*, Vol. 7 (Summer, 1968), pp. 22–28. See also Melford E. Spiro, *Kibbutz: Venture in Utopia* (New York: Schocken Books, 1967).

First of all, the key word will be *temporary:* Organizations will become adaptive, rapidly changing temporary systems. Second, they will be organized around problems-to-be-solved. Third, these problems will be solved by relative groups of strangers who represent a diverse set of professional skills. Fourth, given the requirements of coordinating the various projects, articulating points or "linking pin" personnel will be necessary who can speak the diverse languages of research and who can relay and mediate between various project groups. Fifth, the groups will be conducted on organic rather than on mechanical lines; they will emerge and adapt to the problems, and leadership and influence will fall to those who seem most able to solve the problems rather than to programmed role expectations. People will be differentiated, not according to rank or roles, but according to skills and training.

Adaptive, temporary systems of diverse specialists solving problems, coordinated organically via articulating points, will gradually replace the theory and practice of bureaucracy.[10]

This is certainly not a portrait of all organization men, in all kinds of work, now or ever. But it is a characterization of more and more members of a growing number of organizations.

The details will differ, of course, but Bennis's characterization applies more rather than less to a wide variety of life situations. The range extends from low-affect organizations like those Bennis sees as becoming more important, to high-affect situations like friendship[11] and even sexual liaisons.[12] Temporary is *the* word for more and more of life, though hardly for all of it.

b. Demography Is Destiny:
Some Trends and Their Probable Consequences

A recent book on voting announces that "demography is destiny" and, if it is, the character of the future is implicit in a few broad trends. Consider only these summaries of major demographic trends of the recent past which, if anything, are intensifying worldwide:

- A far greater proportion of the population is exposed to far more schooling than ever before.

10. Warren G. Bennis, "A Funny Thing Happened on the Way to the Future," *American Psychologist,* Vol. 25 (July, 1970), p. 598.
11. Courtney Tall, "Friendships in the Future," quoted in Alvin Toffler, *Future Shock* (New York: Random House, 1970), p. 97.
12. Staffan B. Linder, *The Harried Leisure Class* (New York: Columbia University Press, 1970).

- The population is "younging" in unprecedented ways, while people also are living longer than ever.
- Rapid increases are occurring in professional and service employment.
- Larger segments of the population are more mobile than probably ever before, geographically but also in various socioeconomic senses.

These demographic trends portend profound consequences for a wide variety of life situations, as in the case of mobility. Both the new demands and the new costs seem clear enough. Observers like Courtney Tall see one of the major demands of mobility expressed in terms of a substitution of "many close relationships of shorter durability for the few long-term friendships formed in the past." He explains:

> Stability based on close relationships with a few people will be ineffective, due to the high mobility, wide interest range, and varying capacity for adaptation and change found among the members of a highly automated society. . . . Individuals will develop the ability to form close "buddy-type" relationships on the basis of common interests or sub-group affiliations, and to easily leave these friendships, moving either to another location and joining a similar interest group or to another interest group within the same location . . . Interests will change rapidly . . .
>
> This ability to form and then to drop, or lower to the level of acquaintanceship, close relationships quickly, coupled with increased mobility, will result in any given individual forming many more friendships than is possible for most in the present. . . .[13]

The adjustment will not come easily, at least for some people. Not only do people mourn a friend left behind, and sometimes intensely. There are also apparently growing numbers of people who are mobile and who also mourn the lost place as they might mourn a lost person. Marc Fried notes that: "It is quite precise to speak of their reactions as expressions of *grief*." He concludes that these mournful reactions are manifest "in the feelings of painful loss, the continued longing, the general depressive tone, frequent symptoms of psychological or social or somatic distress . . . the senses of helplessness, the occasional expressions of both direct and displaced anger, and tendencies to idealize the lost place."[14]

As these demographic tendencies imply demands on people, so also do they mean that man's institutions must respond to a broader range of

13. Tall, *op. cit.*, p. 97.
14. Marc Fried, "Grieving for a Lost Home," in Leonard Duhl, *The Urban Condition* (New York: Basic Books, 1963), pp. 151, 160.

human needs. The growing professionalization and education of organization members, for example, both imply significant changes in the values of work. Thus growing numbers of people may seek greater involvement in their work, as well as enhanced control over their worksite environment. This is the essence of Bennis's guess that a prime effect of the "increase in educated persons, whose status is less dependent on property, will likely increase the investment of individuals in having autonomy and a voice in decision making" at work.[15] Such new needs might be variously expressed, as in a preference for patterns of organizational influence and authority that are consistent with the values of growing numbers of organization members. Uniformly, however, these various expressions will in most cases differ from the values of bureaucracy. Such needs might be responded to within the chain of command or via such bypasses as unionization for managers or greater concern for organizational due processes.[16]

c. Sustaining and Extending an Unprecedented Affluence: The Dynamics of Rising Expectations

The dynamics of our kaleidoscopic future will be generated in important ways by efforts to sustain and extend the unprecedented if relative economic affluence that much of the Western world has experienced over the past several decades. The point has both obvious and subtle aspects. Consider the former first. Since more people have partaken of the horn of plenty, and perhaps even more have come to aspire to partaking therefrom, there is potential social dynamite aplenty in threatening what some have come to enjoy and what others have come to believe is either within their reach or should be, by right. Without much doubt, then, considerable effort will be devoted to sustaining and extending affluence. Or else.

The point has a subtler aspect. There is a common developmental pattern in all economic systems, that is. Early on, the emphasis is on accumulation by the few, whether they be capitalists or socialist bureaucrats. Put otherwise, some form of saving and reinvesting by those with a low propensity to consume seems necessary for early economic development. The many get exploited in the process, at least in the short run, whether willingly or because they have no alternative. In Havighurst's terms, the emphasis in early economic development is on *opportunity* and *production*. Somewhere down the track, the emphasis shifts to *consumption*.[17] Beyond some point in economic development, as it were,

---

15. Bennis, "A Funny Thing Happened on the Way to the Future," p. 603.
16. William G. Scott, *The Management of Conflict: Appeals Systems in Organizations* (Homewood, Ill.: Richard D. Irwin, 1965).
17. R. J. Havighurst, "The Social and Educational Implications of Interinstitutional Cooperation in Higher Education," in L. C. Howard (ed.), *Interinstitutional Co-*

mass demand is increasingly necessary to sustain and expand important segments of the industrial and service apparatus. Some kind of fundamental redistribution of income becomes increasingly necessary as the emphasis shifts toward *consumption,* which certainly in major senses underlies the unprecedented affluence of at least the recent American experience.

There are powerful implications for huge segments of life in this shift to distribution. Consider only appropriate responses to unemployment. With emphasis on opportunity and production, nonworkers historically have been treated with the absolute minimum consideration, and even that as a matter of privilege only. Substantial harshness, in fact, was often prescribed as just the right medicine to motivate some nonworkers into the labor force. The person is treated not as a human but as a factor of production, in sum. With a growing emphasis on consumption, however, major changes tend to occur. Cushions against unemployment are developed, and various programs are as a matter of right extended to various classes of nonworkers. Whether the motivation is to preserve human dignity or to induce some base level of consumption, the guiding notion is that the society owes its members more than a direct economic reward for exploiting an opportunity or for adding to production.

There is no assumption in this broad sketch that some kind of invisible hand preserves equity in the allocative processes. But the sketch should suggest two points. Our recent spreading affluence implies that consumption has come on stream in a major way as a broad determinant of economic activity. Once resorted to, moreover, the engines of consumption are extremely difficult to turn down. Hence our economic future probably will see some frantic running, if only in order to stand still with respect to the accumulating aspirations whose frustration can be socially dangerous.

d. Shifting Patterns of Needs and Motives:
Changes in Some Internal Stimuli of Behavior

One significant product of this economic affluence seems clear enough and should become more of a factor if that affluence persists and is extended. That product is the shifting of needs and motives, at least among certain segments of the population, which implies changes in behavior as responses to a new set of internal stimuli. The focus is on what moves modern women and men, in short.

No few data can establish such a fundamental conclusion, but some evidence supports the common observation that for some growing num-

---

operation in Higher Education (Milwaukee: University of Wisconsin Press, 1967), pp. 508–23.

ber of people the times really are a-changin' in the matter of which motives and needs induce behavior.[18] If the sketch above is anywhere near the mark, for example, the opportunity and production themes should find less acceptance now than before. Some selective data do not violate this expectation. Thus the attractiveness of business careers seems to be falling, perhaps precipitously. In one leading university, for example, 70 percent of the students in 1928 were planning business careers. By 1962, the percentage had dropped to 24; and five years later, the figure had plummeted to 19 percent.[19] A similar pattern appears in changes in themes that characterize children's stories.[20]

Such findings suggesting changes in motives and needs are easy to interpret as responses to affluence, and they also imply a broad range of effects in many life situations. In Abraham Maslow's terms,[21] economic affluence may be said to have substantially satisfied the needs that economic deprivation could activate. The relatively satisfied needs, as a consequence, are relatively ineffective motivators of behavior.

All institutions feel the consequences of changing patterns of motives and needs. For example, major direct changes at work seem to be occurring. Thus two observers note that: "Extrinsic rewards such as pay, job security, fringe benefits, and conditions of work are no longer so attractive. Younger people are demanding intrinsic job satisfactions as well. They are less likely to accept the notion of deferring gratifications in the interests of some distant career."[22] Changes in motives and needs seem to underlie such effects. "In most organizations today," these observers conclude, "the dominant motives of members are the higher-order ego and social motives—particularly those for personal gratification, independence, self-expression, power, and self-actualization. . . ." Noting that the newly-aroused motives can take a variety of forms, many of them already familiar, they explain:

> First there is the emphasis upon self-determination or self-expression, or "doing one's thing." Second is the demand for self-development and self-actualization, making the most of

---

18. Generally, for specific data about such changes in attitudes and values, see John B. Miner, "Changes in Student Attitudes toward Bureaucratic Role Prescriptions during the 1960s," *Administrative Science Quarterly,* Vol. 16 (September, 1971), pp. 351–64. Daniel Katz and Basil S. Georgopoulous, "Organizations in a Changing World," *Journal of Applied Behavioral Science,* Vol. 7 (May, 1971), esp. pp. 349–51, provide a broad perspective.
19. Katz and Georgopoulous, *op. cit.,* p. 350.
20. Richard de Charms and Gerald H. Moeller, "Values Expressed in Children's Readers," *Journal of Abnormal and Social Psychology,* Vol. 64, Nov. 2 (1962), pp. 136–42.
21. Abraham H. Maslow, *Motivation and Personality* (New York: Harper & Row, Publishers, 1954).
22. Katz and Georgopoulous, *op. cit.,* p. 350.

one's own talents and abilities. Third is the unleashing of power drives. The hippies represent the first emphasis of self-expression, some of the leftist leaders the emphasis upon power. Fourth is the outcome of the other three, a blanket rejection of established values—a revolutionary attack upon the existing system as exploitative and repressive of the needs of individuals.

With the need for self-expression goes the ideology of the importance of spontaneity; of the wholeness of human experience; the reliance upon emotions; and the attack upon the fragmentation, the depersonalization, and the restrictions of the present social forms. It contributes to the anti-intellectualism of the student movement and is reminiscent of the romanticism of an older period in which Wordsworth spoke of the intellect as that false secondary power which multiplies delusions. Rationality is regarded as rationalization.[23]

e. Changing Patterns of Authority: External Controls as Causes and Consequences

Significant changes in prevailing patterns of authority also contribute momentum to, and derive impetus from, the above contributions to a kaleidoscope in our future. The old verities have been variously questioned, or discredited, or even hooted down, in short. The new truths are but vaguely perceived, at best, if the very search for them is not rejected by those who still prefer the old ways. And all institutions have to do the best they can, and somehow muddle through, while the very bases for collective action are being given a thorough going-over.

There is no overestimating the impact of such changes in patterns of authority. Perhaps the impact is greatest on such institutions as the Roman Catholic Church, whose authority structure was considered as ultralegitimate by many, and not very long ago. Now the concern is whether the church has "lost its soul" along with losing the sense of the order-and-obey authority relations that were accepted by many as the essence of their religious experience.[24] On the secular side, the impact is equally profound. As Daniel Katz and Basil Georgopolous explain in their "Organizations in a Changing World," order-and-obey authority was the glue of the old order. To the degree that the traditional concept of authority is superseded, flexibility may possibly be gained, but comfortable certainty is clearly lost. They conclude:

The break with the older pattern of authority has eroded some of the formerly dependable maintenance processes of organiza-

23. *Ibid.*, p. 351.
24. "Has the Church Lost Its Soul?," *Newsweek*, October 4, 1971, pp. 80–84, 87–89.

tions. Bureaucratic systems had long profited from the socialization practices of traditional society, in which values and
legitimacy had a moral basis of an absolutist character. It was
morally wrong to reject in word or deed the traditional teach-
ings about American institutions. It was wrong to seek change
other than through established channels. . . .

There was an all-or-none quality about virtue, honesty, and
justice, and these values were not seen as relativistic or empirical generalizations. Member compliance with organizational
norms and values no longer can be sustained on the basis of
authority. . . .[25]

Only two broad facts seem incontestable about the changes in patterns
of authority that are influencing so many institutions. First, the changes
began slowly, and they seem to be intensifying in numerous ways. It does
not seem likely that the high-water point is already behind us, in short.

Second, the changes in patterns of authority were induced by multiple
sources, and it is meaningful to speak only of interacting elements rather
than of causes and effects. For example, there no doubt has been an ongoing "transformation of the American middle-class family,"[26] and it
contributed to changes in the concept of authority while it also drew
sustenance therefrom. It is not possible to specify the magnitude of the
interacting effects, but they are undeniably there. Children have been
given greater opportunities for expression and greater support for autonomous behavior, both of which imply changes in authority just as
much as does the probably increased equality between husbands and
wives. And such effects also have multiple causes. Given expanded educational opportunities and growing obsolescence of skills, for example,
many parents might have felt adequate only to permit their children to
drink heavily of the new wines. The children may have perceived either
estrangement or coercion in such an act; and many children certainly felt
in the possession of a new power. Both features would have stressed
authority relations. Similarly, the greater mobility and employability of
females encouraged a change in patterns of husband-wife dominance,
with direct implications for traditional patterns of authority.

On a different front, similar effects corroded the linkages once provided with certainty by command/obey authority. For example, Bennis
saw changes occurring in the basic philosophy of managerial behavior.
This philosophy had profound implications for authority, in at least
three of its essentials. Bennis described them as:

---

25. Katz and Georgopoulous, *op. cit.*, p. 347.
26. Richard Flacks, "Protest or Conform: Some Social Psychological Perspectives on
Legitimacy," *Journal of Applied Behavioral Science,* Vol. 5 (April, 1969), pp.
127–50.

(a) a new concept of man, based on increased knowledge of his complex and shifting needs, which replaces the oversimplified, innocent push-button concept of man; (b) a new concept of power, based on collaboration and reason, which replaces a model of power based on coercion and fear; and (c) a new concept of organizational values, based on humanistic-democratic ideals, which replaces the depersonalized mechanistic value system of bureaucracy.[27]

Again, a wide range of interacting factors contributed to such changing elements in managerial philosophy. These impacted on the basic concept of authority, to a degree which can with safety be identified only as accelerating from a low base. The separation of ownership from control, for example, certainly served to take some of the edge off command/obey authority. But this effect, in turn, was but one sign of complex social, economic, and political forces. No doubt more than ever before, more and more people and institutions are having an impact on a widening range of topics in the full panoply of organizations. The list includes labor unions, government agencies, civil rights associations and other specialized interests, courts, staff personnel and professionals, and so on. Command/obey authority was less and less appropriate as the parties to authoritative sequences grew more numerous and more impactful on each other. Concept simply followed practice in this case, taking on a complexity far beyond command/obey authority. Command/obey authority did not disappear, of course, but it was substantially diluted even in such rather extreme life situations as boot-camp training for the U.S. Marines.

f. From Exploitative Particularism ⟷ Integrative Allocation: A Response to Shrinking/Shifting Resources

A rough-and-ready distinction adds to the discussion of changes in patterns of authority. The growing scarcity of resources, coupled with growing demand, encourages what might be called "integrative allocation," an increasingly explicit statement of goals against which alternative uses of resources must be traded off. Epigrammatically, low costs of plant operations are increasingly being balanced against costs of polluting natural resources and man's environment. In contrast, "exploitative particularism" characterized a simpler age with more abundant untapped resources. At one time, to illustrate, cost considerations of harvesting a forest were likely to be narrow enough to exclude all but the immediate

---

27. Bennis, "A Funny Thing Happened on the Way to the Future," p. 597.

costs of exploiting the opportunity provided by a stand of timber. Polluted streams and endemic unemployment after the cut-off would not be part of the calculations. Not so now, of course, although perfection awards are premature.

At least two conclusions can be drawn without straining the point. First, there has been some movement from exploitative particularism to integrative allocation, on balance. No doubt, the movement is clearer and more advanced in the case of Pennsylvania strip-mining than in other states which still permit extractors to gouge the earth and run. But the movement seems undeniable, if only because (illustratively) it is no longer possible to massacre buffalo because there are so few of them left.

The second conclusion is that, as integrative allocation is emphasized, so is a command/obey concept of authority less tenable. That is, integrative allocation means bringing a broadening range of interests into decision-making situations. These interests include organizational "outsiders," such as consumer groups, labor unions, government agencies, and so on. And these interests include diverse "insiders," often professionals in budgeting or planning or whatever, who are attempting to bring to bear perspectives and skills that will enhance integrative allocations in the present sense. The concept of authority had to bend or break, as a consequence.

3. OD AS AN INTEGRATOR OF FUTURISTIC DIVERSITIES: SOME GUIDELINES EMERGING FROM THE CRUCIBLE OF EARLY EXPERIENCE

Given these futuristic probabilities, organization development faces huge challenges in integrating diversities that can safely be expected to grow more profound and complex. The focus here is on the preparedness of OD to accept such challenges, specifically on guidelines that have emerged from the early experience with OD. That experience is seen as a crucible for testing initial notions, as well as for mothering more useful concepts where the old are found wanting. Note that the guidelines below are intentionally prescriptive, and they reflect both value considerations and pragmatic judgments about what seem useful perspectives and approaches.

Basis in Appropriate Concept of Man

Paramountly, OD efforts must be imbedded in an appropriate concept of man. This is a matter of avoiding extremes, and also of leaning more in one direction than another. Attaining and maintaining this in-tension view of man will be no easy matter, for man's attachment to concepts tends to be characterized more by a widely swinging pendulum than by a balance.

Specifically, the appropriate view of man is boundedly optimistic. The optimism has several facets. Thus optimism is appropriate that man can become less imperfect, that most people are not so fragile that they cannot look at themselves and their behavior without disintegrating or being grievously shaken as persons, that some things *can* be done to induce satisfying growth in all but the most frozen personal and in the most reactionary organizational systems.

What are the appropriate bounds of this core optimism? Specifically, it is also clear what the appropriate concept of man should not be. The crucial challenge is to avoid two extremes, while inclining more to one than the other. On the one hand, the appropriate concept of man must reject a view of man as basically bad and incorrigible. As Robert Tannenbaum and Sheldon Davis sketch the underlying rationale, "When people are seen as bad they need to be disciplined and corrected" only on specific issues and can otherwise be left alone. Dynamically, this is perverse. "Avoidance and negative evaluation can lead individuals to be cautious, guarded, defensive," they conclude. "Confirmation can lead to personal release, confidence, and enhancement."[28] On the other hand, there are dangers in assuming too much about man's perfectibility, and especially about his existing perfection.

An appropriate concept of man, then, seeks to avoid the traps of two simple definitions of human nature, of man as basically "good" or "bad." Thomas A. Greening frames the issue well and also reflects the in-between concept of man emphasized above. He notes:

> One school of thought holds that man is basically good, self-actualizing, and cooperative, if only we can help him let down his barriers. On the other hand, there are those who argue that man is basically an amoral, irrational animal who must be kept in check by external restraints and a self-deluding veneer. Personally, I prefer the position I once heard Martin Buber take in a discussion with Carl Rogers: "Man is basically good—and bad."[29]

Basic early OD concepts tended to fall into one of the traps to be avoided, and en masse. Their common view of man was boundlessly optimistic, even perfectionistic. For example, a dominant OD view held

---

28. Robert Tannenbaum and Sheldon A. Davis, "Values, Man, and Organizations," in Warren H. Schmidt (ed.), *Organizational Frontiers and Human Values* (Belmont, Cal.: Wadsworth Publishing Co., 1970), p. 134.
29. Thomas C. Greening, "Sensitivity Training: Cult or Contribution?" *Personnel*, Vol. 41 (May, 1964), p. 21.

that bureaucracy was the basic blight in what was otherwise man's garden of paradise. Loving and trusting man would overcome it in 25 to 50 years at the outside. Indeed, Bennis and Slater informed us, "democracy was inevitable."

The brilliance of the initial OD vision dimmed quickly, and the disappointment no doubt added impetus to an ongoing trend in managerial thought toward a darker view of man.[30] Not long after the declaration of the inevitability of democracy, for example, at least Bennis has changed his mind about the difficulty of the task, and he has recognized the simplicism his earlier enthusiasm encouraged. Bennis's goal remains unchanged, however, although his confidence in achieving it has been seriously shaken. Basically, Bennis seems to recognize the profound limitations on man's existing and future states of perfection, especially what Alexander Winn called "the irrational and destructive impulses in man."[31] For example, Bennis epigrammatically observes that the issue is no longer whether democracy is inevitable, but whether it is sexy enough to attract and retain enthusiastic support in competition with atavistic and authoritarian alternatives. He believes that democracy is not sexy enough, on balance. Specifically, Bennis emphasizes these four factors as new limits on his earlier vision of the organizational tomorrow:[32]

- the recent widespread dislocations, if not breakdowns, in the perceived legitimacy of a broad range of traditional authority figures and institutions
- the growing evidence of tension between the elitist and populist functions of our institutions, as in universities which can be conceived as elite centers of disinterested inquiry and criticism as well as populist centers of mass education, service, socialization and politicization
- a heightened awareness of "the discontinuities between microsystems and macrosystems," which Bennis notes was a painful discovery for him

---

30. Bennis's change in viewpoint suggests the sharper reaction and seems similarly motivated by the turbulence of recent years. His earlier optimism was based on his perception that large masses of men were prepared to work collaboratively for broad common goals. That perception diminished as the 1960s spasmodically were lived through and man's focus swung toward short-run, individualistic goals. Bennis explains: "we can observe a growing uncertainty about the deepest human concerns: jobs, neighborhoods, regulation of social norms, child rearing, law and order. . . ." "A Funny Thing Happened on the Way to the Future," p. 603.
31. Alexander Winn, "The Laboratory Approach to Organization Development." Paper read at Annual Conference, British Psychological Association, Oxford, September 1968, p. 3.
32. Bennis, "A Funny Thing Happened on the Way to the Future," pp. 509–602.

- the recognition of a basic "structural" weakness of democratic ideology, especially as applied to large aggregates of people, in that it is strong on individual rights but ambiguous as to collective obligations

The sense of Bennis's new view is illustrated by a response to a letter in which Carl Rogers stressed that an increased concern with human relationships was perhaps *the* prerequisite for managing our institutions. The letter writer was of two minds:

> Though I agree with [Rogers] heartily, I have some very strong questions about whether, indeed, this kind of future is in the cards for us. I raise this primarily because out of my experiences working in the U.S. Department of Housing and Urban Development and out of experiences working in and with cities, it is clear that in the basic decision making that takes place, the values Dr. Rogers and I hold so dear have an extremely low priority. Indeed, the old-fashioned concerns with power, prestige, money and profit so far outdistance the concerns for human warmth and love and concern that many people consider the latter extremely irrelevant in the basic decision making. Sadly, it is my feeling that they will continue to do so.[33]

The choice of a concept of man has myriad implications for the laboratory approach. For example, an heroic concept of man would encourage learning designs of maximum power and would require no special concern about transfer of any learning into various back-home situations. Oppositely, the concept of man as "good—and bad," as having "irrational and destructive impulses" and other fragilities that set real limits to his perfectibility, encourages concern about both learning designs and transfer of learning. For example, such a concept of man implies the need for designs with a margin of safety. Such a concept also suggests the value of family groups, which highlight the long-run responsibility of the individual for the specific and continuing impact of his contributions. As Richard E. Parlour details the tradeoffs:

> The people in the organization have to live with what they do. It is true that in some ways people will be cautious in self-expression in such situations because of possible repercussions from the other group members who have the power to do harm. Each person also has a vested interest in making the organization successful and reducing the unnecessary obstacles to smooth cooperation resulting from faulty self-evaluations and misunderstandings between the members. Reality cannot be well-confronted without including the power factor. . . .

---

33. Quoted in *ibid.*, pp. 601–2.

We cannot know a person until we see what he does in real-life situations where he must bear the responsibility for his actions.[34]

For stranger groups, relatedly, the balanced concept of man urges the expenditure of considerable energy in both design and training to raise the probability that desired outcomes do occur. For example, feedback and disclosure processes might be variously structured to assure desired outcomes. The guidelines for feedback sketched above in Section A of Part II, for example, are one such way to increase the probability of desired outcomes. To be sure, a person using the guidelines might be spared the experience of how punishing he can be otherwise. But that is a small loss indeed.

To complete the point, choice of a concept of man as basically bad also would have a direct implication for the laboratory approach. That implication: Forget about the laboratory approach for, given that concept of man, it would be mischievous if not dangerous.

Basis in Social Contract

OD activities or programs should be imbedded in a social contract of reciprocal obligations appropriate to the situation. Two kinds of such social contracts can be distinguished.[35] Each theory has profoundly different implications for the character of the commitment required of participants, as well as for the details of the learning design.

Most OD efforts assume what might be called a "comprehensive social contract" theory. This kind of contract is a pervasive and binding one, the typical details of which are suggested by Figure 3. Figure 3 is drawn from the work of Tannenbaum and Davis, whose basic proposition is that OD should work away from "a view of man as essentially bad toward a view of him as basically good." The authors qualify their effort in these important terms:

> We clearly recognize that the values to which we hold are not absolutes, that they represent directions rather than final goals. We also recognize that the degree of their short-run application often depends upon the people and other variables involved. We feel that we are now in a period of transition, sometimes slow and sometimes rapid, involving a movement away

34. Richard R. Parlour, "Executive Team Training," *Journal of the Academy of Management,* Vol. 14 (September, 1971) , p. 343. His emphasis.
35. For one discussion of the contract notion in relation to sensitivity training, see Gerald Egan, *Encounter: Group Processes for Interpersonal Growth* (Belmont, Cal.: Wadsworth Publishing Co., 1970) , pp. 25–67.

from older, less personally meaningful and organizationally relevant values toward these newer values.[36]

The vitals of the comprehensive social contract theory can be indicated briefly. In total intention, the goal is to create a specific social order so as to change and guide behavior, and perhaps even to contribute to "personal development." The commitment required of participants is consequently a pervasive one indeed. The learning designs

Figure 3. Some Basic Values in a Comprehensive OD Social Contract

Organization Development should work:

- away from avoidance, or negative evaluation, of individuals, and toward confirming them as human beings. This does not refer "to the excessively neurotic needs of some persons for attention and response, but rather to the much more pervasive and basic need to know that one's existence makes a difference to others. . . . Confirmation can lead to personal release, confidence and enhancement."
- away from a view of individuals as fixed, and toward seeing them as in the process of becoming
- away from resisting and fearing individual differences, and toward accepting and utilizing differentiated people
- away from utilizing an individual primarily as a job-holder, and toward viewing him as a person
- away from suppressing the expression of feelings, and toward making their expression appropriate and their use effective
- away from maskmanship and game-playing, and toward greater mutual authenticity
- away from the use of status for maintaining power and personal prestige, and toward the use of status for organizationally relevant purposes, such as intervening when lower levels are in conflict as to a course of action
- away from distrusting people, and toward trusting them
- away from the avoidance of facing others with relevant data, and toward confrontation
- away from avoidance of risk-taking, and toward a greater willingness to risk
- away from a view of interpersonal and intergroup processes as being nonrelevant, and toward seeing them as essential to effective performance
- away from a primary emphasis on competitive or distributive strategies, and toward a growing emphasis on collaborative or integrative strategies.

Source: Based on Robert Tannenbaum and Sheldon A. Davis, "Values, Man, and Organizations," in Warren H. Schmidt (ed.), *Organizational Frontiers and Human Values* (Belmont, Cal.: Wadsworth Publishing Co., 1970), pp. 132–44.

illustrated in Section F, Part II, are appropriate when the comprehensive social contract theory provides guidance for an OD program.

Despite the likelihood that comprehensive social contracts are implied by most OD programs, in most cases it is just so much long-range hoping. Clearly, only a mature OD program can provide any realistic basis on which organization members can opt for the comprehensive social contract.

This is not to say that it has to be all or nothing, as far as OD goes. Indeed, given only those two choices, it commonly would be nothing.

---

36. Tannenbaum and Davis, *op. cit.*, p. 131.

Alternatively and practically, "limited exchange contracts" can also characterize OD efforts. In essence, this kind of social contract implies a strictly bounded rationale. Every relationship implies an exchange, goes that rationale; each exchange has a certain balance of costs/benefits for individuals and for their organizations; and at least some of these exchanges can be singled out for attention without doing major violence to the truism that every exchange is related to every other exchange in a huge nest of ever-more comprehensive systems. Assume that in the case of relationship A, the costs are too great relative to the benefits. Is there something that can be done to make the ratio more favorable? And without first creating appropriate superordinate systems? The commitment to find out is a far narrower one than Figure 3 requires.

No general rules apply, but designs can commonly be developed that safely meet the sense of "limited exchange contracts." The point applies in at least three senses. *First,* many OD designs based on the laboratory approach can be limited as to participants and subject matter. For example, third-party consultation requires a deep commitment but it involves only the pair, and thereby avoids some sticky issues. Similarly, some varieties of process observation or team development—such as the "mirror" exercise—can be useful while intendedly limited in subject matter, time, and so on.

Second, many OD designs following the limited exchange contract can be designed so as to be relatively or even substantially private.[37] Many career-planning designs have such a character, for example, as do many designs for eliciting feedback from among large cadres of organization members.

Third, for a wide range of organizationally relevant issues, even public OD designs can be limited in ways that avoid the comprehensive social contract implicit in a design that (for example) uses T-Group training in family groups. Such designs focus on work relations in terms of the values of the laboratory approach, rather than on the personal impact of the experience. Friedlander's organizational training laboratories described in Section D, Part II, used such a design, as did some innovative OD work in schools headed by Richard Schmuck.[38]

The logic and thrust of Schmuck's OD design can be illustrated usefully and economically. At the level of broad strategy, we are told that:

> In designing this intervention, we made strong use of the laboratory method. . . . The training often called for conscious observation of the group processes of the faculty. The design required the actual practice of new behaviors before

---

37. For an example, see Subsection 4 below.
38. Richard A. Schmuck and Matthew B. Miles (eds.), *Organization Development in Schools* (Palo Alto, Cal.: National Press Books, 1971).

using them in daily work. Although the design made use of the school as its own laboratory, we made use of laboratory groups in ways very different from those associated with sensitivity training or the T-group. Personal development was not our target. We did not attempt to improve the interpersonal functioning of individuals directly; when this occurred, it was incidental. Our targets were the faculty as a whole and several subgroups within it. We sought to increase the effectiveness of groups as task-oriented entities. We tried to teach subgroups within the school and the faculty as a whole to function more effectively as working bodies carrying out specific tasks in that particular job setting.[39]

Somewhat more specifically, the entire faculty and staff constituted the total training population, and design elements rotated sizes and memberships in such ways that each participant worked with every other participant in at least two subgroups. Early on, subgroups worked on a variety of games, such as the NASA Trip to the Moon exercise. The games were chosen so that they emphasized the role of clear and effective communication and decision-making. The common thrust was from an analysis of the results of each game-play, to a search for similarities or differences between the game dynamics and real-life experiences at school. A number of such exercises followed the same pattern, with consultants encouraging adherence to laboratory values and planning supplementary learning experiences in listening, in describing the behavior of another, and so on. The concluding two thirds of the training experience—four days—completed the thrust of the training design. Their focus was on "a problem-solving sequence, working on real issues that were thwarting the organizational functioning of the schools." Several reinforcing experiences were also held later. A broad range of indicators strongly suggests the value of such a design, using three other schools as comparison groups.[40]

These design alternatives come to an obvious if often-neglected point. The nature of the problem, the learning goal, and the characteristics of participants as well as their environment, should interactively determine the appropriate social contract. This "rule" is often breeched, however, due to the common but usually implicit acceptance of the general appropriateness of a comprehensive social contract and the typical prescription of the T-Group as the learning vehicle appropriate to that contract.[41]

39. *Ibid.*, p. 52.
40. *Ibid.*, esp. pp. 59–61.
41. Sylvia A. Joure, Roland L. Frye, Paul C. Green, and Frank P. Cassens, "Examples of Over-Use of Sensitivity Training," *Training and Development Journal*, Vol. 25 (December, 1971), pp. 24–26.

The interaction of social contract and problem can be illustrated. Consider the case of a small public agency experiencing some run-of-the-mill adjustments, even though the work was still being done efficiently and effectively. The supervisor's goal was "to quickly get over the hump" of these adjustments, a sentiment shared by all. These adjustments centered around: a new head, a young and attractive female at that who was somewhat unsure of her new role; a previously all-male group, on the older and somewhat stodgy side, and a little threatened by several recent personnel changes; and several new employees who were definitely mod-squad aspirants if not aficionados, both male and female subtypes. The overkill prescription for this new group was three week-ends of family T-Grouping. The result: the revelation of nonwork material that would have tested even a far more stable group that was certain of its relations. The long-run outcome: strong feelings of guilt due to cross-pressures involving peak work demands and the humanitarian impulse to provide emotional support at work to several colleagues. The work demands tended to win out, but at substantial cost of feelings of guilt for most members and abandonment for others.

This seems a case of design overkill, for more limited designs seem appropriate to the modest initial learning goals. The design chosen rested on a comprehensive social contract of obligations, for which the group was ill-prepared.

Bias toward Participant Choice, not Change

Whatever the specific social theory of obligation bounding any OD activity or program, the consistent bias should be toward participant choice and not necessarily change. The value of this bias is multidimensional, suggested perhaps most forcefully by the data in Section A, Part II, about the association of psychiatric casualties in T-Groups and trainers who demand change rather than offer choice. Frank Friedlander eloquently explains his emphasis on choice in this way:

> In a larger sense, OD provides for the organizational member the opportunity for exploration and choice—of his values, of the structures in which he is living, and of the tasks upon which he is working. I am personally far more concerned with providing people with an awareness of who they are, of what they are doing with who they are, and of the choices they have in these areas—than I am with changing them in some way. My own energies, then, are directed toward helping the individual encounter or experience his own values, needs and skills; the kinds of tasks to which he is devoting his organizational career; the structures and relationships he has with his work and with

559

the people with whom he works; and finally how these all interact upon his sense of fulfilment and task competence.[42]

This view clashes head on with charges that the laboratory approach,
and especially the T-Group, is an engine for conformity, group-think,
and lockstep. And that clash is intentional. In its broadest sense, that is,
the laboratory approach seeks to blend groupiness and individuality.
The essence of the blend is straightforward. Group contexts can be
useful, even indispensable, for a variety of purposes. They can facilitate
the cross-validation of perceptions of individual behavior, the development of norms that may persist after a group's membership has changed
many times over, a locus for exchanging emotional support, and so on.
Even in the T-Group, however, it is nonsense to argue that "the group"
(for example) always makes better decisions than individuals, whatever
that really means. Only individuals make decisions, although various
group contexts can bring out the best (or the worst) in any collection
of individuals.

The laboratory approach variously seeks to provide group environments that facilitate decision-making by individuals, who as a consequence can psychologically own the decision and its consequences. Necessity dictates the blend. On the one hand, individuals are variously
involved in group contexts, and elementary common sense urges making
the best of ubiquity. On the other, no group can make a decision for an
individual, even though a group's members can coerce or cajole apparent
ownership in other members. Ideally, in sum, the laboratory approach
uses groupiness to foster individual growth and responsibility. Spencer
Klaw captures much of this essence in his account of a T-Group experience. He observes:

> . . . it is a fact that, for better or worse, many people do have
> to spend a lot of time working with groups. And it can be
> argued that someone who has been in a T-Group is likely to
> find his ability to resist group pressures strengthened rather
> than weakened. Furthermore, even though T-Grouping tends
> to emphasize such qualities as modesty, sensitivity, and group-
> mindedness, members of a T-Group may also gain some notion
> as to why many people are *not* sensitive and modest and group-
> minded—and thereby become more ready to listen to the ar-
> rogant boor who nevertheless happens to know what he's talking
> about.[43]

42. Frank Friedlander, "Congruence in Organization Development" (Paper presented
   at the Annual Meeting, Academy of Management, Atlanta, Ga., August 17–18,
   1971) , p. 6.
43. Spencer Klaw, "Two Weeks in a T-Group," in Robert T. Golembiewski and
   Arthur Blumberg (eds.) , *Sensitivity Training and the Laboratory Approach* (Itasca,
   Ill.: F. E. Peacock Publishers, Inc., 1970) , p. 37.

Adjustment to Models of Change

OD activities and programs must be appropriately adjusted to various possible models of change. The point can be approached in terms of the contrast between mechanical and organic systems in Figure 4. The development of organic systems is the recognized *summum bonum* of OD, and the "truth-love" model is the accepted vehicle for achieving that highest good. As Winn notes: "Most of the organization development practitioners rely almost exclusively on . . . the 'truth-love' model, based on the assumption that man is reasonable and caring and that once trust is achieved, the desired social change within the organization will take place with no other sources of influence required."[44] The

Figure 4. Some Points of Comparison between Mechanical and Organic Systems

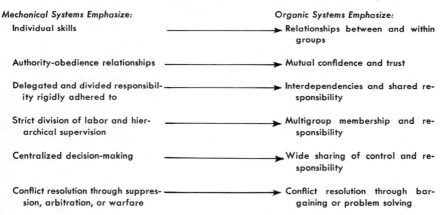

Mechanical Systems Emphasize:

Individual skills → Relationships between and within groups

Authority-obedience relationships → Mutual confidence and trust

Delegated and divided responsibility rigidly adhered to → Interdependencies and shared responsibility

Strict division of labor and hierarchical supervision → Multigroup membership and responsibility

Centralized decision-making → Wide sharing of control and responsibility

Conflict resolution through suppression, arbitration, or warfare → Conflict resolution through bargaining or problem solving

Organic Systems Emphasize:

Source: Herbert A. Shepard and Robert R. Blake, "Changing Behavior through Cognitive Change," cited in Robert T. Golembiewski and Arthur Blumberg (eds.), *Sensitivity Training and the Laboratory Approach* (Itasca, Ill.: F. E. Peacock Publishers, Inc., 1970), p. 309.

"power-coercive" model is seen as the base technique of the contra-ideal, the mechanical system.

There can easily be too much definitional tidiness about such distinctions, which is not to say that truth-love and less power-coercion should be less fervently desired and sought after. The more relevant question is this. Where power-coercion does exist, can its patterns be modified enough to permit some movement toward truth-love? The question is of enormous moment. For power-coercion is everywhere, and it is very

---

44. Alexander Winn, "Reflections on the T-Group Strategy and the Role of Change Agent in Organization Development." Unpublished Ms., February 1971, p. 1. The paper has been published as "Réflexions sur la stratégie du T-Group et le rôle l'agent de changement dans le developpement organisationnel," *Bulletin de Psychologie,* Vol. 25, No. 296 (1971–72) , pp. 250–56.

likely to be for an extended time to come. That is, the relevant concerns are: where is it reasonable to increase the incidence of truth-love, and how much? Everywhere, and to the maximum extent, are not meaningful responses to these central concerns.

Bowers usefully frames the point in terms of the needed sensitivity of the change agent's style to the general level of preparedness of the host organization. Overall, he recommends that the change agent's style of approach "should be determined by the degree of irrationality and resistance to change in the client system." More specifically, he adds:

> Where the client system is quite irrational, rigid, and resistant, or where it is lacking in structure, purpose, energy and force, the change agent's style should be that of *Direct Intervenor*. Where the client system is moderately resistant or defensive, his style should be that of the *Non-Directive Responder*. Where the client system is open to change, rational, and reasonably flexible (but lacking in the necessary information, skills, or resources), his style should be that of an *Indirect Structuror*.[45]

This situational flexibility has deep roots. Perhaps most basically, mechanical systems in the sense defined above will be with us for a very long time indeed, because much work now is and will continue to be such that mechanical approaches to organizing are at least convenient and may in fact be necessary. The relevant issues, in sum are: How big a dent can be made in the more extreme varieties of power-coercion, and what departures from the mechanical system are at once possible and at least comparable to it in overall outcomes?

The implied picture deserves specific statement, for there is significant meaning in it at the practical level even if the conceptual issue might appear exotic and elusive. Directly, OD designs have strongly tended to be based on the truth-love model, to the neglect of alternative models. Schmuck and Miles develop the point persuasively, and their argument can be sketched here. Their characterization of the truth-love model provides a convenient starting point. They note:

> Such a "tender" model states that shared expectations involving trust, warmth, and supportiveness are formed as the members of a working team gain confidence and skill in communicating clearly and openly. These norms and skills, in turn, support

45. David G. Bowers, "Perspectives in Organizational Development" (CRUSK-Institute of Social Research, Working Paper, University of Michigan, 1970), pp. 40–41. This material is reprinted herein with the permission of the author, David G. Bowers, and the publisher, the Institute for Social Research, The University of Michigan. This material may not be used without permission of the author. Copies of the working paper are available from the Institute for Social Research. More broadly, see Paul Lawrence and Jay W. Lorsch, *Organization and Environment* (Boston, Mass.: Division of Research, Harvard University Graduate School of Business Administration, 1967).

collaborative problem-solving and the rational use of information in making decisions. This model assumes, . . . that the work of schools is carried on through interpersonal interactions and that heightening abilities for problem-solving must commence with new norms for interpersonal openness and helpfulness.[46]

So dominant has been the truth-love model, and so powerful have T-Groups been in inducing positive affect and strong loyalty, that OD often has been strongly associated with (if not actually viewed as the same as) T-Grouping or sensitivity training. Such association is reinforced by ideological factors. For example, most OD programs assume comprehensive social contracts with organic systems as their ultimate goal. The truth-love model well fits those critical assumptives. At still another level, the focus on truth-love may discourage emphasis on alternative models which may be as technically attractive and which may also have a sequential priority. Schmuck and Miles direct very preliminary attention to one such alternative model of OD as power-conflict. To them, early stages of OD programs in schools are in major senses

> . . . centrally a matter of clarifying and strengthening expressions of the conflicting interests of diverse groups, and of radically redistributing decision-making prerogatives so that low-power groups can have more influence over an organization's fate. . . . those low-power clients who are usually somehow allotted the back seat in educational OD programs. The authors, in effect, argue not only that students ought to have more power in schools, but that they are in a much better position than educational professionals to transform schools in desirable ways.[47]

This implies an advocacy role for OD.

The point is not a quibble. In concept, if all the bases really are touched, truth-love will do the complete job. In practice, however, where you start makes a critical difference. Note, for example, the impressive difference between assumptives versus actuals as a point of departure. The common OD approach makes a spectacular leap toward an ideal but gives too little attention to the reality of the differential launching platforms of specific organizations as they diversely exist.

A rough contrast illustrates the broad point. The position here is that, given a continuing commitment to the values of the laboratory approach, the key issue is the design of diverse learning experiences that are sensi-

---

46. Schmuck and Miles, *op. cit.*, pp. 234.
47. *Ibid.*, p. 185. See also in that volume, Mark A. Chesler and John E. Lohman, "Changing Schools through Student Advocacy," pp. 185–212.

tive to where the client system is initially. If the client system is character-ized by blatant self-interest, narrowly defined, or coercive power, or what-ever, that is where the OD program must start. And the appropriate initial design may be to openly counter that self-interest with other in-volved self-interests to force the issue of the kind of system that would result if all parties sought to marshall their forces for win/lose games. The stage might also be set for bargaining about mutual adjustments,[48] even if no major changes in the opposed self-interests are possible due to persisting differences in class, status, formal power, and so on. Epi-grammatically, the initial basic OD commitment is to an open con-sideration of the factors influencing interpersonal and intergroup relations, whatever those factors are. With only a little qualification, more or less oppositely, much OD work has used the T-Group as a standard learning design consistent with where an organization should ideally be: trusting, problem-solving, moving to consensus. It does make a profound difference, whichever approach one chooses. The former ap-proach risks compromising the ideal; and the latter approach might effectively demand that the system in responding to an early learning design be what it only might potentially become.

A final variation on the theme of the limits of applications of the truth-love model is perhaps most impactful. Especially in the early stages, for a wide variety of reasons, an OD program is likely to stress love somewhat more than truth. Substantial mischief inheres in this tendency, as can be suggested from two points of view. For example, OD designs have emphasized integration far more than separation, even though both are organizational truths that require confronting. Dealing with separa-tion, as in the OD design involving the demotees reported in Section B, Part II, is still unusual and almost unique. Separation is not such a rarity in nature, however, as in the case of reorganizations. And too much emphasis on the latter theme of the truth-love model can complicate dealing with that reality. In one case, to illustrate, conditions required differentiating parts of a large industrial firm in which T-Groups had been widely used. Reality proved difficult to accept, and at least one observer credits the earlier training for part of that difficulty. Two dis-tinct sets of operations were reorganized out of the original whole, we are told, but the "departure was perceived as 'abandonment' with en-suing feelings of resentment and guilt. They were leaving the 'one big family,' which the prior reliance on the extensive T-Group strategy had helped to foster."[49]

That OD programs typically accent the latter theme of the truth-love

---

48. C. Brooklyn Derr, "Surfacing and Managing Organizational Power," *OD Practi-tioner*, Vol. 4 (No. 2, 1972), pp. 1–3, presents a model for such a power-oriented intervention in an OD program.
49. Winn, "Reflections on T-Group Strategy. . . ," p. 8.

model also can be suggested in a second, more obvious way. That is, OD programs are likely to be triggered by a vivid concern by superordinates about their *responsibility toward subordinates*. Occasionally, the stimulus is a dramatic one, such as the subordinate who collapsed outside his boss's office after a "chewing out" by his superior who blamed himself and his insensitivity for that tragic consequence. More than one OD program had its proximate beginning in a deeply-felt resolve never to allow such a tragedy to occur again. Most often, the stimuli triggering a superordinate's sense of responsibility are less tragic, but still troublesome. Thus superordinates might reflect on how easily they can turn off subordinates, constipate upward channels of communication, or bind subordinates into ineffectiveness.

Accepting what Herman calls the "myth of omnipotence," the superordinate takes full responsibility and thereby overdoes it. A manager may initially inspire an OD program to undo the dysfunctional consequences of his own omnipotence, as he views it. Immediately thereafter, the manager typically keeps himself under tight rein so as to preserve the delicate new relationships that early OD activities often help induce. Under such circumstances, the essential strategy is likely to be one of Attitudinal Change, as described above. Themes of warmth, support, and positive identification tend to dominate. At the same time, some aspects of truth—e.g., those related to differences in formal authority and power—are likely to be deemphasized. A kind of gentle nurturance model of leadership is implied.

A number of signs support the aptness of the characterization above. Note, for example, the contemporary swing of the pendulum back toward the needs and concerns of superordinates as well as subordinates. The "gestalt orientation," for example, urges the instability of the binds sketched above into which superordinates can place themselves, with the help of their subordinates. Assume that subordinates are doing the "poor, little, powerless me" role-play, for example. The superordinate who has recently got a little religion, laboratory style, but who still fancies his own omnipotence, is likely to take the easy way out. Such a superordinate will hold a tight rein on himself, and in the process will induce a variety of dysfunctional effects. These effects include: the superordinate's own nagging discomfort; a condescending or paternalistic attitude toward his subordinates, whom he basically perceives as too fragile to confront with his power, which they probably are not; and concern among subordinates that their superior is withholding data from them, which he is. Stanley N. Herman encourages an emphasis on this variety of "truth," even at some potential cost to "love." He concludes:

> I believe it is worthwhile to urge ourselves and others to take
> new risks—risks of greater self assertion, more spontaneity, and

565

more willingness to experiment with power and aggression as well as trust and love. If we in O.D. do indeed believe in a wider distribution of power it would be well for us to stop trying to deny power's existence, muffle it, wish it away, or disguise it under velvet wrappings. Rather we can encourage as many people as possible at *all* levels of the organization from highest manager to lowest subordinate to discover his own power and use it.[50]

The point may be put briefly. Later OD stages should tend toward the Problem-Solving strategy, as defined above.

Adjustment to Decision-Making Conventions

OD activities and programs must be appropriately adjusted to various organizational conventions for making decisions. Consensus has been the implicit or explicit ideal convention for decision-making in much OD ideology, the rationale for which is plain. Consensus as a decision-making convention increases the probability that participants will internalize the decision because of their involvement with it. Once internalization occurs, then, self-controls can be basically relied on to produce behavior consistent with the decision. In such a case, systemic controls are congruent with personal freedom. This seems an attractive state of affairs, at least from many perspectives.

Some finer discriminations seem necessary, however. As vital as consensus may be in the case of comprehensive social contracts, and as much as widening involvement is desirable in all OD efforts, both may still be counterproductive for many OD activities. At their worst, they may imply that no action will occur until risk $= 0$, or thereabouts, which means that not much is likely to happen, ever. At the very least, most formulations of consensus or near-consensus emphasize the usefulness of expert power, referent power, and value power, as described above. And useful they are. But it is unrealistic to neglect legitimate authority or coercive power. For they still exist. And although the nurturance model of leadership is a significant one, normatively, there are times when very direct roles also are appropriate.

This is no call for the emergence of organizational Genghis Khans. Rather, it directs attention to a base reality that is neglected only at one's peril.

The vision of consensus as a kind of social Holy Grail has faded, moreover, which merely adds urgency to the present point that OD

---

50. Stanley N. Herman, "Gestalt Orientation to Organization Development" (Paper presented at NTL Conference on New Technology in Organization Development, New York, October 8–9, 1971), p. 26.

activities should be sensitive to various conventions for making decisions. Consider the change in view experienced over the past few years
by Warren Bennis, perhaps *the* early ideologue of organization development. "There was a time when I believed that consensus was a valid
operating procedure," he recently explained. "I no longer think this is
realistic, given the scale and diversity of organizations. In fact, I have
come to think that the quest for consensus, except for some microsystems where it may be feasible, is a misplaced nostalgia for a folk
society as chimerical, incidentally, as the American search for 'identity.' "[51]

What is meant by "appropriate adjustment" of OD activities to conventions for decision-making other than consensus is not always clear, of
course. But some examples come to mind. Consider an organization re-
nowned for its unrelenting use of the power-coercive model. A number
of OD interventions still could be useful in it: various privatized inter-
view-*cum*-feedback designs, with the change agent providing the feedback; a wide range of career-planning designs with minimal public
sharing; and even such confrontive designs as third-party interventions,
which are public but narrowly so. Other OD designs, such as a family
T-Group, might be disastrous in an organization with a dominant power-
coercive model. The disaster could take at least two forms: a closed,
suspicious, "nothing" experience; or an openness that might later be
relentlessly punished because the system had only a temporary tolerance
for it.

Level of Intervention as Determinant of Model

*The level at which any specific OD intervention is made—at the level
of interaction or behavior, task, or macro-structure of the organization—
will be a critical variable in determining the appropriate model of
change and the appropriate set of conventions for making decisions.*
This point is intimately related to the two points above, which concern
OD adjustments to alternative models for change as well as to different
conventions for decision making.

Stanley Herman's graphic concept of OD as dealing with an "organizational iceberg" will help develop the point. As Figure 5 suggests,
OD deals with both formal and informal aspects of organization. As with
real icebergs, a good part of the bulk of organizational icebergs is below
the surface and traditionally is examined only in part. This traditional
neglect implies a practical priority for OD, of course. As Wendell French
notes: "Organization development efforts focus on both the formal and
the informal systems, but the initial intervention strategy is usually

---

51. Bennis, "A Funny Thing Happened on the Way to the Future," p. 602.

through the informal system in the sense that attitudes and feelings are usually the first data to be confronted."[52]

For a variety of reasons, the reasonable priority of dealing with the covert aspects of the iceberg has dominated the early development of OD. This is true in two related senses. Thus the basic focus has been micro-

Figure 5. The Organizational Iceberg

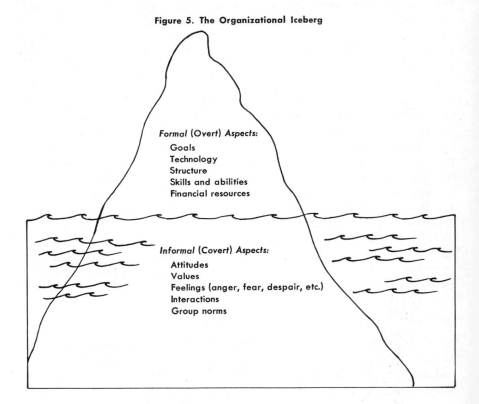

Formal (Overt) Aspects:
   Goals
   Technology
   Structure
   Skills and abilities
   Financial resources

Informal (Covert) Aspects:
   Attitudes
   Values
   Feelings (anger, fear, despair, etc.)
   Interactions
   Group norms

Source: Based on an address by Stanley N. Herman, of TRW Systems, at an OD conference sponsored jointly by the Industrial Relations Management Association of British Columbia and NTL Institute for Applied Behavioral Science, Vancouver, B.C., Canada, 1970.
   See also Herman, "What Is This Thing Called Organization Development?" *Personnel Journal,* Vol. 50 (August, 1971), pp. 595–603, for a useful elaboration of the notion.

level: on interpersonal versus intergroup phenomena, on interaction versus structure, and so on. Relatedly, the favored learning design has been the T-Group or sensitivity training group, which of course highlights interpersonal interaction. As Winn concludes:

52. Wendell French, "A Definition and History of Organization Development" (Paper presented at the Annual Meeting, Academy of Management, Atlanta, Ga., August 17–18, 1971) .

. . . far too many consultants confuse organization development with T-Group or sensitivity training. Thus, they limit
their intervention almost exclusively to the interpersonal
model. They pay lip service to some of the important variables
of organizational effectiveness, like work flow, basic organizational design, tasks, technology and environment. It is not surprising then that many organization development programs
based exclusively on the T-Group strategy fell short of the
expected objectives, just as "Human Relations" training programs did some twenty years earlier. . . .

The underlying assumption of this strategy is the belief that
what the classical theorists missed, i.e. the motivational and
collaborative issues, should get prominence in the consultant's
intervention. Thus, the T-Group approach aims at organizational climate, the "ambience," a system of beliefs, values and
attitudes which determines the way people relate to each other
and to authority figures. The emphasis is on openness, authenticity and confrontation.[53]

There are numerous attractions in this bias toward the interpersonal
and toward interaction. For example, the truth-love model and consensus
are clearly more applicable at the level of interpersonal interaction than
in larger systems. Given the broad commitment to truth-love and consensus, it is not surprising that many OD practitioners chose a congenial
context for emphasis. Applications to intergroup and structural issues
are at least more complex and chancy. Consider Section E in Part II.
For a variety of practical and technical reasons, two regularities characterize the several OD efforts reviewed there. Thus the learning designs
became safer and less intense as the size of the training population increased. Relatedly, truth-love and consensus became somewhat attenuated as the size increased. Not that fantasy-hate was glorified and coercion was endemic. But the acceptable definition of consensus was eased
as the intensity of the design was diminished.

Despite the attractions of the bias toward interpersonal and interaction
data, however, data of crucial interest to OD are found at other levels of
organization. At these other levels, an insensitive emphasis on truth-love
and consensus may not only be less appropriate, it might be seriously
counterproductive.

Three illustrations should suggest the fullness of the point. *First,* all
organizations are wheels within wheels, and typically an individual has
memberships in several simple systems. In Figure 6, for example, X is
a subordinate of A and a member of A's team. But he is also the superordinate as well as the delegate of the p's, in complex and shifting

---

53. Winn, "Reflections on T-Group Strategy. . . ," pp. 2–3.

senses. Consequently, any intensification of collaboration at Team Level I may bring mixed results. More effective performance may result at Level I. But the same intensified collaboration at Team Level II may be perceived as a threat by the p's. That is, the intensification may suggest that X is being co-opted. This is an implied encroachment on the autonomy of Team Level II, and may also be a dilution of the legal or traditional prerogatives of Team Level II. The situation is perhaps clearest in university administration, involving deans and department chairmen. But most supervisors are variously "in the middle" as superordinate/delegate/subordinate. Even more complex is the case in which A does not have clear authority but still must work closely with X, Y, and Z, who are superordinates/delegates in the sense above. And there can be numerous levels of such linkages, both of the straightforward and the subtle variety.

Figure 6. Two Interlocking Teams

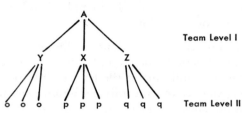

The moral should be clear. Truth-love and consensus at one level may inspire power-coercive reactions and dissensus or opposition at other levels. Powerful designs oriented toward truth-love and consensus at one level, then, might inspire equal but opposite reactions at other levels. Hence OD programs—which typically deal with interaction, task, or macro-structure in complex combinations—have to be sensitive to different models of change and different conventions for decision-making. And all this while seeking to more closely approach OD values.

Second, designs for micro-level interventions may have serious unanticipated consequences when the focal issue really resides at another level of organization. Winn gives the example of a West African plant of a multinational corporation. Considerable unrest existed in the plant, due to a volatile mixture: native blacks and expatriate whites in an environment of obvious and sharp status differences, with a vivid history of "colonial" practices. The design to reduce the unrest emphasized interpersonal interaction: a series of T-Groups were to be formed, each with six black and six white supervisors, and with one white and one black North American trainer. Winn comes down hard on the design and its inappropriate level of focus:

570

The consultant obviously did not even attempt to diagnose the situation. Had he done so, he would hopefully have questioned the usefulness of the T-Group strategy in the situation. The pathology was evident on the macro-social level, and the major problems were only tangentially related to the interpersonal or inter-group issues. The T-Group strategy would have set the stage for frustration and have been perceived as a manipulation, an attempt to have the Negro supervisor accept that his White colleague should have special privileges in terms of salary, home leaves, etc.[54]

Third, at least the strong possibility exists that substantial and perhaps unavoidable constraints inhibit building truth-love and consensus into at least some organizations. This is the thrust of the "contingency theory of organization" developed by Paul Lawrence and Jay W. Lorsch, for example. Epigrammatically, attempting to build very many opportunities for consensus into a plant organized to produce cardboard cartons may be disingenuous, or even counterproductive. As Lawrence and Lorsch describe them, the cardboard carton markets and technology are such as to make high degrees of centralization convenient, and perhaps indispensable. Somewhat the same argument might be made concerning such specialized agencies as the Strategic Air Command.

Whatever the example, the import is similar. Some organizations may require mechanical systems, or the functional model of organization. Inducing aspirations about consensus in such organizations, consequently, may be foolhardy. Or inducing such aspirations may even be cruel, if compelling considerations require structure within which only centralized conventions for decision-making are realistic.

This is not to say that OD interventions are impossible in such organizations; rather, those interventions will tend to be consistent with the initial style of the host organization, while working toward laboratory values. Specifically, an appropriate OD intervention in an organization with a highly centralized pattern of decision-making might reasonably deal primarily with the structure of the organization or of its tasks, rather than with interaction. The prime OD challenge will be to demonstrate that alternative "organic" structural arrangements consistent with the values of the laboratory approach generate results equal to or better than the "mechanical system" or the functional model. This is the approach sketched in Subsection 5 of Section D, which argues for a kind of guided participative approach to job enlargement. Highly technical and interdependent operations, or those requiring experimental verification of effects, however, may have to be approached dif-

---

54. *Ibid.,* pp. 9–19.

ferently. In such cases, job enlargement may need to take on an even more elitist character. As Frederick Herzberg argues, for example:

> . . . So far as the process of job enrichment itself is concerned, experimental constraints in the studies dictated that there could be no participation by jobholders themselves in deciding what changes were to be made in their jobs. The changes nevertheless seemed to be effective. On the other hand, when people were invited to participate . . . results were disappointing. In one case, for example, a group of personnel specialists suggested fewer than 30 fairly minor changes in their jobs, whereas their managers had compiled a list of over 100 much more substantial possibilities.
>
> It seems that employees themselves are not in a good position to test out the validity of the boundaries of their jobs. So long as the aim is not to measure experimentally the effects of job enrichment alone, there is undoubtedly benefit in the sharing of ideas . . .[55]

In either case, the desired outcome is the same. The structural changes in both cases are intended to encourage or permit patterns of behavior and interaction more consistent with the values of the laboratory approach, while they also raise output and motivate effort.

The issue may be framed more broadly by considering the full range of possible OD interventions. Robert A. Blake and Jane S. Mouton provide a convenient place to start in their list of the major kinds of interventions that can facilitate OD programs. Interventions might stress:[56]

- *discrepancy*, which calls attention to contradictions in actions or attitudes
- *theory*, which highlights research findings or insights that might help the client system gain perspective
- *procedures*, with the purpose of analyzing methods or processes of problem-solving
- *relationships*, so as to focus attention on the quality of interpersonal, intragroup, and intergroup life
- *experimentation*, which involves testing several alternative actions before a decision is made

---

55. William Paul, Keith Robertson, and Frederick Herzberg, "Job Enrichment Pays Off," *Harvard Business Review*, Vol. 47 (March, 1969), p. 75.
56. Robert A. Blake and Jane S. Mouton, "A 9,9 Approach to Organization Development," cited in Warren G. Bennis, "The Change Agents," in Golembiewski and Blumberg, *op. cit.*, p. 307.

- *dilemmas,* which seek to point up choice points and potential conflicts between alternative sets of assumptions and potential solutions
- *perspective,* so as to provide situational or historical understanding of problems
- *organization structure,* which seeks the sources of problems in structural arrangements of tasks of organizations
- *culture,* which focuses on traditions, norms, and values

OD activities with an emphasis on interaction would stress these interventions: discrepancy, relationships, dilemmas, and culture. OD activities with an emphasis on structure would focus on: theory, procedures, experimentation, perspective, and organization structure.

Integration of Levels

Whatever the level an OD activity or program initially stresses—behavior or interaction, the task, or macro-organization structure—all levels need to be integrated to reinforce lasting change. Preaching in this regard is easy enough, but the practice has been most uneven. As Friedlander notes, the issue is less whether the initial level of intervention should be interaction, task, or structure. The critical point is the failure to follow through on the other two levels, whatever the level of initiation. He observes:

> The assumption of the behavioural scientists, for example, would seem to be that behavioural change (derived from training sessions) will automatically lead to structural change in the organization. Similarly, the assumption of the technology based change-agent seems to be that changes in the task processes will automatically lead to structural change as well as change in the individual's behaviour. And finally, those who would change the structure of the organization seem to assume that changes in both the task and human processes will conveniently follow structural change.[57]

Degree of Emphasis on Integration

OD activities and programs should stress integration, but to degrees that are consistent with such factors as the nature of the problem situation, the specific social contract of reciprocal obligations, and the level

---

57. Friedlander, *op. cit.*

of the intervention. The point can be put bluntly. The thrust of OD typically is integrative, and should remain so. Commonly, however, a good thing has been overdone. Each conclusion will be considered, in turn.

The bias of OD activities is to integrate that which is disparate. This is meant in social, technical, and moral senses. For example, the underlying model of OD is an organic system, an ongoing process of bringing together people and responsibilities. The people and responsibilities are continually changing and evolving; but they are being brought together nonetheless, even if in the very effort they become quicksilver that ultimately defies the bringing together. Similarly, the integrative structure sketched in Section A, Part III, is more congenial to OD at many stages than is the bureaucratic model. And, at a basic moral level, the OD bias is toward what Walton has called integrative social situations, as distinguished from distributive situations in which what one person gains, some others must lose.

The integrative bias of OD usually comes on very strong. Indeed, perhaps *the* base objective of most OD has been to bring at least major qualities of "primary groups" into the many "secondary groups" of which people are members. Even further, the implicit OD objective in many cases more nearly approximates an attempt to create *Gemeinschaft* out of a *Gesellschaft* world. In this view, large organizations sometimes come perilously close to being conceived of as big T-Groups. The generally unrelieved emphasis in OD programs on comprehensive social contracts, consensus, and truth-love reflects the same bias, if in a less extreme way.

More or less clearly, however, varying degrees of integration are appropriate. Patently, for example, the degree and kind of integration appropriate for a work team are likely to be unnecessary and probably impossible between that work team and the board of directors of their firm. OD designs appropriate for helping integrate the work team, as a consequence, will differ profoundly from the designs applicable to its interface with the board. Perhaps more realistically, only a certain quality of integration is convenient or perhaps even safe between some organization roles, short of the millenium. Consider auditors and line managers, for example. The degree of desired integration follows Beckhard's rule about conflict: little energy should be expended in interpersonal conflict; but the clash of ideas and perspectives and insights should remain high as a sign of a vital but functionally limited interdependency.

Some systems may (or should) overlap substantially, in sum; they might (or should) merely touch from time to time; or some intermediate condition might (or should) be characteristic of two systems. OD designs must be sensitive to the differences.

574

4. ONE CASE OF OD SEEKING FUTURISTIC INTEGRATION: A PROTOTYPE FOR THE FUNCTIONAL INTERFACING OF TWO SYSTEMS

One OD design illustrates the family of designs that fit within the guidelines, while the design also suggests the breadth of OD foci. The design attempts to ease the problems of heavy travel schedules of husbands as they have impact on wives and marriages, certainly a common and probably a growing concern. The overall goal was to develop a more satisfying interface between two systems that impinged on one another only in part, and should be kept that way. The basic value was that involvement of all parties in matters that influence them is desirable, while largely separate spheres for work and family also ought to be maintained. Perhaps the difficulty of drawing the line tends to inhibit efforts at working on the interfaces of work and family. In any case, the plain fact is that organizational issues are not usually defined in ways that emphasize the relevance of family involvement. As Samuel Culbert and Jean Renshaw observe:

> Failure to involve those affected by a decision is particularly prevalent where the family is concerned. The family helps the manager cope with a set of organizational issues including promotion and new managerial responsibilities, changes in geographical location, career planning, personal establishment of criteria for evaluating success, and development of a greater capacity to cope with the stresses of work-related travel. Each of these issues can involve interaction between the organization, the employee and his family, but the organization deals with them as if only the employee has relevant inputs to make.[58]

The interface between work and family systems in this case was bounded in two ways, by restrictive policies as well as by a learning design with a strong privatizing bias. A number of policies defined the restricted interface between the demands of work and of family. An acceptable design would

- restrict attention to the stresses of travel, not the entire marriage; broader family business would remain private
- involve organization members only by their own choice, based on full information about the design

---

58. Samuel A. Culbert and Jean Renshaw, "Searching for Integration: Coping with Stresses of Travel as an Opportunity for Improving the Quality of Work and Family Life," (unpublished MS, 1971), p. 1.

Figure 7. "Limited Exchange Contract" OD Design for Functional Interfacing of Two Systems

Approximate Time (minutes)	Purpose of Design Exercise	Design Steps
15	1. to introduce design	
45	2. to establish individual differences	2a. Each person draws on a sheet of paper his "life-line" from birth to death and indicates his present location on that line. 2b. Separate pairs of spouses share and discuss their life-lines. 2c. All couples share their reactions, in part to legitimate the range of differences.
120	3. to develop awareness of, and empathy for, the different ways in which spouses view themselves as a prelude to later formulating specific strategies for coping with the stresses of travel	3a. Each person takes 10 minutes to reflect on his distinguishing characteristics—a role, idiosyncrasy, or whatever. 3b. Each person writes one of these characteristics on each of 10 slips of paper. 3c. Each person rank orders his own slips of paper from most-essential to least-essential. 3d. Each pair of spouses returns to own motel room to share self-descriptions. 3e. Each spouse takes a turn, with the listening spouse being instructed to ask questions to increase understanding of the self-descriptions but not to try to change them. 3f. Couples reassemble to share reactions.
60–90	4. lunch	4a. Same-sex groups, so as to: 1. provide some relief from design 2. gain perspective from others with a similar role
120	5. to recognize forces acting upon the marriage	5a. A general session of "force-field analysis,"* a method for analyzing complex situations. 5b. Couples return to own room, where each person independently develops a large graphic of those forces driving toward a more satisfying relationship with his wife or husband and those forces restraining such a relationship. 5c. Couples share and discuss with each other their individual force fields.
at least 60	6. to reflect on and integrate the events of the day	6a. "alone time"
	7. dinner and evening	7a. married couples
90	8. to use feelings as data	8a. A fantasy exercise is used to provide an indirect way to express feelings that might be difficult in normal situations, the fantasy being that the husband had just left on a long business trip. 8b. Couples reflect on the emotional experience induced by the fantasy and write each other a letter describing that experience.

576

Figure 7—continued

		8c. Couples return to separate rooms and read aloud the letters they have just written to each other.
90	9. to demonstrate empathy for their spouses	9a. Consultant describes and demonstrates "brainstorming."†
		9b. Each person uses this technique to list all the stresses expected during an upcoming period of peak travel.
		9c. Each person rates intensity of each stress on 1–10 scale.
		9d. Spouses exchange lists, with their focus for analysis being the specific behaviors in terms of which the other partner responds to each specific stress.
		9e. Couples return to separate rooms to discuss the accuracy of their perceptions of the other, as well as their feelings about being understood.
	10. lunch	
90–120	11. to build support, to legitimate the giving and receiving of support by each partner	11a. Using lists of stresses due to travel, each partner develops a list of actions he or she would *like* to take themselves and of the kinds of support they would prefer to receive.
		11b. Discussion by couples of the supporting actions they prefer to give and receive.
30–45	12. closing	12a. reactions to learning design
		12b. recommended organizational changes that would aid coping with stress of travel

Source: Based upon Samuel A. Culbert and Jean Renshaw, "Searching for Integration: Coping with the Stresses of Travel as an Opportunity for Improving the Quality of Work and Family Life" (unpublished MS, 1971).
   * Robert T. Golembiewski and Arthur Blumberg (eds.), *Sensitivity Training and the Laboratory Approach* (Itasca, Ill.: F. E. Peacock Publishers, Inc., 1970), pp. 293–94.
   † Sidney J. Parnes and Harold F. Harding (eds.), *A Source Book for Creative Thinking* (New York: Charles Scribner's Sons, 1962), pp. 251–304.

- not force or pressure participants into discussing subjects they did not wish to discuss
- emphasize the strengthening of current problem-solving capabilities associated with the stresses of travel, as opposed to criticizing deficiencies

The narrow if significant interface of family/work systems also was defined by a design with a strong privatizing bias, as Figure 7 details. Basically, each husband-wife pair worked on the several design elements in a separate motel room, with a change agent available if desired. The several pairs did meet together to get instructions about design elements, and for some minor sharing of reactions. But the design overwhelmingly involved only the private husband-wife pairs. The brevity of the design —two gently paced days—also no doubt contributed to limiting the experience to the individual married pairs.

A variety of considerations urge caution in responding to this prototypical design, but it does seem promising. The considerations urging caution are commonplace ones: the small size (seven couples) of the trained population, which limits the confidence that can be placed in the results; and special conditions—such as the "fairly conservative morality" of the couples—which may account for important effects. Given such factors, however, the design seems to have induced the desired outcomes in the case of most of the couples. Culbert and Renshaw note that an independent research program provides tentative support for the basic hypotheses guiding the design:

- The problem-solving resources of husbands and wives seem to have been augmented, as reflected in self-reports about changes in attitudes, changes in perceptions of norms relating to problem-solving in their marriage, and anecdotes about increased effectiveness in problem-solving.
- The abilities of couples to cope with the stresses of travel seem to have increased, as aided by both greater personal planning and by organizational changes inspired by the learning design.
- Changes seemed to occur which applied to other areas of work, and the easing of family pressures made available more potential energy for dealing with issues at work.

Whatever replications of this design may show, it illustrates the broad family of limited exchange contract OD efforts which are sensitive to the guidelines sketched above. These guidelines seek at once to preserve the sense of the historic development of the laboratory approach and to suggest directions for the future drawn from the experience of the past.

NAME INDEX

Eddy, William B., 71, 82, 84, 88, 89, 90, 97, 197, 231
Egan, Gerard, 64, 82, 89, 218, 222, 225, 226, 241, 555
Eitington, Julius E., 236, 405
Elliott, A. G. P., 263
Ellul, Jacques, 6
Ellis, Albert, 227, 272
Elliss, J. D., 254, 256, 264
Esbeck, Edward S., 136
Evans, Martin G., 406
Ewen, Robert B., 380

Fein, Mitchell, 385
Feinstein, Alvan R., 210
Ferguson, R. Fred, 377
Ferris, Ray, 366
Festinger, Leon, 101
Fine, H. J., 257
Fink, Stephen L., 249, 260, 261, 265
Fisher, John, 196
Flacks, Richard, 549
Flanagan, John C., 308
Flash, Frederic F., 235
Follet, Mary P., 63
Ford, Henry, 4, 182
Ford, Robert N., 380, 381, 383, 385, 386, 512
Fordyce, Jack K., 146, 149, 150, 151, 167, 170, 301
Forer, Bertram, 88, 89, 158
Fosmire, Fred, 332
Fowler, Irving, 392
Frank, Jerome D., 81, 89
French, John R. P., Jr., 249, 265
Fried, Marc, 544
Friedlander, Frank, 32, 33, 233, 366, 367, 368, 371, 373, 374, 395, 557, 559, 573
Frye, Roland L., 558

Gardner, John, 111, 151, 152
Garfield, S. L., 253
Gassner, Suzanne M., 263, 264
Gazda, George M., 268
Geitgey, D. A., 255, 264
Georgopoulos, Basis S., 547, 548, 549
Gergen, Kenneth J., 207

Ghiselli, E. E., 529
Ghorpade, J. V., 535
Gibb, Jack R., 32, 33, 53, 54, 68, 81, 86, 116, 141, 208, 212, 213, 230, 231, 232, 233, 253, 268, 279, 323, 397, 540, 541
Gibb, Lorraine M., 55, 56, 268, 397, 540, 541
Gindes, Marion, 402
Gold, Jerome, 263, 264
Golembiewski, Robert T., 15, 64, 68, 74, 96, 101, 126, 131, 133, 138, 162, 182, 188, 206, 210, 212, 263, 277, 278, 321, 391, 392, 397, 407, 409, 411, 418, 426, 431, 433, 455, 458, 463, 467, 468, 476, 501, 509, 513, 520, 528, 529, 539, 560, 561, 572, 577
Golomb, Naphtali, 543
Gomberg, William, 57, 116
Goode, William J., 392
Goodall, Kenneth, 227, 238
Goodson, Max R., 531
Gottschalk, Louis A., 67, 81, 234, 235, 270
Grater, Harry, 263
Gouldner, Alvin, 60
Grant, Donald L., 309, 316, 317
Green, Paul C., 558
Greening, Thomas C., 552
Greenwood, J. M., 309
Greiner, Larry E., 133, 171, 401
Griffin, Kim, 237
Guest, Robert A., 179
Gunther, B., 87

Hagstrom, Warren O., 531
Haim, A. W., 422
Haiman, Franklyn S., 260
Haire, Mason, 529
Haldane, Bernard, 299, 300, 303
Hall, Jay, 264
Halpin, Andrew W., 125, 461
Hampden-Turner, Charles M., 53, 54, 55, 240
Hanson, Philip G., 272, 463
Hardert, Ronald, 250
Harding, Harold F., 577

582

Valiquet, Michael I., 254
Van Riper, Paul P., 200
Vaughn, James A., 392

Wagner, Alan B., 397
Walton, Richard E., 291, 294, 295, 296, 297, 298, 538, 539
Watson, R. I., 64
Webb, Eugene J., 250
Weber, R. Jack, 207, 220, 221
Weil, Raymond, 146, 149, 150, 151, 167, 170, 301
Wendell, French, 101, 173, 270, 326, 568
Weschler, Irving R., 83, 145
Whitaker, G., 391
Whittaker, James O., 102
White, Robert W., 35
Whitman, Roy M., 231, 232
Wight, A., 395
Williams, Martha S., 264
Whyte, William H., 293, 503

Wiener, William, 484
Wilcox, Herbert G., 530
Wildavsky, Aaron, 196
Winn, Alexander, 75, 112, 122, 123, 124, 390, 398, 506, 526, 553, 561, 564, 569, 570
Wohlking, Wallace, 501
Wolfe, W. W., 255
Wolfson, Alan, 366
Wollowick, Herbert B., 309
Woodward, Joan, 181

Yalom, Irwin D., 81, 236, 238, 239, 240, 242, 246, 248, 249, 267, 268, 272
Young, Oran, 293
Yablonsky, Lewis, 541

Zalkind, Sheldon S., 401
Zand, Dale, 32, 33, 35, 212
Zirnet, C. N., 257
Zuckerman, Marvin, 234, 237, 251, 284, 285, 286

SUBJECT INDEX

586

Feelings, 23–28, 44–52, 105–110, 227, 234–41; and affective range of laboratory approach, 105–110; and emotional arousal, 105–110, 234–41; and feel wheel, 227; and group development, 44–52; as central in laboratory approach, 23–28; *See also* Disclosure; Feedback; Laboratory Approach; and T-Group

FIRO-B, 45–489

Fishbowl technique, 476, 496–97

Future shock, 1–4; and culture shock, 3–4; and illness severity, 3

Futuristic analysis, 533–74; dominant environmental features in, 542–51; major probable characteristics in, 533–42; OD as an integrator in, 551–74

General Accounting Office, 199

Grid design, 170–72

Griggs et al. vs. Duke Power, 317

Group Behavior Inventory, 368–69

Group development, 39–52; and authority, 44–50; and intimacy, 44, 50–52; and modalities of interaction, 39–52; central problems in, 45; *See also* Laboratory Approach; and T-Group

Group dynamics, principles of, 321

Group-level interventions, 319–32, 356–66, 455–63; and team development, 326–32, 356–66, 455–63; two phases of development in, 320–26; *See also* Process Orientation; and Team Development

Group-observing-group formation, 476, 496–97

Group, orientations toward, 320–24; as agent of change, 322–24; as medium of control, 320; as target of change, 320–22

Group therapy, as distinguished from T-Groups, 80–83

Growth, organizational, 181–83; implications for OD programs, 182–83; stages of, 181–82

Guilt, 221

"History," or pseudo self-disclosure, 225

Hydro-Electric Power Commission of Ontario, 254

Hygiene factors, 379–80

Identity stress, 230–31

In-basket, 310–312

Incentive systems, 527

Individual development, 53–58, 105–110, 540–42; and affective range of laboratory approach, 105–110; as a cyclical process, 52–53; existential learning theory of, 53–58; futuristic potential for, 540–42

Influence, forms of, 62–63, 537

Instinctoids, 106

Institutional environments of organizations, 186–201; implications for OD programs, 194–201; public sector as example of, 186–94

Interaction, modalities of, 39–52; in group development, 45–52; kinds of, 39–44; confrontation, 39, 42–44; fight, 39, 41–42; flight, 39–41; pairing, 39–40; *See also* Climate, Interpersonal; Group Development; and T-Group

Interaction, systems of, 30–32, 35–39, 53–58, 136–41, 260–61; and individual development, 55–56; and interpersonal competence, 35–39, 53–58, 260–61; degenerative, 30–32; in OD programs, 136–41; regenerative, 30–32, 35–39; *See also* Climate; Interpersonal Competence; Laboratory Approach; Organization Development; and T-Group

Interface Group designs, kinds of, 169

Interface Team-building design, 170

Intergroup relations, win/lose character of, 463–64

Internal consultant, 333–46, 400; illustrative role of, 333–46; schema for world of, 400; *See also* Change-Agent

Internal Revenue Service, 197

Interview-cum-feedback design, 147–48, 357–66; general features of, 147–

Nonreactive research, 250
Non-verbal designs, 85–88
Non-Linear Systems, 402–403

Objective uncertainty vs. social uncertainty, 33
Ohio State Leader Description Questionnaire, 255
Opinions, 108–109
Organization Development (OD), 9–11, 111–19, 128–29, 134–64, 146–201, 273–492, 503–578; and bureaucracy, 158–64; and concept of man, 551–53; and consensus, 552–53, 566–67; and contingency theory, 174–201, 571; and contrasting managerial systems, 161–64, 503–506; and power, 562–64; and regenerative interaction systems, 136–41; and social contracts in, 555–59; and the future, 533–51; and truth-love model, 562–64; and voluntarism, 412–14; definitions of, 111–12; features of, 113–18; internal logic of, 9; limits on applications of, 174–201;

adequacy of models, 176–79, cultural preparedness, 174–76, institutional environments, 186–201, organization missions and stages of growth, 180–86;

models for, 176–79; objectives of, 128–29, 158–64; process orientation as central in, 141–54; some goals of, 158–64; some intended consequences, 134–41; some alternative designs, 146–50, 165–72;

for individuals, 273–318, for groups, 319–86, for large organizations, 387–497, Managerial Grid, 170–172, selected micro-designs, 146–50, 165–70;

strategies for, 9–10; values or norms of, 10–11, 118–19; some guidelines for development of, 551–78; via structural variation, 375–86, 506–531; via variation in interaction, 406–447; See also Feedback, Interpersonal and Organizational;

Organization Development (Continued)
Change-Agent; Laboratory Approach; And Process Orientation
OD cube, 11–12
OD designs, 36–39, 53–58, 74–94, 124–55, 169–70, 209–211, 222–71, 279, 291–98, 318–86, 455–530, 575–78; assessment center, 308–318; career planning, 298–308; confrontation, 463–84; consulting pair, 169; demotee, 279–90; feedback, 124–55, 356–66, 455–84; interface group, 169; interface team building, 170; interview-cum-feedback, 147–48, 357–66; job description, 375–78, 494–95; job redesign, 379–86; merger, 484–97; mirror, 169–70; organizational training laboratory, 366–77; role negotiation, 375–78; structural variation, 374–86, 506–530; team development, 142–55, 327–86, 455–84; T-Group, 36–39, 53–58, 74–94, 121–28, 209–211, 227–71; Third-party consultation, 169–70, 291–98; Work/marriage interface, 575–78
Organizational training laboratory design, 366–77; dimensions to be affected by, 367–69; issues related to, 372–75; rationale for, 366–67; some consequences of, 369–72
OSS Assessment Staff, 308
Ownership, psychological, 209–214, 232–33; and climate, 211–13, 232–33; and feedback, 209–14

Position classification, 527
Problem-Analysis Questionnaire, 263
Process orientation, 12–13, 142–55; an illustration of, 152–55; characteristics of, 142–46; guidelines for, 146; indicators of healthy states of, 150–52; six major perspectives on, 143–44; some methods for, 146–55; See also Laboratory Approach; and Organization Development
Project ACORD, 190, 492
Project organization, 521–22

591

Projective hypothesis, 231–32
Psychological safety, as central in laboratory approach, 218
Psychological success, 38–39, 212–14; as central in laboratory approach, 38–39; conditions for, 212–14

Rational Encounter, Weekend of, 227
Regression in T-Groups, 230–32
Renewal and revolution, as alternative strategies, 5–6
Research designs, issues concerning, 422–25, 437
Risk, 30–33; in interpersonal theory, 30–31; in regenerative and degenerative systems, 30–32; *See also* Interaction, Systems Of; and Trust
Role negotiation design, 375–78

Scapegoating, 211
Schedule C, 193
Self-acceptance, 36–37, 260–61; as central in laboratory approach, 36–37; as result of T-Grouping, 260–61
Self-actualization, 106
Self-perception, clarity of, 263–64
Sensitivity training group, 74–94, 121–28, 209–211, 227–71; *See also* T-Group
Set, or frame of reference, 109
Simulation, general business management, 124–26
Situational testing, 308–310
Smith, Kline and French Laboratories, 300, 303
Socio-technical systems, 375–86, 395, 404–405; and OD history, 404–405; as affected by structural variation, 375–86
Stranger experiences, 120–28; as a basic paradigm in OD programs, 120–21; testing usefulness of in OD programs, 124–28; *See also* Organization Development
Structural variation, 374–86, 506–530; and contingency theory, 174–201, 571; and degenerative interaction,

Structural variation *(Continued)*
513–15; and start-up, 515–18; by redesigning jobs, 379–86; in job descriptions, 375–78; some consequences of, 515–30; two models for, 509–512; underlying polarities of, 506–509, 518–30;
differentiation/integration, 507–508, 518–22, function/flow of work, 509, 527–30, repression/wriggle room, 508, 522–24, stability/newness, 509, 524–27;
See also Bureaucracy; Job Redesign; and Organization Development
Survey feedback design, 147–48, 357–66
Systems theory, 207

Team-building design, 169–70
Team development, 142–55, 327–86, 455–84; and structural variation, 375–86; at start-up, 332–33; designs for, 147–49, 356–74, 455–84;
confrontation design, 149, 463–84; interview-cum-feedback, 147–48, 356–66; managerially-oriented, 455–63; organization training laboratories, 366–74; process observation, 366–74; work/family interface, 575–78;
effects of, 142–55, 346–53; emphases in, 327–28; examples of, 333–46; foci of, 328–31; on a mass scale, 455–63; intergroup aspects of, 331; some common features of, 353–55; *See also* Disclosure; Feedback; Laboratory Approach; Organization; Development; and Process Orientation
Temporary systems, management of, 524–31
Tennessee Self-Concept Scale, 257
Tennessee Valley Authority, 137
T-Group, 36–39, 53–58, 74–94, 121–28, 209–211, 227–71; and interpersonal competence, 36–39, 53–58, 260–61; anxiety or threat in, 229–31; as matrix vehicle of laboratory approach, 73–85, 227–71; basic com-

T-Group (*Continued*)
monalities in, 74–77; distinguished from group therapy, 81–83; distinguished from some encounter groups, 88–94; family variety of, 79–80, 121–28; goals of, 243; kinds of learning in, 77–80; record of traumatic effects in, 234–40; realistic expectations about, 240–42; research on effects of, 242–52; stranger variety of, 76–78, 120–28; three kinds of, 83–85, 209–211; underlying assumptions of, 244–46; *See also* Laboratory Approach; and T-Group, Research On

T-Group, research on, 254–72; and average members, 264–68; and characteristic specific outcomes, 259–64; and lack of change in basic personality, 256–59; and permanence of change, 268–71; and resulting behavioral change, 254–56; some guidelines for, 271–72

Theory X, 503

Third-party consultation, 169–70, 291–98; and ubiquitous conflict, 291–93; conditions for, 296–98; design for, 169–70, 293–96; some effects of 294–95

Three-dimensional images, 466–68, 486–88; in confrontation design, 466–67; in merger design, 486–88; properties of, 466–68

TORI group, 540–41

Trainer, T-Group, 83–85, 227, 237–40; and psychological trauma, 237–40; and self-disclosure, 227; role of, 83–85, 237–40; styles of, 237–40; *See also* T-Group

Transfer of learning, 254–57, 269–90, 325–27; centrality of, 325–26; research about, 254–57, 269–70, 274–90, 327; *See also* Laboratory Approach; Organization Development; and T-Group

Transference, 210–11

Trauma, psychologic, 75, 234–40; and regression in T-Groups, 75; and T-Group experiences, 234–40

TRW Systems, 401

Trust, interpersonal, 30–35, 55–56; a mini-theory of, 32–35; and individual development, 55–56; and interaction systems, 30–32; and managerial effectiveness, 33–35; model of, 33–35; significance of, 32–33; *See also* Disclosure; and Feedback

Unfreezing, 97–100, 219–20; in change, 97–100; in feedback, 219–20

Unobtrusive measures, 250

U. S. Civil Service Commission, 194, 200

U. S. Department of State, 195–96, 198

Upward feedback design, 147

Values, 10–11, 60–72, 105–110; as desired or desirable, 10–11; as related to affective range of laboratory approach, 105–110; in OD, 10–11; of laboratory approach, 60–72; acceptance of inquiry, 60–61; authenticity in interpersonal relations, 65–66; collaborative concept of authority, 62–63; expanded sense of choice, 61–62; mutual helping relationships, 64; *See also* Laboratory Approach; and Organization Development

Word association, 232

Work Group Description Questionnaire, 126

Work/marriage interface design, 575–78; properties of, 576–77; travel as a mutual issue in, 575–76

YMCA, 235–36

BOOK MANUFACTURE

Renewing Organizations: The Laboratory Approach to Planned Change was typeset, printed by offset, and bound by Kingsport Press, Inc. The paper is Perkins & Squier Company's Glatfelter Special Book. Internal design was by John Goetz. Cover design was by Charles Kling & Associates. The type is Baskerville, with tables in 20th Century Medium and table numbers and titles in Spartan Heavy.